DON'T MISS . . .

"The Last Word on the Lost Order" by STEPHEN W. SEARS
A Confederate messenger riding out of Robert E. Lee's Maryland
headquarters dropped a sealed envelope wrapped around a gift of
cigars. An Indiana corporal named Barton P. Mitchell spotted the
package in a clover field. He delivered it into the hands of General
George B. McClellan. It contained Lee's Special Orders No. 191—and
the strategy that might have handed victory to the Confederacy was
lost. Civil War historian Sears reveals the famous mystery of the Lost
Order and how this spectacular coup changed the course of war. . . .

"Guernica: Death in the Afternoon" by DAVID CLAY LARGE
Picasso's most famous painting immortalized the terror and tragedy of
Hitler's bombing of the holy city of the Basques. But General Francisco
Franco's government first tried to deny that the bombing had taken
place. Later it charged that Red arsonists had destroyed Guernica.
Professor David Large tells us not only of the horrors, but of the ironies
of what really happened on the evening of April 26, 1937. . . .

"A Lousy Story" by VLADIMIR LEMPORT
A remarkable memoir translated from the Russian brings us a former
second lieutenant's account of life (and needless death) on the Don and
Stalingrad fronts in the summer and fall of 1942. A rare eyewitness
report, these "notes" by the much-decorated Vladimir Sergeyevich
Lemport give a scathing view of the murderously detached way in
which Stalin conducted the war.

. . . AND FORTY-EIGHT MORE FASCINATING AND
THOUGHT-PROVOKING ARTICLES

EXPERIENCE OF WAR

An Anthology of Articles from
MHQ: The Quarterly Journal of Military
History

EDITED AND INTRODUCED BY

ROBERT COWLEY

A LAUREL TRADE PAPERBACK
Published by
Dell Publishing
a division of
Bantam Doubleday Dell Publishing Group, Inc.
1540 Broadway
New York, New York 10036

The trademark Laurel® is registered in the U.S. Patent and Trademark
Office.

The trademark Dell® is registered in the U.S. Patent and Trademark Office.

ISBN: 0-440-50553-4

Reprinted by arrangement with W.W. Norton & Company, Inc.

Printed in the United States of America

Published simultaneously in Canada

July 1993

10 9 8 7 6 5 4 3 2 1

RRH

Contents

Introduction

When we started *MHQ: The Quarterly Journal of Military History* in 1988, we did so as unabashed enthusiasts. We also felt strongly that there was a need for such a magazine, and not one that dealt merely with shoot-'em-ups (or, if you will, spear-'em-ups). As we come to the end of our fourth year, we feel that more strongly than ever. Military history matters because wars matter. Wars—and the threat of wars—have changed all our lives. I am not the first to point out that the history of war is the history of humankind. The Spanish philosopher José Ortega y Gasset once wrote an essay called "Against the Economic Interpretation of History," and he proposed instead that we should pay much more attention to the military interpretation. The study of arms would reveal one of the dominant mechanisms of history—if not the most dominant. "According to such a theory, life in each epoch would be determined not by what the instruments of production were, but what the instruments of destruction were." I think, too, of the words of the late British military historian Cyril Falls:

> What I want to urge is that all men, common and uncommon, great and small . . . have been profoundly and unceasingly influenced by wars. Our literature, our art and our architecture are stamped with the vestiges of war. Our very language has a thousand bellicose words and phrases woven into its fabric. And our material destinies, our social life and habits, our industry and trade, have assumed their present forms and characteristics, largely as the result of war. . . . We are, all of us, indeed, the heirs of many wars.

History starts with war. Among the first written records to come down to us are accounts of assaults upon, and defenses of, that relatively new phenomenon, the organized community. Literature, too, starts with war: The Epic of Gilgamesh, the Iliad, and the Odyssey—and, indeed, much of the Old Testament—all tell of war and its aftermath. In these pages, Robert L. O'Connell examines some of the most plausible current theories about the origins of war. And if credence is to be given to the recent arguments of Francis Fukuyama, history will, in effect, "end" with the end of organized armed combat. But we won't conclude *Experience of War* with a prediction that we are on the stultifying verge of a "posthistorical period" in which market-system self-gratification expands to fill a conflictless vacuum. That is perhaps too much to hope for. It seems more reasonable to end with Martin van Creveld's "The Gulf Crisis and the Rules of War," which touches on certain historical precedents for, and the possible consequences of, one of the world's most recent—and certainly the most visible—clashes of arms. We are far from seeing the last of war, and that is another reason why military history can't be ignored.

Lord knows we've done our best to deny its validity in recent years. But military history is coming back, both as an academic discipline and as a serious popular diversion. "Rediscovered" or "rehabilitated" might be more apt: During much of the sixties and seventies military history was regarded a bit like a madman who deserved to be chained in the attic. The Vietnam War took a dreadful toll on the study of military history in particular and history in general. I sometimes think the most lasting—and unfortunate—legacy of the youthful radical movements that coalesced around the anti-Vietnam cause was a disdain for history. History, in the hands of the elders in Washington, was one of the tools that wrought Vietnam. History gave legitimacy to the efforts by that same cabal to pinch off the buds of tomorrow. History really was, as Henry Ford once put it, "the bunk." And military history was identified with discredited patriotism, to be trashed with a vengeance.

All this has changed as the sour memory of Vietnam has receded. The huge success of Ken Burns's television series on the Civil War, and that of the book based on it, by Geoffrey C. Ward, is an undeniable measure of military history's return to public favor. I could point to other influential best-sellers, such as Paul Kennedy's *The Rise and Fall of Great Powers,* or James M. McPherson's *Battle Cry of Freedom.* (McPherson's moving judgment on the memoirs of U.S. Grant is one of the articles anthologized here.) But beyond those conspicuous *succès fous* are other equally remarkable scholarly studies that have broken genuine ground in recent years. At the risk of sounding cataloguey, I'll cite such books as Victor Davis Hanson's *The Western Way of War,* William McNeill's wide-ranging *The Pursuit of Power,* Martin van Creveld's *Supplying War,* and Geoffrey Parker's *The Military Revolution;* all of these authors are represented in this volume.

The return to favor of military history in academic circles is to the good, but there is something we can never let ourselves forget. *MHQ* is, after all, a magazine for the general reader, and our mission is not just to inform, instruct, and provoke—which we make every effort to do—but to entertain. Not "mere" entertainment. History at its best can be a literary art. You will find here essays as diverse as David Quammen's article on the relationship of man and horse in war or Michael Howard's thoughts on the coming of World War I that remind us that history is not just a matter of collating facts—and arcanely disputing someone else's collating of similar facts—but of elegance of thought and word. G.M. Trevelyan spoke of the "poetry of history" and indeed the past has its own special images, its truths, its clarifying moments that could be called epiphanies. History has its own inner rhythms. Listen to that fine historian Simon Schama: "History needs to declare itself un-apologetically for what it is: The study of the past in all its splendid messiness. It should revel in the pastness of the past, the strange music of its diction."

There is a savage, messy, and frequently epic poetry to military history. The further we get from the Civil War, for example, the more it takes on the quality of an American Iliad, and the fact that subdivisions now proliferate in the Wilderness can never diminish those heroic—and undeniably poetic—proportions. Troy will forever be more than just a mound. For the British, the First World War has begun to loom with similar epic menace. Its heroes may not be the larger-than-life leaders like Grant or Lee or Stonewall Jackson but common men, their grandfathers and great-grandfathers, who suffered through another siege that promised no end. Twenty-odd years ago when I first visited the battlefields of the Somme, the graves registers showed a couple of signatures per year—if that. Now buses daily unload throngs of tourists and schoolchildren, who clamber up the once deadly and still slippery fifty feet of the Butte de Warlencourt or wander the placid avenues of Delville Wood where, in 1916, not even the hard summer rains could quench the raging fires. The consolation of a shared ordeal in the past has replaced the imperial promise that once was England's future. Memories in common define nations as surely as boundaries.

But there is another aspect to military history that will forever defy those who seek merely to quantify and compartmentalize the study of war. That is its natural attraction to narrative. Crisis and confrontation are the heart of military history; they are also the essence of plot. It is no accident that many of our best military historians are natural storytellers.

Narrative abounds here, and for good reason. But narrative, you might say, is not the whole story. Essays that account for and illuminate the study of arms, Ortega y Gasset's dominant mechanism of history, are an *MHQ* staple. Geoffrey Parker's "Taking Up the Gun" or William McNeill's "The Gunpowder Revolution" or Charles Strozier's "The Tragedy of Unconditional Surrender" are noteworthy examples. What accident of history may have brought about European domination of the world? How did the Far East adapt to the military revolution of the period we now call Early Modern? (Did you know that the late-sixteenth-century Koreans had the first ironclads—so-called turtle boats—and used them successfully against the Japanese?) How, and why, did FDR deliberately misinterpret U.S. Grant's policy of unconditional surrender?

I think of this anthology as less a "best of" *MHQ* than a representative collection of what is best about the magazine. The organization is chronological, and on purpose. I mean to give some feeling of the way arms and combat have evolved, and of the varying ways that human beings have reacted to the stress of war. As John Keegan has taught us, the experience of battle is the key to so much else. If the American Civil War marks the rough halfway point in the book, that is on purpose, too. You can contend that the Civil War is either the last Napoleonic conflict or the first modern one. Williamson Murray, in "What Took the North So Long?," argues for the latter conclusion, and convincingly. Last or first: Take your choice. But it seems indisputable that what comes after 1865 is markedly different from what comes before.

Finally, I should admit that some of my own views about military history have changed since I began editing *MHQ*. In my first "Note to Our Readers," I wrote that "Maybe we have been too quick to discredit the old concept of the 'decisive battle.' " I take this opportunity to retract, and if the phrase crops up in these pages, I apologize. Decisive battles rarely decide. Industrial and matériel superiority does. Exhaustion does. Politicians do. Revolutionary fervor can. Is there any better example than Cannae, so terrifyingly described here by Victor Davis Hanson? It was history's ultimate spear-'em-up, as tactically brilliant a battle as has ever been fought, and one that military commanders have sought to emulate for centuries. And yet, Hannibal was unable to follow through with the capture of Rome itself. Waterloo was a "decisive" battle, but only, I suspect, because after almost a quarter century of Continental civil war no one had the will or the energy to keep on fighting. For Napoleon, a far worse catastrophe, the winter retreat through Russia in 1812, did not end his ambitions: He was back trying to restore his fortunes within a few months. The 1967 Israeli preemptive air strikes, which Abraham Rabinovich describes, may have ended a war almost before it began, but they left Israel with little more than temporary breathing room. There are exceptions. One that comes to mind is the Battle of Mohács in 1526, in which a Turkish army erased an entire nation, Hungary, from the map of Europe in a single afternoon. But in the main, decisive battles tend to be like children's peg benches. What you pound in always comes out on the other side, and the pounding process only begins again.

Too, when we started *MHQ*, another phrase came too readily to my lips: the lessons of history. If I now feel uncomfortable with the notion, it is because I find myself having increasing reservations about it. In deriving conclusions about the processes that have occurred in history and applying them to our times, we must exercise care. Nowhere is that more true than in military history. How often have nations come up short because they entered a new war still fighting the last one? Neither Vietnam nor Kuwait was a Munich by any stretch of the historical imagination. Which is not to say that we can't, or shouldn't, make comparisons, or attempt to place an event, or events, in the context of the past. We do that all the time in *MHQ*. At least one version of Alexander's victory over the Indian king Porus by the Hydaspes River has overtones of Desert Storm, as does Stonewall Jackson's miraculous left hook at Chancellorsville.

We would do well to remember the caution of that most respected of modern military historians, Michael Howard, on the subject of lessons. "The first lesson that historians are entitled to teach is an austere one: Not to generalize from false premises based on inadequate evidence. The second is not more comforting: The past is a foreign country; there is very little we can say about it until we have learned its language and understood its assumptions."

The chief lesson of military history may be that there are few lessons, and that even those are intimidatingly elusive. History no more repeats itself than snowflakes replicate. The past is a foreign country, and we probe its frontiers at our risk. That is where the real adventure begins.

Acknowledgments

There are three people who have made *MHQ: The Quarterly Journal of Military History* possible. Byron Hollinshead, our publisher, and Elihu Rose, the chairman of our Advisory Board (who also teaches an immensely popular course in military history at New York University), created the magazine. Their enthusiasm has never slacked. Without Barbara Benton, our managing editor, the magazine—*MHQ*—quite simply wouldn't exist: I can't think of a better way to describe the part she has played. There are other people on our small, overworked, and always resourceful staff whom I want to thank profusely, all of whom have contributed in various important ways to the making of this book: Douglas Hill, Diana Perez, Richard Slovak, Suzanne Wise, Linda Sykes, Marleen Adlerblum, Joyce Parente, Brigitte Goldstein, and Edna Shalev. Bruce Macomber copy-edited Experience of War—talk of indispensable people—and Vantage Art (and Douglas Hill) were responsible for the maps. Finally, I want to thank Starling Lawrence and Richard Halstead of W.W. Norton, who have been more helpful than they possibly know.

I'd also like to take this opportunity to thank the members of *MHQ*'s Advisory Board: Elihu Rose, David S. Croyder, Thaddeus Holt, Samuel Hynes, Paul Kennedy, William McNeill, Allan Millett, Al Silverman, and Norman Tomlinson. They not only were immensely helpful with the starting of *MHQ* but have weighed in with suggestions and—sometimes more important—criticisms. Our contributing editors have played a similar role. They have given us some of our most memorable articles, as well as shared their considerable knowledge. I name them with thanks: Stephen E. Ambrose, Caleb Carr, David Chandler, Arthur Ferrill, Thomas Fleming, Victor Davis Hanson, David Kahn, John Keegan, Richard H. Kohn, David Clay Large, Jay Luvaas, John A Lynn, Williamson Murray, Geoffrey Norman, Robert L. O'Connell, Geoffrey Parker, Rod Paschall, Stephen W. Sears, Ronald H. Spector, and Geoffrey C. Ward.

For information about *MHQ: The Quarterly Journal of Military History*, write or call

MHQ: The Quarterly Journal of Military History
29 West 38th Street
New York, NY 10018
(212) 398-1550

Credits

"The Athenian Century," adapted from *The Influence of Sea Power on Ancient History* by Chester G. Starr, © 1989. Reprinted by permission of Oxford University Press, Inc., New York. · "The Masada Myth," adapted from *Between Past and Present* by Neil Asher Silberman, © 1989. Reprinted by permission of Henry Holt and Company, Inc., New York. · "The Gunpowder Revolution," adapted from a portion of the American Historical Association (AHA) pamphlet *The Age of Gunpowder Empires, 1450–1800* by William McNeill, © 1989. Reprinted by permission of the AHA. · "George Washington, General," by Thomas Fleming, © 1990. Reprinted by permission of The Helen Brann Agency, Inc. · "Europe 1914," adapted from *The Lessons of History* by Michael Howard, © 1991. Reprinted by permission of Yale University Press, New Haven, Conn. · "Jutland," adapted from *The Price of Admiralty* by John Keegan, © 1988. Reprinted by permission of Viking Penguin, a division of Penguin Books USA Inc., New York. · "FDR's Western Front Idyll," adapted from *A First-Class Temperament: The Emergence of Franklin Roosevelt* by Geoffrey C. Ward, © 1989. Reprinted by permission of Harper-Collins Publishers, New York. · "Gamblers on the Turkish Brink," adapted from *The Peace to End All Peace: Creating The Modern Middle East 1914–1922* by David Fromkin, © 1989. Reprinted by permission of Henry Holt and Company, Inc., New York. · "Guernica: Death in the Afternoon," adapted from *Between Two Fires: Europe's Path in the 1930s* by David Clay Large, © 1990. Reprinted by permission of W. W. Norton & Company, Inc., New York. · "They Can't Realize the Change Aviation Has Made," adapted from *The Borrowed Years 1938–41: America on the Way to War* by Richard M. Ketchum, © 1989. Reprinted by permission of Random House, Inc., New York. · "From Light to Heavy Duty," adapted from *Wartime: Understanding and Behavior in the Second World War* by Paul Fussell, © 1989. Reprinted by permission of Oxford University Press, Inc., New York. · "The End in North Africa," adapted from *Panzer Commander* by Hans von Luck, © 1990. Reprinted by permission of Praeger Publishers, a division of Greenwood Publishing Group, Inc, Westport, Conn. · "When the Maquis Stood and Fought," adapted from *An Uncertain Hour: The French, the Germans, the Jews, and the City of Lyon, 1040–1945* by Ted Morgan, © 1990. Reprinted by permission of William Morrow & Company, Inc./Publishers, New York. · "Casey's German Gamble," adapted from *The Lives and Secrets of William J. Casey from the OSS to the CIA* by Joseph E. Persico, © 1990. Reprinted by permission of Viking Penguin, a division of Penguin Books USA Inc., New York, and Curtis Brown, Ltd., New York. · "Thats Ocay XX Time Is on Our Side," adapted from *Bouncing Back* by Geoffrey Norman, © 1990. Reprinted by permission of

EXPERIENCE OF WAR

The Origins of War

by ROBERT L. O'CONNELL

Let's start at the beginning, with a question that is basic not just to military history but to all history. Do we, like the ants, have organized aggression embedded in our genes? Is it a part of human nature? Or is war learned behavior—a relatively recent phenomenon in our development? If so, what was the change in the way we lived that made cooperative mass killing—as opposed to mere fighting—an essential part of our political agenda? Can we say when war began, and where? Robert L. O'Connell, whose *Arms and Men* (Oxford University Press) is a notable exposition of the history of weaponry, presents the latest findings on the controversial origins of war. O'Connell's most recent book is *Sacred Vessels: The Cult of the Battleship and the Rise of the U.S. Navy* (Westview Press).

By dawn the warriors had assembled outside their quarters. Either by signal or by common understanding, they began the march to the colony they were going to raid. Upon reaching the territory of their victims, they were met by defenders, who put up a tremendous fight, cutting relentlessly at the legs of the attackers. The raiding warriors, however, were bigger and better fighters and soon were piercing the armor of the defenders at will. Yet their primary aim was not to kill, but to steal the defenders' infants and carry them back to their own colony. There the youngsters would grow up to be slaves, spending their lives finding food for the warriors and even feeding them. Meanwhile the warriors—like proud imperial paladins—would dedicate themselves to an endless search for more slaves.

Here we find the origins of true war. Virtually all the prerequisites are present: a complex social structure, coordinated aggression, political and territorial overtones, and a lust for property. Yet the practitioners are only a few centimeters long. They are *Polyergus ruféscans*—Amazon ants. For between 50 million and 100 million years, members of this species and their cousins *Myrmica*, *Formica*, and the rapacious *Eciton* and *Dorylus* have lived by fighting. The manner in which they fight defines what we now call warfare.

These ants have no choice—their genes predestine them for a martial existence. Is this also the case with humans? If it is true that the martial impulse resides in our genes—that we are in effect born warriors drawn irresistibly to war—there is little hope for the future of our species in a time of nuclear weapons. On the other hand, if it can be shown that we learned to wage war, there is reason to hope that we can learn not to. For now there can be no definitive answer, nor can we expect one until the science of genetic mapping becomes far more advanced. Nonetheless, we can glimpse outlines of a solution by studying the past. There is considerable disagreement as to how human warfare began, but if we look carefully and selectively at the main arguments, and are precise about what we define as "war," then the origins of war can be approached, if not exactly pinned down.

"Nothing in the habits of man seems more ancient than war," the military historian Bernard Brodie has written, and until very recently the history of thought had produced little to contradict this notion. The ancient Greeks, the world's first self-consciously analytic people, simply took wars for granted, assuming that men had always fought them. Even Plato and Aristotle, who did consider the origins of city-state rivalries, declined to treat warfare as a subject in and of itself. Wars were important; war was not. Similarly, Leonardo da Vinci denounced warfare as *bestialissima pazzia* (the most bestial madness) but did not question its age or inevitability. Indeed, until the nineteenth century, Western cultures fatalistically included war, along with famine, death, and pestilence, as one of the Four Horsemen of the Apocalypse, scourges that had always been and always would be.

Only the coming of the concept of evolution caused people to question this basic assumption in any systematic fashion. Appropriately, it was Charles Darwin who suggested, in his 1871 book *The Descent of Man,* that rather than being innately blueprinted, war was subject to manipulation and improvement. In fact, Darwin considered war the prime driver of cultural evolution. In his view each martial innovation "must likewise to some degree strengthen the intellect. If the invention were an important one, the tribe would increase in numbers, spread, and supplant other tribes." By 1896 Darwin's follower Herbert Spencer went even further, arguing that the basic leadership/subordination behavior patterns necessary for centralized political systems first developed in primitive military organizations. However, by 1911 this assumption and the implied primacy of warfare as a force in the development of complex societies were cast aside by William Graham Sumner, who said war and peaceful pursuits developed side by side.

The most important thing about this intellectual give-and-take is not who was right or wrong but that war was no longer being treated like glaciation or the formation of mountain ranges. Rather, it had become for these evolutionary thinkers essentially a cultural institution whose roots could be discerned and whose development was primarily a function of learning. This was an important change, and it is probably not accidental that it coincided with the rise of the idealistic pre-1914 peace movement, which assumed that war could be progressively mitigated and eventually outlawed.

Meanwhile, the serious study of man's cultural beginnings had just gotten under way. Darwin had performed field studies in the course of his animal research, but when it came to human societies the evolutionists were mostly armchair theorists, relying on written sources and their own intellects. Field anthropologists would later test these theories against hard evidence.

Basically, research relevant to the origins of war proceeded in three directions: ethnography (the observation and reporting of a people's way of life), physical anthropology (essentially archaeology applied to the remains of humans and their precursors), and historically oriented studies (including philology, comparative government, and a more traditional form of archaeology that focused on what humans built or manufactured). In the case of ethnography, European travelers had for centuries been gathering information on societies that were discovered as Western culture expanded, but they had done so randomly and based on anecdote. Now, at the beginning of the twentieth century, a group of pioneering anthropologists, among them W.H.R. Rivers and Franz Boas, produced careful and systematic studies of non-Western cultures, basing their findings on intimate familiarity with their subjects and on long and direct observation. Since the ultimate intent was to understand the evolutionary roots of our own cultural institutions by analogy with simpler societies, the bulk of subjects prior to World War II belonged to tribal groups, particularly tribal hunter-gatherers.

Ethnographers made several discoveries of real significance to our understanding of man's attachment to warfare. First, they found that hunting-and-gathering cultures generally led a relatively low-key existence in which teamwork within the groups was paramount and hostility and aggression were muted. It has been argued that the apparent gentleness of contemporary hunting-and-gathering groups resulted largely from natural selection, whereby less aggressive groups became concentrated in remote locations, where they continued to pursue very basic life-styles. Nevertheless, the behavior of these people toward one another did much to undermine stereotypes of both the savage "savage" and his brutal ancestors.

Affability aside, these people, or at least the males among them, were still hunters by occupation and were found to be suitably equipped. Virtually without exception they possessed weapons. Indeed, in the entire course of ethnographic research, investigators have found only two small groups that lacked even weapons to hunt with—the Fhi Tong Luang of Southeast Asia and the Tasaday, a group of about twenty-five individuals living what appeared to be a peaceful arboreal existence in the Philippines. (The Tasaday life-style is now thought by some to have been a hoax perpetrated by the Marcos regime to boost tourism.)

As for the other groups studied, ethnographers found weapons to be not only the tools of the hunter but the means to manslaughter: Intergroup violence was observed to be part of the hunting-and-gathering existence. It was certainly not universal—and this is important—but lethal fighting between tribal groups did go on. Such combat took the form of extended blood quarrels, sporadic and highly personalized affairs, homicidal in intent and, occasionally, in effect, but lacking a sustained economic and political motivation. The goals of combatants were typically revenge and the capture of women. Ambush and raiding were the preferred modes of operation, and the target was frequently a single "enemy." Pitched battles, when they occurred, represented tactical failure. The object was rout, not prolonged combat. Thus the attacking party would come close only if surprise was reasonably certain; otherwise the aim was to stay at long range and exchange missiles.

From the perspective of the participants, this made perfect sense. Combat was really only an extension of personal disputes. Armies were little more than collections of individuals, in most cases fighting more out of loyalty to some injured party than to the group and its aspirations. Because the participants lacked a stronger, more unifying purpose, the fighting potential of such a force was limited by the participants' willingness to assume risk. Since the degreee of such willingness was usually low, this type of combat was inherently indecisive and produced few casualties.

All of this was duly noted by the ethnographers, who were nothing if not accurate observers. Yet they were also human beings, at times living in the midst of, or at least confronted with, the results of this mayhem. Even if casualties were few, they did occur. People they may have known were being killed, often horribly. The attacks and counterattacks persisted in a hopeless chain of violence, which must have suggested to these Westerners the futility, if not the true character, of their own culture's martial conflagrations. Consequently, it is not hard to understand why ethnographers persisted in labeling these quarrels among their subjects as "wars." Yet in doing so, they set the stage for later confusion. Ethnographers and those in related fields, such as sociobiology and physical anthropology, adopted an exceedingly inclusive definition of *war*, while historians and political sciencists were generally more selective. The two sides were not talking about the same thing, but at times this was not very obvious.

Meanwhile, ever since Darwin had set forth his theory explaining how life developed, a major element of evolutionary studies had been devoted to defining better the process by which man emerged from his primate ancestors. The first discoveries in the late nineteenth century of the fossilized remains of Neanderthal and then so-called Java man—both apparently transitional beings with apelike features—raised the hope of actually establishing physical proof of man's evolution and transformed anthropologists into burrowing creatures digging for bones at the slightest provocation.

This prolonged search bore fruit first in 1924 and again in 1959 with discoveries of *Australopithecus africanus,* an apelike creature later established as a key figure on the evolutionary trajectory that led from apes to humans. *Australopithecus* was not very impressive to look at. Slight of build and probably no more than five feet tall, these hominids (as such ape-people are commonly called by anthropologists) was virtually without natural armaments, lacking even a decent set of canine teeth such as those of baboons. Yet they did possess one remarkable feature: All the physical data indicated that these nearly 4-million-year-old protohumans walked upright, probably as easily as we do. There is general agreement that their unique posture—which, among other things, freed their hands—was the critical break that separated them from the apes and set them on their own evolutionary way.

Yet the evidence also indicated that they were not walking on familiar ground. Found in association with the little hominids were the remains of antelope and other mammals specialized for life on grasslands. This indicates strongly that *Australopithecus* lived not in the tropical rain forests that are the customary homes of the great apes but on the savannas, with the teeming herds of herbivores and the big cats and other carnivores that preyed upon them. Why they left their ancient forest home is not clear, but it appears that they began their stay in this new and inhospitable environment as vegetarians. Perhaps they eked out a living gathering seeds, an occupation that would have made use of and improved their digital coordination. Still, food was probably scarce, and the danger from big predators virtually constant.

Hunger and fear drove them to change. It may have begun modestly with digging for grubs and progressed gradually to scavenging. But these human ancestors developed a taste for meat, and, of equal importance, at some point they learned to use weapons. It could well have happened in the scavenging stage, possibly in defense of carcasses brought down by a larger predator. Gradually the little hominids realized that previously useless objects such as sticks or bones, taken up in a hand preshaped for grasping, could be thrown or wielded with deadly effect. From then on, they took the offensive. The hominids became hunters.

It was an amazing transition. Although the weapon may not have been the first tool, it did mark the hominid line's first great success with tools. Combined with *Australopithecus*'s unique posture and superior intelligence, weapons transformed the little ape-people into truly dangerous beings. Once they began hunting, our ancestors moved quite quickly to big game, prey much larger than themselves. In conjunction with the remains of *Australopithecus,* anthropologists have found numerous skulls fractured by blunt instruments, indicating that the hominids attacked and killed the now extinct giant baboon. They also numbered among their victims antelope, giant sivatheres (horned giraffes), elephantlike deinotheriums, and other large mammals. They became, in short, accomplished and voracious killers.

So voracious, in fact, that a number of researchers concluded that Australopithecus and their hominid descendants employed violence with nearly equal ardor against each other. M.K. Roper, for example, analyzed the remains of 169 pre–*Homo sapiens* and concluded that one out of three in the sample had suffered injuries from armed aggression. Raymond Dart, the earliest discoverer of *Australopithecus* remains, went even further, calling our predecessors "confirmed killers." Dart maintained that "the loathsome cruelty of mankind to man forms one of his inescapable, characteristic and differentiative features; it is explicable only in terms of his carnivorous and cannibalistic origin. . . ."

Significantly, this vision of human nature was passed to a brilliantly persuasive writer, Robert Ardrey, who, while on assignment in Africa, met Dart and was mesmerized by his version of the emergence of humans. The result was a series of compelling books published in the 1960s and 1970s— *African Genesis, The Territorial Imperative*, and *The Social Contract*—which popularized the accomplishments of physical anthropology. They also, incidentally, established in the public mind Ardrey's theme that war was based on "a human instinct [territoriality] probably more compulsive than sex" and fueled by a genetic urge to "design and compete with our weapons as birds build distinctive nests."

Ardrey made some good points, but most experts agree that his case was entirely overstated. For one thing, the whole concept of innate territoriality among humans or prehumans falls apart when subjected to close scrutiny, and while there may be some reasons to suspect that weapons development could have a genetic component, that is little more than a possibility. There is an even more fundamental objection to this blood-soaked picture of our prehuman ancestors: The studies on which it is founded use very small samples of very old and incomplete evidence. One can easily read a good deal more into these data than can be logically supported by practical models of the hunting-and-gathering way of life. Certainly it is possible, even likely, that there was some lethal violence among hominids. The animal behaviorist Konrad Lorenz has theorized that since our progenitors were once not dependent upon killing for a living, the need for special inhibitory mechanisms against intramural bloodshed, present in a number of predators, was not anticipated in the ancestral gene pool. It follows that the introduction of armaments, with their death-dealing capacity, must have posed a great challenge to the primitive hominid social structure. Yet the survival of the strain from which humans evolved is prima facie evidence that they learned to keep the violence within acceptable limits.

Economic reality, if nothing else, must have set some limit on the duration and intensity of the bloodshed. The hunting-and-gathering way of life simply does not afford the long-term food surpluses necessary for extended military campaigns. Nomadic shifts in hunting grounds also precluded all but the simplest, most easily portable material goods, removing one major motive for armed aggression. Furthermore, the population density of prehumans was very low, hence contact between bands was probably limited and could be quickly broken off in case of hostilities. Unlike today's hunter-gatherers locked in perpetual feuds with neighbors, early humans always had someplace else to go.

Even when fight rather than flight was the choice, it is logical to assume (for the economic reasons cited above) that the violence was analogous to the sporadic forays observed by contemporary ethnographers. Probably as weapons were improved—slowly during the Lower and Middle Pleistocene (from 1 million to 35,000 years ago) and then more rapidly in the Upper Paleolithic (35,000 to 10,000 years ago)—the deadliness of interpersonal combat did increase. But there is no reason to assume that it changed qualitatively or in terms of motivation, for it was hunting, not fighting, that drove improvements in weaponry.

Most important was the introduction of the bow. Deadly against game as large as antelope, the bow was also well suited to the hunter-gatherer's brand of fighting. At once safe and lethal, it was the ideal weapon of harassment. A combatant might spend an afternoon shooting away at long range with little fear of injury. Yet if the opportunity presented itself, he could move in for a swift, silent kill. Therefore it comes as no surprise that the earliest surviving image of combat, a Mesolithic cave painting at Morella la Vella in Spain, depicts men fighting with bows. The picture seems familiar, for it is difficult to see the action as anything but confused and fleeting. The participants appear to be on the run, perhaps hoping to rip off a few quick shots before retreating. Indeed, the scene captures in a single visual metaphor the essence of primitive combat. But is this warfare?

Some would have it so. The military historian Arther Ferrill, for example, sees evidence of disciplined fighting forces attempting a double envelopment (a tactic that uses a weak center to lure an opponent into a trap between two strong wings) in the Morella la Vella cave painting. Once again this seems to read more into the data than can really be supported. Even more fundamental is the problem of definition: What is being called "warfare"? In large part physical anthropologists have adopted the very broad use of the term favored by ethnographers. Thus fighting of the sort seen among hunter-gatherers is usually referred to as war, although it is clearly more akin to the random violence that takes place within a number of species, particularly higher mammals. With the exception of weapons use, the lethal violence between rival champanzee groups observed by Jane Goodall bears a remarkable resemblance to the fighting of contemporary hunter-gatherers and, presumably, early humans.

Ants, on the other hand, exemplify the kind of warfare that has been the driving force of our own political history and now poses such a challenge to our survival. The Amazon ants described earlier were not incited randomly by their passions; they were highly organized, in a genetic sense political, and their motives were economic (the acquisition of slaves). All of this requires a complex and stratified social structure, which ants have had for millions of years and which humans have achieved recently. The critical difference is that ants evolved these things genetically, whereas humans clearly learned them. War is a case in point.

For the most part scholars oriented toward political and historical studies have been more attuned to the differences between fighting and warfare; their own professional interests are often the very things that lead them to differentiate between the two. For example, forty-five years ago Quincy Wright, although imprecise in his terminology—calling everything from animal and primitive human aggression to imperial aggrandizement "warfare"—was able to see clearly what separated fighting from true war and warned his readers not to carry analogies between them too far. Although historians lacked, until recently, a clear idea of the role of weapons and hunting in early human development, a number of them have correctly and consistently identified the organizational requirements for true warfare, even if they remained somewhat fuzzy as to its motivational basis.

How then did it actually start? The scholarly mainstream dates the inception of true war among humans to somewhere between 7,000 and 9,000 years ago, not as an aberration of the human psyche (as followers of Freud and Jung, such as Sue Mansfield, suggest) but as the culmination of a revolutionary change in economic and social life. Prior to this major transition, humans had been peripatetic beings, going where the game went. However, as early as 20,000 years ago, for reasons that are as yet unclear, scattered groups of humans began settling down and intensifying their efforts at foraging. Shelter and personal possessions no longer had to be portable but could become more substantial and elaborate. Food was stored, and there is evidence of social differentiation.

Several such complex foraging communities have been unearthed from this very early period; they seem to have evolved, collapsed, and disappeared. The primary food they were storing was still meat, which spoils easily, and it seems these societies simply could not perpetuate themselves on this resource base. It is also possible that violence, intramural or from the outside, played a role in their extinction, for the bases of societal conflict—property and politics—were in place in a primitive form.

Somewhat later, groups that had never stopped depending on big game for sustenance began to make the transition from hunting to herding. Though they continued to move as nomads, they now controlled the movement of their food supply, not vice versa. Control, moreover, implied ownership. Thus, flocks were transformed into property to be protected.

True war, however, probably required a more robust economic engine than either early settlement or pastoralism could supply. Agriculture provided it. The roots of agriculture appear to go back 13,000 or 14,000 years, to a few Middle Eastern cultures based on the harvesting of abundant wild grains that could be stored for long periods. Gradually, over the next 3,000 or 4,000 years, the deliberate practice of planting and cultivating grains took hold, and as agricultural techniques improved, fertile, well-watered land began to produce regular and substantial surpluses. By degrees, a nexus of property grew up around the agricultural communities. Wealth accumulated, and it fueled the growth not only of a much more complex social structure but of covetousness and the will to power.

War may well have begun, as Jacob Bronowski suggests, when nomads, having learned to steal from one another's flocks, swept down on the farmers to take their surpluses—a major theme of aggression until at least the time of Genghis Khan. It was the response of the farmers, however, that would provide the major substance for our warlike past. As farmers learned to defend themselves, it became apparent that the more bountiful agrarian economic system imparted certain advantages in terms of resources and time available for martial activities. These could be turned against fellow plant growers to obtain land, women, possessions, and even political dominion.

Archaeologically, these changes are reflected in two ways: the appearance of such weapons as the mace and later the battle-ax, clearly specialized for combat, not hunting; and the introduction of massive walls encircling centers of population. In the latter case, the discovery and subsequent excavation of the fabled walls of Jericho in the mid-1950s revealed that such fortifications were a good deal older (c. 7000 B.C.) and more advanced than anyone had suspected. Moreover, their size (up to twenty-seven feet tall) and sophistication implied the capacity to engineer an equally potent means of attack.

Nor was Jericho unique. Its very early, elaborate fortifications were clearly a reaction to the danger that would later be posed to city dwellers generally by calculated aggression from the outside. Thus around 6300 B.C. the rich and remarkable settlement of Çatal Hüyük, in what is now Turkey, employed the interconnected outer walls of its individual structures to produce what is generally regarded as a continuous defensive front. At Hacilar and Mersin, also sites in Turkey dating to the seventh and sixth millennia B.C., this arrangement was supplemented by a strong, separate encircling wall. As time went on, virtually every population center became a Jericho, outer walls and towers being at once the preservers and the price of civilization.

Once plant growers realized the possibilities for gain inherent in organized, premeditated, and economically purposeful aggression, they had only to look to themselves to find the means to create effective fighting forces. The behaviorial basis of soldiering had already been established, perhaps less by man's previous experience with intraspecific combat, which after all was largely individualized, than by the lessons in cooperative mass killing that he had learned as a hunter. As much as anything, hunting had prepared man for war. The two main styles of war until the advent of the gun—close-in combat, exemplified by the phalanx; and long-range combat, conducted by military archery—both had their roots in the Pleistocene chase, the former in the hand-to-tusk spearing of big game and the latter in the shooting of small animals from a distance. Further, it seems likely that the stealth and cooperation required to kill animals efficiently was later reflected in the tactics and leadership that would usually spell the difference between victory and defeat in war. It was the cool ruthlessness of the hunt that would help make armies such effective killing instruments, allowing men to commit acts of mass butchery unprecedented except for the slaughter of antelope run off a cliff.

Whether one accepts or rejects Karl Wittfogel's thesis that the organization of agriculture and irrigation provided the model for military command, it is clear that disciplined, hierarchical fighting forces, once developed, were not only ideal means of aggression but imposing instruments of social control.

So man's first political agenda was set; he became an imperial ape and a soldier, a conqueror and an organizer. And this, it would seem, is how and why war was born.

Yet we should not forget that man was required to learn his new roles; he was not born into them. It was social innovation, not evolution, that drove the process. War is and always was a cultural phenomenon among humans. What we learned to do, we can choose to stop doing. We may not so choose, but it *is* possible. Our fate is in our own hands. Technology, particularly nuclear technology, has rendered war, man's most powerful social institution, obsolete. If we recognize this in time, we will probably remain alive to watch as the ants carry on the tradition. For they have no choice.

Amazons

by ADRIENNE MAYOR
and JOSIAH OBER

The ancient Athenians were convinced that Amazons had once laid siege to the Acropolis. Hitler had nightmares about them. California was named after one. What explains our perpetual fascination with the idea of women warriors? What does the Amazon myth say about the ancient Greeks? As the authors write, the kind of "alternate universe" of the Amazons, with its elaborate details about their conquests and way of life, "offers us a strongly distorted mirror image of actual Greek military society." That alternate universe also reveals some of the tensions within Greek culture. All that may be true, but a question remains: Does the Amazon legend have any foundation in reality? (The notion of Amazon single-breastedness doesn't—it originates, the authors say, in an etymological misreading.) Adrienne Mayor is a folklorist and Josiah Ober is a professor of classics at Princeton University. He is coauthor, with Barry S. Strauss, of *The Anatomy of Error: Ancient Military Disasters and Their Lessons for Modern Strategists* (St. Martin's Press).

Amazonomachy is a Greek word meaning combat between male and female warriors. In literature such scenes always take place far from the here and now: either "once upon a time" in the mythic past or beyond the bounds of civilization. Amazonomachies are common in modern pulp fiction; they usually go something like this:

> She shouted with glee, leaping into the fray. Panic and confusion seized the men. . . . She darted about, wielding her dagger with deadly effect. Three men fell in the first minutes. . . . She was tall, slender, yet formed like a goddess: at once lithe and voluptuous. Her only garment was a broad silken girdle, a quiver at her back. Her whole figure reflected an unusual strength. Her strong limbs and the ivory globes of her breasts drove a beat of fierce

passion through the Cimmerian's pulse, even in the panting fury of battle. ... Bright metal whirled ... parried ... flashed ... slashed ... plunged and ripped ... through leather, flesh, and bone. ... Her companions advanced, weapons crimson to the hilt—the warriors froze in fear. In the tempest of blood and iron, an arrow-storm whizzed through the air. . . . The plain became a scarlet morass. . . .

Such imagery is typically associated with modern fantasy fiction, but it would be familiar to a much earlier audience. The Greek hoplites would recognize in these passages their supposed archenemies, the original women warriors—the Amazons. In Greek legend and in modern adventure tales alike, the Amazon dwells at the distant frontier—at the edges of geography or time. Whether in the glorious past of Greek myth or the lurid pages of pulp fiction, the life-and-death struggle between the fierce woman warrior and a valiant male is fraught with suspense. And whether it is Conan the Barbarian and Red Sonya of the Hyborian Age or Achilles and Penthesilea on the plains of Troy, we know that the encounter will end in death or love—sometimes both.

The word *Amazon* is often used today, either negatively or positively, to describe a physically or willfully strong woman. Most people know that the Amazon story goes back to ancient Greek myth, and many have heard that the name comes from the "fact" that they cut off one breast in order to shoot arrows more efficiently. This "fact" is actually based on a false etymology (taking *a-mazon* to mean "without breast"). No ancient artist ever depicted this sort of self-mutilation. The Greek word probably really meant "those who were not breast-fed," a definition supported by ancient stories that the women warriors fed their babies mare's milk.

What explains our perpetual fascination with images and stories of war-making women? The female warrior narrative seems especially compelling for cultures in which men pride themselves on military prowess and attribute weakness to women and foreigners. Ancient Greece was just such a culture: It was the war-loving Greeks of the sixth to fourth centuries B.C. who, in art and literature, gave the image of the Amazon its enduring form.

The classical Greek Amazon legends were detailed and complex; taken as a whole they created a kind of "alternate universe." The writers of Greek legend recorded dozens of names of individual Amazons and speculated on their feats of arms, motives, sex lives, and methods of raising children and making war. Greek writers and artists described Amazon weapons, clothing, military training, and battle tactics and charted the topography of their conquests. The Amazon offers us a strangely distorted mirror image of actual Greek military society: In Amazonia, warriors were women instead of men; they used arrows instead of spears, cavalry instead of infantry. The reversal of Greek norms reveals some of the tensions within Greek culture—a warlike, xenophobic culture that has remained vital in Western tradition, yet never resolved questions of its own identity. Who were these female, barbarian alter egos that the Greeks created as dream opponents for their own ancestors?

For the early Greeks—before Herodotus invented history in the mid-fifth century—there was no formal distinction between myth and history. But such a distinction is obviously crucial for modern readers. We can learn much about Hellenic warrior culture by looking at legends, but we keep wondering, "Could this really have happened? Were Amazons *real?*"

The earliest mention of Amazons in Greek literature occurs in Homer's *Iliad,* written down in the eighth century B.C. But the myth is far older than that, going back to the Greek dark ages (c. 1100–750 B.C.) and perhaps even to the Bronze Age (c. 1600–1100 B.C.). Homer referred to ancient legends about Amazon strongholds in Lycia and Phrygia, and noted that the Amazon queen Myrina, renowned for the speed of her chariots, was buried on the Trojan plain.

Amazonomachy was depicted in Greek art as early as the seventh century B.C., and the image of heroes combating armed women became very popular in the Golden Age. Herodotus detailed the life-style of Amazons in the fifth century B.C. According to him, they were a bellicose and barbaric tribe of horsewomen who inhabited the wilderness beyond the known world. Various legends placed them in North Africa or, more plausibly, on the Steppes of south Russia. Yet as the known world expanded, the territory of the warrior women receded, always just out of reach.

Their legendary arms and armor were just as exotic as the locales they inhabited. Some Amazons killed giant pythons and fashioned the tough snakeskins into body armor. They wielded bows, javelins, and battle-axes with terrible efficiency. All Amazons disdained the domestic chores performed by Greek women; instead, like Greek men, they gloried in sexual pleasure, hunting, and fighting.

The Greeks imagined the Amazons as warriors who, like male hoplites, regarded personal bravery, loyalty to fellow soldiers, and battle prowess as paramount virtues. Yet the Amazons were very different from hoplites in their way of fighting: Instead of phalanxes of heavy-armored infantrymen who marched and fought in close ranks with interlocked shields and thrusting spears on the open plains, the Amazons relied on light armor, ambush, lightning cavalry raids, and arrows that could kill from afar. Although the Greeks considered the bow the weapon of cowards, they were terrified of arrows that rained death on vulnerable hoplite ranks. For the Greeks, the barbarian Amazons were the perfect "other": In their love of war, they were the opposite of Greek women; and in their practice of war, they were the opposite of Greek men.

By the first century *B.C.,* the legend of the fighting women had amassed many more details. According to the Greek historian Diodorus of Sicily, who wrote a "history of the world," the original Amazon homeland was Libya. Their land was rich in fruit and game, so they were free to eschew agriculture and concentrate on warfare. Diodorus points to a key factor in the Greek legends: the blatantly imperialistic character of the women warriors. According to him, the warrior queen Myrina began the process of empire building: Her armies of women defeated the neighboring cities and the nomad tribes of

North Africa, and she founded an imperial capital at Chersonesus.

Queen Myrina's forces emphasized light cavalry—the army consisted of 30,000 horsewomen and 3,000 infantrywomen, all of them armed with bows and swords. Enemies in pursuit discovered that Amazon arrows were deadly even in retreat; the women (like the real-world Parthians of Iran) were such skilled riders and archers that even at a gallop they were able to turn in the saddle and aim their bows.

Eventually, Myrina and her army invaded the "most civilized nation west of the Nile," Atlantis, the legendary island utopia so admired by Plato and other Greek philosophers. The bloodthirsty women soon overran the Atlantean capital, Cerne, slaughtering every man and capturing the women and children. Having destroyed the city, Myrina allowed the rest of the Atlantean men to surrender. As a good empire builder, the queen consolidated her conquest and established a new city on the site of Cerne, settling there all the Atlantean captives and "anyone else desirous of living there."

Since they were now part of the Amazonian empire, the defeated Atlanteans were entitled to protection from their traditional enemies. Myrina launched a preemptive strike on the neighboring tribe of hostile Gorgons. In a spectacular battle, the Amazons cut down countless Gorgon warriors and took 3,000 prisoners. But at the victory feast, the Amazon guards were lax. Long after nightfall, the prisoners managed to snatch up swords and signal to companions who had been routed earlier that day and were still hiding in the wooded hills. At a sign from the prisoners, the Gorgon troops descended from the hills and massacred the sleeping Amazons.

Myrina and some followers escaped. She now headed east, and somehow gathered a huge new army of women. At this point the story moves from the mythic landscape of Atlantis into the real geography of eastern North Africa. When she arrived at the border of Egypt, the most powerful state of North Africa, the pharaoh allowed her army safe passage through his lands to Arabia—which the Amazons conquered.

The women then steamrolled through Syria to Asia Minor, subduing the countryside and founding great cities: Myrina, Cyme, Pitane, and Priene (each named for an Amazon commander), Cyrene, Gryneion, Smyrna, Anaea, Thebe, Sinope, Pygela—most, incidentally, real cities with complex and often contradictory foundation legends. At Ephesus, another Amazon city, warrior women built a magnificent temple to Artemis, goddess of the hunt. Later this temple would be regarded as one of the Seven Wonders of the World. At Ephesus the women performed their war dances, rattling their shields and quivers, beating the ground to the music of pipes.

Meanwhile, Amazon sailors were winning important Aegean islands for the great empire. Myrina's sister Mytilene was a leader in the naval campaigns: The fine harbor town of Mytilene, on Lesbos, was named for her. The red earth of the island of Samos was explained by ancient tourist guides as the blood-soaked site of a great battle between the forces of the god Dionysus and the Amazons.

Like all ancient navies, the Amazon fleet had as much to fear from foul weather as from enemy ships. During Myrina's sea campaigns, a sudden storm blew the women's ships north. The Amazon navy managed to land safely on the island of Samothrace, where Myrina built altars to Artemis and offered splendid sacrifices in gratitude. But her imperial ambitions now led her to invade mainland Thrace. The Thracian king called on his allies, the Scythians from the Black Sea region, and a pitched battle commenced. Diodorus notes that "it was a fair fight, and Myrina was killed." The Amazons continued to wage a vigorous Thracian campaign but suffered a series of decisive setbacks. They eventually withdrew to their strongholds in Asia and North Africa.

Other Greek traditions, perhaps closer to reality, maintained that the original Amazons lived in south Russia, beyond the Scythians, a real tribe of archers who fought on horseback. According to Herodotus, the Scythians knew the warrior women as *Oiorpata* (Mankillers). These Russian Amazons were just as aggressive as their Libyan sisters. Led by Queen Lysippa, they swept down from the river Don, surging south around the Black Sea, defeating every tribe they met. With her spoils, Lysippa erected temples to Ares, god of war, and to Artemis. Her people eventually settled along the southern coast of the Black Sea, forming three independent tribes. This pattern of a great unitary empire splitting into three successor states parallels the fate of the very real empire founded by Alexander the Great.

The Black Sea Amazons were highly innovative in military technology: The legend claims that they were the first people to forge iron weapons and the first to use war-horses. They fought with bows, javelins, and battle-axes, using half-moon Thracian-style shields covered with hide; horses carried quivers full of arrows. Unlike the python-armored women of North Africa, they wore fur tunics, with knitted wool sleeves and leggings in wild geometric designs, leather helmets, studded belts, and high boots.

Like Myrina, Queen Lysippa died on the battlefield after an illustrious career of war, conquest, and empire. Her three Amazon tribes were then led by the warrior queens Marpesia, Lampado, and Hippo, who expanded Amazonian culture west to the borders of Thrace and to Phrygia, even capturing the great city of Troy when the Trojan king Priam was a boy. Jason and the Argonauts were careful to avoid Amazon territory on their expedition to obtain the Golden Fleece. As they sailed past the Amazon port of Themiscyra on the Black Sea, the Argonauts could see the women arming for battle: These "brutal and aggressive girls were in love with fighting."

The burgeoning Amazon empire and the fame of the women's war exploits cried out for a counterattack led by heroic men. When Hercules set out on his Ninth Labor, the ostensible reason was to capture the golden "belt of Ares" worn by Hippolyta, the reigning Amazon champion. But the expedition, which included a band of virile Greek heroes, was clearly an excuse to quench Amazon power, now in the hands of Queens Hippolyta, Antiope, and Melanippa.

Hippolyta herself rode out to meet the adventurers when they landed at Themiscyra. Some say the queen was attracted by Hercules' muscles and reputation, and that she offered him the belt as a love gift, but the rumor

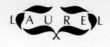

DON'T MISS . . .

insects, they too thrashed about helplessly, baring their throats to the victors. All were similarly dispatched as Hannibal gave free rein to his men to execute the wounded while they scavenged and rummaged among the dead. The August sun, remember, made it necessary to act quickly if the bloating bodies were to be stripped and collected for burial.

Thousands of Romans fled or were taken prisoner—nearly all of them horsemen, light-armed skirmishers, and some infantry who escaped the encirclement. The struggle, of course, did not end here—it raged on and off for another fourteen years. Finally, young Scipio and the orphans of the Trebia, Trasimene, and Cannae brought the war home to Africa and caught Hannibal's infantry in a ring of their own at Zama (202 B.C.), mercilessly butchering 20,000 Carthaginians in the process and ending for good Hannibal Barca's ideas of conquest.

The Masada Myth

by NEIL ASHER SILBERMAN

Scholars and archaeologists are reexamining Israel's most powerful political metaphor. Nobody doubts the spectacular evidence of siege and slaughter on the rocky heights of Masada; the giant ramp that the Romans built in A.D. 74 has become a permanent part of that barren desert landscape. But the grim arithmetic of the famous mass suicide by Jewish Zealots doesn't add up, and there is now a real question as to whether it ever happened. Was the story the product of the creative imagination of an ancient Jewish historian? What really took place when the Romans stormed the plateau stronghold? "A people often chooses their past," Neil Asher Silberman says, "by the way they see their present." Silberman's controversial article is adapted from his recent book, *Between Past and Present* (Henry Holt), an explanation of the uses politics has made of archaeology in the Middle East.

Although almost twenty-five years have passed since the end of Israel's most ambitious archaeological undertaking, the name of the site where it took place—Masada—still exerts romantic appeal. For many Israelis and visitors to Israel, that isolated, flat-topped rock in the Judaean Desert remains the most visible symbol of the power and significance of modern archaeology.

Excavations there from 1963 to 1965 revealed the magnificent fortress-palace of King Herod the Great of Judaea (37–4 B.C.) and evidence of the later, tragically unsuccessful attempt by Jewish rebels at the end of their Great Revolt against Rome to prevent Masada's capture by the Romans in A.D. 74. For modern Israelis, deeply concerned with issues of sovereignty and independence, the findings at Masada offer a tangible link between the present and the past. That Jews returned after nearly 2,000 years of exile to reveal the splendor and the tragedy of an earlier national existence at that remote mountain in the Judaean Desert has made Masada a powerful political metaphor. Yet in focusing almost entirely on the defenders, the modern archaeological explorers of Masada may have overlooked its true historical significance—as the scene of a brutal, efficient, and cruelly successful exercise in the techniques of Roman siege warfare.

In the years since the end of the excavations, Masada has become one of Israel's most popular tourist attractions. Easily accessible from Jerusalem by a scenic highway that winds along the western shore of the Dead Sea, it is maintained by the Israel National Parks Authority as a historical monument, and the visitors' complex at the foot of the mountain now includes a youth hostel, a museum, a cafeteria, and a row of the inevitable souvenir shops. Sightseeing buses, rented cars, and vans fill the parking lots at the foot of the mountain on almost any day of the year. Cable cars carry people to the summit, although the hardiest visitors and student groups can make the difficult climb up Masada's steep eastern slope on foot.

Guides at the summit continue to tell the story of Masada's ancient rise and fall in much the same way it was presented to the public at the time of the excavations, even though on an archaeological level some of the original evidence has since been questioned or reinterpreted. Now doubt has been cast on the central event of the Masada story, the mass suicide of the Jewish Zealots. Did 960 defenders submit willingly to executioners chosen from their own number by lot, preferring death to surrender?

Yet it may be that historical facts are only a small part of Masada's mystique. Masada's story remains such a meaningful parable for the modern, besieged state of Israel that it seems to have a life of its own. It may even be that the discovery, preservation, and presentation of the mountain's archaeological remains can reveal as much about modern as about ancient Israeli history.

There's no question that Masada was an archaeological achievement. From a purely logistic standpoint, the excavations were a triumph of organization and determination over the most difficult natural conditions. Masada is a remote and isolated plateau, cut off by precipitous ravines from the towering limestone cliffs that line the western shore of the Dead Sea. The excavations were undertaken on the mountain's summit and steep slopes, hundreds of feet above the surrounding terrain. What's more, the climate of this region is brutal and sometimes violent: dry and extremely hot in summer; subject to high winds and flash floods in winter. Yet beyond the physical obstacles lay the legend, for the same factors that made Masada's modern excavation so difficult also made its reputation as an impregnable fortress unparalleled in antiquity.

Physical difficulties did not deter the dig's director, the late Professor Yigael Yadin. As a former chief of the general staff of the Israel Defense Forces, he saw Masada as both an archaeological and a national challenge, and by gaining financial support and publicity from private and public institutions both in Israel and abroad, he was able to marshal enough public interest to see that the challenge was met. With the support of the Israeli army to clear a campsite at the foot of the mountain, and with the assistance of engineers from the National Water Authority to pipe drinking water to the site, Yadin and his staff supervised the work of hundreds of volunteers from twenty-eight countries through two digging seasons stretching over one and a half years. Due to their efforts and the discoveries they made, Masada became the most famous project in the history of Israeli archaeology and—perhaps second only to the tomb of Tutankhamen—the most publicized excavation in the twentieth century.

Beyond the natural setting and the enthusiasm of the volunteers, there was, of course, the ancient story of Masada that set it apart from most other archaeological digs. Few other sites in Israel—or for that matter in the entire eastern Mediterranean—could boast such a colorful cast of characters or such a spectacular closing scene. According to the first-century Jewish historian Josephus Flavius, whose writings are the main source of our knowledge about Masada's history, this mountain was chosen by the Roman client-king Herod as a secure place of refuge in case of either popular uprising or dynastic intrigue. Herod had ample reason to fear for his safety, for many Judaeans considered him a usurper. With Roman help, he had snatched the throne of Judaea from the local Hasmonaean, or Maccabean, dynasty.

Building on the foundations of a small outpost established in the first century B.C. by his Hasmonaean predecessors, King Herod spared no expense in the construction of a desert pleasure palace and secure asylum, a Judaean Xanadu. His court architects, engineers, and master builders—not to mention a huge force of laborers—transformed the remote mountain in the wilderness into a luxurious, self-supporting residence for the king. Josephus showed obvious admiration for this massive construction project in his detailed description of the lavish reception rooms, bathhouses, colonnades, and living quarters—as well as vast storerooms and giant water cisterns—that permitted Herod and his royal entourage to live elegantly and securely in otherwise impossible terrain.

Yet the focus of Josephus's description of Masada was not the opulence of Herod's palace but the role that the desert fortress played in the great Jewish revolt against the Romans between A.D. 66 and 74. That revolt against the world's mightiest empire was to be a turning point in Jewish history, and Josephus was himself a major participant. His writings tell how, after the death of Herod and the brief, incompetent rule of his immediate successors, Judaea was transferred to the direct rule of Roman governors; and during the decades that followed, how economic, social, and religious tensions between various strata of Judaean society and the Roman administration finally built to the breaking point.

The explosion came in the autumn of A.D. 66, sparked by an anti-Jewish riot at the administrative capital of Caesarea on the Mediterranean coast. Word of the killing of Jews by Caesarea's pagan, pro-Roman population spread quickly to Jerusalem, which was crowded with Jewish pilgrims for the Feast of the Tabernacles. The religious rites at the Temple soon served as a focus of nationalistic fervor and resistance to foreign rule. The small Roman garrison at Jerusalem was overpowered, and radical priests ordered that the daily sacrifices at the Temple in honor of the emperor Nero be halted immediately as a sign of open revolt.

The Roman governor of the province of Syria, Cestius Gallus, quickly marched southward to Jerusalem with reinforcements to put down the rebellion, but his threatening advance unexpectedly turned into a rout. After destroying a number of Jewish villages in the surrounding districts, he met stiff resistance within the walls of Jerusalem. The rebels successfully fought off the Roman forces, and when Gallus ordered his troops to retreat, they were ambushed by Jewish guerrilla forces and suffered humiliatingly heavy casualties.

With the withdrawal of Roman forces from Judaea, the leadership of the rebellion—drawn increasingly from the lower classes of Judaean society, who had suffered most from the abuses of both the Romans and the local Judaean aristocracy—attempted to prepare for the inevitable Roman counterattack. Even some of the country's aristocrats joined the rebellion now that events had made a military confrontation with Rome inevitable. Josephus, the son of a wealthy Jerusalem family of priestly descent, was one of these uncomfortable, aristocratic rebels. Although he had not received any formal military training, he was dispatched by the rebel leadership in Jerusalem to strengthen the defenses of Galilee.

No amount of preparation or hurried fortification, however, could repel the coming Roman attack. Judaea, lying on vital routes of land and sea communication in the eastern Mediterranean—and dangerously close to the Roman Empire's eastern frontier with the Parthians—could not be allowed to proclaim its independence. So in the spring of A.D. 67, Nero appointed a seasoned commander who had participated in the subjugation of Britain—Flavius Vespasianus—to bring the Jewish revolt to a quick and brutal end.

Vespasian, at the head of three legions and auxiliary forces (amounting to approximately 60,000 troops), landed on the northern coast and began a methodical campaign of reconquest. Josephus, the rebel commander of Galilee, was the first to face the full power of the Roman army. After a forty-seven-day siege of the Galilean city of Jotapata, he surrendered to the Romans (rather than take his own life, as many of his rebel colleagues suggested) and became Vespasian's local interpreter, adviser, and confidant.

Galilee fell quickly, and Vespasian moved southward to Judaea, the heartland of the Jewish revolt. Unfortunately for the Romans, however, political intrigue at the highest levels of the empire diverted attention from strictly military operations. In A.D. 68 Nero was ousted, to be replaced on the throne by a quick succession of provincial military commanders: Galba, Otho, Vitellius—and finally Vespasian himself. Departing Judaea to become emperor, Vespasian left his son Titus with the task of conquering the Holy City of Jerusalem and putting an end to the Jewish revolt.

Josephus was an eyewitness to the destruction of Jerusalem—to the brutal siege tactics that first isolated and starved the local population and then to the bloodbath that accompanied the leveling of the ancient city and the destruction of the Temple in the summer of A.D. 70. Judaeans unlucky enough to fall into Roman hands were either massacred or condemned to slavery. Those who escaped began the painful process of reconstructing Jewish life and religion without a central temple and under the harsh military rule of the Roman occupation force. The Tenth Legion was now permanently stationed in Jerusalem, and with the departure of Titus, the subsequent governors of Judaea devoted their attention to tracking down and eliminating the few remaining rebel strongholds.

Masada was the last of these strongholds to be taken. In A.D. 66 a small group of Jewish rebels had captured it—and its precious arsenal of weapons—from the small Roman garrison that had been posted there since Herod's death. The rebels may have used the remote, self-sustaining fortress as a secure base of operations throughout the course of the revolt, and they continued to hold it for more than three years after Jerusalem and the Temple were destroyed. This undoubtedly caused the Romans some embarrassment, and by the autumn of 73, seven years after the start of the revolt, they decided to put an end to it.

The new Roman governor of Judaea, Flavius Silva, marched on Masada at the head of the Tenth Legion, the powerful force of veterans that had besieged and conquered Jerusalem. After establishing his field headquarters at the foot of Masada and making sure that his troops were properly provisioned, Silva ordered the construction of a siege wall around the entire mountain. Siege warfare had been a characteristic of Roman strategy in Judaea, but Silva had no intention of waiting patiently and starving the Masada rebels into submission. The mountain fortress was to be taken as soon as possible; the siege wall was to make sure that none of the defenders escaped.

With a slave force of captured Jewish rebels, Silva's engineers began constructing a massive earthen ramp up the western slope to provide a means of approach for the piece of equipment that would end the rebels' resistance: a 100-foot-high ironclad siege tower and battering ram. When the siege tower was finally rolled up the steep ramp toward Masada's fortifications, it seemed that the conquest of the fortress would be quick. Indeed, the huge battering ram made short work of the stone defensive wall built around the edge of the summit by Herod. But the Romans then discovered that the rebels had constructed a second defensive wall. Just inside the line of the old Herodian fortifications, they had laid down a double row of heavy timbers, between which they piled freshly dug earth. This pliable wall proved far more resistant to the battering ram, for repeated pounding of the wood and its earthen filling merely strengthened it.

But Flavius Silva would not be turned back so easily by this makeshift defensive stratagem. He ordered his troops manning the siege tower to hurl torches and shoot burning arrows at the timbers so the wooden wall would be set on fire. At first the flames and smoke blew into the faces of the Romans, but then—"as if by divine providence," Josephus notes in his account of the final stage of the battle—the wind suddenly shifted and the Zealots' last, hastily built line of fortifications was destroyed.

Confident now of triumph, the Roman forces reportedly returned to their camps for the evening, intending to administer the coup de grace at dawn the following day. Yet the defenders of Masada found a way to make the Roman victory a hollow one. In a stirring and now familiar passage,

Josephus vividly describes how the 960 men, women, and children holding out on Masada refused to die at the hands of the Romans—or, even worse, suffer the horrible fate of Roman captivity that had already befallen so many of their countrymen—preferring instead a mass suicide.

As reconstructed in Book VII of Josephus's *Jewish War,* the leader of the Masada rebels, Eleazar ben Ya'ir, assembled his comrades in Herod's once magnificent palace and convinced them that death was preferable to Roman slavery; God, he told them, had forsaken their cause and they must now pay for their hubris in declaring holy war on the mightiest power on earth. To reassure the more fainthearted that suicide was not really self-destruction, Ben Ya'ir gave an eloquent speech on the immortality of the soul. So, with the conviction that they were taking the only honorable course available to them, the Jewish defenders of Masada went off to slay their families. And when that was done, they gathered all their supplies and personal possessions together and set fire to the pile so the Romans would know that their own free choice—not starvation—had led them to take their own lives. The heads of families then chose ten men by a grim lottery to slay all the others, and by yet another fatal lottery the ten survivors chose one man to slay the other nine and himself.

The following morning, Josephus tells us, when the Romans stormed the fortress expecting fierce resistance, they encountered only the silence of death. Informed of what had happened by two women and five children who had hidden in an underground aqueduct, the Romans, says Josephus, did not gloat over their victory. But "encountering the mass of slain, instead of exulting as over enemies, they admired the nobility of their resolve and the contempt of death displayed by so many in carrying it, unwavering, into execution." So ended, according to Josephus, the last episode of the Great Revolt.

That was the dramatic story behind the Masada excavations—and the evidence that Yadin and his staff uncovered seemed to corroborate it to a degree that surpassed even the most optimistic expectations. Josephus's descriptions of the physical layout of Masada proved uncannily accurate. Beneath the rubble of collapsed walls at various places on Masada's summit, the excavators uncovered the reception rooms, bathhouses, and storerooms of the luxurious Herodian palaces, substantially as Josephus described them. The most elaborate structure, the northern palace—apparently unknown to Josephus—was built on three levels on the dizzying heights of Masada's sheer northern face. The arid climate had preserved the vivid frescoes and carved plaster that had decorated its various rooms. But even more meaningful to the members of the Yadin expedition were the many archaeological indications of the concluding chapter of the Great Revolt.

Throughout the Herodian palaces and administrative buildings, the excavators found evidence of a later, far less opulent occupation. Crude mud-and-stone walls partitioned the halls and large rooms of the royal residences into smaller, less elegant chambers. In many of these makeshift rooms, the team found clay ovens and collections of personal possessions that indicated occupancy by individual family groups. The most evocative evidence came from the dozens of small cells built into the Herodian casemate wall. Clearing the debris from the floors of these small chambers, the diggers found cooking vessels, combs, coins, baskets, and even scraps of wool fabric and leather sandals. "As we excavated these casemate rooms," Yadin later reported, "we found ourselves recapturing the daily lives of the Zealots, and we stood awed by the evidence of what had taken place in the final moments before their suicide."

Previous archaeological surveys of the surrounding area had already identified the remains of the six Roman siege camps at the foot of the mountain and the Roman siege ramp on the western slope. As early as the mid-nineteenth century, European and American explorers had noted that the ruins of the Roman siegeworks corresponded to Josephus's descriptions, and a series of aerial photos taken by the Royal Air Force in the 1920s provided scholars with incredibly detailed information on the remains of Flavius Silva's camp, the siege wall, the "engineers' yard" where the ironclad siege tower was assembled, and the still impressive siege ramp.

But it was Yadin's 1963–65 excavations on the summit itself that brought to light the ultimate effects of the Roman siege. There, throughout the rooms that the Zealots lived in, the excavators noted thick layers of ash, charred beams, and blackened stones—traces of an intense conflagration that marked the end of the squatter occupation. There was little question that those squatters were Jewish, as indicated by their construction of a synagogue and ritual baths and by their use of biblical scrolls, among them copies of Psalms and Leviticus. And there was no doubt that the destruction of their settlement had taken place at the end of the Great Revolt, as indicated by the catapult stones, Roman-period arrowheads, and coins found in the destruction debris. The latest of those coins bore a date in Hebrew characters equivalent to A.D. 70—the year in which the city and Temple of Jerusalem were destroyed.

Even more striking evidence came from the lower terrace of Herod's northern palace. Beneath the collapsed rubble of the Herodian colonnade, Yadin and his staff found the skeleton of a young man, surrounded by scales of armor and fragments of a prayer shawl, and the skeletons of a young child and a young woman, whose leather sandals and long plaited hair were perfectly preserved after 2,000 years in the arid desert. "There could be no doubt," Yadin later stated, "that what our eyes beheld were the remains of some of the defenders of Masada."

In a cave on the southern face of the mountain, another group of excavators came upon an even more grisly scene: a heap of twenty-five skeletons, jumbled with the remains of clothing and personal possessions. Later anthropological analysis at the Hebrew University Medical School indicated that these were probably not the remains of Roman soldiers or Byzantine monks, who were known to have later occupied the same area, but perhaps more of the Masada defenders. The skeletons in the cave were the remains of a surprisingly heterogeneous collection of people who met their deaths suddenly— men, women, and children ranging in age from eight to seventy, as well as the skeleton of an unborn child.

But the most dramatic discovery of all came during the clearance of debris near Masada's storerooms, where the volunteers discovered eleven unique *ostraca*—inscribed potsherds. Ostraca were relatively common finds at Masada, for it seems that the last occupants used them as coins or tokens for the efficient distribution of food and other supplies. But these ostraca were different. Instead of the usual letter or symbol, each of them bore a personal name. And since one of the names was Ben Ya'ir, the name of the commander of the defenders according to Josephus, Yadin and his staff felt sure they had found the lots cast by the last Jewish rebels at Masada at the time of their mass suicide.

In 1965 the Masada excavations finally came to an end. For scholars who had long speculated on the reliability of Josephus, the discoveries were truly astonishing in their quantity, state of preservation, and close correspondence to his account of the Masada siege. For the people of Israel, who had watched the difficult undertaking with fascination, Yadin's finds seemed nothing short of a national miracle.

On an archaeological level, however, the Masada story didn't end in 1965. Despite the emotional, almost religious, veneration that came to be associated with Masada in the years that followed Yadin's excavations, doubts began to arise in some scholarly circles about the significance of his finds. The famous ostraca, for instance, presented a numerical problem: The ones bearing personal names were eleven in number, not Josephus's explicitly stated ten. Perhaps, after all, these were more of the tokens commonly used for distributing supplies. The fact of the names could mean many things besides a lottery for suicide. And there were also some troubling questions with regard to the human remains. Josephus had reported that the mass suicide of all 960 defenders took place in Herod's palace, yet the excavators found only three of the skeletons there. As for the other twenty-five, found in the cave on the southern slope, although Yadin identified them as the remains of the rebels, there is some indication that he himself wasn't so sure. In an interview he gave to the *Jerusalem Post* nearly twenty years after the excavations, he admitted he couldn't even vouch for their being Jewish, since they had been found with the bones of pigs. Most likely they were, in fact, some of the defenders who were killed in battle with the Romans and tossed into a cave that the conquerors later used as a kitchen dump. But of planned suicide, there were no clear archaeological indications, save those that an imaginative faith in the literal truth of Josephus's account could provide.

This is not to say that much of Josephus's account wasn't accurate; regarding the dimensions and physical layout of the fortress, the excavations proved him substantially correct. But while the remains of the siegeworks and ramp also validated his account of the Roman conquest, his narrative of the grim decision taken by the defenders on the eve of their defeat still seemed open to dispute. Indeed, finding bodies in several places, scattered traces of burning, and small heaps of personal possessions all over the summit contradicted Josephus's account of unified action—of all the supplies piled together as an act of defiance toward the enemy, and of the palace set afire by the last survivor before he took his own life. These discrepancies eventually led one

American scholar, Shaye J.D. Cohen, to suggest a new interpretation of the evidence, based less on archaeology than on a reexamination of Josephus Flavius's personal motivations for composing his tale.

Cohen's credentials as a scholar of Josephus are impeccable. His book on the author's life and background, *Josephus in Galilee and Rome*, has become a standard in the field. In it, Cohen describes how Josephus, scion of a prominent Jerusalem family, was placed in charge of the defense of Galilee at the outbreak of the revolt against Rome in A.D. 66, and how he defected to the Roman side a year later when his troops were brutally defeated and it became clear to him that the rebel cause was doomed. Becoming the personal protégé of the emperor-to-be Vespasian, he adopted the family name of the Flavians, and after the war was over he was set to work in comfortable surroundings in Rome to write the definitive history of the Jewish revolt. His purpose was apparently not only to record the events but to demonstrate to the Roman reading public that the uprising in Judaea was not an expression of the entire Jewish people; that it was the misguided work of irresponsible troublemakers who called themselves Zealots and Sicarii (Knife-wielders), and it was the latter group who made their last stand at Masada.

The Sicarii adopted their name from their favorite means of political persuasion, and their reputation was anything but heroic in their own time. According to Josephus's testimony, they used assassination, arson, and theft to terrorize members of the Judaean populace who opposed the rebellion. After killing the Roman garrison and taking control of the fortress at Masada at the outbreak of the revolt, they continued their violent ways. They did not come to the aid of their rebel colleagues in Jerusalem when the city was under siege by the Tenth Legion, but preferred to remain at their desert hideaway, maintaining themselves by preying on the surrounding populace. During the festival of Passover in A.D. 68, for example, they raided the nearby settlement of Ein-Gedi, carrying off the inhabitants' crops and livestock. Their victims in this encounter were not the hated Romans but, according to Josephus, more than 700 innocent Jewish men, women, and children.

This criminal background is not what might be expected of national heroes, but Cohen explains why Josephus gave the story the dramatic ending so beloved of visitors to the site today. According to Cohen, the tale of the mass suicide served Josephus's polemical purpose: to have the Sicarii make a collective admission of guilt. The theme that Josephus wanted to make clear to his readers was that rebelling against Rome was a tragic mistake, and that the Sicarii, after coming to that realization, felt compelled to accept the verdict of history.

Of course, one might legitimately ask how Josephus could have known the precise text of Ben Ya'ir's speech if his only informants were the two women and five children who had been hiding in an underground aqueduct at the time. Or how, for that matter, he could have known the precise order of the casting of the lots and the killing of the families if all the participants in that grisly ritual had died. But all these components of Josephus's story are easily understandable, Cohen argues, when they are viewed in their proper literary context. He points out that far from being a unique event, the story of the collective suicide on Masada was only one example of what had become, by Josephus's time, a common—even hackneyed—literary motif.

In his article "Masada: Literary Tradition, Archaeological Remains, and the Credibility of Josephus," published in the 1982 volume of the *Journal of Jewish Studies*—a volume intended as a tribute to Professor Yadin—Cohen presented some highly persuasive literary evidence. To show the popularity of the suicide theme in antiquity, he assembled sixteen other incidents strikingly similar to the Masada story that were recorded by such prominent classical authors as Herodotus, Pliny, Appian, Plutarch, Xenophon, and Polybius. Spanning a period from the sixth to the first century B.C., these historians described how in desperate circumstances such diverse peoples as Lydians, Phocians, Taochians, Sidonians, Cappadocians, Isaurians, Spaniards, Greeks, Gauls, and Illyrians sacrificed their lives and their property rather than allow them to fall into the hands of their victorious enemies. Cohen examined the doubtful authenticity of several of his examples and pointed out that the "ancient historians regularly sacrificed 'historical truth' for the sake of art and effect."

For Josephus, basing his own history on such classical models, the use of this collective-suicide motif must have been an obvious way to end his account of the great Jewish revolt. The other stories, which may have served as his literary models, were always highly elaborated with gruesome details of death and dedication, and served to underline the heroism of the defenders, even if their cause was misguided or doomed. Therefore, after placing the blame for the Great Revolt on the irresponsible Sicarii, Josephus may have decided at least to endow them with a final act of collective heroism as an elegant and literarily acceptable climax.

One glaring inconsistency in the story seemed to Cohen the key to understanding what actually took place at the climax of the siege. Just as the final line of the Zealots' fortifications was destroyed in the conflagration, the Romans unexpectedly returned to their camps for the night. "Why withdraw when victory was so close?" Cohen asked. The answer, to his mind, was simple: They didn't—they pressed on and conquered the fortress immediately, killing every rebel they could find. It was Josephus the historian, taking literary license, who inserted the dramatic pause so the Masada defenders could discuss and decide on their fate.

The slaughter on Masada was undoubtedly horrifying. Few of the defenders could have escaped, and some of them may well have taken their own lives as *individuals*. Cohen sincerely doubted, however, that the speeches, the lottery, and the calculated killing of whole families ever took place. The real course of events was probably chaotically violent, with no time for romantic, impassioned speeches, much less for carefully premeditated mass suicide. As the Romans stormed the desert stronghold, after finally breaching its fortifications, they would most likely have vented their fury for the months of privation and isolation they had suffered, so far from their relatively comfortable headquarters. While a significant number of the Masada defenders may have been taken into brutal slavery, most were probably killed. The Roman infantry, with their short swords unsheathed for the final assault on this last remaining nest of Jewish rebels, would quickly have hacked to death any of the defenders who offered resistance. The bodies of those Sicarii already killed in battle—and of the few that may have committed suicide—were probably tossed over the steep sides of the mountain, together with the bodies of the fresh victims of the assault.

In sum, according to Cohen, the story of the mass suicide on Masada was the product of the creative imagination of a Jewish historian who sought to impress his educated audience with a chronicle written in an acceptable literary style. "Josephus needs no apology for these inventions and embellishments," Cohen noted, "since practically all historians of antiquity did such things." But seen in that light, the Masada story today takes on a new meaning, as a literary device, well known in the first century, that has perhaps been taken far too literally in modern times.

In 1968, three years after completion of the Masada excavations, the Israeli government reburied the twenty-eight skeletons found on the mountain with full military honors under headstones used for the fallen of the Israel Defense Forces in the recent Israeli-Arab wars. The summit of the mountain itself became the scene of an annual swearing-in ceremony for the new recruits of the Israeli tank corps, who vowed every year under the light of torches that "Masada shall not fall again." Stamps, coins, and posters were issued to commemorate the achievement of the excavations and their importance to modern Israeli society. Yigael Yadin, the director of the excavations, was well aware of the significance of this juxtaposition of the present and the past. "The echo of your oath this night," he proclaimed at one of the armored-division ceremonies at Masada, "will resound through the encampments of our foes! Its significance is not less powerful than all our armaments!"

Yadin's personal account of the Masada excavations quickly became a best-seller. The site of Masada was restored and opened to the public, a symbol of the rebirth of the modern nation and its connection to a heroic past. Yet in time, voices of criticism began to be heard, especially in the years after the 1967 war, when Israel was no longer seen so clearly as an underdog.

The initial uncritical acceptance of the Masada story began to give way to new interpretations, not all of them strictly archaeological. And in a 1971 article in *Newsweek* magazine, the American columnist Stewart Alsop used the term "Masada complex" to describe what he saw as Israel's emerging diplomatic inflexibility. Writing at a time of diplomatic and military deadlock between Egypt and Israel, Alsop called for a spirit of compromise, implying that under the dangerous conditions of the Middle East, the national acceptance of suicide rather than survival might become a tragically self-fulfilling prophecy. But by the early 1970s, Masada had gained almost mystical significance in the Israeli consciousness, and many Israelis did not take his observation as constructive criticism.

In 1973, on an official visit to Washington to celebrate the twenty-fifth year of Israel's existence, Prime Minister Golda Meir finally had her chance to confront Alsop directly. The matter of Masada came up unexpectedly during a lunch followed by questions and answers at the Washington Press Club. After responding to some routine reporters' questions, the prime minister of Israel turned toward Alsop and spoke her mind. "And you, Mr. Alsop," she said from the podium, "you say that we have a Masada complex. It is true. We do have a Masada complex. We have a pogrom complex. We have a Hitler complex." Alsop was temporarily silenced. To challenge the significance of the Masada story as revealed by the excavations was seen at the time as tantamount to challenging Israel's right and reason for national existence in the modern world.

Today, nearly twenty years after that encounter, and more than twenty-five years after the end of Yadin's excavations, the "Masada complex" is no longer mentioned so frequently, and at least for some scholars, the initial interpretations of the archaeological finds at Masada are no longer such persuasive proof of the historical accuracy of the mass-suicide story. But that is of little concern to the visitors who still flock to the site, for the symbol and slogan "Masada Shall Not Fall Again"—now mass-produced and offered for sale on sweatshirts, coffee mugs, and ashtrays in the souvenir stands at the foot of the rock—have a life of their own.

At the time of the excavations, Masada served to provide Israelis with a self-image of heroism and sacrifice when the country felt threatened by imminent attack. And although times have changed and Israel now faces different challenges, Masada's impressive position, its vista over the Dead Sea, and the well-practiced story all conspire to exert their effect. A people often chooses their past by the way they see their present, and in such cases scholarly doubts have little influence in undercutting the popularity of a dramatic story that once seemed so much in tune with its time. The tale of mass suicide on the remote mountain in the Judaean desert therefore continues to be both a complex historical problem and a clear manifestation of a modern state of mind.

The Ineffable Union of Horse and Man

by DAVID QUAMMEN

Touching, uncanny, and all but symbiotic, that relationship was the central fact of mounted warfare. "As many grains of barley as thou givest thy horse, so many sins shall be forgiven thee," said Muhammad, who was no mean judge of equestrian bonding, especially when it came to sending horsemen and their horses to battle. But, asks David Quammen, to what extent did the development of cavalry also depend on the saddle, the rein, the stirrup, and the long, heavy lance known as the sarissa? They were all important to varying degrees, but there remains something that defies explanation. What was it that allowed the Prussian regiments of Frederick the Great to sustain a charge over a mile of bad ground, taking the last 800 yards at a full gallop? Surely not discipline alone. What drove the riderless horses of the Light Brigade forward into the midst of the Russian artillery? Surely not just instinct. Quammen is a novelist and science essayist, and the recipient of the 1987 National Magazine Award in essays and criticism.

It's such a long, tangled story, spread out across centuries and continents, fogged by legend and romantic delusion, gaudy with anecdote, stinking of horse sweat and leather and adrenaline, impossibly rich in its cultural ramifications, that we might do best to begin at the end. On the evening of July 14, 1916, at the Somme, General Douglas Haig decided that he wanted a cavalry charge.

This was to be one of the last of its kind. Two squadrons each of the 20th Deccan Horse and the 7th Dragoon Guards were sent up across sloping ground, through wheat fields, toward a German infantry position in a copse known as High Wood. Also in place among those trees, although Haig didn't foresee it or didn't care, was a machine gun. "You know there's nothing like a lance against machine guns," a French infantry officer had said, mordantly pitying, as he watched some cavalry lancers forming up on another occasion two months earlier. Cavalry had been standing available on the western front for two years, but this charge at High Wood seems to have been the first time since the war settled into trenched lines that they were actually thrown forward. Now it happened: Up through the wheat they galloped, in all their Napoleonic flash and clatter; and as they came out of the fields, the German machine gun laid into them. Losses were heavy. In hindsight, a horse charge against machine guns seems amazingly lunkheaded, even for that war. Also amazing is that remnants of the 20th Deccan and the 7th Dragoon did succeed in taking a part of High Wood. They held it one night, futilely, before falling back.

Eight weeks later the first tank assaults began and the word *cavalry* entered its age of metaphor.

After three millennia of intimate partnership, warriors and horses had been separated. But a question remains: What was it that bound them together so efficaciously and so long?

Somewhere around eight or nine centuries before Christ, one group of nomadic horsemen from the grasslands of southwestern Asia, the Scythians, developed a useful device. It consisted of two cushions stuffed with animal hair and connected along one edge by straps. It could be draped over the back of a horse like a pair of tea bags and sat on, so that the rider's weight rested over the mount's dorsal muscles and ribs rather than chafing against the spine. It mitigated discomfort for both horse and man, and therefore increased the range of travel. Today we would call it—but only barely—a saddle.

Some physical evidence of the early saddle comes from the remarkable frozen graves uncovered at Pazyryk in western Mongolia by the Soviet archaeologist S.I. Rudenko sixty years ago. This complex of burials by some tribe of equestrian nomads had been locked in a matrix of icy ground, and therefore nicely preserved, for more than two millennia. Among other odd treasures, Rudenko and his team found sixty-nine horses, evidently sacrificed and interred as part of a funerary rite. They were so well preserved—skin, flesh, and organs—that the excavators could tell stallion from gelding, and analysis of stomach contents showed signs of grain feeding. Two styles of saddle were also found. One was the simple saddle of the Scythians, a pair of stuffed cushions connected by straps. The fancier version included a padded wooden frame, hinting incipiently at pommel and cantle.

To the history of mounted warfare, this device brought convenience but not revolution. Men had been riding horses for hundreds of years by then, even fighting from horseback, without any gewgaw to mediate the intimacy of their seat. And for hundreds more years after these burials at Pazyryk, some of the proudest of the world's mounted armies carried on without saddles.

The Assyrians, for instance, had regular cavalry archers back in 850 B.C. The Hittites, the Israelites under Solomon, and the Chorasmian people of central Asia had all put part of their armies on horseback, also armed with bows, by roughly the same period. The devilish flexibility of these mounted warriors—their ability to advance and reverse quickly, whirl and maneuver amid the chaos of a battle, fire an arrow or two and then dash safely away—was what had made war chariots obsolete. By 750 B.C., as shown in a bas-relief from the reign of Tiglath-pileser III, the Assyrians even had lance-carrying cavalry armored in shirts of mail. Except for the Scythians, though, it seems that none of them bothered with true saddles. That same bas-relief clearly shows an Assyrian lancer riding bareback. His horse wears bridle and bit and decorative tassels, but not so much as a pad over the midsection. The reins lie ignored on the horse's neck; and the rider, busy aiming his lance, seems to keep himself seated by nothing but sheer force of leg.

Quilted saddlecloths and simple horse blankets of fur were optional for Assyrian cavalry (or at least for Assyrian artists depicting cavalry), evidently, because other bas-reliefs from about the same time show this sort of minimal padding. The saddlecloths were held in place by breastbands and girths, and it might seem logical that the use of girth straps would have invited that next technological leap, the real saddle. But the Assyrians never leaped. They developed a heroic tradition of military equestrianism that shows itself boastfully in their friezes—light cavalry fighting with bows, armored cavalry charging with lances—yet their horsemen stayed aboard without saddles. In fact, from the evidence of their art, the closest thing to a saddle among the Assyrians may have been a pack frame strapped onto a baggage mule.

The Greeks of the classical period were also indifferent to saddles. They had adopted an Assyrian type of bit, but several more centuries may have passed before they cared to take on so much as the padded saddlecloth. Until the fourth century B.C. (according to J.K. Anderson's authoritative book *Ancient Greek Horsemanship*), all the horsemen on vase paintings and other monuments from Corinth, Athens, Sparta, and elsewhere on the mainland were shown riding bareback. On the Parthenon frieze, too, the riders are parading their horses bareback. Even Xenophon, the first great authority of cavalry literature, gave short shrift to saddles. What he did say, in his treatise *On the Art of Horsemanship*, was:

> When [the rider] is seated, whether on the bare back or on the cloth, we would not have him sit as if he were on his chair, but as though he were standing upright with his legs astride. For thus he will get a better grip of his horse with his thighs, and the erect position will enable him, if need be, to throw his spear and deliver a blow on horseback with more force.

If the handling of cavalry weapons while mounted bareback presented special problems, Xenophon was one of many experienced riders who had learned to cope.

A packsaddle loaded with baggage might need to be fixed to the animal with straps, but a man had his horse sense and his legs. Of course the saddle would eventually make riding easier. It might even make a mounted soldier more dangerous. The point here is that for the estimable cavalry troops of antiquity, it was no necessity.

The stirrup came later and caused (at least among historians, possibly also among cavalry troops and tacticians) more fuss.

The preeminent study here is a famous essay by Lynn White, Jr., "Stirrup, Mounted Shock Combat, Feudalism, and Chivalry," which appeared in 1962 as a chapter of his *Medieval Technology and Social Change*. White makes large claims for the significance of this particular technological innovation. The addition of stirrups so greatly increased the potency of a charging cavalry lancer, according to White, as to revolutionize not only warfare itself but also the way society was organized toward financing it. White describes how the first revolutionary stirrup appeared, in India, as a small loop for the big toe alone and was therefore workable only in warm countries where the equestrian class went barefoot; how the Chinese developed that into full-foot stirrups; how the idea came so late, and spread so slowly, that neither the Greeks nor the Romans exploited it; how eventually, around the seventh century, stirrups started turning up in Europe; how Charles Martel either had stirrup-equipped cavalry troops at Poitiers or realized soon afterward that he wanted them; and how the stirrup, through Martel and his offspring, invented feudalism.

The logic behind this argument is that stirrups were so drastically advantageous when two lancers charged at each other, or when one charged at a formation of infantry, that the invention brought on a new sort of arms race. Armor became more crucial and heavier, horses were bred bigger, cavalry equipage was therefore much more expensive. Horse soldiering became a profession (known as knighthood) that only landed aristocrats could afford. These horse soldiers owed their estates and their service to the Carolingians, and their continuing income to serfs. In White's view, the whole system had raised itself into position—like a jockey galloping down the stretch—on the firm support of its stirrups.

"The stirrup," White proposes, "by giving lateral support in addition to the front and back support offered by pommel and cantle, effectively welded horse and rider into a single fighting unit capable of a violence without precedent. The fighter's hand no longer delivered the blow: it merely guided it." He is referring primarily to shock combat, especially the headlong charges of cavalry lancers, and neglecting in this argument all the functions of skirmish and harassment performed by mounted archers and swordsmen. Nevertheless there's hyperbole here that we'll question more closely in a minute: *The fighter's hand no longer delivered the blow; it merely guided it.*

"The stirrup thus replaced human energy with animal power," White continues, "and immensely increased the warrior's ability to damage his enemy. Immediately, without preparatory steps, it made possible mounted shock combat, a revolutionary new way of doing battle."

It's an ingenious theory, nicely shaped and comprehensive, supported by shreds of far-flung evidence raked together from archaeology, art history, documentary testimony, and philology. For example, at just the time that the Carolingians were consolidating their cavalry-based power among the Franks, the verbs *insilire* and *desilire* (as applied to mounting and dismounting a horse) started being replaced by *scandere equos* and *descendere,* which suggested an act of stepping rather than of leaping. Also at that time the Frankish taste in weaponry changed, according to White, with the battle-ax and the barbed javelin disappearing and the long, heavy lance coming into favor. The lance's blade included a crosspiece that would prevent penetrating too deeply, and White argues that this crosspiece is intelligible only if the lance was designed for stirruped shock combat in which a hell-bent cavalry lancer might otherwise have skewered his opponent like a gobbet of lamb kabob and been forced therefore to abandon the weapon. From this whole impressive gathering of negative and positive evidence, White concludes that "it was the Franks alone—presumably led by Charles Martel's genius—who fully grasped the possibilities inherent in the stirrup and created in terms of it a new type of warfare supported by a novel structure of society which we call feudalism." The period of consolidation of that technocultural revolution, in western Europe anyway, is neatly bounded by the battles of Poitiers and Hastings.

Hastings is White's great test case, best explicable (so he argues) in light of the stirrup. The Normans and the Saxons both rode stirruped horses, but only the Normans knew what they had. Harold and his few horsemen dismounted to fight. The main body of their force consisted of infantry armed with axes, spears, and shields. The Norman knights charged repeatedly at this shield-wall formation of infantry during the day of October 14, 1066, failing repeatedly to break the Saxon line. But then the Saxons made a tactical mistake, dissolving their own formation to chase the withdrawing cavalry downhill. The Normans saw opportunity, swung their horses around, pressed forward against their stirrups, and now trampled and lanced the Saxons decisively, in what Lynn White would have us take as "the classic example in European history of the disruption of a social order by the sudden introduction of an alien military technology."

An alien military technology, that is, if we ignore the fact that the Saxons did have stirrups. A classic example, that is, if we consent to dismiss the importance of William's large numerical advantage in archers. There are other interpretations of Hastings, but none so sleek and ingenious, so crisply technological, as White's. Near the end of the essay, carried away, he claims: "The Man on Horseback, as we have known him during the past millennium, was made possible by the stirrup, which joined man and steed into a fighting organism." In many ways his "Stirrup" is an intriguing and closely argued piece of work. But at a certain point overstatement becomes bad logic.

If it was only the stirrup that "welded horse and rider," if it was only the stirrup that kept mounted swordsmen from taking pratfalls, and if it was only the stirrup that could add linear momentum to the force with which a cavalry lance struck, then eleven centuries of cavalry actions begin to seem not only clumsy but inexplicable. For a case in point, there is Chaeronea.

The work of Minor M. Markle III on the Battle of Chaeronea (in central Greece, 338 B.C.), and on the Macedonian sarissa that may have won it, is narrower and more obscure than White's on the stirrup. But no one should be too quick to accept White's grand argument without at least considering

Markle's small one. In essence Markle proposes that Macedonian cavalry, lacking stirrups and probably even saddles, but armed with long, heavy lances known as sarissae, gave Philip of Macedon this decisive victory over the Athenian and Theban infantry.

The accounts of Chaeronea are patchy. Markle assembles his evidence in a number of tiny scraps, some textual, some archaeological, some from art, some from inspecting the topography of the battlefield at Chaeronea as it is today. He quotes from Plutarch that all the men of the Sacred Band, the elite unit of Theban infantry, were eventually found dead on the battlefield by Philip at a place "where they had faced and met his sarissae. . . ." He cites evidence from excavations, too, showing that sarissae were definitely used at Chaeronea. Those sarissae may have been infantry pikes rather than cavalry lances, since both infantry and cavalry fought here on the Macedonian side. From the texts of Diodorus and others, however, Markle argues that Philip himself was on the right wing, commanding an infantry maneuver against the Athenians, while the young prince Alexander was given command of the left wing. That put Alexander opposite the Thebans of the Sacred Band, on level ground along the Cephisus River, which would have been much better suited to cavalry than would the foothills and gullies on the Macedonian right. Again from Diodorus, Markle shows that there were 2,000 Macedonian cavalry, who certainly wouldn't have been left idle. From the physical specifications of the weapon itself (fifteen to eighteen feet long, weighing about fourteen pounds), Markle argues that a sarissa-armed formation of infantry, whacking each other like stooges with stepladders each time they tried to turn, couldn't possibly have executed the well-timed reversal attributed to Philip's wing in the midst of the battle and that therefore the sarissae must have been in the hands of Alexander's horsemen. Finally, Markle points to the Alexander mosaic from Pompeii for a vision (despite the tantalizing lacuna) of what Alexander may have looked like, at Chaeronea and other battles, fighting on horseback with a sarissa.

Of course the chain of evidence and deduction is drastically truncated here. Markle's own two long papers, published a decade ago in the *American Journal of Archaeology*, offer it in elaborate detail. In the second of those, titled "Use of the Sarissa by Philip and Alexander of Macedon," he concludes:

> If one assumes that Alexander led a cavalry charge [at Chaeronea], then a straightforward interpretation of these sources would be that the Macedonian cavalry charged an unbroken front of hoplites armed with spears. In this event, when Plutarch wrote that the Sacred Band "had faced and met his [Philip's] sarissae," he meant the sarissae of the Macedonian cavalry.

Markle is saying that the best of the Theban infantry were shattered by riders who, despite the lack of stirrups, managed to deliver through their fourteen-pound lances effective jolts of linear momentum. His view of Chaeronea and White's view of Hastings collide here like a pair of jousters.

Markle isn't alone, furthermore, in his respect for the unstirruped lancer. Coins and tomb art throughout the Hellenistic period suggest that such combat wasn't illogical. A painting from the Kinch Tomb near Naousa, dated about 300 B.C., gives a persuasive glimpse of a Macedonian cavalry lancer blasting through shield-bearing infantry. The bas-relief mentioned above shows that as far back as Tiglath-pileser III, shock cavalry tactics were valued by the Assyrians. Plutarch describes Parthian cavalrymen with steel helmets, breastplates, and long lances. In the third century, the Sarmatians, also from western Asia, were so deadly with their heavy lances that the Romans labeled that weapon *contus Sarmaticus* and eventually copied it.

The Roman result was a new sort of cavalryman known as the *contarius*, armed with a sword, darts, and ("above all," says John W. Eadie, the leading authority on this subject) a heavy lance. When these contarii and their horses were both outfitted with armor—possibly in imitation of the Sarmatians, or the Chorasmians, or (still another group of horsey interlopers from the barbarian East) the Sassanids—Rome called them *cataphractarii*. Each Roman cataphract was so heavily metal-encased that, like a medieval knight, if he was knocked off his horse he might be helpless to remount, or even to get up off the ground.

It seems obvious, therefore, that he was not expected to be easily knocked off his horse.

We have saddles and stirrups and lances and reins and mass times velocity and cataphractarian armor. Now let's try to consider the intangible.

The close relationship between humans and horses is at least 4,000 years old, perhaps even half again older—no one can ever know precisely. The best guess is that it began somewhere out in those grasslands of southern Asia (stretching from the Ukraine through Kazakhstan to Mongolia) that get offhandedly labeled "the steppes." Before domestication, the original animal was most likely a small, ponylike thing, twelve or thirteen hands high, possibly with a thick neck and a short, stiff mane like Przhevalski's horse, which is a wild subspecies that survived in Mongolia into modern times. To the Asian nomads who first tamed and bred it, the horse may have signified chiefly a source of convenient meat on the hoof, an alternative to cattle, goats, and deer. Then they began drinking mare's milk. Eventually they discovered that the beast would also accept them as passengers on its back, could carry loads of baggage, and could even be made to drag sleds and carts. The genes that made some horses wildly intractable, crazy for independence and uninterested in exploring this symbiosis with the two-legged species, were bred out. (Among the early Asian horse cultures, there may also have been some human genes that were maladaptive to a life of horse-centered nomadism. Those genes, too, would have been bred out.) The relationship grew into something deep and broad and complicated, definitive of whole patterns in human history. It grew into something without parallel in any act of domestication ever committed by *Homo sapiens*. The dog has *never* really been man's best friend. That was the horse.

For centuries, into millennia, the relationship continued refining itself.

Horse and human converged, genetically and by acquired skills, toward horse-manship. Becoming a part of all life, this relationship became also a part of war. In successive waves the Scythians, the Sarmatians, the Huns, the Goths, the Magyars, the Mongols of Genghis Khan, and other nomadic tribes came out of temperate Asia on horseback to harrow the more sedentary cultures of Europe and the Middle East with their astounding cavalry prowess. True, some of these Asian tribes possessed the important technological innovations (the saddle, the stirrup, possibly the snaffle bit) before Assyria and Greece and Rome. They also possessed something that had to have been equally crucial: a tradition of thoroughgoing familiarity with horses.

Of the Huns, for instance, the Roman historian Ammianus Marcellinus wrote: "There is not a person in the whole nation who cannot remain on his horse day and night. On horseback they buy and sell, they take their meat and drink and there they recline on the narrow neck of their steed and yield to sleep so deep as to indulge in every variety of dream." These Huns even slaughtered and ate the horses themselves when necessary, and did their bingeing on a fermented drink made from mare's milk. They sacrificed horses to their war god, read omens from the charred bones, raised horse skulls and manes as totems over their camps. Horses, not bread, were their staff of life. Maybe the animals weren't loved or coddled—sometimes, no doubt, they were brutalized—but as a class, they were treasured. Most important, the Huns must have *known* their horses, in a way that we of the automobile age can hardly imagine; and their horses must have known them. It doesn't re-quire sentiment, or anthropomorphism, to conclude that under these circum-stances an ineffable but very firm bond would have formed.

And it wasn't just the Huns. Similar claims are made for the Mongols, six centuries later: male children riding before they could toddle, weaned on mare's milk, qualified for cavalry warfare by age sixteen, drinking horse blood from a tapped vein when rations were running low.

Something about this ethos was apparently irresistible. It spread. The Greeks came late and a little warily to mounted horsemanship, but eventually they learned to idealize the horse, and the unification of horse and rider, in their art. Theirs was the mythological imagination, after all, that dreamed up a creature called the centaur. The pre-Islamic literature of the Arabs also celebrated (with good reason, since they were probably already riding the classic Arabian breed) the nobility of the war-horse and the inseparability of horse and horseman:

> *Lo, the mares we bestride at the dawn of battle!*
> *Sleek coat mares, the choice ones; ourselves have reared them.*
> *Charge they mail-clad together, how red with battle,*
> *Red the knots of their reins as dyed with blood.*
> *Are not these the inheritance of our fathers?*
> *Shall we not to our sons in turn bequeath them?*

Muhammad himself later learned the value of cavalry (initially by a defeat) and moved quickly to bring good horsemanship into both his army and his moral hierarchy: "As many grains of barley as thou givest thy horse, so many sins shall be forgiven thee."

The forcefulness of this equestrian bonding can be traced up and down through the column of time, back and forth across Europe and Asia, to America with Cortés (whose own favorite horse was eventually deified) and down into Sudanese Africa with such people as the Angass (who, also lacking stirrups and saddles, chafed the horse's back till it bled and then let themselves be glued into position by the drying blood, if one traveler's account can be believed). It can be traced from the stiffly disciplined New Model cavalry of Cromwell through the hussar regiments of Frederick the Great (so well conditioned and trained that they could sustain a charge over a mile of bad ground, taking the last 800 yards at full gallop), to the romantically doom-hungry Light Brigade at Balaklava, where the riderless horses of men who had been blasted from their saddles continued charging with the other cavalry, heedless and lathered and probably god-awful confused, straight at the Russian artillery. It can be traced right up to those 20th Deccan Horse and 7th Dragoon Guards at the Somme, men and animals galloping together toward a machine gun. In some sense they were all glued together in intimate pairings, rider to horse—not just the Angass of the Sudan, and not just by contrivances of scab or tack. What sort of bonding was it?

We come back to Alexander the Great, for a parable that may or may not contain literal truth but clearly displays one potent idea about cavalry horsemanship, an idea in which humanity has always desired to believe.

Bucephalus was the crazy-wild horse that no one could ride until the boy Alexander cured him of being spooked at his own shadow by facing him into the sun. Bucephalus lived to an advanced age, pampered a little in his later years, attended by grooms at the rear of the Macedonian march, but always (as Plutarch testifies) called forward in time to carry Alexander into each battle. At the Hydaspes River, against the Indian king Porus, Bucephalus carried him again. In the ugly mayhem of the battle, arrows and javelins flying every which way, Alexander himself was invincible but Bucephalus took some bad wounds. Old and exhausted, losing blood, fading, Bucephalus carried Alexander out of the center of the fight and when they were both on safe ground—so goes the story—lay down and died. Alexander ordered that a city be built on the spot, and named the place Bucephala.

What held man and horse together? Certainly it must have been more than the stirrup.

The First Crusade

by NORMAN KOTKER

The confrontation between the West and the Near East is practically as old as recorded history. What may be regarded as the world's longest-running conflict is as impervious to solution now as it ever was. The story of the First Crusade has more than a little in common with Desert Storm or the sad subplot of the hostages of Iran and Lebanon. For the armies of Christian faithful who came to the Holy Land at the end of the eleventh century, it was an epic journey full of danger and hardship, the like of which had not been witnessed since the time of that earlier Western conqueror, Alexander the Great. Eight more crusades were to come, but this was the only one to gain the ultimate prize—Jerusalem. A regular contributor to *MHQ,* Norman Kotker is a novelist who frequently writes on the subject of the Near East.

Someone called out, "God wills it!" Then everyone took up the cry: "God wills it! God wills it!" The entire congregation—310 bishops and abbots assembled before Pope Urban II at France's Clermont cathedral in November 1095—believed that what God willed was the capture of the holy city of Jerusalem. Christian pilgrims had been welcome in Jerusalem since Muslims first conquered the city some four centuries earlier. But now they were being harassed by the city's new Muslim masters, the Seljuk Turks. "Oh, race of Franks!" the pope exhorted his listeners. "You murder and devour one another. . . . Let your quarrels end; let wars cease. . . . Wrest that land from the wicked race and subject it to yourselves."

The pope's words and the preaching of his emissaries found enthusiastic response, not only in France but throughout western Europe. People everywhere pinned crosses of red cloth to their garments and determined to go on crusade. The pope had urged them to begin their journey on the following August 15, on the Feast of the Assumption, but many couldn't wait and started right out. Urban issued further pleas calling for noncombatants to stay home, but he was too late. Thousands of pious peasants—women and children among them—set out, without supplies or proper planning. They were led by a French monk named Peter the Hermit, who had reportedly witnessed Muslim atrocities in the Holy Land, and whose stories had helped convince Urban of the need for a crusade. They traveled overland, trying to live off the countryside, plundering and massacring Jews along the way. Most were killed or died of starvation before they even got near the Holy Land.

But real soldiers took up the cause, too: mounted knights and infantrymen under experienced military leaders. By August 1096, four separate armies had started for Jerusalem. One, mostly men from southern France, had been mustered to follow Raymond, count of Toulouse. His army had plenty of money and food, and although it traveled by a difficult route along the mountainous coast of modern Yugoslavia, it reached Byzantine territory safely.

The other armies were led by feudal lords from France and Italy—notably Godfrey of Bouillon, duke of Lower Lorraine (whom legend calls the perfect crusading knight), Bohemond I of Taranto (who proved to be the Westerners' most successful general), and Robert II of Flanders (one of the most charismatic and devout of the crusader leaders). These three crusader armies had a more difficult trip than Raymond's. Some were shipwrecked sailing from Italy; others followed the route taken by the uncontrolled, voracious hordes of the Peasants' Crusade and were attacked by wary natives.

The vast majority of the crusader soldiers were infantry, many armed with bows or spears and wearing metal helmets and leather or metal armor. A favored weapon was the arbalest, a crossbow that could hurl rocks as well as arrows. It wasn't only their religious devotion that inspired them to walk thousands of miles from France to Jerusalem. Most owed their lords military duty in return for tenure on the land they worked. Others, mainly from southern and western France, were peasants or citizens mustered to fight at the behest of towns or local magnates.

Then there were the knights—mounted warriors who owned enough land to support them while they trained for war and went off to crusade. Carrying kite-shaped shields, they wore knee-length coats of mail and conical steel helmets, with a bar across the nose to protect the face and a mail panel hanging down in back to protect the neck. In battle, they arrayed in formation behind a screen of foot soldiers. Then, with heavy lances held under their right arms, they charged at the enemy *"vehementer,"* and, as chroniclers wrote, *violenter, strenue,* and *velocissime.*

Chronicles of the Crusades are filled with accounts of the skirmishes these men fought before arriving at Constantinople. They were mostly local raids for provisions, but they took on more significance as the soldiers neared the city, perhaps as many as 100,000 strong; for here they came into conflict with troops of the Byzantine Empire. The Byzantine emperor, Alexius Comnenus, who had encouraged the expedition in order to strengthen his hand in the East, at one point ordered his soldiers to demonstrate a little, but to avoid killing any Crusaders. He also had prepared the Crusaders' reception: Supplies were waiting for them, as were troops to ensure that the newcomers didn't disturb the local population.

The Byzantine Empire was the eastern remnant of the Roman Empire. In 330 Constantine the Great had constructed a new capital for the empire on the ancient site of Byzantium. When the Roman Empire was officially divided into two parts in 395, Constantinople became its capital in the East. It remained tied to Rome by heritage and religion, but over the centuries divisions grew. To the Byzantines, Constantinople was the equal of Rome in church matters. By 1054 the schism over religious doctrine had widened considerably. The two seats of the Church regarded each other respectfully but mistrustfully. It was in this light that the Crusaders came requesting supplies and free passage, and Alexius wondered—prophetically—what the armies would do with them if the requests were granted. Each side was prepared to show some strength before greeting the other.

An accord was reached: Alexius supplied the Crusaders and they swore fealty to him, promising to repatriate any territory they captured. The oath later caused acrimonious debate among the Crusaders. But it was no wonder they had agreed to it: They had just completed an arduous journey and needed an ally. The emperor commanded able and disciplined troops. And he had Constantinople, the wealthiest city in Christendom. At its center was the vast open space of Constantine's Hippodrome, with its numerous columns and an enormous Egyptian obelisk. The city's lavish palaces and churches included the Basilica of Saint Sophia, with its elaborate mosaics and 180-foot domed ceiling. Wonders of engineering such as its intricate water system and four-mile triple walls added to Constantinople's splendor.

Constantinople may have been an awesome sight, but to the Crusaders the city's grandeur was hollow. The Byzantine Empire was fighting for its life. Nomadic Turkish tribes from north of the Black Sea were eager to expand, as were the Normans, who had recently grabbed Byzantine lands in southern Italy. Emperor Alexius had only recently managed to repulse both of these invasions of his Balkan territories, but the empire had lost its authority in most of Asia Minor to the Seljuk Turks. It was in hopes of expelling them that Alexius had appealed to the pope to send an army to free Jerusalem—and, incidentally, Asia Minor as well. And Pope Urban, too, saw an opportunity beyond liberating Jerusalem: He might bridge the gap between the Eastern and Western churches.

If the Byzantines were embattled, the Crusaders were on the rise, or perhaps it's fairer to say on the make. Bohemond of Taranto was among the Normans who had recently invaded the Balkans. Other Normans among the Crusaders were hunting for domains as well. Only thirty years earlier some of their kinfolk had mounted the largest amphibious operation since Roman days to conquer England. Around the same time, Normans had established principalities in southern Italy and the kingdom of the Two Sicilies. Now they hoped to do as well in the East.

Before they could attack Jerusalem the Crusaders had to form into a single army, learn new tactics, and cross hostile territory controlled by the Seljuk Turks. The Byzantines, who had had ample—and often humiliating— experience dealing with Turkish tactics, warned the Crusaders that they must always make sure to cover their flanks. They must try to get the Turks to mass close together, preferably on a field where hills or a lake or river would protect flanks.

The crusader armies left Constantinople, stopped off to besiege and expel a Turkish garrison from the ancient Byzantine city of Nicaea, then set off eastward under their several commanders. Many of the major Byzantine roads in Asia Minor went through Dorylaeum—near present-day Eskişehir, some 120 miles southeast of Constantinople—where the Turks were well established. The crusader commanders, managing to control their rivalries, conceived a plan for approaching the site. They divided their forces into two fairly equal columns and proceeded on parallel courses. The left column, led by Bohemond and Robert, set out first. The right, under Godfrey and Raymond, followed. This arrangement made it easier for the entire company to march through a land so grievously desolated by Turkish raids that it offered few provisions.

In the July heat, near the ruins of the ancient city of Dorylaeum, Bohemond's column began to be harassed by parties of Turkish horsemen. The Turks would ride in to the attack, pick off any stragglers outside the line, then take cover in the low, rolling hills. Nevertheless, Bohemond decided to pitch camp and made no effort to join with the rest of the crusader army. The next morning, as his column moved again, his scouts reported an enormous army of Turkish horsemen ahead—about 150,000 strong, according to later accounts. It was under the personal command of Kilij Arslan, the Seljuk sultan of Rum and ruler of much of Anatolia.

Although he had had ample warning, Bohemond was startled to see the entire Turkish army on horseback. His Byzantine hosts had told him of the Turks' reliance on mounted archers in battle, but he had expected to encounter a line of spear-carrying foot soldiers massed in front of horsemen in European fashion. Equipped with heavier armor and initially with bigger horses than those of the Turks, he had expected to benefit from what today might be called a "weight advantage." He had persisted in this expectation even though many of his army's European horses had died and been replaced by lighter mounts.

Bohemond had to rethink his situation immediately. He dispatched messengers to find the other crusader army and summon reinforcements, and he sent his foot soldiers to the rear with orders to pitch camp at a site protected on one side by a marsh. But before his knights could form their battle line, waves of attacking Turkish bowmen were upon them, galloping in from all directions, howling, whistling, and shouting, shooting arrows and then riding off again as another wave swept in. Although they had started out in their usual crescent-shaped line, the Turks fell out, adopting no formation that the Crusaders could oppose directly.

Bohemond waited for the Turks to form ranks so he could attack, but they didn't oblige him. As swarm after swarm rode in, he remained reluctant—probably wisely—to order an attack on an unreachable enemy. If his charge was unsuccessful, he would be unable to get his men into a useful formation again—that trick wasn't in the medieval military repertoire. Finally, despite orders, small bands of crusader knights, frustrated by passivity, sallied out to chase the enemy. But as soon as a few of them became separated from the line, Turkish horsemen swarmed over them.

With the infantry waiting in the camp, virtually unused in the battle, mounted knights had to play a role unsuited to cavalry: maintaining a defensive position. After several hours of this, Bohemond's defensive line grew ragged and his flanks began collapsing inward on the main force. His entire army gradually edged backward, toward the camp. The left flank and rear of the Turkish army had begun to attack the camp, when suddenly, as in a cowboy movie, the cavalry came to the rescue.

The second column of Crusaders, under Godfrey and Raymond, had been six or seven miles back. Moving slowly, they had finally reached a ridge overlooking the battle—and saw that the Turkish army, now concentrated in the crusader camp, was susceptible to a charge. Before the Turks were even aware that another army had arrived, they were engaged with it. As most of the second crusader column galloped over the ridge, Godfrey in the lead and Raymond close behind, Kilij Arslan's troops found themselves crushed between two armies. The two crusader forces joined into one long formation and advanced against the Turks, who were unable to rally and form a front to meet their attack. When yet more Crusaders, in a planned diversion, came charging over a ridge toward them, the Turks panicked and fled.

It was a crusader victory, but an expensive one. Five hours of steady barrage had cost them 4,000 men and an even greater number of horses, which, unlike the knights riding them, were not protected by armor. In fact the toll among the knights was lower than among the foot soldiers protecting the camp and the unarmed camp followers who attended the Crusaders, neither of whom were engaged for long. The Turks lost fewer men, about 3,000.

Events at Dorylaeum—the sudden appearance of crusader reinforcements in their nearly invincible armor—convinced the Turks that they should not oppose the crusader march across Asia Minor. Still, the Crusaders took until October to reach the Orontes River in northern Syria. There, just south of the river, the way was blocked by the great fortress city of Antioch, inhabited for the most part by Christians but controlled by the Turkish emir Yagi Siyan. The Crusaders established a secure camp outside Antioch's formidable walls, blockading all but two of the city's gates. Their task was made harder by the fact that the walls climbed partway up a mountainside. Five months elapsed before they succeeded in blocking one of the remaining city gates and building a tower to control the other. But the Turks still found ways to get in and out of the city.

Though skirmishing was frequent outside the walls, there were only two noteworthy engagements—the Battles of Harenc. Twice, the Crusaders trapped Syrian relief forces on narrow battlefields where their horsemen had no room to maneuver. But Antioch, whose walls were extensive enough to enclose gardens and pasture lands, couldn't be starved into submission. In

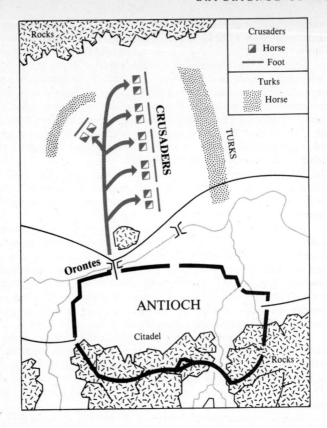

tact, the Crusaders, running low on supplies, were themselves threatened by starvation and defeat. Without materials to construct towers and ladders, it seemed as though the siege would get nowhere. Then, providentially, six Christian ships anchored at St. Simeon at the mouth of the Orontes, some ten miles from Antioch. They carried everything the Crusaders needed: food, rope, bolts, and nails. So the siege continued.

The Crusaders' dilemma was eventually solved—by treason: A renegade Turkish captain let them into the city. The timing seemed lucky because an enormous Turkish army, led by Emir Kerboga of Mosul, was en route from Iraq to relieve the siege. But perhaps it wasn't so lucky after all: Now, instead of besieging Antioch, the Crusaders themselves were besieged within its walls; and Yagi Siyan still held out in the citadel high up on the mountainside. But on June 15, 1098, there was a miraculous discovery—or so it was reported. The Holy Lance, the spear believed to have pierced Jesus' side when he was on the cross, was found in Antioch. Though even many of the Crusaders doubted its authenticity, it provided a rallying symbol and the hope of victory.

On June 28 the Crusaders left the shelter of Antioch's walls to battle the Turkish army, which was drawn up on a plain north of the city. To reach it, they had to cross the Orontes by a bridge that opened directly at one of the city gates. Bohemond, who commanded the entire army, arranged the battle plan. He divided his army into seven groups, six to fight and one to guard the city. There is much disagreement over the number of Crusaders who fought and the precise order in which they arrayed themselves; but it is clear that each of the groups consisted of both foot soldiers and knights on horseback. The infantry line was stiffened by the presence of many knights equipped with armor and swords but largely without horses, which had been lost during the journey across Asia Minor. All in all there were probably 25,000 to 30,000 Crusaders on the battlefield, 90 percent unmounted.

The army, in column, marched through the gate and over the fortified bridge, deploying across the plain in a two-mile line perpendicular to the river. As each group marched from the city, it turned to face the enemy, placing infantry to the front and mounted knights to the rear. This enabled the next formation to march from the city under cover. The infantry probably stood six deep—experience had shown that a line only three or four deep tended to give way too easily. Guarding the rear was a reserve of both infantry and mounted men led by Bohemond himself.

One of Kerboga's commanders urged him to attack the van of the crusader army and engulf it while the rear was still emerging from the city. Kerboga refused. He allowed his entire army to form up on the plain, assuming he could then outflank the Crusaders with customary Turkish tactics. "The farther out they come," he reportedly said, "the more they will be in our power."

As more and more Crusaders emerged from the city, Kerboga realized he was wrong: The Crusaders would stretch all the way across the plain to a range of hills on the north, making it impossible to outflank them. Since there had been disaffection in his own army and he wasn't eager to face an enemy so numerous, he sent a herald to offer a truce. The Crusaders ignored the offer and continued to move toward the hills. Kerboga finally ordered his men to block the Christians' left wing and keep them from reaching the hills. But the movement failed. Although the Turks tried their usual envelopment tactic, attempting to surround the Provençal and Aquitainian troops at the front of the crusader column, the French fought their way through and succeeded in getting into line—cutting the Turkish army in two. At the rear of the crusader line, 15,000 Turkish horsemen were now on one side, while the bulk of Kerboga's army was on the other. The reserve unit under Bohemond quickly deployed behind the main line, placing itself back to back with the other crusaders.

The Crusaders now stretched across the plain from the hills to the river. And as they had done in the Battles of Harenc, they left the enemy horsemen no room to maneuver. As Bohemond's line advanced, the Turks had to re-treat. Several detachments of Kerboga's army, led by the ruler of Damascus, suddenly defected. To slow the Crusaders' advance, Kerboga set fire to the summer-dry grass between the two armies, but the advancing Christians' horses trampled out the flames. Kerboga tried to rally his troops, but with part of his army already fleeing, their spirit had broken; the retreat became a rout.

At the rear, however, it was a different story. There, the 15,000 Turkish cavalrymen who faced Bohemond's smaller force still had to be dealt with. Bohemond's infantry withdrew into a tight circle, but the Turks, uncharac-teristically, came at them not just with arrows but with swords. Perhaps they were beginning to learn how to deal with these heavily armored Westerners. Not until a detachment from the Crusaders' already victorious main army came over to help did the Turkish attack flag. When they realized that the rest of their army was in full retreat, these Turks followed. And high above the action, in the citadel, Yagi Siyan dispatched a herald to surrender the city of Antioch. After being allowed to leave unharmed, he and many of his men became Christians. Some even joined the crusader army.

The Crusaders who had not left for home or lucrative conquests else-where remained at Antioch for seven months, raiding the vicinity. When they finally set out for Jerusalem, it was without Bohemond. After a heated debate, he had decided not to abide by his oath: He would not return Antioch to Alexius, but instead proclaimed himself its prince. Raymond left first, in January; Godfrey and Robert followed a month later. The Crusaders traveled down the coast past Beirut into territories recently recaptured from the Turks by the Fatimid rulers of Egypt. The enemies they encountered here were not just Turks but Syrians and Kurds, Egyptians and Sudanese. The Crusaders called them all Saracens and so shall we—though the term more accurately describes the pre-Islamic tribes of Syria and Arabia.

At the site of present-day Tel Aviv, the army turned inland to climb toward Jerusalem. By June 7, 1099, they had completed their encampment to the north and west of the holy city's walls, wherever the ground was fairly level. They numbered at most 1,500 knights and 12,000 infantry. Within the city, the Saracen commander prepared for a siege. He expelled all Christians, ridding himself both of possible traitors and of extra mouths to feed. He pushed sacks of cotton and hay against his towers to strengthen them. He gathered sheep within the walls and poisoned most nearby wells. The Crusad-ers would have to travel six miles for water.

On June 12, crusader leaders on a pilgrimage to the Mount of Olives were advised by a hermit to assault the city at once. Armed with faith rather than siege engines, they went ahead. After heavy losses, they withdrew.

The Crusaders needed lumber to make siege engines. Jerusalem's envi-rons were almost treeless, but there were plenty of trees miles to the north and plenty of captured Muslims to haul them. The hapless prisoners were made to "work as if they were . . . serfs," wrote one chronicler. Fifty or sixty of them would carry a beam on their shoulders that couldn't have been dragged by eight oxen.

When word came that an Egyptian army was en route to relieve the city, the Crusaders decided to act quickly. Two great siege towers, covered with ox and camel hides, were almost finished. (The supply ships had followed them down the coast to Jaffa.) Solemnly, the entire army fasted and, as Muslims stood on the walls laughing, marched in barefoot procession around the city. Then they ascended the Mount of Olives to listen to exhortatory sermons. In the next two days they finished the two great siege towers and a third, smaller one. Finally, after the ground where the towers were to rest had been leveled, they were rolled into place.

The appearance of the siegeworks surprised and worried the Saracens. Even before the towers were in place, they started bombarding them with rocks and what the Crusaders called "Greek fire"—an incendiary mixture. The Crusaders put their mangonels into action. These were catapults that used twisted torsion ropes to hurl rocks, flaming cotton-wrapped arrows, bales of burning straw, or fiery, iron-banded bundles of wood and straw that had been dipped in pitch, wax, and sulfur. These projectiles couldn't breach the walls, of course, but they did clear them of defenders. The Saracens countered by sending two witches out to hex the Christians, but both women were killed by crusader rocks.

In any case, their hex was ineffective. Although the attackers at the city's southwest wall made no headway, around noon on July 15 Godfrey, commanding the northeast tower, succeeded in lowering a gangplank onto the wall. A detail of Flemish troops, led by two knights, got across it and onto the wall and managed to hold their position, enabling others to lean scaling ladders against the wall without being attacked. Soon dozens of Crusaders were fighting their way through the narrow streets of the city toward the Gate of the Column in the northern wall. They opened the gate and let the rest of the army in.

Crusaders rushed through the streets and into house after house, killing and looting indiscriminately. Muslims who sought refuge in the Mosque of al-Aqsa were hacked to death. Jews who closed themselves into the Great Synagogue were burned alive. The slaughter was terrible, and total. A small detachment of defenders shut itself into the citadel called the Tower of David, which still stands at the western side of Jerusalem. Its commander, who agreed to surrender the tower and all its treasure to Raymond, was allowed to go free with his soldiers. But no one else in the city survived the siege.

It had taken the Crusaders almost three years to conquer Jerusalem. Now they had it. First they recited their prayers. Then they cleared away the corpses. And then they dealt with the problem of trying to hold on to it. The first challenge came almost immediately, when a Saracen army marched up from Egypt to retake the city. Though that army was defeated in the Battle of Ascalon, Jerusalem's Christians had to keep fighting off Muslim attacks.

Urban II died before hearing the news, but he had recaptured the Holy Land for Rome. Bohemond—and many others—had found wealth and power (though for Bohemond it was short-lived; he was captured and held prisoner by the Turks for three years, then returned to Italy to fight the Byzantine Empire). Robert was anxious to get home, and left for Flanders very quickly. Peter the Hermit and others from the Peasants' Crusade had accompanied the soldiers to the Holy Land; Peter saw Jerusalem, but few peasants did. Raymond was offered the "kingdom of Jerusalem," but he refused. He took control of the county of Tripoli and headed several military campaigns in the area. Godfrey also declined the offer of a crown, ruling Jerusalem only as "protector of the Holy Sepulchre." He died one year later.

In 1187, after ninety years of warfare, Muslims under Saladin succeeded in retaking the city. Despite successive crusades and many other Christian attempts to get the city back, the Muslims held it for centuries thereafter.

The Life and Hard Times of the Crossbow

by ROBERT L. O'CONNELL

"The crossbow," as Robert L. O'Connell points out, "is usually thought of as a medieval weapon, invented around the time of the Crusades. But in fact it appears to have been developed around 500 B.C., almost simultaneously in China and Greece. Yet its subsequent history in each theater differed remarkably." The Chinese changed the way they waged war to suit the crossbow. But the Greeks, rather than give up their confrontational style of warfare, got rid of it. Ruling classes in the Middle Ages similarly distrusted a device that profoundly threatened the social order. King and commoner were equally vulnerable to the killing power of this equalizing weapon. In the end, though, that was not what doomed the crossbow. The following article originally appeared as one of O'Connell's frequent contributions to the *Arms and Men* department of *MHQ*.

The crossbow is a weapon that most of us recognize but don't really know much about. The term conjures images of Hollywood extras in chain-link suits and conehead helmets taking potshots at Ivanhoe. But the truth is much more intriguing. For the crossbow marks a significant departure from the usual relationship of arms and men—at times it has been a veritable stick in the spokes of Western military history.

To understand why, it is helpful to look first at how the crossbow works. Mechanically, the crossbow improves on the mostly efficient simple bow, which has two weaknesses. First, if you pull a bowstring back to your ear, you quickly realize that you have to shoot almost immediately or risk a very sore, shaky arm. Second, if a bowstring offers too much resistance, drawing the bow becomes impossible. The solution to both problems lay in attaching the middle of the bow to the end of a right angle. Around A.D. 1200 the stock was equipped with a mechanical trigger that held the cocked bowstring in place until released. A metal stirrup projected from the front of the stock, enabling the bowman to use the strength of his entire body when cocking the string. With his foot in the stirrup, he could hold the crossbow steady and pointed downward with his leg muscles while drawing the string with his back and arm muscles. As the bows grew stouter, bowmen were aided in drawing the string by a series of devices, added between the mid-fourteenth and fifteenth centuries. With successively stiffer bows and stronger, more ingenious mechanisms for cocking, crossbow performance improved.

In almost any form, however, the weapon was powerful and easy to use. The operator had merely to lay a quarrel (shorter and heavier than an arrow, but retaining its essential shape) in front of the drawn bowstring atop a groove running lengthwise down the stock. He then raised the bow, aimed it like a gun, and released the trigger. Because this involved negligible effort and coordination, a soldier required little training to shoot a crossbow accurately. Moreover, the greater weight of the quarrel and the inherent strength of the bow made a force at impact much greater than that of an ordinary arrow. The rate of fire was certainly much lower than for a simple bow, and prior to the introduction of the steel bow section (around A.D. 1400), the maximum range was shorter; nonetheless, from the beginning the crossbow was a very significant weapon, since it could pierce personal armor at a range of perhaps sixty yards.

In the context of Western military history, *that* degree of effectiveness was not altogether welcome. Until the invention of the gun, nearly every battlefield was dominated by highly trained, armored warriors—typically of high social standing—dedicated to fighting it out at close quarters, but not necessarily dedicated to killing each other: Taking prisoners to be ransomed later was often preferred. Such practical fellows, when confronted by crossbowmen whom they could not reach without being shot at, understandably felt very vulnerable. In seconds an amateur with a crossbow could wipe out years of costly training, to say nothing of generations of noble (even royal) breeding. When commoners on foot could so easily kill their social betters, the fabric not only of warfare but of European society began to fray. That is why the crossbow had such a checkered history in the West.

The crossbow is usually thought of as a medieval weapon, invented around the time of the Crusades. But in fact it appears to have been developed around 500 B.C., almost simultaneously in China and Greece. In both places the impetus for its invention was probably the same: The crossbow is a formidable improvement over the ordinary bow. Yet its subsequent history in each theater differed remarkably.

In China, the crossbow was quickly adopted by fighting forces and became a major individual weapon. Until then, warfare in China had been highly individualized and dominated by chariots. The ability of crossbowmen to shoot through body armor and shields probably drove the Chinese chariot off the battlefield and into obsolescence. But the crossbow's influence was even more far-reaching—extending to the very heart of Chinese military thinking. The strategy of war, exemplified by the writings of the great military theorist Sun-Tzu, became more subtle, emphasizing maneuver and psychological advantage. Indeed, to describe the essence of his combat philosophy, Sun-Tzu resorted to analogy with the weapon: "When the strike of a hawk breaks the body of its prey, it is because of timing./ Thus the momentum of one skilled in war is overwhelming, and his attack is precisely regulated./ His potential is that of a fully drawn crossbow; his timing, the release of the trigger."

The Greeks, on the other hand, rather than cast aside their confrontational style of warfare, got rid of the crossbow—by improving it out of existence. The first detailed description of a *gastrophetes* (belly-bow) can be found in Hero's *Belopoeica* of 399 B.C. It depicts a simple crossbow that, while rather large (over five feet long), almost certainly could have been wielded by a single man due to its concave stock. From this point, however, the weapon grew steadily into what in essence became a piece of artillery, the *euthytonon*. Its bow section was even replaced by two vertical, wooden propelling arms embedded in skeins of tightly packed fibers. When the fibers were twisted tightly, the bowstring between the two vertical arms gained the tension needed to shoot the weapon. As this and other large engines took their place in Hellenistic siegecraft, portable one-man weapons such as the gastrophetes slipped conveniently out of sight, not to be heard of in the West for nearly 1,300 years.

Around A.D. 950, writers began to refer to the crossbow again, although for the most part as a hunting instrument. We know from the writings of the Byzantine princess Anna Comnena that the first Crusaders brought it to the Holy Land, though perhaps only as an intimidating novelty. (The princess herself was repulsed by it, calling it "a weapon of the barbarians, . . . a truly diabolical machine.") By the time of the Third Crusade, its ease of use, accuracy, and ability to knock a man out of the saddle at considerable distances made it a key element of the sophisticated combined-arms forces crafted by Richard the Lion-Hearted to fight on the march.

What had proved so useful abroad would hardly be ignored at home. By A.D. 1100 the quarrel had become commonly available and was being used in Europe to shoot down knights. While the crossbow's rate of fire remained slow (about one shot per minute), its psychological impact was swift. Military prepotency was no longer reserved for one class, a fact dramatized when Richard the Lion-Hearted himself was shot down by a crossbow as he cavorted before a besieged castle.

Rather quickly the Church stepped into the breach. In A.D. 1139 the Second Lateran Council outlawed the use of the crossbow among Christians (though not against Muslims). The Church was not alone. The English aristocracy also banned the offending instrument in the Magna Carta of 1215.

The crossbow survived such decrees nicely. Indeed, according to crossbow specialist Sir Ralph Payne-Gallwey, it continued to be the favorite weapon on the Continent from the thirteenth century well into the fifteenth. As one might expect, given its slow rate of fire, the crossbow was most effective during sieges. Yet it was also used to good effect in set-piece battles, particularly by companies of Genoese mercenaries who had made it their specialty. Soon enough, they would wish they had specialized in something else.

For as old and overshadowed as the simple bow was, the English were bringing it back to prominence. By fashioning bows out of yew, a strong and elastic wood whose unique combination of heartwood and sapwood resembled composite construction, and by extending the length of the bows upwards of six feet (hence the term *longbow*), British bowyers dramatically improved both range and power. In the hands of highly trained and motivated English yeomen, these longbows proved exceptional weapons at the very outset of the Hundred Years' War in 1337. And they were truly devastating in their first real Continental test—on the fated field of Crécy in 1346. While the battle is remembered today chiefly for the lemminglike performance of the French heavy cavalry in the face of these longbowmen, it was the Genoese crossbow corps who first felt their sting. Their predicament was analogous to matching—at the limit of each weapon's range—flat-trajectory tank guns against howitzers. Rushing forward to let loose a salvo that fell short, the Genoese, struggling to reload their rain-soaked weapons, were hit by wave after wave of longbow arrows, a barrage that soon drove them from the field. Though the crossbow remained a weapon of choice into the next century, Crécy was a rout that, in a sense, signaled the crossbow's end.

For also present at Crécy was a curious fire tube, brought to life by gunpowder, that was apparently shot but had no effect on the battle. It may have been useless that day, but its loud report was the sound of the future. Within two centuries, this fire tube's hand-held cousin, the harquebus, would drive both longbow and crossbow from the ranks of European armies. It has frequently been noted by supporters of the crossbow and the longbow that they were much more accurate and had a longer range than the harquebus. In fact, they argue, the longbow could be shot much faster than the harquebus and even the eighteenth-century musket. They see it as illogical, even unjust, that the military careers of bow weapons were terminated. Yet they miss an important point. Much of warfare is psychological. As the noted strategic analyst and military historian Bernard Brodie explains, the shattering report of a harquebus, the smoke, and the flame were much more frightening than the twang of a bowstring, and the wounds it inflicted were not neat punctures but mutilating gouges that, if they did not kill immediately, quite probably would do so later through infection. This is why the gun prevailed.

Yet if the crossbow vanished from the battlefield, it lived on in the imaginations of weapons designers. Around 1485, Leonardo da Vinci sketched an enormous crossbow, designed to be forty feet long with a bow section about thirty-six feet wide—beyond the capacity of contemporary engineers to construct. More than 400 years later, British soldiers would find in the trenches of Ypres a German grenade launcher in the form of a crossbow.

Old weapons die hard.

The Gunpowder Revolution

by WILLIAM McNEILL

If the crossbow was the harbinger of vast social and political change, gunpowder was its implementer. Gunpowder, too, was invented in China and arrived in Europe in the fourteenth century. Gunpowder weapons were at first curiosities, but as Professor McNeill points out, "the balance of power among peoples was suddenly altered to favor those who owned or controlled the new artillery, first in western Europe, where these guns were primarily developed, and then in all the other parts of the civilized world. Indeed, the spread of big guns inaugurated what may be called the age of gunpowder empires." Gunpowder left one continent, Europe, in control of the rest. William McNeill, professor emeritus of history at the University of Chicago, is the author of such major works as *The Rise of the West* (University of Chicago Press), a National Book Award winner for nonfiction. This article is adapted from an essay originally written for the American Historical Association.

Any big change in weapons and military organization affects politics and society because it helps some people attain their ends more easily than before, while it puts new, perhaps insuperable obstacles in the way of others. The advent of guns was such a change.

Gunpowder weapons appeared as curiosities in Europe in the fourteenth century, then became devastatingly effective in sieges by about the middle of the fifteenth century. The balance of power among peoples was suddenly altered to favor those who owned or controlled the new artillery, first in western Europe, where these guns were primarily developed, and then in all the other parts of the civilized world. Indeed, the spread of big guns inaugurated what may be called the age of gunpowder empires.

Whenever they managed to monopolize the new artillery, central authorities were able to unite large territories into new, or newly consolidated, empires. This took place in the Near East, in Russia, in India, and, in a considerably modified fashion, in China and Japan as well. The Spanish empire of the Americas, together with the Portuguese empire of the Indian Ocean, also relied on artillery, though the most important Spanish and Portuguese guns were on ships, not on land.

But in western Europe, the original home of these guns, the response was different. No single ruler was ever able to monopolize siege cannon, and no gunpowder empire ever emerged.

Gunpowder was invented in China shortly before A.D. 1000 and was first used in war as an incendiary. That, at least, is a plausible interpretation of a text that tells how in A.D. 969 an emperor of the Sung dynasty awarded a prize to officers who had invented a new "fire arrow." The arrow probably carried a charge of gunpowder. Further development of gunpowder weaponry was inhibited by the fact that the Chinese style of warfare under the Sung dynasty (960–1279) was defensive, and since the emperor's troops usually fought from behind defensive walls, they had absolutely no incentive to invent guns that could attack such walls.

This state of affairs changed, however, when the Mongols conquered China, between 1205 and 1279. The horsemen who followed Genghis Khan and his successors were accustomed to attacking, but they could not hope to capture forts and walled cities from horseback. For this reason, they welcomed anything that would allow them to break through defensive walls quickly. Catapults had been used for that purpose since Roman times, and the Mongols took to them eagerly. But the explosive force of gunpowder seemed promising as well, and Mongol armies routinely used lengths of bamboo filled with gunpowder in order to blow open city gates. In this primitive form gunpowder weapons reached Europe in 1241, when Mongol armies ravaged Poland and Hungary.

The Chinese also pioneered the next improvement in firearms. If, instead of allowing the powder to shatter its bamboo container, a stronger vessel, open at one end, were constructed to hold the powder, then the exploding gases could be made to launch a missile placed over the vessel's mouth. Chinese texts from 1290 seem to show that this sort of "gun" was in use.

News of China's new weapons reached Europe quickly. The first known portrait of the new contrivances, dated 1326, comes from western Europe in the form of a crude manuscript painting preserved at Oxford. It shows a vase-shaped container lying on its side, with a touchhole on top and a large arrow affixed to a circular base closing off the mouth. A Chinese drawing just six years later shows a very similar vase-shaped receptacle for the powder, with an arrow-shaped projectile. The resemblance between the two drawings is so close that a common origin seems certain, and Chinese priority is hard to doubt.

What is clear about the early history of artillery is that Europeans soon outstripped the Chinese and others by building bigger and bigger guns. One reason was that Europeans had access to more metal than did other civilized peoples (with the possible exception of the Japanese), thanks to developments in hard-rock mining that dated back to the eleventh century. Methods for cracking bedrock and for ventilating and draining mines allowed Europeans to follow metalliferous lodes deeper into the earth than was done elsewhere.

A second reason for European artificers and rulers to build more-powerful guns was that they had a clear idea of how bigger and better guns might make their owners more powerful. Initially, the idea far outran reality. Early guns were mainly good for scaring horses, and should have scared the men who risked firing them. They were not efficient weapons; most of the force of the explosion was wasted because the expanding gases simply rushed around the sides of the projectile, so that aiming was extremely inaccurate. Nevertheless, the awesome noise and obvious force of exploding gunpowder promised truly superhuman results, if only it could be harnessed effectively. Guns, if powerful enough, might even be capable of destroying the enemy's best-built stone fortifications with just a few shots, thereby abruptly altering the balance between defenders and attackers.

Soon after 1400 this vision of the possible took firm hold on the imaginations of a few rulers and artisans in western Europe. Substantial resources were therefore lavished on building gigantic "bombards." These weapons differed from the vase-shaped gun of 1326 in being cylindrical tubes, closed at one end. Instead of firing an arrow, poised at the lip of the gun, they shot spherical stone balls, propelling them the length of the tube before allowing the exploding gases to disperse in thin air. This assured more accurate aim and much more effective use of the explosion's force to accelerate the projectile. Guns, as we know them, were on their way, and Europeans soon were making bigger and better guns than anyone else, including the Chinese. For the first time, western Europeans outstripped other civilizations in at least one important respect.

By about 1430, European-made bombards were twelve to fifteen feet long, fired a projectile up to about thirty inches in diameter, and had become truly formidable engines. They were so heavy and so awkward to move that on some occasions artisans actually cast the big guns on the spot, instead of trying to transport them to the site of the siege. Yet such weapons did accomplish their purpose, causing stone fortifications to crumble and allowing a besieging army to storm through the breach after only a brief bombardment.

The capture of Constantinople by Sultan Mohammed the Conqueror in 1453 is the most famous example of how such clumsy weapons could make a decisive difference, allowing a field force to overcome otherwise invulnerable defenses. That the sultan hired Christians from Transylvania to build and operate the cannon attests to the skill that European metalworkers and gunsmiths had achieved, as well as to his eagerness to acquire what was clearly a superior weapon.

The speed with which the Turks reacted to the novelty is striking, for such guns had not existed before about 1430. The first Western ruler to use them systematically was the king of France, who in 1450 set out to drive the English from the Continent. His new guns made old fortifications quite useless. Consequently, English garrisons throughout France surrendered so rapidly that the hitherto interminable Hundred Years' War came to an end in

1453—the same fateful year in which Mohammed captured Constantinople.
Historians have often used that year to divide medieval from modern history,
and not without reason, since the advent of the new weapons system, signal-
ized by the twin events for which 1453 is famous, did alter the way political
and military power was distributed, not just in Europe but around the world.

After defeating the English in 1453, the king of France still faced a
formidable rival in the form of an overmighty subject—the duke of Burgundy, who had accumulated territories stretching from the Low Countries at
the mouth of the Rhine to the border of Switzerland in the south. As it
happened, the most skilled gunmakers of the age inhabited his territories.
Therefore, when the Burgundians decided they must arm against the French,
lest the French king do to them what he had done so successfully to the
English, they had an ample technical base for improving upon the gun design
of the 1450s.

The Burgundian-French rivalry promptly precipitated an arms race of
the sort so familiar to us today. Metalworkers on both sides aimed at a single
goal: to make guns mobile without sacrificing their battering power. Between
1465 and 1477, designers solved their problem brilliantly by resorting to
smaller, denser projectiles. They discovered that a comparatively small iron
cannonball could strike a more damaging blow than a stone projectile (which
fractured on impact) ever could, no matter how large. This meant that guns
could be made smaller but had to be stronger, too.

The trade-off was favorable, for even with thicker walls, the new guns
weighed a lot less than the great bombards and became genuinely mobile.
Mounted on wheels, a gun six to eight feet long, capable of firing an iron ball
eight inches in diameter, could travel wherever a heavy wagon could go.
Simply by unhitching the trail from a forward pair of wheels and planting it
on the ground, these guns were ready for action; and having been fired, they
could be moved on, if needed, to some new vantage point—all in a matter of
minutes. Moreover, when it came to knocking down stone walls, these cannon were just as effective as the monster guns of the previous generation.

A gun park with a few such weapons allowed a ruler to threaten his
subjects or weaker neighbors with speedy and assured destruction of defenses
behind which, in earlier times, they might have sheltered for weeks and
months—until starved out by besiegers. Keeping even a superior force on
enemy territory for a long time had always been difficult because supplies were
hard to deliver in sufficient quantity. With the new guns, that was no longer
necessary; a few hours' bombardment would now suffice to bring down the
most formidable walls wherever guns could be brought to bear. The balance
of power between central and local authorities was thereby transformed, making whoever controlled the new siege cannon into a sovereign and reducing
those who could not afford them to a subjection they had not previously
experienced.

As it happened, the Burgundians, though they had taken the lead in
perfecting mobile siege artillery, were not destined to profit from it. Instead,
Charles the Bold, duke of Burgundy, being too impatient to await the arrival

of his guns on the battlefield at Nancy, led a cavalry charge against a massed formation of Swiss pikemen who had dared to oppose him, and met his death on the point of a pike in 1477. Burgundian lands were then swiftly partitioned between the French king, Louis XI, and the Habsburg heir, Maximilian, who married Charles the Bold's daughter and only heir.

Even after Maximilian was elected and crowned Holy Roman emperor of the German nation in 1493, he lacked a bureaucracy and army with which to exploit the possibilities of the new artillery. The French kings Louis XI and Charles VIII were better situated in this respect, and proceeded to consolidate their kingdom as never before. Then in 1494 Charles VIII, after annexing Brittany, decided to use his new military power for ventures abroad. He invaded Italy, the richest and most sophisticated part of western Europe, in order to enforce his dynastic claim to the Kingdom of Naples. This required him to march the length of the peninsula, bringing his big guns with him and using them to threaten anyone who dared oppose his passage. On the rare occasions when he met resistance, his cannon demonstrated their devastating force by reducing famous fortresses to rubble at the word of command.

In 1494 the Renaissance rulers of Italy had long since developed a professionalized art of war, combining cavalry, pikes, and crossbows. They were accustomed to setting the pace for all of Christendom in war as well as in peace. To be so suddenly outdistanced by the French was therefore a great shock, which was not diminished by the fact that the French invasion inaugurated a long series of wars (1494–1559) in which foreigners—French and Spanish primarily—and sometimes the Italian states themselves fought over Italy. Even the largest Italian states, dwarfed by the newly consolidated kingdoms of France and Spain, proved incapable of defending themselves or of driving the attackers away.

The reason the Italian wars were so long-drawn-out was that early in the conflict military engineers discovered a way to make fortifications safe from the new guns. In 1500 Florence attacked Pisa, using heavy guns to break through the ringwall, only to find that the Pisans had erected a new earthen wall inside, behind the threatened breech. Moreover, to get earth for their emergency wall, the Pisans had scraped out a ditch in front of it that blocked a direct, running assault. But the important thing was this: Cannonballs fired into the earthen wall buried themselves in the soft soil without doing much damage. As a result, the Florentine attack was foiled and Pisa retained its independence.

In light of this experience, Italian military engineers saw quickly how to make fortifications safe again. All they had to do was protect brittle stone walls with a sloping layer of earth to absorb cannon fire, while obstructing access to such revetted walls by carving out ditches in front of them, just as the Pisans had done. In a sense the new design turned ordinary fortifications upside down, making empty ditches the principal obstacle an attacker had to traverse, while walls became merely an aid to the defenders in protecting the ditch.

The advantage of a ditch, of course, was that it was completely unaffected by cannon fire, and earth-covered walls were nearly as secure. Yet the new style of fortification did not make cannon useless; rather, guns emplaced on projecting bastions were needed to defend the ditch, and others had to be hidden behind the main ringwall, ready to attack besieging artillery. Careful geometry could assure clear lines of fire for guns of every caliber, making a well-designed and adequately garrisoned city or fortress impregnable to sudden attack.

By 1520 the refinements of building cannonproof fortifications were well understood, and what came to be called the *trace italienne* made it possible for anyone who could afford the new style of fortification to erect a stronghold that was effective in resisting cannon fire. The siege therefore again became a feature of European warfare, because comparatively small garrisons, protected by the new style of fortification, were capable of holding off a superior attacker for months at a time. But there was a difference: The new fortifications were expensive to construct and required even more of the big guns than attackers did. Only states and rulers that had access to artillery and enough money to pay for an ample stock of the new weapons could hope to compete in European war and diplomacy.

As a result, urban wealth and skills became more decisive than before in military matters. Without access to the products of urban workshops, and without money to pay for them, no government and no military captain could expect to succeed. Capitalist enterprise and military enterprise were wedded together more closely than in any earlier age or anywhere else in the world. Each nourished the other, making European armies, navies, and governments much more powerful than before.

But precisely because several European armies and governments mobilized greater and greater resources for war and defense, no single empire succeeded in uniting western Europe. Big guns were never monopolized. By 1519 the Habsburg heir, Charles V, Holy Roman emperor and king of Spain, had gathered together all the diverse territories he had inherited and appeared to have a real chance of establishing hegemony over all of western Europe by defeating the French. But it was already too late for the new siege guns to have the sort of effect that they had in some other parts of the civilized world. By then the trace italienne was available, so that even when Charles did drive French forces from the field in Italy, he was unable to press ahead, invade France, and expect to see the French king's fortresses crumble as soon as they were attacked.

In 1450 that could have happened, but not in 1525 or subsequently. Instead, a defeated army could expect to withdraw into prepared defenses and hold off attackers as long as food stocks allowed. Quick and easy conquest had become impossible. The window of opportunity for consolidating western Europe into a single gunpowder empire had closed. One may even speculate that it was the division of the Burgundian lands after the death of Charles the Bold in 1477 that assured this result.

To begin with, gun-casting skill was concentrated in the Low Countries near the mouths of the Scheldt and Rhine rivers. If a single ruler had continued to control that region and been able to monopolize the new guns for as long as a generation, he might have been able to use his mobile wall destroyers to achieve hegemony wherever the new siege guns could reach. Instead, the kings of France and the Habsburgs of Germany divided up the Burgundian guns and gunmakers along with Burgundian lands, assuring a standoff, which became permanent, thanks to the swift improvements in fortification after 1500.

A balance of power therefore persisted, keeping Europe divided among dozens of sovereigns. Perennial rivalries among neighboring states and rulers continued to put a forced draft under the evolution of the art of war in Europe across the ensuing centuries, and a long series of improvements in organization, armament, training, and supply raised the effectiveness of European armies to ever greater heights.

Nothing of the sort occurred anywhere else. Big guns of the type used in Europe did spread very rapidly throughout Asia after 1499 when European ships began to stop at Asian ports, with heavy guns on board for protection. Asian rulers without exception recognized the advantages of owning such guns and took steps to obtain them, sometimes by trade, sometimes by learning how to cast such weapons for themselves. As this transfer of weapons took place, old imperial centers of power were able to secure new authority over potentially unruly local magnates, whose strongholds now became vulnerable to gunfire wherever the guns could be dragged.

In this fashion a newly consolidated empire of India arose after 1526, when Bābur founded the Mughal dynasty; the Ottoman and Safawid empires divided the heartlands of Islam between them after 1499; and a great new empire arose in Muscovy, tied together by the elementary fact that the grand duke of Moscow could move his big guns up and down the Russian rivers on barges, bringing under fire every Russian city that dared to oppose him. In China the Ming emperors did not alter their military establishment very much, since the Chinese already had long practice with guns and Ming forces were, as before, interested in defending walls, not in destroying them. The Japanese, however, took to the new weaponry with abandon, as local rulers competed for access to Portuguese suppliers after 1542, when the first Europeans reached Japan.

For the next half century, Japanese warlords fought one another, using ever larger numbers of guns. Castles had to be rebuilt to resist gunfire, using principles similar to the trace italienne, except that the Japanese preferred revetments of stone, loosely laid one on another, with a moat of water in front. But no permanent balance of power emerged, and when first Toyotomi Hideyoshi and then Ieyasu established effective sovereignty throughout the islands, the new Tokugawa rulers decided to abandon the gun, fearing that such weapons in the hands of commoners would undermine the privileges of the sword-wielding samurai class, upon whose loyalty they depended. In a truly remarkable fashion, therefore, a nation that at the height of the civil wars had been more heavily armed with handguns than any European state was induced and then compelled to give up the gun in order to assure the security of Tokugawa and samurai rule.

Thus, for Japan as well as for the other empires of Asia, the effect of gunpowder weapons was to consolidate central power over comparatively vast territories. Once a ruler had monopolized big guns or, in Japan, disarmed the whole nation, there was no incentive to continue experiments with improvements either in weaponry or in the organization and command of armies. Nevertheless, among the rival states of Europe, such experimentation continued, and at a very rapid pace.

The result was that by about 1700, European military (and naval) skills had outdistanced those of all the great empires of Asia, making those proud civilizations vulnerable to even small expeditionary forces, either dispatched from Europe or armed and trained on the spot by European commanders. The amazing imperial successes of European nations in the eighteenth and nineteenth centuries resulted—and all because in 1477 the Burgundian lands were divided between French and German rulers, and because Italian engineers were so swift to find out how to make walls safe again, even against powerful, mobile artillery.

Truly, the course of history, even on a world scale, sometimes turns on single events, and on a skilled (or lucky) response to a moment of crisis.

Apocalypse at Münster

by JON SWAN

There is no war quite so unpleasant as a religious war, and the Reformation's butcheries in the name of God still have the power to shock. In 1534 an unlikely combination of German Catholics and Lutherans laid siege to Münster, a city under the spell of an actor turned Hitler-like messiah. King Jan, as he styled himself, was capable of personally beheading one of his own wives (he married sixteen during his brief reign), but his brutality was nothing compared to that of his opponents, who slaughtered an entire city. Two things should be noted. When the religious threat proved serious enough—and the nonconformist Anabaptists offended Catholics and Protestants equally—there could be a brief outbreak of ecumenicalism between them. That had happened just five years earlier when the infidel Turkish armies of Süleyman the Magnificent reached the walls of Vienna. (The Turks retreated and the squabbling began again.) And, according to the military etiquette of the time, once surrender of a city was demanded, and refused, and once siege artillery was in place, no quarter would be given if the place was taken by storm. Beyond those considerations, the extirpation of the Anabaptists at Münster and elsewhere would have unfortunate repercussions in our own century, as Jon Swan makes clear. Swan is a poet, translator of Dutch and German, and a free-lance writer.

Throughout northern Europe in the early sixteenth century, just as among born-again Christians of the twentieth century, belief in the imminent end of the world—or something like it—was widespread. First there would be a time of troubles, a time of wars and other calamities, as Satan and the Antichrist sought to obtain total domination of the world. Thousands upon thousands of people would die. Ultimately, however, the forces of evil would be destroyed. Christ would then return to judge the quick and the resurrected dead; and the holy city of God, the New Jerusalem of the Book of Revelation, would be established on a transformed, purified earth. Only the pure, the people of God, would dwell in this city.

In the early 1500s the air was full of signs that the Last Days had begun. The one true Church broke in two in the 1520s—a traumatic sundering— and to Martin Luther and the German nobles who supported him, it was self-evident that the pope in Rome was that very Antichrist whose appearance was a sure sign that the end was nigh. Another clear sign was the astonishing advance of the infidel armies of Süleyman the Magnificent: from Belgrade, taken in 1521, through Hungary, and on to Vienna, before whose walls the Turkish cavalry arrived in September of 1529, their pikes raised and, at the end of each pike, the head of an Austrian. Everywhere, it seemed, the evil empire was on the march.

Meanwhile, within Germany, or that great squabble of principalities and duchies that constituted the Holy Roman Empire, thousands of peasants and weavers and miners—some of them incited by preachers who, unlike Luther, questioned the right of princes to rule—rose up in a series of revolts known collectively as the Peasants' War. It is estimated that some 100,000 people were slaughtered in the year 1525 as German nobles brought cannon, cavalry, and disciplined troops to bear on the untrained, inadequately armed throngs of the poor.

In general, then, it was a dangerous time in which to live—and particularly dangerous for those who managed to arouse the hatred of both Lutherans and Catholics, perhaps by some doctrinal difference or by refusal to swear an oath, carry a weapon, or kill their fellow men, including Turks. These people were called Anabaptists, or rebaptizers—a misnomer because these Christians who had been baptized as infants believed that infant baptism was a meaningless "dipping in the Romish bath." A true Christian had to be born again in Christ as an adult; baptism was a sign of this rebirth. Anabaptists called themselves simply Baptists.

The Anabaptist movement spread rapidly, in part because every member—male and female alike—was regarded as a missionary. Sects proliferated until there were altogether some forty of them, each led by a preacher who claimed to be a prophet. All of the sects shared a belief in divine inspiration and a deep distrust of civil authority. The authorities, for their part, gave these nonconformists ample reason to distrust them. In 1525 the Protestant city fathers of Zurich made death by drowning the penalty for being an Anabaptist. Four years later the Imperial Diet, meeting at Speyer, in Germany, and attended by both Catholic and Lutheran electors, decreed that Anabaptists should be put to death throughout the empire.

Thousands of Anabaptists perished. As Menno Simons—a Dutch Anabaptist whose followers became known as Mennonites—wrote:

> Some they have executed by hangings. . . . Some they roasted and burned alive. Some they have killed with the sword. . . . Some they have cast to the fishes. . . . They are hated, abused, slandered, and lied about by all men.

For the Anabaptists, then, the times were truly apocalyptic. How long could such suffering last? Melchior Hofmann, a south German Anabaptist preacher and pamphleteer, was sure the millennium would begin in 1533—to mark the fifteenth centennial of Christ's death. It would begin in Strasbourg, from which 144,000 virgin apostles would march out to gather God's people. Hofmann traveled widely—as far north as Stockholm—but was most enthusiastically received in Holland and Friesland, where an old man prophesied that the preacher would lie in prison for half a year, after which the invincible army of God would set forth to claim the world for Christ. Thus, when in 1533 Hofmann was arrested and imprisoned in Strasbourg, he and his Dutch and Frisian followers believed that the Last Days had begun in earnest.

By this time, however, Hofmann had moved away from the pacifism practiced by most Anabaptists: Before Christ's kingdom could be established on earth, he said, there would be a great slaughter of all who had not been born again in Christ. This new readiness to take up the sword was soon to make itself manifest, not in Strasbourg but well to the north, in the Westphalian city of Münster.

The story of what happened in Münster—the takeover of the city by Anabaptists, the establishment there of a communist regime, the efforts of mercenary troops hired by the bishop-prince of Münster to regain his stolen city—is at once a military tale and a kind of hallucinatory parable reminiscent of the paintings of Hieronymus Bosch. For what began as an attempt to establish the New Jerusalem on earth ended in the creation of a hell from which, for most, there was no escape except by violent death.

Over the years historians and others have been fascinated, or appalled, by what one mid-nineteenth-century German called "the only genuine and complete revolution on German soil." Different writers in different times see different things in the same event. At the end of the last century, for example, the Marxist writer Karl Kautsky saw the Münster Anabaptists as "forerunners of socialism," because in the New Jerusalem all things were held in common, at least theoretically. Half a century later, the German essayist Friedrich Percyval Reck-Malleczewen, who was to die in Dachau, saw the eloquent immigrant who ruled over Münster as a forerunner of Adolf Hitler—a charismatic opportunist, an actor who loved pomp and circumstance, an amateur general who, for a time, showed an uncanny ability to rout the professionals.

In the fall of 1533, the man who was destined to become king of Münster was running a tavern in Leiden. His name was Jan Bockelszoon; also known as John of Leiden, he was twenty-four years old and strikingly good-looking. A tailor by trade, he had spent four years in London, presumably as an apprentice, before returning to Leiden, where, at the age of twenty, he married a widow several years older than he was. Using money left to his wife by her first husband, he set himself up as a traveling salesman and journeyed far—south to Lisbon, north to the Hanseatic city of Lübeck. His voyages were not profitable, however, and on returning to Leiden he dipped into his wife's inheritance once again and opened a tavern—the White Lily.

Bockelszoon seems to have had a knack for acting—or at least for the kind of declamatory performance favored by the *Rederijkers,* or rhetoricians. He was, at any rate, invited to join one of the rhetoricians' chambers in

Leiden. Since the yearly competitions held by the chambers throughout the Netherlands were major social and cultural events, it would seem that Jan Bockelszoon, born illegitimate, had at last found a means of distinguishing himself. Then, at age twenty-four, he encountered Jan Mathys, an Anabaptist preacher and visionary described by a contemporary as "a great long man" who had "a great black beard and was a Hollander" from Haarlem. Mathys, a follower of Melchior Hofmann, preached the imminent end of the world with such power that Bockelszoon asked to be baptized and became an "apostle." The great long man then sent him out, together with another apostle, to baptize and proselytize throughout the provinces on their way to their final destination: Münster.

Münster was, at the time, one of the most volatile cities in western Europe. It was a bishopric, but one whose powerful guilds had, in 1532, forced the councilmen to install Lutheran preachers in all of the city's churches except the cathedral. It was, moreover, a bishopric that had changed hands three times that same year. One bishop, seeing that the Lutherans were gaining adherents, had resigned, and a second had drunk himself to death at his inaugural banquet. His successor, a petty prince named Franz von Waldeck, was annoyed that the capital of his ecclesiastic state had turned Lutheran and he insisted that the change was illegal. To cow the city into abandoning its new faith, he paraded troops outside the city walls. This show of force served only to provoke the leading citizens of Münster. On Christmas Eve of 1532, the militia was sent out and, in a bold raid, the city's soldiers seized several of the bishop's officers, who were then held as hostages. In early 1533 Waldeck officially recognized Münster as Lutheran.

By this time, however, the city was starting to fill up with Anabaptists. Some slipped in from the nearby duchy of Jülich-Cleve, from which they had been abruptly expelled; others, from the Netherlands and Friesland. By the end of 1533, when Jan Bockelszoon and his fellow apostle started out from Leiden, an extremely popular Münster preacher named Bernt Rothmann had abandoned Lutheranism and become an Anabaptist. An educated man who had won the respect of both Luther and his close friend and associate Philipp Melanchthon, Rothmann had become radicalized through conversations with several Dutch Anabaptists. He began to preach that the priest who does not work does not deserve to eat; that the rich should share their riches with the poor; and that all things should be held in common, as the apostles had done after the crucifixion.

A kind of religious frenzy seized the city. Townspeople were secretly baptized, thus forming a secret society, which added to the allure of the new doctrine. Then, on January 5, 1534, the first of Jan Mathys's apostles arrived in Münster. The reaction was astounding: Within eight days, 1,400 people— out of Münster's total population of about 15,000—were baptized. On the eighth day, Jan Bockelszoon and his fellow apostle arrived. Appearing at a moment of high hopes and expectations, the handsome actor, who was said to be a spellbinding orator, and his less-charismatic companion were at first taken to be Enoch and Elijah, whose return portended the Second Coming.

Less than two months later, the Anabaptists controlled the city—and the siege of Münster had begun.

What took place in those early months of 1534 was, in effect, a putsch. The city became a vortex, pulling in hitherto-hidden Anabaptists from near and far. In and around Münster, nuns, especially young ones, began leaving their convents as the eloquent Rothmann denounced virginity: Was it not a young woman's duty to "be fruitful and multiply"? Whole crowds saw visions. Religious fervor was turning into something akin to mass hysteria.

Feeling threatened, Münster's Lutherans and Catholics drew together. They began stockpiling weapons in a convent—now all but emptied of nuns—on the far side of the river Aa. Members of the coalition then met with officers in the service of the bishop and drew up a plan: On a certain night, two of the city's ten gates would be opened to admit the bishop's troops; the Anabaptists would be driven out of the city, and peace would be restored.

But things did not go according to plan. On the night of February 10, sensing that something was afoot, the Anabaptist men armed themselves and threw barricades up around the main square in preparation for battle. It was a time of terror and exaltation. A fire was seen in the sky. A figure out of Revelation—the man on the white horse—was seen riding through the fire and brandishing a sword.

But there was no battle that night. Some of the bishop's officers entered the city, bringing news that the bishop was on his way to Münster at the head of a force of 3,000 armed peasants. On hearing this, the Lutherans and Catholics—proud of their city's freedom—decided to come to terms with the Anabaptists rather than let the bishop back into Münster. The two sides then negotiated a kind of peace treaty: Religious liberty would be guaranteed to all parties, and all parties would obey the civil authorities in all temporal matters. When the bishop arrived, he found the city closed to him.

In the following days, the Anabaptists claimed, with some justice, that they had won a great victory. Now many more people accepted baptism in Münster. Letters were sent out to surrounding towns and to Holland and Friesland describing the recent triumph over evil and urging all Anabaptists to come to this place from which, shortly, the saints would go marching out to claim the world for Christ.

In mid-February, Jan Mathys, the chief prophet of the Münster Anabaptists, arrived in the city with his beautiful wife, Differe (or Divara), a former nun. By this time, what with the influx of Anabaptists from the outside, the conversion of hundreds of townspeople, and the flight of others who had grown alarmed by the constant turmoil, the Anabaptists constituted a majority. This was made clear—alarmingly so to the Lutherans and Catholics—when on February 23 a new town council was elected and a majority of the seats were won by Anabaptists. Now, at last, the Reign of the Saints could begin.

The beginning was ominous. Four days after the election, Mathys called for the expulsion of all "the ungodly" from the New Jerusalem. At 7 A.M. on February 27, bands of armed Anabaptists started going from door to door, rousing all the Lutherans and Catholics. As Meister Heinrich Gresbeck, an eyewitness, wrote, those who refused baptism "were forced to leave behind all they had . . . and leave then and there" on a cold day "with rain and snow and a great wind." Those who agreed to be baptized—or, rather, rebaptized— were allowed to remain, and became known as "Friday Christians."

On Saturday, February 28, 1534, peasants conscripted by the bishop-prince started digging trenches and throwing up earthworks outside the city walls. The siege had begun.

To raise money for his siege operation, including the payment of his field officers, Waldeck not only imposed a special tax but also took from several churches their most precious religious objects and then forced the towns to buy them back. This netted him more than 12,000 guldens; it also turned the looted towns against him.

Meanwhile, inside Münster, heads of households were ordered, on pain of death, to deliver up all the gold, silver, coin, and jewels in their possession; these were henceforth to be used for "the common good." Like Protestant iconoclasts in other cities before them, the Münster Anabaptists went about the edifying business of smashing statues and stained-glass windows. Then they went a step further: It was decreed that all books save the Bible must be burned—and this was done.

One night, serving watch duty on the city wall, a man named Hupert Smit made some caustic cracks about the preachers who were running the town: They preached so long that they must have a devil inside them, he said, and he called Jan Mathys a "shit prophet." Already, people were being encouraged to inform on one another, and the following day Smit was hauled before Mathys and other preachers and sentenced to death for mocking God. Reck-Malleczewen observes that his execution marked "the beginning of the Terror." From then on no one dared to grumble or protest.

It wasn't long after this that Jan Mathys himself met his doom. One day in early April the prophet attended a wedding feast. In the midst of the festivities, Meister Gresbeck tells us, he was seized by "the baptists' spirit . . . and sighed deeply, just as if he was about to die," and cried out to God, "Not my will but thine"—Christ's words in Gethsemane.

Mathys had received a divine command: He should go out against the enemy as David had gone out against Goliath. This latter-day David, however, was accompanied by a dozen or so volunteers. Confident that God would go with them, they ventured forth—and were slaughtered. Mathys, in fact, was butchered. The mercenaries drove their pikes through the prophet; then they cut his head off; and, finally, by night they nailed his genitals to the door of one of the city's ten gates.

Bockelszoon put what today would be called positive spin on the prophet's death: He had foreseen it, he said; it was God's will, he said; "God will raise up another for us, who will be even greater than Jan Mathys," he said.

The people quickly recognized the eloquent Bockelszoon as this greater God-given man. Practically overnight the disciple became the master. Swept up in a fresh wave of religious enthusiasm, women and girls danced through the streets crying, "Father, father, give us light!" until they could dance no more. In May, Bockelszoon himself danced in the streets, naked, then fell silent for three days, after which he called the people together to announce that God had spoken to him. The divine message was that the traditional town council must be disbanded; the New Jerusalem, the New Israel, should, like the old, be ruled by twelve elders, whom Bockelszoon then named.

It was at about this time—in the spring of 1534—that Bockelszoon took as his wife the fallen leader's beautiful widow, making himself a bigamist—as, in fact, Mathys had been (he, too, having had a wife at the time he married the former nun). But bigamy was hardly a Münster novelty. Chief among Bishop Franz von Waldeck's allies in his effort to recapture Münster and stifle the communist revolution that threatened to spread throughout northern Europe was Landgrave Philip of Hesse, a powerful supporter of Luther and, as it happened, a bigamist.

Philip, who had earlier dispatched two preachers to Münster, hoping they could convert the Anabaptist leaders to Lutheranism, would soon send up siege cannon, including two huge pieces known as the Devil and His Mother. Meanwhile, from March through June the bishop was relying on the Catholic princes of Cologne and Cleve to help him retake his city. First he got them to agree to lend him some cannon—which they did only after he had posted security for the pieces and had promised to repair any damage done to the cannon. Next he persuaded each to send him two companies of landsknechts, or mercenary foot soldiers (a company consisting of 100 to 200 men), and later 400 armed horsemen.

All this while the levies of peasants continued to dig—the circumference of the city was roughly ten miles—and the bishop, for his part, continued to pay out fifty gold guldens a month to his various field captains and thousands more for the gunpowder and other supplies that had to be brought in from Amsterdam and Cologne and Trier.

Inside the city, men, women, and children were organized for defense. Churches served as quarries while walls and bastions were reinforced. The lead linings of coffins were melted down to make bullets. At night, small bands of Münster's citizen army would steal out of the city, spike the enemy cannon, seize prisoners, and seize as well some pieces of light field artillery— demiculverins and falconets—then slip back into the city. (The raiders had at least one advantage over the mercenaries: They were sober. The mercenaries seem to have been almost perpetually drunk—at night, anyway.)

Once brought back into the city, the cannon were lugged up to the top of Münster's wildly iconoclastic but highly effective gun platforms—the result of another of those divine revelations that became almost commonplace within that apocalypse-minded city. On April 9, Bockelszoon's close friend, the Münster cloth merchant and patrician Bernt Knipperdollingk, had been seized by the prophetic spirit: "The high must be brought low," he said. Accordingly, the steeples of every church in the city but one—Saint Lambert's, used as a watchtower—were brought crashing down into the streets. The platforms from which the steeples had risen were converted into gun platforms.

But perhaps the most impressive project undertaken to strengthen the city's defenses was the digging—in the Dutch manner—of a double ring of water ditches outside the city walls, into which the river Aa was then diverted. (One of the bishop's field commanders, the burgomaster of Frankfurt, was so impressed by the Anabaptists' innovations that he urged his hometown's city council to send up an engineer to study Münster's defenses.) That this prodigious feat could be carried out within firing range of the bishop's troops says as much, perhaps, about the generally low morale of the mercenaries as it does about the effectiveness of the covering fire provided by the Anabaptists, as well as their readiness to work day and night until the job was done.

The Anabaptists also conducted a fairly effective propaganda war, using catapults and arrows to hurl messages at the mercenaries, urging them to leave the service of "a powerless and lousy bishop who doesn't have any money" and to serve "the brotherhood of Christ gathered in Münster" and be paid regularly. Desertion in the ranks was fairly common; several mercenaries, tempted by the promise of prompt payment, changed sides. (One of these turncoats, interestingly, was nicknamed the Smoker—a reminder that the use of New World tobacco was beginning to spread throughout Europe.)

The bishop's forces mounted their first serious attack in May. The bombardment began on May 22, the primary goal being to smash holes in the gates or to breach the walls so that the troops could rush in and overpower the defenders. But the Anabaptists were so well disciplined that the moment a hole was made in a wall, a gang of men, women, and children started filling it with stones and beams and dirt and dung. Meanwhile, other work parties gathered the incoming cannonballs and stacked them in the main square.

One night Preacher Rothmann and a band of volunteers took the offensive. After slipping out of the city through a secret exit, they surprised and killed a watch party, spiked several cannon, then set fire to powder kegs, timing one explosion so that the powder blew up the soldiers pursuing them.

On the evening of May 25, a company of drunken mercenaries, apparently eager to get the first crack at the loot and the women inside the city, staged a disorganized assault. The Anabaptists—sober, as usual—killed or wounded 200 of them, losing only two of their own. According to Meister Gresbeck, who had himself served as a landsknecht, the Anabaptists fought "as if they had been waging war for twenty years, and all that they did they did with cleverness and with skill and with sober sense." In any case the bishop's spring offensive was a fiasco.

In June some 200 mercenaries came over to the Anabaptist side, presumably because they wanted to be paid for their services and perhaps also because they were no longer sure that the bishop would emerge the victor in the conflict. In June, too, a lovely young Frisian woman named Hilla Feicken said she was told by God that she should kill the bishop, following the Old Testament example of Judith, who, by slaying Holofernes, had saved the besieged

Jewish city of Bethulia. But the bishop learned of this plot and the young Frisian was seized on her way through the enemy camp and, after being interrogated "under pain," was beheaded.

In July Jan Bockelszoon received a revelation of a different sort: To truly obey the Lord's command to be fruitful and multiply, a man should follow the example of the Old Testament and take more than one wife—indeed, the more wives, the better the Christian. The elders then set about explaining the new law to the townspeople: that all the women must marry, upon pain of death. Married women whose husbands had left the city had to accept another spouse. Even girls of eleven and twelve were compelled to marry—and, in fact, of the five new wives Bockelszoon acquired before October of that year, at least one was a mere girl.

The new doctrine almost resulted in the overthrow of the whole regime. On July 30, while the city slept, a smith named Heinrich Mollenhecke and a group of more than 200 men, including several former mercenaries fed up with life inside the New Jerusalem, seized the entire Anabaptist leadership and locked them up in the town hall jail. At this point all that the insurgents would have had to do to return the city to the bishop was open a gate and call in the troops. But greed undid them. Instead of letting in the bishop's men, they broke into the treasure room in the town hall. After gazing at all the gold and jewels and coins stored there, they spotted the bottles of wine—and started drinking.

The following morning, when the townspeople learned what had happened, they freed their leaders and seized the insurgents. About eighty of them were executed. Bernt Knipperdollingk served as the principal executioner, but, as Meister Gresbeck points out, after the burly patrician had killed several men, "whoever wished to kill somebody, he could take one and kill him. . . . The killing lasted three or four days." After this, he adds, nobody dared speak out against the doctrine of holy polygamy.

On August 24, less than a month after this abortive uprising, a council of war was held outside the city walls. The siege cannon promised by Philip of Hesse—including the Devil and His Mother—had arrived and the city was ringed with artillery. The bishop and his allies were now confident that they could smash their way in, but Waldeck, wanting to regain his city without destroying more of it than need be, first tried diplomacy. He assured the Anabaptists that if they simply went home he would consider the matter closed. If they refused, however, he would have no choice but to force his way in and, once victorious, execute the troublemakers. Bockelszoon and the other elders spurned this offer.

A shot fired by the Devil on August 31 at five in the morning signaled the beginning of the attack. Then all the cannon fired, concentrating on six of the city gates. Bombardments in those days were undoubtedly noisy and frightening, but they also involved long intermissions. The Devil and His Mother, for instance, could be fired only five or six times a day; between firings, the cannon barrels had to be swabbed out—to remove any remaining powder that might cause an explosion—and then dried out.

There seem to have been three major cannonades at the most, after each of which the landsknechts rushed the gates. The defenders were ready for them. Each time the soldiers came up, the women lining the walls threw buckets of seething lime and wreaths of burning pitch onto them, while men tipped boulders over the walls and other men and boys shot arrows down at them. Bockelszoon, in charge of the defense, dispatched troops to one gate after another as needed.

When the landsknechts withdrew, the Anabaptists jeered at them from the walls: "Come back! Leaving already? An attack should go on for at least a whole day!" A broadsheet put the casualties at forty-two officers and hundreds of men on the bishop's side, as against only fifteen or sixteen Anabaptists.

Almost every historian who has dealt with the Münster revolution—from Leopold von Ranke in the nineteenth century to Norman Cohn, author of *The Pursuit of the Millennium,* in the twentieth—holds the opinion that if, following this defeat of the bishop's forces, the Anabaptists had sortied out, they might well have routed the enemy and captured some of the bishop's chief officers. The reasons they failed to do so appear to have been twofold: They lacked a sufficient force of cavalry; and, although confident that God would protect them as long as they were inside the New Jerusalem, they were less certain about enjoying his protection outside its walls.

In any event, instead of attacking, the Anabaptists contented themselves with repairing and reinforcing the damaged walls and gates. In front of each gate, they built "a great earth house"—a semicircular earthwork—"and made the city as strong as it had been before." Now more than ever they believed that God was on their side. Their preachers assured them, Meister Gresbeck wrote, that "God would come out of heaven and save them, and Christ would come out of heaven and reign on earth for one thousand years."

It was during these heady days that a lame goldsmith named Johan Dusentschur made a startling declaration in the main square: God, he said, had revealed to him that Jan Bockelszoon was to be king of the New Israel and of the whole world. The elders discussed this wonderful revelation among themselves and, after prayerful deliberation, named Jan king "until God reclaims dominion." Jan's acceptance speech, as recalled by Meister Gresbeck, was a classic of sanctimoniousness:

> Now God has chosen me to be a king over the whole world. But I tell you, dear brothers and sisters, I would much rather be a swineherd and would much rather hold the plow or dig than be such a king. What I do I must do because God has chosen me to do so. For this, dear brothers and sisters, let us thank God.

A king must have his court and trappings. Jan's chief wife, Differe, became the queen; Knipperdollingk, lord chamberlain and executioner; Rothmann, royal orator; and so on. Thrones, crowns, orb, scepter, robes, royal coaches, seals, coins to be used in the fallen world outside—for such purposes as buying provisions and paying mercenaries—all these things were made quickly so that a proper coronation could take place in early September. By that time King Jan had taken unto himself ten more wives, all under the age of twenty, bringing the count to sixteen, not including his long-since-forgotten wife back in Haarlem. Knipperdollingk and Rothmann also increased their count of wives.

Thrice weekly, fanfare would resound through the city and the court officers would march into the main square, followed by King Jan—wearing his triple-tiered crown, carrying his scepter, and, unlike the others, on horseback. He would take his place on the throne, a page standing on either side, one holding the Old Testament, the other a sword. The sometime actor appears to have played his role with conviction. He also appears to have begun to fear an uprising, because he selected the strongest of the men who could ride a horse and made them an elite mounted bodyguard.

In the weeks following Jan's coronation, the leaders of the Münster revolution seem to have realized that the only way they could win their battle with the bishop and his allies was to attract to their New Jerusalem the thousands of Anabaptists who lived in nearby cities and villages and as far away as Amsterdam to the west and Friesland to the north and west. Rothmann thus wrote various treatises and these were distributed far and wide, as well as by arrow and catapult to Münster's besiegers. The message of all these writings was, in essence, the following: For fourteen centuries Christendom has suffered in a Babylonian captivity; now, in preparation for his return, Christ has established his kingdom in Münster, and soon it will be time to set forth and claim the whole world for him.

In October the goldsmith-turned-prophet, Dusentschur, had another revelation. God had told him, he said, that the trumpet of the Lord would sound three times in Münster, and at the third blast everyone should gather on Mount Zion (i.e., the renamed cathedral square), the men armed. From there everyone would march out, right into and through the enemy camp, and God would make them invincible. Five would slay a hundred and, by visionary progression, ten would slay a thousand.

Some days thereafter a horn did sound—blown not by God nor by some angel but by the limping prophet himself. Two weeks later, at the third blast of the prophet's horn, everyone gathered in the main square. King Jan—armed, armored, wearing his crown, and surrounded by his retinue—rode into the square and there appointed officers to lead the army of God. Drills and maneuvers were performed and a mock battle was staged. The air was filled with expectancy: Something miraculous was about to happen. Knipperdollingk assured a lame man that he would walk, a blind man that he would see. But as Meister Gresbeck dryly noted, "the lame and the blind remained just as they were."

Something truly astonishing did happen, however: The king called the whole thing off. The call to arms, he explained, had been simply a test of faith. He invited one and all to share in a banquet in the main square. Tables were set up, a meal presented, and—in a touching display of Christian humility—both the king and his queen helped to serve. After the banquet, communion was served, hymns were sung, and sermons preached. Then, in an abrupt change of mood, Jan ordered a prisoner—a recently captured landsknecht—to be brought before him. "And bring my sword of justice, too," he called out. The prisoner was fetched; Jan beheaded him. It was God's will that he should do so, he said.

The madness of that October night was not yet over. Close to midnight the limping prophet got up on a chair and announced that once again God had spoken to him—in considerable detail, naming names: Twenty-seven men were to leave the city within the hour; they were to go out into the world and prepare the way for the king, who would follow, sword in hand, and punish those who mocked his apostles. God would protect them.

There was no arguing with this prophet who presumed to speak for God—and to whom the king owed his high station. That very night the twenty-seven men, including Dusentschur, bade farewell to their 120 wives and, armed with nothing but their faith, set out to prepare the way for their king. All were captured. Some were used as decoys to lure out into the open the hidden Anabaptists within a given city; all were killed save one—Heinrich Graes, a schoolteacher. Graes struck a deal with the bishop: If his life was spared, he would go back into the city and serve as a spy.

When he returned to Münster and was asked what had happened to him and the others, he replied that the others had all died martyrs' deaths; as for himself, an angel of the Lord had freed him from prison. Perhaps for political reasons—the story of divine intervention lent weight to the preachers' assurances that God would not fail the faithful—or perhaps because they truly believed the man, King Jan and his court officers not only accepted Graes's tale but raised him to the status of prophet and henceforth included him in their innermost councils.

The bishop, for his part, needed all the help he could get during the autumn of 1534. Some contagious disease—possibly typhoid fever—had struck the Cleve contingent. When the bishop ordered the officers to burn the infected camp and move to new quarters, large numbers of men deserted instead, looting farms and villages as they slipped away.

Then there were the usual money problems. In September, Cleve and Cologne, which had already pledged to supply 8,000 troops between them, plus 1,000 sappers for a month and 20,000 guldens each for pay and supplies, reluctantly agreed to raise another 50,000 guldens to defray the cost of constructing blockhouses around Münster. There were strings attached: The bishop had to promise to pay the money back after he had retaken the city. Also, it is doubtful that more than 4,000 troops were ever encamped before Münster at any one time.

Shortly after Graes the apostle returned to Münster as Graes the spy, the king and his council tried a new tactic to gain support outside the city walls. First, a good deal of gold and silver was smuggled out in what proved to be a vain attempt to raise an army of mercenaries big enough to take on the bishop's army. Second, thousands of pamphlets written by Rothmann were smuggled out of the city—and this propaganda effort proved more effective.

In January 1535, captured Münster couriers revealed that four large groups of armed Anabaptists were to form up somewhere in the area between Aix-la-Chapelle and Amsterdam. In late January, a stadtholder (viceroy) reported that a host of 1,000 Anabaptists had gathered in the province of Groningen in preparation for a march on Münster; an even larger host was said to be gathering in Utrecht. There were serious riots in Amsterdam and Leiden.

It was in January, too, that Graes left Münster, having concocted a convincing reason to leave: God had instructed him to go forth and bring back to Münster a great host of armed men from Wesel and Amsterdam and Deventer. He headed straight for the bishop, whose headquarters were in nearby Iburg. There, Graes wrote up a detailed report, including passwords, defenses, secret passages, number of armed men, and quantity of ammunition and food supplies. He also constructed an earth-and-clay model of the defense system to show the would-be attackers its strengths and weaknesses and its several passages. Among other things, he told the bishop that King Jan had announced publicly, after beheading his barber for lying, that his own head should be cut off if deliverance had not come by Easter.

If the thousands of Anabaptists who yearned to reach Münster saw it as a heavenly city, its roughly 10,000 inhabitants were living through a kind of purgatory that was rapidly degenerating into sheer hell. Practically every offense was a capital crime—the possession of money, the failure of a wife to show proper respect for her husband or to allow him his "marital rights," the mocking of a preacher. Knipperdollingk seemed to relish beheading people; when one of his wives was sentenced to death and the executioner was a bit slow about his job, the lord chamberlain wrested the sword from his hands and beheaded her himself. The number of executions had been increasing ever since Jan's coronation, and the pace quickened during the winter of 1534–35.

To add to the horrors of this reign of terror (carried out, of course, in the name of Christ) there was the pain of hunger. Rationing of sorts had been imposed almost as soon as the city found itself at war with the bishop, back in February and March 1534. A year later, with the circumvallation of the city nearly completed, the situation became desperate—at least for the common people.

King Jan had had the foresight to store up provisions for a full year, so when he and his sixteen wives dined, they ate well. Those who did not belong to the privileged court, however, were reduced to eating horsemeat, and when the horsemeat was gone, Meister Gresbeck wrote, they ate "all sorts of beasts"—rats, mice, cats, hedgehogs, water snakes—and finally boot leather, bootlaces, grass. The atmosphere became that of a Poe horror story, with the king and his court trying to distract the people's attention from the ghastliness of their condition by putting on plays and by holding a mock mass with dead cats and mice taking the place of the Eucharist.

Easter—which in 1535 fell in March—came and went without deliverance. After withdrawing from public view for some days, King Jan emerged with an explanation: He had meant internal, *spiritual* deliverance, not deliverance by the arrival of troops or anything worldly like that. The people had passed the spiritual test; the more mundane form of salvation would come in due course. One must be patient.

In fact, help had been on the way. Three ships loaded with Dutch Anabaptists had been hurrying to lift the siege of Münster, but all were sunk in the IJssel River; farther to the west, Anabaptists had seized a fortified monastery and fought a vicious battle in which some 800 people on both sides were killed. Later, in May, Anabaptists would once again run riot in Amsterdam, briefly taking over the town hall.

It was in May that King Jan divided Münster into twelve sectors, appointing a "duke" to rule over each and granting to each a portion of the German empire, which would be theirs following the promised victory over the forces of evil. It was in May, too, that King Jan beheaded one of his wives (the crime was gross insubordination) in the presence of his other wives, who then joined in the singing of the hymn "To God in the Highest Alone Be Praise."

Forced to face up to the disintegration of morale among the townspeople, Jan began granting "leave" to those who cared to try their luck outside the walls. But the minute they received permission to go, they found there was a catch: Their houses, goods, and all their clothes save those they were wearing—everything they owned was confiscated. When they finally walked out into no-man's-land, these living skeletons whose skin was "white as linen cloth" and "ears, cheeks, lips, and noses were more transparent than a sheet of paper" were so dazed and demoralized that according to the bishop's field commander, Wirich von Dhaun, "they would rather be killed, would much rather die, than go back into the city."

On May 23, five men—among them Meister Gresbeck—managed to escape the nightmare of Münster. They explained to the mercenaries that now, with the city's watch parties decimated by sickness and starvation, it would be no difficult matter to storm the walls. Yet the field officers, having experienced two defeats at the hands of the Anabaptists, suspected a trap, and a month passed before an attack was launched. On June 22 Wirich von Dhaun demanded the surrender of the city—a demand that court orator Rothmann rejected. The following day a tremendous storm broke over the landscape, the loud thunder and the rattle of hail covering the sounds of preparations for the assault.

An hour before midnight, Gresbeck and others swam across the moat, trailing ropes to which ladder bridges were attached. The earthen outerworks in front of the two gates on which the attack was to be concentrated were sparsely manned and the sentries were swiftly silenced. The Anabaptist password—Earth—was given, a door swung open, and into the city swarmed thirty-five officers and some four hundred men.

Then, as once before, fatally, they forgot all about tactics. Instead of leaving behind a body of men to hold the gate or sending a scout back to alert the commander to the fact that the defenses had been breached, officers and men rushed to seize their prime objective—the treasure stored in the town hall—before any of their comrades could get their hands on it.

Belatedly alerted to this host in their midst, the Anabaptists quickly converged on the main square, drove the mercenaries out of it, and finally cornered them. King Jan came to discuss a truce with them—a truce that he probably would not have honored—but at first light a mercenary standard-bearer who apparently had slipped away during the confused street fighting shouted out over the city wall to the main force, "Waldeck! Waldeck! Münster is ours!" Waving his banner, he urged the army to move at last.

The men surged forward—a force of about 3,000 against frantically fighting bands of Anabaptist men and boys whose numbers had dwindled to only a few hundred. One of the largest bands threw up a barricade of over-turned carriages and fought so bravely that, at last, the mercenaries agreed to a truce. A contemporary "True Account of the Wonderful Affair of the Baptists in Münster" relates what then happened:

> It was agreed by both parties that everyone should go to his own home again till the coming [of] his grace the bishop, when the matter should be further handled . . . and every man went to his own home again. But as the landsknechts had suffered great and notable losses, they fell with furious rage on the houses, and where they found anyone they dragged him by the head out of the house into the street, hacked him to pieces or stabbed him dead.

Women and children were generally spared—that is, if the women re-canted their heretical beliefs. King Jan and his lord chamberlain, Bernt Knip-perdollingk, and an elder named Bernt Krechting were taken alive. No one knows what happened to the court orator, Rothmann, who had in a sense started it all in 1533 with his radical preaching. According to some reports, he was speared through the chest, his arm was nearly lopped off, and he died. Yet years later, sightings of Rothmann were reported in various cities and a "Wanted" poster was circulated. It described him as "a solidly built, thickset man . . . with black-brown straight hair; usually wears a Spanish cape."

The searching and stabbing and hacking and killing went on for ten days. The streets were clogged with the dead. "And then the peasants were let back into the city," according to a contemporary account,

> to bury the corpses on account of the great stench. The peasants stripped the corpses and robbed them, dug deep pits in the cemetery and threw the corpses, naked, into the pits, one on top of the other, just as if they were beasts.

As for the treasure stored in the town hall, it proved not to be as fabulous as everyone from the bishop on down had hoped. Rumor had made it huge, and many officers and men had run up sizable debts on the assumption that once the city was taken they would be rich. As a result, when word went out that the most an ordinary landsknecht could hope to be paid at the sharing out of the booty was sixteen guldens, there was widespread rioting. A gang of fifty landsknechts broke into the treasure room to see for themselves how much gold there was; seven of them were executed, the rest driven out of the city.

Captured in June, Jan Bockelszoon had another six months to live. The authorities seemed in no hurry to kill him. Many people came to visit him in the various prisons in which he was kept, and he proved to have a sense of humor he had not previously revealed. When, for example, the bishop complained to him about the grievous expenses incurred in the siege operation, Jan came up with an extraordinary solution to his captor's financial problem: The bishop should put him—Jan—in a cage and take him around the countryside, charging a fee for a view of him. (The bishop did have his prize captive carted around in a cage, but the show was free of charge.) Again, when the bishop complained that Jan had "ruined me and my poor people," Jan replied that he hadn't ruined him at all, but had "handed over to you a strong city, proof against everything."

Among other visitors the deposed king received were two preachers dispatched by the ever-humane Landgrave Philip of Hesse (to whom Jan as king had written letters, addressing him familiarly as "Dear Phil"); their mission was, as earlier, to convert Jan to Lutheranism. They were about to leave his cell, having failed in their attempt, when Jan called them back. He had a proposition to make: If he was allowed to live, he said, he would agree to travel—together with Melchior Hofmann (still in prison in Strasbourg) and his wife Differe (who, unknown to Jan, had been killed shortly after her capture)—to all the Anabaptist communities in Holland and Friesland and England, preaching obedience to the authorities and other nonrevolutionary virtues. This offer was declined.

On January 22, 1536, Jan Bockelszoon, Bernt Knipperdollingk, and Bernt Krechting were brought to Münster's main square, where only a few months earlier Jan had sat on a throne, a triple-tiered crown on his head. The three men were tied to stakes. Their punishment was to be tortured with hot tongs until death. The tongs were heated in the coals of two field kitchens. Jan was the first to be tortured, the red-hot tongs being used to pull chunks of flaming flesh from his body. The terrible torture lasted nearly an hour. According to a broadsheet, "while the king was being martyred, he neither spoke nor screamed, but after [the torture was over] repeatedly called out such words to God as, 'Father, have mercy on me.'" Finally, to put an end to his suffering, one of the executioners drove a dagger into his chest.

Knipperdollingk, who presumably had to watch all this, tried in vain to strangle himself by straining against his neck iron, and was tortured even more horribly than Jan. Then it was Krechting's turn.

Only in death did Jan get his wish of being placed in a cage and exhibited. Three iron cages had been built in Dortmund for the express purpose of holding the corpses. When the three men had been killed, the doors to these cages were opened and the corpses tossed inside; then the cages were hoisted to the top of Saint Lambert's Church as an example to one and all. The corpses were removed later that year because of the stench; the cages themselves were left in place and, indeed, they hang there to this day.

In his fury, the bishop revoked the city's privileges and made Münster officially Catholic once again. Meanwhile, throughout the Holy Roman Empire, the excesses of this single, exceptional sect of Anabaptists were used as an excuse to drive out, forcibly convert, or kill all Anabaptists, even though the vast majority of them were known for their piety, simplicity, and probity—as well as for their unwillingness to yield on matters of conscience.

The Reformation historian Roland Bainton has called the virtual extirpation of the various Anabaptist sects throughout the empire "one of the greatest tragedies of German history"; it meant that the emergent Lutheran church would never be subjected to criticism as it allied itself with and became part of the established order. Conscientious dissent came to seem suspect, un-German, even un-Christian. (It was in England, to which many Anabaptists fled following the fall of Münster, and eventually in America that the descendants of sixteenth-century nonconformists—the Amish, the Mennonites, the Hutterites, and the Quakers—would come into their own.) Because his actions gave religious dissent a bad name, the sixteenth-century actor who saw himself as ushering in the thousand-year reign of Christ on earth helped prepare the way for the rise to power, four centuries later, of the demagogue who foresaw a Third Reich that would last a thousand years.

The Great Wall of China

by DAVID CLAY LARGE

Robert Frost said it: "Something there is that doesn't love a wall." A case in point is the Great Wall of China. Forget everything you have learned about it. The wall can't be seen with the naked eye from the moon. Much of China's "Earth Dragon" was built early in the seventeenth century—which makes it about as ancient as the city of Boston. "Before I built a wall," the poetic narrator of Frost's "Mending Wall" says, "I'd ask to know / What I was walling in or walling out . . . ?" Exactly. The Great Wall of China did a better job of keeping people in than invaders out—in fact it seemed to attract them like a magnet. Its "very elaborateness," David Clay Large writes, "was its main weakness, and the huge costs involved stirred up rebellion at home. A defensive system like this . . . was a provocation to the human spirit." (The same might be said of the late Berlin wall.) But the myths of the Great Wall of China are, apparently, as formidable as its battlements, Large concludes. He is a professor at Montana State University and is the author of *Between Two Fires: Europe's Path in the 1930s*, published by W. W. Norton.

"Every wall in the world, whether German or Chinese, begs to be overcome."

—PETER SCHNEIDER,
New York Times, June 25, 1989

We all know, or think we know, what the Great Wall of China is: the world's most stupendous engineering marvel, a great stone rampart snaking across the mountains and plains of northern China, hoary with age but fastidiously maintained over the millennia by xenophobic rulers determined to seal off their sophisticated civilization from the barbarous nomads of the steppes.

Those of us anxious to learn more could turn to one of our trusted repositories of practical wisdom and discover that it was completed in just fifteen years during the third century B.C. by China's first emperor, Ch'in Shih Huang Ti (c. 259–210 B.C.), who, according to *Ripley's Believe It or Not!*, buried a million men in the walls "to make them strong." From *Reader's Digest* we could learn that this vast structure contains enough building materials "to girdle the globe at the equator with a barrier eight feet high and three feet thick."

According to *National Geographic*, an eighteenth-century British visitor estimated that the wall was composed of "more brick and stone [than] all the buildings in the United Kingdom." (No wonder Dr. Johnson told Boswell that a trip to the wall "would be of importance in raising your children to eminence. . . . They would at all times be regarded as the children of a man who had gone to view the Wall of China.")

Estimations of length are unfortunately less precise: According to a 1982 *Reader's Digest* article, it is 3,700 miles long, which means that "if straightened out, it would span the United States from New York to San Francisco, and back to Salt Lake City." A *National Geographic* article (1923) put the length, minus zigs and zags, at 2,000 miles, meaning that it "would stretch from Portugal to Naples or from Philadelphia to Topeka. . . ."

As for the human energy required to build such an edifice, an early-twentieth-century American account notes that Ulysses S. Grant—who had never seen the wall—"estimated that it took as much work as would have built all our railroads, all our canals, and nearly all our cities." Equally astonishing, we learn, is the wall's durability; this "Eighth Wonder of the World has survived all the others save one, the Great Pyramid of Kufu at Gizeh," *National Geographic* observes. Yet the pyramids are mere pimples on the desert sands compared to the Great Wall, which, according to astronomers quoted in the article, is "the only work of man's hands which would be visible to the human eye from the moon."

Unfortunately, the Great Wall's popular image is essentially a literary and historical myth. When Richard Nixon made his heralded trip to China in 1972, he planned to tell the Chinese that the Apollo astronauts had seen the wall from the moon. Since his staff could not confirm this, however, he had to settle for the somewhat pallid "This is a great wall, and it had to have been built by a great people."

Actually, although the section of wall northwest of Beijing that Nixon saw—and that thousands of American tourists have since visited—is certainly great, it is not terribly old. It was built early in the seventeenth century during the late Ming period. Virtually nothing survives of Ch'in Shih Huang Ti's original Great Wall. Nor, in fact, was that wall a single rampart at all; it was a series of fortifications and walls connecting earlier barriers thrown up by preimperial feudal states. Post-Ch'in emperors sometimes refurbished the earlier wall system but often built new complexes in different places and in different styles. In their various manifestations, the Chinese walls undoubtedly contained prodigious amounts of stone and brick (and bones) and stretched over great distances. But we will never know their precise dimensions—no reliable physical surveys of them were ever made. We do not even know exactly how long the currently extant Great Wall is, for the present Chinese estimate—8,494 li, or 2,633 miles—is based on maps, not physical measurements.

The same is true of the figures provided in 1971 by the sinologist Joseph Needham in his *Science and Civilization in China:* 3,930 miles if all branch walls are included, 2,150 if one counts the main line alone. There seems to be some confusion, moreover, regarding just which ramparts, forts, mounds, and roads constitute the "Great Wall." In 1987 a British ultra-marathoner claimed to have run its entire length, but he admitted later that at times he didn't know where the "wall" was.

Perhaps all we can say with certainty is that the Great Wall *cannot* be seen with the naked eye from the moon.

Putting aside the mythology about the Great Wall's size and age, there are also controversial questions about its military functions and utility. Was Edward Gibbon, the historian of ancient Rome's decline, correct in asserting that "this stupendous work, which holds a conspicuous place in the map of the world, has never contributed to the safety of an unwarlike people"? And which of Voltaire's assessments was right? At one time he insisted that the wall was a highly practical edifice, compared to which the pyramids were "merely childish and useless heaps." On another occasion he denounced the wall as a "useless" monument to fear, as the pyramids were monuments to vanity and superstition.

National Geographic seemed to have no doubts on this score. Its 1923 article stated confidently that the Great Wall "had a mighty purpose, serving as a barrier to keep the barbarians of the north from overrunning China, whose fertile plains invited them." The barbarians in question were the Hsi-ung-nu, the dreaded "Huns." Were these fierce nomads, as Needham contends, effectively repelled by the wall and obliged to visit their destructive predations elsewhere? Was the Chinese wall system truly an ever-vigilant "Earth Dragon," as the Chinese called it, or was it more like a paper tiger—an ancient harbinger of that twentieth-century barrier against modern Huns, the Maginot Line?

The first Chinese walls, like early walls in ancient and medieval Europe, were ramparts of tamped earth built around villages and cities as protection against intruders. Yet it may be that the Chinese were particularly obsessive about walls, for they went on to wall off everything they could—houses, palaces, gardens. Then they encircled inner walls with outer walls, so that their villages resembled those wooden dolls that enclose numerous replicas of themselves in gradually diminishing sizes. The ancient Chinese even had a god of walls and moats, whose primary duty was to guard the dividing line between the familiar Inner and the hostile Outer.

During the Chou dynasty (c. 1122–255 B.C.), rival feudal states built walls along their borders to impede invasions not just from nomads but from each other as well. When faced with a particularly severe outside threat, the feudal regimes sometimes pooled their resources to build longer fortifications.

Thus the Ch'i, Sung, and Chao states built an extensive northern wall in what is now Hopei Province.

The evidence suggests that these early walls proved to be a poor defense, for the enemy simply went around them or, if they were low enough, over the top of them, as if they were no more than ancient speed bumps. This was the fate of the wall built by the state of Wei in 353 B.C. It was easily breached by the Ch'in, a semibarbarous Chinese people whose armies copied nomadic cavalry techniques. Soon the Ch'in skirted and jumped other walls as well, pulling the conquered territories into their own domain.

Despite the ease with which they had crossed other states' walls, the Ch'in began building walls themselves along their new borders. Their ruler, King Chao-hsiang (306–251 B.C.), built a wall to fence out the Hu, a people even more barbarous than his own. But the creators and perpetuators of the Great Wall myth invariably credit the Ch'in king and first Chinese emperor, Ch'in Shih Huang Ti, with the momentous decision to build the continuous long wall that allegedly protected China's northern border for centuries to come.

Ch'in Shih Huang Ti is believed to have been a paranoid megalomaniac who was constantly plagued by a fear of death. In addition to walling off his empire, he searched for an elixir of immortality, buried alive 500 scholars who had criticized him, burned all the Confucian Classics he could get his hands on, constructed a mile-long palace stocked with 3,000 concubines, and finally had himself buried in an enormous tomb defended by an "army" of 6,000 soldiers cast in terra-cotta.

For his accomplishments as conqueror and builder, Ch'in Shih Huang Ti has been labeled by a French sinologist the "Napoleon of China" and an "administrator of genius," comparable to Caesar and Alexander the Great. But while many modern accounts analyze his acts and motives as if he had died only a few years ago, leaving behind detailed records, actually we know little about what made him embark on his monumental projects. The *Shih Chi*, the main contemporary account of his wall-building enterprise, says only:

> [The emperor] dispatched his general [Meng T'ien] to lead a force of a hundred thousand men north to attack the barbarians. He seized control of all the lands south of the Yellow River and established defenses along the river, constructing forty-four walled district cities overlooking the river and manning them with convict laborers transported o the border for garrison duty. . . . Thus he utilized the natural mountain barriers to establish the border defenses, scooping out the valleys and constructing ramparts and building installations at other points where they were needed. The whole line of defenses stretched over ten thousand li (3,125 miles) from Lin-t'ao to Liao-tung and even extended across the Yellow River and through the Yan-shan and Pei-chia.

When the Ch'in dynasty began constructing its fortification system, the empire's northern frontier was not particularly threatened, Ch'in's armies having massacred or semicolonized the nomadic tribes near that border. It is therefore possible that as well as seeking long-term security, the Ch'in regime intended to mark more closely the division between China and the barbarous steppes and to delineate the outer limits to which the Chinese people should expand.

Perhaps there was yet another, internal motive. Ch'in Shih Huang Ti may have used this vast building project to employ surplus workers and recalcitrant scholars—thus anticipating both the WPA and the gulag by well over 2,000 years. For this purpose, the enterprise was conveniently labor-intensive, and the workers who dropped from exhaustion or illness could simply be bricked up in the structure as extra ballast or as "guardian spirits" of the wall.

These guardian spirits had little opportunity to guard, however, for within a few years the Ch'in regime fell victim to internal rebellion—a threat that no wall, however ambitious, could ward off. Neglected after the fall of the dynasty, the Ch'in wall—a discontinuous system of earth, stone, and brick ramparts—soon fell under the control of the Hsiung-nu, Huns who penetrated deep into China proper.

By the latter part of the Han period (206 B.C.–A.D. 220), the original wall was a line of rubble, though it survived in the Chinese consciousness as a symbol of despotism and cruelty—"the longest cemetery on earth," according to a modern historian. A peasant song of the Han era warned: "If a son is born, mind don't raise him! / If a girl is born, feed her dried meat. / Don't you just see below the Long Wall / Dead men's skeletons prop each other up?"

However ominously the Ch'in walls may have loomed in the Chinese consciousness, they were apparently rather rudimentary in design compared to the ramparts constructed by the next dynasty, the Han, which set about fortifying the northwestern regions it gradually reconquered from the Hsiung-nu. More extensive contemporary evidence allows us to describe in some detail the Han defenses and the garrisons that manned them.

Like the Ch'in, but more elaborately and extensively, the Han built a defensive system consisting of guard towers connected by a causeway along which archers and guards could be stationed. The square brick towers, of varying thickness and height, were situated to allow their occupants the maximum view of the terrain below. Therefore the distance separating them differed considerably, in some areas less than a mile, in others as much as five miles.

Just outside the ramparts lay sandbanks that were smoothed regularly to reveal evidence of nocturnal intruders, whether man, beast, or disease-ridden Hunnish prostitutes. One of the least popular garrison duties was that of patrolling the sandbanks in search of footprints, for of course whatever had made the prints might be lurking nearby.

Surviving readiness reports on the border defenses give a good indication of the military hardware and supplies with which the Han wall was equipped. The watchtowers were armed with heavy crossbows (a Chinese invention) on revolvable mountings. Ammunition consisted of two types of arrow held at the ready in large quivers attached to the walls. There were supplies of helmets and armor, as well as grease and glue for the weapons. Dogs, useful in patrolling the sandbanks (and also as delicacies at ceremonial banquets), were lodged in tower kennels. There is no evidence that the ramparts possessed any of those vats of boiling oil said to have enlivened defensive operations in European fortifications.

Signaling devices were important parts of the wall's equipment. Each tower had a pole up which flags, fire baskets, or smoke pots could be hoisted to send messages like "No Huns in sight" or "We're in trouble here—send men fast!" Posted above tower doors were elaborate instructions concerning the standard signaling procedure for various emergencies. Here is one example that puts Paul Revere's "One if by land, two if by sea" to shame:

> If one or more enemy are seen to penetrate the defenses, light one woodpile and raise two flags, or two torches by night. If ten or more enemy are seen outside the defenses, light a wood-pile and raise signals as in the case of . . . one man. If five hundred enemy or more are observed; if they attack the post's defenses, light one wood-pile and raise three flags, or three torches by night; in the case of twenty men or less, light wood-piles and raise signals as in the case of . . . five hundred men. If the enemy are in occupation of the defenses of a post, raise flags over the post by day, or a [call and return] signal by torch at night; and the next post shall forthwith acknowledge by lighting wood-piles or raising signals, in accordance with the code.

Unfortunately the code did not say how many flags to raise or woodpiles to light if 5,000 Huns had disemboweled most of the garrison. But perhaps this was seen as irrelevant. Indeed, the posted operating procedure might have been largely irrelevant anyhow, since most of the tower guards apparently could not read.

Aside from their illiteracy, what do we know about the forces manning the Hans' border fortifications? The rank and file in the garrisons consisted of volunteers, conscripts, and convicts, the latter brought in mainly during emergencies. Conscripts, the largest contingent, were generally of peasant stock. According to one authority, they were "marched from their farmland . . . to serve their emperor in the harsh conditions of a largely barren country, where they could expect neither the comforts and pleasures of sophisticated city life nor the stability of a well-established tradition of civil government."

These conscripts unquestionably resented a duty that took them away from their fields and families. On the other hand, few of them could have pined for the refinements of "sophisticated city life"; they were rustics, used to a primitive existence. A snobbish Chinese proverb says: "One doesn't use the best metal to make nails, nor the best men to make soldiers."

Service in the border forts was no doubt psychologically harder on the officers, who often came from privileged backgrounds, yet—unlike their modern equivalents—had to live and work under almost the same conditions that their men did. We do know that the officer classes regarded border duty "as a form of living death" and—this time not unlike their modern counterparts—tried to avoid it when they could.

Life on the wall must have oscillated between the tedium typical of guard duty in most military installations and those adrenaline-filled moments when the enemy appeared. Unfortunately, we have only the sketchiest accounts of actual skirmishes in the Han border regions, but they cannot have been pleasant if the following description of the Huns' military prowess is even close to accurate. The observer here is the Chinese minister of war under Emperor Wen Ti (180–157 B.C.).

> The Hsiung-nu scale and descend even the most precipitous mountains with astonishing speed. They swim the deepest torrents, tolerate wind and rain, hunger and thirst. They can set off on forced marches unhindered even by precipices. They train their horses to cope with the narrowest trails, and are so expert with their bows that in a surprise attack they can fire their arrows at full gallop. Such are the Hsiung-nu! They attack, recoil and rally again, and if ever they do suffer a setback they simply disappear without a trace like a cloud.

Formidable as the Hsiung-nu undoubtedly were, they seem to have made few serious assaults against the Han northern border defenses. A major reason is that the Huns were gradually becoming less Hunnish; they were undergoing a process of partial sinicization that made them inclined to wear silks rather than skins, and sit on cushions rather than saddles.

In fact, during the reign of Wen Ti, the high point of the Han Empire, the wall was less important as a defensive barrier than as a bridgehead for Han military forays into Mongolia and Manchuria. These expansionist operations were generally unsuccessful, since the Chinese were not good at fighting on the nomads' home turf. The wall's employment as an offensive bridgehead, moreover, was rather ironic, since its raison d'être was to guarantee perpetual tranquillity for China.

As it declined in defensive significance, the Han wall assumed another function performed by many other walls (including a prominent modern one): that of keeping people *in*, rather than out. Around 33 B.C., Emperor Yüan Ti's counselor explained:

> Besides serving as a bulwark against invaders, the frontier posts are kept on constant guard to stop the escape of traitors from our country. Many of the subjects of northernmost China are descendants of barbarians, and therefore have to be watched extremely carefully if treachery is to be avoided.

Emperor Yuan Ti himself observed, perhaps tongue in cheek, that his armies had to "hold back our people from invading the territory of friendly neighbors." He said that the wall "was built not so much to protect the Empire against the outside world, as to protect the outer world from the ever-enterprising Chinese." This was a questionable statement, since the Han continued to pursue expansionist policies beyond the wall.

The Han wall was designed to control the passage not just of people but also of goods. It became a gateway for trade with the Hsiung-nu, who, according to a Chinese official, could be induced to exchange "articles worth several pieces of gold" for one "piece of Chinese plain silk." From their wall the Chinese could control the transfer of products on which the empire levied customs duties, and also commodities of possible military utility whose "export" was prohibited.

Under the Han empress Lü, the sale to outsiders of horses and metal products was banned, not to mention such high-tech items as crossbows. In 82 B.C. the horse-and-crossbow ban was lifted for unstated reasons. Perhaps it was because the nomads were no longer so feared, or perhaps the crossbow manufacturers had a powerful lobby at the imperial court.

Whatever the reasons behind such a surprising lapse in vigilance, it was indicative of a growing degeneracy in the Han Empire, which soon affected the border defenses. In A.D. 9 a usurper named Wang Mang pronounced himself Son of Heaven and provoked such internal discontent that he had to withdraw his armies from the frontier to put down a rebellion. Border fortifications were neglected and a recent western extension of the wall system was allowed to fall victim to desert sandstorms. The sinicized Hsiung-nu, awakening slightly from their own torpor, made a few opportunistic raids across the border. What finally finished Wang Mang, however, was not the Huns but an internal revolt led by members of the former royal family.

Yet Wang Mang's elimination did not end the imperial decline and internal strife. The last Han emperor was a nine-year-old boy who was a pawn in the hands of various warlords. His realm was divided into three parts, the northernmost ruled by a barbarian despot who also controlled the Han "Great Wall"—or what was left of it.

The fate of the wall in Han times is instructive. It suggests that as long as internal conditions allowed this elaborate and costly system to be well maintained and amply garrisoned, it could serve a host of useful functions, including imperial defense. However, in addition to providing no protection against domestic chaos, the wall presented a twofold danger to the state it was meant to secure.

On the one hand, it fostered complacency among the citizenry and officials, which led them to neglect other dimensions of defense, including military staffing and training. At the same time, faith in an impregnable defense promoted the belief that China could go on the offensive, could attempt to sinicize Asia from Mongolia to Korea and Vietnam. Unquestionably, China's so-called border wall fed an expansionist urge and the (now familiar) affliction of "imperial overstretch."

The period from the collapse of the Han dynasty to the beginning of the Six Dynasties (A.D. 220–589) is sometimes called China's Dark Ages. Certainly it was a dark era for the northern wall system, which fell into severe disrepair. This was significant, since powerful new nomad tribes were replacing the sinicized Hsiung-nu on the northern steppes and casting a greedy eye on the Middle Kingdom. Around A.D. 265 an emperor named Tsin Wu Ti decided to restore the border fortifications, though a trusted adviser warned, "Trust in Virtue, not in Walls!" Tsin Wu Ti should have heeded this advice, as the barbarians were now firmly ensconced on *both* sides of the barrier.

China's next major dynasty, the resplendent T'ang (618–907), showed little interest in the wall. An early T'ang emperor, Li Shih-min, believed that the best defense against barbarians was a good offense. He told a general who had launched a successful attack against the Turks: "You are a more efficient Great Wall than that built by [the last Dark Ages emperor] Yang Ti."

Li Shih-min and his successors deliberately let the wall fall to ruin as a monument to the inferior past. The T'ang instead focused their energies on scientific and cultural matters. It was in this era that the Chinese invented printing, shorthand, and fingerprinting. Their poetry often spoke of the futility and horror of war. Li Po's "Fighting South of the Rampart" said wearily:

> Men die on the battlefield to the sound of
> clashing swords,
> While the horses of the vanquished neigh
> piteously to Heaven.
> Crows and hawks peck around for human
> guts,
> Carry them off in their beaks, and hang
> them on the branches of withered
> trees.
> Captains and privates [the rank] are
> smeared across the bushes and grass.
> The generals schemed for nothing. The
> sword is but a cursed thing
> That a wise man employs only when he
> must.

Another poem, "Under a Border Fortress," directly addressed the futility of the Great Wall:

> Of old the battles along the Great Wall
> Were spoken of with lofty praise,
> But antiquity has now been transformed to
> yellow dust
> White bones jumbled amongst the grass.

Luckily for the T'ang, the barbarian tribes of their era were not particularly warlike, but this changed dramatically during the next major dynasty—the Northern Sung (960–1126), whose early rulers faced the emergent Khitan tribe. The fierce Khitan armies, which boasted highly trained mounted archers called "ordos" (the source of the word *hordes*), stormed across the decrepit wall system and occupied much of northern China. In their wake emerged an even rougher group called the Juchen, who founded the Jin dynasty (1126–1234). The rule of the steppes seemed to be "You think this lot is ugly? Wait till you see the next!"

As if aware of this progression of ferocity, the Jin began restoring the line of walls, which now ran across the middle of their empire, and built new fortifications along their northern and western frontiers. This was of little avail, however, for the next barbarians to howl down out of the North were the nastiest creatures ever to appear on the steppes: the Mongols. Their most famous warlord, Genghis Khan, summed up the Mongol code when he said: "The greatest joy a man can have is victory: to conquer one's enemies, to pursue them, to deprive them of their possessions, to reduce their families to tears, to ride on their horses and to make love to their wives and daughters."

Showing their contempt for the "Great Wall," the Mongols in 1211 selected an invasion route to the Jin capital (Yencheng) that led through the main wall's most heavily fortified gate, at Chü Yung Kuan. When the gate resisted the Mongols' initial assault, they simply moved farther west to a section of the wall whose defense the Jin had entrusted to a barbarian "ally," the Ongut tribe. The Ongut promptly made a pact with the Mongols and let them pass through the wall to plunder Jin territory.

After this first successful raid, the Mongols returned booty-laden to the steppes, but the riches of China soon enticed them to renew their pressure. Significantly, Genghis Khan again chose the Chü Yung Kuan gate as his point of attack, though in the interval its doors allegedly had been "sealed with iron." Seeing that the gate was well guarded, and again disinclined to lay siege to what he might outflank, Genghis quickly shifted a small force to a weaker gate, broke through it, stormed Chü Yung Kuan from behind, and opened its "sealed" doors to the main body of his troops.

Once they had conquered China, the Mongols saw no reason to maintain the northern wall system. During their rule in China (1260–1368), the border defenses moldered away. (Therefore it is not so surprising that Marco Polo, who visited China in the late thirteenth century, neglected even to mention the Great Wall in his *Travels.*) Instead of walls, the heirs of Genghis Khan built canals, roads, and a fast postal system, as if to show that they were a people of action, not of sedentary habits. Yet even they eventually became corrupted by the soft delights of Chinese civilization and gradually allowed real power to fall into the hands of rival warlords. One of these warlords, Chu Yüan-chang, chased the Mongols back to Mongolia in 1368 and established a new ruling dynasty, the Ming.

Although the Great Wall had meant little to the Mongols, it gradually came to mean much to the Ming (1368–1644), the last Chinese dynasty to take it seriously as a defensive system. Initially the Ming tried to emulate the Han and early Mongols by sending expeditionary forces into the northern steppes. Only when these offensives failed did the Ming revert to defensive tactics, first of piecemeal wall building, then of the elaborate construction project that ultimately yielded most of the Great Wall we know today.

In this regard the Ming experience anticipated the trench system of World War I, another elaborate defensive response to the failure of offensive operations. But the Ming defenses were more impressive in appearance than the filthy mudholes of Flanders and northern France. Now underlaid with a foundation of huge granite blocks and equipped with a sophisticated drainage system, the main wall boasted eight to twelve towers per mile, spaced from 100 to 200 yards apart, which meant that every foot along the structure was within bowshot. The top of the wall was thirteen to sixteen feet wide, allowing five horses or ten men to patrol abreast. Crenellated battlements were raised along the outer edge. From the late fifteenth century on, the towers were stocked with cannon, first glorified peashooters, then twenty-foot Portuguese behemoths that had to be hoisted up the wall with pulleys.

Needless to say, all this was costly to build and maintain. Ming rulers justified the special taxes they imposed to pay for the border defenses by pointing out that the Mongols remained an ever-present threat to China's tranquillity. Nevertheless, the new wall was so expensive and required so many men to garrison it that the Ming (like previous dynasties) began entrusting the defense of parts of it to "friendly" barbarian tribes.

Unfortunately, the Ming wall, imposing as it was, could be easily penetrated. The wall's very elaborateness was its main weakness, and the huge costs involved stirred up rebellion at home. A defensive system like this, moreover, was a provocation to the human spirit, for there is something about a wall, especially an allegedly impenetrable one, that makes a person want to go over it, around it, under it, or through it any way he can. Certainly the Mongols—who by now, back in the hardy atmosphere of the steppes, had recovered their lust for rape and pillage—saw the Ming wall as a challenge rather than a deterrent. Starting in 1439 they repeatedly assaulted it, generally with success. Another group of barbarian tribes related to the Mongols, the Manchus, also saw the wall as something to be breached. Exploiting the rebellious disaffection of the Ming citizenry, especially the angry peasants, they opened a full-scale crusade against the dynasty. By 1644 the Manchus had stormed through weak sections of the wall and finished off the Ming.

The Great Wall never again played a role in the defense—or lack thereof—of China. The Manchus (Ch'ing dynasty, 1644–1912) had no military use for it, since they controlled both sides of the structure; only a few gates were maintained as customs points. Like Parisians dismantling the Bastille following its fall in 1789, Chinese peasants carried away Great Wall stones and brick to build their houses.

Oddly enough, it remained for the People's Republic of China to "rediscover" the Great Wall—not, of course, as a military defense but as a national symbol and an imposing tourist attraction. Travelers to the wall today find parts of it, particularly the section near Beijing, handsomely restored. Visiting it in 1985, the American novelist and travel writer Paul Theroux found that it "swarmed with tourists," who "scampered on it and darkened it like fleas on a dead snake." Souvenir shops along its length sell plastic replicas of the wall and "scholar bones" supposedly excavated from its foundations. As another

Chinese proverb has it, "We can always fool a foreigner."

Reduced to a tourist's photo opportunity though it may be, the Great Wall is not devoid of meaning for the modern era. Considering the long history of China's "Earth Dragon" may serve to remind us that a wall, *any* wall, "begs to be overcome."

The Maiden Soldier of Picardy

by JOHN A. LYNN

If the army of Louis XIV allowed only men to serve, how could a woman be punished for desertion? And why would she masquerade as a man in the first place? John A. Lynn unearthed the curious case of Marie Magdelaine Mouron while examining military trial records at the French war archives in Vincennes. Her decision to dress as a man and serve as a soldier may have been unusual, but in the seventeenth and eighteenth centuries it was hardly unprecedented, having less to do with sexual confusion than with the plight of working-class women. Professor Lynn teaches European and military history at the University of Illinois at Urbana-Champaign.

Major Rochepierre was obviously confused as he wrote from St.-Omer to the French war ministry on May 28, 1696, for instructions. "All the ordinances against desertion make no mention of women," he complained. Therefore he did not know what to do, for in an army that recruited only men, a woman had deserted from the service of Louis XIV. Disguised as a man, she had enlisted under the name of La Garenne in the Régiment du Biez. Only when she was charged with desertion was her true sex discovered.

To give the ministry a basis for a just decision, Rochepierre enclosed the record of her trial along with his note. Some diligent clerk in the war office dutifully filed away this correspondence, so that today we can reconstruct the story of this formidable woman who soldiered in three different regiments under as many different names before her arrest.

The trial record reports that under questioning the woman admitted "her true name is Marie Magdelaine Mouron, daughter of Louis Mouron of the town of Desvres" near Boulogne. Her father, a butcher in that town, later moved to Trépied in Picardy, where he was a minor functionary of the royal salt monopoly. By her account, her widowed father married a vile woman whom he had been keeping for some time. This new stepmother plagued Marie Magdelaine, who "suffered such chagrin . . . that in the end she resolved to abandon the place of her birth five or six years ago." Buying men's clothing at the nearby town of Montreuil, she "there engaged herself as a soldier under the name of Picard" in the company commanded by a Captain Destone of the Royal Walloon Regiment.

The recruiter must have been eager to enlist "Picard"; by 1690 the French were mired in the Nine Years' War (1688–97)—also known as the War of the League of Augsburg—and were hard put to find enough recruits to mount an army of 400,000, the largest that Europe had seen since the days of Imperial Rome.

With this regiment she marched south to Provence. In garrison at Sisteron, she "had a quarrel with one Blondin, [a] soldier in [another] company of the same regiment." For reasons left unclear in her testimony, the trouble with Blondin "obliged her to leave and to retire to Avignon where she signed up with . . . the company of [Captain] de Pressée in the dragoon Régiment de Morsan, where she served about one year and a half under the name of St. Michel." Although her trial record makes no mention of combat service by Marie, the Régiment de Morsan did take part in the successful siege of Rosas, in Catalonia in the summer of 1693.

The strong-willed Marie apparently could not avoid confrontations, however, and while encamped at Collioure near Perpignan after the siege, she tangled with a dragoon named St. Jean. "She finally fought with St. Jean on the day when they were to pass in review on the glacis of Collioure before the Marshal duc [Anne-Jules] de Noailles their general." She was wounded by "a sword blow in the side" so seriously that she "lost blood without the power to stop it by all the bandages that she . . . made herself."

At this point she decided "to make a declaration of all her adventures" to the duc de Noailles and trust in his mercy. She had little choice in the matter, since "she found herself reduced, either to letting her sex be known by those who" could give her medical attention "or to letting herself die in maintaining" her secret. Noailles took pity and arranged for "the wife of an artillery officer in Collioure to keep [Marie] in her house during the space of two or three weeks, during which time she was well cared for, well fed, and well clothed."

At the end of her convalescence, "following the orders and the care of the said general, she was taken to Perpignan [and placed] in a house which held girls in order to instruct them." There she remained for about six months, but "at the end of this time, having quarrelled with the Superior, by whom she had often been mistreated," Marie was piqued "to the point of throwing a plate of salad at [the Superior's] head."

Marie fled the school and decided "to return to her country," the province of Picardy. But even this would not be easy for her. While on her way "she was obliged to stay at the hospital of Montpellier during several months because of a very grave illness for which she was bled thirteen or fourteen times."

After an unspecified number of weeks en route, she reached home, "where it is true that she again signed up as a soldier under the name of La Garenne . . . in the company of de Brière in the Régiment du Biez." She signed up "about the commencement of last March [and] served . . . in the said company during all that month and that of April." Apparently she was stationed at St.-Omer in the neighboring province of Artois.

According to her testimony, two reasons drove her to desert. First, "she realized day by day that many of the soldiers of the same regiment understood the truth of her sex, saying loudly that she was not a man, which she did not want known." Second, she learned that two of her companions planned to desert.

She "found herself drinking many times with Lagenois and Languedoc, her comrades in the same company, who had taken her into their confidence concerning the design that they had made . . . to desert." Although she tried, "she had not been able to detour them," and she thought that perhaps she ought not "to remain in that company after them, for fear of being bothered and perhaps mistreated because of their desertion."

Marie "abandoned the said company the first day of the month of May" and went "away the same day to Aire," some twelve miles from St.-Omer. "After having hidden [her] regimental jacket [*justaucorps*] and stockings in some undergrowth," she "offered to enlist in the company of de la Bussière, lieutenant colonel of the Régiment de Sanzay, who having suspected that she was not a man wanted to have [Marie] visited [examined] which would oblige the so-called La Garenne to confess that he was a woman." In addition, "la Bussière . . . recognized that the vest of the so-called La Garenne was of the régiment du Biez." Backed into a corner, "La Garenne . . . confessed that 'he' truly had just deserted from the said regiment. . . .

"And after having been visited by the female jailor who declared that Marie was of the feminine sex, she confessed that it was more than six years since she had attended any sacraments." However, she insisted, "affirming every time by oath, that she had never had carnal affairs with any man, although she had almost always bunked with some comrade [soldiers regularly shared tents and beds] having, according to what she said, always done it so well that she never had been recognized for what she was, which seemed truly so by the account that was made of her conduct."

After her arrest, Marie was cooperative, even aiding the investigation of her comrades' desertion.

When, one afternoon in July 1989, I unearthed Marie's file at the French war archives, buried in carton MR 1785, I had never seen anything like it. Certainly, to my knowledge, the extraordinary tale of Marie Magdelaine Mouron has never before appeared in print. However, I have since learned that the phenomenon of women dressing as men and serving as soldiers was anything but unprecedented during the seventeenth and eighteenth centuries.

Rudolf Dekker and Lotte van de Pol, in their fascinating book drawn from Dutch records on the subject of women who chose to live as men, counted 110 cases in the Netherlands between 1600 and 1800. The overwhelming majority posed as soldiers and sailors, and the authors theorized that the practice occurred most commonly in the Netherlands, northern Germany, and Britain. But of course the very nature of sexual disguise makes it impossible to arrive at authoritative figures. The only certified instances were those that reached, and were recorded by, public authorities.

Still, known cases and anecdotal evidence suggest that the phenomenon was widespread, even if it remained unusual. An eighteenth-century piece entitled "The Female Warrior," attributed to Oliver Goldsmith, suggested that since so many women masqueraded as men in the British army, they ought to form their own regiments. While French records are rare, two noblewomen who dressed as men gained notoriety: Christine de Meyrac, whose fictionalized biography *L'Héroïne mousquetaire* appeared in 1679; and Geneviève Prémoy, who, as the chevalier de Baltazar, was decorated for bravery by no less than Louis XIV.

While the exact circumstances of Marie's odyssey were unique, she had much in common with other working-class girls who enlisted. Popular ballads told of young women serving in order to follow their lovers or husbands, but the more common story of what Dekker and van de Pol label the "tradition of female transvestism in early modern Europe" was of women seeking to escape an intolerable daily existence.

For women of the lower classes at that time, life was onerous and choices were few. In an age when the poor married late and died young, the death of a parent frequently brought a stepparent into a household where there were still young children to be reared. In fact as in fiction, such interlopers all too often became the wicked stepmothers—or stepfathers—of fairy tales. Driven from her home, a poor girl with no marketable skills could turn to only the lowest occupations, if she could find work at all. Some girls saw prostitution as the sole work open to them. But stories of cross-dressing were common enough to make it clear that some women recognized this as an alternative—one that offered them the broader horizons enjoyed by men.

Marie mentioned no work experience outside the home, so she probably faced such harshly limited opportunities. And although the testimony does not specify her age, she seems to have first signed on in her late teens—again fitting the mold. Dekker and van de Pol found twenty to be the average age when a woman made the decision to live as a man.

The accounts of these women suggest that often they looked better in men's than women's clothing. Marie Magdelaine Mouron was almost certainly a robust and large young woman. Her enrollment as a dragoon indicates greater than normal stature even for a man, as by custom cavalrymen were larger than infantrymen. She was also strong-minded and quarrelsome, traits common among women masquerading as men. Women who adopted such an unorthodox career were likely to be fiercely independent, brave, and assertive. Marie did not shy away from a fight. In fact, a frequent way in which such women were discovered was through the treatment of wounds, and here again she was typical.

Perhaps surprising to the modern reader, Marie was also representative in that she was not guilty of sexual license with men, and neither is there any record of her being actively homosexual. While her gender was obviously an issue in an army that didn't recruit females, her sexual conduct was apparently beyond reproach. She allegedly remained a virgin.

We may well wonder how a woman could conceal her womanhood while living for any length of time in close quarters with men. The answer, according to Dekker and van de Pol, is that strong gender stereotypes went a long way toward protecting her secret. Someone dressed as a man and doing a man's work was simply assumed to be a man. Marie would have been accepted as male until she demonstrated that she was not. Her higher-pitched voice and lack of facial hair need not have given her away, since she could pretend to be a mere lad. Women often claimed to be much younger than they really were when they signed on. This subterfuge could not last forever, but it could work for some time.

Seemingly more difficult would be the problem of disguising anatomical differences and bodily functions. But since people rarely removed their clothes in front of one another at that time, an impostor might have been able to avoid discovery indefinitely. Marie supplied no information on this matter, but records report that other women pretended to be male by urinating through a small silver tube or other hollow device. There are no records of how these women dealt with menstruation, but apparently they managed to conceal it.

Marie avoided the brutal fate prescribed by French regulations for desertion in the late seventeenth century. The nose and ears of a convicted deserter were lopped off; then he was branded on the cheek with a *fleur de lis* and condemned to life service on the galleys. Major Rochepierre made it clear that he never expected Marie to suffer such punishment.

The reluctance to deal harshly with this particular deserter may reflect a sense of chivalry on the part of the men in charge, or perhaps it was because the case against her rested on something other than the fact that she had left the service. After all, she would have been discharged anyway if it had been known that she was a woman. The trial record specifies that before her desertion she received two months' pay, and while the report fails to mention it, or to concern itself at all with her earlier enlistments, she almost certainly pocketed a recruitment bounty from the Régiment du Biez and would have gained another one from the Régiment de Sanzay. This was taking the king's money on false pretenses, making Marie a thief.

Rochepierre believed that only a prison sentence awaited Marie, but did she serve one? It would seem so. One of the documents in her file bears marginal comments written in a spidery, barely legible hand—apparently instructions from an official at the war ministry. "It is not difficult [to determine] that she is liable only to [a] prison [term], but it is necessary to hold her there for a long time."

Since she was more victim than villain, I find myself wishing that the maiden soldier could have been spared even this.

Taking Up the Gun

by GEOFFREY PARKER

It may come as a surprise that the military history of the Orient is so varied and full of innovation. Gunpowder is of course a Chinese invention. But how many know that the world's first ironclads were Korean, or that it was the Japanese who originated the technique of musketry salvos? The list goes on. The oriental powers also made decisions that puzzle us, and they should not. Our Eurocentrism is such, Geoffrey Parker writes, that we often mistake measures that were eminently sensible in the context of their time for weakness. The sophistication of oriental arms and tactics goes far to explain why the European military techniques that had subjugated the Americas and much of India failed so completely against China and Japan. Those states not only adapted to the Western military revolution of the sixteenth and seventeenth centuries but remodeled it to their own ends—and occasionally bested would-be European conquerors at their own game. Why, though, were the Europeans finally able to gain the upper hand? Professor Parker's article is adapted from *The Military Revolution* (Cambridge University Press), a book that has radically changed our view of the period historians call Early Modern. Parker teaches at the University of Illinois at Urbana-Champaign.

Many excellent books have been written about "the rise of the West," most of them devoting much attention to the contribution made by military technology. Understandably, however, most of these studies deal with the modern period, covering the extraordinary story of how the Europeans extended their control over the globe from 15 percent of the total land area in 1750 to 84 percent in 1914. The rapidity of that process left even contemporaries breathless and bewildered. When, for example, Edmund Burke spoke in December 1783 in the English House of Commons on Charles Fox's India reform bill, he interrupted his vitriolic tirade on the injustices and humiliations inflicted upon the Mogul emperor by officers of the Honourable East India Company to say:

It is impossible, Mr. Speaker, not to pause here for a moment to reflect on the inconsistency of human greatness and the stupendous revolutions that have happened in our age of wonders. Could it be believed, when I entered into existence or when you, a younger man, were born, that on this day, in this House, we should be employed in discussing the conduct of those British subjects who had disposed of the power and person of the Grand Mogul?

No, indeed—in 1727, the year of Burke's birth, it *had* been unimaginable, for the Europeans in India were still confined to a handful of fortresses and factories huddled around the coasts of the subcontinent. And that was still the situation in East Asia a century later. In the 1820s in Japan, the Europeans remained confined to Deshima, a small, unfortified island, carefully cordoned off from the rest of the country; in China they possessed only the precarious coastal promontory of Macao; in Korea, not even that much. Moreover, their seaborne commerce in the area was closely controlled and subject to periodic disruption. But why? Why did the military techniques that had subjugated the Americas in the sixteenth and seventeenth centuries, and much of India in the eighteenth, fail so completely—by both sea and land—against the states of East Asia until the mid-nineteenth century?

The first European empires in Asia were seaborne, depending therefore on control of the sea rather than of the land, and at their heart lay the naval gun. But herein lurks a great irony, for it is now beyond dispute that the entire development of firearms was originally Asian—from the first discovery of the correct formula for gunpowder (which is now thought by Joseph Needham and his associates to have occurred as early as the ninth century A.D.) to perfection of the metal-barreled gunpowder weapons in mid-thirteenth-century China. A hundred years later, when the iron cannon is first mentioned in Arabic as well as European sources, China already possessed a sophisticated arsenal of both iron and bronze ordnance. Pictorial and archaeological evidence indicates that artillery was used (perhaps for the first time) for the ill-fated second seaborne invasion of Japan in 1281 by Kublai Khan.

This early use should not surprise us, for firearms were fully compatible with the traditions of Chinese warfare at sea. From the eighth century A.D., at least, Chinese naval commanders had preferred fighting from a distance with projectiles to close combat and boarding. In Sung times, war junks with catapults and their more powerful cousins, trebuchets, became the staple of the navy. In the 1350s, the fleet of the founder of the Ming dynasty, Chu Yüan-chang, carried artillery. The Peking military museum possesses a bombard with an inscription stating that it was cast in the year 1372 for the "Left naval station" near Nanking. It also bears the number 42, which suggests that naval guns were by then standard issue. In the early fifteenth century, every imperial warship was required to carry fifty firearms of various sorts, with 1,000 bullets. This was probably the armament deployed some years later aboard the seven great expeditions sent into the Indian Ocean under the command of the Muslim admiral Cheng Ho, which took the Chinese as far as

Mogadishu and Aden and involved the invasion of Ceylon. Guns were still in use on ships of the Ming navy in the 1520s; naval artillery helped defeat a Portuguese flotilla off Canton in 1522, delivering the Europeans aboard to imprisonment and eventual execution.

However, as we shall see, to possess guns is one thing; to use them effectively is quite another. Ultimately, in the 1550s, the Chinese imperial authorities concluded that their naval artillery was of little value against bands of Japanese pirates known as *wakō* (literally "dwarf pirates") who were terrorizing the coasts of China. According to an illustrated treatise of naval warfare, published in 1564 by Cheng Jo-tseng (a protégé of the Chinese supreme commander), the pirates were defeated not by naval means but by a combination of three things: intrigue designed to divide the Chinese from the Japanese groups among them; diplomatic pressure on the pirates' supporters in Japan; and overwhelming military assaults on their land bases in China. And even those assaults were conducted without firearms. Ming commanders did not rely on muskets or cannon, whether by land or by sea, because they found them too difficult to supply with shot of standard caliber and too prone to explode when fired. They also dismissed proposals for reinforced, shot-resistant junks, on the grounds that such craft would be far too cumbersome, and they deprecated shipborne artillery as too inaccurate. Instead, they defeated the wakō in the traditional Chinese manner: by concentrating vastly superior numbers of troops armed with bows, lances, and swords. Although Chinese war junks continued to carry some guns, they were only light, antipersonnel pieces. The principal weapon of the imperial navy remained, even in the 1630s, the fire ship: a vessel loaded with combustibles that could be floated into an enemy's fleet.

The Europeans pursued a very different strategy in Asian waters. The instructions given by King Manuel I of Portugal to Portuguese navigator Pedro Álvares Cabral in 1500 for his voyage to India, for example, specified: "You are not to come to close quarters with [Muslim ships] if you can avoid it, but you are to compel them to strike sail with your artillery alone" so that "this war may be waged with greater safety, and . . . less loss may result to the people of your ships." The next fleet, sent under the command of Vasco da Gama in 1502, defeated a large Muslim fleet in a pitched battle off the Malabar Coast by sailing "one astern of the other in a line" and by keeping up rapid artillery fire, the gunners making "such haste to load again that they recharged the guns with bags of powder which they had ready for this purpose, made to measure so that they could load again very speedily."

But we must not exaggerate the Europeans' reliance on naval gunnery at that time. Vasco da Gama destroyed the fleet of Calicut in 1502 with eighteen ships, it is true, but his flagship carried only sixteen guns—none of them large—and the others carried still fewer. And even in 1525, at the height of its power, the Portuguese Estado da India—the State of India, its Eastern empire—was defended by a mere 1,073 artillery pieces shared among six fortresses and sixty ships—and not always effectively used. In an encounter in 1510 between the 400-ton flagship of Viceroy Afonso de Albuquerque and a large Sumatran merchantman in the Straits of Malacca, the entire Portuguese fleet closed in for the kill and

> started shooting at her; but this did not affect her in the least; and she went on sailing. . . . The Portuguese ships then shot at her masts . . . and she dropped her sails. Because she was very tall . . . our people did not dare to board her, and our artillery did not hurt her at all, for she had four layers of planking on her side, and our biggest cannon would not penetrate more than two.

In the end, after two days and nights of fruitless bombardment, the gallant and resourceful Albuquerque decided to pull off his adversary's two rudders. Only then did she surrender.

So it is imprudent to ascribe too much power to the Europeans in Asian waters during the earlier sixteenth century. By 1600, however, the situation had changed somewhat—East Indiamen now resembled floating fortresses. The flagship of the first fleet sent to Asia by the Dutch East India Company—the *Dordrecht* in 1603—weighed 900 tons and carried six 24-pounders and eighteen 8- or 9-pounders. The *Dordrecht* and other ships like her were clearly more powerful than any other vessel in Asian waters. But this would not be the case for long.

Cheng Ch'eng-kung, better known in Western sources as Coxinga, grew up near the Dutch factory at Hirado in southern Japan, where his father was an interpreter for the Europeans. In the 1620s his father also began to act as a pirate in Dutch service, modifying Chinese junks along European lines, with decks strengthened and adapted to carry heavy artillery, and with better sail plans to improve maneuverability. After 1644 and the collapse of Ming power before the Ch'ing onslaught, Coxinga established a powerful army and navy along the coasts of Fukien, dedicated to restoring the heirs of the Ming. But where the Cheng family had commanded only three junks and a force of about 100 pirates in the 1620s, by 1655 Coxinga commanded some 2,000 warships and well over 100,000 troops, making admirable use of European-style weaponry—whether imitated, captured, or purchased.

The financial and commercial organization that underpinned this powerful military machine in the 1650s was unprecedented, and it even alarmed the Dutch. "He is now the man who can spit much in our face in Eastern waters," the Dutch governor-general reported from Batavia in 1654; and the next year he warned that "Coxinga has become a terrible thorn in our flesh here." These sentiments were by no means exaggerated. In 1655 Coxinga informed the Dutch that he regarded their trade as a threat: "Such places as Batavia, Taiwan, and Malacca are one inseparable market and I am master of this area. I will never allow you to usurp my position," he told them. In 1657 he sent forty-seven junks to Nagasaki alone, with cargoes worth more than double those of the eight Dutch ships that year.

Coxinga's commercial empire, however, had a crucial weakness: It relied on control of the Fukien coast and its offshore islands; without them, his ships had no access to the Chinese luxuries he exported or to the Chinese supplies on which his ships and men depended. In 1656–58, his armies advanced triumphantly to the Yangtze, reclaiming almost all of southeast China for the Ming; but in 1659 his attempt to take the southern capital of Nanking failed disastrously, and the Ch'ing forces rolled forward to the coast of Fukien. The Ch'ing had eventually been forced to adopt the strategy used by the Ming against the wakō a century before: With irresistible force they subjugated the land bases of an adversary they could not defeat at sea. But Coxinga was resourceful: Early in 1661 he decided to shift his headquarters to the largest of the offshore islands—Taiwan (Formosa).

Taiwan, however, was fast coming under European control. The Spaniards maintained forts in the north between 1624 and 1642, and the Dutch developed a colony around Fort Zeelandia in the southwest (on the site of modern T'ai-nan) after 1624. By 1660, thanks to the labor of perhaps as many as 50,000 mainland Chinese, whose immigration was encouraged by the Dutch, Taiwan had become one of the most prosperous parts of the Dutch overseas empire. But the colony was still defended by only two small fortresses when, in April 1661, Coxinga led a major expedition to the island and called on the Dutch to surrender. He claimed that they had only been allowed to trade there under license from the Ming; that license he now revoked.

The Dutch, not surprisingly, rejected this argument, and Fort Zeelandia was blockaded. After a nine-month siege, in which twenty-eight Western artillery pieces were deployed, it fell and Taiwan was organized as an "imperial prefecture" under Ming rule. Envoys demanding tribute were sent to the Spanish governor of the Philippines in preparation for further expansion. Since there were fewer than 600 Spanish soldiers in Manila, and scarcely 500 more in the rest of the archipelago, the governor panicked and ordered both the withdrawal of all troops from the outlying islands and the massacre of all Chinese residents near his capital. But in the event, Manila was saved, in June 1662, when death (probably by suicide) ended Coxinga's remarkable career. He was just thirty-seven.

Although Coxinga's son carried on resistance for another twenty years, it was a hopeless task. Taiwan was not Fukien; it lacked the food supplies, the population, and the shipbuilding facilities to sustain resistance to the Ch'ing on the mainland, and thereby to preserve access to the Chinese luxury goods that were essential for trade. Gradually the Ch'ing built up a navy of their own, and from time to time the Dutch assisted them. Coxinga's son suffered a catastrophic naval defeat in 1681, and Taiwan surrendered two years later. The Europeans could at last breathe again, and the China Sea came back under the traditional system of imperial control for the next century and a half.

The response of early modern Japan to Western maritime power was strikingly different: Where Coxinga emulated the Europeans, the Japanese embarked on an alternative course. The crucial influence here appears to have been the unsuccessful invasion of Korea in the 1590s by the forces of Toyotomi Hideyoshi, who had just completed the unification of Japan.

Hideyoshi was of course fully aware of the need to control the seas during the invasion, and he attempted to hire two Portuguese galleons to help him do so. When this failed, he increased the size of his own fleet to 700 vessels, on the assumption that the Koreans would fight hand to hand and be overwhelmed. In fact the invasion force landed at Pusan without meeting any Korean ships, and the Japanese forces began their lightning march north, reaching Seoul within twenty days on May 2, 1592.

But the Korean navy was not idle. In May and June, in a series of actions, a small Korean fleet commanded by Yi Sun-sin destroyed several minor Japanese flotillas—in all perhaps seventy-two vessels were sunk. Then, on July 8, in a decisive battle, Admiral Yi destroyed the main enemy fleet in Hansan Bay; and on the following day, he defeated a relief expedition sailing up from Japan. There were two main reasons for these victories. In the first place, the defeat of the wakō by the Chinese in the 1560s seems to have eliminated numerous experienced Japanese naval personnel, who were not replaced. Certainly the sailors aboard the invasion fleet were mostly conscripts provided unwillingly by the lords of Kyūshū and Shikoku, who had only recently been conquered by Hideyoshi's armies. The second decisive factor in Admiral Yi's victory was his use of the famous "turtle ships," about 110 feet long and 28 feet wide, entirely encased in hexagonal metal plates so that they could be neither boarded nor holed. They had twelve gunports and twenty-two loopholes per side (for small arms), plus four more ports at each end, together with firepots and toxic smoke. Sometimes the turtle ships came up close, just like modern torpedo boats, and fired broadsides; sometimes they used their metal rams to hole the enemy, leaving the other warships to close in for the kill. Their armament outweighed that of the Japanese by about forty to one.

But Hideyoshi and his commanders learned fast. The Japanese were not unfamiliar with the idea of proofing their ships with iron. In 1578 General Oda Nobunaga had deployed on the Inland Sea "iron ships so arranged that guns would not penetrate them." Probably they were ordinary ships plated with iron, for they heeled over and sank when the enemy tried to board at one side and everyone rushed over to repel them. Even so, in 1592 Hideyoshi ordered his generals to supply him with iron plates, no doubt intending to create ships equal to the turtle squadron. Meanwhile, at Pusan, the surviving Japanese warships took aboard some heavier guns and clustered beneath the harbor's defenses. Even Admiral Yi could not make any impression on them.

Nevertheless, the Japanese attempt to conquer Korea failed, and was abandoned after the death of Hideyoshi in 1598. A period of peace began not only in Japan but in the surrounding seas as well. The wakō did not reappear, and the Korean turtle ships did not go into action again. Instead, a new form of maritime enterprise grew up in Japan. A fleet of large merchantmen, averaging 300 tons each, was constructed locally and the ships were entrusted by their merchant owners to European pilots or, less often, to European crews. By the 1600s one or more of these great ships sailed annually to each of nineteen destinations in Southeast Asia. They were known as *shuinsen* ("red-seal ships") because they were protected only by a passport bearing the shogun's *shuinjo* ("red seal"). Since, from 1531 onward, every Portuguese vessel sailing south for Asia was required by law to carry artillery, it may seem incomprehensible that the shogun did not allow his merchantmen to arm themselves. But that just goes to show how "Eurocentric" naval history has become. The Japanese government considered it cheaper and more effective to persuade the Europeans to allow the safe passage of unarmed Japanese merchantmen than to invest in new ship designs and massive armament (which might, after all, fail to save the merchantman's cargo from damage) and to retaliate for any offense at sea with sanctions against the Europeans' access to the Japanese market.

Until the shuinsen themselves ceased to trade in the 1630s, the system worked well. When, for example, a red-seal ship arrived at Manila in 1610 in the middle of a sea battle between the Dutch and the Spaniards, hostilities had to cease while the Japanese neutral sailed serenely through. On the rare occasions when a European ship—almost always Dutch—did attack or plunder a red-seal vessel, the Japanese aboard made no attempt to defend themselves, but instead returned to Nagasaki and reported the incident to the magistrates. Thereupon all Dutch goods and ships in the port were impounded until the charge could be investigated, restitution made, and punishment meted out. The shuinsen may have lacked heavy armament, but they were protected by legal remedies that were remarkably effective. Anyone who wished to share in the lucrative Japanese trade was compelled to regard the shogun's passport as sacrosanct.

The naval balance between early modern Europe and East Asia was thus far more nearly equal than it has usually been portrayed. On the one hand, the Asian states had more powerful weapons at their disposal than is sometimes supposed; on the other, the Europeans had less. This contrast, however, does not by itself explain the divergent maritime development of the two continents. The difference lay not so much in means as in aims.

The voyages of Cheng Ho in the fifteenth century, the defeat of the wakō in the sixteenth, and the overthrow of Coxinga's forces in the seventeenth show beyond all question that Imperial China had the capacity to rule the seas around her coasts whenever she wished. But clearly, once the immediate occasion for doing so was gone, the effort was discontinued. This should not surprise us. After all, the only real justification for creating a vast and permanent navy was (and still is) the need to match and parry a vast and permanent naval threat. Regional empires able to secure total and continuous local ascendancy do not need to maintain great battle fleets, and both the Ming and Ch'ing navies were able during most periods to maintain regional supremacy at sea by traditional methods. The Japanese, in their own way, did the same. It was only the introduction of steam-powered ironclad warships into Asian waters by the Europeans and Americans in the nineteenth century that made it impossible for the two empires to rule the waves around their shores. On one day in February 1841, for example, on her way to Canton during the First Opium War, the two pivot-mounted 32-pounders of the East India Company's steamer *Nemesis* destroyed nine war junks, five forts, two military stations, and one shore battery. Imperial China had no answer to that.

The dominant states of East Asia were no less attentive to Western military technology on land. Firearms, fortresses, and standing armies had long been part of the military tradition of China, Korea, and Japan; indeed, as has already been noted, both bronze and iron artillery were fully developed in China before the gunpowder revolution spread westward to Europe. However, after the mid-fourteenth century, contact between the Far East and the Far West diminished, and the subsequent evolution of firearms in the two areas took somewhat different courses. By 1500 the iron and bronze guns of Western manufacture—whether Turkish or Christian—proved to be both more powerful and more mobile than those of the East, so that when the soldiers of the former transported them to the Orient, they attracted attention and prompted imitation. The guns may have arrived in China as early as the 1520s, perhaps accompanying one of the numerous Ottoman diplomatic missions to the Central Kingdom; but, if so, knowledge of them seems to have remained confined to government circles. For most Chinese, Western-style firearms were first encountered in the hands of the wakō who were operating against Fukien in the late 1540s.

Although guns were not widely used by the Ming forces against the wakō, they were introduced only a short time afterward on the empire's northern frontier against the nomads of the steppe. In 1564, for example, the Peking garrison replaced their clay-cased cannonballs with lead ones; and in 1568 these were in turn abandoned in favor of iron. In the 1570s, under the direction of Ch'i Chi-kuang (who had masterminded the defeat of the wakō), the Great Wall was equipped with pillboxes to shelter musketeers, and reserve units of the northern army were strengthened with small carts known as "battlewagons" that each carried breech-loading light artillery and twenty men.

A remarkable source showing the degree to which Western weaponry had been adopted under the late Ming is the illustrated *T'ai-tsu Shih-lu* (Veritable records of the great ancestor), compiled in 1635 to commemorate the deeds of Nurhachi, founder of the Ch'ing dynasty. It is significant that in the pictures of the "Great Ancestor's" early victories, all the guns are on the side of the Ming: The imperial armies are shown deploying field guns, mounted either on trestles or on two-wheeled battlewagons, while the northern warriors seem to rely on their horse archers. But in 1629, Nurhachi attacked and annexed four Chinese cities south of the Great Wall; in one of them, Yung-p'ing, a Chinese artillery crew "familiar with the techniques of casting Portuguese artillery" was also captured. By 1631 some forty of the new European-style artillery pieces had been made by the captives, and, directed by men who had received either first- or secondhand training from Portuguese gunners, they were soon in action against Ming positions. Gradually, as shown in later illustrations from the *T'ai-tsu Shih-lu*, they appear on the Ch'ing side, too.

Still, firearms remained only a minor part of the armament of Chinese armies. After all, the Ming supported, in theory at least, some 500,000 men and 100,000 horses on the northern frontier, while the Ch'ing army that entered Peking in 1644 probably numbered 280,000 warriors. It would have been almost impossible to equip all these troops with Western-style firearms, so the soldiers of the new dynasty continued to fight in the traditional manner until the nineteenth century. It is true that in 1675 the Chinese Imperial Army was supported by 150 heavy guns and numerous batteries of field artillery, cast under the direction of Jesuit missionaries in Peking. But this was a specific campaign against dangerous domestic enemies (the "Three Feudatories" and their supporters); at other times the main strength of the Ch'ing remained the overwhelming numbers of their armed forces. A dynasty that was capable of sustaining a campaign army of 150,000 men for up to eight months in the field, and of throwing 40,000 men (when necessary) into a battle, had little need of expensive European military techniques.

Although their armies were considerably smaller, the Japanese made far more use of Western firearms. It is generally accepted that they were first introduced by Portuguese castaways in 1543 on the island of Tanegashima south of Kyūshū, and that they were quickly copied by local Japanese metalsmiths. For this reason the weapons themselves came to be called Tanegashima. There is less agreement about the date these muskets were first used effectively in battle. The honor has plausibly been claimed for the powerful warlord Takeda Shingen, who in 1555 deployed 300 musketeers at the Battle of Shinano Asahiyamajo, but there is general agreement that the first spectacular demonstration of the power of Japanese musketry occurred on May 21, 1575, at the Battle of Nagashino. Oda Nobunaga deployed his corps of musketeers (who may have numbered 3,000 men) in three ranks in this action, having trained them to fire in volleys so as to maintain a constant barrage. The opposing cavalry—ironically of the same Takeda clan that had pioneered the use of the gun—was annihilated. The battle scene in Akira Kurosawa's film *Kagemusha* (The shadow warrior) is a credible reconstruction of the action at Nagashino.

The originality of Japan's rapid adoption of the gun has perhaps not always been fully appreciated. In the first place, whereas Europeans concentrated on increasing the speed of reloading, the Japanese were more interested in improving accuracy. Western military manuals therefore explained primarily how a soldier could recharge his weapon more rapidly, while Japanese treatises offered instruction on how he could take better aim. The Tanegashima were, for their day, remarkably accurate, but a smooth-bore weapon can be made to hit the mark more often only by making the ball fit more tightly in the barrel, and this automatically increases the length of time required for reloading. The only way to overcome this disadvantage was to draw up the musketeers in ranks and have them fire in sequence, so that the front rank could reload while the ranks behind were firing. This solution was not even suggested in Europe until 1594, by a commander of the Dutch army, and it did not come into general use there until the 1630s. Yet Oda Nobunaga had experimented with musketry salvos in the 1560s, and won a decisive victory with the technique in 1575—twenty years before the Europeans made the same discovery.

By the time Nobunaga was assassinated in 1582, he had conquered about half the provinces of Japan. After a brief hiatus of disorder, the work was continued by two of his most brilliant generals, first Toyotomi Hideyoshi and then Tokugawa Ieyasu. As further provinces were brought under central authority, the size of the main army was swollen by contingents from Hideyoshi's new vassals and allies. In 1587, when he decided to invade the island of Kyūshū, almost 300,000 troops were mobilized. The island was conquered in a matter of weeks. As late as 1610 Tokugawa Ieyasu was trying to acquire firearms and powder from any possible source. In one memorable letter, he wrote that "guns and powder . . . are what I desire more than gold."

It is possible that the "three unifiers of Japan" would have achieved their goals without the gun, but the ability to turn large numbers of their subjects into effective musketeers certainly accelerated the process. In this respect Europe's "military revolution" was not only adopted by the Japanese with enthusiasm but remodeled.

Nobunaga and his contemporaries also saw the usefulness of the heavier guns used by the Europeans, and they seem to have realized immediately that artillery would render indefensible almost every existing castle and fortress in Japan, since (as in Europe) any wall built high to keep besiegers out was thereby made vulnerable to artillery bombardment. A new sort of defensive fortification therefore emerged, situated on a ridge that was surrounded by the walls in such a way that they could be backed by rock and soil, creating a solid complex that extended over several square kilometers. Nobunaga himself built a prototype beside Lake Biwa at Azuchi, between 1576 and 1579, using the combination of hilltop and thick stone walls to produce a virtually solid bailey surrounding a seven-story keep of unparalleled beauty. Azuchi was almost totally destroyed after its creator's murder (although the ruins of the outer walls and the surviving foundations of the keep are still impressive). Even less remains of another massive fortress of this period: Odawara, the stronghold of the Hōjō clan, large enough to shelter 40,000 warriors and surrounded by twenty outlying forts. It required an army of 100,000 men to starve it out in the summer of 1590 and was destroyed after its capture by Toyotomi Hideyoshi—giving rise to a popular doggerel the following year: "So what's the use of hauling rocks and building castles? Just look at Azuchi and Odawara!"

Rather more exists today of the even greater citadels built by Hideyoshi and his followers, who preferred to fortify isolated hills on the plain. There is a remarkable homogeneity about the sixty or so surviving castles built between 1580 and 1630 from Sendai in the north to Kagoshima in the south, even though some works were bigger than others. The castle at Kumamoto, for example, was twelve kilometers in circumference, with forty-nine turrets and two keeps. The beautiful "White Heron Castle" at Himeji, almost as large, was constructed with an estimated 103,000 tons of stone. The walls of the vast citadel at Osaka extended for over thirteen kilometers. Some of the stones used for the main defenses at Osaka weighed 120 to 130 tons each and were brought to the site from all over Japan by feudatories anxious to prove their loyalty to the regime. Even today the lords' marks can be seen affixed to "their" rocks (which were each given special, auspicious names). With such blocks, more appropriate to a Pyramid than to a castle, walls were built that were in places nineteen meters thick—far thicker than those of any Western fortification. Quite possibly, as Professor J.W. Hall pointed out some years ago, these Japanese castles had "no peers in terms of size and impregnability" in the early modern world.

Japanese leaders were perfectly prepared to take over Western military innovations, although they always adapted them to local conditions in a distinctive way. Early modern China, however, had no need of Western examples in the art of defensive warfare, for her rulers had been living with gunpowder for centuries, and the massive fortifications erected under the Ming dynasty had been designed to resist both artillery bombardment and mining. It is true that the Chinese had few castles, preferring to fortify whole towns—indeed the Chinese use the same character (*ch'eng*) for "walled city" and "defensive rampart." These towns were surrounded by massive walls (fifteen meters thick in places) that could withstand even modern shells. Thus in 1840, during the Opium War, a two-hour battery from a seventy-four-gun Royal Navy warship on a fort outside Canton "produced no effect whatever," according to an eyewitness. "The principle of their construction was such as to render them almost impervious to the efforts of horizontal fire, even from the 32-pounders." Likewise, the British expeditionary force sent to China in 1860 found the walls of Peking impregnable. In describing them, the British commander, General Henry Knollys, said:

> Ancient history tells us the walls of Babylon were so broad that several chariots could be driven abreast on top of them; but I really think those of Peking must have exceeded them. They were upwards of 50 feet in breadth, very nearly the same in height, and paved on the top where, I am sure, five coaches-and-four could with a little management have been driven abreast.

The scale of fortification in East Asia in effect rendered siege guns useless, and that may be why indigenous heavy artillery was never really developed there. In Japan it was seriously deployed only against Osaka in 1615 and against a rebellion at Shimabara in 1636–37 (and on both occasions it proved indecisive); in China it was seldom used offensively except during the 1670s. In both empires, sieges were usually decided by mass assaults, mining, or blockades rather than by bombardment. Heavy guns, both of traditional and of Western manufacture, were certainly employed to defend the massive walls, but otherwise the use of artillery in the land warfare of East Asia was confined to the field.

Even so, the great states of East Asia paid more attention to the military innovations of the Europeans than to any other aspect of Western culture (with the possible exceptions of astronomy and the clock). This paradox, however, is easily explained when it is remembered that the seaborne arrival of the Europeans in the Far East coincided with a period of sustained political disintegration in both China and Japan. In China, instability lasted roughly from the renewal of pirate attacks on Fukien in the 1540s to the suppression of the last of the Ming loyalists in the 1680s. In Japan, an era of almost continuous civil war began with the Onin War in 1467 and lasted until the fall of Odawara in 1590. Throughout this lengthy period, every military innovation was naturally accorded close attention; but once stability was restored, the value of such things as firearms became diminished. In China, they were largely confined to the frontiers; in Japan, most were kept in government arsenals, and throughout the century the production of guns (which could be manufactured only under license) was steadily reduced.

But Japan did not merely "give up the gun." After 1580 the central government carried out a series of "sword hunts" aimed at removing *all* weapons from the temples, the peasants, the townsmen—from anyone who might try to resist the administration's taxes or policies. Some of the confiscated swords were melted down to make a great metal Buddha at Kyōto, while others were kept in state arsenals for use in emergencies, until in the end wearing the sword was largely confined to the hereditary arms-bearing class— the samurai. But though the samurai kept their swords, they lost most of their castles. Starting (again) in 1580, the central government began to systematically destroy fortifications belonging to its defeated enemies. Then, after the fall of Osaka in 1615, the shogun decreed that each lord could thenceforth maintain only one castle; all the rest should be destroyed. Thus in the western province of Bizen, for example, where there had been over 200 fortified places at the end of the fifteenth century, there were only ten by the 1590s, and after 1615 only one—the great "Raven Castle" at Okayama. The "demilitarization" even affected literature: For some decades after 1671, the importation of all foreign books concerning military matters and Christianity was forbidden; and the *Honcho Gunki-ko* (On the military equipment of our country), completed in 1722 and published in 1937, contained only one brief chapter on firearms.

By that time the West had also largely lost interest in Japan, for the European presence in East Asia had changed substantially. The Dutch had lost Taiwan in 1661–62, and their factory in Japan no longer yielded huge profits; the Iberian powers had lost much of their trading empire in the Orient; and the English East India Company still traded relatively little in the Far East. China and Japan thus remained largely unchallenged by the Europeans until the early nineteenth century; neither did they threaten each other. The distinctive "world order" of both nations endured intact until the industrial nations of the West deployed steel artillery and steamships against them. The impact of the *Nemesis* in 1840 has already been noted: It resulted in the opening of China to Western trade on Western terms. In 1863 it was Japan's turn. An attempt by the shogun to exclude Western warships from Japanese waters ended in catastrophic failure, with the French, Dutch, American, and British navies combining to silence the modern gun batteries in

Shimonoseki Strait, and the Royal Navy closing in (despite a typhoon) to destroy all shipping (and large parts of the town) at Kagoshima. The states of East Asia, which had so brilliantly adapted and modified the Military Revolution, could not withstand the Industrial Revolution.

George Washington, General

by THOMAS FLEMING

Thomas Fleming, who is the author of several notable books on the American Revolution, here evaluates an overlooked aspect of George Washington's career: his record as a general. "The great captains of history," Fleming writes, "are rated on their ability to conceive a winning strategy and devise tactics to execute it. Does Washington, the man the British called 'a little paltry colonel of militia' in 1776, belong in this select group?" Fleming's answer is yes, even if Washington's won-lost percentage was at best mediocre—in fact, he never did win a major battle. But Washington was one of history's great revolutionary generals: He fought a new kind of war in which his strategy was less to engage the enemy than to outlast him. In an age when, time and again, supposedly "decisive" battles settled nothing, George Washington, who avoided more battles than he fought, came away with a permanent victory.

How good a general was George Washington? If we consult the statistics as they might have been kept if he were a boxer or a quarterback, the figures are not encouraging. In seven years of fighting the British, from 1775 to 1782, he won only three clear-cut victories—at Trenton, Princeton, and Yorktown. In seven other encounters—Long Island, Harlem Heights, White Plains, Fort Washington, Brandywine, Germantown, and Monmouth—he either was defeated or at best could claim a draw. He never won a major battle: Trenton was essentially a raid; Princeton was little more than a large skirmish; and Yorktown was a siege in which the blockading French fleet was an essential component of the victory.

Most contemporary Americans, even if unacquainted with these statistics, are inclined to see General Washington as a figurehead, an inspiring symbol whose dedication and perseverance enabled his starving men to endure the rigors of Valley Forge and Morristown winter quarters. He wore the British out by sheer persistence, with little reference to military skill, much less genius. The recent spate of books devoted to how Washington's image was invented either by himself or by skillful propagandists bolsters this idea. Almost as misleading is our post-Vietnam fascination with guerrilla warfare and comparisons of our defeat in Southeast Asia with the British failure in America. If American guerrillas defeated the British, Washington the general seems almost superfluous.

A general's ability to inspire his men is not, of course, to be discounted, and Washington unquestionably had this gift. But in the final analysis, the great captains of history are rated on their ability to conceive a winning strategy and devise tactics to execute it. Does Washington, the man the British called "a little paltry colonel of militia" in 1776, belong in this select group? The answer is complicated by Washington's character. He was, as the historian J.A. Carroll has pointed out, "not an architect in ideas; he was essentially a man of deeds." He never set down in a neat volume his military (or political) principles. The best way to grasp his superior qualities, Carroll maintains, is to examine his thoughts and actions at climactic moments of his career.

To judge his generalship this way requires a look at the strategy of the Revolutionary Army when Washington became its commander on July 3, 1775. By that time the Americans had fought two battles, Lexington-Concord and Bunker Hill, from which their politicians and soldiers drew ruinously wrong conclusions. At Lexington-Concord they saw proof that militia could spring to the defense of their homes and farms and rout British regulars on a day's notice. At Bunker Hill they thought they had found a secret weapon, the entrenching tool, that would enable them to inflict crippling casualties on the attacking British even if, at the very end of the battle, the Americans ignominiously ran away.

In fact, the minutemen who fought at Lexington and Concord were a well-trained rudimentary army that had been drilling and marching for six months. They outnumbered the British five to one and knew it—a fact that added immensely to their élan. At Bunker Hill the overconfident British commander, William Howe, ordered a frontal assault on the entrenched colonials. Why the Americans assumed he would repeat this mistake in the future remains a mystery. As early as March 17, 1776, when the Americans outflanked the British defenses in Boston by seizing Dorchester Heights and fortified them with cannon dragged from Fort Ticonderoga in New York, Howe demonstrated he had learned his lesson by evacuating the city—something he had planned to do anyway.

A corollary to these ideas was the conviction that the war would be settled in one tremendous battle—what in the eighteenth century was called "a general action." Thus there was no need to sign men up for long enlistments—a year was considered more than enough time. There was even less need for a large regular army, which might endanger the liberties of the embryonic republic. Militia could operate as well as regulars from behind Bunker Hill–like barricades. As Israel Putnam, the commander at Bunker Hill, summed it up: "Cover Americans to their chins and they will fight until doomsday."

Still another corollary—though the term may be paying too much of a compliment to the Continental Congress's foggy military thinking—was the idea that if the Americans could push the British off the continent, the war would be won. So Washington obediently detached some of his best regiments and officers, such as Daniel Morgan and Benedict Arnold, to wrest Canada from royal control—a campaign that consumed close to half the 20,000 regulars Congress had empowered him to enlist. And the British evacuation of Boston was hailed as a stupendous victory, for which Congress issued Washington a medal.

Washington did not question these strategic assumptions—or Congress's order to abide by a majority vote of his generals in councils of war— until mid-1776, when the main theater of conflict shifted to New York. Congress told him to defend the city; he did it Bunker Hill–style. On Brooklyn Heights and at various points around Manhattan, his men expended immense amounts of energy building forts on which the British were expected to impale themselves. One, on the corner of Grand and Greene streets, was appropriately named Bunker Hill.

Meanwhile, in mid-July, William Howe proceeded to land 25,000 men unopposed on Staten Island, underscoring the idiocy of Congress's continental redoubt strategy in a war with the world's dominant sea power. Washington had only about 10,000 regulars to defend a city surrounded by rivers that permitted the enemy to land where and when they chose. The rest of his 23,000-man army was militia.

A few weeks later Howe shifted his field army to Long Island and defeated the Americans in a battle of feint and maneuver. Faking a frontal assault in order to pin Washington's men in their entrenchments, Howe swung half his army in a night march around the exposed American left wing, creating rout and panic.

A shaken Washington was able to move his surviving troops to Manhattan by night. But a few weeks later Howe outflanked the American forts on lower Manhattan, landing at Kips Bay (now Thirty-fourth Street) after a ferocious naval bombardment. The Connecticut Militia guarding the shore fled without firing a shot. Washington, watching this stampede, cried out, "Are these the men with which I am to defend America?" Again, mostly thanks to British sloth, Washington managed to extricate the bulk of his army, this time to strong positions on Harlem Heights, where a brisk skirmish with British patrols temporarily steadied their collapsing morale.

During "hours allotted to sleep," Washington began rethinking the strategy of the war in a series of letters to the president of Congress. Henceforth, he wrote, the Americans should "avoid a general action or put anything to the Risk, unless compelled by a necessity into which we ought never to be drawn." Their goal should be "to protract the war."

In cutting terms, Washington demolished congressional prejudice against a large standing army. It was imperative to recruit regulars committed to serve for the duration, and end their dependence on militia. "Men just dragged from the tender Scenes of domestick life, unaccustomed to the din of arms," had no confidence in themselves or their officers on a battlefield. They were impatient, impossible to discipline, and they infected the regulars with similar vices.

But Washington and his generals were themselves still infected with the Bunker Hill virus, which they now called "a war of posts." When Howe outflanked him again, landing troops on the Westchester shore of the Hudson who threatened to trap the Americans on Manhattan Island, Washington retreated to the hills around White Plains. Behind him he left almost 3,000 regulars in Fort Washington, overlooking the Hudson at present-day 181st Street. These men were supposed to deny the British full use of Manhattan Island and the river.

At White Plains, Howe did little more than feint an attack, then detached a hefty portion of his army to assault Fort Washington. Masterfully combining artillery with flank and frontal attacks, the British took the fort in two hours, bagging irreplaceable regulars and scores of cannon. A chagrined Washington confessed there had been "warfare in my mind" about whether to evacuate the place. He had let Major General Nathanael Greene, at this point one of the leading Bunker Hillists, talk him into leaving them there.

That bitter pill purged the last vestige of entrenchment-tool illusions from Washington's mind. Two weeks later General Greene was across the Hudson River in Fort Washington's New Jersey twin, Fort Lee, when he learned from a local farmer that four or five thousand British troops had crossed the river at Dobbs Ferry, a few miles to the north, and were marching on the fort. Greene rushed a dispatch to Washington in Hackensack, asking for instructions. Should he stay and fight it out? Instead of a written answer, he got General Washington in person on a lathered horse. His instructions were one word: Retreat. Cannon, food, ammunition—everything was abandoned.

That was the day Washington began fighting a new kind of war in America. He was just in time, because in New Jersey the British, too, had some new ideas. Having demonstrated their ability to defeat the American army almost at will, they launched a campaign to win what post-Vietnam Americans would call hearts and minds. Along their line of march, they distributed a proclamation offering rebels pardons and guaranties against "forfeitures, attainders and penalties." All they had to do was appear before a British official within sixty days and sign a statement promising to "remain in a peaceable Obedience to His Majesty." New Jersey, the British hoped, would become a model of how to defuse the Revolution. It had a large percentage of Loyalists who would support a restoration of royal government and back the king's troops against "the disaffected."

At first Washington thought he had a good chance to defend New Jersey. He had brought 2,500 regulars across the Hudson with him, leaving some 7,000 men in Westchester to bar the British from the Hudson highlands and New England. New Jersey had 16,000 militiamen on its muster rolls. He asked Governor William Livingston to call them all out. He told the commander of the Westchester force, Major General Charles Lee, to cross the Hudson and join him for a stand on the Raritan River around New Brunswick.

These hopes rapidly unraveled. The British reinforced their invading army until it was 10,000 men strong, under the command of one of their most aggressive generals, Charles, Lord Cornwallis. Charles Lee, a headstrong compound of radical political opinions and careening military ambition, ignored Washington's request to join him. Meanwhile New Jersey's militia declined to turn out. Not a single regiment responded to the governor's call. Only about 1,000 individuals showed up at mustering sites, almost as useless as none at all. It was grim evidence of the power of Britain's shrewd combination of carrot and bayonet.

On November 29, Washington was in New Brunswick with an army riven by three months of retreat and defeat. Some militiamen broke into stores of rum and got drunk. Others, mostly Pennsylvanians, deserted in droves, although they had been paid to stay until January 1. Those whose contracts expired on December 1 announced they were going home then, no matter what was happening to the glorious cause.

Soon down to 3,000 men, and with the British crunching toward the bridges over the Raritan, Washington told Congress, "We shall retreat to the west side of the Delaware." Although New Jersey and the rest of the country saw this decision as mere flight, Washington was still thinking strategically. He wrote Charles Lee that he hoped the British would pursue him and attempt to pacify New Jersey by detaching garrisons across the state. He planned to "lull them into security" and, when he saw an opportunity, "beat them up."

The Revolution in New Jersey slid toward collapse. The legislature disbanded. As many as three to four hundred people a day flocked to British army posts to renew their allegiance. Brigadier General Alexander McDougall wrote from Morristown: "This state is totally deranged, without Government or officers, civil or military . . . that will act with any spirit." Another contemporary observer remarked that at this point the British could have bought New Jersey for eighteen pence a head.

Finally realizing that the fate of the infant nation was at stake in New Jersey, Charles Lee crossed the Hudson into Bergen County. He was not encouraged by what he encountered along his line of march: The mass of the people were "strangely contaminated" with loyalty to the king. He urged Congress to recruit a new army immediately by drafting every militiaman they could find. A few days later Lee was captured by a British cavalry patrol and the remnants of his force straggled across the Delaware to join Washington's handful.

Major General Israel Putnam, the architect of Bunker Hill, was also wandering through New Jersey telling everyone the war was lost. The current army was about to disband, he said, and even if Congress could raise another one, there was no hope of resisting the British "in the plain country to the southward." Without a hill to fight from, Putnam was devoid of ideas.

Washington took a different view. In a letter to General William Heath, who was guarding the Hudson highlands, the American commander in chief wrote that "the defection of the people . . . has been as much owing to the want of an Army to look the Enemy in the face, as any other cause."

In this offhand, intuitive way, Washington enunciated the central idea of the strategy that would win the American Revolution. It merits his inclusion in the select circle of great revolutionary generals who invented a new kind of war—with an additional laurel for conceiving this winning strategy while most of the others around him were losing their heads.

This central statement coincided with the rest of the new strategic ideas Washington had enunciated in the previous chaotic months of defeat and disillusion: recruiting a regular army for the duration, protracting the war, never risking a general action, retreating until the enemy exposed a part of their army to insult or destruction.

Washington swiftly demonstrated his ability to implement tactics to match his strategy. He ordered General Heath to invade northern New Jersey from the Hudson highlands, seize arms, and intimidate the many Loyalists the British had encouraged to come out of hiding there. He gave Alexander McDougall three of Charles Lee's continental regiments to support a fairly good turnout of militia in Morris County. Finally, he marshaled the 2,500 shivering regulars under his command and led them across the ice-choked Delaware River on Christmas night of 1776 to kill or capture two-thirds of the 1,500-man royal garrison at Trenton.

A few days later, Washington again invaded New Jersey. Cornwallis came at him with 9,000 men. On January 2, 1777, Washington wheeled his army around the British left flank by night and chewed up three regiments at Princeton, then headed for the Royal Army's main base at New Brunswick. The frantic British abandoned west Jersey and marched all night to get there first. They flung themselves into defensive positions around the town—only to discover that Washington had slipped away to winter quarters in Morristown. There, he coolly issued a proclamation announcing that anyone who had switched sides could return to the cause by showing up at any American post and pledging fresh allegiance to the United States.

With an army to look the enemy in the face and British power reduced to a narrow enclave along the Raritan, New Jersey's revolutionary ardor underwent a magical revival. British commissaries and foraging parties were ambushed on the roads. Loyalism beyond the army's enclave collapsed. Brilliantly combining military force and patriotic persuasion, Washington had rescued the state—and the country.

Recruiting for a new army revived in the rest of the nation, and General Howe glumly reported to London that he now saw no hope of ending the war "but by a general action." Here was irony indeed: Washington had maneuvered the British into adopting the flawed strategy with which the Americans had begun the war.

Washington had already decided that a climactic battle was precisely what Howe was never going to get. And for the next five years he stuck to his strategy despite criticism from hotheads in Congress and in the army, who still envisioned a general action as the answer to everything. In early 1777 Congressman John Adams, who fancied himself a military expert, was still drinking toasts to "a short and violent war."

When the British tried to advance across New Jersey that summer to assault Philadelphia, they found Washington's army on the high ground in the center of the state, waiting to pounce on them—and absolutely declining to come down from the hills to give all-out battle. A disgusted Howe abandoned the stunned Loyalists of east Jersey as he had deserted those in the west after Trenton and Princeton, marched his army to Perth Amboy and sailed them down the coast, then up Chesapeake Bay to attack Philadelphia in a roundabout fashion.

Howe found the hard-marching American army waiting for him in line of battle on Brandywine Creek, apparently ready to offer him the general action he wanted. But Washington positioned his men to give them the whole state of Pennsylvania into which to retreat if—as it transpired—victory eluded them. He followed the same policy a few weeks later at Germantown. Retreat, a dirty word in the American vocabulary in 1776, was no longer considered disgraceful. When the frustrated Howe settled into winter quarters in Philadelphia, former Bunker Hillist Nathanael Greene exulted that British rule in America did not extend beyond "their out-sentinels."

Meanwhile, to make sure the British did not conquer America piecemeal, Washington was extending his central strategic concept of an army to look the enemy in the face. When a British army under General John Burgoyne descended from Canada in 1777, Washington sent some of his best troops, in particular a regiment of Virginia riflemen under Daniel Morgan, to help Major General Horatio Gates's northern army. These men played a crucial part in the victory at Saratoga, inspiring thousands of militiamen to turn out to support the regulars. Although the regulars did almost all the fighting, the militia blocked Burgoyne's line of retreat and destroyed his supply lines, giving him no alternative but surrender.

Washington followed the same strategy in the South when the British shifted their main effort to that region in 1779. They swiftly pacified Georgia and ensconced a royal governor in Savannah. Washington detached one of his most dependable generals, Benjamin Lincoln, and some of his best regiments to meet the threat, but the British trumped this hand by trapping Lincoln and his army in Charleston and forcing them to surrender—a victory that more than balanced Saratoga.

Grimly, Washington detached more regulars he could not spare and assigned them to an army led by Horatio Gates, the victor at Saratoga. They inspired another good turnout of militiamen, but Gates made the mistake of putting the amateurs into line of battle alongside the regulars at Camden. A bayonet charge routed them, exposing the regulars to defeat.

This time Washington riposted with his best general, Nathanael Greene, who had learned a great deal about the art of war at Washington's side since sponsoring the disaster at Fort Washington in 1776. Although he began with barely 800 ragged regulars, Greene adapted Washington's strat-

egy to the South, summing it up admirably in a letter to the guerrilla leader
Thomas Sumter:

> The salvation of this country don't depend upon little strokes nor should
> the great business of establishing a permanent army be neglected to pursue
> them. Partisan strokes in war are like the garnish of a table, they give
> splendor to the Army and reputation to the officers, but they afford no
> national security.... You may strike a hundred strokes and reap little benefit
> from them unless you have a good army to take advantage of your success.
> ... It is not a war of posts but a contest for States.

Greene soon demonstrated what he meant. He dispatched 350 regulars
to South Carolina under Daniel Morgan when the state was on the verge of
total surrender. These regulars rallied enough militiamen to win a stunning
victory at the Cowpens and reverse the momentum of the war.

While Washington supported armies to the north and south, he never
forgot New Jersey. The state remained the cockpit of the Revolution for him.
In three out of five years, he made it the site of his winter quarters. In the
other two years, the ones he spent at Valley Forge and at Newburgh in
Westchester, he was never more than a day's march away. The payoff came in
June 1780, when swarms of New Jersey militiamen turned out to join 3,500
continentals in stopping a 7,000-man invading army. After two bloody collisions at Connecticut Farms and Springfield, the British withdrew and never
invaded the state again.

One thing should now be apparent: Washington's strategy was far more
complex than guerrilla warfare. Instead, it posited a regular army as an essential force to sustain a war, aided when necessary by guerrilla elements. In spite
of his criticism of militia, Washington used them throughout the war. He had
no other choice. He soon resigned himself to never achieving the 40,000-man
army Congress voted him in the aftermath of Trenton and Princeton. For
most of the war, he was lucky to have a fourth of that number under his
command. He called out militia again and again to flesh out his forces, but he
never depended on them the way he and his fellow generals had in 1776. In
1780 he told the president of Congress that militia were useful "only as light
troops to be scattered in the woods and plague rather than do serious injury to
the enemy." This kind of fighting, which he called *petite guerre*—a first
cousin of the Spanish word *guerrilla*—was, as his lieutenant Greene made
clear, never decisive.

In 1778 Washington met the greatest challenge to his strategy. It came
from Charles Lee, who returned from British captivity with a plan to disband
the regular army and commit the country to a guerrilla war. Washington
rejected the idea as firmly as he turned aside proposals for summoning all the
militiamen within reach and hurling them and the regulars at the British for
the one big battle John Adams and other fire-eaters wanted.

Washington got the most out of his thin line of regulars because he
seldom used them in a European way—and because he was generously en-

dowed with a trait essential to a great general: audacity. It runs like a bright thread through his whole career, beginning with his dawn attack on a French patrol on Virginia's frontier in 1754, a burst of gunfire that started the Seven Years' War. Even in early 1776, during the stalemated siege of Boston, he startled his Bunker Hill–infatuated colleagues by proposing a dawn assault across the ice of Back Bay on the entrenched British—a gamble that might have ended the war on the spot. A council of war voted him down.

Trenton and Princeton were, of course, masterpieces of audacity, but not enough credit has been given to Germantown. Here, just four weeks after losing a major battle on the Brandywine, he hurled his entire army in four columns at the main British camp. Only the confusion generated by an early-morning fog prevented him from winning. In Europe, it was Germantown as much as Saratoga that convinced France the Americans were capable of winning the war and were worth the risk of an alliance.

Even after he went into winter quarters at Valley Forge, Washington's audacity continued to manifest itself. He insisted on constant skirmishing and harassment of the enemy in Philadelphia. Although driven to cries of exasperation and despair at the way Congress failed to feed and clothe the army, he found time to plan a winter attack on the British, which Nathanael Greene narrowly persuaded him was too "hassardous."

By this time Washington had stopped paying much attention to Congress's military thinking. He refused to split up his army to give various parts of the country an unfounded feeling of security. Not even the president of Congress could persuade him to station some units closer to the politicians' 1778 headquarters in York. "It would give me infinite pleasure to afford protection to every individual and to every spot of ground in the whole United States. Nothing is more my wish . . . [but] I cannot divide the army. If this is done I cannot be answerable for the consequences," Washington wrote. For the same reason he vetoed a plan to give the marquis de Lafayette a chunk of the main army and let him invade Canada in 1778.

But Washington never stopped looking for a chance to strike at an exposed British position. In July and August of 1779, when the war in the north seemed stalemated, he struck two ferocious blows. First, bayonet-wielding light infantry under Anthony Wayne killed or captured the entire garrison at Stony Point on the Hudson. A month later Washington's favorite cavalryman, Light-Horse Harry Lee, repeated the performance against the smaller British outpost at Paulus Hook in present-day Jersey City.

Surprize [sic] was one of the favorite words in Washington's military vocabulary, and he was constantly studying ways to improve his technique for achieving it. Because the enemy expected surprise attacks at dawn, he recommended midnight. "A dark night and even a rainy one if you can find the way, will contribute to your success," he told Anthony Wayne, advice Wayne put to good use at Stony Point.

But Washington tempered his audacity with caution. When Benedict Arnold wanted to organize an assault on British-held Newport in 1777, Washington told him to forget it unless he had "a moral certainty" of succeeding.

More and more, as the war dragged on, he sought to avoid giving the British even the appearance of a victory. He was ever aware of the importance of maintaining popular support. This not only was important politically but was a vital part of his military strategy. Militia would not turn out for a loser.

In this context, Brandywine, which seems at first glance to contradict Washington's determination to avoid a general action, fits his strategy of maintaining an army to look the enemy in the face. He recognized that in the struggle for hearts and minds up and down a 2,000-mile-long continent, there were times when the Americans had to fight even if the odds were heavily against them. To have allowed the British to march into Philadelphia without a battle would have ruined the patriots' morale.

A similar blend of pugnacity and public relations motivated the last major battle under Washington's command—Monmouth in June 1778. The French had entered the war, and the panicky British abandoned Philadelphia to retreat to New York. Now more than ever Washington was disinclined to risk everything in a general action. But he sensed the need to strike a blow. After a day of ferocious fighting in nightmarish heat in the New Jersey Pine Barrens, satisfied that he had won the appearance of a victory, he let the redcoats continue their retreat.

To maintain civilian morale, Washington at one point suggested Congress provide the army with "a small traveling press" to supply "speedy and exact information of any military transactions that take place." When the bankrupt Congress refused, Washington did the next best thing. He furloughed an ex-newspaperman, Lieutenant Sheppard Kollock of the continental artillery, and set him up as editor of the New Jersey *Journal,* which at least stabilized public opinion in the cockpit state.

On another front Washington displayed an audacity—and an imagination—few generals have matched. Throughout most of the war, he was his own intelligence director. He proved himself a master of the game, running as many as a half dozen spy rings in Philadelphia and New York, and constantly urged his fellow generals to follow suit. "Single men in the night will be more likely to ascertain facts than the best glasses in the day," he wrote to Anthony Wayne in 1779.

One of the keys to his victory at Trenton was his use of a double agent, John Honeyman, to give him a thorough briefing on the enemy's defenses— and to lull the local commander with stories of the American army's collapse. At Valley Forge, Washington manufactured documents in his own handwriting full of returns from imaginary infantry and cavalry regiments. Double agents handed those documents over to the British in Philadelphia, convincing them that the main army had been reinforced with 8,000 men and was too strong to molest.

In July 1780 Sir Henry Clinton decided to launch a preemptive attack on a French army that had just landed at Newport. A brilliant idea, it might well have succeeded if one of Washington's best New York agents had not rushed him news of the plan. Clinton actually had his men aboard ships when he was distracted by the capture of some "secret" papers that showed Washington was planning an all-out attack on New York. The jittery British general reluctantly abandoned his coup de main.

The Yorktown campaign was the ultimate proof of the genius of Washington's generalship. The idea of trapping Cornwallis in the little tobacco port came from the French commander, the comte de Rochambeau; Washington was skeptical of its chances for success. But the execution of the plan depended totally on Washington's tactics and strategy. First he befuddled Sir Henry Clinton with a veritable blizzard of false information about an attack on New York. Then he took the huge gamble of marching his men south in a long, exposed line through New Jersey. Benedict Arnold, by that time a British general, begged Clinton to attack, but Sir Henry declined another encounter with "the bold persevering militia of that populous province" and let Washington march to victory.

Perhaps the most appealing thing about Washington's strategy was its strong link to freedom. It eschewed the militaristic idea of hauling every man into the ranks at the point of a gun. It rested instead on faith in the courage of free men. It was a realistic faith: He did not expect men to commit suicide in defense of freedom, but he did believe men would take grave risks if they thought they had a reasonable chance of succeeding.

Looking back later, Washington, an innately modest man, was often inclined to attribute victory to the "interposition of Providence." But those who study the evidence, and ignore the statistics, are inclined to think Providence wore the shape of a tall Virginian who had the brains to conceive a way to win a war when it was on the brink of being lost—and the ability to provide the leadership that converted this strategy into a military victory won by free men.

Berezina

by I R A M E I S T R I C H

Napoleon's Russian calamity is the stuff of military nightmares, but in fact it could have been even worse. As his Grande Armée, now no longer grand, staggered home from Moscow at the end of November 1812, he faced the specter of total annihilation on the banks of the Berezina River. Assuming that any river would be frozen that late in the year, Napoleon had ordered the burning of most of his pontoon boats, to speed his retreat; an unseasonal thaw had turned the tiny Berezina into a torrent. Three Russian armies were closing in for what seemed to be a sure kill. Then, for a crucial moment, the audacious energy that had once served Napoleon so well surged back. Did that save him? Ira Meistrich asks. Or was it simply the inability of the Russians to seize a final advantage? Meistrich, a television producer, writes frequently on Napoleonic subjects.

The Battle of the Berezina, which lasted for three late-November days in 1812, was the climactic event in Napoleon's catastrophic retreat from Moscow. Surrounded by vastly superior forces, his army disorganized and demoralized by cold and hunger, faced with a river to cross and only the most rudimentary bridging equipment, the emperor assessed his chances: "This time," he said, "only the brave will survive."

That he did survive, with even a fraction of his original force, was an epic confirmation of his own dictum: "In war men are nothing; one man is everything." For the outcome of the battle—a blindfolded slugging match of senseless actions and irrational decisions on both sides—was finally determined by one man, Napoleon, behaving rationally, if only for a brief time.

Napoleon invaded Russia in June 1812 with more than 500,000 men (including over 80,000 cavalry) and 1,300 cannon. He had hoped to smash the Russian armies quickly in a single decisive battle and optimistically had issued troops rations for only twenty-four days. But the Russians refused to oblige. As the weeks wore on and the distance from Paris increased, Napoleon complained bitterly of the ongoing Russian withdrawal: "After throwing up earthworks, batteries, and redoubts, and after announcing their intention of holding them, the enemy, as usual, have shown the white feather." Count Louis de Narbonne, one of his aides-de-camp, observed, "Sire, this is the kind of war of time and space that we were promised."

In early September Napoleon got his chance for a "decisive" battle at Borodino. But his performance that day was tenuous and the Russian army was able to withdraw, battered but intact. The road to Moscow lay ahead, and by mid-September the Grande Armde was in the city, more than 1,500 miles from Paris.

For five weeks Napoleon paced the Kremlin, utterly convinced that at any moment the czar would negotiate. While he waited for an envoy who would never arrive, Moscow burned and the Grande Armé's morale deteriorated. Yet Napoleon refused to concede that he might have to abandon his prize.

Others knew better. Armand de Caulaincourt, his former ambassador to Czar Alexander I, was more familiar with Russia than was the emperor, but his intimations of "difficulties" only irritated Napoleon, and his warning that "[w]inter will come like a bombshell" was ignored.

While Napoleon frittered away precious days in Moscow, the Russians bided their time. Fifty miles to the southwest, at Tarutino, Field Marshal Mikhail Kutuzov, commander in chief of the czar's forces, vowed to make the French eat horseflesh. Carefully preserving the illusion that an armistice was in effect, he rebuilt his army. The last thing he wanted was for Napoleon to awaken prematurely from his dreams of a peace dictated from Moscow to the reality of his increasingly desperate position.

Napoleon was unable to force a decisive conclusion to the campaign, and when the Russians attacked south of Moscow, he realized the czar would not negotiate a peace. On October 19 he ordered the Grande Armé out of Moscow. The weather was fine, and after five weeks of lax discipline, the troops, camp followers, horses, and wagons streamed out of the city looking more like a carnival than an army. To General Philippe de Ségur, a member of Napoleon's staff, the column "resembled a horde of Tartars after a successful invasion." According to de Ségur:

> It consisted of three or four files of infinite length, in which there was a mixture, a confusion of chaises, ammunition wagons, hansom carriages, and vehicles of every kind. Here trophies of Russian, Turkish, and Persian colours, and the gigantic cross of Ivan the Great—there, Russian peasants with their beards carrying or driving along our booty, of which they constituted a part: others dragging even wheelbarrows filled with whatever they could remove.

Despite the festive atmosphere, things began to go wrong almost immediately. With no one in overall charge of the withdrawal, chaos soon spread through the lines, snarling traffic. "Most of the carts were already shattered," recorded Adrien Bourgogne, a sergeant of the Imperial Guard, "and others could not move, the wheels sinking deep in the sandy road. We could hear screams in French, oaths in German, entreaties to the Almighty in Italian, and to the Holy Virgin in Spanish and Portuguese."

On October 24, in the bloody Battle of Maloyaroslavets, Kutuzov barred the French from retreating along a southern route that would have taken them through fertile, unspoiled land. Napoleon knew that from here on his forces would only get weaker. Each of his men was irreplaceable, whereas the Russians could continue to draw on the countryside. So rather than renew the battle the next day, he resorted to the safer, if already despoiled, route he had taken into Russia.

Kutuzov, for his part, was in no hurry to confront the French. The Russian general, sixty-eight years old at the time, has been described as lazy, cowardly, and deceitful. But among the czar's commanders and confidants he had the most comprehensive overview of the consequences should Napoleon fall in Russia. He considered Europe's liberation solely the business of Europe, and did not relish the idea of the Germanic states freed of the Napoleonic yoke. As for the English, Kutuzov was quoted by Robert Wilson, a liaison officer on his staff, as saying, "I am by no means sure that the total destruction of the Emperor Napoleon and his army would be such a benefit to the world; his succession would not fall to Russia or any other continental power, but to that which already commands the sea whose domination would then be intolerable." Accordingly, he had built what he called a "golden bridge" out of Russia for Napoleon: He would hound the retreating emperor and make him pay for the invasion, but he would let him escape in the end. Although Kutuzov's staff and the czar himself might fume, the general was determined to have it his way.

On October 28 Napoleon's army, already dispirited by several days of rain, was distressed at having to recross the Borodino battlefield. To Eugène Labaume, a staff officer of IV Corps, "most horrible was the multitude of dead bodies, which, deprived of burial fifty-two days, scarcely retained the human form. . . . The whole plain was entirely covered with them."

That night, part of the army bivouacked on the battlefield, making its campfires with the shattered remnants of muskets, carts, and gun carriages. But they had no water, as the nearby stream was polluted by decaying bodies. Morale continued to plummet.

By October 30, wrote Bourgogne,

> the road had become very heavy, and many carts laden with booty had the greatest difficulty in getting along. . . . The road was heaped with valuable things—pictures, candlesticks, and quantities of books . . . books such as Voltaire, Jean-Jacques Rousseau, and Button's *Natural History,* bound in red morocco and gold.

The nights grew colder, food scarcer. Camaraderie vanished. The men were sustained only by the thought of Smolensk, where they were to rest and

receive rations and clothing. Many believed they would go into winter quarters there. But on November 6, when they were only fifty miles from the city,
a three-day march, "the heavens declared against us," wrote de Ségur.

> The army marched enveloped in cold fogs. These fogs became thicker,
> and presently an immense cloud descended upon it in large flakes of snow. It
> seemed as if the very sky was falling, and joining the earth and our enemies
> to complete our destruction.

Now the cold turned bitter. Said Bourgogne, "Our lips were frozen, our
brains too. To Labaume, "the country around, as far as the eye could reach,
presented, unbroken, one white and savage appearance."

The army began its descent to Smolensk on November 9. For five days
Napoleon tried to concentrate his depleted forces, while his famished men
looted a city that had already been burned and looted the previous summer.
Colonel Raymond de Fézensac of III Corps described the chaos:

> Abuses of every sort were exercised with impunity; the magazines were
> broken into and plundered; and, as always happens in such cases, the re-
> sources of months were destroyed in twenty-four hours. In the midst of
> pillage men died of hunger.

While this went on, Napoleon received alarming reports that proved the
impossibility of remaining at Smolensk. In the north, a Russian army under
General Ludwig Adolph Wittgenstein had captured Vitebsk and was now
within range of the Berezina River—which Napoleon needed to cross in order
to reach some of the stockpiles he had left behind on his trip into Russia.
Meanwhile, the Army of Moldavia under Admiral Pavel Tchitchigov was
moving northeast toward Napoleon's main column. Thus Napoleon's forces
not only were unable to hold Smolensk but also found their escape routes to
both the north and the south threatened by Russian armies; in addition,
cossacks were harrying the length of his communications. So eager was Kutuzov to push Napoleon across the "golden bridge" that he failed to recognize
how close it was to collapse.

The emperor needed a place to rest, rally, and reorganize his troops. He
chose Minsk, a depot city with an enormous stockpile of rations—unaware
that Tchitchigov's army was moving on that city. But Napoleon was still some
200 miles away from Minsk. The retreat had to continue.

He also needed to reinforce his ranks by joining with Marshal Nicolas-
Charles Oudinot's II Corps and Marshal Claude P. Victor's IX Corps. The
two commanded some 25,000 badly needed, well-disciplined troops who so
far were unaffected by the army's collapse. They began to move south toward
Borisov, where Napoleon planned to link up with them.

The cold worsened, on some nights reaching thirty degrees below zero.
The survivors dragged themselves along as best they could, their faces
smeared with blood from the little horseflesh there was to be had, their beards

stiffened with icicles. One unpublished memoir tells of soldiers "walking barefoot, using pieces of wood as canes, but their feet were frozen so hard that the sound they made on the road was like that of wooden clogs." Flocks of ravens followed the line of the retreat, and the route was marked by thousands of snow-covered hillocks—the graves of the fallen. To de Ségur, the snow "was like a vast winding-sheet which Nature had thrown over the army."

Even now, many soldiers refused to abandon their booty and struggled to drag it through the snow. Labaume described how curious it was "to see those who were dying with hunger, laden with more riches than they could possibly carry."

Sometimes Napoleon marched along with them, iron staff in hand. Although he might have been said to be the author of all their misfortunes, he alone was spared their reproaches. According to Caulaincourt,

> As the Emperor passed through that ill-starred multitude, there was not a murmur or groan to be heard. How generous those Frenchmen in their misfortune! They cursed the elements, but . . . [n]ot one murmur against the Emperor was heard in the whole course of this disastrous retreat.

The French were not the only ones suffering the effects of winter—Kutuzov's army was freezing too. The Russians had received no shipments of winter clothes or boots, and after mid-November they had little fodder for their horses. In the first weeks of the pursuit, their casualties were probably about 30,000 out of 110,000. A Russian hussar general wrote that to keep his feet from freezing, he "stuck them in the fur caps of the French grenadiers, which littered the road."

On November 16 Tchitchigov's Army of Moldavia captured Minsk with all its supplies, so Napoleon had to alter course yet again. Vilna seemed the next-best option, and the most expeditious route lay through Borisov, a hamlet of 350 houses on the left bank of the Berezina. French and Russian attention now focused on this little place and its 600-yard bridge across the river.

But Napoleon was still more than eighty miles from Borisov, twice as far as Tchitchigov, and the very real danger existed that he would be cut off on the east bank of the Berezina. He needed to speed the retreat. Arriving at Orsha on November 19, he ordered many of the carriages and extraneous vehicles burned so the army could move faster. And assuming that rivers and streams would be frozen, he added two pontoon trains of sixty boats to the pyre; the horses that had pulled them were turned over to the artillery. Certainly he could not have known that an unseasonal thaw had already turned the Berezina into an impassable torrent.

The French position was further complicated by news received on November 22: The day before, Tchitchigov's advance guard had captured Borisov, and the main body of his army was moving on the town. Napoleon was then at Toloczin, still forty miles from the Berezina. The situation was critical. Tchitchigov was sitting athwart the main escape route with 34,000 men.

Wittgenstein was pressing from the north with 30,000 more. Within two days Napoleon would march through the snowfall to the accompanying growl of Marshal Victor's cannon, struggling to fend off Wittgenstein. Kutuzov was right behind, with the main Russian force of 80,000 men. In all, more than 140,000 enemy troops were converging on a Grande Armé of some 25,000 battered men.

Yet even as he lost one bridge and burned two pontoon trains, what Napoleon would have called his star provided another means of crossing the river. At midnight on November 22, Brigadier General Jean-Baptiste Juvenal Corbineau, trying to rejoin the main body of II Corps, came across a peasant who, judging from his wet horse, looked as if he had just crossed the Berezina. The peasant guided Corbineau's unit to fords between the villages of Studianka and Vesselovo, about eight miles north of Borisov, and they crossed to the east bank.

It has been said that the loss of time is irreparable in war. And in fact time was the key issue throughout this battle. The Russians had made an unintentional gift of time to the harried French, and the French constantly squandered the gift.

Even after he heard about the Studianka ford, Napoleon vacillated. This was no simple solution. Without bridging equipment, he would be crossing a river in spate, its currents laced with ice floes. Also, the thaw had made the river overflow, creating 500 yards of marsh on the far bank, in which troops, horses, vehicles, and artillery would surely bog down. And all these obstacles would have to be overcome under the fire of a well-entrenched enemy in a commanding position.

On November 24 the emperor learned that Oudinot had recaptured Borisov, which only prolonged his indecision. After taking Borisov, Tchitchigov had sent his advance guard out on reconnaissance. They were routed by a patrol of Oudinot's chasseurs and rode back to warn Tchitchigov. The admiral assumed that Napoleon's main force was about to descend on the town and hastily ordered a withdrawal, barely escaping across the bridge, which he cut in two places.

Napoleon reached Borisov around 3 P.M. on November 25. Around 11 P.M. he and Armand de Caulaincourt walked out onto the ruins of the bridge. It is possible that even at this late stage Napoleon had not fully abandoned the idea of crossing here. But standing at the very ends of the shattered timbers, he could see that the river at this point was substantially wider than at Studianka. Finally convinced, he now turned all his energies toward the task ahead at the Studianka ford.

He ordered Oudinot to stage a series of diversionary actions to the south. The idea was to direct Tchitchigov's attention anywhere but to Studianka. In the interim, materials would be gathered with which to construct bridges over the river. Victor's IV Corps and Marshal Louis Nicolas Davout's I Corps would form the rear guard around Borisov, holding off Wittgenstein and Kutuzov as long as they could and allowing the army, its equipment, and as many stragglers as possible to reach the bridges.

Napoleon had managed for a long time to conceal the magnitude of his army's collapse—especially from Oudinot and Victor, but to some extent even from the marshals who accompanied him. The shock was therefore all the greater when Victor's corps first laid eyes on the survivors of Moscow outside of Borisov. According to General de Ségur, they "perceived behind Napoleon only a trail) of spectres covered with rags . . . marching confusedly with their heads bent, their eyes fixed on the ground, and silent, like a troop of captives." To Caulaincourt the reinforcements seemed "like men belonging to another race. They were alive, we were shadows."

These were the men with whom Napoleon would face a comparatively fresh enemy opposing his passage of the Berezina. Since November 23 he had been preparing himself for a desperate struggle. The regimental eagles had been buried or destroyed so that they would not fall into enemy hands. Standard-bearers had removed flags from their staffs and wound them around their bodies. Some 1,800 dismounted cavalrymen had been formed into two battalions, although they could muster only 1,150 muskets. The state archives had been burned. According to the emperor's aide-de-camp, General Jean Rapp, "the situation was frightful, and unheard of. . . . [N]o Frenchman, not even Napoleon, could expect to escape."

Indeed, all Tchitchigov really had to do was wait where he was, on a long front on the west bank of the Berezina, while Wittgenstein fell upon Napoleon's right. Success was virtually guaranteed. But indecision plagued the Russian effort as much as it did the French. Tchitchigov had received a dispatch from Wittgenstein expressing the opinion that Napoleon would head for Bobruisk, south of Borisov. Slightly earlier, Kutuzov had sent a warning to Tchitchigov to guard his southern flank against a surprise crossing. Napoleon, he said, "is sure to make a demonstration of crossing at one point in order to attract your attention, while he crosses at another. . . ."

On the morning of November 25, Tchitchigov had been warned by the commander of a light horse detachment that the French appeared to be putting up a bridge over the river at Studianka. Tchitchigov, knowing that the spot was marshy and unfavorable, concluded that this had to be the diversion Kutuzov had cautioned him about. If Napoleon was feinting to the north, Tchitchigov reasoned, he must really be moving south, as Kutuzov and Wittgenstein had warned.

He decided that Napoleon was headed for Berezino, twenty-five miles south of Borisov, where there was a solid bridge with a good road. He ordered his troops to make all possible speed south. Opposite Borisov he left only General Comte Louis de Langeron—a French emigré, one of the many foreign commanders in the czar's army—with one division of 4,000 men. General Yefim Tchaplitz was left to cover the rest of the western bank from Zembin to the river opposite Studianka with a few scattered detachments.

Tchitchigov was right about those marshes at Studianka. They could be crossed only by a series of twenty-two wooden bridges that led to Zembin, five miles to the northwest. According to Colonel Jean-Baptiste de Marbot of the 23rd Chasseurs, when the admiral withdrew his forces, he committed a blun-

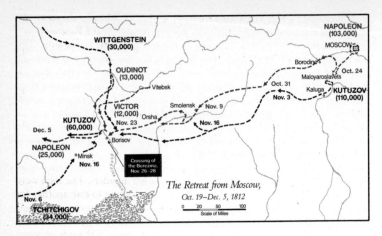

The Retreat from Moscow,
Oct. 19–Dec. 5, 1812

der that "any sergeant would have avoided, and for which his government never forgave him": He neglected to burn these bridges. "Had [he] taken this wise precaution," continued de Marbot, "the French army must have been irrevocably lost. To cross the river would have done it no good, since it would have been stopped by the deep marsh which surrounds Zembin."

That very night, as Tchitchigov hustled most of his troops away from Studianka, construction began on Napoleon's bridges over the river. General Jean-Baptiste Eblé had arrived at Studianka at 5 A.M., bringing with him a modest treasure that—by an act of inspired disobedience—he had withheld from the pyre at Orsha and that was suddenly more precious than all the loot taken from Moscow. De Ségur inventoried this treasure as "two field forges, two wagons of coal, six covered wagons of utensils and nails." To put all of it to use, Eblé had with him some companies of *pontonniers*.

At dusk the French started dismantling the houses of Studianka for construction materials. After days of thaw, a frost had hardened the boggy riverbanks, slightly easing the task of the pontonniers as they positioned the first of twenty-three trestles for two bridges.

The bridging operation was slowed during this early stage by a bizarre competition between Eblé's pontonniers and General François de Chasseloup-Laubat's engineers. They stubbornly obstructed each other's efforts until at last Napoleon decreed that each corps should build one bridge. Then, according to de Marbot,

> those brave men gave a proof of devotion. . . . They leapt into the cold water of the Berezina and worked there for six or seven hours, though there was not a drop of spirits to give them, and they had no bed to look forward to for the following night, but a field covered with snow. They nearly all died when the great frost came.

Working through the night, the French were mystified by the inactivity of the Russians. In fact, confusion and discord reigned in the Russian ranks. Tchaplitz was unable to get a clear picture of what was happening. The eastern bank of the river was higher than the western, and he could not see over the crest to where Eblé and his men were stockpiling materials. But his suspicions had been aroused by the number of French officers watering their horses at the spot, and on the evening of November 25 he sent a party of 300 cossacks across the river on patrol. Before they returned, Tchaplitz was ordered by de Langeron to move south and take up new positions opposite Borisov. Despite his pleas to be allowed to continue to observe the situation at Studianka, he was forced to leave.

Napoleon had reached the bridging site just as construction was beginning. He inspected the terrain and encouraged the builders. The men were working up to their chins in the freezing water, clinging to one another for balance on the slippery riverbed, struggling to prevent themselves and their fragile handiwork from being swept away by chunks of ice. Napoleon's survey of the opposite bank was not encouraging. There were 500 yards of soggy marsh, and beyond that a line of woods. If the Russians were there, they would surely foil any attempt to cross.

Just after dawn, he reviewed the situation at the headquarters of Marshal Oudinot. It was time to consider extraordinary remedies.

Joachim Murat, king of Naples and Napoleon's brother-in-law, suggested the emperor abandon the army and make a flat run for it, crossing the river a few leagues away and heading for Warsaw with just a detachment of Polish lancers. Napoleon refused even to consider it. A few days earlier, overhearing some officers wishing for a balloon to carry him away, he had said to Caulaincourt, "If we cannot cross, we shall try what our pistols can do. . . . [M]ake sure that my weapons and yours are in good condition. . . ."

General Jean Rapp described the atmosphere at Oudinot's headquarters:

> Napoleon was uneasy: we had neither a bridge-train nor subsistence. The main [Russian] army was advancing, and the troops from Moldavia blockaded the passage: we were surrounded. . . . Ney . . . said to me, in German, "Our situation is unparalleled; if Napoleon extricates himself today, he must have the devil in him."

But even while this conversation took place, Rapp reported, the unbelievable happened:

> While conversing, we perceived the enemy were filing off; their masses had disappeared, the fires were extinguished. . . . I went to Napoleon, who was conversing with Marshal Oudinot. "Sire, the enemy have left their position."—"That is impossible." The King of Naples and Marshal Ney arrived, and confirmed what I had just announced. The Emperor came out from his barrack, cast his eye on the other side of the river. "I have outwitted the Admiral. . . ."

Napoleon's eyes, Rapp continued, "sparkled with joy and impatience." To another observer he remarked, "I have been Emperor long enough, it is now time that I acted as a general."

Napoleon the general moved decisively to exploit this unexpected opportunity. He swiftly mounted a battery of forty-four cannon on the riverbank to cover the operation, and sent a force of 400 men across the rising river. In a short time the few remaining cossacks were driven off.

The effort to complete the bridges was redoubled. Napoleon spent much of the day building morale in the ranks. De Marbot describes him as "striding about, accompanied by Murat, going from one regiment to another, and talking to men as well as officers."

Building the two bridges—one for infantry and one for artillery, cavalry, and all wheeled traffic—required a heroic effort by Eblé and his 400 sappers, and the results were unavoidably flimsy. Even so, once the bridges were ready, Napoleon ordered them to be in constant use, day and night.

Oudinot's relatively fresh II Corps (13,000 men) was to cross first and secure the bridgehead. The Imperial Guard (8,500 men) and headquarters (2,500 men) would come next, forming a reserve force for Oudinot. Victor's IX Corps, supported by Marshal Andoche Junot's Westphalians (a total of 13,500 troops), was to form the rear guard at Borisov, slowly contracting the bridgehead around Studianka and Vesselovo, and crossing last. In between, the other corps, too devastated to be effective, would file through Victor's position to the bridges. No plan was made for the thousands of stragglers— the camp followers, Moscow's French community, and tens of thousands of disbanded soldiers who no longer had units to report to—who encumbered the army's movements.

By 1 P.M. on November 26, the first bridge was completed. With cries of "Vive l'empereur!" II Corps crossed the Berezina, joined by General J.P. Doumerc's cuirassier division and some light guns. As soon as he saw them in possession of the ford, Napoleon cried, "Behold my star again appears!" Very quickly, Oudinot established himself in a strong position only six miles from Borisov. A few hours later, the second bridge was completed, and the artillery of Oudinot and that of the Imperial Guard crossed.

Napoleon's star may have reappeared, but the Russians did not.

The Russian commander closest to the scene, Admiral Tchitchigov, had reached Berezino on the morning of November 25 to find no French. That afternoon an aide-de-camp of de Langeron arrived, warning Tchitchigov that Napoleon was constructing bridges north of Borisov. Exhausted by an all-night, thirty-mile trek through bitter cold and over atrocious roads, Tchitchigov's men turned right around and marched back north.

Wittgenstein, too, was struggling with bad roads. On that day he was still twenty-five miles away at Kolopenitchi.

But more than the condition of the roads accounted for the slackness of the Russian pursuit. Tchitchigov had been confused by the incorrect assumptions inflicted upon him by Kutuzov and Wittgenstein. As for Wittgenstein, he had never been too highly thought of as a commander and was terrified by the prospect of facing Napoleon. And what of the commander in chief, Kutuzov? He believed that the objective of the campaign—the expulsion of Napoleon from Russia and the destruction of the emperor's army—had been achieved. He saw no need to continue to shed Russian blood when it was clear that the French were finished. He simply waited.

De Ségur reports that the French at the Berezina "had everything to conquer but the enemy." With temperatures at twenty below zero, and the bridges wide enough for only two or three men abreast, the crossing proceeded with agonizing slowness. Then, pummeled by the ice, the artillery bridge gave way at 8 P.M. Eblé's exhausted men had to plunge back into the frigid water and wrestle new trestles into place. By dawn the bridge had collapsed twice more, and twice more the exhausted pontonniers had gone back into the water.

So far, the crossing had proceeded without a single shot fired. Hurrying back to Studianka, Tchitchigov still lost most of November 27 while he was forced to rest his exhausted troops some miles to the south. Meanwhile, in an effort to surprise Victor, Wittgenstein left the good road to Vesselovo, using instead the poor back roads to Stari-Borisov—which actually eased the pressure on Napoleon's rear guard.

At daybreak on November 27, Marshal Ney's III Corps crossed the river in support of Oudinot, taking up a position on II Corps's left. Napoleon transferred his headquarters to the west bank at 1 P.M. The Imperial Guard followed and formed itself as a reserve for Oudinot near Brilli. Discipline at the approach to the bridges was strict: A semicircle of immaculately uniformed *gendarmes d'élite* allowed no unarmed man to pass, despite the surging pressure of the stragglers.

But at 4 P.M. three trestles of the artillery bridge collapsed, and the first panic began. The columns instantly turned into a frenzied mob, all scrambling for the one intact bridge. Eyewitness Eugène Labaume wrote:

> Now began a frightful contention between the foot soldiers and the horsemen. Many perished by the hands of their comrades, but a great number were suffocated at the head of the brigade; and the dead bodies of men and horses so choked every avenue that it was necessary to climb over mountains of carcasses to arrive at the river.

Eblé's men got the bridge back into operation again by evening, but the carnage had been terrible. In order to clear a pathway for I and IV corps, the engineers had to hew their way with axes through the dreadful palisade of abandoned vehicles and hundreds of corpses.

The situation became calm again by nightfall—too calm: After the panic, the mob's hysteria slid into apathy. Desperately, Eblé and others tried to rouse the listless men as they settled around their campfires for the night. De Marbot described the scene:

> At that moment, no one was crossing, while a hundred paces away I could see by the bright moonlight more than 50,000 stragglers and soldiers sepa-

rated from their regiments. . . . These men, sitting calmly in front of enormous fires, were grilling horseflesh without a notion that they had in front of them a river, the passage of which would cost many of them their lives on the next day, while they could at the present time cross it without hindrance in a few minutes, and finish preparing their supper on the other bank.

November 27 had been a good day for the French: Most of the army was now across, except for the rear guard formed by IX Corps. All Russian attempts to foil the crossing had been repelled. Greatly pleased, Napoleon remarked, *"Voilà comment on passe un pont sous la barbe de l'enemi"* ("This is how to pass over a bridge under the enemy's nose" [literally "beard"]). But there were to be no more reprieves. Wittgenstein reoccupied Borisov that evening, repaired the bridge, and established communications with Tchitchigov's forces. A joint assault was planned for the next morning. Wittgenstein would attack Victor's rear guard while Tchitchigov attempted to seize or destroy the Zembin bridges spanning the marshland west of the Berezina.

Events that night greatly aided the Russian plans. General Louis Partonneaux, the commander of Victor's 12th Infantry Division, had been ordered to abandon the final positions held in Borisov and to fall back on Studianka. Moving out at 3 A.M. on November 28, Partonneaux took a wrong turn in the darkness and marched his division straight into Wittgenstein's I Corps. Some 4,000 troops, including 500 cavalry, and four guns were lost to the Russians. Only 160 Frenchmen who had accidentally taken the right road escaped and were able to rejoin Victor's main force.

Although Victor had at last been ordered across the Berezina, he delayed, waiting for Partonneaux, little suspecting how untenable his position had become. But Wittgenstein was well aware of Victor's weakness. At 8 A.M. he launched a heavy assault against the French left, toward the gap left by Partonneaux's division. Very quickly, Victor was in serious trouble, with Russian troops pressing on the approaches to the bridges. Napoleon learned at 1 P.M. of Partonneaux's surrender and the resulting crisis. Furious, he moved to reinforce Victor, ordering a General Hochberg to recross the Berezina with his Baden brigade.

But chaos had taken over on the east bank. Exploiting the gap in Victor's lines, Wittgenstein had maneuvered some batteries within range of the stragglers. As the first Russian cannonballs began to plunge amid the mob, another panic erupted. They swamped the bridge approaches, packing themselves into a dense mass three-quarters of a mile wide and 200 yards deep. Men on horseback or in wagons lashed their horses straight through the crowds. Thousands reached the bridges only to be pushed off and swept to an icy death. To make matters worse, the artillery bridge collapsed once more at the height of the panic. Those still on the riverbank made for the infantry bridge.

The Baden brigade struggled desperately to come to Victor's aid but could make little headway against the human tide. Ultimately, although Hochberg's infantry succeeded in forcing its way back across, his guns had to be left behind. Napoleon ordered a massive battery into position on the west bank to counter Wittgenstein's bombardment. They poured a heavy fire onto the Russian guns until forced to withdraw. Victor, finally reinforced by Hochberg, continued stubbornly to resist Wittgenstein. The 350 survivors of General Frangois Fournier-Sarlovése's cavalry charged the Russian flank and halted its advance, further stabilizing their positions. Now drawn into a narrow enclave around the bridgehead, IX Corps held the Russians at bay until nightfall.

On the west bank, heavy fighting took place most of the day. Tchitchigov launched a weak attack at dawn with 9,000 infantry and 1,500 cavalry. Ney held the left, Oudinot the center and right along a front of one and one-quarter miles. But Oudinot's lines were weakening, and under steady pressure from Tchitchigov it looked as if they might break. Napoleon himself came to their support at the head of the Imperial Guard. Oudinot managed to rally his forces before the Guard intervened, but was severely wounded.

Napoleon ordered Ney to take over Oudinot's command, and at 10 A.M. Ney promptly counterattacked the Russian left. Doumerc attacked the Russian 18th Division with the 4th, 7th, and 14th regiments of the 3rd Cuirassiers, about 4,000 men. In a sparkling action they inflicted 600 casualties and took 2,000 prisoners and a few guns. The Russians staggered back. A flank attack by General Pierre Berthezène's brigade of the Young Guard reduced 4,000 Russians to 700 battered survivors in minutes, and Tchitchigov showed little inclination to renew hostilities that day.

At 9 P.M. Victor, still holding his bridgehead on the east bank, got his order for the final withdrawal. Once more Eblé's men had to carve a path through the grisly obstacles at the bridge approaches. Eblé himself spent another frustrating night pleading with the stragglers to take advantage of the lull to get safely across. Once again he was unable to move them.

By dawn of November 29 the entire combat strength of the army was across, and at 7 A.M. Eblé received orders to burn the bridges. He eked out every possible minute for the stragglers, who, once more in a frenzy, were trying to battle their way across. But at 9 A.M., with Russian troops now at the approaches, Eblé could delay no longer and fired the bridges. Instantly they became a hellish mass of screaming humanity. Thousands died in the final panic, whether in the flames, the river, the crush, or from the Russian lances. For weeks the river was blocked with frozen corpses.

Carl von Clausewitz, who came to Russia with Napoleon's army but then defected to the other side, wrote:

> Bonaparte had escaped with about 40,000 men, as if some higher power had decreed not to destroy him utterly on this occasion. He had been forced into a situation in which it appeared he must be lost. Had Admiral Tchitchigov only held on to his position at Zembin . . . with 10,000 men he could not have been forced out of it, and it was then too late for the French to retreat by any other road. In twenty-four hours, hunger, a more potent commander than even Napoleon, would have exercised its sway, and the French army must have been lost.

Even a hostile observer like Clausewitz had to conclude that at the Berezina, Napoleon had "not only completely saved his honour but acquired new glory." But was this entirely merited?

Although Napoleon certainly was entitled to claim some sort of victory, the credit (or blame) rightfully should be shared. It was Napoleon's audacious plan that got the army across the Berezina River in the face of seemingly insuperable odds. However, the energy that he displayed came dangerously late and flickered out too soon when he left the scene. A younger Napoleon would not have wallowed in indecision about his route. He would have personally reconnoitered the situation and then made his decision.

This indecision characterized much of his performance throughout the campaign, from his stopping short of bold maneuvers during the Battle of Borodino to his paralysis in Moscow. Napoleon had said after the Battle of Austerlitz in 1805 that "one has only a certain time for war. I shall be good for six years more; but after that even I must cry halt." By his own estimation, in 1812 he was one year past his limit.

Napoleon's vacillations should have enabled the Russians to seal his fate at the Berezina, but again, precious time was lost in confusion and inactivity. Tchitchigov has been assigned the bulk of the blame for Napoleon's escape, but this is not entirely fair. He had been totally confused by the flow of inaccurate dispatches from Wittgenstein and Kutuzov, as well as by Napoleon's deceptive maneuvers. Wittgenstein's terror of Napoleon prevented him from moving briskly to mount a challenge. His appearance at the battle was tardy at best, and his pursuit of Victor's rear guard was tentative.

Kutuzov moved the slowest of all. Aside from some elements of the advance guard, none of his soldiers took part in the fighting at the Berezina. True, his army had suffered severely during the campaign, but that does not fully justify his absence. Kutuzov subordinated his military actions to his political judgment: He did not agree that it was in Russia's best interests to topple Napoleon from his throne.

But Kutuzov was also worn out. Within four months Czar Alexander 1, who was once his bitter foe, would approach the old general's deathbed and beg his forgiveness. "I forgive you, Sire," Kutuzov is said to have responded, "but Russia never will."

If the Russians had no lack of scapegoats at the Berezina, the French had an excess of heroes. These included Oudinot, whose II Corps located the crucial ford, secured the bridgehead, and held the southern flank; and Victor, whose IX Corps fought a valiant rearguard action against overwhelming five-to-one odds, allowing the French combatants and all but twenty-five guns to cross the river safely. Both of these commanders came to the Berezina with intact corps; both lost more than half their effective strength.

Beyond a doubt, however, the most credit goes to General Eblé and his 400 pontonniers, whose selfless devotion built the vital bridges and kept them functional despite brutal conditions and keen exhaustion. Only forty survived their ordeal, and within a few weeks Eblé himself died, worn out by the Herculean effort. Without the total dedication of Eble and his engineers, the human cost would have been far higher. It is possible that Napoleon himself would not have survived.

That cost was frightful as it was, although the actual number of casualties cannot be known. French combatant casualties had to be near 30,000, with the majority suffered by II and IX corps. The Russians lost at least 10,000 killed, and many thousands more were wounded. Finally, at least 30,000 French noncombatants and stragglers died during the battle or in its aftermath. Napoleon amply deserves censure for not taking more interest in the fate of these wretched souls. He could have pursued other crossing options—Murat proposed lashing carts together—or at least could have delegated authority for the stragglers' crossing.

While he was personally present at the crossing, discipline was fairly well maintained. His departure to establish headquarters on the west bank on November 27 was taken as a signal that it was now every man for himself. By the time the retreat was over, the Grande Armé had lost more than 200,000 horses, 1,000 cannon—and 570,000 men. De Marbot, in concluding his account of the action, wrote:

> Thus ended the most terrible episode of the Russian campaign, an event which would have been far less disastrous if anyone had known how to make use of the time which the Russians allowed us after reaching the Berezina, and had chosen to do so.

Stalking the Nana Sahib

by ANDREW WARD

While we're on the subject of calamities, let's not forget one of the bloody low points of the British tenure in India: the siege of Cawnpore during the Great Mutiny of 1857. The atrocities committed by the native sepoy troops who rose up against the British East India Company were more than matched by the reprisals of their colonial masters. Of the personalities who achieved brief notoriety that murderous summer, none is more enigmatic than the Nana Sahib, rajah of Bithur, the grim bumbler who for forty days ruled the Upper Provinces of India and then disappeared. It was he who presided over the massacre of hundreds—women and children as well as British solders—trapped behind crumbing walls and a shallow trench at the Cawnpore barracks. Their suffering became, as Andrew Ward writes, "a kind of imperial sacrament." Ward, a novelist and commentator for National Public Radio who grew up in India, describes his haunting visit to the site of the massacre.

Leaf through almost any Anglo-Indian family album of the late 1800s and amid the inevitable pictures of the Taj Mahal, the bungalow, the tiger shoot, you will come upon an icon of the Memorial Well at Cawnpore: a marble angel standing within a pierced Gothic screen.

And if you look closely enough, and the mildew and white worms that afflict the libraries of the raj haven't yet destroyed it, you might make out an inscription:

> Sacred to the perpetual memory of a great company of Christian people, chiefly women and children, who, near this spot, were cruelly massacred by the followers of the Nana Dhundu Pant of Bithur, and cast, the dying with the dead, into the well below, on the 15th of July, 1857.

In 1985 I published *The Blood Seed,* a novel masquerading as the memoirs of Balbeer Rao, an Indian Hindu servant born in the ashes of the Great

Mutiny of 1857. You may wonder how a thirty-three-year-old American could have presumed to write the ostensible memoirs of a ninety-year-old, nineteenth-century Indian Hindu, and I'll admit that I sometimes wondered, too.

But the story of Balbeer Rao arose out of the dust and color of my own boyhood in India. Even before my father brought us to India in 1954, we already had a little Indian dust in our lungs. My great-grandfather Ferdinand Ward was a missionary in Madras back in the 1840s, and on his return lectured on the heathen evils of the subcontinent to incredulous congregations all through New England. And my mother's aunt Nancy Spencer was a Presbyterian missionary who died of the ague on her way to a sanatorium in the Himalayan foothills.

My family lived for four years in a compound with an imperial complement of servants on what were then the outskirts of New Delhi. A fox lived in the brush across the street, jackals yipped at night beyond the compound gate, poised lizards clung to the high walls of my bedroom. For a time I attended an Anglo-Indian school and learned the British version of Indian history sitting in a tented classroom on a broad, tended lawn. During the summers we lounged in Kashmiri houseboats, from which I would venture forth in a kayak to explore the ruined, half-submerged English bungalows along Nagim Lake's shore.

The result of my Indian boyhood is that all my life I will be homesick: for India when I'm here, for America when I'm there. To dull the pang, I returned to India for a couple of years after college, and then spent the intervening years reading everything I could find on the British raj, whose ghosts still haunted the India of my childhood.

Sometime in the 1970s it dawned on me that my homesickness might not have been for India herself but for the days of the white man's burden, when I was a *chota sahib* and grown men were deferential in my path. (See glossary, page 173, for Hindi terms.) So I began to read and reread through Indian eyes, or as Indian as I could approximate. And that was when Balbeer emerged, filling in the blanks, solving the mysteries for me that still hover over the history of the raj like monsoon clouds.

Of all the epilogic mysteries of the raj, none tantalized me more than the brief reign and strange disappearance of the Nana Sahib, who for forty summer days in 1857 ruled the Upper Provinces as the Mutiny's Hindu king. Variously known as the Nana Sahib, Nana Rao, the Nana Dhundu Pant, the Last Peshwa, the Beast of Cawnpore, the Fiend of the House of Ladies, for decades he was a kind of all-purpose bugaboo for the raj, roaming the corridors of the imperial subconscious and savoring his bloodstained infamy.

During the hiatus before the Mutiny, no one could have seemed a less likely candidate for archvillainy than this pliable, stuttering young prince. The Nana Sahib claimed to be the adoptive heir to the throne of the Maratha, the great Hindu warriors who dismembered the Mogul Empire before themselves succumbing to British might in the early 1800s. But he was notable chiefly as a host to the Europeans of Cawnpore, for whom he threw open the doors of his palace in the neighboring town of Bithur. No reliable portrait of the Nana Dhundu Pant survives, but those who dined off his mismatched china and joined him for billiards in his gaming parlor remembered him as plump, with slightly protuberant lips beneath an elaborate, upended moustache. Though the *Illustrated Times* described him at the time as "one of the best and most hospitable natives in the Upper Provinces," he did not mix much with his guests, and when he did he could wax rather tiresome about his grievance with the East India Company, which had come to rule India under the protection of the British crown.

The previous governor general, the dogmatic Lord Dalhousie, had recently introduced the Doctrine of Lapse, whereby the regency of any native prince who had no natural issue would redound to the Company upon his death. The British therefore not only refused to grant the adopted Nana Sahib his father's pension but even disallowed his use of the diminished sobriquet "maharaja of Bithur," forbade a salute, and denied him the use of his father's seal.

Thus he was left with a shrinking treasury and a deck of promissory notes with which to support his father's extravagant, bickering widows; his grand palace with its gardens and menageries; and his idle retinue, including 300 horse guard and infantry, variously armed with lances, pikes, and dragon-shaped blunderbusses.

Ever since the British had gained suzerainty over India with their victory at Plassey in 1757, Indian astrologers had predicted that the East India Company's reign would last for only one century. The Company was impatient to expand its markets and instruct the heathen in Christian civics, and its agents had inevitably trod on the bejeweled toes of the rajas, nizams, and begums who had ruled India in the vacuum of Mogul dissolution. No less dangerously, they had alienated the powerful priests and mullahs who steered the subcontinent's soul.

The city of Cawnpore was a Company invention, arising in the late 1700s on the banks of the Ganges, a thousand navigable miles inland from Calcutta. What began as a garrison became a tabula rasa for Anglo-Indian industrialists, whose woolen mills and leatherworks sprouted up around the outskirts, adding their smoke and stench to the dust of the North Indian plains.

Distinct from the crowded city of factories and bazaars was the military cantonment, a mock suburbia of verandahed bungalows and dusty gardens. Within its walls were British officers' clubs, a racecourse, a Freemason's Lodge, a racket court, a library, even a small theater, where junior magistrates took the stage "to represent female whims and graces."

The commander of the Cawnpore garrison, General Hugh Massey Wheeler, had spent all but a few of his sixty-seven years in India and doted on his sepoys, whom he believed he could protect from the contagion of mutiny. But as the centennial of the British victory at Plassey approached and mutinies broke out at Meerut and Delhi, delegations of merchants and missionaries finally persuaded the old general to construct an entrenchment. Perhaps to demonstrate how little weight he gave their apprehension—and also to avoid provoking the sepoys—Wheeler chose for his position not the garrison's heavily fortified magazine by the river but a little row of cantonment barracks, into which his officers and a group of *boxwallahs* and missionaries began to move their families.

On the night of June 4, 1857, two sepoy regiments sacked the Treasury. Amid the alarms and confusions, British officers opened fire the next morning on orderly, if irascible, assemblies of native troops. As a result, all but a few sepoys marched off that same day to join the rebels gathering in Delhi.

They were met on the road by a delegation from Bithur. Some say it was the Nana Sahib himself who coaxed the sepoys to rally around his throne, promising them gold anklets, plunder, and easy victory over the "yellow-faced monkeys" trapped in the entrenchment. Others say it was Hindu sepoys, in search of a monarch, who gave the temporizing Nana a stark choice between glory and extermination. This last scenario, and the Nana Sahib's ready acquiescence, was at least in character. Though many later contended that the Nana Sahib had hatched the entire mutiny on his own, those who knew him felt that only the haplessness of his subsequent regime gave his "vulgarity the appearance of design."

In either case, over the next forty days he warmed to his reign. As if to make up for his paucity of titles, he proclaimed himself Sri Munt Maharaj Dheeraj Dhundu Pant Nana Sahib Pant Padhan Peshwa Bahadur. He arranged protocols for his court, down to the disposition of priests and astrologers at *durbar*, with stations reserved for the ambassadors of China, Siam, and Rome, among other nations, from which he would exact a yearly tribute of 100 million rupees. Plans were made for an invasion of England, and for an alliance with the czar, from whom a force of Muslims was expected.

But in military matters the Nana Sahib proved a vacillating amateur. His disenchanted forces quickly became divided by caste and religion, and some days almost as many of his soldiers straggled home to their villages as marched into the city to join the rebellion. Those that remained, some 8,000 at most, took turns as snipers along their lines but did not press the assault, most preferring the sherbet shops, courtesans, and less hazardous plunder of the bazaars.

Not that the entrenchment posed much of a hazard. It was a single acre surrounded by a crumbling mud wall and a shallow trench. Within this small enclosure, almost a thousand people were jammed, nearly 400 of them women and children, housed with sick and wounded soldiers in two single-story barracks. Under the intermittent bombardment and "iron hail" of sniper fire, the garrison held out for three weeks, and its suffering became a kind of imperial sacrament. Bulls, horses, and even dogs that strayed close were shot by the British and dragged inside the walls to be turned into soup. Babies were born in 138-degree heat, only to be killed by sniper fire. A grandmother was decapitated by round shot where she sat. Fever, dysentery, cholera, and apoplexy claimed daily victims. Some died of thirst, for the only well with potable water was exposed to sniper fire. There was nowhere to deposit the bodies of the dead except a second well used only for that purpose beyond the entrenchment walls. By the end of the first week, the stench of excrement and death was so great that women sought refuge in shell holes, where many died of sunstroke.

But it was not until June 23, Plassey's centennial day, that the Nana Sahib managed to persuade his divided army to mount a full-scale assault, for which many trapped in the garrison had prepared by scratching their own memorials into the barrack walls. Even this was repulsed, and there was some feeble rejoicing in the entrenchment. But with the monsoon due and their stores running out, the garrison's situation was hopeless. And so on June 26 Wheeler and his officers warily accepted the Nana Sahib's unexpected offer of safe passage by boat to Allahabad.

The next morning the tattered garrison staggered out of the entrenchment to Sati Chaura Ghat, a small landing at the base of an old fishermen's temple, where twenty-four boats awaited them. Believing themselves saved, women and children sang hymns and men put down their muskets and loosened their shirts to pitch in with the boats. But when the last of his command had embarked and Wheeler himself began to step aboard, a sepoy's bugle sounded.

As the native boatmen set fire to the boats' thatched canopies and swam for shore, the British shot at them. Hundreds of muskets opened fire from the surrounding scrub, and swordsmen swooped down the riverbank. Wheeler may have been the first to die, struck in the neck by a sepoy's saber. Men, women, and children flung themselves out of the burning boats, only to drown or be hacked to death in the shallows. A little girl was seen pleading for mercy from a sepoy she recognized, but as he turned away, a villager splashed forward and clubbed her to death.

Only two boats got away, but one of them was soon sunk by round shot and the other was overtaken farther downriver. Of the seventy or so officers in this boat, only four finally made it to safety. Those who survived in the shallows by the ghat were dragged back to the riverbank, where the men were separated out and executed, after prayers. The women and children were then marched back as derisive crowds reached out and snatched away their earrings and wedding bands.

The survivors were transferred to a bungalow called the *bibighar,* which in the Mutiny's aftermath came to be known as the House of the Ladies. They were joined there by other prisoners, including a group of women and children from Futtehghar who had stumbled into the city seeking protection. And there, more than two weeks later, on the night of July 14, 1857, all 210 were hacked to death and cast the next morning, "the dying with the dead," into a nearby well.

The Nana Sahib's culpability for the massacres at Cawnpore remains obscure. He had been so plaintive and indecisive a monarch that by the time the British retook Cawnpore on July 17, the Hindus among the sepoys had already pledged their allegiance to his brother, Bala Rao, and the Muslims had turned to a local *nawab.*

There had been atrocities on both sides all summer. The God-fearing

Scotch colonel James Neill had quelled a mutiny in Benares by hanging virtually every native suspected of collaborating with the small boys who "had flaunted the rebel colors and gone about beating tom-toms." Proclaiming that "the Word of God gives no authority to the modern tenderness for human life," Colonel Neill had burned down whole villages along his march to Allahabad, and had encouraged his troops to plunder the city, where many houses containing women and children were put to the torch. During a reign of terror that would last three months, the dead-carts of Allahabad made their runs from dawn to dusk "to take down corpses hung at the cross-roads, and the marketplaces."

Word of these atrocities had reached Cawnpore during the siege, and by some accounts the massacre in the House of the Ladies was conceived as retribution. It appears that Tantya Tope, the most able of the Nana's commanders, may have masterminded the massacre at the ghat. But it has always seemed to me that responsibility for the slaughter at the House of the Ladies rests more squarely on the Nana Sahib's shoulders. Whether his sin was one of omission or commission, he was present at the meeting where their fates were decided. He reportedly weighed Bala Rao's argument that the British forces converging on Cawnpore would not fight so savagely if there were no women and children left to save. In one of the Nana's later missives to Queen Victoria, he claimed that the massacre was the work of her mutinous sepoys. But by all other accounts, the sepoys who had been ordered to carry out the execution only fired their rifles into the ceiling, and among the five men who finally hacked the women and children to death was a member of the Nana Sahib's own guard.

British retribution was fearsome. Neill marched his men past the bloody well to fire them up for battle, and then loosed them on the countryside, where, clad in their Highlanders' kilts, they were mistaken for the wrathful ghosts of the slaughtered ladies. Amid the clutter of torn Bibles and babies' dresses, natives suspected of collaboration were forced to lick the caked blood from the floor of the House of the Ladies before being blown from cannon or hanged in rows from a nearby banyan tree. The bodies of condemned Muslims were burned and the Hindus buried, thus relegating their respective souls to either hell or an eternity of monstrous incarnations.

After waging intermittent war on the pursuing British, the Nana Sahib fled into the swamps of the Tarai. The British pursued him into the foothills of Nepal, but he was never captured, and his mysterious fate provides a hook upon which more than one writer—myself included—has hung a tale.

A mutineer claimed that the Nana had died of malaria in 1859, and in fact a bone reputed to be the Nana Sahib's was sent to Benares for immersion. But then it was said that the bone was merely a knuckle of his little finger, which he had cut off to propitiate the goddess Kali.

The sightings lasted for forty years. The most reliable witnesses placed the Nana Sahib north of the Tarai, where he was said to live as a mendicant under the furtive protection of the king of Nepal. In 1863 a *sadhu* suspected of being the Nana Sahib turned up in Ajmer, but the survivors of the siege who came to identify him did not recognize him and he was let go.

The maharaja Sindhia of Gwalior, a childhood friend of the elusive prince, was approached in 1874 by a *sadhu* who claimed to be the Nana Sahib, and Sindhia was apparently convinced by the man's story. Newspapers throughout the empire were already trumpeting the capture of the Fiend of Cawnpore when the *sadhu*'s masquerade began to crumble. There were stories that the Nana Sahib had surrounded himself with look-alikes to bewilder his pursuers, and it was suggested that Sindhia had given one of these over to the British, meanwhile providing his friend safe escort out of the kingdom. In any case no one chose to investigate and the little mendicant was released.

As the Mutiny receded, Nana sightings grew sparser and more preposterous. In 1877 it was rumored that he was about to invade India with the Russian army. Then someone claimed to have found him in Constantinople, living with an English girl captured during the outbreak, but a civil servant of that city reported to his Indian counterparts that local Hindus believed that the Nana Sahib was in Mecca, plotting with a descendant of the last Mogul to conquer India. As the decades passed he became the raj's bogeyman. One biographer described him as a scented sybarite "who read Balzac, played Chopin on the piano, and lolling on a divan, fanned by exquisite odalisques from Cashmere, had a roasted English child brought in occasionally on a pike."

In 1895, when the Nana Sahib would have been about seventy, an addled old man dressed as a *sadhu* was found in a northern station being pestered by children. Placed in protective custody, he confided to a young British police officer that he was the Nana Sahib and wished to place himself under the protection of the king of Nepal.

The police officer telegraphed district headquarters. "Have arrested the Nana Sahib. Wire instructions."

"Release at once" came the weary reply.

And so the file was closed. A trial would have been a travesty after all those years, and might have stirred whatever embers remained of the rebellion itself. It was best to let him die, if he yet lived, "old, discredited, half-witted . . . still clawing to the horrible honor of being himself."

The Mutiny changed the nature of British rule forever. Not only was India immediately brought under the direct rule of the queen herself, but the Company's initial attitudes of tolerance and assimilation were discredited.

After the last of the mutineers had been cut down from the gallows and hanging trees, the British leveled the House of the Ladies and in 1863 installed a marble angel carved by the Italian sculptor Carlo Marochetti over the well. Memorials were erected beside the graves and execution grounds of the outbreak's European victims, and the site was enclosed by an iron picket fence, beyond which no Muslim or Hindu was allowed to step.

A vast Gothic church arose near the entrenchment, its apse lined with a dado of stones listing the Cawnpore dead, and its clerestory punctuated by stained-glass panels emblazoned with the names of prominent victims of the Mutiny. But the entrenchment itself was not preserved until the Prince of Wales came to visit in 1875 and directed that stones be laid out to mark its vanishing boundaries. The only memorial erected at the Massacre Ghat was a small marble cross bearing the legend "In Memoriam/June 27th/1857."

Some Indian historians now refer to the Sepoy Mutiny of 1857 as the first Indian War of Independence. Whether it was really a national revolution or the last throes of Muslim and Brahmin feudalism, it was swift and savage and poisoned the dialectic of British India. For almost a century the raj waved the atrocities of the mutineers in the face of any Indian who strove for freedom from British rule. A people capable of such outrages do not deserve independence, went the argument, and even the most moderate Indians bitterly resented the raj's remembrance of what it called the "Epic of the Race."

When my research for *The Blood Seed* finally brought me back to India in November of 1982, I did not know what I might find of the old Mutiny sites in Cawnpore. A friend had told me that during the last days of the raj, Cawnpore was a center of radicalism and union upheaval, so it seemed to me as I rode in on the Grand Trunk Road that I was going to have to use my imagination; no memorials to the summer of 1857 could have survived.

Cawnpore is now spelled Kanpur. As I pulled up to my hotel I could see that the city was still the smoky, belching progenitor of Indian industrialism that Gandhi warned against. In fact Kanpur seemed to me to be the provincial paradigm of Uttar Pradesh itself: crowded, divided, transient, hostile.

My first stop in Kanpur was what the British called the Memorial Gardens, the Indian government now calls Nana Rao Park, and the locals have always referred to as Company Bagh. I wandered around awhile, past picnickers and *pahn* sellers, along the gaily painted wrought-iron perimeter of a park that was no longer in mourning.

In the center of the gardens, I stumbled upon a blank sandstone circle occupied by a few children performing tricks on bicycles. I asked one of the gardeners if this was all that remained of the Memorial Well. He didn't know, and had to summon his most senior colleague, a grizzled old *mali* named Kishan Lal.

Assuming, I think, that I was British, Kishan Lal made a great show of regret as he informed me that when independence was achieved in 1947, a mob burst in, toppling Marochetti's angel and breaking up half of its surrounding Gothic screen with hammers before the police could stop them.

So there was nothing left of the angel? I asked him.

"No, sahib," he said, sadly shaking his head. It was dust.

I thanked him and strolled around a while longer. New nationalist memorials had been installed around the park, including a multicolored statue of Dr. Amvede Kar, the austere architect of the Indian constitution, and a bust of Tantya Tope, the mastermind of the massacre at the ghats, surrounded now by plaster frogs. I noticed that shards from the well's rim were being used by the Kanpur Municipal Corporation as benches and potstands. I remembered reading that the British had preserved one of the original banyan trees from which scores of mutineers had been hanged, and eventually I found it, the hollows of its trunk occupied now by a Shivaite altar made of shards from the angel's pedestal.

I drove out in the evening to the Nana Sahib's abandoned palace at

Bithur. In the little town, a place of Hindu pilgrimage, people spoke of the Mutiny as though its ashes were smoldering. Much of the town still lay in ruins from British cannonfire, for the town and the palace had been used as artillery targets long after the Mutiny.

But I found that a crumbling portion of the palace still survives, suggesting, amid the vines, vast arched colonnades and elaborate stone- and plasterwork. Some descendants of the Nana Sahib's garden shrubs remain, and part of the menagerie wall. At the end of an alley, the government has set a heroic bust of the Nana Sahib himself, freshly garlanded, jowly, defiant, and implausible, like a costumed Walter Slezak.

The Indians I spoke to were hard put both to deny the Nana Sahib's culpability and to cite his specific military accomplishments, but his reputation basks in the indiscriminate glow of Indian nationalism. Regarded by local historians as India's founding father, he is now such a revered figure in Kanpur that an elderly journalist I chanced upon in an optician's shop forbade me even to include him in my fiction. "How would you like it," he said, shaking his finger at me, "if an Indian were to write a novel about your esteemed founding father, saying that Mr. Abraham Lincoln, beloved of millions, was kissing his stenographer?"

I ended my visit to Kanpur with a stroll through the cantonment. The Indian army, like armies everywhere, yearns for continuity, but I was still astonished by how much of the cantonment had been left undisturbed since the days of the raj. I was amazed to find not only that the old spelling of Cawnpore was still in use but that the cantonment's spacious lanes and boulevards were still named for British generals, even including Sir Henry Havelock, whose subordinates oversaw the retributive slaughter of native Indians before he died fighting at Lucknow, thirty miles north of Cawnpore.

Nor was I prepared for the apparition that confronted me as I walked up the drive to All Souls' Church, for there in the twilight stood Marochetti's angel, the most hallowed icon of the British raj, shimmering like a small stone ghost. Even the old gate to the memorial screen was there, cast from cannon found at the entrenchment. A young Indian Anglican escorted me around and told me that in 1949 the pastor at All Souls' had retrieved what was left of the old Memorial Well from the gardens and had it hauled by bullock cart to the churchyard.

Several other resurrected Mutiny memorials stood in its vicinity, and the walls of the church itself were covered with plaques and memorial stones honoring the British soldiers and civil servants who fell during the rebellion. I noted down one for John Robert Mackillop of the Bengal Civil Service who "nobly lost his life when bringing water from the well for the distressed women and children." Hindi services are held every evening at seven, and according to a nineteenth-century guidebook, the echoing acoustics still "bewilder the clergyman and astonish his hearers."

The exposed well is all that remains of the entrenchment itself. Prince Albert's stones continue to mark its outline, under which a mysterious tunnel was recently unearthed, presumed to have been dug by sappers from the garrison but now overrun by snakes.

My final pilgrimage was along the garrison's path from the entrench-ment to Sati Chaura Ghat. Back in the 1800s the Ganges was navigable from Cawnpore to the Bay of Bengal, 1,000 miles away, and travelers wrote of a riverfront choked with budgerows. But now trains and trucks carry the city's wares to the rest of India, and the river, choked with silt, has been diverted away from many of the old ghats.

Though Indian historians deny that the Nana Sahib was responsible for the assault on the embarking garrison, Massacre Ghat has been renamed Nana Rao Ghat, and the memorial cross broken off and left leaning beneath a banyan tree. For all that, the bullet-pocked ghat remains the most pristine and haunting of Kanpur's Mutiny sites.

The last few hundred yards of the route the garrison took to the river— what the British called the "Via della Rosa of Empire"—remains a small dirt lane running along a culvert, where sacrosanct monkeys gather to be fed. At the steps a boat is kept to take visitors on tours of the neglected riverfront, and as the boatman helped me aboard and showed me to my seat beneath the roof's damp thatch, I caught myself scanning the scrub and listening a mo-ment for a sudden bugle call.

Glossary of Terms

Ajmer   A hill station in Rajputana (now Rajasthan)
Anglo-Indian   any Englishman residing in India
ayah   Indian nursemaid
bagh   a garden
begum   a Muslim queen
bibighar   the house of a European's native mistress (bibi)
boxwallah   a derisive army and civil-service term for a European merchant or peddler
Brahmin   the highest Hindu priestly caste
budgerow   a large, keelless barge
burra sahib   the title given to a British master of the house
chota sahib   a little master
durbar   a royal assembly
East India Company   the trading company that conquered India under the protection of the British government, often referred to simply as the Company
ghat   a boat landing
Gwalior   a wealthy central Indian principality ruled by the Scindhia dynasty
mali   a gardener
Moguls   the Turkestani Muslim emperors of India, at one time perhaps the richest and most powerful monarchs in human history
mullah   an Islamic priest
nawab   a petty Muslim prince
nizam   originally a Muslim governor, then an autonomous king after the dissolution of the Mogul Empire

pahn   a betel leaf, usually wrapped around a nugget of betel nuts, anise, and other spices, chewed as a digestive aid

Plassey, Battle of   the British victory over Tipu Sultan, the ruler of Bengal, that marked the beginning of the East India Company's rule; the final battle took place on June 23, 1757

raj   the British Empire in India

raja   a Hindu prince

sadhu   a Hindu holy man

sepoy   a native trooper in the East India Company's army

Tarai   the pestilential swamp that occupied the area between Nepal and the Upper Provinces before it was drained by the Indian government

Uttar Pradesh   the modern name for the Upper Provinces

What Took the North So Long?

by WILLIAMSON MURRAY

This is a question often asked, given the natural advantages the North enjoyed. Williamson Murray's answer is that the American Civil War could hardly have taken less than four years. He quotes the British general James Wolfe before the First Battle of Quebec in 1759: "War is an option of difficulties." Few wars before the Civil War had presented quite so many. There was, to begin with, a Confederacy inflamed by revolutionary nationalism and determined to outlast the North by any means possible. It was the strategy that had paid off for George Washington, and it might have been successful if the North hadn't possessed an even greater staying power. (Let's not forget that it had a certain revolutionary fervor of its own.) There were, too, the difficulties of geography. Just consider that the distance from central Georgia to Richmond is approximately the distance from East Prussia to Moscow. But in the end, Professor Murray writes, the length of the war had less to do with the supposed superiority of Confederate manhood and the competence of its generals than it did with the formidable strategic complexities that the North's leaders so brilliantly overcame. Murray teaches military history at Ohio State University and is the author of *The Change in the European Balance of Power, 1938–1939* and *Luftwaffe*.

The Civil War devastated the South and savaged the armies of both sides, exacting a casualty toll that made it one of the costliest wars in modern times and the worst in American history. At the heart of the bloody struggle lay the grand strategy of the North. As with grand strategy throughout history, Northern strategy emerged only gradually. The strategic path to victory was not clear on either side in 1861. Nor was the outcome of the war preordained. Political and military leaders on both sides enjoyed few of the prerequisites in education, inclination, and background to wage a war of this magnitude and intensity.

The North was eventually victorious because its leadership learned from its mistakes and adapted to the "real" conditions of war. In particular, Abraham Lincoln, a backwoods Illinois lawyer with only ninety days of militia experience in the Black Hawk War of 1832, and Ulysses S. Grant, perhaps the clearest-thinking general in American history, solidified Northern strategy and grasped victory from the wreckage of the early days.

The North, of course, relied on its great superiority in population, industrial resources, financial reserves, and agricultural production. Why, then, did it take so long for the federal government to achieve victory? We might begin by examining several popular explanations for the length of the war. The most persistent is that Southern soldiers, largely drawn from a yeoman class of farmers, had spent their lives shooting game and inuring themselves to hardship in a healthy outdoor environment. The Northern population, on the other hand, condemned to work in dark, dank factories, supposedly had developed few of the attributes that an army requires. Such a view, however, flies in the face of social evidence and the testimony of those who fought. One Southern officer, writing to a Northern friend immediately after the war, put the case differently. "Our officers were good," he commented, "but considering that our rank and file were just white trash and they had to fight regiments of New England Yankee volunteers, with all their best blood in the ranks, and Western sharpshooters together, it is only wonderful that we weren't whipped sooner." The fact is that nearly 80 percent of the Northern population lived in rural areas, like their Southern counterparts, and it is hard to see much difference in the social composition of the armies.

A corollary argument holds that the crucial factor in the war's length lay in the natural superiority of Southern officers and generals, an aristocratic group of West Point cavaliers who had been raised in the antebellum South to appreciate warrior values. The legends surrounding Robert E. Lee, Stonewall Jackson, and Jeb Stuart lend a certain plausibility to the argument, and the dismal record of the Union Army of the Potomac in the eastern theater of operations supports it. With two victories (Gettysburg and Five Forks), twelve defeats, and one draw (Antietam), the Army of the Potomac had a record of unambiguous failure matched by no other unit of equivalent size in the history of the United States Army. But historians have for too long overemphasized the war on the eastern front.

In fact, in the West, the reverse was true: There, Confederate forces fared just as badly as their counterparts in the Army of the Potomac and as a result of the same kind of wooden-headed leadership. Floyd, Pemberton, Bragg, and Hood on the Confederate side in the West fully matched the incompetence of McDowell, McClellan, Hooker, and Burnside in the Army of the Potomac. In his memoirs, Ulysses S. Grant recounts one anecdote from the prewar army that captures the nature of Bragg's leadership:

On one occasion, when stationed at a post of several companies commanded by a field officer, [Bragg] was himself commanding one of the companies and at the same time acting as post quartermaster and commissary. He was first lieutenant at the time, but his captain was detached on other duty. As a commander of the company he made a requisition upon the quartermaster—himself—for something he wanted. As quartermaster he declined to fill the requisition, and endorsed on the back of it his reasons for doing so. As company commander he responded to this, urging that his requisition called for nothing but what he was entitled to, and that it was the duty of the quartermaster to fill it. As quartermaster he still persisted that he was right. In this condition of affairs Bragg referred the whole matter to the commanding officer of the post. The latter, when he saw the nature of the matter referred, exclaimed, "My God, Mr. Bragg, you have quarrelled with every officer in the army, and now you are quarrelling with yourself."

One of the soldiers in the Army of Tennessee reflected a perfect understanding of Bragg's leadership when asked whether he was in the general's army. "Bragg's army? Bragg's got no army. He shot half of them himself up in Kentucky, and the other half got killed at Murfreesboro!" The superior command skills of the Confederate generals in the East were more than counterbalanced by the quality of Union leadership in the West.

As for the romantic image that clings to eastern Confederate generals, one might well remember Jackson's and Lee's ruthless brand of leadership. The former's marches up and down northern Virginia were frequently punctuated by summary executions of deserters; under his cold-eyed Presbyterian command, there was nothing cavalier about serving in his army. As for Lee, he was as ferocious a combat leader as the American army has produced. At Malvern Hill he brashly threw his men against a Union artillery concentration deadlier than any in the war. He won the day, but only at tremendous cost. War is a nasty business, and the Confederate generals in the East were extremely good at it.

The length of the war has far more to do with the immensity of the geographic arena and the complexities of modern war than with the supposed superiority of Southern manhood and the competence of Southern generals. Geography offers a major clue as to why the North found it so difficult to project its industrial and military power into the Southern states and end the rebellion. Taken together, Mississippi and Alabama are slightly larger than present-day West Germany. The distance from central Georgia to northern Virginia is approximately the distance from East Prussia to Moscow. The distance from Baton Rouge to Richmond exceeds the distance from the Franco-German border to the current Soviet-Polish frontier. Considering that it took Napoleon from 1799 to 1807 to reach the frontiers of czarist Russia, one should not be surprised that it took the North so long to conquer the South. Exacerbating the challenge was the fact that primeval wilderness covered substantial portions of the South, particularly in the western theater of operations. While the eastern theater was relatively close to the centers of Northern industrial power, the starting point for the western armies—Cairo, Illinois—was nearly a thousand miles from the North's industrial center. Without railroads and steamships, the North would not have been able to bring its power to bear and probably would have lost the war.

The first formidable problem confronting the North in the Civil War lay in mobilizing its industrial strength and population and then deploying that power into the Confederacy. The problems of mobilization were daunting. The regular army was little more than a constabulary designed to overawe Indians on the frontier; it was certainly not prepared for large-scale military operations. Nowhere was there a body of experience from which to draw in solving the issues that now arose; the armies and their support structure had to come from nothing. The politicians knew nothing about war. The military leaders may have read a little of Baron de Jomini's works on the Napoleonic Wars, but the knowledge they derived was probably more harmful than helpful. Certainly no one had read Clausewitz; and though by 1864 Lincoln and Grant were to evolve an approach resembling Clausewitz's, their success resulted more from trial and error and common sense than from military history or theory.

The South did possess one significant advantage at the beginning of the war. Since it had no regular army, officers who resigned their commissions in the federal army to return home and serve the Confederacy found themselves spread throughout the newly formed state regiments, where their experience could at least provide an example to others.

But in the North, since regular units continued to exist, the experience of those within the professional officer corps was not used to best advantage in creating the Northern volunteer armies. Grant records the value of just one experienced officer—himself—in training the 21st Illinois. "I found it very hard work for a few days to bring all the men into anything like subordination; but the great majority favored discipline and by the application of a little regular army punishment all were reduced to as good discipline as one could want." The 20th Maine, trained by another lone regular officer, Adelbert Ames, also suggests the importance of experience in the training process. Not only did Ames turn out one of the best regiments in the Army of the Potomac, but Joshua Chamberlain, second-in-command of the regiment and up to July 1862 a professor of Greek at Bowdoin College, arguably became the best combat commander in the Army of the Potomac by the end of the war. All too often Union regiments did not have that one officer and therefore had to learn on the battlefield—which was an expensive process.

The armies themselves, whichever side one describes, retained a fundamentally civilian character. Photographs of even the units of the Army of the Potomac, supposedly the most spit-and-polish of all the Civil War armies, suggest a casualness that perhaps only the Israelis have exemplified in the twentieth century. When properly led, however, these troops were capable of sacrifices that few units in American military history have equaled. The performance of the 1st Minnesota at Gettysburg is only one case among hundreds. Although it sustained 80 percent casualties on the second day, it was back in the line receiving Pickett's charge on the third.

The whole first year of the war largely revolved around the complex task of raising, equipping, training, and deploying the forces that the strategic and political requirements of the war demanded. These problems presented themselves concurrently, not sequentially. Nor could Civil War military leaders depend on former certainties of war. The rifled musket had drastically altered combat. With killing ranges extended by 300 to 400 yards, Napoleonic set-piece tactics were no longer valid. Through a process of learning on the battlefield, Civil War armies substantially changed the manner in which they deployed and defended themselves as the war proceeded. How to wage offensive warfare against modern long-range firepower, however, remained an unsolved problem. Ultimately it would require the four long years of the First World War before answers to this question began to appear.

The initial strategic moves of the war turned out entirely in favor of the federal government. Above all, Lincoln's political acuity brought the all-important border states over to the Union camp. Ruthless action secured Maryland and Missouri, while cautious maneuvering led the South to mistakes that tipped Kentucky to the North. Gaining Maryland secured Washington; Missouri represented the first step down the Mississippi; and the securing of Kentucky would in early 1862 allow an obscure Union brigadier general to move against Forts Donelson and Henry. The latter success may have been among the most decisive in the war; the Tennessee and Cumberland rivers were now open to federal naval power as far as they were navigable. In effect Grant not only captured an entire Southern army but also made Tennessee indefensible by the South, while affording the Union the opportunity to cut the only east-west railroad that the Confederacy possessed.

However, the North's grand strategy took considerable time to emerge, at least in its fullest, winning form. The federal government's senior commander at the start of the war, General Winfield Scott, had a three-point strategic framework, the famous Anaconda Plan: (1) to blockade the South, (2) to capture its capital, and (3) to open up the Mississippi. It was a start, but only a start; the North would have to add a number of elements to achieve victory. The Battle of Shiloh in April 1862, which underlined how drastically the tactical game had changed, should have warned how difficult this war would prove to be. The federal government was going to have to break the will of a population—a population, moreover, inflamed by nationalism and possessing both a huge territory on which to draw and a Confederate government willing to take drastic measures to keep shirkers in line. Little of that was clear in April 1862; thus Grant was widely criticized in the North when Shiloh's casualties became known. But Grant at least sensed the depth of Southern hostility and its implications after the slaughter of Shiloh:

> Up to the battle of Shiloh, I, as well as thousands of other citizens, believed that the rebellion against the Government would collapse suddenly and soon, if a decisive victory could be gained over any of its armies. Donelson and Henry were such victories. An army of more than 21,000 men was captured or destroyed. Bowling Green, Columbus, and Hickman, Kentucky, fell in consequence, and Clarksville and Nashville, Tennessee, the last two with an immense amount of stores, also fell into our hands. The Tennessee

and Cumberland rivers, from their mouths to the head of navigation, were secured. But when Confederate armies were collected which not only attempted to hold a line farther South, from Memphis to Chattanooga, Knoxville and on to the Atlantic, but assumed the offensive and made such a gallant effort to regain what had been lost, then, indeed, I gave up all idea of saving the Union except by complete conquest.

Grant's emergence in 1862 was seemingly one of the great surprises of the war; certainly the vicious backbiting that characterized Major General Henry Halleck's reports on the future Northern commander did little to speed the process. Nevertheless, one should not assume that Grant was entirely an unknown quantity. Confederate General Richard S. Ewell wrote in spring 1861: "There is one West Pointer, I think in Missouri, little known, and whom I hope the Northern people will not find out. I mean Sam Grant. I knew him in the Academy and in Mexico. I should fear him more than any of their officers I have yet heard of. . . ."

Grant, of course, exercised little influence over Union grand strategy at the beginning; that was left to supposed prodigies such as George McClellan, whose sense of personal importance came close to losing the war in the East. Grant's conquest of the Mississippi in 1862 and 1863 opened up the great inland waterway, split the Confederacy, and cemented the alliance of the eastern and western states that would ultimately crush the Confederacy. His opening move at Forts Donelson and Henry exposed the one crucial geographic weakness of the Confederacy: the fact that its rivers in the West allowed Northern armies to penetrate into the very heartland of the Confederate nation. Tennessee, northern Alabama, and northern Georgia were all now within reach of invading Union troops. But under the constraints of Halleck's insipid leadership and Brigadier General William Rosecrans's tardy drive, the Union push took a considerable length of time to develop. There were some in the Confederacy who recognized how dangerous this threat might become, but Jefferson Davis continued to emphasize the eastern theater at the expense of the West and to support the inflexible and incompetent leadership of Braxton Bragg.

Unfortunately, Grant's second great victory—and his second battle of annihilation—at Vicksburg never realized its full potential. Once the Mississippi had been opened, his victorious army dispersed and the Union high command wasted Grant during the summer of 1863. The humiliating September defeat at Chickamauga, however, forced the high command to reorganize the western theater under Grant's control, sending him considerable reinforcements from the East. Lincoln and Secretary of War Edwin Stanton redeployed two corps from the Army of the Potomac, moving 25,000 men, along with their artillery and horses, over 1,200 miles in less than two weeks. This awesome logistic accomplishment underlines how far the North had advanced in its ability to mobilize and utilize its resources. Grant more than repaid the trust of the Lincoln administration with his smashing victory at Chattanooga in late November. His devastating defeat of Bragg's army solidified the Northern hold over Tennessee and established a solid base from which the Union's western armies could break the South apart at its very heart: Georgia. None of this had been imaginable at the onset of war. By now the North could logistically deploy, maintain, and put into battle an army of 100,000 men in the very center of the Confederacy.

Chattanooga set the stage for the Lincoln-Grant partnership—and the full evolution of Northern grand strategy—that saw the war through to its victorious conclusion in spring 1865. By the beginning of 1864, the Anaconda Plan had for the most part been realized: The Mississippi was open; the blockade was largely effective; and only Richmond remained untaken. Northern strategy moved in new directions. Lincoln had seen early in the war that a concerted, concurrent Union effort in all theaters would be required to break the outer ring of Confederate resistance. But George McClellan had babbled about the foolishness of such an approach and had contemptuously dismissed Lincoln's proposal. McClellan, as a disciple of Jomini, could think only in terms of capturing the enemy's capital or seizing some central position that would lead to a decisive battle. Lincoln thought in far broader terms. He would learn, while McClellan, like the Bourbons who briefly regained power between the reigns of the two Napoleons, learned nothing.

Both Lincoln and Grant looked beyond the eastern theater. Grant's grand strategy for 1864, after being made commander of all the U.S. armies, aimed to crush the Confederacy with thrusts from a number of different directions. His instructions to General William Sherman (similar orders were given to General George Meade) made his intentions clear.

> It is my design, if the enemy keep quiet and allow me to take the initiative in the spring campaign, to work all parts of the army together and somewhat toward a common center. For your information I now write you my programme as at present determined upon.
>
> I have sent orders to [Major General Nathaniel P.] Banks by private messenger to finish up his present expedition against Shreveport with all despatch. . . . With [his] force he is to commence operations against Mobile as soon as he can. It will be impossible for him to commence too early.
>
> [Major General Quincy] Gillmore joins [Major General Benjamin F.] Butler with 10,000 men, and the two operate against Richmond from the South side of the James River. . . . I will stay with the Army of the Potomac, increased by [Major General Ambrose E.] Burnside's corps of not less than 25,000 effective men, and operate directly against Lee's army wherever it may be found.
>
> [Major General Franz] Sigel collects all his available force in two columns . . . to move against the Virginia and Tennessee. . . .
>
> You I propose to move against [Joseph E.] Johnston's army, to break it up and to get into the interior of the enemy's country as far as you can, inflicting all the damage you can against their war resources.
>
> I do not propose to lay down for you a plan of campaign, but simply to lay down the work it is desirable to have done, and leave you free to execute in your own way.

Grant concluded by telling Sherman that Sigel probably had the smallest chance of achieving his objective, but, as Lincoln had suggested during the strategy briefing, "if Sigel can't skin himself, he can hold a leg whilst someone else skins." There is no clearer, more concise strategic conception in American military history. It spelled the end of the Confederacy by 1865.

Why it did not spell defeat for the Confederacy in 1864 is worth examining. Failure to achieve victory before 1865 reflected the extraordinary difficulty in planning, coordinating, and executing military operations, as well as the inevitable impact of political reality on the world of military operations. Unfortunately, two key elements in Grant's strategy—Banks's move against Mobile, and Butler's move from Bermuda Hundred to cut the Petersburg–Richmond railroad—failed to materialize. Banks remained tied to the disastrously inept Red River campaign; consequently his move against Mobile, which would have tied one corps of the Army of Tennessee to Alabama, did not occur and that unit reinforced Johnston's defense of Atlanta. Butler's attack from Bermuda Hundred collapsed in a welter of incompetence rarely seen this late in the Civil War. As Grant noted in his memoirs, Butler "corked" himself and his army into a position where he could exercise no influence on the unfolding campaign. Had he succeeded, Lee would have been forced to divide his forces against two foes. As it was Butler's army was simply subsumed into the Army of the Potomac. The results of these failures prevented victory in 1864. Sherman faced far more effective resistance in his offensive against Atlanta, while the Army of the Potomac confronted an Army of Northern Virginia that was able to devote full attention to the defense of northern Virginia.

Significantly, Grant did not complain in his memoirs that the great spring offensive failed because of the incompetent leadership of "political" generals. He was well aware that Lincoln needed the support of "war Democrats" in the upcoming presidential campaign and that keeping Butler and Banks in positions of high responsibility was therefore essential for political reasons; both were "war Democrats." Good strategy, as with all things in war, is a fine balance of choices. As the British commander James Wolfe commented before Quebec in 1759: "War is an option of difficulties." The delicate coalition that Lincoln was holding together in the North was essential to the successful settlement of a war that had opened wounds not only between the North and the South but also within the North itself. To risk damaging that coalition by removing Banks and Butler was to risk losing the presidential election, and defeat in November might well have eviscerated whatever battlefield successes the Union army would achieve in 1864.

In assuming his position as commander of all Union forces, Grant was initially inclined to remain in the West. But his justified trust in Sherman's competence led him to change his mind: He would accompany the Army of the Potomac. Meade's competent but hardly driving brand of leadership in the last half of 1863 suggests that the Army of the Potomac's commander required the support of a more senior officer upon whom he could rely in moments of crisis. Grant would provide that support. He understood, however, that as an outsider he was not in a position to replace that army's senior leadership. He therefore was compelled to fight the coming battles of spring 1864 with a fundamentally flawed instrument—a military organization whose cohesion, willingness to sacrifice, and dogged determination were second to none in American military history, but whose repeated failures to seize the initiative, incapacity to take risks, and sheer bad luck resulted in a long record of defeat and reversal.

Thus, the Army of the Potomac fought the spring and summer battles in Virginia at appalling cost to itself and the nation. As a brigadier in the Army of the Potomac wrote his wife after Spotsylvania Court House: "For thirty days it has been one funeral procession past me and it has been too much." However, while Grant pinned Lee and the Army of Northern Virginia to Richmond, Sherman battled General Johnston back in Atlanta. The pressure on Lee prevented the Confederate government from reinforcing Johnston. Jefferson Davis then made the fatal mistake of replacing Johnston with General John B. Hood. Hood's slashing attacks from Atlanta wrecked his army, lost Atlanta, and opened the way for Sherman's March to the Sea. The march again allowed Union forces to bisect the Confederacy and further fragment the span of Southern control, while opening up the last undamaged areas of the South to attack.

It also opened the way for the final chapter in the evolution of the war's strategy: a straight-out Union policy aimed at breaking the will of the Southern population by destroying the property, homes, and sustenance on which the survival of the South rested. In May 1864 Sherman had already confided to his wife his perplexity that the Southern population had not yet given up: "No amount of poverty or adversity seems to shake their faith. . . . [N]iggers gone, wealth and luxury gone, money worthless, starvation in view, yet I see no sign of let up—some few deserters, plenty tired of war, but the masses determined to fight it out." Sherman's frustration in front of Atlanta had led to bombardment of the city irrespective of the danger to civilians or to its military usefulness. The March to the Sea had taken place soon afterward, and while Sherman's progress through Georgia was not aimed directly at civilian lives, its "collateral" effects—the ruthless destruction of homes and foodstuffs and the starvation and disease that followed in its wake—indicated how far the North was willing to go in this war. As Sherman warned in a letter to the citizens of northern Alabama in 1864:

> The government of the United States has in North Alabama any and all rights which they choose to enforce in war, to take their lives, their houses, their land, their everything, because they can not deny that war exists there, and war is simply power unconstrained by constitution or compact. If they want eternal warfare, well and good. We will accept the issue and dispossess them and put our friends in possession. To those who submit to the rightful law and authority all gentleness and forbearance, but to the petulant and persistent secessionists, why, death is mercy and the quicker he or she is disposed of the better. Satan and the rebellious saint[s] of heaven were

allowed a continuance of existence in hell merely to swell their just punishment.

Sherman then noted that the American Civil War, unlike traditional European warfare, was "between peoples," and the invading army was entitled to all it could get from the people. He cited as a like instance "the dispossession of the people of North Ireland during the reign of William and Mary."

General Philip Sheridan's conduct of the Shenandoah campaign suggests that Sherman's treatment of Georgia, Alabama, and South Carolina was not a matter of idiosyncratic choice but rather represented a larger strategic and policy design of the authorities in Washington and the Union high command. Clearly indicating this were Grant's instructions to Sheridan to turn the Shenandoah into "a barren waste . . . so that crows flying over it for the balance of this season will have to carry their provender with them." Sheridan followed his orders. His remark to the Prussians during the Franco-Prussian War of 1870–71 that they were "too humanitarian" in their treatment of the French population suggests how far the Union's strategy had descended into a relentless crushing of popular resistance. As he added to his European listeners, "Nothing should be left to the people but eyes, to lament the war!" Admittedly, neither Sherman nor Sheridan reached the level of Bomber Command's "dehousing" campaign of World War II. But Northern military forces were on the ground; they could spare the inhabitants their wretched lives while destroying the economic infrastructure, homes, foodstuffs, and farm animals far more effectively than "Bomber" Harris's force could ever dream of in World War II.

The Civil War was the first modern war, one in which military power, built on popular support and industrialization, and projected by the railroad and steamships over hundreds of miles, approached the boundary of Clausewitz's "absolute" war. Neither the strategic vision nor the military capacity to win the war existed at the onset. The mere creation of armies and their requisite support structure created problems that were neither readily apparent nor easily solved. The Union leadership did evolve a strategy that at last brought victory, but the cost was appalling: somewhere around 625,000 dead on both sides, equaling the total losses of all our other conflicts up to the Vietnam War. A comparable death toll in World War I would have been about 2.1 million American lives. Given what we now know of the cost of war in the modern world, we should not be surprised at the cost of this terrible conflict. We should, rather, wonder how the leaders of the Union—unversed in strategy at the beginning of the war, masters by its end—were able to see it through to its successful conclusion.

The Stonewall Enigma

by JOHN BOWERS

In times of crisis democracy has a way (at least it once did) of creating unexpected leaders, personages who, like characters from popular fiction, emerge from obscurity to take sudden charge when others, supposedly more competent, have failed. That was particularly true of the Civil War, and except for Robert E. Lee, whose leadership qualities were established well before the country broke apart, all its most effective military commanders seemed to have suffered from long periods of debilitating eclipse. Stonewall Jackson fitted the pattern to a T. Gifted, complex, and enigmatic, Jackson may have been the only authentic tactical genius the war produced (though one might reserve a vote for Sherman on the strategic side). John Bowers, author of a memorable recent biography of Stonewall, frames the question that may have no certain answer: "How could Jackson—a valetudinarian in peacetime, a poor excuse for a professor at VMI—have proved to be one of the most daring, brilliant, and tenacious generals on the battlefield?" And where did the frontier eccentric find the unending supply of lemons he sucked?

In Stendahl's novel *The Charterhouse of Parma,* the young hero, Fabrizio, is caught smack-dab in the middle of the Battle of Waterloo. Fabrizio is bright, romantic, fearless, and ready to experience the glories of war to the fullest. He expects to find what he has read in books. Yet when he looks around, through the dust and din, the plundering, the screams and carnage, the sutlers plying their trade amid the slaughter, he can find no rational master plan for it at all. It seems like pure chaos.

So it is with battles. So it appears to most men in combat. The duke of Wellington himself remarked that battles, indeed history itself, can never be recalled with total accuracy. He compared the past to a grand ball, where everyone in attendance sees small moments only. After a battle, though, when tolls have been taken, when ground has been won or lost, there is the victor and there is the vanquished. If anyone should have an inkling of what is happening in a battle—or what is supposed to be happening—it is the commanding general of each side. We say Napoleon lost Waterloo—not General Ney, nor anyone else.

We say that Stonewall Jackson won at Chancellorsville; Robert E. Lee lost at Gettysburg (for which he more than once took complete blame); Ulysses S. Grant won at Fort Donelson; and so on. It is the commanding general who finally, everlastingly, takes the blame or the credit for how a battle turns out.

Thomas Jonathan ("Stonewall") Jackson was a general who won. He commanded the 1st Virginia Brigade and then the Army of the Valley, CSA, in the Civil War. He took a ragtag band of Virginia farmers, some of his former students at the Virginia Military Institute, a preacher or two, and some neighbors from Lexington and fought off a superiorly numbered Northern army that intended to invade his home state.

He fought in the snow, on scorching summer days, in a blinding rainstorm, up a mountain and down in valleys, through a cornfield and by split-rail fences. He knew how to win. He had an abundant amount of ambition (which he usually kept out of sight), and the hallmark of his character was his single-mindedness in impressing his will upon and prevailing over whatever task and enemy faced him.

He was not a "parade general" like General George ("Little Mac") McClellan, commander of the Army of the Potomac. Little Mac loved spit and polish, the plumes that bobbed in review, the snapping of bright flags. Jackson, who was at West Point with McClellan, went off to fight the Yankees wearing the frayed blue tunic of a VMI professor and the kepi of a student. He preferred the kepi pulled forward until it nearly covered his eyes and he had to tilt his head upward to see. Jackson never tried to look like a general.

Once, a captured Washington official, his leg broken, lay in agony on a stretcher near some Confederate troops. He noticed a strange figure by a campfire. A surgeon said proudly that this was Stonewall, Old Jack. The official asked to be carried nearer so he might have a look. It was a once-in-a-lifetime chance. He saw an improbable figure in a grimy uniform, enormous mud-caked boots, and tiny, filthy cap. The man was hunkered down over the fire like a lowly private. The official looked in wonder, then disbelief, finally in disenchantment. He moaned, "O my God! Lay me down again!"

Word of his reaction spread, and Jackson's troops picked up on the prisoner's words. From that time on, during long forced marches, extra picket duty, and needless drilling, the cry went out: "O my God! Lay me down again!" But though Jackson might push them beyond their endurance, goad them to superhuman efforts, in the end he saved them from the worst of all fates for a soldier: He saved them from defeat; he saved their blood. They held him in absolute affection.

Jackson's most important characteristic was his taciturnity. He did not believe in divulging secrets. At times this trait—and some others—reached a level of obsession. Rarely did he discuss his military credo, his general military thinking. Early in the war he told John Imboden, a comrade-in-arms:

There are two things never to be lost sight of by a military commander, always mystify, mislead, and surprise the enemy if possible; and when you strike and overcome him, never let up in your pursuit as long as your men have strength to follow; for an army routed, if hotly pursued, becomes panic stricken, and can then be destroyed by half their number. The other rule is, never fight against heavy odds, if by any possible maneuvering you can hurl your own force on only a part, and that the weakest part, of your enemy and crush it. Such tactics will win every time, and a small army may thus destroy a large one in detail, and repeated victory will make it invincible.

This straightforward prescription, with its emphasis on action, was vintage Jackson. He never intellectualized the game of war, never thought in terms of a grand design. He simply acted in response to whatever immediately faced him.

Jackson came by his famous nickname, and his reputation for tenacity, at First Manassas. When the federal assault there reached its apogee on that hot, dusty afternoon of July 21, 1861, only Jackson and his 1st Virginia Brigade stood on Henry House Hill to bar a complete breakthrough by the Union soldiers. If Irvin McDowell's Federals had broken through, the path to Richmond would have lain open and a rebel rout surely would have ensued. The rebellion, the whole new Confederacy, stood poised at this moment on the brink of near-annihilation. Rebel troops were falling back and were close to panic when General Barnard Bee called to his South Carolinian troops, "Look! There's Jackson standing like a stone wall! Rally behind the Virginians!"

Jackson and his men stood—then charged with an eerie, high-pitched shrieking and whooping that later came to be known as the Rebel Yell. The hapless Federals under McDowell began moving back, finally breaking into a run. Jackson wanted to chase them all the way to Washington, thirty miles down the pike. At this early moment in the war, he wanted to descend on the now defenseless U.S. capital and capture it. Make a bold move, do the completely unexpected, risk all when he knew he had the enemy at his mercy, when its ranks were demoralized and fatigued and beaten.

That was typical Jackson. Press your advantage for all it was worth! He thought he could end the war—surely come by a peace settlement, which was the aim of this new Confederacy. But everyone else, from Jefferson Davis on down, said the battle was over, that everyone needed to rest and regroup for tomorrow. A golden opportunity for the Confederacy thus slipped away.

Remember, though, that Jackson was defending his own soil. He was thinking up ways and means to block the invader. History shows that the one being invaded can be a fierce foe, inspired to come up with unorthodox and imaginative tactics. Jackson was defending Virginia against a horde of "foreigners" from New York, Ohio, and Massachusetts. He did invade Maryland later, and while there took part in what has been called "America's bloodiest day," the Battle of Sharpsburg at Antietam Creek. When it was over, he took his battered and weary troops back across the Potomac onto the home soil of Virginia.

Jackson was not a natural leader. He was not a Napoleon who could digest reams of intelligence and carry in his head a political program for settlement after the furor of battle ended. In fact, Jackson probably had what we now call a learning disability. At West Point he could learn only by rote—by memorizing his lessons word for word. He was not intuitive and could never afford to cut corners. He had to try ten times harder than the next cadet just to keep up. But he had in spades what far more gifted students lacked—the discipline to impress his will and to succeed. He lay by the fire at West Point, long after taps, studying by the flickering light while his fellow cadets slept. He was near the bottom of his class his first year, and near the top his last (not far behind George McClellan, who placed second in Jackson's class of 1846).

At VMI Professor Jackson taught artillery tactics and natural philosophy in much the same way as he had studied—by rote. He would memorize wide swatches of text and then lecture his fidgety students with it. If a student broke in with a question, Jackson stopped, rewound his recitation to the preceding paragraph, then continued, word for word. He seemed incapable of answering questions off the cuff or indulging in personal anecdotes to enliven his speeches.

Jackson suffered from a variety of physical complaints. His main source of discomfort was his digestive tract, possibly as a result of a spastic colon. His suffering was genuine, but from all accounts of those close to him, he was also a hypochondriac. When he had time and leisure he tended to suffer a great deal more than when he was under extreme pressure and danger—to wit, in war. In peacetime he sought out doctor after doctor, cure after cure.

Many of Jackson's famed eccentricities stem from his unorthodox schemes to ward off these maladies. He would raise an arm suddenly in the midst of conversation and keep it raised as if he were a schoolboy trying to be called on in class. He once explained this habit to a friend: "One of my legs is bigger than the other—and so is this arm. I raise my arm so the blood will run back in my body and lighten its load. It's a cure I've discovered. Everything has a cure."

He sat bolt upright in chairs, not allowing his spine to touch the back. Only that way, he believed, would his internal organs rest properly one on top of another and his digestion be accomplished. He thought he was losing his hearing; that his eyesight was failing. He used a chloroform liniment and swallowed a concoction containing ammonia. He sought out health spas, "taking the waters" at popular resorts, North and South.

When war came in 1861, his ailments and complaints suddenly vanished. He caught what little sleep he needed outdoors on the ground, his saddle for a headrest. He once rode fifty miles, without stopping, to have an hour's secret meeting with Lee, then fifty miles back to his troops, going over twenty-four hours without sleep. It was not unusual for him to place such demands on his 165-pound body then, and he made equally stringent demands on his men.

Jackson had the stomach, metaphorically speaking, for taking extremely harsh measures to enforce his brand of discipline. He brought court-martial charges against General Richard B. Garnett and relieved him of command because Garnett had ordered his greatly outnumbered brigade to retreat at the Battle of Kernstown. No matter that Garnett's troops probably would have been slaughtered if they had stayed in place; no matter that, by retreating, Garnett could cover other Confederate troops and allow their escape from ambush. They had retreated, Jackson hadn't authorized it, and no one on earth could placate Stonewall's anger. It shone with a fine blue light.

Garnett was a noble and brave officer, scion of landed Tidewater gentry. Still smarting from the humiliation of Jackson's charges even after Jackson's death at Chancellorsville, Garnett volunteered to join a doomed charge at Gettysburg and met his death.

The question is, how could Jackson—a valetudinarian in peacetime, a poor excuse for a professor at VMI—have proved to be one of the most daring, brilliant, and tenacious of generals on the battlefield? In searching for the key to personality it is necessary to consider the beginning. Jackson was not of landed Southern gentry; he was not accustomed to tall, cool drinks on a veranda. Tom Jackson was born in what is now Clarksburg, West Virginia, and grew up on what was then the western frontier. The last buffalo in his region was killed the year of his birth, 1824.

It was Calvinistic country, hardscrabble, and Jackson's life was made even harder by his being orphaned: His father, a lawyer and a veteran of the War of 1812, died when Tom was two; his mother died when he was seven. The boy was shunted among a collection of relatives and then put under the wing of a bachelor uncle, Cummins Jackson, on Cummins's frontier farm, which featured a gristmill and was known as Jackson's Mill.

Cummins Jackson was well over six feet tall, strong as an ox, and had robust appetites. Legend has it that he could pick up a whiskey barrel by himself and let the amber liquid squirt into his mouth. He was known locally as a man who struck sharp deals but was fiercely loyal to friend and family. Throughout his life Tom Jackson showed a tolerance, if not a weakness, for wild, flamboyant characters. He had a softness of heart for Jeb Stuart, and his quartermaster in the Valley Army, John Harman, was a man who swore a blue streak and couldn't be tamed.

The frontier that nurtured Jackson was cruel toward failure and the weak. Only the strong survived. Jackson showed a survivor's instinct throughout his life; but perhaps because he'd been orphaned and displaced, he also showed surprising kindness at times toward those who needed aid. He would quick-march his men thirty miles and then stand guard over them while they slept. He thought nothing of shooting deserters or bringing down brave enemy soldiers who were trying to escape. Yet at West Point he went out of his way to care for cadets who were sick or homesick, and on the streets of Lexington he doffed his hat to passing blacks—a courtesy unheard of in the antebellum South. Deeply sympathetic to the troubles of slaves, he bought the freedom of two and started a "colored" Sunday school in his Lexington Presbyterian Church.

Jackson married twice, both times to women whose fathers were Christian ministers and college presidents. His first wife, Elinor, was the daughter of the Reverend George Junkin, president of Washington College in Lexington (later Washington and Lee); Jackson had done his shy, stiff courting while he himself was a professor at nearby VMI and, marching to his own drummer, as ever, took Elinor's sister along on their honeymoon to Niagara Falls. When Elinor died delivering a stillborn daughter a year later, Jackson became inconsolable, almost suicidal. Only a solitary trip to Europe finally lifted his depression. He kept on close terms with the Junkins for the rest of his life even though several—including Dr. Junkin—fled to the North and joined the Union side.

Jackson's second wife, Mary Anna (known as Anna), was the daughter of the Reverend Robert Hall Morrison, first president of Davidson College. Jackson settled comfortably again into well-regulated domesticity with an overlay of religion. He demanded punctual morning prayers in his home, and in Lexington he was also in the habit of taking a quick cold bath every morning followed by a three- or four-mile walk.

Yet from Anna Morrison Jackson's memoirs and other accounts, we know that Jackson was not the dour Presbyterian some might think. Anna, who is shown as a bright-eyed, dark-haired woman in the few pictures we have of her, could be mischievous with her husband. There was a teasing, bantering, fun-loving side to their marriage. He affectionately called her his *esposa,* a word he had picked up in the Mexican War. She never remarried after he died in 1863, living on in Charlotte, North Carolina, until her death in 1915, and receiving almost daily visits from Confederate veterans who called to pay their respects.

Jackson was as much an enigma in his private life as on the battlefield. His private persona bore no perceptible relation to his reputation in war as a stern, unmerciful foe. Next to Lexington, New York was his favorite city, and before the war he enjoyed dropping in on publishers there and selecting books. He read Melville. On his trip to Europe, he covered a lot of ground and brought back many souvenirs. In his Lexington home, preserved today much as it was when he lived in it, there is a doll he purchased in Germany. At a museum in Chancellorsville, there is a well-thumbed map that he used as he sought out Renaissance art in Florence. In civilian life Jackson was receptive to new ideas, particularly those having to do with science. He owned one of the first iron stoves in Lexington.

Jackson was simple and complex by turns, and so were the battles he faced in the Civil War; he brought his genius to bear on all of them. In the winter following Manassas, he fought the Romney campaign in the western Virginia mountains in bone-chilling weather. Horses slid off the side of icy treacherous roads. Wagons stuck. His men suffered frostbite. Still he pressed on. Supporting generals nearly mutinied, and among troops who were serving for the first time under Jackson the cry went up that the man must be mad. How could human beings march in such weather, in such conditions, and, above all, not knowing where they were going or for what purpose?

True to form, Jackson did not divulge his plans: If his troops didn't know what he was up to, surely the enemy never would. He pressed on, sucking lemons, putting his shoulder behind caissons and wagons to free them from mud and snow. He took the strategic hamlet of Romney before the might of the federal army could get in place there. Federals could well have used Romney as the springboard into Winchester and the whole of the important Shenandoah Valley. Jackson cut them off and served notice by his presence that they had to be mightily concerned with this fidgety and unpredictable commander. They could never overlook him in their strategy—and thus he kept thousands of Federals occupied when they could have been used much farther east, in McClellan's push on Richmond.

The Valley campaign began on March 23, 1862, with the Battle of Kernstown, into which Jackson threw some 2,700 Confederates against perhaps 11,000 Federals. Technically he lost (barely)—one of the few fights he ever lost—but as a result Lincoln sent three whole armies after him, 60,000 Union troops. Jackson fought through the Shenandoah in the summer of '62, using lightninglike tactics and completely befuddling his enemy.

Although he was a brilliant tactician and a master of ambush who could seemingly spring from nowhere, Jackson actually had little knowledge of geography and a poor sense of direction or of the lay of the land. In many ways, like many successful people, he was plain lucky. He was particularly lucky to come by one of the greatest mapmakers the Civil War produced—Jedediah Hotchkiss. Hotchkiss was an ex-New Yorker who had fallen under the spell of the Shenandoah on a summer walking tour. He did not believe in the Southern cause, did not believe in slavery, but he believed in supporting the people and land he had become smitten with and he fought for them. When Jackson found out that Hotchkiss was a master cartographer, he put him to work without a pause. It was Hotchkiss who laid out the maps that Jackson followed to surprise his enemy.

In the Mexican War, particularly in the Battle of Chapultepec, Jackson had learned the value of taking the high ground. As a trained artillerist, he also knew the importance of placing heavy guns on an elevated plateau. If he had lived to fight at Gettysburg, no doubt he would have strongly advised against George Pickett's doomed charge of shoulder-to-shoulder infantry against fortified Cemetery Ridge. He himself probably would have found a way to circle behind George Meade and surprise him mightily from the rear.

But of course he did not live to fight in the most critical battle of the war. He died right after his most stunning victory, at the crowning moment of his military career, at Chancellorsville. There he circled around General Joseph Hooker's right flank and launched a surprise attack from the rear.

Hooker, known for good reason as "Fighting Joe," was certain that his defenses were impregnable and was relaxing in the late afternoon on the veranda of Chancellor Mansion, when suddenly a soldier on the road outside cried, "Here they come!"

First came Hooker's own troops, running at full throttle, among them some German mercenaries shouting in broken English that they needed pontoons to cross the river. Behind the blue-clad Federals came in full stride scrawny soldiers in gray—Jackson's troops. Hooker flung himself onto his white steed and rode into the melee, exhorting his men to stand fast and fight, but he changed not one man's mind. The confusion was so complete, the dust and noise and powder smoke so overpowering, that Hooker got swallowed up. Ignored by the onrushing Confederates, he escaped. Jackson, meanwhile, kept pressing toward the ever-receding front. True to his belief in relentless pursuit, he urged his men and officers to cut off escape routes, to press forward—to punish.

It was around nine at night on May 2, 1863, in growing darkness that some of his frontline troops, North Carolinians, mistook him and his party for a Yankee patrol and shot him. Eight days later, on Sunday, May 10, he died quietly, his wife and daughter and a few of his staff beside his bed. Before the end, delirious, he had called out battlefield commands: "Order A.P. Hill to prepare for action! Pass the infantry to the front!" Then a calmness passed over him and he uttered his final, famous words: "Let us cross over the river and rest under the shade of the trees."

Of all those who missed Jackson's presence in battle, Robert E. Lee undoubtedly led the list. Jackson was his right-hand man, the one soldier who could take a general plan of attack and brilliantly devise a method to execute it. No other general worked anywhere near as closely with Lee as Jackson did. The two of them were a perfect symbiosis: Lee, a tidewater patrician with courtly manners and an engineer's mind; and Jackson, the self-made frontiersman who simply willed himself to make up for natural deficiencies. Lee was the only commanding officer with whom Jackson felt totally in tune, with whom he got along.

As a rule, Lee's orders to Jackson were loosely put and circumspectly offered. Jackson would take Lee's vaguely articulated wishes and carry them out with devices of his own making and with his own personal stamp on them. Lee told Jackson early in the war that he wanted him to hold the Shenandoah Valley and keep the Federals' hands tied there. Lee didn't tell him how. It was Jackson who came up with the lightninglike surprise assaults; it was Jackson who pursued crippled and battered enemy troops, inflicting as much damage as possible to make sure they wouldn't attack him the next day.

At heart Jackson was a loner. Only once, at Winchester, did he call his staff to a war council—and he rued the day. On that occasion he had wanted to attack the Union army under General Nathaniel P. Banks, after dark, even though he would have been outnumbered ten to one. His staff, however, advised him to retreat. As he rode out of Winchester, one of the last to leave, he stopped at the top of a hill and turned to look back at the sleepy little Southern hamlet, pinpoints of light showing in a few homes. Dr. Hunter McGuire, his personal physician, stopped beside him. McGuire, who idolized Jackson, later wrote that at that moment Jackson had a look of unholy ambition on his face, which was enough to frighten McGuire. "That is the last council of war I will ever hold!" Jackson said. And it was.

Jackson was rather like a warrior from the Old Testament, a devout

Christian who sought mightily to keep the Sabbath holy and to obey the Ten Commandments. A man who didn't even like to mail a letter on Sunday, he was forced to fight some of his major battles on the sabbath—the Battle of Kernstown, for one—and, of course, the commandment concerning killing had to be overlooked. But in peace and in war, the general did not like to hear the Lord's name taken in vain, and hardly anything pleased him as much as seeing his troops at revival services in the field. Some of his soldiers later confessed that they attended these services simply because they knew it would please Old Jack, not because they felt religious stirrings.

Jackson's life was relatively short. He had been seasoned in the Mexican War, as had Grant, Sherman, and Lee, but unlike them he never lived to become an elder statesman. Because of his dark, full beard and also because of his deep imprint on the Civil War and his reputation as a leader of men, one tends to think of him as older. But in fact Jackson was only thirty-nine when he died, and he fought a young man's war. His stamina, his daring, his uncompromising stances came in part from a young man's makeup. Old men tend to compromise, to delay, to be prudent rather than rash. Not Jackson.

The quality, though, that made Jackson a great general—perhaps the greatest of the Civil War—is an intangible one that defies definition and can't be taught. He personified the word *indomitable.* He would not accept defeat and had a way of coming back, prevailing no matter what was thrown at him. Many of these setbacks would have caused others to lose heart. He came through—despite an apparent learning disability, despite an undermanned army and inferior arms (when bullets ran out, he cried, "Charge them with the bayonet!"), and despite gargantuan demands on his mind and body. When the Battle of Cedar Mountain was being lost, bluecoats storming over Stonewall's regiments in a clatter of musket fire, Jackson himself galloped into the maelstrom, drew his sword, and rallied his retreating troops back into the fight. "Rally, brave men, and press forward! Your general will lead you. Jackson will lead you! Follow me." The tide turned, and Cedar Mountain was won.

In the Seven Days' Battle he suffered what we now might call a nervous breakdown, or shell shock—but somehow, in a near-trance, carried on, though not as the fearsome Jackson he was before, or would be later. He was assigned by Lee's roundabout orders to cross Grapevine Bridge and pursue the Federals. For once, however, he couldn't act. He stared off into space, mumbling. Without his orders and directions, Stonewall's army stalled and the enemy was able to get away. At a camp table, he fell asleep with a biscuit in his mouth.

Without aid from anyone or anything, Jackson willed himself back into the fray. After the Seven Days' he won again at Manassas, invaded Maryland, and gave the South its crowning glory (and final unmistakable victory) at Chancellorsville. Confederate army general Richard Taylor, son of the former U.S. president Zachary Taylor, said the bullet hadn't been molded that would kill Stonewall Jackson. He felt safe in his presence, for Jackson seemed protected by Providence from the lead and iron that screamed and whined and buzzed around him. Shells would crash into trees and miss Jackson by inches. He was shot in the finger at First Manassas, was thrown off a horse in Maryland, but suffered no other injury until a round of musket fire found him and brought him down at Chancellorsville. Like the rest of us, Jackson proved in the end to be neither immortal nor invincible. However, when the guns at last became silent and a reckoning took place, Jackson came to be thought of as arguably the most formidable general in the conflict.

Over an archway to the barracks at VMI is a saying found in the commonplace book of Stonewall Jackson. Those who knew and cherished him chose this sentence to personify and honor him. It reads, "You may be whatever you resolve to be."

The Last Word on the Lost Order

by S T E P H E N   W .   S E A R S

Has there ever been a military might-have-been quite the equal of the famous Lost Order of Antietam? A Confederate messenger riding out of Robert E. Lee's Maryland invasion headquarters presumably dropped a sealed envelope wrapped around a gift of cigars, and nobody realized it was missing. But in the days after an overage Indiana corporal named Barton W. Mitchell spotted the package in a field of clover on September 13, 1862, the Civil War truly hung in the balance. General George B. McClellan, commanding the Union Army of the Potomac, now knew his opponent's most secret plans, and had an opportunity to destroy him. But then, if Special Orders No. 191 had not been lost, Lee might well have lured McClellan into a battlefield of his own choosing and have destroyed him, guaranteeing independence for the Confederacy. Instead, Corporal Mitchell's discovery brought about the bloodiest single day of the whole war—a reprieve nevertheless, and one that just may have saved Lee's army. Stephen W. Sears tells how the Lost Order changed nothing—and everything. (Poor Mitchell did not even get to keep the cigars.) Sears is the author of *Landscape Turned Red: The Battle of Antietam* and *George B. McClellan: The Young Napoleon,* both published by Ticknor and Fields.

In the annals of military intelligence, there is nothing quite like the Lost Order. Even the most spectacular code-breaking accomplishments of World War II never handed one general's army to another "on a silver platter," as one chronicler of the Lost Order puts it. Civil War historians grope for superlatives to describe this opportunity of a lifetime, this hit on "the all-time military jackpot."

At the time, however, there was an astonishing lack of interest in how the Lost Order was lost, in how it was found, even in what it meant in the larger scheme of things. It was one of the pivots on which the course of the Civil War turned, yet it was some time before that notion sank in. Even today, tellings of the story of the Lost Order have been marked by mystery and misunderstanding.

Special Orders No. 191—the Lost Order's official designation—was key to Robert E. Lee's strategic plan for the fall campaign of 1862. He composed S.O. 191 on Tuesday, September 9, at his headquarters at Frederick in western Maryland, where he was resting his army and contemplating nothing less than winning independence for the Confederacy. General Lee was on a winning streak and had no intention of letting his opponent up. In June he had beaten George McClellan outside Richmond; and in August he had beaten John Pope at Manassas outside Washington; and now, learning that McClellan was once again opposing him, he intended to deliver a knockout blow on Northern soil.

This instinct for the kill was an important element of Lee's genius, as was his intuitive reading of the man he was fighting. Only the day before, he had been heard to describe McClellan as "an able general but a very cautious one." (He repeated that characterization on another occasion, except then he labeled McClellan "timid" instead of "cautious.") Lee's entire design, as he spelled it out that Tuesday, was carefully calculated with General McClellan's shortcomings in mind.

It was Lee's intention, in crossing the Potomac into Maryland, to draw the federal army after him and away from its Washington base. In due course, somewhere off to the north and west in the Cumberland Valley of Pennsylvania, he would maneuver McClellan into a finish fight. He was very clear on that point: "I went into Maryland to give battle," he said in discussing the campaign after the war, and had it all gone as planned, "I would have fought and crushed him."

To clear the way for this march westward, he had to establish a new line of communications to Virginia through the Shenandoah Valley, and to do that he had to dispose of the federal garrisons guarding the Shenandoah at Harpers Ferry and Martinsburg. S.O. 191 was designed for that purpose. He assigned six of his nine divisions to the operation, under the overall command of Stonewall Jackson.

In dividing his army in the face of a superior foe, Lee was violating a military canon, but it gave him no concern. He had done it twice before, against McClellan in June and against Pope in August, and twice it had brought him victory. The Federals were reported to be advancing from Washington with great caution and were several days' march away. Jackson would be back and the army reunited before McClellan caught on to what was happening; in ten days they would be in Pennsylvania, Lee said, with "a very good army, and one that I think will be able to give a good account of itself."

During the afternoon of September 9, his headquarters staff busied itself making copies of S.O. 191 for the generals involved and dispatching them by courier. Each copy was on a single sheet, written front and back, and listed in detail the assignment of every major command in the Army of Northern Virginia. Each was marked "Confidential" and signed "by command of Gen. R.E. Lee" with the name of R.H. Chilton, Lee's chief of staff. Each was delivered in an envelope that was to be signed by the recipient and returned by the courier as proof of delivery.

All the deliveries but one were made without event. The exception was the copy addressed to General D.H. Hill, which someone at headquarters had wrapped around three cigars, for Hill was known to enjoy a good smoke. The packet with Chilton's copy of S.O. 191 never reached Hill or anyone at his headquarters with the authority to sign for it.

What General Hill received instead that day was a copy of S.O. 191 in the handwriting of Stonewall Jackson himself. To this point in the campaign, Hill had been under Jackson's orders, but now he was reassigned as the army's rear guard. Consequently, when Jackson received the copy of S.O. 191 addressed to him, he made a copy of it to inform his former subordinate of the change. Hill thus received his new orders from the same source he had been receiving orders from for the past week, and thought nothing of it.

For some reason that no one at Lee's headquarters could ever explain, no alarm was raised on September 9 over the lack of a delivery receipt for the copy of S.O. 191 Chilton had addressed to D.H. Hill. No one in the chain of command that Tuesday suspected, as Hill later phrased it, "that there was something wrong in the manner of transmitting it. . . ."

The next morning, September 10, at his customary starting time of first light, Stonewall Jackson led the way westward on the National Road out of Frederick and across South Mountain. Through the day the rest of the army followed, division by division, until only a cavalry picket remained at Frederick. Over the next three days, three of Jackson's divisions, varying their route from what was specified in S.O. 191, crossed the Potomac at Williamsport and, pushing the Yankee garrison from Martinsburg ahead of them, closed in on Harpers Ferry from the west. Jackson's two other columns, adhering exactly to the plan, marched by separate routes to complete the encirclement of Harpers Ferry.

Meanwhile, in a second deviation from S.O. 191's order of march, Lee took James Longstreet's two divisions with him to wait at Hagerstown, near the Pennsylvania border. D.H. Hill's single division remained at Boonsboro, on the National Road beyond South Mountain, to act as rear guard. Jeb Stuart's cavalry patrols, continuing their watch on federal movements, reported nothing untoward. Except for the fact that it was running twenty-four hours behind schedule, the Harpers Ferry operation was proceeding smoothly.

"As soon as I find out where to strike I will be after them without an hour's delay," General McClellan promised Washington when he moved into Maryland on the trail of the enemy. But finding out where to strike was proving uncommonly difficult. His cavalry, under Alfred Pleasonton, was unable to break through Jeb Stuart's troopers for a firsthand look at Lee's Army of Northern Virginia. Pleasonton's intelligence-gathering was therefore limited to interrogating rebel prisoners and deserters and questioning civilians, who picked up what they knew from Confederate soldiers passing through their towns or stopping at their farms.

The result was an intelligence Babel. Reports handed to McClellan had enemy columns marching toward every point of the compass, even eastward straight toward him, which caused him to halt his own columns for a time and prepare to receive an attack. The Confederates planted stories wherever they went, so that Stonewall Jackson was "reliably reported" to be where he was and where he wasn't in about equal measure.

Mixed in with these tales from talkative clergymen and boastful prisoners and credulous country folk was some highly accurate intelligence. But all of it arrived at headquarters in an indiscriminate jumble, so McClellan could make little sense of it. As late as September 12, it was his best guess, he told his wife, that "secesh is skedadelling & I don't think I can catch him. . . . I begin to think that he is making off to get out of the scrape by recrossing the river at Williamsport. . . . He evidently don't want to fight me—for some reason or other." On that day, as on previous days, the average march in his Army of the Potomac was six miles.

McClellan was especially befuddled about the size of Lee's army. It was an article of faith with George McClellan that he was fated to be the underdog in any contest against Lee, and the intelligence reaching him in Maryland reinforced that delusion. He finally settled on a count for "the gigantic rebel army before us" of 120,000 men, "numerically superior to ours by at least twenty-five per cent." That this calculation multiplied every Confederate soldier facing him by three was a truth quite beyond his imagining. On Saturday morning, September 13, when he arrived in Frederick with the Potomac army's headquarters, he was acting every inch the cautious captain that General Lee believed him to be.

The federal XII Corps also advanced to Frederick that morning, with the 27th Indiana Regiment in the lead. The column splashed across the Monocacy River at Crum's Ford and went on two miles along a back road to the outskirts of town. There the order came back to halt and make camp. Company F of the 27th appropriated a clover field alongside the road for its bivouac. Later it would be said that this field was where D.H. Hill's division had camped during the Confederate occupation of Frederick, but that was simply speculation. Hill's division had been posted several miles away on the Monocacy. There is no certain evidence than any Confederate troops had camped in this particular clover field.

Company F had the odd distinction of having the largest contingent of tall men in the regiment—two-thirds of the company stood six feet or more—and the unique distinction of having the tallest man in the entire Union army, Captain David Van Buskirk, who was half an inch shy of being seven feet tall. Corporal Barton W. Mitchell was about to give Company F another mark of distinction.

Corporal Mitchell was himself unusual in that he was much older than almost all his fellow soldiers. He was a man in his forties, a farmer in civilian life, who had volunteered to go to war in 1861 despite having a wife and four children to support. Patriotism ran strongly in his family: His oldest son had recently enlisted in another Indiana regiment.

Company F stacked arms, and Mitchell was relaxing and chatting with Private John Campbell when he noticed a bulky envelope in the clover nearby. Curious, he picked it up—and found it contained a document of some sort wrapped around three cigars. The cigars were a find, but Corporal Mitchell had the intelligence and the maturity to investigate as well the document they were wrapped in. While he read it through, Private Campbell (as Campbell later testified) "looked over his shoulder and read it with him."

The paper was marked "Confidential" and was headed "Hd Qrs Army of Northern Va Sept 9th 1862 Special Orders No 191." It was studded with names and places that Mitchell immediately recognized—Jackson, Longstreet, Stuart, Lee, Harpers Ferry, Martinsburg, Boonsboro, Hagerstown. It was signed by R.H. Chilton and labeled "For Maj Gen D.H. Hill, Comdg Division." By sheer chance, by fantastic good fortune, Corporal Mitchell had in his hand the missing copy of S.O. 191, and furthermore he recognized it as something important.

Mitchell took his find to his first sergeant, John M. Bloss, and together they went to the company commander, Captain Peter Kopp. Kopp took one look at the paper and told them to find the regimental commander, Colonel Silas Colgrove. Colgrove read it and, as he later said, "was at once satisfied that it was genuine." He sent Mitchell and Bloss back to their company (presumably with thanks, but apparently not with the cigars; Colgrove's recollection of the cigars is the last mention of them, and who finally smoked them will probably never be known). Then he set off for higher command.

Colgrove skipped brigade and division, the next links in the chain of command, and rode straight to XII Corps headquarters and Brigadier General Alpheus S. Williams. Williams and his adjutant, Colonel Samuel E. Pittman, scanned the paper. As Colgrove remembered their conversation, Pittman said he had served with R.H. Chilton in the old army in Michigan before the war and recognized his handwriting. But Colgrove's recollection was faulty; Pittman had not entered the army until September 1861, six months after Chilton resigned his U.S. commission to join the Confederacy. By Pittman's own postwar recollection, he simply recognized Chilton's name as the army paymaster stationed in Detroit when he lived there.

In any event, General Williams was persuaded that the order was authentic. He sent Pittman with it to army headquarters, along with a brief note for General McClellan: "I enclose a Special Order of Gen. Lee commanding Rebel forces which was found on the field where my corps is encamped. It is a document of interest & is also thought genuine." In a footnote he added, "The Document was found by a corporal of 27 Ind. Reg, Col. Colgrove, Gordon's Brigade."

Colonel Pittman delivered the envelope containing the Lost Order, along with General Williams's covering note, to McClellan's adjutant, Seth

Williams. McClellan was in his headquarters tent discussing details of the army's occupation of Frederick with a delegation of local citizens when adjutant Williams interrupted to hand him the find. McClellan scanned the paper and the note with it and suddenly, according to one of his visitors, threw up his hands and exclaimed, "Now I know what to do!"

This description of his reaction is entirely credible in light of the telegram he sent a few minutes later, at noon, to President Lincoln. No doubt he first ushered his visitors out with the explanation that he had urgent army business to attend to. Usually McClellan's dispatches to Lincoln were stiff and militarily formal, for usually the two were at odds over one thing or another. But this dispatch was like none he had sent before. He boasted:

> I think Lee has made a gross mistake and that he will be severely punished for it. . . . I hope for a great success if the plans of the Rebels remain unchanged. . . . I have all the plans of the Rebels and will catch them in their own trap if my men are equal to the emergency.

In his elation he became almost giddy, presenting his respects to Mrs. Lincoln and exclaiming over the enthusiastic welcome he had received from the ladies of Frederick that morning. "Will send you trophies," he promised.

What so excited McClellan about the Lost Order was its revelation that General Lee had divided his army into four widely separated segments, at least two of them so isolated from the others as to be fair game for total destruction. (In fact, the rebel army was even better game than he thought, for Longstreet's move to Hagerstown had divided it into five segments, the largest of which were twenty-five miles and a river crossing apart.) No general could hope to know more about his opponent's most secret plans: McClellan knew Lee's objective; his dispositions for taking that objective; his routes of march; his timetable; and most important, how vulnerable he was to the tactic of divide and conquer.

There is no doubt that McClellan grasped his unique good fortune. That evening he would take the Lost Order from his pocket and tell brigade commander General John Gibbon, "Here is a paper with which if I cannot whip Bobbie Lee, I will be willing to go home. . . . Castiglione will be nothing to it." Castiglione was the 1796 military classic in which Napoleon crushed General D. Wurmser's divided and overextended Austrian army. To act on this opportunity, however, required General McClellan for once in his life to throw caution to the winds. Time was critical; the Harpers Ferry operation outlined in S.O. 191 was already in its fourth day.

His time clock of opportunity began ticking at noon on September 13, when he sent his exuberant telegram to President Lincoln. Sounds of gunfire could be heard from Harpers Ferry, indicating that the garrison there still held out. The Lost Order told him that one rebel division had crossed the Potomac to invest Harpers Ferry on the south and east. Two more divisions, under the command of Lafayette McLaws, were still in Maryland, holding Maryland Heights overlooking the town on the north. According to S.O. 191, Jackson's "command," its forces unspecified, was at Martinsburg, eight miles beyond the Potomac, to prevent the Yankee garrison's escaping to the west. At Boonsboro, across South Mountain from Frederick, the Lost Order placed D.H. Hill's division and Longstreet's "command," his forces, like Jackson's, unspecified.

Just then at Frederick, McClellan had four army corps—thirteen divisions—with which to cross South Mountain and attack Hill and Longstreet at Boonsboro, fifteen miles distant. A half dozen miles south of Frederick, the army's left wing, three divisions under William B. Franklin, was also fifteen miles distant from its quarry, McLaws's two divisions at Maryland Heights.

It might be supposed that any general presented with such an opportunity would put his troops on the march without a moment's delay, taking advantage of the seven hours of daylight remaining that Saturday to close up to the base of South Mountain and be ready to force the passes in the range at dawn the next morning. General McClellan marched to a different drum: He could never act until all plans were complete, all details perfected, all potential surprises disarmed before they occurred—and the more he studied the Lost Order, the more uneasy he became. He later testified that he gave no thought to its being a *ruse de guerre*—it explained too much to be a plant, and General Williams's note suggested it was found by accident rather than by the enemy's design. Yet be began having worrisome second thoughts about it. He would have to ponder the whole matter before acting.

The Lost Order confirmed some of the intelligence received over the past few days but seemed to contradict other reports. He had been told of a substantial rebel force at Hagerstown, and of a major crossing of the Potomac at Williamsport, yet neither place was on the routes of march prescribed in S.O. 191. He told the president he hoped for success "if the plans of the Rebels remain unchanged," but now it looked as if they had been changed. He worried that question for three hours, then at 3 P.M. sent a copy of S.O. 191 to his cavalry chief, General Pleasonton, with instructions to find out if the routes of march it contained had actually been followed.

Pleasonton knew little enough about the matter but replied that he thought Lee's instructions had been followed. That was the wrong answer, but it reassured McClellan; thereafter he regarded everything in the Lost Order as revealed truth. With that settled, he determined to begin his movements the next morning, September 14. "My general idea," he told General Franklin, "is to cut the enemy in two & beat him in detail." Reaching that decision cost eighteen hours of his golden opportunity.

The other factor giving him pause on September 13 was the enemy's numbers. In a dispatch to Washington that night, he listed eight generals in Lee's army, commanding a total of "120,000 men or more . . . & they outnumber me when united." From the Lost Order and other sources, he knew that six of these generals led single divisions, and that gave him a problem with his arithmetic. To make his figures come out, he gave the two "commands" of Jackson and Longstreet a kind of "grand corps" rating, so that in advancing across South Mountain to do battle with Longstreet and Hill at Boonsboro, he anticipated meeting a very substantial force.

That prospect instilled in him further caution. With two days' hard marching, he told General Gibbon that evening, "I will put Lee in a position he will find hard to get out of." By that timetable he budgeted an additional forty-eight hours to gain his reward from the Lost Order. If the loss of S.O. 191 "was a shabby trick for fate to play us," as a Confederate officer said, fate contrived to even the balance by handing the find to General McClellan.

It might also be supposed that army headquarters, with General Williams's note as a guide, would have made an effort to identify the discoverer of the Lost Order and reward him—a field promotion, a mention in dispatches, perhaps nomination for the newly authorized Medal of Honor. Instead the discovery went entirely unremarked; literally, no one gave it another thought. When he was asked about it after the war, General McClellan confessed he knew next to nothing about how the Lost Order reached him.

Only in 1886, twenty-four years after the event, was an account of the finding published in *Century* magazine, whose editors had sought the details from Colonel Colgrove for their "Battles and Leaders" series. There for the first time Barton Mitchell was identified as the finder of S.O. 191—and in Colgrove's account demoted to private. In 1892 Sergeant Bloss, to whom Mitchell had taken the find, further diminished Mitchell's role by manufacturing an account in which he was the actual discoverer, having simply asked Mitchell to pick up the envelope and hand it to him. Bloss had risen in the world to be a school superintendent, and his self-importance had risen as well.

This credit, imperfect as it was, came too late for poor Corporal Mitchell. For him the Lost Order was simply a jinx. The fruit of his discovery, the Battle of Antietam, was fought four days later, and in it he suffered a severe leg wound from which he never really recovered. (Antietam cut a terrible swath through the 27th Indiana and especially through Company F. Of those linked to the Lost Order, Corporal Mitchell, his friend Private Campbell, and Sergeant Bloss were all wounded, and Captain Kopp, to whom they took the find, was killed. In all, Company F took 40 percent casualties at Antietam.)

Mitchell spent eight months in the hospital, then was forced by disability to transfer to the ambulance corps. After his discharge his disability grew progressively worse, until he was bedridden. He died early in 1868, not yet fifty. His widow did not succeed in obtaining a survivor's pension until 1890. The army's Pension Office was not moved to act sooner by the claim that it was her husband who had found the famous Lost Order.

It is clear enough how the Lost Order was found, but it is still not clear how it was lost. The best hope is to narrow the possibilities. One certainty is that D.H. Hill was entirely innocent in the matter. Hill spent a quarter of a century vigorously defending himself against those who would make him the guilty party. In 1867 Richmond editor E.A. Pollard charged him with tossing the order away in a fit of petulance at its contents. In 1876 the count of Paris, pretender to the French throne, wrote in his history of the Civil War that Hill carelessly left his copy of S.O. 191 on a table in his headquarters. In 1884 former Confederate general Bradley T. Johnson retailed a story that the paper was seen to fall from Hill's pocket as he rode through Frederick.

Where Pollard and Johnson and the count heard these tales is anyone's guess. All of them were refuted by the *Century* article and by Hill's repeated declaration that he never saw the copy of S.O. 191 that the Federals found; he had instead the copy Jackson sent him.

What these theories (and others like them, then and since) fail to account for is the fact that the copy of S.O. 191 addressed to Hill was found in its delivery envelope. When Hill learned from McClellan after the war that he had preserved in his private papers both the Lost Order and the envelope in which it left Lee's headquarters that September 9, he put the case with perfect clarity: "If the envelope was with it, the paper was never received."

The fact that the order was found not in Hill's former encampment but some miles from it is further evidence that it never reached its destination. Finally, the fact that the discovery represents the workings of pure chance, that the envelope containing the copy of S.O. 191 and the three cigars could just as easily have been overlooked in that clover field near Frederick on September 13, is evidence that its loss was as much an accident as its finding.

Before the account of Corporal Mitchell's discovery appeared, General Hill suggested treachery as the cause of the loss. He was supported in this by his adjutant, Major J.W. Ratchford, who noted in a memoir of his service with the general that not long afterward, during the Harpers Ferry operation, a headquarters courier was unmasked as a Yankee spy and summarily hanged.

The problem with the treachery theory is the place where the Lost Order was found. Surely a traitor to the Southern cause would have found a better way to make certain so important a piece of stolen intelligence reached General McClellan than to drop it in a meadow alongside a back road—not even along one of the major highways in the region—in the hope that at some future time the Federals just might come that way, discover the packet, recognize its importance, and get it to the high command in time to do some good. It is impossible to imagine so naïve a spy, or (as it turned out) one so lucky.

The likeliest explanation for the loss of S.O. 191 is the simplest one: It was accidentally dropped by Lee's courier—whose identity remains unknown—on his way to deliver it to Hill. At some point he would have discovered his loss and probably backtracked in search of it. Perhaps he continued his search as far as Hill's command and found they already had their orders (unbeknownst to the courier, from Stonewall Jackson); perhaps he assumed the order he lost had been found and delivered. Back at army headquarters, he must have contrived some excuse for lacking a delivery receipt, or perhaps he even forged a receipt.

However it happened, it must have happened something like this, and the careless courier, thinking or hoping no real harm had been done, covered his tracks well enough to escape detection and punishment. Remarkably, Lee's headquarters would never investigate the matter at all, even after learning that a copy of S.O. 191 had been found by the enemy.

Nothing in the tangled story of the Lost Order is more misunderstood than just when General Lee discovered that his opponent had a copy of S.O. 191. Following the lead of Lee's biographer Douglas Southall Freeman, many historians have assumed that within some twelve hours of the time McClellan was handed the Lost Order, Lee learned that McClellan had it. That is a false assumption. One of the highest trump cards that fate dealt General McClellan that day was the advantage of surprise, for at no time during the Maryland campaign did Lee (or any other Confederate) know about the Lost Order. Not until January 1863, at the earliest, and probably several months after that, did he learn of the loss, and the finding, of S.O. 191.

When he did learn of it, it was through the Northern press. The order was first printed (from a copy made by General McClellan himself) in the

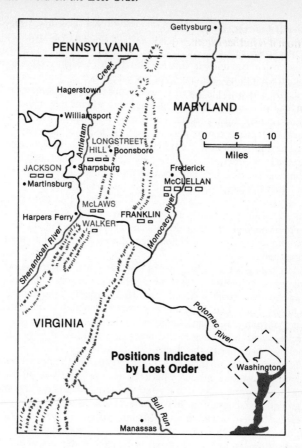

Positions Indicated
by Lost Order

New York Journal of Commerce on January 1, 1863. In March McClellan testified to a congressional committee that "at Frederick we found the original order issued to General D.H. Hill by direction of General Lee, which gave the orders of march for their whole army, and developed their intentions," and a month later his testimony was put into print by the committee and by the newspapers. General Lee, always a careful reader of Northern papers passed through the lines, thus learned for the first time of the loss of S.O. 191.

The misunderstanding on this point stems from a misreading of what Lee himself said about the Lost Order after the war. In 1868, in reviewing the Maryland campaign, Lee recalled that on the night on September 13–14 he received a dispatch from Jeb Stuart with information from a civilian who had been at General McClellan's headquarters in Frederick that morning. The civilian, a Confederate sympathizer, said that during their meeting McClellan was handed a paper by an aide and seemed excited by it and exclaimed, "Now I know what to do!"

The civilian had hurried off to tell Stuart of McClellan's response and to report that something—he could not say exactly what—had energized the Federals. On his way, he had seen Yankee troops advancing beyond Frederick toward South Mountain. (In fact this was only a routine movement, ordered some hours earlier, but the civilian tied it to what he had seen at McClellan's headquarters.) Stuart reported this development to Lee at Hagerstown.

In recounting the story, Lee phrased it as McClellan's reaction on being handed the Lost Order, which was true enough but was a fact supplied by Lee from hindsight knowledge. The amateur spy did not know—could not have known—that the paper McClellan read in his presence was a copy of Lee's plans. Neither McClellan nor his staff would be so careless as to reveal that fact to a civilian, particularly a civilian in Maryland, where loyalties were known to be divided. Stuart made no mention in his report of any Confederate plan, lost or found; Lee said nothing of it to Longstreet that night when they discussed their next move.

Most telling is the testimony of Lee's aide Charles Marshall, who was explicit about the matter. "I remember perfectly," he told D.H. Hill, "that until we saw that report"—McClellan's 1863 account of the finding of the Lost Order—"Gen. Lee frequently expressed his inability to understand the sudden change in McClellan's tactics which took place after we left Frederick. He regarded the finding of that order by McClellan as a complete and satisfactory explanation of the change."

As important as anything else, Lee's actions over the next several days were hardly those of a general who knew his opponent had all his plans. Rather than ordering Jackson to give up the siege of Harpers Ferry and find safer ground, he allowed him to continue it. Instead of instantly marching from Hagerstown to block the South Mountain passes, he waited until morning to move. Rather than prudently withdrawing across the Potomac to reunite his scattered forces, he ran an immense bluff by standing at Sharpsburg and then challenging McClellan to fight there. His actions were simply those of a general reacting to an opponent who was now advancing (as he told Jefferson Davis) "more rapidly than was convenient. . . ."

To be sure, the Army of Northern Virginia survived these various perils to fight again on other fields, but it survived only because McClellan squandered his golden opportunity. However little General Lee thought of McClellan's abilities, not even he would have dared to count on that happening.

On Sunday, September 14, Hill had time enough to cobble together a defense of Turner's Gap in South Mountain, with assistance late in the day from Longstreet's column from Hagerstown, against McClellan's belated offensive. To the south at Crampton's Gap, Franklin's equally sluggish advance got no farther that day than the crest of South Mountain. McClellan proclaimed a great victory, but his dream of cutting the enemy in two and beating him in detail—of winning another Castiglione—was fading rapidly.

The next day, September 15, Lee with Hill and Longstreet fell back behind Antietam Creek at Sharpsburg. Lee took his stand that day with hardly 15,000 men of all arms, but McClellan's pursuit was slow and cautious. According to the headquarters journal kept by his brother, Captain Arthur McClellan, the general believed he was facing 50,000 rebels. Franklin's feeble effort to advance toward beleaguered Harpers Ferry was blocked by McLaws. On September 15, too, General McClellan put the Lost Order aside. Whatever advantage he thought he had gained from it, he now decided its usefulness was at an end.

The narrator of this final twist in the story is Captain William J. Palmer, who visited McClellan's field headquarters a mile or so from Antietam Creek the night of the 15th. Palmer, a scout for Pennsylvania's forces and easily the best intelligence gatherer on the Federal side, had an inside look at the view from headquarters. General McClellan, he reported to Pennsylvania's governor, believed that the Harpers Ferry garrison had surrendered to the rebels that morning, and by nightfall "Jackson re-enforced Lee at Sharpsburg. . . . Rebels appear encouraged at arrival of their re-enforcements." By McClellan's train of thought, the scattered elements of the Army of Northern Virginia were now reunited, he was once more outnumbered, and the Lost Order was no longer of any use as a blueprint of his opponent's operations.

This final twist presents another irony, for it was thanks to the Lost Order that General Lee was granted the reprieve that saved his army. Despite conflicting evidence, McClellan seems to have concluded that Stonewall Jackson spent the siege of Harpers Ferry on guard duty at Martinsburg, where S.O. 191 placed him; and that on learning of the garrison's surrender that morning, he made the easy march to Sharpsburg to join Lee. To be sure, McClellan had not a scrap of evidence to confirm this—he had none because there was none; even the cheering he had supposed greeted Jackson's arrival was merely Lee's men reacting to the news of the capture of Harpers Ferry. He simply deduced it from his blind faith in the Lost Order.

The first of Jackson's footsore troops did not reach Sharpsburg until noon on September 16, and they continued to trail into the lines throughout the afternoon. Even then just three of his divisions were at hand; fully a third of Lee's army was still absent. Two more divisions reached the field at dawn on September 17, the day McClellan finally chose to offer battle, and the last division arrived only at the last moment during the battle. McClellan spent September 16 pondering his fate and "the gigantic rebel army" facing him.

In the end, the Battle of Antietam represented his final opportunity to profit from the Lost Order. For four days he had wasted glittering chances to divide and conquer his foe, yet at Antietam he still had odds that were greatly in his favor. By Lee's own testimony, he fought there with less than 40,000 men, leaving him outnumbered two to one. Lee's position was a good one, but his back was to the Potomac, inviting certain destruction if his line was breached and he had to fall back. But at this climactic moment, General McClellan could not rid himself of his fears and delusions: On September 17 he could not force himself to seek victory for fear of courting defeat. And so it ended. In the bloodiest single day of the war, he did not win the victory, but he was not defeated, either.

After defiantly holding his position for another day, Lee returned with his battered army to Virginia. At Antietam he had inflicted one-fifth more casualties than he suffered, and in the campaign as a whole he showed a profit—27,000 Federals (including the Harpers Ferry garrison) and substantial captures of arms and supplies against a loss of 14,000. But he failed in the task he had set for himself. He might claim Antietam as a narrow tactical victory, but he did not win a campaign that was decisive for the war.

And in the end that is how the impact of the Lost Order is measured. Lee termed the loss of S.O. 191 "a great calamity"; to his mind it was of crucial importance to the Maryland campaign because it enabled McClellan "to discover my whereabouts . . . and caused him so to act as to force a battle on me before I was ready for it."

It is permissible to speculate (as General Lee speculated) that had the Lost Order never been lost, then sometime during the latter half of September 1862 a great battle would have been fought in the Cumberland Valley of Pennsylvania—the Battle of Greencastle, perhaps, or the Battle of Chambersburg, or even the Battle of Gettysburg—in which "I would have had all my troops reconcentrated, . . . stragglers up, men rested and *intended then to attack McClellan*. . . ." Lee admitted it was "impossible to say that victory would have certainly resulted," but on one point he was very clear: "the loss of the dispatch changed the character of the campaign."

The Fiery Trail
of the *Alabama*

by J O H N   M.   T A Y L O R

About the time that Lee's orders were being lost, another extraordinary story was unfolding off the Azores. There, on September 5, 1862, the British-built Confederate raider *Alabama* captured and destroyed a Martha's Vineyard whaler called the *Ocmulgee*. It was the first of sixty-five victims that the *Alabama* would claim in the next twenty-two months, a time in which it ravaged the North's merchant fleet from Newfoundland to Java. The *Alabama,* captained by Raphael Semmes (nicknamed Old Beeswax, for his carefully cultivated mustache), was the first commerce raider to operate in the age of steam. But when Semmes's ship finally encountered the Union cruiser *Kearsarge* off Cherbourg in June 1864, their meeting would establish not a first but a notable last—the last one-on-one duel between two wooden ships. John M. Taylor is a frequent contributor to *MHQ.* His most recent book is a biography, *William Henry Seward: Lincoln's Right Hand* (HarperCollins).

Workers in the John Laird shipyard at Birkenhead, near Liverpool, watched attentively on the morning of May 15, as a handsome steam bark slid into the waters of the Mersey River. The vessel was known to them as No. 290, for hers was the 290th keel laid at the Laird yards. Upon launching, she was named the *Enrica,* but the identity of her owners remained a subject of speculation, for No. 290 was being built to the specifications of a Royal Navy cruiser. As May turned into June, the new vessel sprouted three tall masts that would enable her to carry a broad spread of canvas, and took on two 300-horsepower engines for steam propulsion.

In the waterfront bars of Liverpool, it was said with a wink that the actual purchaser of the *Enrica* was the Southern Confederacy, then locked in a war to establish its independence from the United States. For once, the tipsters were right on the mark. The possibility that No. 290 was destined for the Confederacy had not been lost on the U.S. minister in London, Charles Francis Adams, who was bombarding the Foreign Office with demands that the ship be seized. By mid-July, James Bulloch, the adroit Confederate naval agent who had supervised construction of the *Enrica* for the government in Richmond, knew that time was growing short.

The ever-imaginative Bulloch arranged for the *Enrica*'s departure from England in the guise of a gala trial run. On the fine morning of July 29, the new bark sailed down the Mersey with local dignitaries on board. At dusk, however, Bulloch and his guests returned to Liverpool on a tugboat, leaving the *Enrica* off the coast of Wales at Moelfra Bay. British authorities had in fact been attempting to detain the *Enrica,* and Bulloch had thwarted them by the narrowest of margins.

On Sunday, August 10, the *Enrica* arrived at the island of Terceira in the Azores. Eight days later the *Agrippina,* a tender under charter to Bulloch, showed up with equipment for the Confederate cruiser, including a 100-pound Blakely rifle, an 8-inch smoothbore, six 32-pounders, and provisions. That afternoon a second vessel, the *Bahama,* arrived with officers and hands for the new vessel. Thanks to Bulloch, the complicated logistics of equipping and manning a cruiser outside British waters were carried out without a hitch. On Sunday, August 24, in the presence of the crews of the *Enrica* and the *Bahama,* the Union Jack fluttered down from the the mainmast, to be replaced immediately by the Stars and Bars of the Confederacy. A band played "Dixie," and the mystery ship was officially christened the Confederate steamer *Alabama.*

The cruiser's designated commander was fifty-two-year-old Raphael Semmes, a Maryland native who had taken up residence in Alabama. Semmes had entered the U.S. Navy in 1832 and by 1861 had achieved the rank of commander. He was widely read in naval history and marine law and had written several books, including a lively narrative of his naval service during the Mexican War. A strong advocate of states' rights, Semmes had resigned his federal commission even before the firing on Fort Sumter.

In April 1861, Confederate secretary of the navy Stephen Mallory gave Semmes command of one of the South's first warships, the 437-ton screw steamer *Sumter.* The *Sumter* and its more powerful successors were intended to tackle one of two missions that Mallory had established for the Confederate navy: to attack the North's merchant marine, so as to increase the cost of the war to the enemy and thus encourage Lincoln to acknowledge Southern independence. The navy's other mission—to construct a fleet of ironclads capable of breaking the federal blockade—was beyond Confederate capabilities, but the first was not.

It had taken Semmes two months to convert the *Sumter* into a vessel of war, but he was able to gather around him a nucleus of able officers—no mean feat in the agrarian South, with its limited seafaring tradition. The *Sumter* broke the federal blockade off New Orleans on June 30, 1861, and reached the open sea. Thereafter, during a six-month cruise, the little raider burned eight Northern ships and released ten others on bond—a procedure under which the owners of an American ship's neutral cargo were expected to reimburse the Confederacy for goods not destroyed.

Eventually, boiler problems and a need for coal obliged the *Sumter* to call at Gibraltar. There she was blockaded by three federal warships, with no prospect of escape. Having made the most of his ship's limited capabilities, Semmes directed that the *Sumter* be sold, and set out for Britain with most of his officers. There, to the disappointment of Bulloch, who had hoped for the command, Semmes was given the far more powerful *Alabama.*

Semmes's first challenge in the Azores was to persuade enough British sailors to sign aboard the *Alabama* so that he could take his new command to sea. Semmes assured the hands of both the *Alabama* and the *Bahama* that they were free to return to Britain if they chose, but he then painted a glowing picture of life aboard the *Alabama.* He offered good pay—£4 10s. a month in gold for seamen, and £7 for firemen—plus grog twice a day and the prospect of prize money. He touched only briefly on the issues of the American war, but promised excitement and adventure. To his considerable relief, Semmes was able to sign on eighty British crewmen—enough to take the *Alabama* to sea. As time went on, he would supplement this nucleus with recruits from captured vessels.

Once Semmes had his officers and crew, he turned his attention to his ship. The *Alabama* represented the zenith of a hybrid marine form: ships powered by both sail and steam. She measured 220 feet in length, had a beam of 32 feet, and displaced 1,040 tons. She carried enough coal for eighteen days' steaming and had an innovation found on few ships of her day—a condenser that provided a gallon of fresh water per day for everyone on board, enabling her to remain at sea for extended periods. Her two-bladed screw could be raised into a well when she was under sail, thus posing no drag in the water. She could make about twelve knots under sail alone, to which her engines could add another three knots. She came with a year's supply of spare gear. In the words of one of her officers, Lieutenant Arthur Sinclair, the *Alabama* "was at the same time a perfect steamer and a perfect sailing vessel, each entirely independent of the other." The ship's armament also was impressive, comprising six 32-pounders and two pivot guns. A visitor to the *Alabama* would comment, "What strikes one most . . . is to see so small a vessel carrying such large metal."

Semmes was under orders to avoid engagements with enemy warships, for his was a special mission. The *Alabama,* as her commander wrote later, "was the first steamship in the history of the world—the defective little *Sumter* excepted—that was let loose against the commerce of a great commercial people." And Semmes set to his mission with a vengeance.

The *Alabama* had been at sea for only ten days when, on September 5, she sighted the first of the sixty-five victims she would claim over the next twenty-two months. The ship was a whaler—the *Ocmulgee,* of Edgartown, Massachusetts—and the capture was easy, for the *Ocmulgee* had a whale lashed alongside when the *Alabama* approached. The raider had been flying the American flag—an accepted ruse in war—and in Semmes's recollection, nothing could exceed the Yankee skipper's "blank stare of astonishment" when the *Alabama* finally ran up the Confederate ensign.

The *Ocmulgee*'s crew was transferred to the *Alabama,* along with some provisions; officers were permitted to bring one trunk with them, others a single bag. Semmes prepared to burn the whaler, but with the guile that would become his trademark, he postponed the firing until daylight: He knew that whalers operated in clusters, and he did not want to scatter them with an unexplained fire at night.

The *Alabama* spent two months in the Azores, burning eight vessels in all. The American whaling fleet—or what was left of it—returned to its home ports in New England, where shipowners filled the Northern press with tales of the "pirate" Semmes. The *Alabama,* too, worked her way westward. Semmes briefly considered throwing a few shells into New York City, but he thought better of it and instead seized several grain carriers off the Newfoundland banks.

The *Alabama*'s captures followed a pattern. The raider would hail a ship on sight. If she did not heave to, Semmes would fire a blank cartridge. If she still failed to respond, he would send a shot from a 32-pounder across her bow, and that would bring her to a halt. While the prize was boarded, Semmes remained in his cabin, and the skipper of his victim was taken to him there. Any ship whose papers showed her to be of neutral ownership was released. When a ship was found to be U.S.-owned, Semmes transferred her crew to the *Alabama.*

For a commerce raider, the *Alabama* operated under an unusual handicap: Because of the Federal blockade, she had no home port to which Semmes might send prizes. As a result, he was obliged to burn most of the ships he captured. After appropriating any provisions he could use, a rebel boarding party would pile up furniture and mattresses, douse them with lard or some other flammable substance, and fire the ship. Semmes's first officer was another veteran of the "Old Navy," John McIntosh Kell. The tough, red-bearded Kell later wrote:

> To watch the leaping flames on a burning ship gives an indescribable mental excitement that did not decrease with the frequency of the light, but it was always a relief to know that the ships were tenantless as they disappeared in the lonely grandeur, specks of vanishing light in the "cradle of the deep."

Between captures, the crew of the *Alabama* had ample opportunity to take the measure of their skipper. Semmes had just turned fifty-three and was not physically imposing; in the view of some, he was past his prime for sea command. His one idiosyncrasy was a carefully cultivated moustache that led his sailors to call him "Old Beeswax," but he was a tough disciplinarian; in his postwar memoir he outlined his command pbilosophy:

> On week days . . . about one fourth of the crew was exercised, either at the battery or with small arms. This not only gave them efficiency in the use of

their weapons, but kept them employed—the constant employment of my men being a fundamental article of my philosophy. . . . My crew were never so happy as when they had plenty to do, but little to think about.

Whatever the hands may have thought of Old Beeswax, Semmes appears to have enjoyed the respect of virtually all his officers. First Officer Kell worshiped his commander. And Lieutenant Sinclair later wrote that "Semmes [understood] just how to keep himself near the hearts and in the confidence of his men, without in the slightest degree descending from his dignity, or permitting direct approach." Semmes also impressed everyone with his professionalism. He was a student of every facet of seamanship—he digresses in his memoirs to discuss how variations in temperature affect the currents—and he had a childlike wonder at the natural beauty of the sea.

Probably only Kell glimpsed the virulent hatred that Semmes nourished for his enemy, the Yankees. Of them Semmes had written in his journal, "A people so devoid of Christian charity, and wanting in so many of the essentials of honesty, cannot be abandoned to their own folly by a just and benevolent God." Yet not even his loathing for Northerners as a class could totally destroy his admiration for them as seamen, and as the war went on the task of burning their ships became less satisfying to him.

Semmes dealt with his prisoners as humanely as conditions permitted. Captured crews were usually housed on deck but were afforded some protection from the elements. When the prisoners included women passengers, Semmes's officers turned over the wardroom for their use. Prisoners received full rations, and cooks among their number had access to the *Alabama's* galley. Officers were occasionally placed in irons, generally after Semmes had heard reports of mistreatment of Confederate prisoners. Because prisoners were a nuisance, Semmes got rid of them as rapidly as possible. Sometimes he landed them at a neutral port, but more often he transferred them to a captured ship whose cargo he had bonded.

From Newfoundland the raider worked her way south to Jamaica, where, on their first liberty, crewmen got so drunk that Semmes put some twenty sailors in irons. The incident was a reminder that while most of the *Alabama's* officers were reliable seamen, committed to the Confederate cause, most of the British crewmen were not. Much as the duke of Wellington once called his army the scum of the earth, Semmes called his crew

a precious set of rascals . . . faithless in . . . contracts, liars, thieves, and drunkards. There are . . . exceptions to this rule, but I am ashamed to say of the sailor class of the present day that I believe my crew to be a fair representation of it.

Kell, who supervised the boarding of every prize, had a firm rule that no member of the *Alabama's* crew could board a captured vessel until any supply of spirits was thrown overboard. Even with such precautions, he and Semmes were constantly on the alert for smuggled liquor.

Semmes had passed up the temptation to show his flag off New York City the previous fall, but in the Caribbean he was inclined to stretch his orders and play a role in the ground campaign along the Texas coast. A federal force under General Nathaniel P. Banks had captured Galveston in October 1862. Confederate forces had subsequently recaptured Galveston, but the city was blockaded by five federal warships when the black-hulled *Alabama* arrived there on January 11, 1863.

Semmes considered his options. The city that he had contemplated bombarding was now in friendly hands, and he could hardly take on five enemy warships. While he deliberated, the Federals detached one of their fleet, the gunboat *Hatteras*, to check out the new arrival. It was a fatal error. Semmes set out toward open water, steaming slowly, luring his pursuer away from the other federal warships.

Night had fallen by the time the *Hatteras* reached shouting distance of the *Alabama*, and Semmes, in reply to a hail from the Yankee, identified his ship as the HMS *Petrel*. While the federal captain dispatched a boat to check out his story, Semmes ran up the Confederate ensign and loosed a broadside at point-blank range.

The *Hatteras* was an underpowered side-wheeler that had no business engaging the powerful *Alabama*. The U.S. gunboat struck her flag after an exchange that lasted only thirteen minutes, and a few minutes later she sank in the shallow waters of the gulf. Two of her crew had been killed and three wounded. Semmes rescued the survivors and set course for the Atlantic.

The *Alabama* stopped again at Jamaica, where Semmes paroled his prisoners and partook of the hospitality that he would encounter in British possessions throughout the *Alabama*'s two-year cruise. Then he turned his ship southeast around Brazil to work the heavily traveled trade routes of the South Atlantic. Four more ships were stopped and burned in the first weeks of 1863, raising the *Alabama*'s total to thirty.

Coaling the raider, however, was proving to be a problem. She still had the services of the *Agrippina* as a tender, but it was difficult for Semmes to anticipate every supply requirement, and he had little confidence in the master of the *Agrippina*. In southern latitudes, moreover, coal was scarce as well as expensive. Fortunately for Semmes, he had a generous supply of gold for payment of ship's bills in remote corners of the world.

In June 1863, off the coast of South America, Semmes captured the American clipper *Conrad*, bound for New York with wool from Argentina. He had been waiting for such a prize, and rather than burning the clipper, he commissioned her as a Confederate cruiser, the *Tuscaloosa*. This was one more example of Semmes's creative approach to commerce raiding; but the *Tuscaloosa* had little success.

From South America, Semmes set sail for the Cape of Good Hope. In August 1863, the *Alabama* reached Cape Town, where Semmes supervised some badly needed repairs on his ship. The Confederate commander found himself a celebrity in the British colony, in part because his latest seizure—the *Sea Bride*, from Boston—had taken place within sight of the cape. As in

Jamaica, the officers of the *Alabama* were exhaustively entertained. Semmes held a shipboard "open house" that produced, in his view, "a generous out- pouring of the better classes." He also came within a day of encountering a federal warship that had been dogging his trail, a well-armed paddle-wheeler, the *Vanderbilt.*

For all the outrage in the Northern press concerning the *Alabama*'s depredations, pursuit of the raider was disorganized and ineffectual. This was to some degree inevitable. The Confederacy never had more than a handful of commerce raiders at sea, and of these only the *Florida*—commissioned around the same time as the *Alabama* and destined to destroy thirty-eight ships—was in the *Alabama*'s class. The Lincoln administration regarded the maintenance and strengthening of the blockade of Southern ports as its first priority; it was not willing to weaken the blockade to track down the *Alabama*, the *Florida,* or one of their lesser consorts.

Even making allowances, however, federal pursuit of the *Alabama* showed little imagination. The U.S. Navy dogged Semmes's trail as if con- vinced that the raider would remain in the area of its most recent capture. After the war, Semmes wrote that had Navy Secretary Gideon Welles sta- tioned a heavier and faster ship than the *Alabama* along two or three of the most traveled sea-lanes, "he must have driven me off, or greatly crippled me in my movements."

From Cape Town, the *Alabama* worked its way eastward across the Indian Ocean. There, most of the ships encountered proved to be neutral, and friendly captains warned Semmes that the Federals had a warship, the *Wyoming,* patrolling the Sunda Strait. Nevertheless, Semmes seized and burned a New York clipper, the *Winged Racer,* off Java, and set off in pursuit of another, the *Contest,* the following morning.

The pursuit of the *Contest* proved to be an omen. For the first time, the *Alabama,* employing both sail and steam, was initially unable to overtake her prey. But the sun rose higher, the morning breeze died, and the Confederate raider eventually closed in. The *Contest* was captured and burned—not with- out regret, for several of the *Alabama*'s officers vowed that they had never seen a more beautiful vessel. Only the failing wind had enabled the *Alabama* to make the capture, however, and Semmes realized that eighteen months at sea had taken a toll on his ship.

On December 21, 1863, the *Alabama* dropped anchor at Singapore. There Semmes saw new evidence of the effectiveness of his campaign: Singa- pore harbor was filled with American ships that had taken refuge there rather than chance an encounter with the *Alabama.* Within days of her arrival, about half of these were sold to neutral nations and could be seen flying new flags. The *Straits Times* estimated that Singapore was playing host to seven- teen American vessels aggregating 12,000 tons, some of which had "been lying there for upwards of three months and most of them for at least half that period."

On Christmas Eve 1863, the *Alabama* set course westward. Pickings were predictably slim, but the crew had their hands full with their own ship.

The raider's boilers were operating at reduced efficiency, and some of her timbers were split beyond repair. First Officer Kell observed that the *Alabama* "was loose at every joint, her seams were open, and the copper on her bottom was in rolls." For all of Semmes's skill at improvisation, nothing but a month in drydock could restore the raider to fighting trim.

By early March the *Alabama* was again off Cape Town, but because a belligerent vessel could provision at the same neutral port only once in a three-month period, she had to pass ten days offshore before docking. After coaling at Cape Town, Semmes turned northward. He intended to put his ship into dry dock in France, but he must have realized that the time necessary for repairs made it likely that the *Alabama* would be blockaded in port as the *Sumter* had been.

On April 22 the raider made the second of only three captures during 1864, the *Rockingham,* carrying a cargo of guano from Peru to Ireland. After the crew was taken off, Semmes directed that the prize be used for target practice—the raider's first live gun drill in many months. Sinclair later recalled that the sea was smooth and that the gun crews "amused themselves blithely" at point-blank range. Semmes thought his gun crews fired "to good effect," but Kell was less impressed: Of twenty-four rounds fired, only seven were seen to inflict damage. Ultimately, Semmes had to burn the *Rockingham.*

On April 27 the *Alabama* made her final capture, the *Tycoon,* out of New York with a mixed cargo. Semmes burned the Yankee vessel and resumed his northward course. He later wrote:

> The poor old *Alabama* was . . . like the wearied fox-hound, limping back after a long chase. . . . Her commander, like herself, was well-nigh worn down. Vigils by night and by day . . . had laid, in the three years of war he had been afloat, a load of a dozen years on his shoulders. The shadows of a sorrowful future, too, began to rest upon his spirit. The last batch of newspapers captured were full of disasters. Might it not be that, after all our trials and sacrifices, the cause for which we were struggling would be lost?

On June 11, 1864, the *Alabama* docked at the French port of Cherbourg. Word of her arrival was telegraphed all over Europe, and three days later the U.S. Navy ship *Kearsarge* appeared off the breakwater. Semmes had not yet received permission to make repairs at the French navy docks at Cherbourg, but he was allowed to disembark his prisoners and to take on coal.

The Confederate commander faced a crucial decision. He knew that his ship was in need of a refit, and he probably realized that the prudent course would be to do as he had done with the *Sumter:* put his ship up for sale and fight another day. But his fighting blood was up, and he had no great respect for his enemies. Nor was he inclined to solicit recommendations from his officers; as skipper of the *Sumter* and then the *Alabama,* he was accustomed to making his own decisions. Shortly after *Kearsarge* appeared, he called Kell to his cabin and explained his intentions.

"As you know, the arrival of the *Alabama* at this port has been telegraphed to all parts of Europe. Within a few days, Cherbourg will be effectively blockaded by Yankee cruisers. It is uncertain whether or not we shall be permitted to repair the *Alabama* here, and in the meantime, the delay is to our advantage. I think we may whip the *Kearsarge*, the two vessels being of wood and carrying about the same number of men and guns. Besides, Mr. Kell, although the Confederate States government has ordered me to avoid engagements with the enemy's cruisers, I am tired of running from that flaunting rag!"

Kell was not sure the decision to fight was wise. He reminded his skipper that in the *Rockingham* gun drill only one in three fuses had appeared effective. But Semmes was not to be deterred. He sent a message to Captain John A. Winslow of the *Kearsarge*, whom he had known in the Old Navy: He intended to fight.

Sunday, June 19, 1864, was a bright, almost cloudless day off Cherbourg. Aboard the *Alabama*, boilers had been fired at daybreak, and Semmes had inspected his crew at muster. Decks and brasswork were immaculate, and the crewmen were dressed in blue trousers and white tops. By 9:45 the cruiser was under way, cheered on by the crews of two French warships in the harbor.

The clash between the *Alabama* and the *Kearsarge* was, among other things, pure theater. It seemed that everyone in France wanted to watch what would prove to be the last one-on-one duel of the era of wooden ships. Excursion trains brought the curious to Cherbourg, and throngs of small craft hovered outside the breakwater. Painter Edouard Manet, with brushes, paints, and easel, was on one of them.

The two ships were almost equal in size and armament. Both were hybrid steamers of about the same tonnage. The *Alabama* carried 149 crewmen and mounted eight guns; the *Kearsarge* had a crew of 163 and mounted seven guns. The outcome of the battle would depend largely on the skill of the gun crews and the condition of the ships, but the *Kearsarge* had an ace in the hole: The enterprising Winslow had made imaginative use of his ship's chains, draping them along vulnerable parts of the hull as impromptu armor and concealing them behind wood paneling. Semmes later denied knowledge of the chains, but there is evidence that he was warned about them.

After the *Alabama* entered the English Channel, Semmes steered directly for his antagonist, some four miles away. He rotated his two pivot guns to starboard and prepared to engage the enemy on that side. The *Alabama* opened fire at about 11 A.M., and soon both ships were exchanging shots from their starboard batteries. The Kearsarge sought to run under the *Alabama*'s stern, but Semmes parried this move by turning to starboard.

The two antagonists thus fought on a circular track, much of the time at a range of about 500 yards. They made seven complete circles during the course of the action, reminding one Northern sailor of "two flies crawling around the rim of a saucer." Semmes may initially have wanted to put his ship alongside the *Kearsarge* for boarding, but the Yankee's greater speed ruled out this option.

From the first, the firing from the *Alabama* was rapid and wild. The Confederate cruiser fired more than 300 rounds, only 28 of which struck the *Kearsarge*, many of them in the rigging. In their excitement, the *Alabama*'s gunners fired some projectiles without removing the caps on their fuses—preventing them from exploding—and in other cases fired ramrods as well. It was not a disciplined performance. One of the *Alabama*'s crew conceded that the Confederate batteries were badly served; "the men all fought well, but the gunners did not know how to point and elevate their guns." In addition, the dark smoke emitted by the *Alabama*'s guns lent credence to Kell's fear that the raider's powder had deteriorated.

In contrast, Winslow and his crew fought with disciplined professionalism. Kell later conceded that the Yankee guns were "aimed with precision, and deliberate in fire."

"The firing now became very hot," Semmes related, "and . . . soon began to tell upon our hull, knocking down, killing and disabling a number of men . . . in different parts of the ship." Semmes ordered his gunners to use solid shot as well as shell, but to no effect. Meanwhile, the *Alabama*'s rudder was destroyed, forcing the Confederates to steer with tackles. In desperation, Semmes offered a reward to anyone who could put the *Kearsarge*'s forward pivot gun out of action.

Sinclair recalled how an 11-inch shell from that weapon entered the *Alabama* at the waterline and exploded in the engine room, "in its passage throwing a volume of water on board, hiding for a moment the guns of [my] division." With his fires out, Semmes attempted to steer for land, only to have the *Kearsarge* station herself between the *Alabama* and the coast.

Shortly after noon, Semmes gave the order to abandon ship. The *Alabama* had suffered only nine killed in the battle, but some twenty others, including Semmes, had been wounded, and twelve more would be drowned. Semmes and Kell, along with about forty others of the *Alabama*'s complement, had the good fortune to be rescued from the water by a British yacht, the *Deerhound*, which took them to England rather than turn them over to the *Kearsarge*. Seventy more were picked up by the *Kearsarge*, and another fifteen by excursion boats.

Semmes was lionized in England—British admirers replaced the sword that he had cast into the English Channel—but he was bitter over the loss of his ship, blaming the debacle on his defective powder and the *Kearsarge*'s protective chains. In point of fact, the battle off Cherbourg was the Civil War in microcosm: the gallant but outgunned South, ignoring its own deficiencies, heedlessly taking on a superior force.

During her twenty-two months at sea, the *Alabama* had burned fifty-four federal merchant ships and had bonded ten others. When, after the war, British and U.S. negotiators determined that Britain owed the United States a total of $15.5 million for damage caused by ships sold to the Confederacy, the amount charged to the *Alabama*—$6.75 million—was much the highest. In addition to its remarkable toll in merchant shipping, the *Alabama* had sunk an enemy gunboat, the luckless *Hatteras*, and had brought untold embarrassment to the federal navy. Semmes's record with the *Alabama* would not be approached by any raider in modern times.

Yet the raider's influence on the outcome of the Civil War was almost imperceptible. Its toll, however remarkable, represented only about 5 percent of U.S. shipping; the bulk of the U.S. merchant fleet stayed in port, transferred to neutral flags, or took their chances on the high seas. After all, the Confederacy's three or four commerce raiders could not be everywhere. Soaring rates for marine insurance added to the North's cost of waging war, but such economic damage was insignificant alongside the cost of the ground fighting in terms of both lives and matériel. The Northern states—economically self-sufficient—could ignore the depredations of Confederate raiders.

After the war, Semmes suggested that the North at first could not comprehend the threat posed by Confederate commerce destroyers. Yet when the threat materialized, he noted ruefully, the North was "too deeply engaged in the contest to heed it."

By the summer of 1864, there was no possibility of a replacement for the *Alabama,* and Semmes could have lived out the war comfortably in England. Instead, he made his way back to the Confederacy, by way of Cuba and Mexico. In Richmond he was promoted to admiral and assigned to the command of the James River squadron in Virginia. Following the evacuation of Richmond, he burned his boats and formed his men into a naval brigade that served under General Joseph E. Johnston in the final weeks of the war. After the war Semmes was briefly under arrest, but he was never brought to trial and supported himself with a small law practice until his death in 1877.

Raphael Semmes was not the first commerce raider in the history of naval warfare, but he was the first to operate in the age of steam and he may have been the best of all time. Nothwithstanding the unavailability of any home port, he managed to keep a wooden ship at sea for nearly two years without an overhaul and without losing either a crewman or a prisoner to disease. As a strategist, he demonstrated that a nation with a weak navy could nevertheless inflict great damage on any foe with a substantial merchant fleet. It is hardly surprising that Kaiser Wilhelm II made Semmes's postwar memoirs required reading for his admirals. In both world wars, German submarine and surface raiders would refine the qualities of speed, surprise, and endurance demonstrated by the *Alabama,* but with little of Semmes's regard for the lives of passengers and crew.

In taking on the *Kearsarge,* however, Semmes had let his emotions control his judgment. His gun crews were insufficiently trained, and he committed a cardinal sin: He didn't keep his powder dry.

Ulysses S. Grant's Final Victory

by JAMES M. McPHERSON

According to F. Scott Fitzgerald's too-often quoted dictum, there are no second acts in American lives. That hardly seems to have been the case with Ulysses S. Grant. Few lives, American or other, have added up to such a complete drama, and the last act may have been the most triumphant. Twenty years after the Civil War, Grant's reputation and his fortunes were in tatters. Great men do not always make great presidents; he had been one of our worst. Soured stock-market deals had left him deep in debt. Then, as he set out to recoup by writing his memoirs, he learned that he was suffering from incurable cancer. Grant soldiered on. "I was reduced almost to the point of death," he wrote, "and it became impossible for me to attend anything for weeks. I have, however, somewhat rejoined my strength. . . . I would have more hope of satisfying the expectation of the public if I could have allowed myself more time." That was Grant all over. James M. McPherson tells the story of his literary race with death—and how he created in the process what may be his most enduring monument. It is a story, McPherson suggests, that may go far to explain why the North won the war. McPherson, a professor of history at Princeton, is the author of the Pulitzer Prize–winning history of the Civil War *The Battle Cry of Freedom,* and *Abraham Lincoln and the Second American Revolution,* both published by Oxford University Press.

When I put my pen to paper I did not know the first word that I should make use of in writing the terms. I only knew what was in my mind, and I wished to express it clearly, so that there could be no mistaking it.

So wrote Ulysses S. Grant in the summer of 1885, a few weeks before he died of throat cancer. He was describing the scene in Wilmer McLean's parlor at Appomattox Court House twenty years earlier, when he had started to write the formal terms for the surrender of the Army of Northern Virginia. But he could have been describing his feelings only one year earlier, in July 1884, as he sat down to write the first of three articles for *Century* magazine's "Battles and Leaders" series on the American Civil War.

These articles were subsequently incorporated into Grant's *Personal Memoirs,* two volumes totaling nearly 300,000 words written in a race against the painful death that the author knew would soon overtake him. The result was a military narrative that Mark Twain in 1885 and Edmund Wilson in 1962 judged to be the best work of its kind since Julius Caesar's *Commentaries,* and that John Keegan in 1987 pronounced "the most revelatory autobiography of high command to exist in any language."

Grant would have been astonished by this praise. He had resisted earlier attempts to persuade him to write his memoirs, declaring that he had little to say and less literary ability to say it. There is no reason to doubt his sincerity in this conviction. Grant had always been loath to speak in public and equally reluctant to consider writing for the public. As president of the United States from 1869 to 1877, he had confined his communications to formal messages, proclamations, and executive orders drafted mainly by subordinates.

In 1880, after a postpresidential trip around the world, Grant bought a brownstone in New York and settled down at age fifty-eight to a comfortable retirement. He invested his life's savings in a brokerage partnership of his son and Frederick Ward, a Wall Street high roller. Ward made a paper fortune in speculative ventures, some of them illegal. In 1884 this house of cards collapsed with a crash that sent Ward to jail and left Grant with $180 in cash and $150,000 in debts.

It was then that he overcame his literary shyness and accepted a commission to write three articles for the *Century.* They revealed a talent for lucid prose, and although the $3,000 he earned for them would not begin to pay his debts, it would at least pay the bills.

While working on the articles, however, Grant experienced growing pain in his throat. It was diagnosed in October 1884 as cancer, incurable and fatal. Grant accepted the verdict with the same outward calm and dignity that had marked his response to earlier misfortunes and triumphs alike. To earn more money for his family, he almost accepted an offer from the *Century* of the standard 10 percent royalty for his memoirs. But his friend Mark Twain, angry at being exploited by publishers, had formed his own publishing company, and he persuaded Grant to sign up with him for 70 percent of the net proceeds of sales by subscription. It was one of the few good financial decisions Grant ever made. *The Personal Memoirs* earned $450,000 for his family after his death, which came just days after he completed the final chapter.

Grant's indomitability in his battle against this grim deadline attracted almost as much attention and admiration as his victory over rebellion twenty years earlier. Both were triumphs of will and determination, of a clarity of conception and simplicity of execution that made a hard task look easy. To read Grant's memoirs with a knowledge of the circumstances in which he wrote them is to gain insight into the reasons for his military success.

In April 1885, when Grant had written a bit more than half the narrative—through the November 1863 battles of Chattanooga—he suffered a severe hemorrhage that left him apparently dying. But by an act of will, and with the help of cocaine for the pain, he recovered and returned to work. The chapters on the campaign from the Wilderness to Petersburg, written during periods of intense suffering and sleepless nights, bear witness to these conditions. The narrative becomes bogged down in details; digressions and repetition creep into the text. Just as the Union cause had reached a nadir in August 1864, with Grant blocked at Petersburg and Sherman seemingly stymied before Atlanta while war-weariness and defeatism in the North seemed sure to vanquish Lincoln in the presidential election, so did Grant's narrative flounder in these chapters.

As Grant's health temporarily improved in the late spring of 1885, so did the terse vigor of his prose. He led the reader through Sherman's capture of Atlanta and his marches through Georgia and the Carolinas, Sheridan's spectacular victories in the Shenandoah Valley, and the Army of the Potomac's campaign to Appomattox. These final chapters pulsate with the same energy that animated Union armies as they delivered their knockout blows in the winter and spring of 1864–65. Just as he had controlled the far-flung Union armies by telegraph during those final campaigns, Grant once again had the numerous threads of his narrative under control as he brought the story to its climax in Wilmer McLean's parlor.

Grant's strength of will, his determination to do the best he could with what he had, his refusal to give up or to complain about the cruelty of fate, help explain the success of both his generalship and his memoirs. These qualities were by no means common among Civil War generals. Many of them spent more time and energy clamoring for reinforcements or explaining why they could not do what they were ordered to do than they did in trying to carry out their orders. Their memoirs are full of self-serving excuses for failure, which was always somebody else's fault.

Early in his memoirs Grant described General Zachary Taylor, under whom he had served as a twenty-four-year-old lieutenant in the Mexican War. Taylor's little army won three battles against larger Mexican forces. Fearing that the general was becoming too popular and might win the Whig presidential nomination, Democratic president James Polk transferred most of Taylor's troops (including Grant's regiment) to General Winfield Scott's campaign against Mexico City. This left Taylor with only a handful of veterans and a few raw volunteer regiments. Nevertheless, he won the Battle of Buena Vista against an army three times larger than his own—and thereby ensured his election as the next president. Grant wrote nearly forty years later:

> General Taylor was not an officer to trouble the administration much with his demands, but was inclined to do the best he could with the means given him. . . . If he had thought that he was sent to perform an impossibility with the means given him, he would probably have informed the authorities of his opinion and . . . have gone on and done the best he could with the

means at hand without parading his grievance before the public. No soldier could face either danger or responsibility more calmly than he. These are qualities more rarely found than genius or physical courage.

Whether subconsciously or not, with these words Grant described himself as much as he described Taylor. Old Zack became a role model for young Ulysses. "General Taylor never made any show or parade either of uniform or retinue." Neither did Grant when he was commanding general. "In dress he was possibly too plain, rarely wearing anything in the field to indicate his rank." Nor did Grant. "But he was known to every soldier in his army, and was respected by all." The same was true of Grant in the next war. "Taylor was not a conversationalist." Neither was Grant. "But on paper he could put his meaning so plainly that there could be no mistaking it. He knew how to express what he wanted to say in the fewest well-chosen words, but would not sacrifice meaning to the construction of high-sounding sentences." This describes Grant's prose perfectly, his memoirs as well as his wartime orders to subordinates.

This question of "plain meaning" is no small matter. There are many Civil War examples of vague, ambiguous, confusing orders that affected the outcome of a campaign or battle in unfortunate ways. Grant's orders, by contrast, were invariably clear and concise. Many of his wartime associates commented on this. George B. Meade's chief of staff wrote that

> there is one striking feature of Grant's orders; no matter how hurriedly he may write them on the field, no one ever has the slightest doubt as to their meaning, or even has to read them over a second time to understand them.

Unlike many other generals, Grant did not rely on staff officers to draft his orders and dispatches; he wrote them himself. Horace Porter of General George Thomas's staff first met Grant at Chattanooga in October 1863. After a daylong inspection of the besieged Army of the Cumberland, which was in dire condition, Grant returned to his headquarters and sat down to write. Porter was impressed

> by the manner in which he went to work at his correspondence. . . . His work was performed swiftly and uninterruptedly, but without any marked display of nervous energy. His thoughts flowed as freely from his mind as the ink from his pen; he was never at a loss for an expression, and seldom interlined a word or made a material correction.

After a couple of hours, Grant gathered up the dispatches and had them sent by telegraph or courier to every point on the compass from Vicksburg to Washington, giving orders, Porter said, "for the taking of vigorous and comprehensive steps in every direction throughout his new and extensive command." These orders launched the movements that opened a new supply line into Chattanooga, brought in reinforcements, and prepared the Union armies for the campaigns that lifted the sieges of Chattanooga and Knoxville and drove Braxton Bragg's demoralized Army of Tennessee into Georgia after the assault on Missionary Ridge.

Porter, amazed by Grant's "singular mental powers and his rare military qualities," joined Grant's staff and served with him from the Wilderness to Appomattox. His own version of those events, entitled *Campaigning with Grant*, is next in value only to Grant's memoirs as a firsthand account of command decisions in that campaign.

Porter had particularly noticed how Grant never hesitated but wrote steadily, as if the thoughts flowed directly from his mind to the paper. How can this be reconciled with Grant's recollection that when he sat down to write out the surrender terms for Lee's army, he had no idea how to start? How can it be reconciled with his initial reluctance to write his memoirs because he thought he had no literary ability? The truth is, as he admitted in his account of writing the surrender terms, "I only knew what was in my mind."

There lies the explanation of Grant's ability as a writer: He knew what was in his mind. That is a rare quality in a writer or a general, but a necessary one for literary or military success. Once unlocked by an act of will, the mind poured out the words smoothly.

Grant had another and probably related talent, which might be described as a "topographical memory." He could remember every feature of the terrain over which he traveled, and find his way over it again; he could also look at a map and visualize the features of terrain he had never seen. Horace Porter noted that any map "seemed to become photographed indelibly on his brain, and he could follow its features without referring to it again."

Grant could see in his mind the disposition of troops over thousands of square miles, visualize their relationships to roads and terrain, and know how and where to move them to take advantage of topography. Most important, he could transpose this image into words that could be understood by others—though the modern reader of his memoirs would be well advised to have a set of Civil War maps on hand to match the maps in Grant's head.

During the last stages of his illness, unable to speak, Grant penned a note to his physician: "A verb is anything that signifies to be; to do; to suffer; I signify all three." It is not surprising that he would think of verbs at such a time; they are what give his writing its terse, muscular quality. As agents to translate thought into action, verbs offer a clue to the secret of Grant's military success, which also consisted of translating thought into action. Consider these orders to Sherman early in the Vicksburg campaign:

> You will proceed . . . to Memphis, taking with you one division of your present command. On your arrival at Memphis you will assume command of all the troops there . . . and organize them into brigades and divisions in your own army. As soon as possible move with them down the river to the vicinity of Vicksburg, and with the cooperation of the gunboat fleet . . . proceed to the reduction of that place.

In the manner of Caesar's *Veni, vidi, vici,* these sentences bristle with verbs of decision: "Proceed . . . take . . . assume command . . . organize . . . move . . . proceed to the reduction. . . ." Note also the virtual absence of adverbs and of all but essential adjectives. Grant used these modifiers only when necessary to his meaning. Take, for example, his famous reply to General Simon B. Buckner's request to negotiate terms for the surrender of Fort Donelson: "No terms except an unconditional and immediate surrender can be accepted. I propose to move immediately on your works." Not an excess word here; the adjectives and adverb strengthen and clarify the message; the words produce action—they become action.

The will to act, symbolized by the emphasis on active verbs in Grant's writing, illustrates another crucial facet of his generalship—what Grant himself called "moral courage." This was a quality different from and rarer than physical courage. Grant and many other men who became Civil War generals had demonstrated physical courage under fire in the Mexican War as junior officers carrying out the orders of their superiors. Moral courage involved a willingness to make decisions and initiate the orders. Some officers who were physically brave shrank from this responsibility, because decision risked error, and initiative risked failure.

This was George B. McClellan's defect as a commander: He was afraid to risk his army in an offensive because it might be defeated. He lacked the moral courage to act, to confront that terrible moment of truth, to decide and to risk. Grant, Lee, Jackson, Sheridan, and other victorious Civil War commanders had moral courage; they understood that without risking defeat they could never achieve victory.

Grant describes how he first confronted that moment of truth and learned the lesson of moral courage. His initial Civil War command was as colonel of the 21st Illinois. In July 1861 the regiment was ordered to find Tom Harris's rebel guerrilla outfit in Missouri and attack it. Grant says:

> My sensations as we approached what I supposed might be "a field of battle" were anything but agreeable. I had been in all the engagements in Mexico that it was possible for one person to be in; but not in command. If some one else had been colonel and I had been lieutenant-colonel I do not think I would have felt any trepidation. . . . As we approached the brow of the hill from which it was expected we could see Harris' camp, and possibly find his men formed ready to meet us, my heart kept getting higher and higher until it felt to me as though it was in my throat.

But when the 21st reached Harris's camp, they found it abandoned. Wrote Grant:

> My heart resumed its place. It occurred to me at once that Harris had been as much afraid of me as I had been of him. This was a view of the question I had never taken before; but it was one I never forgot afterwards. From that event to the close of the war, I never experienced trepidation

upon confronting an enemy, though I always felt more or less anxiety. I never forgot that he had as much reason to fear my forces as I had his. The lesson was valuable."

Grant may have taken that lesson too much to heart; he forgot that there were times when he *should* fear the enemy's intentions. This lesson he learned the hard way, at both Fort Donelson and Shiloh. After the failure of the Union gunboats to subdue the Donelson batteries on February 14, 1862, Grant went downriver several miles to consult with Flag Officer Andrew Foote of the gunboat fleet. Grant was therefore absent on the morning of February 15 when the Confederate garrison launched its breakout attack. He confessed that "when I left the National line to visit Flag-officer Foote, I had no idea that there would be any engagement on land unless I brought it on myself."

It took one more such experience to drive this lesson home. This time it was the Confederate attack at Shiloh on April 6, 1862, when Grant was again absent at his headquarters seven miles downriver. "The fact is," he admits in the memoirs, "I regarded the campaign we were engaged in as an offensive one and had no idea that the enemy would leave strong intrenchments to take the initiative." Thereafter he had a healthier respect for the enemy's capabilities.

But this never paralyzed him or caused him to yield the initiative. At both Fort Donelson and Shiloh, Grant's recognition that the enemy still had as much reason to fear him as he to fear the enemy enabled him to wrest the initiative away and grasp victory. Upon returning to his troops at Donelson after a fast ride over icy roads, he calmly took charge and re-formed his broken lines. After hearing reports of the morning's fighting, he told a member of his staff: "Some of our men are pretty badly demoralized, but the enemy must be more so, for he has attempted to force his way out, but has fallen back: the one who attacks first now will be victorious and the enemy will have to be in a hurry if he gets ahead of me." Suiting action to words, he ordered a counterattack, drove back and penned in the Confederate forces, and compelled their surrender.

At Shiloh, Grant conducted a fighting fallback until dusk stopped the Confederate advance. His army was crippled, but he knew that the Confederates were just as badly hurt and that he would be reinforced during the night. Thus he replied to one subordinate who advised retreat: "Retreat? No. I propose to attack at daylight and whip them." And he did.

One of Grant's superstitions, described in the memoirs, was a dread of turning back or retracing his steps once he had set forth on a journey. If he took the wrong road or made a wrong turn, he would go across country or forward to the next turn rather than go back. This superstition reinforced his risk-taking inclination as a military commander. Crucial decisions in the Vicksburg and Wilderness campaigns illustrate this trait.

During the winter of 1862–63, Grant's river-based campaign against Vicksburg bogged down in the Louisiana and Mississippi swamps. While criticism mounted to an angry crescendo in the North, Grant remained calm and carefully worked out a daring plan: to run the gunboats past Vicksburg; cross his army to the east bank; cut loose from his base and communications; and live off the land while operating in Vicksburg's rear.

This was the highest-risk operation imaginable. Grant's staff and his most trusted subordinates, especially Sherman, opposed the plan. Sherman "expressed his alarm at the move I had ordered," wrote Grant, "saying that I was putting myself in a position voluntarily which an enemy would be glad to manoeuvre a year—or a long time—to get me in." Go back to Memphis, advised Sherman, establish a secure base of supplies, and move against Vicksburg overland, keeping open your communications—in other words, wage an orthodox campaign by the book.

But Grant threw away the book. He was confident his army could live off the land and substitute mobility for secure communications. "The country is already disheartened over the lack of success on the part of our armies," he told Sherman. He goes on to explain in the memoirs:

> If we went back as far as Memphis it would discourage the people so much that bases of supplies would be of no use: neither men to hold them nor supplies to put in them would be furnished. The problem for us was to move forward to a decisive victory, or our cause was lost. No progress was being made in any other field, and we had to go on.

Go on he did, to what military historians almost universally regard as the most brilliant and innovative campaign of the Civil War.

As Grant departed Washington a year later to set forth on what became the campaign from the Wilderness to Appomattox, he told President Lincoln that "whatever happens, there will be no turning back." What happened in the Wilderness, however, might have caused other Northern commanders to turn back; indeed, similar events in the same place had caused Joe Hooker to turn back exactly a year earlier.

On May 6, 1864, the second day of the Wilderness, Lee attacked and bent back both of Grant's flanks. That evening a distraught brigadier galloped up to Grant's headquarters to report disaster on the right. "I know Lee's methods well by past experience," panted the officer, in words recorded by Horace Porter. "He will throw his whole army between us and the Rapidan, and cut us off completely."

Grant slowly removed a cigar from his mouth and fixed the man with an icy stare. "Oh, I am heartily tired of hearing about what Lee is going to do. Some of you always seem to think he is suddenly going to turn a double somersault, and land in our rear and on both of our flanks at the same time. Go back to your command, and try to think what we are going to do ourselves, instead of what Lee is going to do."

Once again Grant suited action to words. He ordered preparations for a movement. Men in the ranks who had fought the Battle of Chancellorsville in these woods thought it was another retreat, but when they realized that this time they were moving south, the scales fell from their eyes. It was not "another Chancellorsville . . . another skedaddle" after all. "Our spirits rose," wrote a veteran who recalled this moment as a turning point of the war. "We marched free. The men began to sing." When Grant cantered by one corps, the soldiers recognized him and sent up a cheer. For the first time in a Virginia campaign, the Army of the Potomac was staying on the offensive after its initial battle. Nor did it turn back or retrace its steps until Appomattox eleven months later.

These incidents in the Wilderness do not come from the memoirs. Though Grant keeps himself at the center of the story, his memoirs exhibit less egotism than is typical of the genre. Grant is generous with praise of other officers (especially Sherman, Sheridan, and Meade) and sparing with criticism, carping, and backbiting. He is also willing to admit mistakes, most notably: "I have always regretted that the last assault at Cold Harbor was ever made. . . . No advantage whatever was gained to compensate for the heavy loss we sustained."

But Grant did not admit culpability for the heavy Union casualties in the whole campaign of May–June 1864. Nor should he have done so, despite the label of "butcher" and the subsequent analyses of his "campaign of attrition." It did turn out to be a campaign of attrition, but that was by Lee's choice. Grant's purpose was to maneuver Lee into an open field for a showdown; Lee's purpose was to prevent this by entrenching an impenetrable line to protect Richmond and his communications. Lee was hoping to hold out long enough and inflict enough casualties on attacking Union forces to discourage the people of the North and overturn the Lincoln administration in the 1864 election.

Lee's strategy of attrition almost worked; that it failed in the end was due mainly to Grant, who stayed the course and turned the attrition factor in his favor. Although the Confederates had the advantage of fighting on the defensive most of the time, Grant inflicted almost as high a percentage of casualties on Lee's army as vice versa. Indeed, for the war as a whole, Lee's armies suffered a higher casualty rate than Grant's. Neither commander was a "butcher," but measured by that statistic, Grant deserved the label less than Lee.

On one matter Grant's memoirs are silent: There is not a word about the rumors and speculations concerning his drinking. On this question there continues to be disagreement among historians and biographers. Most of the numerous stories about Grant's drunkenness at one time or another during the war are false. But drinking problems almost certainly underlay his resignation from the army in 1854, and he may have gone on a bender once or twice during the war—though never during active military operations. In any event, I think, his silence on the subject reflects his sensitivity about it, not his indifference.

That sensitivity is indicated by Grant's curious failure to mention John A. Rawlins in the memoirs except twice in passing and once in a brief paragraph of opaque praise. Yet as his chief of staff, Rawlins was both Grant's alter ego and his conscience. So far as was possible, Rawlins kept him away from the temptations of the bottle. Grant may have been an alcoholic in the modern medical meaning of the term, but that meaning was unknown in his time. Excessive drinking was in those days regarded as a moral defect and was a matter of deep shame among respectable people. Grant himself doubtless so regarded it.

If Grant was an alcoholic, he should have felt pride rather than shame, because he overcame his illness to achieve success and fame without the support system of modern medicine and organizations like Alcoholics Anonymous. But lacking our knowledge and perspective, he could not see it that way. His support network consisted mainly of his wife, Julia, and John Rawlins. Grant, a happy family man, did not drink when his wife and family were with him. And when they were not, Rawlins guarded him zealously from temptation. Many contemporaries knew this, but to give Rawlins his due in the memoirs would perhaps have seemed a public confession of weakness and shame.

And, of course, the memoirs are about triumph and success—triumph in war, and success in writing the volumes in a race against death. They are military memoirs, which devote only a few pages to Grant's early years and to the years of peace between the Mexican War and the Civil War. Nor do they cover his less-than-triumphant career after the Civil War. But perhaps this is as it should be. Grant's great contribution to American history was as a Civil War general. In that capacity he did more to shape the future of America than anyone else except Abraham Lincoln. He earned a secure place as one of the great captains of history, an "unheroic" hero, in John Keegan's apt description. Both in their substance and in the circumstances of their writing, the personal memoirs of Ulysses S. Grant offer answers to that perennial question of Civil War historiography: Why did the North win?

"The Man of Silence"

by CALEB CARR

If the American Civil War was the first modern conflict, who was the first truly modern general? Caleb Carr argues that it was not Grant or Lee or Sherman but their contemporary, the admirable but elusive Prussian, Helmuth von Moltke. Moltke, he writes, "was able to address the military challenges brought on by the Industrial Revolution and devise a system of mobilization, organization, and command that . . . would remain unmatched until the outbreak of the Second World War." Modern Germany is as much Moltke's creation as Bismarck's. Hardly the harsh stereotype of Prussian militarism, he also had considerable literary talent—but then that seems appropriate for a man who viewed the conduct of war more as an art than as a science. Protracted violence was not his way, and he feared for the future: As he warned the Reichstag the year before his death, "Woe to him who sets fire to Europe, who first puts the flame to the powderkeg!" An *MHQ* contributing editor, Caleb Carr is the author of the recently published *The Devil Soldier: The Life of Frederick Townsend Ward* (Random House).

The century following Napoleon's defeat at Waterloo in 1815 produced three military leaders of the first rank: Robert E. Lee and Ulysses S. Grant, the immortal antagonists of America's savage Civil War, and Helmuth von Moltke, the architect of Prussia's victories over Denmark in 1864, Austria in 1866, and France in 1870–71. Of the three, Moltke has proved the most troublesome for posterity. Lee, the consummate gentleman warrior and valiant leader of a doomed cause, had an assured place in the pantheon of military heroes almost from the moment he assumed command of the Army of Northern Virginia; and Grant's humble personal style, contrasted with his relentless pursuit of a righteous goal, was strong enough to overshadow the gross political mismanagement of his later life. But in the collective imagination of subsequent generations, Moltke has remained very much as he was in life—subtle and altogether elusive.

Yet this silent, unassuming Prussian affected the conduct of modern warfare to a far greater extent than did either of his American contemporaries. Although Lee was a superb tactician, he never demonstrated the talent for organizational and administrative innovation that modern warfare requires; indeed, failure in these areas contributed weightily to the ultimate defeat of the Confederacy. And Grant, though possessed of a keen understanding of strategy, was unable to find a more sophisticated military use for the new technological and industrial might of the Union than the kind of wholesale destruction that Sherman unleashed in his March to the Sea and Sheridan oversaw in the Shenandoah Valley. Moltke, by contrast, was able to address the military challenges brought on by the Industrial Revolution and to devise a system of mobilization, organization, and command that was far more efficient than anything that had been seen since the Napoleonic Wars. The system he created would remain unmatched until the outbreak of the Second World War.

Moltke's achievements in actual battle were no less striking. All three of his wars were strategic marvels punctuated by tactical triumphs—notably Königgrätz and Sedan, to name but two. Most important, and again in contrast to the American Civil War, the victories were lightning-quick—the fates of both Austria and France, for instance, were sealed within seven weeks of each war's outbreak. Moltke's method in these conflicts was consistent: Like Lee, his goal was to defeat the enemy's army rather than destroy their homeland; but unlike Grant, he knew how to bend the new industrial might of his nation to that purpose with finesse.

Moltke played a key role in changing the political configuration first of Germany and then of Europe. But his importance to military history did not end there, for such was his acumen that later in his remarkable life, which spanned almost the entire nineteenth century, he renounced the practicality of a military solution to Europe's growing problems, and warned that the looming world war would be of protracted length and ungovernable violence—two things he had always abhorred.

There was little enough that was typically Prussian about this man who, together with Otto von Bismarck, would establish his nation as the predominant land power in Europe. In fact, Moltke was not even born within Prussia proper, but in neighboring Mecklenburg, in 1800. The family was of noble lineage, but Moltke's father ran through his inheritance with a speed that indicated something more than simple carelessness. When Helmuth Karl was five, the senior Moltke resettled his family in Holstein, becoming a Danish subject and entering the Danish army. What was left of the family's holdings was lost during the Napoleonic Wars. Their country house was burned by the French, and their town house in Lübeck—where Frau Moltke and her children were staying at the time—was sacked as well.

The experiences of these first fifteen years, including the hard juxtaposition of extreme poverty and a noble name, produced in Moltke a pronounced distaste for the reckless, spendthrift ways of his father, a subsequent inclination toward the quiet gentility and broad learning of his mother, a singular endurance and prodigious energy for work, and finally a deep bitterness toward France. These remained hallmarks of his character until his death in 1891.

Moltke followed his father's path into the Danish army in 1818, but found it dull and unpromising. At twenty-one he decided to join Prussia's 8th Infantry Regiment, although the move entailed a loss of rank to second lieutenant. He attended the Berlin Kriegsakademie, which was then under the direction of Carl von Clausewitz. Moltke did not personally study under Clausewitz, but the latter's preoccupation with the interrelationship between war and politics permeated the curriculum, and Moltke came away indelibly marked by it. His performance during the course of study was brilliant. In 1826 he returned to his regiment, but within two years he had already secured assignment to the Prussian General Staff.

The extracurricular activities that Moltke began to pursue during this period were as revealing as his exemplary work in the Kriegsakademie. He had continued to maintain a deep interest in subjects other than war—indeed, he had acquired, somewhat surprisingly, a traditional German liberal-humanist education. Literature, the classics, history, various sciences, and especially languages were all part of this program. Still feeling the sting of poverty, Moltke began to supplement his army pay through writing, and he did not confine himself to military subjects. Under a pseudonym, he authored installment fiction in popular magazines. He also translated Gibbon's Decline and Fall. In addition, when he journeyed to southeastern Europe and was seconded to the Turkish army for a dismal tour of duty in Egypt in 1835, he wrote letters and made notes about his travels; on his return these resulted in prose works that, according to one German authority, are "still read as literature." Marked by a high level of compositional and artistic excellence, as well as by penetrating—if dryly subtle—humor, Moltke's writing brought him both increased income and recognition outside the army.

Moltke's early military writings—notably The Russo-Turkish Campaign in Europe (1845)—were also extremely well received, and they offer important insights into the evolution of his military doctrines. The same can be said of his technical studies, especially on the subject of railways, whose military and commercial advantages Moltke already could foresee. Largely on the basis of these works, he rose quickly within the General Staff, becoming first adjutant to Crown Prince Friedrich Wilhelm in 1855 and a major general the following year, despite having spent just a few years serving with active units. But Moltke himself spoke little of his achievements—or of anything else, for that matter; his reticence earned him such epithets as "the man of silence" and, perhaps more revealing, "the man who could be silent in seven languages."

Simple humility appears an inadequate explanation for his silence, especially given his remarkable self-confidence. More plausible is the assessment of the French empress Eugénie, who upon meeting Moltke remarked that he appeared to be a man who labored under a constant inner tension. We can only speculate as to the causes of that tension—the pronounced distance from his father, the bitter memories of war during childhood, the physical and emotional distress of poverty, perhaps the simple fact of possessing an artistic temperament in a rigidly practical society—but this much is clear: Strong emotions did move Moltke, and they were not emotions that he could ever comfortably proclaim. Even his literary works (at least those that he authored under his own name) rarely strayed too close to the personal.

Further evidence of this apparent duality of character—the artist paired against the militarist—is provided by Moltke's marriage. That event coincided with the beginning of his rise to eminence in 1842. Moltke's bride was his sister's stepdaughter, an English girl named Marie Burt. She was just sixteen; he was already in his forties. By all accounts his devotion to her throughout a marriage lasting a quarter century (she died in 1868) was as deeply passionate as it was unequivocal. At times he mixed that passion with practicality: When construction of the Berlin–Hamburg railroad got under way shortly after their wedding, he strongly supported it not only for military and commercial reasons but also out of a simple if understated desire to cut the amount of time it would take him to reach Marie.

The fullest expression of the creative side of Moltke's character was unquestionably his absorption in the art of war. Only here could the "inner tension" between private passion and public discipline be resolved. Moltke shared the view of one of the principal formulators of Austria's General Staff system, Field Marshal Count Radetzky, that "war is manifestly an art and not a science, an art by which, as is true of all arts, the sublime cannot be taught." Given such a view, the attempts by many officers—including Clausewitz—to apply extensive "scientific" principles to warfare were futile. "In war as in art," Moltke himself stated, there "exist no general rules; in neither can talent be replaced by precept."

It is ironic that a good many of Moltke's successors, as well as military historians, so misunderstood his character and principles that they could declare, along with J. F. C. Fuller, that Moltke "looked upon war more as a business than as a science or an art." More than ironic, such misconceptions—fostered, it must be said, by the quiet, methodical personal style that masked Moltke's inner workings—were to prove ultimately dangerous. For the war machine that Moltke built (much like the delicate political balance of European power created by Bismarck) required men of the most refined sensibility for its effective operation. When placed in the hands of officers who truly possessed nothing more than businesslike, parochial competence, it was a device filled with a frightening potential for abuse.

Moltke assumed the responsibilities of chief of the Prussian General Staff in 1857. This post had fallen significantly in stature since the days of Scharnhorst and Gneisenau, who had structured the staff to embody the best elements of the Prussian officer corps during and after the Napoleonic Wars. Though still respected, the General Staff in 1857 was not given a place of real authority in the Prussian army—its chief was not able to report directly to the king or even to the war minister. The transformation from subordinate office to that of virtual supreme commander was Moltke's achievement.

Problems with Italy in 1859 and a subsequent mobilization of the Prussian army revealed the organizational and compositional shortcomings of that body. Over the next few years, under the direction of Chancellor-President Bismarck and War Minister Albrecht von Roon, these problems were dealt with by the creation of a truly national army in which universal conscription, long-term service, and reserve activity were all instituted. It was an impressive undertaking and it ensured that, should the need arise, Prussia could immediately raise hundreds of thousands of men. But the question remained—what would be done with them?

Bismarck clearly intended to use the new Prussian army in precisely the manner advocated by Clausewitz—as an instrument of policy, in this case the policy of unifying the various German states and federations under Prussian hegemony. As conceived by Bismarck, this was a two-step process. First, the other great Central European power, Austria, would have to be denied any future voice in German affairs. Second, France would have to be made to recognize the power and legitimacy of the new German Empire. Both of these goals, Bismarck believed, could be convincingly realized only through battle. It was an opinion shared by Moltke. Given Bismarck's remarkable ability to bait an opponent into war, it remained for the chief of the General Staff to ensure that when the Prussian army took the field, it would meet with success.

Moltke knew that unless this new army could be harnessed by an effective command structure and made to operate under new strategic and operational guidelines, it would be merely a wandering mass, a modern army fettered by Napoleonic concepts. That this could lead to wars of devastating attrition was highlighted by the introduction of new technology—not only railways and greatly improved road systems but advances in small arms and artillery (most notably the rifled bore) that made armies far more effective at the job of destruction.

These fears seemed to be confirmed by events in the United States from 1861 to 1865. The armies of North and South were viewed by Moltke as "mere armed mobs" led by men whose understanding of the conduct of war had not advanced appreciably since Napoleon. Among the most stunning aspects of the war was the failure of the Union forces to make creative use of their technical advantages, especially the railways, in order to create greater mobility and hence break the often static lines of conflict. As for leadership, Grant, like Napoleon, attended to the details of the war's prosecution himself; and although Lee's generals were intensely loyal to their commander, the range of territory involved in the conflict often made it difficult for the cavalier from Virginia to manage its overall planning effectively. Indeed, because each man was dealing not with single battlefields but with barely manageable fronts that covered hundreds of miles, the result was a protracted conflict of unimaginable violence.

Moltke's basic theories of command and strategy, evolving as events in America unfolded, were interrelated: In the modern age of wide fronts and rapid movement, greater *decentralization* was required at the command level so that greater *centralization* could be achieved in the field at crucial moments. The new leader of a national army would have to concede his inability to attend to every detail of a campaign. In entrusting more authority to subordinate commanders, he could hope to "open up" the plane of conflict and threaten the enemy at many points, throwing them into confusion. With proper training and coordination, this many-headed modern army could then be made to concentrate quickly—on the very day of battle, it was hoped. Concentration would take place at key points, enveloping the opponent, cutting him off from supply and support, and ultimately crushing him. Moltke developed his policy of General Directives, which stated, "An order shall contain everything that a commander cannot do by himself, but nothing else."

To many traditionalists, including those in the Prussian army, this resembled a blasphemous departure from the eighteenth-century concept in which an inspired general was the ultimate source of control, moving formations of men like chess pieces. But the Industrial Revolution, as well as the rise of nation-states and huge national armies, had forever changed the character of war. Moltke saw this clearly. He also saw that if his theories were to be successfully applied, there would have to be one body of officers—its members placed throughout the army like a nervous system. Their shared values, ethics, and military principles would enable them to coordinate their actions in the field effectively even if they were unable to communicate directly with each other. Moltke set out to make the General Staff just such an organization.

It was in bringing about this transformation that Moltke's artistic genius shone most brightly. The officers of the Prussian General Staff have often been depicted as a group of robots, each interchangeable with the other, all lacking true creativity. It was precisely this danger that Moltke addressed first. "No plan of operations," he wrote in 1865, "can look with any certainty beyond the first meeting with the major forces of the enemy. . . . All consecutive acts of war are, therefore, not executions of a premeditated plan, but spontaneous actions, directed by military tact. . . . It is obvious that theoretical knowledge will not suffice, but that here the qualities of mind and character come to a free, practical and artistic expression, although schooled by military training and led by experiences from military history or from life itself."

In keeping with this philosophy, Moltke personally directed what he believed would be the key element in his new command structure: the training of staff officers. Each year twelve of the finest students from the Kriegsakademie were selected for service with the chief of the General Staff. This service involved far more than mere bureaucratic training—Moltke had already warned of the dangers of relying on simple "precepts." Rather, it became a doctrinal schooling that encompassed the broad range of interests and studies that had marked Moltke's life, and any officers the chief of the General Staff found wanting on any level—including and especially the intellectual and spiritual—were quickly sent packing. During this training, Moltke's more refined and artistic (though intensely demanding) side showed itself, and he attained an almost mythic status within the army and especially among the officers of the General Staff.

It was a role and a process unprecedented in military, and certainly Prussian, history, and it consumed an increasing portion of Moltke's time and energy. Even his physical appearance came to reflect his increasing departure from Prussian military tradition. White-haired, with delicate features unembellished by the whiskers so favored by his fellow generals and counts, Moltke generally dressed his thin frame in an unadorned uniform and plain cap—certainly he looked more the scholar or artist than the warrior. The loyalty he received from his students was in turn of an unprecedented variety. As Michael Howard has written, "The affection and respect in which he was held by his officers was that of disciples and pupils rather than of subordinates."

To make certain that the General Staff never became isolated from the army as a whole, Moltke required each staff officer to do periodic tours of duty with his regiment. The organization thus became both separate and integral, and a natural instrument through which the spirit and doctrines of its chief could permeate the entire army.

Moltke's system was designed to instill strategic boldness in his officers. It led to what came to be called the "flanking and envelopment" strategy—the formalization of Moltke's theories on the decentralization of command and rapid centralization in the field. The superior ability to move and concentrate offered by this doctrine was further enhanced by shrewd use of railways, telegraphs, and modern artillery, all of which opened the field of operations, freeing up movement and making personal initiative, in combination with a shared military philosophy, all the more vital.

That this philosophy was difficult for many Prussian commanders to absorb was demonstrated by the Prusso-Danish War of 1864, basically a conflict over the disputed duchies of Schleswig-Holstein. Moltke devised a plan in which the Danish flanks would be turned before any significant assault was made on the Danish front line. This would allow the Prussians to move behind the main Danish forces and prevent their escape to the powerful fixed fortifications in Düppel and on the island of Alsen. But key elements of Moltke's plan were ignored by Prussian field commanders, and the Danish got away. The war became a protracted, messy affair. Eventually, Moltke was put in charge of it, and within weeks a Prussian victory was assured—all of which seemed to confirm the validity of his new strategic guidelines.

Outside of these general strategic guidelines, Moltke remained remarkably flexible. Although he never discarded Napoleon's basic concept of the "inner line of operations"—by way of which an army concentrated at the earliest possible moment in order to move quickly against a divided enemy—Moltke often employed "external lines of operation" as well. In this scenario, attractive to him largely because of the increased mobility of modern armies, scattered columns would not be brought together until the actual day of decision to destroy the enemy; movement options would thus be preserved until the very last moment. This idea was employed with spectacular results in the Austrian campaign of 1866, which culminated in the Battle of Königgrätz (or Sadowa) and established Prussia as the preeminent German power.

That triumph was achieved over the worried protestations of Bismarck, many of the commanding generals of the armies in the field, and various members of the Prussian royal family. For Moltke's plan of attack defied tradition: He split the Prussians into three army groups, which entered Austria with orders not to concentrate until told to do so by the chief of the General Staff—and those orders to concentrate would come only *after* the Austrians had done so themselves. Previously, allowing an enemy prior concentration had meant disaster; one's own forces could be destroyed piecemeal. Moltke was gambling that the Prussian army's new organization and mobility would bring a favorable number of forces to bear not before the decisive battle but at the instant of engagement.

Such a successful employment of external lines of operation seemed to indicate their further use against France in 1870. But the ever-flexible Moltke was not above employing an inner line of operations if the situation warranted it. Even before the outbreak of war, the configuration of France's railway system planted in Moltke's mind the correct impression that Napoleon III would be forced to concentrate his armies around the fortifications at Metz and Strasbourg—locations separated by the Vosges Mountains. The opportunity to drive a wedge between these two groups and defeat first one and then the other was obvious to the chief of the General Staff. Having, in the minds of many military analysts of the day, effectively killed off the "inner line of operations" at Königgrätz, Moltke apparently intended to revive it in 1870.

Driving hard into France, Moltke engaged the first French army group initially at Vionville-Mars-la-Tour and then at Gravelotte-St.-Privat. During both of these battles, the Prussian field commanders made tactical errors that were counterbalanced by the almost uncanny ability of Moltke's staff officers to sense the plight of their comrades and come to each other's aid. The successful outcome of these engagements forced the first French army group into the fixed fortifications at Metz. The other French group, which escaped Strasbourg, was pursued to Sedan and engaged in a devastating battle of envelopment whose successful outcome had been preordained by Moltke's willingness to shift his overall plan of action to the inner line at the start of the campaign. As the chief of the General Staff himself wrote, "Strategy is a system of ad hoc expedients; it is more than knowledge, it is the application of knowledge to practical life, the development of an original idea in accordance with continually changing circumstances. It is the art of action under the pressure of the most difficult conditions." Here again is the intangible spirit of creativity and spontaneity that was so very characteristic of Moltke's carefully concealed personality.

That spirit, like Moltke's organizational innovations, has often been questioned by historians. Continuing his criticism, J. F. C. Fuller complains that Moltke strayed too far from the Napoleonic ideal of command because he simply "brought his armies to their starting point and then abdicated his command and unleashed them." Yet as Dwight Eisenhower demonstrated during World War II, the success of the modern supreme commander lies in precisely this lightness of control. Others have noted along with Cyril Falls that while Moltke was certainly bold, "his boldness might have led him into the gravest trouble because of his habit of acting on assumptions when in doubt" about enemy movements. Moltke himself admitted that the success of his strategic doctrines depended "not merely on calculable factors, space and time, but also on the outcome of previous minor battles, on the weather, on false news; in brief, on all that is called chance and luck in human life." More than any commander of his century, Moltke believed in calculated risk—the very phrase sums up his character. To note the dangers of such an approach is not to disprove its overall validity.

The Austro-Prussian and Franco-Prussian wars stand as the most sophisticated exhibitions of organizational and strategic brilliance in the century and a half that separated Napoleon and Hitler. Certainly, the lightness of touch involved in Moltke's style of command occasionally created openings for blunders, particularly tactical blunders, on the part of subordinate commanders. But it is a testament to him that none of these blunders ever seriously jeopardized his overall campaigns. Indeed, the constant infusion of spirit into his officers by the chief of the General Staff often allowed the Prussians to turn such blunders into successes, as at Vionville-Mars-la-Tour and Gravelotte-St.-Privat.

Moltke took an interest in politics, of course, but he did not interfere in political matters to any greater extent than delivering speeches in the Upper House of the Reichstag, which were essentially confined to military matters. Nor did he appreciate excessive political meddling in military affairs, as was demonstrated during his famous dispute with Bismarck concerning the bombardment of Paris at the conclusion of the Franco-Prussian War. Moltke argued that bombardment would only prolong resistance, but in the end the chancellor prevailed. Moltke did hold political opinions (they tended toward the more liberal wing of the Monarchist party) and above all he believed in Clausewitz's maxim that war was an instrument of policy. A war without a specific, limited political goal was one of Moltke's nightmares. His assessment of the Austro-Prussian conflict, for example, was typical and shrewd:

> The war of 1866 was entered on not because the existence of Prussia was threatened, nor in obedience to public opinion and the voice of the people: It was a struggle, long foreseen and calmly prepared for, recognized as a necessity by the Cabinet, not for territorial aggrandizement or material advantage, but for an ideal end—the establishment of power. Not a foot of land was extracted from conquered Austria, but it had to renounce all part in the hegemony of Germany.

Similarly, the Franco-Prussian War was undertaken to consolidate the German Empire and to convince the French that Central Europe was no longer an area over which they could hold unquestioned sway. Following that conflict, Moltke based his extensive staff contingency planning on a skilled perception of the shifting realities of political power on the Continent. At times he directed the General Staff to prepare for war with the Western powers, and at times for war with the nations of the East. He regarded a two-front war as anathema, but if it could not be avoided, he said, campaigns in both East and West must have as their goal quick knockout blows; Germany could only lose in a protracted conflict, particularly one that involved an invasion of Russia. This last prospect Moltke saw as ultimately disastrous and of no conceivable political value.

The departure of Bismarck and the accession of Kaiser Wilhelm II to the German throne were matters of deep concern to Moltke: The kaiser was not a man to be persuaded of the value of specific and limited political goals. In a speech before the Upper House of the Reichstag in 1890, the year before his death, Moltke warned the nation's political leaders: "Gentlemen, when the war, which for more than ten years has hung over our heads like a sword of Damocles, when this war breaks out, its length will be incalculable and its end nowhere in sight. . . . Gentlemen, it may be a seven-year, it may be a thirty-year war—and woe to him who sets fire to Europe, who first puts the flame to the powderkeg!"

Perceptive as ever in his ninetieth year, Moltke knew only too well who that culprit was likely to be. He had built the weapon that would allow the rash cult of belligerent militarists around the kaiser to start their total war in the name of goals that were simplemindedly vague. Their failure to understand the subtler points of Moltke's doctrines further ensured that before long the old man's nightmare would become a reality, and that Germany would be the ultimate loser in a protracted war of attrition on two fronts.

In 1891 he died—most typically, in silence, with no last words for posterity, his eyes fixed on a portrait of his long-dead wife. The General Staff and the army it commanded remained behind to ravage Europe. Like Bismarck, Moltke had left an emptiness in German affairs that needed to be filled by men of wisdom and balance. Instead, it was filled by the arrogant and the deluded—men who could never grasp the creative, artistic side of his military philosophy. Silently Moltke had made his name; silently that name passed into the background of history, as the abuses committed by more vociferous men in control of his creations came to the fore and lingered there.

Nevertheless, his legacy was lasting. Within a quarter of a century after Moltke's death, the armies of virtually all the world's major powers had adopted staff systems that were variations of the Prussian model that he devised. If his immediate successors in Germany did not generally share his strategic acumen and his taste for boldness, another generation of German officers, who raced across Poland in 1939 and France in 1940, did. And in the remarkable coordination of frequently feuding Allied field commanders during their campaigns against the Axis powers in the Second World War may be seen the lingering effects of Moltke's organizational and command revolutions.

Moltke's prodigious intellect touched and reshaped nearly every aspect of modern warfare. This achievement even his still-elusive personality cannot shroud.

Crook and Miles, Fighting and Feuding on the Indian Frontier

by ROBERT M. UTLEY

As antiguerrilla fighters, George Crook and Nelson A. Miles have had few peers. By adapting to the tactics of their Indian adversaries in the last wars of the Plains and the Southwest; by making use of Indian against Indian; by relying on small, mobile forces and surprise; and by living off the land when they had to, Crook and Miles were able to bring 250 years of armed conflict between white settlers and Native Americans to an end. But their professional rivalry was something else, epitomizing everything that was bad about the army at the time. Robert M. Utley, one of the most eminent historians of the American West, notes with regret that people may remember Crook and Miles less for what they did than for what they were: vain, petty, obsessed with rank and precedence, and hungry for applause—tireless in-fighters who lobbied and clawed their unseemly way to the top, only to find that time had passed them by.

Crook and Miles. For the Indian-fighting U.S. Army of 1865–90, these names became inseparably linked. Circumstances and personality locked George Crook and Nelson A. Miles in a bitter rivalry that engrossed the army even beyond the death of Crook.

Curiously, it was a long-distance rivalry, conducted chiefly through aides, friends, and sympathetic newsmen. Rarely did the two actually meet, much less face each other down. Yet even an officer corps inured to epidemic bickering found their twenty-two-year feud shocking. The Crook-Miles conflict cast both men in an ugly light and dramatized some of the worst traits of the military profession.

As the years slipped by, however, the linkage between Crook and Miles took on another dimension: They emerged as the regular army's brightest stars in the West. In Indian fighting and "Indian thinking," neither had a peer. Unlike most other frontier commanders, they recognized the military implications of an enemy vastly different from the Confederates and a terrain vastly different from Virginia or Georgia. To their new mission they brought strategic and tactical innovation combined with an energy and persistence unusual in the regular army. Until the frontier disappeared in 1890, they played decisive roles in the most significant collisions between Indians and the army.

George Crook seemed the more personally appealing, an image that he (and his devoted aides) cultivated. An outdoorsman to the core, an accomplished hunter and sportsman, he enjoyed the powerful physique of a hardworking farmer. He looked like one, too. Rarely seen in uniform, he took the field in a serviceable canvas suit and with a pith helmet perched precariously on his big, closely cropped head. His long, reddish blond whiskers parted naturally at the chin, and on campaign he frequently braided each half and tied them behind his neck. For such a figure, a sturdy mule seemed more fitting than a spirited charger.

In the Sioux campaign of 1876, Crook's aide, Lieutenant John G. Bourke, glimpsed a scene that captured the contrast between his chief and other generals. General Alfred H. Terry, immaculately uniformed even in the midst of campaign, chanced on Crook clad only in his underwear and seated in a creek washing his clothes. They looked as if he himself had washed them, noted Bourke, "and also as if he had had a hand in their fabrication."

A soldier's doggerel of 1876 expressed the view from below:

> *I'd like to be a packer,*
> *And pack with George F. Crook*
> *And dressed up in my canvas suit*
> *To be for him mistook.*
> *I'd braid my beard in two long tails,*
> *And idle all the day*
> *In whittling sticks and wondering*
> *What the New York papers say.*

Crook's most pronounced trait was a reticence so extreme that it often spilled into rudeness. The general, commented a subaltern, "has a faculty for silence that is absolutely astonishing." Aides and subordinates found him so infuriatingly uncommunicative that they could only guess at his plans and expectations. Some wondered if he even had any.

Combined with reticence that made him "brusque to the point of severity" was "stubbornness, stolidity, rugged resolution, and bulldog tenacity," said Lieutenant Bourke. "He is a strange man," observed another officer. "He is thought cold and perhaps heartless by many. Certainly his face indicates ambition, determination, and a crafty—almost fox-like—shrewdness." The Apaches, in fact, called him the Gray Fox.

Crook thought well of himself and poorly of others. He could entertain uncharitable opinions of rivals and bear a grudge almost as intensely as Miles, the champion grudge-bearer of the army. Shortly after the death of his one-time friend and West Point classmate Philip H. Sheridan, Crook wrote: "The adulations heaped on him by a grateful nation for his supposed genius turned his head, which, added to his natural disposition, caused him to bloat his little carcass with debauchery and dissipation, which carried him off prematurely."

Beneath Crook's placid exterior boiled anger and resentment, the more ardent because suppressed. He felt his Civil War services were insufficiently appreciated, and he never forgave Sheridan for supposed injustices.

In truth, Crook had not compiled an especially distinguished wartime record. West Point (1852), Indian service on the Pacific coast, and Ohio political connections gained him a colonelcy in the volunteer army. A commander of both cavalry and infantry, he fought in West Virginia, in the Shenandoah Valley under Sheridan, and in the Appomattox campaign. But his best-known exploit, in February 1865, was to get himself captured by Confederate guerrillas while taking his ease at a hotel in Cumberland, Maryland. Crook emerged from the war a major general of volunteers with a brevet of major general in the regular army.

As Colonel Crook marched to war at the head of an Ohio regiment in 1861, Nelson A. Miles, an obscure young Boston crockery clerk who had read deeply in military history and theory, sewed on the straps of a first lieutenant. Courage, leadership, hard work, capacity to learn and grow, and consuming ambition rewarded Miles with rapid advancement. By Appomattox he had made himself a popular hero: four times wounded; veteran of every major battle of the Army of the Potomac except Gettysburg; successful regimental, brigade, division, and corps commander. Like Crook, he ended the war a major general of volunteers with a brevet of major general in the regular army. He was twenty-six years old, a tall, handsome figure with a neatly trimmed mustache and jaunty imperial.

Commissioned colonel of a regiment of black regular infantry, Miles devoted the next forty years to a single-minded quest for fame and rank. In no other officer did the twin drives of vanity and ambition attain greater intensity. They powered a fierce competitiveness that goaded him into shamelessly flaunting his own genuine abilities and successes and tastelessly deriding those of others. Nasty controversies littered his path to the army's top rank. "Brave Peacock," Theodore Roosevelt called him.

"I have known General Miles since he transferred from the web-footed brunettes [black infantry] to the 5th Infantry," recalled a frontier veteran in 1892. "Too much circus, too little brain." The indictment was only half-right: Despite the circus, he had the brain. At the same time, another observer looked on him, accurately, as "a splendid field soldier, prompt, bold, and magnetic. He was always in high spirits."

On the Indian frontier, Crook gained prominence before Miles. Commissioned lieutenant colonel of the regular 23rd Infantry, he was posted to the Pacific Northwest late in 1866. There he conducted a masterly campaign against recalcitrant Paiutes. He had grasped the essence of Indian combat in prewar California, and for two years, at great hardship to himself, his troops, and his animals, he kept after the enemy with such unremitting obstinacy that he won a decisive victory. This earned him the acclaim of his superiors and, in 1871, assignment to command the Department of Arizona in his brevet grade of major general.

That a mere lieutenant colonel could gain such preference aggravated Nelson Miles, commanding the 5th Infantry at Fort Leavenworth, Kansas. If anyone was to be assigned in his brevet grade, he felt he should be the one. He complained, and he complained even more earnestly two years later when he, a full colonel, failed to win assignment to the District of New Mexico as a brevet major general.

Miles enjoyed ideal connections for voicing complaints—or so he thought. His wife's uncle was the four-star commanding general of the U.S. Army, William Tecumseh Sherman. As Miles never seemed to grasp, however, efforts to exploit the family connection did him more harm than good. He tried repeatedly, and year after year the acerbic Sherman turned aside his nephew-in-law's chronic complaints and stoutly resisted advancing his interests even when he deserved it. "I have told him plainly," Sherman exploded in a letter to General Sheridan in 1879, "that I know of no way to satisfy his ambitions but to surrender to him absolute power over the whole Army with President and Congress thrown in."

In his new assignment, Brevet Major General Crook met the toughest challenges the Indian frontier could offer—deserts and mountains that used up troops like no other landscape in the nation, and Apache Indians whose fighting skills surpassed those of all other tribes. In his brilliant Tonto Basin campaign, however, Crook again prevailed. His experience in the Northwest had convinced him that a vigorous and mobile attack would win the day, and by the spring of 1873 all the rebelling Apache bands had surrendered. Arizonans showered the taciturn hero with praise and honors.

More gratifying still, the first message over the newly completed telegraph wire to department headquarters at Fort Whipple brought electrifying news: In a jarring break with the tradition of seniority, President Ulysses S. Grant had advanced Lieutenant Colonel Crook over every colonel in the army, including an outraged Nelson Miles, and awarded him the star of a brigadier general.

In Arizona as in Oregon, the key to Crook's success lay in innovative techniques. He discarded wagon trains for pack mules, developing their management into a science, even an art, and gaining a mobility that almost matched that of his foes. He also made extensive use of Indian against Indian. Indian scouts knew where the enemy was most likely to be found and how he was most likely to be caught. The will to resist, moreover, tended to fade when fugitives discovered their own people on their trail. Crook persisted, preferably in winter, until the quarry despaired of finding relief. "No excuse was to be accepted for leaving a trail," recalled Lieutenant Bourke; "if horses played out, the enemy must be followed on foot, and no sacrifice should be left untried to make the campaign short, sharp, and decisive."

When Crook transferred to the northern Plains in 1875 to head the

Department of the Platte, he was the nation's most successful Indian fighter. No other came close. George A. Custer, Ranald S. Mackenzie, and Eugene A. Carr had all scored successes, but none could boast the repeated achievements that backed Crook's stature.

Nelson Miles had no record at all. But even as Crook settled into his headquarters at Fort Omaha, Miles was well on his way to creating one.

Opportunity finally opened in the autumn of 1874, with the outbreak of the Red River War. Cheyennes, Kiowas, and Comanches fled the reservation agencies at which they were enrolled in the Indian Territory and sought refuge on the Staked Plain of the Texas Panhandle. Miles led one of five columns that Sheridan, the army's sole lieutenant general and commander of the Division of the Missouri, ordered to converge on the Indian sanctuaries.

Typically, Miles complained about the failings of others, but he won a battlefield success and in the end, more than any other commander, won the war. Victory came not through unconventional methods like Crook's but through sheer tenacity. Long after the other columns had returned to their stations, he scoured the wintry plains. In swirling blizzards, bitter gales, and subzero temperatures, his foot soldiers kept pushing, always pushing. "It was quite amusing," Miles wrote to his wife, Mary, "to hear them sing 'Marching Through Georgia' way out on these plains." One by one, the scattered bands of fugitives drifted eastward and surrendered at their agencies. The Red River War ended major hostilities on the southern Plains and brought lasting peace with the Cheyennes, Kiowas, and Comanches.

Just over a year later, opportunity again beckoned—and brought Miles into direct competition with Crook for the first time. The theater of war was Montana's Powder and Yellowstone river country, the enemy the mighty Sioux. Three columns—under Crook, Brigadier General Alfred H. Terry, and Colonel John Gibbon—had converged on the Sioux domain with the mission of driving the "nontreaty" bands of Sitting Bull and Crazy Horse into the Indian agencies along the Missouri River and in northern Nebraska.

In this campaign the Gray Fox's winning streak ran out. Unaccountably, he did almost nothing right. An initial thrust northward from Fort Fetterman, Wyoming, in March 1876 was turned back by numbing winter, and a battle on the Powder River was mismanaged by subordinates. The second advance collapsed on June 17 at the Battle of the Rosebud. Sioux surprised his formidable command during morning coffee break and would have overrun it but for the quick action of his Crow and Shoshoni auxiliaries. In the ensuing fight, he nearly lost control of his units and then, battered and shaken, limped back to his supply base and refused to move again until heavily reinforced. A week later, while he fished in a mountain stream, the Sioux destroyed Custer on the Little Bighorn. Had Crook's vaunted aggressive spirit not deserted him after the Rosebud, he would almost certainly have fallen in with Custer before that fateful June 25 when the 7th Cavalry met disaster.

The loss of Custer, Terry's striking arm, demoralized the forces of Terry and Gibbon, huddled apprehensively on the Yellowstone River a hundred miles north of Crook. Miles and the 5th Infantry were among the reinforcements Sheridan rushed to the Yellowstone.

Terry and Crook finally united on August 10, 1876. It was one of the few times Miles and Crook faced each other in person, though not for long. A disgusted Miles swiftly perceived that the two generals would never catch Sitting Bull and his triumphant Sioux. The combined army force of 4,000 infantry and cavalry was too big, and anyway the Indians had scattered. Seeking escape from a doomed campaign, Miles persuaded Terry to allow him to operate independently along the Yellowstone and try to net any fugitives headed north for the British territory of western Canada.

Miles had predicted accurately. The heavy force wore out in heat and dust, then wallowed in mud as cold autumnal rains drenched the valleys draining toward the Yellowstone. Terry and Crook bickered over what to do and at last went their separate ways. Terry gave up and returned to his headquarters. Crook embarked on a misconceived movement toward the Black Hills. Rain, mud, dwindling rations, and a dearth of wood and grass so punished the command that it could scarcely summon the strength to fight when Sioux turned up in the line of march. The clash at Slim Buttes on September 9, 1876, although nearly barren of results, was the only action of the campaign that could be called a victory.

Miles, by contrast, planted himself on the Yellowstone River and prepared to tough out the fierce Montana winter. "They expected us to hive up," he wrote Mary of the Sioux, "but we are not the hiving kind." From his rude log cantonment at the mouth of the Tongue River, the driven colonel and what the Indians called his "walk-a-heaps" hounded the Sioux all winter and into the summer of 1877. Buried in huge coats of buffalo fur, often mounted on mules or captured Indian ponies, they marched, parleyed, marched, fought, and marched in a repeat of the Staked Plain operation. Noting the cold-weather gear of the soldier chief, the Indians named him "Bear Coat."

Miles did not have the field to himself—although (bypassing Terry and Sheridan, his department and division superiors) he implored Sherman to give him supreme command in the Sioux country. To the south, Crook recovered his offensive spirit and launched a winter operation. On November 25, 1876, his hard-driving cavalry chief, Ranald Mackenzie, fell on the Cheyenne village of Dull Knife in a canyon of the Bighorn Mountains and inflicted a terrible defeat.

More provoking to Miles, Crook sent Indian emissaries to coax the fugitives to surrender. Miles had his own peace feelers out, and he fumed over Crook's effrontery in trying to steal "his" Indians. If the effort succeeded, Miles told Mary, "Crook will go out to meet them and claim the credit of bagging them. Yet he has had no more to do with it than if he had been in Egypt."

As Miles feared, most of the Sioux, including Crazy Horse, gave up to Crook. But some 300 Cheyennes and a handful of Sioux, drawn by the magnetism of their winter adversary, did surrender to Bear Coat on the Yellowstone. Sitting Bull and his immediate following fled across the international boundary.

The campaign of 1876 cast the rivalry between Miles and Crook in personal terms. Miles thought Crook's lamely defensive annual report, exaggerating accomplishments and glossing over failures, "the most extraordinary document ever signed by a Brigadier General." "A man who was a failure during the war and has been ever since," declared Miles, Crook had "accomplished nothing but [to] give the Indians renewed confidence."

Not surprisingly, Miles judged his own role decisive. He had "fought and defeated larger and better-armed bodies of hostile Indians than any other officer since the history of Indian warfare commenced," he boasted to Sherman, whose support he solicited to secure appointment as secretary of war or at least commander of a department.

For all his self-congratulation, Miles had in fact played the decisive role in bringing the campaign to a successful conclusion. Boldness, innovation, hard work, and above all perseverance had yielded impressive results. Crook, on the other hand, had turned in the sorriest performance of his career. "The fact of the case is," Sheridan confided to Sherman, "the operations of Generals Terry and Crook will not bear criticism, and my only thought has been to let them sleep."

For six years Crook remained in virtual eclipse, pursuing the routine duties of departmental command, while Miles went on to greater glory. In the autumn of 1877, Miles interrupted his Sioux operations for a swift dash across Montana to head off Chief Joseph's Nez Percés. Rather than submit to a new reservation in Idaho, the Nez Percés had conducted a heroic fighting retreat across the Rocky Mountains in a desperate effort to find sanctuary in the British possessions. Brigadier General Oliver O. Howard marched hard in pursuit, but could never quite overtake the fugitives. At Bearpaw Mountain, thirty miles south of the international boundary, Miles intercepted the Indians. After a bloody battle and a five-day siege, on October 5 Chief Joseph stepped forward to give up. General Howard had arrived on the field but magnanimously declined to assume command until Miles had accepted the surrender. Even so, Miles claimed all the credit for himself, an act of meanness that infuriated Howard's officers and set off a public controversy.

For three years, 1877-80, Miles and his little command aggressively patrolled the international boundary to keep Sitting Bull off U.S. territory. The colonel ached to dart across the line and smash the Sioux camps, but Sherman warned him that any violation of British sovereignty in these western Canadian territories would land him in deep trouble.

Throughout his Montana years, Miles agitated ceaselessly for promotion to brigadier general. Montana and Massachusetts interests urged President Rutherford B. Hayes—ironically a close friend of Crook's—to give the next vacancy to Miles. The marriage of Mary's sister to Senator Don Cameron brought a muscular Pennsylvania political machine to the effort. In 1880, creating a vacancy (and bitter resentments) by forcibly retiring Edward O.C. Ord, an old comrade and West Point classmate of Sherman's, President Hayes awarded the star of a brigadier to Nelson Miles.

In another irony, the promotion sent Miles into an eclipse even deeper than Crook's. Assigned to command the Department of the Columbia, he was not present at Fort Buford, Dakota, a few months later to receive the surrender of Sitting Bull. He would have immensely enjoyed that ceremony, which marked the end of the Sioux Wars, for more than any other officer he had brought it about. Moreover, as Miles fretted in the obscurity of office routine (and mobilized for an assault on the next vacancy in the grade of major general), Crook once more moved to center stage.

The stage, again, was that rocky, cactus-studded land of Arizona, where the Apaches had confounded one after another of Crook's successors and prompted a universal demand for his return. Most of the Apaches had been settled on the San Carlos Reservation, but a handful would not cooperate. When something displeased them, they simply picked up and left, cutting a swath of blood and terror southward to hideouts in Mexico's towering Sierra Madre. These rebels followed a number of captains, but standing above all was a cunning, ruthless, uncommonly able leader the whites called Geronimo.

When Crook assumed command of the Department of Arizona in September 1882, Geronimo and other "renegades" were in their Sierra Madre lairs. A bloody raid into Arizona in March 1883 set Crook in motion. With Mexican permission, he crossed the boundary on May 1. The campaign demonstrated the efficacy of his peculiar style of Indian warfare. Expertly managed pack trains gave him the mobility to go anywhere the enemy went. Apache scouts led him to hidden enemy camps. Shrewd diplomatic skills combined with rare insight into the Apache mind gave him negotiating advantages. In a critical weeklong parley, Crook persuaded the Apaches to return to their reservation.

"He was a hard fighter," one of Geronimo's warriors recalled of Crook years later, "a strong enemy when we were hostile. But he played fair with us afterward and did what he could to protect the Indians. We actually loved General Crook, and even today think of him, and talk about him, with genuine affection."

When in May 1885 San Carlos again exploded with discontent, and Geronimo and others bolted for Mexico, Crook pursued the same strategy that had won before. Again he enticed Geronimo into negotiations, and on March 25 and 27, 1886, in tense meetings in Canyon de Los Embudos, the Apache leaders allowed themselves to be talked into surrendering. En route northward, however, the Indians chanced on an itinerant whiskey peddler, and after a wild drunk, Geronimo and a small following headed for the mountains once more.

Geronimo's escape brought to a climax disagreements that had been festering between Crook and Sheridan, who had been occupying the commanding general's office in Washington since Sherman's retirement. Sheridan distrusted the loyalty and reliability of the Indian scouts and wanted greater visibility given to the regulars. Crook had resisted, but with Geronimo once again in the Sierra Madre, Sheridan's patience snapped. He ordered Crook to repudiate promises made to Indians who had not bolted with Geronimo, to demand unconditional surrender of those who had, and to go after them with regulars. Tired, discouraged, and certain that his own methods were superior, Crook asked to be relieved. Sheridan lost no time in ordering a replacement to Arizona: Brigadier General Nelson A. Miles.

"General Crook seems very much worried and disappointed," Miles informed his wife after the two men met for a formal transfer of command that must have been strained. In a later letter, Miles, provoked by Crook's remarks to the press, could not resist a parting crack: "I am also annoyed by the statements thrown out by Crook. He made a dead failure of this, as he has of every other campaign."

Reflecting Sheridan's views, Miles turned to the 5,000 regulars under his command. Forming a tightly knit strike force under Captain Henry W. Lawton, he sent it into Mexico. Through the brutally hot summer of 1886, Lawton combed the Sierra Madre, an exhausting and seemingly futile ordeal. Regulars could keep the quarry on the run, Miles discovered, but could not close in a fight. Taking care not to let the shift be too visible, he began to make greater use of Apache scouts. In addition, he summoned Lieutenant Charles B. Gatewood, a Crook protégé experienced in dealing with the Apaches, to seek out Geronimo for peace talks.

Miles also turned his attention to those of Geronimo's people who remained on the San Carlos Reservation. "Crook's policy was to treat those Indians at the Apache reservation more as conquerors than prisoners," he complained. "They have been petted and, if that policy is continued, they will furnish warriors for the next twenty years." The solution was nothing less than the deportation to Florida of all the Chiricahua and Warm Springs Apaches.

Thus when Lieutenant Gatewood finally made contact with Geronimo, he was able to announce the startling news that the reservation no longer contained any of the chief's kinsmen. Disconsolate, Geronimo agreed to talk with the new soldier chief. At Skeleton Canyon, Arizona, on September 4, 1886, Geronimo formally surrendered to Miles. On the Fort Bowie parade ground, the 4th Cavalry band played "Auld Lang Syne" as wagons bore the last Apache holdouts to the railroad for the long journey to Florida.

Once again Miles had won, a victory celebrated by grateful Arizonans and made doubly sweet by contrast with Crook's apparent failure. Again there was controversy, as Miles gathered all the credit to himself and his minions. Lawton was lionized and promoted, while Gatewood was ignored. The Apache exile also brought Crook and Miles into public conflict. Even Crook's faithful Indian scouts had been sent east, and the general fought hard for the return of the Apaches to the West, if not to their Arizona homeland. The crusade solidified Crook's reputation as a leading member of the small fraternity of "humanitarian generals."

In 1888 Crook and Miles competed for a major general's vacancy opened by the retirement of General Terry. Despite the intense lobbying of Miles's partisans, President Grover Cleveland honored the rule of seniority and awarded Terry's two stars to Crook. He and his staff, unobtrusive in civilian clothes, moved into the headquarters of the Division of the Missouri in Chicago. From this base, against vigorous opposition organized by Miles, Crook continued to battle for justice to the Apaches.

With his wife, the general lived in Chicago's Grand Pacific Hotel. On the morning of March 21, 1890, he rose from his bed and began his daily calisthenics. "Exercising with 'Indian clubs' for a few minutes before having breakfast," reported his aide, "he suddenly staggered, gasped for breath, and was dead." He was sixty-one.

As the army's senior brigadier, Miles stood next in line. Powerful supporters besieged President Benjamin Harrison. But the president, reported Senator John Sherman (another of Mary's uncles), thought Miles "a troublesome man to get along with" and resisted. Blaming Crook's friends, Miles rushed to Washington, presented himself at the White House, and talked his way into Harrison's favor. At last he could don the straps of a major general and move into Crook's Chicago headquarters.

That same year of 1890 a new faith, the ghost dance religion, swept the Indian tribes of the West, promising spiritual help in throwing off the white man's yoke. Violence threatened on the Sioux reservations of South Dakota, part of Major General Miles's new jurisdiction. The division commander himself hastened to the scene to oversee the employment of 3,500 soldiers concentrated from all over the nation.

A bloody clash dashed Miles's delicate effort to negotiate a peaceful resolution. On December 29 the 7th Cavalry sought to disarm Chief Big Foot's Sioux village on Wounded Knee Creek. Battle erupted. Troopers and warriors died in vicious fighting at close quarters, and women and children by the score were shredded by Hotchkiss cannon sweeping the village.

Summoning his years of deepening insight into the Indian mind, however, Miles combined force with skilled diplomacy to prod the Sioux into ending the rebellion. On January 15, 1891, 4,000 Sioux streamed into the Pine Ridge Agency as Kicking Bear, chief apostle of the ghost dance, laid his rifle at Miles's feet.

Watching the Indians swarm over the hills on that day, the general recognized the occasion as historic. It was a sight, he told a reporter, "never again to be witnessed in Indian warfare on this continent." He was right. Wounded Knee marked the last major Indian battle in four centuries of Indian-white conflict.

To symbolize the event, a week later Miles staged a grand review. With Sioux stolidly watching from the hills and a winter gale whipping the colored capes of the soldiers, regiment after regiment paraded before the commanding general. His gray hair flying in the wind, an excited Miles took the salute as the 1st Infantry band played "Garry Owen," Custer's rollicking battle song, and the frontier era drew to a close.

This was Miles's grandest moment. What followed, even though he reached the top and received the third star of a lieutenant general, was bitter anticlimax. In the Spanish-American War, his lack of flexibility denied him glory, and his subsequent opposition to the military reforms that introduced the general-staff system brought his career to a painful conclusion. He could not accept the extinction of a post held by Washington, Scott, Grant, and Sherman and retired as the last of the army's commanding generals. In his retirement years, however, controversy and rancor faded, and the portly old general who graced the military ceremonies of the national capital stood as a venerable reminder of the "Old Army."

In the spring of 1925, in his eighty-fifth year, General Miles took his grandchildren to the circus. The band played the national anthem. As he hoisted his ample frame to attention and rendered the salute to the flag, a heart attack felled him as suddenly as one had taken Crook thirty-five years earlier.

In the history of the last Indian Wars, George Crook and Nelson A. Miles are destined forever to be joined. Their professional rivalry engaged the army for two decades. It stamps both as well endowed with characteristics prevalent throughout the officer corps—vanity, pettiness, disdain for peers, hunger for applause, and obsession with rank and precedence. Crook concealed his flaws behind a taciturnity often equated with kindness and generosity, while Miles, adept at Indian diplomacy, proved so inept at human relations as to make himself widely disliked. Professionally and personally, both represented unattractive dimensions of the regular establishment.

At the same time, Crook and Miles were the army's star frontier performers—bold, energetic, innovative, and understanding in their attitudes toward the Indians. Against the Paiutes and Apaches, Crook more than made up for his inexplicable failures against the Sioux. His campaigns against the Apaches, especially, stand as masterpieces of guerrilla warfare. That Miles accepted the surrender of Geronimo does not obscure Crook's decisive contributions.

Overall, however, Miles could claim the more significant record—in the Red River War of 1874–75, the Sioux War of 1876–81, the Nez Percé outbreak of 1877, the Geronimo campaign of 1886, and the final confrontation with the Sioux in 1890–91. Despite an obnoxious personality, Nelson A. Miles must be credited as the most successful and historically significant Indian fighter of the final decades of Indian warfare.

The Kipkororor Chronicles

by ROBERT F. JONES

The name means, in the Nandi dialect, "ostrich feather"—he always wore two plumes in his pith helmet—but he was better known as Captain Richard Meinertzhagen, of the King's African Rifles. He belongs to that small but notable group of British military eccentrics that included Sir Richard Burton, Orde Wingate, and T.E. Lawrence. Meinertzhagen was one of those outspoken loners, the journalist and novelist Robert F. Jones writes, "willing to take any risk, endure any hardship, in any part of the world where duty called—the wilder the better." A soldier foremost (and a good one), Meinertzhagen was also a hunter, ornithologist, adventurer, diarist, Zionist—and killer. ("I was surprised," noted the nephew of the gentle Beatrice Webb, "at the ease with which a bayonet goes into a man's body. One scarcely feels it unless it goes in to the hilt.") Meinertzhagen's most murderously exemplary adventures took place on the remote plains of East Africa at the beginning of this century, a time when, as the saying went, the sun never set on the British Empire.

African memory is long, and up in the Nandi country of western Kenya they still remember the tall, fierce *mzungu* (white man) called Kipkororor. He was the English officer who killed the *laibon* Koitalel in hand-to-hand combat on a thorn-studded slope overlooking Lake Victoria in 1905. And it was his company of King's African Rifles that captured hundreds of Nandi cattle, thousands of their sheep, and shot, clubbed, or speared to death many of the 500 Nandi warriors who died in the subsequent fighting. The laibon was the tribe's chief witch doctor, a spiritual and political leader whose role among the Nandi would be roughly equivalent to that played by the Ayatollah Khomeini in Iran's recent past.

On the KAR muster rolls of the period, Kipkororor—which means "ostrich feather" in Nandi—was better known as Captain Richard Meinertzhagen, who always wore two such plumes around his pith helmet as a form of rude camouflage. There are Nandi even now who would gladly tickle your ribs with a spear for speaking too favorably of Kipkororor.

If Meinertzhagen is remembered at all today in the non-Nandi world, it is as an outstanding ornithologist. His *Birds of Arabia* is the standard work on that subject, and falconers claw like stooping kestrels for copies of his *Pirates & Predators,* a definitive text on the Old World raptors. In his soldiering days, however, Meinertzhagen ranked with such notable British military eccentrics as Sir Richard Burton, Orde Wingate, Wilfred Thesiger, and T.E. Lawrence as a controversial, outspoken loner willing to take any risk, endure any hardship, in any part of the world where duty called—the wilder the better.

Yet by today's "enlightened" standards, these men were monsters. Fearless and full of good intentions—after all, they were making the world's dark corners safe for Christianity and trade—British colonial officers were at the same time capable of racism, religious bigotry, sexism, and bloodlust. Rather than feeling remorse over killing their enemies, many of them exulted in wholesale slaughter. They could show kindness, generosity, and love to the tribes they dealt with on one day, and the next day butcher them. There is a word in KiSwahili, the lingua franca of East and Central Africa, that best exemplifies this bloody-minded quality: *kali,* which means strict to the point of ferocity. Richard Meinertzhagen was as *kali* as they come.

Moreover, he looked the part. He was a whipcord-lean, broad-shouldered and muscular six-footer with close-cropped dark hair and a long, often saturnine face adorned by a tidily trimmed mustache. He had fiery, close-set dark eyes, a saber slash of a mouth that only occasionally relaxed in a wry smile, and an aquiline nose that lent him a resemblance to the hawks and eagles he had admired since childhood. Even T.E. Lawrence, who befriended him in the Near East during World War I, was more than a little awed by him. He described Meinertzhagen as "a student of migrating birds" who "drifted into soldiering" and whose "hot immoral hatred of the enemy expressed itself as readily in trickery as in violence." Meinertzhagen, said Lawrence,

> knew no half measures. He was logical, an idealist of the deepest, and so possessed by his convictions that he was willing to harness evil to the chariot of good. He was a strategist, a geographer and a silent, laughing, masterful man; who took as blithe a pleasure in deceiving his enemy (or friend) by some unscrupulous jest, as in spattering the brains of a cornered mob of Germans one by one with his African knobkerrie. His instincts were abetted by an immensely powerful body and a savage brain, which chose the best way to its purpose, unhampered by doubt or habit.

Those qualities were evident, if only in embryo, during Meinertzhagen's first posting to British East Africa (as Kenya was then known) from 1902 to 1906; they would reach fruition in World War I, when he served with distinction as an intelligence officer in Africa and Palestine.

Fortunately for posterity, Meiner—as he was known to his messmates— was an inveterate diarist, and a candid one. Running from 1884, when he was six, to the mid-1960s, his journals would ultimately comprise some seventy volumes of typescript, all of it literate, colorful, and uncompromisingly honest. His *Kenya Diary,* first published in 1957 and not yet available in an American edition, is a blunt, fast-paced, cleanly written book studded with strong opinions, gruesome scenes of tribal warfare, sharply observed nuggets of social and natural history, and enough big game hunting to make Hemingway's *Green Hills of Africa* read like pastoral poetry. More important, it opens a window on the day-to-day workings of British colonialism in Africa both at its worst and at its best.

The self-described "black sheep" son of a London merchant banker of Danish descent, and a nephew of the Fabian socialists Sidney and Beatrice Webb ("Aunt Bo" in the diaries), Meinertzhagen was a twenty-four-year-old lieutenant in Burma when he was detached to British East Africa from his battalion—the 1st of the Royal Fusiliers—in April 1902. He didn't care to "stagnate in the narrow groove of regimental soldiering," and he took the first opportunity to leave it.

That opportunity came when his commanding officer in Mandalay invited himself along on a Sunday snipe shoot, adding, "You bring the lunch and cartridges." Meiner killed masses of snipe; the major hit scarcely any but expended well over a hundred of the shotgun shells paid for out of the young subaltern's pocket, "drank vast quantities of beer at my expense," and took a two-hour snooze in a paddy field after devouring Meiner's sumptuous lunch. Rank may have its privileges, but when Meinertzhagen was upbraided by the major the next day for missing Church Parade, he had had enough. He volunteered for service with native troops in East Africa.

Eventually posted to the 8th Company of the KAR in Nairobi, Meiner soon made enemies. He fumed in his diary:

> My brother officers are mainly regimental rejects and heavily in debt; one drinks like a fish, one prefers boys to women and is not ashamed. On arrival here I was amazed and shocked to find that they all brought their native women into mess; the talk centres round sex and money and is always connected with some type of pornography.

When the newcomer confronted his superiors with his outrage, they laughed and told him to go back to Burma. He wrote out an official complaint and threatened to send it in unless they reformed. "They were furious but complied. Row No. 1."

But Meinertzhagen also had a wry sense of humor. Immediately following the above diary entry comes this bit of self-deprecating doggerel:

> *They say I'm a quarrelsome fellow.*
> *God rot it, how can that be?*
> *For I never quarrel with any,*
> *The whole world quarrels with me.*

He was equally horrified by the poor state of readiness in his company of Africans: 125 coastal Swahili, a few tough Sudanese, and four Masai—"the

latter being useless." Their rifles—outmoded single-loading, .45-caliber Mar-
tini-Henrys—were choked with rust and in one case a rag. But it didn't
matter, because there was no musketry range and there was hardly any ammunition to spare for such frivolities as rifle practice. The men were equipped
with boots ("which they always take off on the slightest excuse") and the
heavy East African machetes known as pangas—considered "ideal for close
fighting."

Meinertzhagen vowed to shape them up in a hurry, but promptly got
into a second row with his superiors over questions of discipline. When one of
his men was called up for insubordination—"he told his sergeant that his
mother was a crocodile and his father a hyaena"—the company commander,
a certain Captain Bailey, sentenced the man to twenty-five lashes. And as the
man's platoon officer, Meinertzhagen had to witness the punishment.

"The culprit was lashed to a triangle, his breeches were removed, and he
was then flogged by a hefty Sudanese with a strip of hippopotamus hide; he
was bleeding horribly when it was over and I was nearly sick."

Raging with resentment, Meinertzhagen told Bailey that such brutal
punishment should be ordered only for crimes of violence or cruelty, and
should be followed immediately by a discharge from the service. "[H]ow can a
man have any self-respect left after a brutal public flogging? Bailey . . . gaped
in astonishment, told me I was squeamish, that I did not understand the
African and that it was gross impertinence questioning an orderly room punishment."

Not surprisingly, Meinertzhagen soon found himself ordered up to Fort
Hall in the Kikuyu country near Mount Kenya to take command of a small
outpost in the heartland of a warlike, troublemaking tribe. He didn't miss
Nairobi—then just a tin-roofed whistle-stop on the Mombasa–Uganda railroad, known far and wide as the Lunatic Express—but he would miss hunting
on the Athi Plain. There, today, jumbo jets take off and land at Nairobi's
Embakasi Airport, but at one time the plain swarmed with great herds of
zebra, wildebeest, kongoni, gazelles, eland, and Masai cattle. Lions roared at
night on the outskirts of town and sometimes prowled the main street.
Meiner enjoyed watching ostriches—"the cocks running off with flapping
wings and zigzag run, look like a lot of ballet girls with their naked pink
legs"—but feared he was developing a "blood thirst." Still, there would be
plenty of game up near the big mountain, and better yet the prospect of war.

Fort Hall was a typical frontier outpost of empire—just a collection of
scruffy grass huts surrounded by a ditch and a low stone wall—and bush
warfare proved to be brutish. Bands of Kikuyu raided one another constantly
for cattle and women. They also sent "insolent" messages to the civil authorities, destroyed caravans, and slaughtered mail parties and the occasional white
settler with virtual impunity. Punishment for these crimes amounted to confiscation of a certain number of cattle, sheep, and goats—but not without a
fight.

One murder in particular revolted Meinertzhagen. A white settler who
was attempting to barter for sheep from the Kihimbuini band of the Kikuyu

tribe was set upon. "[T]hey dragged him to a village near the forest, where they pegged him down on the ground and wedged his mouth open; then the whole village, man, woman and child, urinated into his mouth till he was drowned."

Meinertzhagen reacted with equal savagery. Following a night march to surround the village, his troops attacked at first light. "I gave orders that every living thing except children should be killed without mercy. I hated the work and was anxious to get through with it," he wrote later. "Every soul was either shot or bayoneted, and I am happy to say that no children were in the village. . . . We burned all the huts and razed the banana plantations to the ground."

Later, assigned to "punish" the Tetu Kikuyu for massacring an Indian caravan, Meinertzhagen's men trekked through the forest to the Aberdare Range, probing for pitfalls lined with sharpened stakes and avoiding ambushes by Tetu armed with poisoned arrows that flew from point-blank range in the dense bamboo thickets. A typical diary entry reads:

> Yesterday's patrol came into camp soon after dawn with their stock, having had some hard fighting. They had a 4 hours' running fight in the bamboos, losing 3 of their number and being hampered by 11 wounded. They then had to guard their captured stock throughout a pitch-dark night. . . .
> Before dawn this morning it was evident that a considerable body of savages were in the vicinity of my camp. Now the Wakikuyu have the habit of entering our old camps as soon as we leave, digging up the dead, and mutilating them. So I decided to teach them a lesson.

Sending the column ahead, Meinertzhagen remained behind in ambush with fifteen Masai spearmen. "We were successful beyond our wildest dreams." Sure enough, the Tetu came in—forty-nine of them—and began to dig for the dead. Meiner and his Masai sprang from their hiding places in the thornwood *zariba* surrounding the camp, and the slaughter began.

> The Masai were out like lightning and began to kill at once. The whole affair was quick and quiet. . . . I held the entrance with my bayonet, being shielded on either side by two Masai with their massive shields of buffalo hide. A good number of the enemy bolted for the door, but none got past me. I was surprised at the ease with which a bayonet goes into a man's body. One scarcely feels it unless it goes in to the hilt. But one frequently has to make a desperate tug to get it out. . . .
> The Masai fought with their shields in front of them and used their spears as stabbing weapons. . . . Once their man is down they use their short sword, inserting it on the shoulder near the collar bone and thrusting it down, parallel to the longer axis of the body, through the heart and down to the bladder. The length of the sword is such that it does not protrude.
> I doubt if the people of Tetu will worry us again for some time.

Like most British officers, Meinertzhagen sometimes had trouble controlling his African *askaris* (Swahili for troops) in the heat of battle. Training maneuvers with blank ammunition frequently devolved into tribal warfare between units of the KAR. He reports one such incident with amusement:

> The dummy enemy was represented by Maycock's Masai company. Their position was assaulted by Barrett's Sudanese company, who in the excitement of the moment fixed their bayonets and charged. The Masai also lost their heads and fixed their bayonets; a few men produced ball ammunition, which was fired at the Sudanese, wounding two men. The position became most realistic, the Sudanese freely bayoneting the Masai and killing three of them. The Masai eventually fled, with the Sudanese in pursuit.

In a campaign against the Irryeni Kikuyu, Meinertzhagen warned his men beforehand that anyone guilty of killing women or children would be shot. "My men are mere savages in the laws and customs of war," he noted, "and the Masai are bloodthirsty villains to whom the killing of women and children means nothing."

Rushing a small Irryeni village, his troop soon cleared it of warriors—

> then I heard a woman shriek. . . . I ran back to the village, where I saw two of my men and three Masai in the act of dragging a woman from a hut, and the body of a small boy on the ground, one of the [Masai] being in the act of withdrawing his spear from the little body. Another . . . was leading a small girl by the hand and was about to knock her in the head with his knobkerrie. I yelled at him to stay his hand, but I suppose his blood was up, for he paid no attention to me and killed the child. Meanwhile one of my own men bayoneted the woman within 30 yards of me. Putting up my rifle I shot the man dead, and then his companion, who I think contemplated having a pot shot at me. The [Masai] bolted, but I bagged them all three. . . .
>
> The two men of my company whom I shot were . . . men whom I personally liked.

But it was not all warfare. Meinertzhagen had ample occasion between punitive expeditions to indulge his love of hunting and natural history. An appendix to his diary scrupulously lists the weight and height at the shoulder of 506 animals he killed during his tour of duty. They range from lions (nineteen) through rhinoceroses (sixteen), leopards (seven), and buffalo (six), down to the diminutive dik-dik, weighing only six pounds and standing thirteen inches at the shoulder, of which he "collected" three. He was the first white man to kill a giant forest hog, then unknown to science, and earned the honor of having the animal named for him: *Hylochoerus meinertzhageni.*

The only member of Africa's "Big Five" (leopard, lion, buffalo, rhino, and elephant) spared from the sting of his light 6.5mm Mannlicher-Schoenauer rifle was the elephant. "It is a pity," he noted, "that an intelligent creature like the elephant should be shot in order that creatures not much more intelligent may play billiards with balls made from its teeth." In hunting as in most matters, Meiner was quirky.

And nowhere more so than in his relations with civilian authority. The

British high commissioner for East Africa was Sir Charles Eliot, whose amateur enthusiasm was the study of nudibranchs—sea slugs. "Never did a man
more closely resemble the objects of his hobby," Meinertzhagen wrote.

> Eliot thinks there is a great future for East Africa, transforming it into a
> huge white farming and stock area. Perhaps that is correct, but sooner or
> later it must lead to a clash between black and white. I cannot see millions of
> educated Africans—as there will be in a hundred years' time—submitting
> tamely to white domination. After all, it is an African country, and they will
> demand domination. Then blood will be spilled, and I have little doubt
> about the eventual outcome.

The Mau Mau emergency of the 1950s and Uhuru in 1963 proved
Meinertzhagen correct on all but the timetable.

He also predicted that the Kikuyu—"the most intelligent of the African
tribes I have met"—would lead Kenya's movement to independence. "I am
indeed sorry to leave the Kikuyu," he wrote at the time of his transfer from
Fort Hall,

> for I have many friends among them. Their great assets are cheerfulness
> even in adversity, and they bear no grudge after punishment. . . . I found
> them honest and truthful, but behaving quite differently to some of the
> European administrators, who treated them as "bloody niggers." The same
> cheerful young men or girls who visited me would become unscrupulous,
> dishonest and treacherous to the man who behaved badly to them. . . . Yes, I
> definitely like and admire the Kikuyu: they are intelligent, and I can see that
> with education they will turn out to be a great asset to East Africa provided
> we do not let them brood over grievances.

The next tribe he came in conflict with was the Nandi, whom he also
admired—so much so that he tried to spare them the horrors of a British
punitive expedition by nipping a tribal rebellion in the bud. His good intentions ultimately went for naught: By killing the rebellion's chief instigator, the
laibon of the tribe, in hand-to-hand combat, he only brought down the wrath
of Whitehall on his head as well as the lifelong resentment of the Nandi.

A Nilotic tribe of pastoralists, the Nandi resembled the cattle-herding
Masai in their love of warfare and raiding. Soon after he temporarily relieved
the commander of a KAR company guarding the railroad at Muhoroni ("very
hot and unhealthy"), Meinertzhagen received a wire from the town of
Kisumu on Lake Victoria: The Nandi were making trouble at a nearby American mission station, and one of the Americans was missing. He proved to be a
Quaker doctor named Wenthe, who had been murdered—"speared through
and through"—when he ignored warnings and strolled into an area where a
local British administrator named Walter Mayes had illegally seized Nandi
stock in retribution for the theft of two rifles.

"I have seldom taken such a dislike to a man at first sight," Meinertzhagen said of Mayes, blaming him for the missionary's murder. "I do not blame

the Nandi, who acted under the severest provocation."

But orders are orders, and the word from Kisumu was that "murderers must be punished." The Kabwuren section of the Nandi tribe, which had done the spearing, was fined forty-eight head of cattle "(which, by the way, Mayes had taken from them before they killed Wenthe)," and though the immediate matter was resolved without further bloodshed, the Kabwuren Nandi now had a grievance to brood over. The band was put on its best behavior for three months, during which Meinertzhagen's company was to be in their country and keep watch on them.

After six months' leave in England, Meinertzhagen returned to East Africa in March 1905 and was promoted to company commander at Nandi Fort. Meiner's relations with Mayes worsened, and the Nandi increased their cattle-rustling raids. One incident with Mayes is raucously reminiscent of Joyce Cary's African novels:

> This evening he rushed into my house, hair disheveled and in frantic excitement. . . . He screamed out: "A terrible thing has happened; my wife has arrived and upset everything! For Gawd's sake give me a bottle of whisky." I said I would come over and see her. She was a dirty-looking slut of a woman and was weeping. I am not too good on these occasions. She called Mayes Wally and said she was bloody well going to stop here. Apparently Mayes deserted her in Mauritius—she is a Mauritian Creole—and she finally found out where he was and suddenly appeared. It is all a bit difficult, as Mayes has half a dozen Nandi concubines in the house. I left them to fight it out among themselves.

Finally, fed up with Mayes for stealing Nandi "cattle, sheep, goats, and even girls," Meiner reported him to the commissioner's office. Before being transferred, Mayes retaliated by trying to set the Nandi leaders against Meinertzhagen. Meiner noted:

> There have been signs lately that the Nandi are becoming restless. I hear that the Laibon, the chief medicine man of all the Nandi, is busy making medicine against the Government and that various meetings take place regularly among the elders to discuss means by which they can rid themselves of British rule. . . .
> Murders and raids are being reported from every part of the district and the country is undoubtedly in a most disturbed state, which I attribute entirely to Mayes' misrule and dishonesty.

When one of Meinertzhagen's men was ambushed and murdered for his rifle, the situation worsened. Though the rifle was returned, the Nandi felt they had gotten away with something. A colonial administrator complained to Meiner that "scarcely a week passes without some complaint against the Nandi. They are like a troublesome schoolboy, and must be whipped." At one point a group of Nandi spearmen tried to ambush Meinertzhagen's company on patrol in the bush. Finally, after weeks of vacillation, the commissioner received permission from the Colonial Office to mount an expedition against the Nandi. Upon learning that the laibon had ordered his murder, Meiner wrote:

> The situation now resolves itself into a personal quarrel between me and the Laibon, and I will bet a small sum that he falls first. I strongly object to anyone wishing to kill me. . . . When 25,000 people are trying to kill one European in their midst it sounds as though it would be an easy job, but in reality it is going to be difficult. . . .
>
> Ever since I came here I have been organising an intelligence service. The men I have employed are taken from a small colony of Uasin Gishu Masai who live not far from my house. They hate the Nandi but can pass to and fro unmolested. I have them scattered about the country, a few living in some capacity with the Laibon and most of the larger chiefs. . . . But the Laibon himself has not neglected to play the same game on me, his agent being the official interpreter at the civil lines. This glib-tongued fellow is a member of the Laibon's family and keeps this wicked medicine man supplied with all the latest information about me and our doings in Nandi Fort. I find his presence convenient, as it gives me an excellent means of conveying false information to the Laibon.

Meiner soon learned that the laibon, Koitalel by name, about forty years old, had told his warriors that he could render British bullets harmless

> if only he can get bits of my anatomy for his medicine, especially my brains, heart, liver, palms of the hands and eyes. He would mix all these with certain plants, bring the whole thing to a boil, and sprinkle his warriors with the broth. . . . He is going to pose as a peacemaker, entice me out to an ambush and secure the necessary parts of my anatomy. As he shakes hands with me, he will pull me over towards him and a man near him will spear me.
> . . .
>
> My main reason for trying to kill or capture the Laibon is that, if I remove him, this expedition will not be necessary and the Nandi will be spared all the horrors of military operations. But both the civil and military authorities in Nairobi are intent on a punitive expedition. The military are keen to gain a new glory and a medal and the civil people want the Nandi country for the new proposal of the White Highlands—just brigandage.

Plans for the expedition moved ahead inexorably. Martial law was declared, and settlers and traders were cleared from the country while troops moved in from Nairobi. A peaceful Nandi widower, fearful of the violence to come, sent his three daughters to live in Meiner's household for the duration of hostilities. (Meinertzhagen nicknamed them "Maggie, Baggie, and Scraggie" and took them under his wing.) When the colonel who was in command of the KAR arrived to lead the expedition, Meinertzhagen broached a plan to meet the laibon and turn the tables on him in what would amount to a double ambush. The colonel hesitated but finally granted permission.

The meeting was arranged for the morning of October 19, 1905. The night before, Meinertzhagen wrote that the laibon jumped at the suggestion but asked me to come with only 5 men. . . . If he attacks me at our meeting I know how to defend myself. However, come what will, I meet him tomorrow, and during the next 24 hours I suspect that either he or I will have said goodbye to this world; I do not really very much care which of us it is.

Meinertzhagen left Nandi Fort at 5 A.M. with eighty men and a machine-gun team under the command of another British officer, his friend Lieutenant "Sammy" Butler. It was a twelve-mile hike to Kaidparak Hill and the rendezvous. Arriving at 8:47 A.M., Meiner deployed his company in heavy cover along a ridge and glassed the bush for Nandi. The *bundu* (thorn scrub) glinted with spears, and Meinertzhagen estimated that fully 300 tribesmen were waiting in ambush.

The Nandi interpreter, whom he already had tagged as the laibon's agent, was all smiles. Meinertzhagen sent him off to see if the laibon had arrived, then told Butler to commence firing with the Maxim if it appeared that he, Meiner, was being overwhelmed, and not to bother retrieving his body. The laibon arrived at 10:30 with an escort of twenty-two spears, "entirely contrary to our agreement." But there was nothing for it: Meinertzhagen had to trust in his reflexes and superior firepower.

"At 11.15 I left the column accompanied by a native officer, Mbaruk Effendi, Corporal Simba Manyema and 3 men," he wrote in his official report.

We approached with rifles at full cock and loaded, also with bayonets fixed. I told my men to fire the moment treachery was apparent. . . .

On advancing into full view of the Laibon it was clear that he had some 50 armed men around him. One man standing on the Laibon's right even had an arrow placed in his bow. The bush all around bristled with spears and shields. I halted my small party within four paces of the Laibon and asked him to come forward and shake hands. He replied that the sun was too hot, which, of course, was a ridiculous statement from a native. I also considered it wrong that a white man should have to make advances to a native, so I replied, "Very well, we will conduct our conversation at this distance. Shall we sit down?"

No sooner was this interpreted than the Laibon made a quick sign with his spear and an arrow pierced the sleeve of my shirt. The interpreter wheeled round on me, making as if to strike me with his spear, but was instantly shot by my corporal. I seized the Laibon and dragged him forward, getting scratched by his spear, and an arrow knocked off my helmet. The Laibon wrenched himself free, but by dragging him towards me I had prevented having spears thrown at me, as they would most certainly have hit him. Both I and my party at once opened fire. I am unable to state with certainty what followed. The Laibon was shot simultaneously by myself and my native officer, and several dead were left at the meeting place, including several of the Laibon's near relations. I took 2 stone-headed knobkerries from the Laibon's belt.

With the Nandi stunned by the laibon's death, Meinertzhagen's force beat a hasty retreat to the fort, the last seven miles a running fight in which they nearly ran out of ammunition. "So may all the King's enemies perish," Meinertzhagen exulted in his diary.

> As both he and all his successors male were gathered today, I much regret that the dynasty must stop from today. The only people I am sorry for are his wives, for they most certainly will be buried with him as is the custom. It is their own choice to be interred dead or alive.

Though Meinertzhagen won the fight, he ultimately lost the battle. The British punitive expedition that he'd hoped to forestall went ahead anyway, killing some 500 Nandi warriors and capturing 10,000 cattle and 70,000 sheep and goats. The cost to the KAR was only ninety-seven killed and wounded. Meinertzhagen was one of the latter, taking a poisoned arrow through the hand during an ambush that killed two of his men and a number of porters.

> I quickly fastened my whistlecord round my wrist as a tourniquet to prevent the poison running up my arm. My hand went black in about 10 minutes. . . .
> We had been issued with strychnine for injections if hit by a poisoned arrow. Mine was definitely poisoned, so I gave myself an injection. These arrows are barbed, and if one is hit in the leg or arm one must push it through; if in the neck or body, one must cut it out. Rather painful whichever happens.

While the expedition was still rampaging through the Nandi country, securing it for eventual white settlement, Meinertzhagen's old enemy Wally Mayes—who had returned as assistant political officer—began spreading rumors that Meiner had deliberately lured the laibon into a trap. "They say that I invited the Laibon to a friendly conference and shot him as he was shaking hands with me, and that afterwards I shot the Government interpreter to keep his mouth shut."

Though three official courts of inquiry requested by Meinertzhagen cleared him of any dishonorable behavior in the incident, and although his KAR peers recommended him for the Victoria Cross, the Colonial Office in Whitehall eventually decided it would be best for him to leave East Africa. Embittered, he returned to the "narrow groove of regimental soldiering."

But World War I allowed him to vindicate himself. As chief intelligence officer of the British forces facing General Paul von Lettow-Vorbeck in German East Africa, he distinguished himself in the field by solo reconnaissance behind German lines and by establishing a reliable spy network employing loyal African tribesmen. On one occasion he denied vital water holes to the Germans by making it appear that the water was poisoned: He scattered the carcasses of plains game shot by his men around the waterholes and posted signs in Swahili warning against drinking there. On another occasion, when a German agent proved uncatchable, Meinertzhagen allowed a courier to be captured by the enemy along with a letter signed by him praising the spy for his work as a double agent and enclosing a hefty payment.

The result was that my letter fell into the hands of the German officer commanding at Mwanza who at once tried his faithful servant for supplying information to the enemy and with the damning evidence of my letter convicted him and shot him. So I am rid of the fellow.

Even more than such trickery, though, Meinertzhagen delighted in direct action. Witness this passage from his Army Diary dated May 9, 1916, at a place called Kondoa Iringa:

We were sitting having supper when quite suddenly the loud rattle of musketry electrified us. The whole camp blazed and we could see the spiteful little flashes of rifles and hear the cheering of troops on the ridge to the south-east. Night work has always fascinated me, for I have especially good sight by night and never feel so much at home as when working in the dark. So I rushed out and made my way towards the firing. . . . I was just bursting for a bayonet charge. An enemy machine gun crept up to within thirty yards of us and opened from behind some rocks and we could not dislodge it so we led out a platoon and smothered it, bayoneting all its personnel. I ended up by using my rifle as a club—with disastrous results for the stock broke, but it was great. . . .

There was a bayonet scrimmage and I crept along a bit of trench, but this time having nothing but my fists and boots, when I suddenly realised there was another man close to me. Thinking he was a native . . . I said in Swahili, "Who are you?" just in case it might have been one of our own men. His reply was a smart blow, meant for my head, which landed on my shoulder and then we closed and had a rough and tumble in the trench. He was carrying a native knobkerrie which I finally wrenched out of his hand, got my knee well into his stomach and then set to on his head with the knobkerrie until he was silent. . . .

As soon as we could see, I returned along the trench to examine my victim and was surprised to find he was a German officer whose papers showed he was a man called Kornatsky, a company commander. His head was well battered in and I retained his knobkerrie, a handsome bit of native work, half black and half brown and beautifully balanced . . .

Lumme, I'm tired.

Later, while he was interrogating German prisoners, Meinertzhagen learned that the late captain von Kornatsky "had taken the knobkerrie from a big native chief at Iringa during a fight in which Kornatsky had killed the chief with his own knobkerrie and had learned that whoever carried that weapon would be killed by it. Maybe my time has not yet come."

Transferred to General Edmund Allenby's staff in 1917, he used the false-letter trick again to eliminate an Arab who was spying for the Turks out of Beersheba, and came within an ace of killing the notorious German spy "Fritz" Franks in a gun duel among the bleak dunes of the Sinai. His major coup in Palestine was the masterful "loss" of a haversack containing false British battle plans near the lines: He rode out on horseback, drawing enemy fire, dropped the haversack, and barely escaped to safety. In consequence, the Turks were unprepared for the sudden attack that carried Beersheba and eventually all of the Gaza front. "This officer has been largely responsible for my successes in Palestine," Allenby was later to write.

As the war ground to an end, Meinertzhagen, now a full colonel, finally got to France. During the British breakthrough on August 8, 1918, east of Amiens, he thumbed a ride with some Canadian armored cars near Marcel-cave and had the time of his life. "I seldom enjoyed myself so much," he records in his *Army Diary,*

> chasing the Hun in standing corn. We got in advance of our infantry and came up with tanks and cavalry, but many Huns who had left their trenches on the approach of the tanks still hid in shell-holes. . . . On our getting near their hiding-places they would bolt like rabbits and the game was not without its element of sport. I was given a Hotchkiss gun in one of the cars and accounted for twenty-three Huns during the day, besides taking part in the utter destruction of the headquarters of a German battalion as they sat at breakfast under a small shelter. I witnessed the overhauling of a Hun car containing two officers. As we approached, these two commenced firing with their pistols, till finally one dropped dead and the other ran off. I leaped out of my car and gave chase with my knobkerrie and was catching the fellow up when my companion in the car bowled him over with a shot from the other Hotchkiss. I was furious at being baulked of my prey, for I should most certainly have had him on the head in another yard.

After the war Meinertzhagen, always an ardent Zionist, played an active part at the Paris Peace Conference, argued for the honoring of the Balfour Declaration (which promised the establishment of a Jewish national home-land in Palestine), and cemented strong friendships with Jewish leaders such as Chaim Weizmann and David Ben-Gurion. By 1948, when Israel achieved statehood, Meinertzhagen—who had retired from the army in 1925—was returning from a trip across Arabia to write his book on the peninsula's bird-life. He embarked at Alexandria with a company of Coldstream Guards headed for embattled Haifa. His son, Daniel, had served with the Guards in World War II and been killed in a mortar barrage near the Maas River in Holland, so the colonel was welcome in their mess.

At Haifa, where Palestinians and the Israeli Haganah were engaged in vicious street fighting, Meinertzhagen borrowed a rifle and uniform from a Guardsman and went ashore. He was seventy years old at the time, but he walked toward the sound of the guns and joined the Haganah in a trench. There the old soldier smelled the perfume of cordite one last time, killing Arabs until he was ordered back aboard ship. He dutifully cleaned the rifle and split a bottle of champagne with the Guardsman who'd lent it to him. "Altogether I had a glorious day," he noted in his diary. "May Israel flourish!"

Meinertzhagen died on June 17, 1967, in his ninetieth year, an unregenerate warrior to the end.

Mutiny on the *Potemkin*

by ELIHU ROSE

Accidents are bound to happen. That may be one of the few sure rules of that blessedly unscientific discipline known as history. Take the mutiny on the Russian battleship *Potemkin*. The actual event turns out to be less driven by immutable forces, and less exalted, than the revolutionary paragon the Communists and the moviemaker Sergei Eisenstein made of it—but more dramatic as a study of human behavior and the anatomy of mutiny. Meat that was supposedly maggoty was the cause of a protest from the ranks; but the uprising itself had more to do with an unpredictably harsh overreaction by the ship's officers. In 1905, to be sure, political turbulence was everywhere in the Russian air, and when the *Potemkin* and her crew, by now officerless, steamed into Odessa looking for food and supplies rather than for radical support, a major, and totally unlooked for, revolutionary happening took shape. Elihu Rose, who is chairman of the *MHQ* Advisory Board, teaches military history at New York University.

utiny was in the air. Nothing specific; nothing tangible. Only a vague uneasiness, a climate of foreboding, like the milling of cattle before a stampede. This sense of apprehension among the 8,000 sailors of the Black Sea Fleet mirrored the general despair festering throughout Russia.

For the previous fifteen years a belated industrialization had generated enormous social dislocation; discontent seethed in the squalid countryside and in the pestilential slums. These accumulated stresses and tensions in Russian social and political life had been brought to a head in 1904 by war with Japan, a war fought for obscure policy objectives in the remotest corner of the empire. A fleeting burst of patriotic fervor that greeted the outbreak shortly dissolved into apathy, then hostility, as a quick and easy victory failed to materialize. The Bloody Sunday massacre of 4,600 civilians, shot down by soldiers in the streets of St. Petersburg, shattered beyond repair the politico-social myth of the czar as the "Little Father" of all Russians. On the military front, one debacle followed another with depressing regularity, culminating in the humiliating annihilation of an entire fleet, twenty-three major ships, at the hands of the Japanese navy in the Straits of Tsushima.

The Black Sea sailors played no part in those momentous events. Reduced to the role of a nautical constabulary, they passed most of their time ashore in crowded barracks, relieved only by occasional routine maneuvers, patrols, or port calls. But their professional quarantine did not insulate them from the political turbulence beginning to sweep the country, and a loosely organized cabal of ships' representatives had gone so far as to call for a general mutiny to take place the first week in July, when all major units of the fleet would be gathered for the annual maneuvers. The plan of action was left vague: Following the mutiny, the fleet would sail to Odessa or, perhaps, the Caucasus, there to provide the vanguard for the anticipated revolution in southern Russia.

On Saturday, June 25, 1905, the armored cruiser *Kniaz' Potemkin Tavrichesky,* Captain Eugene Nickoliavich Golikov commanding, left the Imperial Naval Base at Sevastopol. In company with her escort, Torpedo Boat N267, she was bound for Tendra Strait to test her recently overhauled main guns before joining the rest of the fleet for the planned exercises. Only a year in commission, the *Potemkin* was the most powerful ship in the entire Black Sea Fleet: 12,500 tons water displacement and 350 feet long, with guns of every caliber bristling from her armored turrets and casemates.

The *Potemkin* was neither a happy nor an unhappy ship, nor was she any hotbed of revolutionary ardor. Thirty percent of the crew was illiterate; another 20 percent could do little more than write their names. But if most of the ship's company were political innocents, it was not due to lack of effort on the part of the *Potemkin*'s revolutionary agitators: Two of these were Engineer Quartermaster Ananasi Matushenko and Gunner Grigori Vakulenchuck. Both had come from humble beginnings, both became exposed to political radicalism via the technical education they received in the navy, and both were to play key roles in the *Potemkin* mutiny: Matushenko by living, Vakulenchuck by dying.

Early on the morning of Wednesday, June 27, as the *Potemkin* lay at anchor a few miles off the uninhabited island of Tendra, word spread throughout the ship that maggot-ridden meat was being used to prepare the sailors' staple meal of meat borscht. The ship's senior surgeon, Dr. Smirnov, when called upon to render a professional opinion, certified that the meat was edible. Whether it was edible or not, Matushenko and the other agitators regarded the incident as a heaven-sent opportunity to create a protest. Under their prompting, the entire crew refused to eat the borscht when it was served at the midday meal.

It is a moot point whether or not the brief hunger strike actually constituted an official breach of military regulations, but, as an act of defiance, it distressed the ship's executive officer, Commander Ippolit Giliarovsky. He brought the matter to the attention of Captain Golikov, who pointedly reminded the assembled ship's company that hanging was the traditional penalty for so blatant an insubordination.

Discipline is one of the enduring themes of military life, but it is easier to define than to understand. Troops comply with orders because they have the *habit* of compliance; officers expect compliance because, like the troops, they have the habit of expecting compliance. The system is built upon an expectation of behavior. There are no rules to cover massive noncompliance, no manuals that tell the officer what to do when the troops ignore a command. Shorn of the mystique of discipline and lacking the immediate means of physical coercion, the officers must face the fact that one or two men cannot prevail over 700 who are conscious of their own power. That power may be temporary, but it is no less real.

Captain Golikov may have understood this; however, Commander Giliarovsky most certainly did not. Given the circumstances, the captain prudently decided to put the best possible face on things by announcing that a sample of the meat would be sent ashore for analysis, but he added, for good measure, that the reprehensible behavior of the crew would be reported to the fleet commander. His dignity bruised but intact, Golikov left the deck, apparently convinced that he had done all that he could do.

Commander Giliarovsky thought otherwise. He was, in American naval slang, a "sundowner," a harsh, uncompromising disciplinarian. He was probably appalled by the behavior of his captain and felt that strong, unequivocal action was called for. Instead of dismissing the crew, Giliarovsky acted on his own authority and, without further consultation with the captain, ordered the boatswain to pipe to the deck that traditional agent of warship discipline, the armed marine guard. His reason for doing so remains obscure; execution of troops without benefit of a duly convened court-martial was as unheard of in the Russian navy as in every other armed service. Even corporal punishment was not an everyday occurrence.

Exactly what took place in the next few minutes remains a mystery since no two accounts are in complete agreement. But there is no doubt that the sailors were sufficiently frightened by the *appearance* of imminent violence to be easily aroused by almost any word or movement. Matushenko later wrote that a shout ignited the spark; more likely it was *his* shout. No matter; the mutiny was on.

In an instant some of the crew grabbed rifles from the hands of the firing party while others rushed below to the ship's armory to collect more guns and cartridges. Commander Giliarovsky, too, had snatched a rifle from one of the marines and immediately exchanged shots with Vakulenchuck, the coleader of the ship's revolutionary cell. Vakulenchuck collapsed, severely wounded, and in the ensuing melee, Matushenko shot and killed Commander Giliarovsky.

On deck pandemonium reigned. Men ran every which way—shouting, pushing, having no clear idea of what was happening, trying to avoid ricocheting bullets. One chronicler, Lieutenant A. Kovalenko, an engineer officer, wrote that he and his fellow officers in the dining room below deck were jolted to attention by a "furious and terrible cry from the sailors that shook the vessel. The truth is that we were stupefied by the unexpectedness of the thing. . . . Savage shouts, the tramping of many feet, the jingle of broken things, and desultory gunshots made an odd medley of sound paralyzing one's will and filling one's mind with a strange torpor."

This paralysis did not prevent some officers from reacting with a mixture of discretion and valor. One lieutenant who went up on deck to reason with Matushenko was shot for his trouble. Other officers locked themselves in their cabins or hid in inaccessible places. A few jumped overboard. Torpedo Boat N267 was anchored less than a hundred yards away and, as the officers attempted the swim, sailors lined the railing of the Potemkin and took pot shots at them. Lieutenant Grigoriev died in the water.

Captain Golikov was found below deck, undressing before attempting the swim to the N267. He was hauled on deck and, according to some accounts, begged for mercy before being shot. His body was unceremoniously flung into the water. The ship's surgeon, who had certified the purity of the maggoty meat, was also thrown overboard where, according to Lieutenant Kovalenko, "close to the vessel were floating confused heaps of hats, boots and clothes and among them men who, although bleeding, were still alive."

While all this was taking place, the officers who survived the swim to the torpedo boat convinced her commander to make way for Sevastopol at top speed. With admirable military precision, the Potemkin sailors put a perfect shot through the funnel of the N267, halting the ship's escape. Other officers who had taken refuge on a floating target were collected and brought back aboard.

The violence stopped as quickly as it had started. The virulent part of the mutiny had taken only forty-five minutes; by a quarter past twelve in the afternoon it was all over. The bedlam having abated, there remained the simple question: What next? The crew was certainly not of one mind. In fact, only a minority of the sailors were comfortable with the idea of a mutiny in the first place.

One participant estimated that 100 or so of the 750 men aboard were committed activists. Some of the crew were intimidated, some were physically coerced, some wanted to settle old scores, some wanted only to conform, some actively connived against the mutiny's success. But most were simply swept up and carried along by events. In the absence of real conviction, the rule of the majority was the ultimate arbiter of the Potemkin mutiny.

In the first of innumerable mass meetings, the crew members assembled on the quarterdeck and elected an executive committee to administer the affairs of the ship. Matushenko was acknowledged as the leader and was called by one sailor "our chief and our commander."

But despite the sovereign powers vested in this executive committee, it rarely exercised them. In the days to come, the entire ship's company discussed and voted upon all substantive issues that arose.

Of immediate concern was the lack of provisions aboard. Odessa, less than thirty miles away, was the logical destination for the procurement of food and supplies, and late in the afternoon the Potemkin weighed anchor. The voyage took only a few hours, during which Vakulenchuck died of his wounds. The death of one of their own shipmates traumatized the crew far more than had the grisly deaths of seven officers. It was to have a decisive effect on the course of the mutiny and on the lives and deaths of thousands of Odessans.

It had now been just ten or eleven hours since the *Potemkin* erupted. Eight men had been killed, the ship's officers were under arrest, and the most modern battleship in the Black Sea Fleet was in the hands of a renegade crew. But the mutiny apparently had been limited in scope to one large ship and one small torpedo boat and seemingly limited in cause to the immediate issues of food and discipline. All this was to change in the next forty-eight hours as the stream of events on the *Potemkin* flowed into the river of turbulence that was the city of Odessa. The confluence was to redirect the course of the 1905 Revolution.

The people of Odessa had no inkling of what had transpired on the *Potemkin,* nor did they have any reason to believe that the ship was on anything but a routine military mission. In any event, the townspeople had other things on their minds. The city was in the throes of a general strike and normal civil life was at a standstill.

The 600,000 Odessans shared with the rest of Russia the dissatisfaction over the repressive nature of the regime and the frustrations of an unsuccessful and unpopular war. In Odessa it was quickened by the gnawing daily reality of extraordinary economic adversity. Odessa was in a depression. Labor strikes had first become serious in the early spring of 1905 and continued, with increasing tension, into the middle of June. Each day additional strikes were called: first the dock workers, then the bakers and the butchers, then the tailors, shoemakers, printers, and textile workers. The labor disturbances spilled over into civil disorders; confrontations between cossacks and civilians became a daily occurrence.

The first casualty had occurred on June 26, the day before the *Potemkin* mutiny, when a cossack officer was wounded by a demonstrator. In a scene familiar to most urban Russians, army and police units roamed the city, shooting and being shot at. Odessa became convulsed in street fighting, with scores of military and civilian deaths. At the very moment that the *Potemkin* was having its revolution at sea, Odessa was in the grip of a full-blown general strike: It was a mixture of work stoppage, political demonstration, general roughhouse, random attacks on police and troops, and counterattacks by cossacks—all taking place in an incongruous holiday mood. Spectators stood on their balconies pelting the demonstrators with towers as rioters overturned streetcars.

The crew of the *Potemkin* knew nothing of this as the ship approached the outer harbor. Early the following morning, Vakulenchuck's body was ferried to the pier and laid in an open coffin under a tent made of spars and sailcloth, and surrounded by an honor guard of *Potemkin* sailors. Almost immediately, news of the mutiny spread and the bier of the martyred sailor became a magnet, attracting thousands of Odessans already agitated by the harrowing events of the preceding days. Vakulenchuck's body now became the backdrop for a succession of orators who harangued the growing crowd from hastily erected platforms.

Meanwhile, out in the harbor, the *Potemkin* pursued her normal military routine. Lieutenant Kovalenko, sleeping on a couch in the wardroom, was shocked awake by the sounds of business as usual: the crew called to morning prayers by the boatswain's pipe, the forecastle bell tolling the hour and summoning the relief watch on deck, the splash of decks being swabbed, drums and bugles sounding honors as the Saint Andrew's colors were hoisted to the masthead. The officers were even served breakfast. If the habit of obedience had broken down, the habit of habit had not.

Among the masses of spectators who thronged the quayside was a militant student activist in his early twenties named Constantine Feldmann. Deeply involved in Odessa's radical politics, he set out at once by boat, with two other revolutionaries, to board the *Potemkin* and place himself at the service of the revolution. Their reception on board was cool, but Feldmann was irrepressible and soon managed to insinuate himself into the inner leadership council of the mutiny.

Hordes of nonradical sightseers and well-wishers also swarmed aboard the *Potemkin,* showering the crew with small gifts and generally making nuisances of themselves. While this was going on, a delegation representing the various revolutionary parties in Odessa also came aboard. Surprised by the *Potemkin*'s unheralded arrival at the height of the riots, the delegation came to plead with the ship's committee to send a detachment of 300 sailors ashore. The local party members were convinced that the sudden appearance of armed sailors, backed up by the guns of the ship, would sway the Odessa garrison to the side of the civil uprising.

The *Potemkin*'s committee demurred. Its members felt that sailors ashore, without a ship, would be powerless. They were also certain that once the rest of the Black Sea Fleet learned of their mutiny, they would follow suit and the long-awaited revolution would start in earnest. But the committee also recognized the weak revolutionary resolve of the majority of the crew, and feared that if so large a group were detached, it might defect once it set foot ashore or, worse, that those remaining on board might defect and take the ship back to Sevastopol. The refusal to send sailors ashore to help Odessa was one point upon which the crew was virtually unanimous, and the departure of the delegation ended all further relationship with revolutionary elements ashore. Feldmann and his two revolutionary companions remained on board, but on their own, without being given the official blessing of the organized revolutionary parties.

In the midst of all this excitement, the unarmed auxiliary vessel *Viekha* approached Odessa harbor carrying the wife and newborn infant of the late Captain Golikov. Feldmann gives a moving account of Madame Golikov's discovery of her husband's fate. In a gesture that tells us something of the sailors' naiveté and goodwill, they presented the widow with an indemnity of 1,000 rubles from the ship's chest. Then she was escorted ashore, along with the captain and officers of the *Viekha* and most of the *Potemkin* officers who had survived the outbreak and now were happy to leave the ship.

On the Odessa dockside the situation had turned ugly. All day the mobs had been surging around Vakulenchuck's improvised catafalque, and two police agents, attempting to divert the attention of the crowd by advocating an anti-Jewish pogrom, were set upon and beaten to death. The cossacks, however, were conspicuously absent, presumably having been frightened off by the prospect of a bombardment from the *Potemkin*'s artillery. Early in the evening, for no apparent reason, the port area suddenly erupted in a spasm of uncontrolled and unfocused violence. It was part revolutionary outrage, part pogrom, part general free-for-all, and, perhaps in the largest part of all, simple criminal arson and looting for personal profit.

At eleven o'clock at night the army moved in. The London *Times* correspondent cabled:

> The rifles of the soldiery and the flames kindled by an incendiary mob have vied with each other in spreading death and destruction. The streets are strewn with killed and wounded, the quays are blinding walls of fire and there is no quarter of the city which has escaped bloodshed and destruction. Firing continued in all directions and everything in the port that will burn is being destroyed while the desperate mobs forcibly prevent any attempt to cope with the conflagration.

Although the newspapers all referred to the "aggravating" effect of the *Potemkin*'s presence, the crew of the ship was aloof from the havoc ashore. Of grave concern was the disposal of Vakulenchuck's now-decomposing body, which had been left exposed and unguarded on the pier throughout the turbulence of that evening.

When Vakulenchuck's funeral was finally held at two o'clock the following afternoon, it was the signal for yet another outpouring of emotion on the part of the townspeople. A procession of several thousand accompanied the coffin, escorted by twelve unarmed sailors. The authorities had prudently withdrawn all army and police patrols from along the route, not wishing to exacerbate an explosive situation. But as the cortege was returning from the cemetery, it was ambushed and fired upon. The timely intercession of hastily dispatched troops restored order.

While the funeral was taking place, several soldiers with revolutionary sympathies brought news aboard the *Potemkin* that a meeting of all senior military officers in the district was being held in the municipal theater. To the mutineers, this presented the perfect opportunity to emphasize the seriousness of their purpose, and they attempted to bombard the theater. However, although the range was less than two miles, the two shells missed. Months later, the gunsighter claimed to have purposely avoided the target; his sabotage was subsequently rewarded by a grateful government.

The mutiny was in its fourth day. The mutineers had buried their comrade and demonstrated their power, but the all-night marathon meetings, the lack of sleep, and the enormous expenditure of physical and emotional energy had all begun to take their toll on the mutineers.

The arrival of the Black Sea Fleet had now become the main topic of conversation on the *Potemkin*, and it is not hard to imagine the mixture of anticipation and apprehension that must have gripped the crew when the telegraphist deciphered fragments of a message between ships of the main fleet. Within a few hours, three battleships and their escorts hove into view. Feldmann and Lieutenant Kovalenko attest to the *Potemkin*'s perfect battle-readiness; even the reticence of the loyal petty officers and uncommitted crew members seemed momentarily to have disappeared as they went to their battle stations. Feldmann notes that this time they were not "worked up by nervous excitement or hypnotized by eloquence . . . [but acted like] veterans, ready for anything."

The anticipated battle never took place. The opposing ships closed with one another and, as Feldmann recorded in decidedly unnautical language, "there was sort of a muddle." A sailor on one of the fleet battleships, *George the Conqueror,* reported that there was virtual panic on his ship, with officers running about in terror. An exaggeration, perhaps, but the battleship squadron did, in fact, reverse course almost immediately and head back to the open sea. The first round of what Russian historians call "the mute battle" had gone to the *Potemkin*. The "victory" had a remarkable effect upon the crew, and eyewitnesses report that lunch was a "jovial affair," even though provisions were so scant that biscuits and water were about all there was to eat.

At noon the fleet was sighted again. Now there were two more battleships, bringing the total to five. Of the fleet, only the *Catherine II* had been left behind at Sevastopol; her crew was believed to be too rebellious to include in so sensitive a mission as this. The *Potemkin* proceeded to sea with all hands at fighting stations. The commander of the fleet telegraphed to the mutinous crew: BLACK SEA MEN . . . APPALLED AT YOUR CONDUCT . . . SURRENDER.

To which the sailors on the *Potemkin* replied with a message of their own: SQUADRON HEAVE TO . . . ADMIRAL TO COME ON BOARD TO PARLEY . . . PROMISE SECURITY.

As the ships continued their approach, the commander signaled again, this time in a more choleric and less military vein: MADMEN WHAT HAVE YOU DONE . . . SURRENDER . . . THE SWORD SPARES THE PENITENT HEAD.

The *Potemkin* repeated the invitation to parley but now added: . . . OR WE SHALL FIRE.

The moment was at hand. Lieutenant Kovalenko describes the next few minutes: "With the range down to a mere three hundred yards, sudden agitation began among the crews of the *George the Conqueror,* the *Twelve Apostles,* and the *Synop*. The sailors were pressing in crowds out of the hatchways, and soon the decks were covered with men . . . in evident confusion. . . . On the decks of the *Ratislav* and the *Holy Trinity* there was an ominous silence." Feldmann relates what happened next: "There arose from the ships a tremendous 'Hurrah'. . . . Caps flew into the water. . . . With all our force we greeted the sailors and shouted to them to settle [sic] their officers." Matushenko, to whom this action must have appeared as the culmination of his dreams, said later that he felt it was "the moment we had been waiting for. It was the beginning of the revolution."

Almost, but not quite.

The *Potemkin* reversed course and headed back through the squadron in order not to be cut off from Odessa, which she still perceived as the source of her strength. This second pass was a repetition of cheering and hat-waving, with the exception of the *Ratislav,* whose crew remained at stations. However, as the squadron headed out to open sea, the *George the Conqueror* dropped out of line and fell astern. By semaphore, she signaled the *Potemkin:* CREW OF GEORGE WANT TO JOIN . . . COME ALONGSIDE. Together, the two ships returned to the Odessa anchorage.

After an hour of discussion by the *Potemkin*'s committee over whether or not the defection might be a ruse, an armed guard boarded the *George.* To its consternation, the group found the ship in a strange state of neither mutiny nor discipline. The officers had been arrested and had surrendered both their epaulettes and side arms. In fact, when Feldmann came aboard, he found them involved in the simple domestic chore of packing their suitcases. The only apparent violence was self-inflicted: One of the officers, unable to accept the humiliation of a mutiny, committed suicide with his service revolver. But the lack of revolutionary zeal on the *George* was palpable: The crew was hesitant and apathetic; the petty officers were agitating for surrender.

On the *Potemkin,* the mood was entirely different. Spirits were high. Even among the lukewarm adherents and outright opponents of the mutiny, there was a sense of pride; they had met the enemy not once, but twice, and had prevailed both times. The accomplishment was even more tangible for the leaders of the mutiny; not only had the emotional potency of the revolution been convincingly demonstrated, but the coming over of the *George* had vastly increased the military power of the rebel force.

During the night, however, irresolute and capricious behavior on board the *George* became a source of concern. At least half the crew seemed in favor of returning to Sevastopol and rejoining the fleet. It was obvious to the *Potemkin*'s committee that the *George* needed the same kind of rhetorical stimulation that had been so effective with its own crew, but the most persuasive orators, including Feldmann and Matushenko, were literally talked out. Before amplified sound, it was not easy to make oneself heard to very large audiences and the speechmakers had been shouting at the tops of their lungs for three days. It seemed as if the *George* mutiny would founder on the simple human failing of laryngitis when Dr. Golenko, the assistant surgeon, volunteered to go aboard the *George* as spokesman. Up to this time, he had confined his duties to the care of the sick and wounded and had taken no part in the mutiny. The committee members recognized Dr. Golenko's limitations as an orator, but they concluded that his rank would lend authority to his exhortations. They could not know, however, that he was a traitor to their cause.

No sooner had Golenko arrived aboard the *George* than he announced to her ambivalent crew that the *Potemkin* had decided to surrender; that only a few men who dominated the crew wanted to fight; that the cause was hopeless; and that the best course of action was for both ships to return to

Sevastopol. This was all that was necessary to convince the anxious and divided *George* crew that the mutiny was over. This change of heart was not suspected by the crew of the *Potemkin,* so it was stunned when the *George* weighed anchor and semaphored: SAILING TO SEVASTOPOL . . . INVITE POTEMKIN ACCOMPANY. The *Potemkin* was just then taking on a load of coal and, lashed to a barge, was unable to get under way. She peremptorily signaled: GEORGE REMAIN AT ANCHORAGE. The George answered: WILL COMPLY. However, as she ran past the harbor entrance, she made a sharp turn and headed toward the shore, where she grounded herself on a mudbank.

The *George's* defection meant the collapse of the *Potemkin* mutiny. The *Potemkin* crew realized it immediately. The tables had been turned, and what had been a position of strength suddenly became one of weakness. Had the *George* not mutinied and remained with the fleet after the previous day's standoff, she would have returned to Sevastopol and, for the moment, presented no danger. But in Odessa, in the hands of the authorities and even in its disabled condition, she could prevent the Potemkin from using the town as a base and a source of supply.

As if on signal, someone shouted: "To Rumania!" In two or three minutes, almost the whole crew picked up the chant, everyone yelling at once. Feldmann and the other die-hards tried to turn the tide, but they were now regarded as responsible for the ship's misfortunes. Even Matushenko took up the cry for Rumania.

The events of the preceding twenty-four hours were incomprehensible to observers on shore. "The situation would furnish the libretto for a comic opera were not the elements of the plot so serious," wrote the *New York Times* correspondent, and his equally baffled colleague from the London *Times* suggested that the circumstances "border on the domain of wonderland." The foreign consuls were as ignorant as everybody else. The cables that were sent by U.S. consul Heenen, for example, were typical in their degree of misinformation: All the *Potemkin* officers had supposedly been murdered and the *Potemkin* herself was reported to have been captured by the Black Sea Fleet.

From the beginning of the entire episode, Russian newspaper censorship was strict. No mention of the mutiny or of the events in Odessa was permitted beyond the cryptic announcement that martial law had been imposed because of an unspecified "disruption in the tranquility of the town." The inference was not lost on most Russian readers and, censorship notwithstanding, a garbled version of what had taken place on the *Potemkin* spread unevenly throughout European Russia within twenty-four hours of the arrival of the ship in port. But as late as June 30, the fourth day of the mutiny, a London *Times* reporter found St. Petersburg "ignorant of all these events. . . . So great is the secrecy, that even officials at the Admiralty are, in nine cases out of ten, unaware of the mutiny." The international audience was better informed than the Russians themselves; since June 29, the mutiny had been front-page news throughout the world.

Back in Sevastopol after his humiliating "engagement" with the *Potem-*

kin, Vice Admiral Chuckhnin, commander in chief of the Black Sea Fleet, contemplated his immediate difficulties. He had not only failed to capture the *Potemkin* but had lost the use of the *George,* one of his five capital ships. He now faced the problem of how to keep his remaining ships from joining the insurgents. The only practical answer was as disabling—and almost as mortifying—as an actual defeat at the hands of an enemy: The fleet was officially disbanded, the ships made inoperative, and all 5,000 sailors sent on immediate leave. But if the Black Sea Fleet now had neither ships nor sailors, it still had officers. Hoping to expunge the disgrace to their service, a hand-picked unit of forty officers put to sea in a fast destroyer with the intention of finishing off the *Potemkin* at any cost. As a beau geste, it was magnificent; as a naval deployment, it was a wild-goose chase.

There was one persistent question on the *Potemkin:* What next? A few hours out of Odessa, on her way to Rumania, a passing ship signaled news of the search by the officer-manned destroyer. If that were not trouble enough, the crew learned from a book of naval regulations that, under international law, deserters faced extradition. This last consideration made surrender to the Rumanian authorities out of the question. It was generally believed on the *Potemkin* that the Caucasus region was in a state of revolt, so mutineers expected that the ship not only would receive a welcome there, but would actually aid and support the revolution. The crew decided to proceed to the Caucasus after provisioning in Rumania.

The *Potemkin*'s uneventful cruise to Constanza in Rumania took less than twenty-four hours. The stay there was brief and disappointing. Fearful of antagonizing Russia, the Rumanian authorities prohibited the *Potemkin* from purchasing fuel, fresh water, or food, all of which were in critically short supply. Even on reduced rations, the *Potemkin* could not expect to survive more than five or six days. It had been a week since any of the crew had tasted meat, even bad meat. For the past three days, it had subsisted on biscuits, porridge, and water, which was hardly enough for the deck crews and certainly not adequate to maintain the energy of the engine-room stokers. The ship's distillation plant could provide only enough fresh water for the crew's personal consumption; the boilers had to be operated on sea water, and the consequent loss in efficiency had already reduced the ship's speed. The coal supply was also running out; even with the most rigid economy, there was barely enough remaining for three or four more days' steaming.

The *Potemkin* left Constanza and headed for Theodosia, a small commercial port in the Crimea whose name had been found in a guide to Black Sea ports. Its attraction lay in its out-of-the-way location, and the committee believed that the ship could fuel and provision there before continuing her voyage to the Caucasus. But there was something pathetic and melancholy in this last cruise—an anticlimax of wandering, of lost initiative, of desperation. The crew clung to ceremony and ritual. The vessel was never permitted to become unmilitary; even in her renegade state, she was always shipshape. In all dealings with the Rumanians on the ship's short visit, no detail of traditional military punctilio was overlooked: Artillery salutes were rendered; the foreign officers were welcomed aboard by an honor guard drawn up at the gangway, and taken below for a ceremonial drink. When the ship entered Theodosia harbor, she was, in naval terminology, "dressed overall," festooned with colorful signal flags, the crew members lining the rails in clean uniforms. They presented themselves as sailors of the Russian navy, not as pirate outcasts.

The treatment of the ship's flag is also revealing. Many accounts of the mutiny speak of the *Potemkin* as "flying a red flag." Feldmann records that it was only after leaving Rumania that the committee decided to fly a red flag. "Though the sailors had, by the very fact of mutiny, exchanged the flag of czarism for the flag of revolution, still they had not come to the point of doing so formally. Many sentiments came into the question: the old superstitious reverence for the flag of Saint Andrew, the close association of the gallows with the red flag in their minds, and perhaps the sailors' dread of clearly and openly putting a name on their own action to themselves, of recognizing the gulf which they had crossed." The flag was made from a giant red cloth stretched on a wooden frame. On one side was painted LIBERTY, EQUALITY AND FRATERNITY; on the other, LONG LIVE THE GOVERNMENT OF THE PEOPLE. It was accorded the same ceremonial respect that had previously been bestowed upon the Saint Andrew's Cross.

Punctilious observance of ceremony may have been a balm to morale, but it could not change the fact that, the instant the *George* had grounded herself, the outcome of the mutiny was ordained. The call at Theodosia only prolonged the inevitable. A landing party from the *Potemkin* was fired upon by a company of troops from the local garrison. Two sailors were killed and Feldmann himself was captured in the abortive foray. It was at Theodosia that the *Potemkin* crewmen learned from a local newspaper that the penitent crew of the *George* had identified and surrendered eighty-seven of its own mutineers to the naval authorities. There seemed no point in continuing the rebellion.

The ending was quick. The *Potemkin* returned to Constanza, where most of the crew accepted the Rumanian government's offer of political asylum; the remainder returned to Sevastopol, content to take their chances before a court-martial. The executive committee saw to the final details: The revolutionary flag was buried at sea; the money in the ship's safe was divided among the crew; and, in a final act of defiance, the *Potemkin* herself was scuttled in shallow water.

In its success and its failure, the *Potemkin* mutiny could be considered a metaphor for the entire Russian Revolution of 1905. Its violence reflected the pent-up rage that had been simmering in Russian society. And the fact that the disaffection was military in nature indicated the erosion of support within an institution that for years had been a mainstay of the ruling autocracy. But even more important, the mutiny's collapse was clear evidence that the rage and disaffection had not yet reached the boiling point. The ambivalence of so many of the *Potemkin*'s crew, the "desertion" of the *George*, the failure of the rest of the fleet to follow the *Potemkin*'s example—all point to the weakness of revolutionary sentiment relative to the strength of the czarist regime. In the months that followed the *Potemkin* uprising, more mutinies took place in both the army and navy, and more civilians were shot down in the streets. Yet the regime prevailed. It took twelve more years and the politico-social trauma of a cataclysmic war finally to topple it.

Veterans of the *Potemkin* affair went their separate ways to their separate fortunes: The senior commanders of the Black Sea Fleet were summarily retired; three of the mutineers who returned voluntarily were sentenced to death (though their sentences were commuted), and many of the others faced long terms of imprisonment; most of the crew settled first in Rumania, then later went on to other countries. The irrepressible Feldmann, apprehended in Theodosia, escaped from prison and made his way to Austria. Matushenko lived for a time in Rumania, Switzerland, and France before returning to Odessa in 1907 to carry on revolutionary work. Within four months of his arrival, he was arrested, tried, and hanged. The last surviving mutineer was Seaman Ivan Beshoff. Presumably, the maggoty meat and other unwholesome inconveniences of life in the Imperial Navy did not permanently impair his health. He died in Dublin in 1987, aged 104.

Europe 1914

by MICHAEL HOWARD

One of the foremost military historians of our time reexamines the fateful decisions taken in the days before the great Continental civil war broke out. What, he asks, did Europeans—governments, armies, and ordinary citizens—think would happen to them if they did not go to war? The answer was that peace presented uncertainties that were at the moment more terrifying than those of war. Since most people believed that a war was inevitable, the sooner it was fought the better. The best chance for victory, military leaders on both sides felt, lay in immediately taking the offensive: To yield the initiative was to court defeat. "The lessons of history," Michael Howard writes, "seemed to reinforce the strategic imperatives of 1914." But how dangerous those "lessons" can be—and how often they have led us to mistake short-term gains for long-term consequences. Howard, former Regius Professor of Modern History at Oxford University, is now Robert E. Lovett Professor of Military and Naval History at Yale University. This article was included in Howard's collection *The Lessons of History,* recently published by Yale University Press.

In a place of honor in the Oxford Examination Schools, there hangs a portrait of Kaiser Wilhelm II of Germany, wearing the robes of the honorary doctorate of civil law bestowed on him by the University of Oxford in November 1907. Seven years after the kaiser received his degree, out of a total of seven Oxford honorands in June 1914, five were German. The duke of Saxe-Coburg-Gotha, Professor Ludwig Mitteis of the University of Leipzig, and the composer Richard Strauss all received their degrees at the encaenia on June 25. Special sessions of convocation were held to bestow honorary doctorates on the king of Württemberg and the German ambassador, Prince Karl Lichnowsky. At a banquet in the latter's honor, the professor of German reminded his audience that the kaiser's great-grandfather, King Frederick William III of Prussia, had also received an honorary doctorate of civil law exactly 100 years before. He welcomed the presence of so many German students in Oxford (fifty-eight German Rhodes Scholars had matriculated over the previous ten years) and expressed the hope that thereby the two nations would be "drawn nearer to one another," quoting the belief of Cecil Rhodes "that the whole of humanity would be best served if the Teutonic peoples were brought nearer together and would join hands for the purpose of spreading their civilization to distant regions."

Three days after this encaenia, Archduke Francis Ferdinand of Austria was assassinated at Sarajevo. When the university reconvened three months later in October 1914, many of the young Germans and Englishmen who had rubbed shoulders at those celebrations had enlisted in their respective armies and were now doing their best to kill one another. The Examination Schools had been turned into a hospital. The number of undergraduates in residence had dwindled by over half, from 3,097 to 1,387. (By 1918 it would be down to 369.) During the vacation over a thousand of them had been recommended for commissions by a committee established under the vice-chancellor, and they were already serving with the army. As yet, only twelve had been killed; the slaughter of the First Battle of Ypres was still a few weeks away.

Several colleges had been taken over to house troops. Organized games had virtually ceased, while the Officers' Training Corps, to which all able-bodied undergraduates now belonged, trained for five mornings and two afternoons a week. As if this were not enough, the Chichele Professor of Military History, Spenser Wilkinson, advertised a course of lectures "for those who are preparing themselves to fight England's battles." The course was to begin with a description of "the nature and properties of the weapons in use—the bullet, the shell, the bayonet, the sword and the lance."

In one way it can therefore be said that the war came out of a clear sky. But these events do not indicate a profoundly pacific community taken totally by surprise and adjusting only with difficulty to astonishing and terrible new conditions. Everyone seems to have known exactly what to do, and to have done it with great efficiency. Arrangements to take over the Examination Schools and colleges had been made by the War Office two years earlier. The OTC was already flourishing: One undergraduate in three belonged to it, and 500 were in summer camp at Aldershot when the news of the assassination came through. And insofar as such iconographic evidence can be legitimately adduced, group photographs of Oxford colleges and clubs show how the lolling dandies of the turn of the century, with their canes, blazers, and dogs, had given way soon after the Boer War to a new generation of muscular young men—fit, serious, short-haired, level-eyed—whose civilian clothes already seemed to sit uneasily upon them. This generation may not have expected war to break out in the summer of 1914 but was psychologically and physically ready for it when it came. The challenge was expected, and the response full of zest.

In this respect Oxford was a microcosm, not only of Britain but of Europe as a whole. Europe was taken by surprise by the occasion for the war—so many comparable crises had been successfully surmounted during the past five years—but not by the fact of it. All over the Continent long-matured plans were put into action. With a really remarkable absence of confusion, millions of men reported for duty, were converted or, rather, reconverted to soldiers, and were loaded into the trains that took them to the greatest battlefields in the history of mankind. It cannot be said that during the summer weeks of 1914, while the crisis was ripening toward its bloody solution, the peoples of Europe in general were exercising any pressure on their governments to go to war, but neither did they try to restrain them. When war did come, it was accepted almost without question—in some quarters indeed with wild demonstrations of relief.

The historian is faced with two distinct questions: Why did war come? And when it did, why was it so prolonged and destructive? In the background there is a further, unanswerable question: If the political and military leaders of Europe had been able to foresee that prolongation and that destruction, would the war have occurred at all? Everyone, naturally, went to war in the expectation of victory, but might they have felt that at such a cost even victory was not worthwhile? This is the kind of hypothetical question that laymen put and historians cannot answer. But we can ask another and less impossible question: What did the governments of Europe think would happen to them if they did *not* go to war? Why did war, with all its terrible uncertainties, appear to be preferable to remaining at peace?

Clausewitz described war as being compounded of a paradoxical trinity: the government for which it was an instrument of policy; the military for whom it was the exercise of a skill; and the people as a whole, the extent of whose involvement determined the intensity with which the war would be waged. This distinction is of course an oversimplification. In all major states of Europe, military and political leaders shared a common attitude and cultural background, which shaped their perceptions and guided their judgments. The same emotions that inspired people were likely also to affect their political and military leaders, and those emotions could be shaped by propaganda, by education, and by the socialization process to which so much of the male population of continental Europe had been subject through four decades of at least two years' compulsory military service at an impressionable age. (It must be noted that the British, who were not subjected to the same treatment, reacted no differently from their Continental neighbors to the onset and continuation of the war.) Still, the triad of government, military, and public opinion provides a useful framework for analysis.

First, the governments. Although none of them could foresee the full extent of the ordeal that lay before them, no responsible statesman, even in Germany, believed that they were in for "a fresh, jolly little war." It was perhaps only when they had made their irrevocable decisions that the real magnitude of the risks came fully home to them. But that is a very common human experience. The Prussian chancellor, Theobald von Bethmann Hollweg, in particular saw the political dangers with gloomy clarity: A world war, he warned the Bavarian minister, "would topple many a throne."

There had indeed been a certain amount of wild writing and speaking over the past ten years, especially in Germany, about the value of war as a panacea for social ills; and the remarkable way in which social and political differences did disappear the moment war was declared has tempted some historians to assume that this effect was foreseen and therefore intended: that the opportunity was deliberately seized by the Asquith cabinet, for example, to distract attention from the intractable Irish problem to Continental adventures, or that the German imperial government saw it as a chance to settle the hash of the Social Democrats for good. One can only say that minute scrutiny of the material by several generations of historians has failed to produce any serious evidence to support this view.

Rather, the opposite was the case: Governments were far from certain how their populations would react to the coming of war, and how they would stand up to its rigors. A whole generation of English publicists had been stressing the social consequences of even a temporary blockade of the British Isles: soaring insurance rates, unemployment, bread riots, revolution. The French army, for ten years the butt of left-wing agitation, hardly anticipated an enthusiastic response from conscripts recalled to the colors, and the French security services stood by to arrest left-wing leaders at the slightest sign of trouble. It was only with the greatest reluctance that the German army forced military service on the supposedly unreliable population of the industrial regions. The Russian government had within the past ten years seen one war end in revolution, and for at least some of its members this seemed good reason to keep out of another.

It was one thing to enhance the prestige of the government and undermine support for its domestic enemies by conducting a strong forward policy, whether in Morocco or in the Balkans. It was another to subject the fragile consensus and dubious loyalties of societies so torn by class and national conflict, as were the states of Europe in 1914, to the terrible strain of a great war. Governments did so only on the assumption, spoken or unspoken, that the war, however terrible, would at least be comparatively short—no longer, probably, than six months, the length of the last great war in Europe in 1870. How could it be otherwise? A prolonged war of attrition, as Count Alfred von Schlieffen had pointed out in a famous article in 1909, could not be conducted when it required the expenditure of milliards to sustain armies numbered in millions. The only person in any position of responsibility who appears to have thought differently was Lord Horatio Herbert Kitchener, a British imperial soldier who had served outside Europe throughout his career and who had never, as far as we know, seriously studied the question at all.

But whether the war proved to be short or long, it was for all governments a leap into a terrible dark, and the penalties for defeat were likely to be far greater than the traditional ones of financial indemnities and territorial loss. So we inevitably come back to these questions: What appeared to be the alternatives? And in the event of victory, what appeared to be the probable gains? Why, in the last resort, did the governments of Europe prefer the terrifying uncertainties of war to the prospect of no war?

Let us begin where the war itself effectively began, in Vienna. Was not the prospect that lay before the statesmen of Vienna, even if this crisis were successfully "managed," one of continuous frustration abroad and disintegration at home? Of a Serbia, doubled in size after the Balkan Wars, ever more boldly backing the claims of the Bosnian irredentists, while other South Slavs agitated with ever greater confidence for an autonomy that the empire would never permit them to exercise? What serious prospect was there of the empire hanging together once the old emperor had gone? A final settling of accounts with Serbia while Germany held the Russians in check must have seemed the only chance of saving the monarchy, whatever Berlin might say; and with a blank check from Berlin, Vienna could surely face the future with a greater confidence than had been felt there for very many years. No wonder Count Leopold von Berchtold and his colleagues took their time drafting their ultimatum: They must have found the process highly enjoyable. A successful war would put the monarchy back in business again, and keep it there for many years to come.

What about the government in Berlin? Was this the moment it had been waiting for ever since the huge expansion of the army resulting from the famous Council of War in December 1912? The controversy about this has consumed many tons of paper and gallons of ink. But if one asks again what the imperial German government had to lose by peace and gain by war, the answers seem very clear. One of the things it had to lose by peace was its Austrian ally, which would become an increasingly useless burden as it grew ever less capable of solving its internal problems or protecting its own (and German) interests in the Balkans against the encroachments of Russia and Russia's protégés.

Another thing Germany stood to lose was her capacity to hold her own against a dual alliance in which French capital was building up a Russian army whose future size and mobility appeared far beyond the capability of any German force to contain. It would not be too anachronistic to suggest that the shadow of Russia's future status as a superpower was already rendering out of date all calculations based on the traditional concept of a European balance. If war was to come at all—and few people in the imperial government doubted that it would—then it was self-evidently better to have it now, while there was still a fair chance of victory. By 1917, when the Russians had completed the great program of rearmament and railway building that they had begun, with French funding, in 1912, it might be too late.

And, for Germany, there was a lot to be gained by war. The domination of the Balkans and perhaps the Middle East; the final reduction of France to a position from which she could never again, even with allies, pose a military threat to German power; the establishment of a position on the Continent that would enable Germany to compete on equal terms with England and attain the grandiose if ill-fated status of a world power—all this, in July 1914, must have appeared perfectly feasible. In September, when the program of her war aims was drafted, it looked as if it had almost been achieved. Even in a less bellicose and more self-confident society than Wilhelmine Germany, the opportunity might have seemed too good to miss.

In Vienna and Berlin then, there seemed much to be lost by peace and gained by war. In St. Petersburg, the ambitions for Balkan expansion and the "recovery" of Constantinople, which had been checked in 1878 and 1885, were far from dead, but they can hardly be considered a major element in Russian political calculations in July 1914. More serious were the costs of remaining at peace: abandoning Serbia and all the gains of the past five years; facing the wrath of the pan-Slavs in the Duma and their French allies; and watching the Central Powers establish and consolidate an unchallengeable dominance in southeast Europe. Even so, these costs were hardly irredeemable. Russia had been humiliated before in the Balkans and had been able to restore her authority. She had no vital interests there that, once lost, could never be recovered. Above all, she had nothing to lose in terms of military power by waiting, and a great deal to gain. Of all the major European powers, Russia's entry into the war can be categorized as the least calculated, the most unwise, and ultimately, of course, the most disastrous.

As for Paris and London, a successful war would certainly remove—as it ultimately did—a major threat to their security. But the advantages to be gained by war did not enter into their calculations, whereas the perils of remaining at peace evidently did. The French government took little comfort from the long-term advantages to be gained from the growth of Russian military power and paid little heed to the consequent advisability of postponing the issue until 1917. It was more conscious of its immediate weakness in the face of the growing German army. In 1914, after the increase of the past two years, German peacetime strength had reached 800,000 men, its wartime strength 3.8 million.

Thanks to their new and controversial Three-Year Law, the French could match this with 700,000 men in peace, 3.5 million in war. But with a population only 60 percent of the Germans', that was almost literally their final throw. Completion of the Russian reforms was three years away. In the long run Russian strength might redress the balance, but in the long run a large number of Frenchmen could be dead and their nation reduced to the status of Italy or Spain. So the French government saw no reason to urge caution on St. Petersburg, and even less reason to refrain from supporting its ally when Germany declared war on her on August 1.

To the British government, composed largely (although by no means entirely) of men to whom the whole idea of war was antipathetic and who were responsible to a parliamentary party deeply suspicious of militarism and of Continental involvement, there appeared nothing to be gained by war. Indeed, perhaps more than any of its Continental equivalents, the British government was conscious of the possible costs, but was equally conscious of the cost of remaining at peace. She had no demands to make on any of the belligerents, no territorial aspirations, no expectation of economic gain. So far as the British government was concerned, Norman Angell's famous book *The Great Illusion* was preaching to the converted. But if the Dual Alliance defeated Germany unaided, the two victors would regard Britain with hostility and contempt. All the perils of imperial rivalry that were temporarily dispersed by the Entente with France in 1904 and the British accords with Russia of 1907 would reappear. If, on the other hand, Germany won and established a Continental hegemony, Britain would face a threat to her security unknown since the days of Napoleon.

Leaving aside any consideration of honor, sentiment, or respect for treaties—and let us remember that that generation of Englishmen did not leave them aside but regarded them as quite central—every consideration of *realpolitik* dictated that Britain, having done her best to avert the war, should enter it on the side of France and Russia once it began.

When the statesmen of Europe declared war in 1914, they all shared one assumption: that they had a better-than-even chance of winning it. In making this assumption they relied on their military advisers, so it is now time to look at our second element in the triad: the soldiers.

The first thing to note about the soldiers—certainly those of western Europe—is that they were professionals, and most of them professionals of a very high order. Those of them who were wellborn or socially ambitious certainly shared the feudal value system so excoriated by Professor Arno Mayer in his book *The Persistence of the Old Regime.* Those who were not probably had more than their fair share of the prevalent philosophy of social Darwinism and regarded war not as an unpleasant necessity but as a test of manhood and of national fitness for survival. In all armies, then as now, there were incompetents who through good luck or good connections reached unsuitably high rank; but a study of the military literature of the period strongly indicates that the military professionals—especially those responsible for the armament, training, organization, and deployment of armies—were no fools, worked hard, and took their jobs very seriously. And they, too, shared certain assumptions.

The first was that war was inevitable. The now much-quoted statement made by General Helmuth von Moltke (namesake of his famous uncle) at the so-called Council of War in December 1912, "I hold war to be inevitable, and the sooner the better," can be paralleled with comparable expressions by responsible figures in every army in Europe. They may have differed over the second part of the sentence—whether it was better to get it over with quickly or wait for a more favorable moment—but from 1911 onward it is hard to find any military leader suggesting that war could or should be avoided any longer.

The change of mood in the summer of that year, provoked by the 1911 Agadir crisis over conflicting French and German interests in Morocco, was very marked. In France a new political leadership appointed a new group of military chiefs, who belatedly and desperately started to prepare their ramshackle army for the test of war. The Dual Alliance was reactivated, Russian mobilization schedules were speeded up, and the Great Program of Russian military mobilization was set afoot. In Germany the agitation began that contributed so powerfully to the German army's massive increase in military strength. In Britain the government gave its blessing to the army's plans for sending the British Expeditionary Force to France, and Winston Churchill was sent to the Admiralty to bring the navy into line.

The extent to which war was generally regarded as inevitable or desirable by the public as a whole is still difficult to gauge—although if the "distant drummer" penetrated into the summer idylls of A.E. Housman's poetry, it is reasonable to suppose that less remote figures found the sound pretty deafening. Certainly the evidence is overwhelming that the question in military minds was not "whether" but "when." They saw their job as being not to deter war but to fight it.

The second assumption, which they shared with the statesmen they served, was that the war would be short. It required exceptional perspicacity to visualize anything else. Ivan Bloch in his work *La Guerre future,* published in 1898, had forecast with amazing accuracy that the power of modern weapons would produce deadlock on the battlefield and that the resulting attrition would destroy the fabric of the belligerent societies. Bloch's thesis was widely known and much discussed in military periodicals. But since he was saying in effect that the military was now faced with a problem it could not solve, it was unlikely that many soldiers would agree with him.

In 1904–1905 Russia and Japan had fought a war with all the weapons whose lethal effects were so gruesomely described by Bloch, and Japan had won a clear-cut victory that established her in the ranks of the major powers. The effect on Russia had been much as Bloch described, but revolution and defeat always stalked hand in hand. The war had indeed lasted well over a year, but it had been fought by both belligerents at the end of long and difficult supply lines. In Europe, where lines of communication were plentiful and short, and armies at hair-trigger readiness, the pattern of the German wars of unification seemed much more relevant: rapid mobilization and deployment of all available forces; a few gigantic battles—battles, indeed, that might be prolonged for days if not weeks as the protagonists probed for a flank or a weak point in the enemy defenses; and a decision within a matter of months. Because that decision would be reached so quickly, it was important that all forces be committed to action. There was no point in bringing up reserves after the battle had been lost. It was even more pointless—if indeed it occurred to anyone—to prepare an industrial base to sustain a war of materiel that might last for years. The idea that any national economy could endure such an ordeal seemed absurd.

This shared assumption—that the war would inevitably be short—led to another: that the best chances for victory lay in immediately taking the offensive. With the wisdom of hindsight, it is easy for subsequent generations to condemn the suicidal unreality of this idea; but in the circumstances of the time, it appeared reasonable enough. An offensive held the best hope of disrupting or preempting the opponent's mobilization and bringing him to battle under conditions favorable to the side taking the initiative. As in a wrestling match, which has to be settled in a matter of minutes, to yield the initiative was to court defeat. The French had remained on the defensive in 1870 and been defeated. The Russians had remained on the defensive in 1904–1905 and been defeated. Those who had studied the American Civil War—including all of the students of the British Army Staff College at

Camberley—concluded that the only hope of a Confederate victory had lain in a successful offensive; and that once Lee passed over to the defensive after the Battle of Gettysburg, his defeat had been only a matter of time. The lessons of history seemed to reinforce the strategic imperatives of 1914.

And let us not forget what those strategic imperatives were. The Germans had to destroy the French power of resistance before the full force of Russian strength could be developed. The Russians had to attack sufficiently early, and in sufficient strength, to take the weight off the French. The Austrians had to attack the Russians in order to take the weight off the Germans. For the French alone a defensive strategy was in theory feasible, but the precedent of 1870 made it understandably unpopular, and the national mood made it inconceivable. The doctrine of the offensive was certainly carried to quite unreasonable lengths in the pre-1914 French army, but that in itself does not mean that a posture of defense would have been any more effective in checking the German advance in 1914 than it was in 1940.

Finally we must remember that the stalemate on the western front did not develop for six months, and that on the eastern front it never developed at all. The open warfare of maneuver for which the armies of Europe had prepared was precisely what, in the autumn of 1914, they got. It resulted in a succession of spectacular German victories in eastern Europe, and given bolder and more flexible leadership it might very well have done the same in the west. The terrible losses suffered by the French in Alsace in August and by the British and Germans in Flanders in November came in encounter battles, not in set-piece assaults against prepared defensive positions; and they were losses that, to the military leadership at least, came as no great surprise.

For this was the final assumption shared by soldiers throughout Europe: that in any future war, armies would have to endure very heavy losses indeed. The German army, for one, had never forgotten the price it paid for its victories in 1870, when the French had been armed with breech-loading rifles that, in comparison with the weapons now available, were primitive. Since then the effects of every new weapon had been studied with meticulous care, and no professional soldier was under any illusions about the damage that would be caused—not simply by machine guns (which were in fact seen as ideal weapons of a mobile offensive) but by magazine-loading rifles and by quick-firing artillery hurling shrapnel at infantry in the open and high explosives against trenches. Their effects had been studied through controlled experiment and also in action, in the South African and Russo-Japanese wars. The conclusion generally drawn was that in the future, infantry would be able to advance only in open formations, making use of all available cover, under the protection of concentrated artillery fire.

But whatever precautions they took, sooner or later troops would have to charge with the bayonet across open ground, and they must then be prepared to take very heavy losses. This had happened in Manchuria, where the Japanese were generally seen as owing their success not simply to their professional skills but to their contempt for death. European social Darwinians gravely propounded the terrible paradox that a nation's fitness to survive depended on the readiness of its individual members to die. Avoidance of casualties was seen as no part of the general's trade, and willingness to accept them was regarded as a necessity for commander and commanded alike. Into the literature of prewar Europe crept a term that was to become the terrible leitmotiv of the coming conflict: *sacrifice*—more particularly, *the supreme sacrifice*.

That may have been all very well for professional soldiers, whose job it is, after all, to die for their country if they cannot arrange matters any less wastefully. But the people who were going to die in the next war would not be just the professional soldiers. They would be the people: men recalled to the colors from civilian life or, in the case of England, volunteering to "do their bit." Would these young men, enervated by urban living, softened by socialist propaganda, show the same Bushido spirit as the Japanese? This question was constantly propounded in military and right-wing literature during the ten years before the war. Kipling, for one, surveying the civilians of Edwardian England in the aftermath of the Boer War, very much doubted it, and the writer taunted his fellow countrymen in a series of scornful philippics:

> *Fenced by your careful fathers, ringed by your leaden seas,*
> *Long did ye wake in quiet and long lie down at ease;*
> *Till ye said of Strife, "What is it?" of the Sword,*
> *"It is far from our ken";*
> *Till ye made a sport of your shrunken hosts and a toy*
> *of your arrièd men.*

In Germany Heinrich Class and Friedrich von Bernhardi, in France Charles Maurras and Charles Péguy, all expressed the same doubts about the capacity of their people to rise to the level of the forthcoming test. But the astonishing thing was that when the time came, they did so rise. Why?

This brings us belatedly to the third element in the triad, the people. Without the support, or at least the acquiescence, of the peoples of Europe, there would have been no war. This is the most interesting and most complex area for historians to investigate. We know a lot—almost to excess—about the mood of the intellectuals and the elites in 1914, but what about the rest? There are now some excellent studies of local and popular reactions in Britain, largely based on the superb sources at the Imperial War Museum. Jean-Jacques Becker had done pathbreaking work for France in his study *1914: Comment les Français sont entrés dans la guerre* (Paris, 1977), but elsewhere there remains much research to be done or, where done, brought together. My own ignorance forces me to treat this vast subject briefly and impressionistically, and I hope that others will be able to correct some of my misconceptions and fill some of the yawning gaps.

What does appear self-evident is that the doubts many European leaders felt about the morale of their peoples proved in 1914 to be ill-founded. Those who welcomed war with enthusiasm may have been a minority concentrated in the big cities, but those who opposed it were probably a smaller minority still. The vast majority were willing to do what their governments expected of them. Nationalistically oriented public education; military service that, however unwelcome and tedious, bred a sense of cohesion and national identity; continuing habits of social deference—all of this helps explain, at a deeper level than does the strident propaganda of the popular press, why the populations of Europe responded so readily to the call when it came. For the "city-bred populations" so mistrusted by right-wing politicians, the war came as an escape from humdrum or intolerable lives into a world of adventure and comradeship. Among the peasants of France, as Becker has shown us, there was little enthusiasm, but rather glum acceptance of yet another unavoidable hardship in lives that were and always had been unavoidably hard; but the hardship fell as much on those who were left behind as on those who went away. The same can no doubt be said of the peasants of central and eastern Europe.

Probably only a tiny minority considered the idea of war in itself repellent. Few military historians, and no popular historians, had yet depicted the realities of the battlefield in their true horror, and only a few alarmist prophets could begin to conceive what the realities of future battlefields would be like. Their nations, so the peoples of Europe had learned at school, had achieved their present greatness through successful wars—the centenaries of the battles of Trafalgar and Leipzig had recently been celebrated with great enthusiasm in Great Britain and Germany—and there was no reason to think that they would not one day have to fight again. Military leaders were everywhere respected and popular; military music was an intrinsic part of popular culture. In the popular mind, as in the military mind, wars were seen not as terrible evils to be deterred but as necessary struggles to be fought and won.

I have touched on the social Darwinism of the period: the view, widespread among intellectuals and publicists as well as among soldiers, that struggle was a natural process of development in both the social and natural orders of the world, and war a necessary procedure for ensuring survival of the fittest, among nations as among species. It is hard to know how seriously to take this. Its manifestations catch the eye of a contemporary historian if only because they are, to our generation, so very shocking. But how widespread were such views, and to what extent were proponents like F. N. Maude, Sidney Low, and Benjamin Kidd regarded as cranks?

The same applies to the much-touted influence of Nietzsche and Bergson among intellectuals—the creed of liberation from old social norms, of heroic egotism, of action as a value transcending all others. How widespread was their influence? Did it make the idea of war more generally acceptable than it otherwise would have been? Intellectuals tend to overrate the importance of other intellectuals, or at best attribute to them an influence that becomes important only among later generations. Webern and Schoenberg may have been composing in prewar Vienna, but the tunes that rang in the ears of the 1914 generation were those of Franz Lehár and Richard Strauss.

And if there was a "war movement," there was also, far more evident and purposeful, a peace movement, derived from older liberal-rationalist roots. It was stronger in some countries than in others; then as now, it flourished more successfully in Protestant than in Catholic cultures, at its strongest in Scandinavia, the Netherlands, and Britain (not to mention the United States), weakest in Italy and Spain. It was indeed the apparent strength and influence of the peace movement, especially at the time of the Hague Conferences, that provoked so much of the polemical writings of the social Darwinians and caused so much concern to nationalistic politicians.

In imperial Germany the peace movement had an uphill struggle; but if Heinrich Class and the Pan-German League were thundering out the dogmas of the war movement, the far larger and more important Social Democratic party rejected them. So did the overwhelmingly dominant Liberal-Labour coalition in England and the left wing led by Jean Jaurès that triumphed at the polls in France in the spring of 1914. Social Darwinism may have been not so much the prevailing zeitgeist as a sharp minority reaction against a much stronger and deeply rooted liberal, rational, and progressive creed whose growing influence seemed to some to be undermining the continuing capacity of nations to defend themselves.

But the events of 1914 showed these right-wing fears to be misplaced. Everywhere the leaders of the peace movement found themselves isolated: small and increasingly unpopular minorities of idealists, intellectuals, and religious zealots. Events made it clear that whatever their influence among intellectuals and elites, both the peace and the war movements were marginal to the attitudes of the peoples of Europe. Those people did *not* reject war. Nor did they regard it as the highest good, the fulfillment of human destiny. They accepted it as a fact of life. They trusted their rulers and marched when they were told. Many did so with real enthusiasm; perhaps the more highly educated they were, the greater the enthusiasm they felt. None knew what they were marching toward, and any romantic notions they had about war shredded to pieces the moment they came under artillery fire. But they adjusted to the ordeal with astonishing speed and stoicism. It was indeed because they adjusted so well that the ordeal lasted as long as it did.

Albert and the Yser

by ROBERT COWLEY

Everyone regards the Marne as the turning point of 1914 (and of the First World War itself); indeed, it was. But it might have been only a temporary reverse if the Germans had managed to breach another river barrier, that of the Yser, little more than a month later. "Surely the most insignificant stream that is assured of an immortality in history," one historian said of the tidal river on the Belgian coast, rarely wider than a lazy stone-toss. For the Germans, the Yser was the turning point that didn't turn: There seemed nothing to keep them from the last genuine prizes of 1914, the Channel ports. But the human factor intervened in a most un-Tolstoy-like way. The inspirational hero of the Yser, the person who elected, first, to make a stand there with an army that had practically ceased to exist—and then to sacrifice part of his own country to the sea—was the Belgian king Albert. But the man who literally turned the tide was an almost illiterate Flemish boatman named Hendrik Geeraert, who resorted to an ultimate weapon, the environment. The story of this key but forgotten episode of the Great War is told by Robert Cowley, the editor of *MHQ* and an authority on the western front.

The war on the western front is a war singularly devoid of "what ifs." You can almost count them on the fingers of your hand. What if one side had penetrated beyond the last line of resistance and had been able to pour its masses through ever-expanding gaps, to achieve not just a tactical but a strategic advantage? A rolling up of the line, an outflanking, a Cannae-like double envelopment? How often between the Marne in September 1914 and the Ludendorff offensives in the spring of 1918 did the outcome of a battle—perhaps of the war itself—hang in the balance, to be tipped this way or that by an unprogrammed confrontation, the fortuitous appearance of reinforcements, or the sudden, daring flash of perception that passes for genius?

The battle that took place near the mouth of the Belgian Yser River in the last two weeks of October 1914 is an exception, perhaps the only one: The "what ifs," the teetering balances of those few miles at the edge of the North Sea, are genuine enough. Here the Germans may have squandered the last real chance for open warfare, allowing the line of trenches that became known as the western front to solidify for good. Here, too, an unforeseen occurrence did change everything—the result of a decision that only one man could have made. Never again in the war would the peculiarities of local topography be used to such advantage.

That man was King Albert of Belgium, who led his country and army—or what was left of them—through the Great War. He is among the handful of genuinely attractive public figures in this century, a tall man with spectacles and a moustache that always seemed too wispy for his personality. If a single individual occasionally does have the power to shape destiny—if a leader's character really can influence his nation's fate—then Albert has to be counted in that select number. *Pace,* Tolstoy. His determined example certainly preserved Belgium in 1914, and a decision acted out on those riverbanks may have done for the Allied cause as well. Of all the presidents, prime ministers, and emperors who presided over the Great War, Albert was the only one who actually commanded his army, even to overseeing its day-to-day operations. He was also the only one who regularly showed up in frontline trenches. That army was, to be sure, small, but its symbolic importance was far out of proportion to its size and the tiny stretch of line it held, about 4 percent of the Allied side of the western front. Belgium and its violated neutrality provided the Allies with the ready-made patina of morality the war otherwise lacked. And Albert, the man who chose against all odds to resist the Hun, approached crusaderhood as nearly as anyone. He became, despite himself, the world's last warrior king.

Albert had been elevated to the throne of Belgium only by the accident of death. He was the nephew brought up in the shadows of the presumptive royal heirs, first the old king's son and then his own brother. Disease, as great a leveler in the nineteenth century as violence is in the twentieth, claimed both lives. Albert quickly established his own style, becoming less like a king than a president for life. He hated pomp, and his only concession to it was to wear his general's uniform at state functions. He often turned up with his family at a favorite country inn, where he insisted on being addressed as "monsieur." This was not Marie Antoinette playing at milkmaid.

Neither the isolation nor the ordinary ceremonial preoccupations of kingship were for Albert. He had a collection of automobiles, which he repaired himself. He experimented with wireless radios, made balloon ascensions, and descended into coal mines. An autodidact whose formal education had been pretty much limited to some nondescript palace tutoring and training as an officer in military school, he became a man obsessed with, but not bowed down by, information. Albert's appetite for books was voracious—Barbara Tuchman rightly used the word *gluttony* in this connection—and he read an average of two a day, in several languages. He never left a waking moment unfilled. "Boredom," the king once remarked—he was standing on the beach at Santa Barbara, California, during a triumphal tour of the United

States after the war—"is the sure sign of a mediocre mind. Such people are weary because, when alone, they are with themselves." He kept a rowing machine beside his desk. It was as if he felt a duty to be compulsive.

Albert was a pioneer ecologist who would later worry about the effects of wartime deforestation. Unlike his royal contemporaries, who, as if participating in some ancient blood rite, slaughtered game by the hundreds and thousands, he refused to hunt. His passion, rather, was for mountains, and he collected them the way Theodore Roosevelt collected trophy heads; he might be heard casually discussing botany as he went up the Jungfrau. "He would have discovered a pretext for scaling something in the flattest and most monotonous stretch of land," one biographer commented. The maritime plain of Flanders, to which his patriotism condemned him for the four years of the Great War, strains even that hyperbole.

There is a monument to Albert across the Yser from the town of Nieuport. In this part of the world, it doesn't take much for a structure to dominate the landscape—and the Albert Memorial does so by virtue of height alone, although it barely rises above a nearby grove. A kind of temple, circular, high-shouldered, and open to the sky, its square pillars and epistyle are built of once-pale brownstone that age and polluted air have treated with sooty unkindness. Its surface is covered with square studs and reminds you a bit of dried alligator hide. Or put it another way: Think of Stonehenge as conceived by the designers of suburban villas. That's the twentieth century for you.

An effigy of Albert sits with blackened, bronzy stiffness astride a horse. Though he was an accomplished rider, this particular genre of monumental sculpture hardly suits a man who spent some of his happiest moments driving a car or motorcycle (the faster the better), or piloting a plane. The warrior king wears a ridge-back French-style helmet. The long, handsome face under it seems too haughty for someone whose instincts were more democratic than royal. It's difficult to imagine Albert in the flesh turning up his nose, except to express an environmentalist's distaste for the traffic noise and the inescapable stench of diesel fumes that wash over his memorial.

You notice a sentence chiseled into a marble plaque: Ils ont Changé l'Yser en Rampart d'Occident (They turned the Yser into a Rampart of the West). The word *rampart,* too, has the ring of hyperbole. Through the pillars you can see the river, an unremarkable tidal stream, narrow but dredged deep enough to accommodate fishing boats. With its concrete banks the Yser has the look of a canal. A couple of miles to the west, between two long fishing piers, it alternately empties into the North Sea at low tide and is emptied into at high. Here the western front petered out in the coastal dunes—but that is getting ahead of the story.

Within easy walking distance of the monument, the river runs up against sluice gates; the bridge to Nieuport crosses over them. When the tide rises, the water, its dirty white foam creating the effect of cheap marbleized wallpaper, fairly boils around those gates. Below them, the channel of the river on the land side is placid and the level of the water conspicuously lower. That is a constant; otherwise the general aspect of the place has changed greatly since 1914. Six creeks and canals emptied into the river above the gates then; with modern reconstructions and hydraulic rearrangements, only two canals remain. Does it seem possible that the history of Europe may have been changed on this spot? You look in vain for more commemorative words. There are none. But then, those dark waters swirling impatiently against the sluice gates are their own best monument. Water was the essential element in the history of this part of the western front, the only element that mattered.

The channel under the sluice gates widens into a small lake whose rectangular banks are obviously man-made. It is a reservoir where the river waters could build up until low tide, when they would be released. Sailboats move effortlessly in the soft, warm wind, blown like parachute clumps of thistle seed. A thousand years ago, the surrounding polders—land reclaimed from the sea—formed an imposing bay into which oceangoing craft could sail as far as Dixmude, ten miles distant. Here, as in Holland, the creation of the polders was the result of the labor of generations, first to contain the flood from the sea, and then little by little to drain the marshes where it had left its brackish residue, to make them not just arable but fertile. Dixmude became the leading agricultural town of the area, and Nieuport served as the port for Ypres, that great cloth center of the Middle Ages.

Even now much of the surrounding maritime plain would be underwater if not for the sluice gates at Nieuport. They hold back the salt water at high tide and let the fresh river water flow out at low. To let in the sea, the process can simply be reversed. If the finger in the dike is one side of the legendary Lowlands coin, deliberate inundation is the other. What the sea could take away, it could also preserve. Flanders has always been a major theater of war, and time and again besieged coastal towns such as Ostend, Nieuport, and Dunkirk have been saved by flooding the surrounding plains. It seems an obvious lesson of history that whoever controls the sluice gates controls the surrounding country as well. But in 1914 that lesson was apparently lost on everyone concerned.

Albert had been king five years when the kaiser's armies breached the Belgian frontier on August 4, 1914. He was not quite forty, the youngest of the rulers of Europe. As a foretaste of what was to happen on the Yser, he ordered the destruction of all bridges and tunnels in the path of the advancing enemy. By October, the only real consolation prizes that still presented themselves to the Germans, temptingly so, were the Channel ports of Dunkirk and Calais. With stalemate spreading like hoarfrost across the autumn landscape of northern France, they now concentrated their efforts in Flanders. Success beckoned, especially on the far wing of the line, the sea end—the same Channel water that, according to the mordant imagery of the original but discarded Schlieffen Plan, the sleeve of the last German soldier had been supposed to brush a month or so earlier. There, somewhere on the maritime plain, the Germans would face the remnants of Albert's Belgian army. If they could break through here, and at Ypres, where another part of their offensive was concentrating, one commentator points out, "the Channel ports might be seized, direct communication between England and the Continent endangered and the left wing of the allies rolled up or forced to fall back. . . . The way for an advance on Paris would once more be open." In those first months of the Great War, only the events along the Marne were more important than those on the Yser.

The Belgian army had just managed to slip the German noose at Antwerp at the beginning of the month. In quick succession Ghent had fallen, and then Bruges and Ostend. It is hard to associate the parochial order and discrete stillness of the modern Flemish countryside with the sights and sensations of those wild days: the singing columns of German soldiers (they sang partly out of enthusiasm, partly because they were ordered to do so), the leaden skies and constant rain, the dust of summer turning into the mud of autumn, the unseasonal rumble of distant cannonfire, the villages burning on the night horizon, and, permeating everything, the rancid odor of thousands of marching men in their woolen uniforms, an odor that lingered in the air, mingling with the pungently familiar barnyard smells, long after the troops had disappeared into the morning fogs. Screens of cavalry swept in front, uhlans searching for the enemy rear guard.

Somewhere ahead were the Belgians. The greater number were refugees, packed into the last trains or fleeing by car, by cart, or on foot, heading for the French border and already crowding into the Channel ports. The exodus of populations on such a grand scale was a new phenomenon—but then, so was the "front" that caused it. Mixed in with the refugees were units of Albert's army, men who, in the apt phrase of a British military historian, were "experienced in nothing but defeat." A contemporary writer described the spectacle of the Belgian troops: "Instead of a haversack, almost all the soldiers carried a 'baluchon,' or kind of sack made of coarse grey cloth. They had all kinds of flasks, bottles, and cans by strings, laces, etc. The uniforms 'had nothing uniform but the name.' The soldiers who had come from Antwerp bareheaded had provided themselves with caps." Others, who had escaped into Holland after the city fell, returned rather than face internment, discarding their uniforms and recrossing the frontier in civilian clothes; many showed up on the Yser wearing *sabots* (wooden clogs).

In the first two and a half months of the war, the Belgian field army had lost well over half of its effectives, and by mid-October it could muster only 48,000 men. "They were almost at their last gasp," Albert's chief of staff admitted. Even the king himself was losing hope. "Situation very bad," his wife noted in her journal on October 15. "Everything seems black to Albert." He would have preferred to continue his retreat, reorganizing his shattered forces behind the French border. But he gave in to French pressure to make a stand on the Yser—though not to their demand that his troops join in the offensive they were planning along the whole Flanders front, as far south as Lille. He pointed out that the Yser position was a poor one because it was impossible to dig trenches in the low-lying, waterlogged soil: To resist the enormous German siege guns, trenches were necessary, and the deeper the better. He warned that his men could not resist here for long. Always a clever negotiator, Albert apparently used those reservations to extract from the French a reluctant promise of reinforcements.

Whatever his private misgivings or his temporary waverings, Albert kept them to himself. Once he had given his word, he held to it. Even as his wife was scribbling that gloomy entry, he issued a general order: "The line of the Yser constitutes our last line of defense in Belgium. . . . This line will be held at all costs." He also added a pointed touch of his own when he informed his division commanders that they should distribute staff officers among the fighting troops. They were to remain there during the battle, "giving fresh inspiration" up front "instead of constantly grumbling" in the rear.

The progress of the Germans had been just slow enough to allow Albert's men an interval of rest. It was at ten minutes after six on the morning of October 17, according to the journal of one of his regimental commanders, Lieutenant Colonel Arsène Bernard, that the first sound of cannonfire was heard along the Yser line. That night Bernard recorded a "small diversion": The cloud cover had temporarily lifted and his men watched the progress of a comet across the sky. Had his family, behind enemy lines in Brussels, also seen it? "Perhaps," he wrote, "our gazes met up there."

Between Nieuport and Dixmude, the two strongpoints that anchored the Belgian line, the Yser describes a knobby arc. A map of the river looks rather like the caricature of a rustic's face, one of van Gogh's potato eaters, perhaps, gaping northward with uncertain pugnacity. The peak of the head, at the sluices, slopes into a low brow; the loop at the halfway point forms a bulbous nose; and the chin juts out at Dixmude. The Yser is really just the largest of the creeks in the area, slinking through pastureland and fields of wheat and sugar beets; it is about sixty feet wide and no more than ten feet deep. Both sides are built up in dikes, the western one (behind which the Belgian troops crouched) commanding the eastern by a few feet. Infrequent bridges span the river. Farms built on barely perceptible hillocks as protection from flooding (a persistent threat in the wet months of fall and winter) can be seen here and there. The few trees and the isolated villages are starkly conspicuous. A couple of miles to the rear, across polders divided and subdivided into an intricate network of canals, creeks, and drainage ditches, is the Nieuport-Dixmude railway. It runs absolutely straight along an embankment nowhere more than five feet high (and sometimes as little as three), the highest elevation in the area. In 1914 everyone recognized that this embankment had to be the Belgian army's last line of defense.

On the morning of the 18th, the Germans attacked. The giant siege guns that had crushed the forts of Antwerp now systematically pulverized the brick walls and tile roofs of the farm villages where Belgian troops sought sanctuary on the right bank. By nightfall only two places on the right bank of the river remained in Allied hands: the outskirts of Nieuport, where shelling from a British flotilla offshore stopped the German advance down the dunes; and Dixmude, where a brigade of French marines, mostly young Breton sailors, wearing caps with red pom-poms, made what was literally a last-ditch stand. It would be another twenty-four days before the Germans finally forced them to retreat across the Yser.

The Germans brought up more heavy mortars and the pounding intensified. Their first attempts to get across the little river failed. The bombardment went on. At Nieuport that night the Belgians made their first experiment with inundation—a local initiative that has since been largely forgotten—opening the weirs of the old and uncanalized Yser channel at high tide. Their aim was to deny the bridges and the hydraulic system to the enemy by flooding. Though they created a considerable watery mess, it was not an impassable one. Their failure did not seem to justify another attempt.

The Germans, too, were busy under the cover of darkness. Just before dawn, at the loop of the river—the nose—they put a makeshift bridge across and established themselves on the left bank. During the night of the 22nd-23rd, the better part of two divisions, perhaps 20,000 men, poured over. Before long they had ruptured the Yser in several other places. It seemed only a matter of time until the Belgian army collapsed.

The Germans advanced by fits and starts; the Belgians and their French allies fell back across the amphibious landscape. Beyond that, it is hard to give coherence to the events of the next days. Attacks and counterattacks were broken as much by the slippery terrain and exhaustion as by artillery and machine guns. Formations melted away, and units, or what was left of them, became mixed up. Men skidded forward or backward in small, uncoordinated groups, taking advantage of whatever cover they could find, flopping in the sodden fields, crouching in frigid, water-filled ditches. Dead cattle littered their once-secure pastureland; corpses of every kind turned into sheltering promontories. The fighting spilled over into the night—and only became more confused. In the darkness, trenches were captured and recaptured; men trampled on the dead and wounded lying in the mud. Not even the constant rain could quench the fires of burning towns. At one place, where tanks along the riverbank went up in flames, spilling oil into the water, even the Yser caught fire.

No one—least of all the idealistic German student soldiers thrown into battle for the first time—was prepared for this sort of war. "In what bitter disappointment I now sit here, with horror in my heart," twenty-three-year-old Alfred Buchalski wrote home during a break in the fighting at Dixmude. "It was ghastly! Not the actual shedding of blood, nor that it was shed in vain, nor the fact that in the darkness our own comrades were firing at us—no, but the whole way in which a battle is fought is so revolting. . . . The attack, which I thought was going to be so magnificent, meant nothing but being forced to get forward from one bit of cover to another in the face of a hail of bullets, and not to see the enemy who was firing them!"

Then, in the sort of logically illogical flourish that might occur to a philosophy student like himself, Buchalski added what must surely be the saddest afterthought of the next four years: "If one could only accomplish something, then, no doubt, the bullets wouldn't hurt so much!"

The Germans, on the 24th, were in fact on the verge of accomplishing something. They now brought heavy artillery across, and its demoralizing effect was immediate. Increasing numbers of Belgian troops drifted to the rear; those who remained to fight dug in along their last line of defense, the railway embankment. A French colonel named Brécard reported: "The front is on the point of giving way on all sides . . . it looks as though it will be impossible to avert catastrophe." The Belgian army prepared to shift its head-quarters from Furnes, a few miles behind the fighting, to a safer spot near the French border. Though roofs were crashing around his command post, Albert elected to remain with his military operations staff. It was the sort of gesture, hardly empty, that was his special knack. Then four fresh battalions of a French division, some 4,000 men, showed up at Pervyse, in the center of the Belgian line. They were enough to check the German advance for that day.

The Belgians were saved again on the 25th. A hard rain blew in from the sea, gradually swelling into a tempest. There was a lull in the fighting: The attackers were as worn out as the defenders; their losses, too, had been heavy, and they no longer enjoyed the numerical advantage they had begun with, a week earlier. The real crisis that day took place behind the Allied line. At dawn the operations staff at Furnes was warned that General Ferdinand Foch, commanding the French armies in the North, contemplated letting the sea into the polders around Dunkirk. The Belgians panicked. A sheet of water spreading across their rear would have cut off their main route of re-treat—and retreat was apparently very much on their minds. The indications, long buried by subsequent official hagiography, are strong that retreat had been all but decided on. It took a direct appeal from Albert to General Joseph Joffre, the French commander in chief, to get the Dunkirk order counter-manded.

But another option, overlooked until then, was left to the desperate Belgians. Foch's understandable intention—somehow the enemy had to be stopped short of the Channel ports—precipitated an inundation plan of their own. It seems that a high-ranking member of the Belgian staff was quartered in Furnes with a local magistrate and antiquarian named Emeric Feys. Feys pointed out to him that deliberate inundation of the Yser had saved Nieuport from invading armies in the past; why couldn't it be resorted to again? The idea of creating a protective lagoon from Nieuport to Dixmude appealed to his guest, and it was seized upon at headquarters. No one in the Belgian army had studied the possibility until the moment he proposed it. Neither had the Germans, for that matter; they might otherwise have been quicker to seize the hydraulic system at Nieuport. History has its uses, after all.

Nieuport and its hydraulic system is "the key to the door," wrote that genius of French military engineers, Vauban, in 1706. He had built much of the Flanders canal network, and defensive inundation was uppermost in his mind. "Once Nieuport and Furnes slip from our grasp, we will soon have the enemy at the gates of Dunkirk."

The decision to return a sizable portion of Belgium to the sea—the watery equivalent of the scorched-earth policy—was one that only Albert could make. He made it without hesitation. The whole operation would have to be improvised, and it would be a tricky one. Most of the men who tended the bridge and canal system had fled to France, and headquarters could not even lay hands on tidal charts. Makeshift preparations had to be made. By that afternoon, soldiers of the engineer corps—sappers—had started to close the twenty-two culverts along the railway embankment. Small creeks ran through these culverts; blocking them would cause the creeks to back up and overflow, and would also prevent the flood from spreading behind the embankment. The sappers worked without letup in the violent rainstorm, often under fire. In places the enemy was only a few hundred yards away now.

On the morning of the 26th, the Germans attacked. Once again the intervention of fresh French battalions prevented a breakthrough at the embankment. But at the same time other French troops, who had no inkling of the contemplated inundations, abandoned the bridgehead protecting the Nieuport hydraulic system. They blew up the so-called Five Bridges there and retreated into the town. Once again, too, the Belgian staff prepared plans for a withdrawal. When he learned of them, Albert had one of his rare fits of anger. The embankment would hold. He was convinced the German offensive was beginning to run down.

As if to bear out his prediction, the Germans did not attack the next day, nor on the 28th. They were gathering their strength for a final assault. Preparation for the inundation went forward. Secrecy was maintained; the Germans suspected nothing. By now, the engineer officers in charge had located the chief lockkeeper of the Furnes canal, Carel-Louis Cogge. He would have nothing to do with the plan at first, and only the promise of a decoration induced him to help. On the night of the 27th-28th, Cogge showed sappers how to open the sluices of an abandoned canal on the sea side of Nieuport. A glance at the map makes it obvious that this was the safest one he could find. Even so, the sappers worked within hearing of the Germans, who had reached the sand flats just across the river. It turned out to be a night when tides were abnormally low, and the sappers were unable to let in much water. Then the sluice gates slammed shut. The second experiment had failed, but Cogge still received his decoration, and more than one history book gives him credit he probably didn't deserve.

Clearly the Belgians would have to try one of the watercourses at the dynamited bridges—which would mean venturing out into what was now a no-man's-land. And they would have to wait another day or two for the return of higher tides. At this point an engineer captain named Fernand Umé found a local Flemish boatman, Hendrik Geeraert. He suggested that Umé try a creek called the Noordvaart, which flowed between the railroad embankment and the Yser before emptying into the main channel at Nieuport. Though Geeraert was not a lockkeeper employed by the government, he claimed that he knew where to find the cranks that controlled the Noordvaart weir gates and how to manipulate them. (A distinction has to be made between sluices and weirs. The place where a canal empties into another stream is closed with *sluice* gates, which open outward to allow boats to pass. In a hydraulic system, creek flow is regulated by *weir* gates, which are raised and lowered.)

Hendrik Geeraert, to whom "the supreme maneuver" was finally entrusted, was a handsome but somewhat somber-looking man with graying hair and a thick, drooping mustache. He is described as being rough-mannered and uncommonly powerful for someone in his late middle age, intelligent but almost illiterate. "It could be said," writes the Belgian historian Henri Bernard, "that this primitive played as decisive a role in the Flanders struggle as any Belgian or Allied general."

At 7:30 in the evening of October 29, Geeraert led Umé and a detachment of sappers over a remaining footbridge that spanned the Furnes canal, the first branch. Covered by a machine-gun section and by carabineers from a cyclist platoon, they moved stealthily, fully expecting to encounter Germans amid the trees of the first little island. They found none. Now they had reached the Noordvaart, with its eight weir gates. On the opposite bank, hidden in a clump of bushes, were the gears that could raise those gates. They crossed the second branch. Again there were no Germans. The tide was already rising, and the wind blowing in from the sea made it even higher. Rain fell ceaselessly. To the east they could hear the sound of shellfire; the German assault on the embankment had started again.

They went to work. The seawater surged forward, soon overflowing the banks of the Noordvaart, which were not built up with dikes, and spreading over the plain. In the next few hours, they managed to let out about 700,000 cubic meters of water. At four in the morning, just before the ebb tide set in, Geeraert and the sappers closed the weir gates and returned to Nieuport.

There is something timeless about the polder landscape, even if most of the buildings date from after the Second World War. More fighting and destruction, as well as another inundation, occurred here then. It is one of those curious coincidences—history seems so full of them—that in 1940 the Belgian army was making a last stand in these parts when Albert's son Leopold decided to surrender. You see pylon-shaped concrete telephone poles and an occasional plaster deer in a front yard. You cross under a new motorway. But otherwise the fields are just as broad (though on closer inspection drainage ditches slice them up into rough morsels), the cows as brown, the dark clayey soil as rich, the richest in Flanders, and the tile roofs and the poppies that swarm along the banks of the Yser as red as they were in 1914. Trees still explode in low, isolated bursts, their growth stunted by the wind. The tallest objects are, as they always have been, man-made: the church steeples that rise above every village cluster, as if endlessly aspiring to defeat the precarious monotony of a country rescued from the sea.

Leaving Nieuport and heading along the left bank of the Yser, you follow a road barely wide enough for your car. But it is the narrowness of the river itself that is so impressive, never more than a lazy stone-toss from bank to bank. "Surely the most insignificant stream that is assured of an immortality in history" is the way the British *Official History* puts it. The waters of the Yser have a sluggish and vaguely chemical opaqueness. Who would suspect that in one of the wettest places in Europe, potable water has always been in short supply? The water near the surface of the polders is likely to be contaminated by animal and fertilizer wastes; deeper down, below that impervious layer of clay, it is brackish, still flavored by the sea. "In the barn and stable of a small farm," notes a contemporary account of the Yser battle, "there were crowds of wounded men. It was impossible to evacuate them, as the enemy was ceaselessly shelling the ground behind the Belgian trenches. The surgeon, the chaplain, and the ambulance staff did their utmost. To quench the thirst of the delirious men in agony they had to boil the stagnant water of the brooks."

You have the feeling that you are intruding on an immense game board, but one from which the pieces long ago vanished. The cows are the main players now. Once, near that noselike bend in the river, you come on a stone commemorating a doomed Belgian counterattack that briefly held the Germans on the 22nd of October.

You wander away from the river. Somewhere in those fields you may have encountered the Noordvaart—one deep ditch seems pretty much like another. With a slight bump, you go over the railroad tracks, which run straight as a gunshot, disappearing into the ever-present haze. What can you say about the famous embankment, its careful steep talus of sharp rocks about like any other you will find in the world, except to note that it is just high enough to give shelter? You catch sight of a squarish, ruined tower with a concrete blockhouse built on top, an observation post throughout the war.

The road leads into Pervyse. If you arrive in the afternoon, you will find its metal shutters drawn against the sun. It is that empty time when all the slops are closed for the afternoon break. About this hour during the crisis of the 24th, the commander of the French reinforcements, a plump, white-bearded gentleman named Paul François Grossetti, ordered a chair brought to the center of Pervyse's principal intersection, the most deliberately conspicuous place he could find. There, with shells exploding around him, the general sat throughout the afternoon, leaning on a cane as he directed the defense of the town and the embankment beyond. His kind was all too rare. History sometimes becomes positively axiomatic: The longer the war lasted, the greater the distance generals seemed to put between themselves and the front.

You turn cautiously into that intersection. The notion of someone today plunking his fat body down in the midst of the ever-dense traffic seems a delicious absurdity. Lord knows, it's not easy to find one in the solid brick of those Flanders towns. The place you are looking for is called Ramscappelle; you have to double back a few miles toward the sea. Just off the main east-west highway, at the entrance to that little town, a hedge surrounds a triangular bit of lawn and flower beds. Its centerpiece is a replica of a windmill, large enough to conceal a transformer station. (*Nothing* is wasted in this country.) The object of your search is a low demarcation stone erected after the war by the Touring Club of Belgium; it is set in a break in the hedge. A sizable chip, knocked off by a direct hit in the Second World War, is missing from the French-style helmet on its top. (This seems to be a feature of western-front monuments.) You try to comprehend the meaning of that stone. Presumably, in 1914, some German soldiers had reached this spot, a half mile beyond the railway embankment and at the edge of open country. The stone commemorates the limit of their advance. On the Yser front, this was as far as the Germans would ever get.

Even as Geeraert and Umé were opening the Noordvaart weir in the streaming darkness of the 29th, the Germans seemed on the verge of success. A few hours before, the young American correspondent Edgar Ansel Mowrer had climbed the damaged belfry at Pervyse—the same one you can see from the road—to watch the Germans attacking "across the soggy fields. I could faintly see them advancing in mass formation, singing as they came." Mowrer wandered north, to be closer to the action, "and was sent to the rear by a French artillery lieutenant whose 'seventy-fives' were 'pouring it on' Ramscappelle. That night the Germans reached the embankment."

They not only reached it but went beyond, fighting through Ramscappelle house by house. At 4:30 on the morning of the 30th, Lieutenant Colonel Bernard noted that he was "woken by the hell-like cannonade." By daybreak the German waves were crashing against the embankment with full force. At Pervyse, the attackers got close enough to lob grenades across and soon had gained a foothold on the other side. Meanwhile, they drove the Belgians completely out of Ramscappelle. The way to Dunkirk and Calais was now open.

And then suddenly, around noon, the firing from the German side began to die down.

The French and Belgian troops could not understand what was happening. In the fields south of Ramscappelle, they re-formed behind yet another insubstantial stream and waited for fresh lines of attackers to emerge from the town. None appeared. The Allied troops crept back after nightfall. Though they did not clean out the town until the next day, it was clear that the main German force had gone. The end came even sooner at Pervyse. There at ten on the morning of the 30th, Bernard was ordered to counterattack; at one o'clock the order was countermanded. His regiment entered Pervyse unopposed. "The smell is putrid," he wrote, "from so many bloated animal carcasses. We discover numerous German corpses as well as some wounded . . . who are made prisoners." The enemy, he said, had fallen back because of the inundation. It was Bernard's first mention of the word. Albert's secret had been well kept.

The inundation had taken effect not a moment too soon. You must not imagine that Geeraert and Umé released an immediate floodlike deluge on the Yser plain, a spreading wave that uprooted trees and swept away houses and men. It was nothing so dramatic. At first the only sign was the desperate agitation of the freshwater fish—the trout, carp, and pike that inhabited the canals and side streams—as the salt water took over. As the hours passed, the meadows turned increasingly boggy. The inundation was, in the grandiose but accurate words of a French account,

> invincible and implacable in its slow progress. It stretched as an immense sheet of water, slightly undulating. . . . It came noiselessly, filling the canals, leveling the ditches, the roads, and the shell holes. It glided, slipped, oozed everywhere. It was a silent conqueror at first scarcely visible. The water surrounded islets of rising ground, whence groups of soldiers fled drenched

to the knees. It murmured patiently along the trenches, it came from the horizon and reached the horizon.

The Germans panicked as they felt the ground disappear under them. They could not get reinforcements forward, and soon it was all they could do to retreat to the safety of the right bank. Guns sank in the mud and had to be abandoned. The water hid ditches and creeks, into which men plunged over their heads, and cut off others dug in before the embankment, forcing them to surrender. Isolated wounded undoubtedly drowned or died of exposure. The Germans never suspected the cause and attributed it to the heavy rains. They made no further attempts to seize the Nieuport hydraulic system; the full force of their offensive was directed now at Ypres. Ypres, too, held—barely. You can argue that the Germans never came as close to a break-through there as some historians, mainly British, would like to make out; the Yser was another matter. If not for Albert's decision to inundate, Ypres might have been taken from the rear in the next few days. Play with that thought.

On the night of the 30th, and the two nights following, Geeraert and Umé went back to work. By the time they were done, they had created an artificial lagoon extending from Nieuport almost to Dixmude, and from the embankment to the Yser—about three miles at its widest point and almost nine miles long. At its maximum, it was the widest no-man's-land on the western front. The areas under water varied from three to ten feet in depth. There were, to be sure, sizable patches not covered by water, but they were mostly impassable marsh. What had once been an estuary of the sea reverted to its original state.

"A strange silence reigned," wrote Lieutenant General Emile Galet, Albert's chief of staff. "The enemy, driven away by the most irresistible of the elements, had vanished." When the mists rose, men standing on the embankment could look across a dead sea to the German shore—you could no longer talk about the "banks" of the Yser. Fence posts and the tops of pollarded willows poked up, as forlorn as the gutted walls of drowned farms; an occasional burned-out church tower cast its dark shadow over the waters. Muddy roads that disappeared into the lagoon seemed already annealed to it. Beyond, and out of reach for the duration, stood empty carts, faint waves lapping at their axles. The light caught the dull white of fish stomachs, and half-starved men scooped up the first victims of the inundation while they were still reasonably fresh. Bodies, human and animal, floated amid a flotsam of leather helmets, knapsacks, and cartridge boxes. Bloated corpses rising to the surface marked the line of yesterday's trenches.

Albert had won the only victory he needed to win.

Nuit calme sur le front de l'Yser. For the next four years, the daily communiqué from Belgian headquarters, its version of "All quiet on the western front," would seldom vary. Some weeks after the battle ended, the Belgians extended the inundation by jamming the culverts in the dikes along the straight stretch of the Yser below Dixmude. The inundation now formed a semicircle of about twenty-two miles. A boot may be a more apt simile—

some might say a skeletal foot—with a high heel at the sharp Dixmude bend and a long toe pointing toward the river's source, just across the French border. The inundation had to be one of the great unnatural wonders of the western front.

The Belgians did not budge beyond its watery confines until late September 1918, when Albert joined the final Allied sweep through Flanders. In the long interim, he steadfastly withheld his troops from the offensive adventures of his allies. With most of his small country behind enemy lines, he recognized that he could not rely on a limitless supply of expendable manpower. Albert's army suffered an average of four to five deaths a day from enemy fire, but lost a larger number to disease. The Yser was the unhealthiest sector of the western front. Surface water was hopelessly contaminated by the waste of the dead and the wastes of the living. At the end of 1914, an epidemic of typhoid fever killed 2,500 Belgian troops, only 600 fewer than their total deaths in the Yser battle.

The dedication date on the memorial at Nieuport is 1933. To begin with, it was merely a monument to the stand along the river—the river that became the westernmost dividing line, a rampart in every sense, of the western front. But one February afternoon the following winter, the king was driven to the Meuse for a solitary climb. On some needlelike rocks eighty feet above the river, he slipped, and apparently without a sound—panic was never part of Albert's repertoire—fell to his death. He was just fifty-eight. So the monument became a memorial. You wonder whether the subsequent history of Europe would have been quite the same if Albert had lived out a normal life span.

All of that, admittedly, is afterthought. As you stroll beyond the temple dedicated to Albert, following the path to the Yser sluice gates, something else strikes you. How curious it is that a memorial to a man who loved mountains, who died scaling a rock face, stands in one of the most low-lying places in Europe—a place that was in fact, within documented memory, under the sea.

The Wreck of the Magdeburg

by DAVID KAHN

The First World War was barely three weeks old when another of military history's predictable accidents happened, and one that had the potential to change its outcome. That was the grounding of the German cruiser *Magdeburg* on a Baltic island off the coast of what is now Estonia. A comedy of errors that was not so comic would give the British the *Magdeburg*'s naval codebooks. It could have given them the edge on Jutland in 1916, but they could never quite believe their luck. For every lost order there will always be a McClellan—or in this case, a Captain Blimp. But less than a year later, those broken codes would provide the British with the propaganda coup that would push the United States to the edge of war with Germany. David Kahn has to be counted the world's leading historian of cryptology; this article was adapted and expanded from his most recent book, *Seizing the Enigma* (Houghton Mifflin).

On the afternoon of August 24, 1914, the German warship *Magdeburg* steamed out of the East Prussian harbor of Memel toward the most fateful accident in the history of cryptography.

A four-stacker, the *Magdeburg* was what the Germans called a small cruiser, different from the larger light cruisers. She was new (three years old), well armed (twelve fast-firing, 4-inch guns), fast (27.6 knots)—and unlucky. Her acceptance test had not gone well. Her commissioning had been delayed several months. She had never participated, as was intended, in the autumn 1912 naval maneuvers. Some equipment was still not in order when she was declared "ready for war" and when the ancient city of Magdeburg, for which she was named, sponsored her in two days of festivities. One of her turbines gave trouble. And unlike her sister ships, which got assignments suitable for cruisers, the *Magdeburg* merely fired test torpedoes.

The *Magdeburg* was part of Germany's Baltic Fleet. When war with Russia, France, and England broke out in August 1914, she dropped her test assignment and undertook more-typical cruiser tasks. These were directed against the Russians, whose empire included Finland, Estonia, Latvia, and Lithuania—the countries bordering the eastern Baltic. In her first operation, the *Magdeburg* and another small cruiser, the *Augsburg,* arrived off Liepāja, Latvia's naval port, to lay mines. They gained an unexpected success: The Russians, thinking the appearance of the two ships portended a major fleet operation, blew up their own ammunition and coal dumps and scuttled ships in the harbor entrances. In the two ships' second and third operations, they shot up some lighthouses and a signal station and laid a minefield not far from the mouth of the eastern arm of the Baltic Sea, the Gulf of Finland, at whose farther end lay the Russian capital, St. Petersburg.

A few days later, on August 23, the commander of a new flotilla ordered his vessels, which included the two cruisers, to assemble for an operation. The *Magdeburg,* in Danzig, then a German port, went first to Memel, at the extreme east of Prussia, for some gunnery exercises to reassure the population, nervous because the Russian border was not far from the city limits. The next afternoon the warship set out for the rendezvous. She joined the *Augsburg,* three torpedo boats, a submarine, and three other warships early on the 25th off Hoburgen lighthouse on the southern tip of the Swedish island of Gotland. There, the officers were told of the plan: The ships were to slip by night behind a Russian minefield believed to protect the entrance of the Gulf of Finland, and attack whatever Russian ships they found.

At 8:30 A.M. that same day, the flotilla set out, moving to the northeast at the fairly high speed of twenty knots. The sailors aboard the *Magdeburg,* who suspected the presence of enemy armored cruisers, thought the assignment would prove to be just a suicide mission.

By 5 P.M., in a calm sea, the air misty, the navigational plots of the *Magdeburg* and the *Augsburg* differed by a mile. But this raised no concern, since the *Magdeburg* was to follow the flagship *Augsburg* by half a mile: If the *Augsburg* struck a mine, the *Magdeburg* had time to avoid hitting any herself.

Soon, however, fog—common in those waters in summer—rolled in. By 9 P.M. it was so thick that even with binoculars an officer on the bridge of the *Magdeburg* could not see the lookout on the stern. At 11 P.M. the *Augsburg,* intending to run along the supposed Russian minefield before swinging east to enter the Gulf of Finland, turned onto a course south-southeast 1/2 point east (151 degrees, 32 minutes, 30 seconds) and ordered the *Magdeburg* to do the same. She did so, maintaining the same 230 engine revolutions per minute, or about fifteen knots, that had kept her at the proper distance from the *Augsburg* during the afternoon. But she was a mile farther south than her plot showed her to be.

Her captain, Lieutenant Commander Richard Habenicht, had soundings taken. These showed the depth decreasing: 190 feet, 141 feet, and, at 12:30 A.M., now August 26, 112 feet. At the same time the radio shack reported that a message from the *Augsburg* was coming in; four minutes later it was decoded and on the bridge. It ordered that her course be altered to east-northeast 1/2 point east (73 degrees, 7 minutes, 30 seconds). The helms-man turned the rudder 20 degrees, and at 12:37, just as he reported that the new course was being steered, still at fifteen knots, the luckless vessel hit something. She bumped five or six times and, shuddering, stopped. The cruiser had run aground. As a consequence of her earlier navigational error, she had struck shallows 400 yards off the northwestern tip of Odensholm, a low, narrow island two and one-half miles long at the entrance to the Gulf of Finland.

At once, Habenicht sought to get his ship off. He reversed engines. The ship stayed stuck. He rocked her with various engine speeds. He assembled the entire 337-man crew on the quarterdeck to push the *Magdeburg*'s stern down and her bow up and then went full speed astern. He had the crew carry munitions aft. The ship didn't budge. Soundings showed that at the bow, where the *Magdeburg* normally drew sixteen and one-half feet, the water to starboard was only nine feet deep; at the stern, with normal draft just under twenty feet, the depth was thirteen feet. The vessel needed to rise seven feet.

Habenicht jettisoned the anchors and their chains. He had the drinking and washing water pumped out. Ash ejectors flung coal into the sea. All but sixty boxes of munitions were dumped over the side. All movable steel parts—the mine-laying rails, bulkhead doors, doors on the forward turrets, steel ca-bles, coaling equipment—were pushed overboard. Habenicht then ran the engines forward and backward at various speeds. The *Magdeburg* moved not an inch.

The Germans' efforts were spurred by the likelihood that the officials on Odensholm, which was Russian territory with a lighthouse and a signal sta-tion, had alerted superiors at the major Russian port of Tallinn, only fifty miles away. Habenicht worried that the cruiser's secret documents might fall into Russian hands. In addition to the charts of German minefields and the ship's war diary, these included the main Imperial German Navy code and the key used to encipher its code words and thus to provide another layer of secrecy.

Lieutenant Walther Bender, who as first radio officer was in charge of destroying these documents, brought one of the codebooks and its cipher key from the steering room to the stokehold and burned it. Sailors did the same for other secret documents. But two codebooks—one on the bridge and one in the radio shack—as well as a cipher key were retained for possible use in communicating with rescuers and higher commands. A fourth lay hidden and apparently forgotten in a locker in Habenicht's cabin.

As dawn approached, the seabed and the stones on which the ship was lying became visible. At 8:30, with the fog lifting, the fast and powerful torpedo boat V-26 appeared, attached a line, and tried to pull the *Magdeburg* off. She failed. Habenicht decided he might as well do some damage and fired about 120 shots at the lighthouse, chipping it, and at the signal station, setting it ablaze. By then the radio shack was picking up many signals from Russian ships; apparently they were on their way. Since all attempts to free the *Magdeburg* had failed, Habenicht regretfully concluded he had to blow her up rather than let her fall into enemy hands.

Charges were set fore and aft. The crew was to get off the ship and onto the V-26, which was to come alongside. But suddenly a shout rang through the ship: "The fuses are lit!" Habenicht had not ordered this; it had been done by mistake. The vessel would blow up in only four and a half minutes.

In the midst of the tumult that ensued, Bender directed the second radio officer, Lieutenant Olff, to have the codebook and cipher key from the radio shack taken off the ship and onto the V-26. On Olff's instructions, Radioman Second Class Neuhaus grabbed the codebook and Radioman Third Class Kiehnert the cipher-key papers. The bridge's codebook was in the hands of Radioman Second Class Szillat. The first officer, unable to find Habenicht as the seconds ticked away, ordered the crew to the afterdeck, where the V-26 was to pick them up. He called for three cheers for the kaiser, had the two ships' boats lowered, and commanded, "All hands abandon ship!"

Upon hearing this, Szillat flung the codebook he was carrying over the side, toward the stern. It splashed into what he said was a "dark" place about fifteen feet from the ship and immediately sank. Then he leaped overboard. Kiehnert, too, jumped into the water, holding the radio shack's cipher key. He was struck by men following him, and when he came to the surface, he noticed that he had lost the key.

At 9:10 the forward charge detonated. It split the vessel in half, tore open the forepart from near the bow to the second smokestack, and hurled huge pieces of steel into the air. They rained down upon scores of men who were trying to swim to the V-26. Neuhaus, carrying the radio shack's code, had been seen in the water before the explosion but was missing for a while later; no one knew what had happened to the codebook.

The V-26 picked up many of the swimming men, including Szillat and Kiehnert. Fear of being destroyed in the explosion of the *Magdeburg*'s after charge—which never fired—kept the torpedo boat from coming near enough to rescue the men still aboard. Meanwhile Russian ships, closing, began to fire at the speedy vessel. One shell swept eight men overboard; another smashed into her starboard side, destroying the officers' wardroom and killing all who were in it, mainly wounded men from the *Magdeburg*. But the V-26 got away.

Habenicht, who had appeared briefly on the bridge when he heard the cheers for the kaiser and then vanished again into the bowels of his cruiser, did not abandon ship but awaited his fate on it, together with a few others. Bender and a few dozen sailors, among them Neuhaus, swam to Odensholm, where they were taken prisoner. One of the Russian ships, the torpedo boat *Lejtenant Burakov,* sent a boat with armed men, led by her first officer, Lieutenant Galibin, to the *Magdeburg.* The crew members still on board offered no resistance and were taken prisoner. Habenicht, whom Galibin thought "a true gentleman," offered the Russian his dagger, which Galibin chivalrously declined. The Germans were rowed from both the ship and the island to one of the Russian cruisers and later sent to a prisoner-of-war camp in Siberia.

Galibin lowered the black-white-and-red German naval war flag and raised the white czarist flag with its light blue cross of diagonals. Then, revolver in hand, he searched the wreck of the *Magdeburg*. He found a locker in Habenicht's cabin and broke it open. Hidden deep within it was the German codebook, forgotten in the excitement of the catastrophe. Galibin removed it, together with other documents, and had it transferred to the *Lejtenant Burakov*. The Allies thus came into possession of the key cryptographic secret of the Imperial German Navy—the one that gave them access to many others.

Knowing that possession of the German code books and its cipher keys would be enormously helpful to Britain's Royal Navy, the Russians loyally notified their allies of the find and said they would give them the documents if the British would send a small warship to escort the officers accompanying the documents to Britain. The Russians courteously set aside for the British the original code, which bore serial number 151, making a copy of it for themselves.

The task of bringing Codebook 151 to England was assigned to two naval captains, Kedrov and Smirnow, and to another naval officer, Count Constantine Benckendorff. A cosmopolitan, moustachioed combat veteran of the Russo-Japanese War, Benckendorff was the son of the ambassador to Great Britain and had served a year as a cipher clerk in the London embassy. He was on watch on the battleship *Poltava* in the Tallinn roadstead, pacing the quarterdeck and listening to the sailors' choir chanting the Russian Orthodox mass on a Sunday morning in September, when a yeoman handed him an order to report to the flag captain. On the flagship, he was "amazed and delighted" to be told he would be going to London.

He was given the precious codebook in St. Petersburg. It was in a satchel with a large piece of lead sewn in to make it sink in case he had to throw it overboard. He took the satchel to Arkhangel'sk, where he boarded a Russian volunteer fleet steamer. The vessel was to meet the British escort, the aging cruiser HMS *Theseus*, at Aleksandrovsk (now Polyarny), a port near Murmansk, whence it had arrived early in September from Scapa Flow, the deep, circular, islands-sheltered bay in the Orkneys just north of Scotland.

Owing to the time needed for copying the codebook and to bureaucratic delays and misunderstandings, the *Theseus* and the steamer did not sail until September 30. After an uneventful crossing over the top of Norway, punctuated only by a few vague U-boat alarms, the *Theseus* arrived in Scapa Flow on October 10; the Russian steamer, with Benckendorff aboard, went on alone to Hull, arriving there a couple of days later.

After a slow night-train ride, Benckendorff reached the Russian embassy at dawn. He greeted his parents, then routed out the naval attaché, and the two went, early on the morning of October 13, to the Admiralty. There, in a moment heavy with history, they handed Winston Churchill, the first lord of the Admiralty, a gift more precious than a dozen jewel-encrusted Fabergé eggs: the big, fat, blue-bound *Signalbuch der Kaiserlichen Marine*.

It went at once to the fledgling group of codebreakers set up at the outbreak of war by the director of naval education, Sir Alfred Ewing, an engineer who had long been interested in ciphers. A short, thickset Scot, given to wearing mauve shirts with white wing collars, he was a good friend of the director of naval intelligence, who had asked him to see what he could do with the encoded German radio messages being intercepted by British stations. Ewing had gathered some instructors in German from the Royal Naval Colleges, sat them around a desk in his cramped office, and, with them, examined the intercepts. But though they classified the messages into different kinds based on their appearance and addressees, they had not been able to read any of them.

Now, two months later, the German naval codebook landed on their desk. It contained hundreds of pages of columns of five-digit groups and three-letter groups standing opposite the German words they were to replace. For example, 63940 or OAX were the secret substitutes for Oktober. The encoder looked up each word of his message in the codebook as in a dictionary and replaced it with the five-digit code number or—more usually—the three-letter code word next to it. The succession of these code numbers or code words formed the secret message, or cryptogram. But British attempts to decipher the intercepts by this simple method still did not work. Some code words could not be found in the codebook, and those that could produced gibberish.

Gradually the British discovered that the *letters* of the code words had also been disguised. Other letters replaced them, so that the codebook's OAX might become the transmitted JVM. By early November the British had worked out the letter substitutes and were able to read many German naval messages.

Among the first were some that dealt with a possible ambush. The German naval commander, encouraged by the success of a bombardment and mine-laying off the British port of Yarmouth, which some Britons feared presaged an invasion, decided to repeat the action with two ports in northern England, Scarborough and Hartlepool. He hoped to lure some British battle cruisers into the arms of his full High Seas Fleet, destroy them, and thus regain at least near-parity with British naval forces. On December 14, 1914, his scouting-force commander, Vice Admiral Franz von Hipper, wirelessed a request for extensive aerial reconnaissance to the north, northwest, and west on the next two days. He added that German forces would sail from their roundish harbor in the estuary of the Jade River at Wilhelmshaven at 3:30 A.M.

The British intercepted and deciphered the message. It went to retired admiral Sir Arthur Wilson, a former first sea lord (equivalent to a U.S. chief of naval operations) who had returned as Churchill's adviser on intelligence and other matters. At 7 P.M. on the 14th, he brought it to Churchill, who summoned the first sea lord and the chief of staff. What did it mean? It specified no objective, but Wilson said that it probably indicated a movement of the German battle cruisers against English coasts and that the High Seas Fleet as a whole seemed not to be involved. The others agreed with his conclusions, though they acknowledged that hypotheses were needed to bridge the gaps in the evidence.

Within hours the Admiralty ordered units of the British fleet to proceed at once to a "point where they can intercept the enemy on his return." But thinking the German battleships were staying in port, the Admiralty refused to let more than a single squadron of British battleships sail from their home base of Scapa Flow. The commander of the British Grand Fleet, Admiral Sir John Jellicoe, chose the perfect intercept point: on an almost direct line between Scarborough and the German island fortress of Heligoland off Wilhelmshaven.

The Germans sailed at 3 A.M. on December 15, the British soon thereafter. By the morning of the 16th, the Germans were bombarding Hartlepool and Scarborough. Churchill, notified in his bath at 8:30, hopped out, put his clothes on over a damp body, and hurried downstairs to the War Room. The admirals assembled there were confident of their dispositions, but they knew that weather in the wintry North Sea could shut down visibility, and thus the possibility of contact, within minutes. What they did not know was that, despite their assumptions, the whole High Seas Fleet had sailed. If it met with the reduced force of British ships, it could destroy the British squadrons and regain the equivalence in forces that could change the course of the naval war.

Indeed, in the predawn blackness of December 16, one of the German destroyers ran into the British advance screen. The contact created the very situation that the Germans had sought since the start of the war. But the German commander did not recognize it. Believing himself to be confronted by the whole of Britain's Grand Fleet, and mindful of the kaiser's fears about losing the navy, he turned for home. He thus lost the greatest opportunity the German navy was ever to have.

Meanwhile, Hipper's forces were likewise racing for home after the bombardment. British intelligence had placed their ships so precisely in Hipper's path that at 10:30 A.M. the light cruiser *Southampton* spotted them. But fog and rain were reducing visibility, and before either the *Southampton* or the heavier British forces could attack, Hipper's ships escaped behind the veils of mist, reaching home safely.

The British were angry and disappointed. Not only had the navy failed to defend Britain's coast, it had failed to sink any Germans. Their anger was compounded by frustration. Churchill later said that he had

> to bear in silence the censures of our countrymen. We could never admit for fear of compromising our secret information where our squadrons were, or how near the German raiding cruisers had been to their destruction. One comfort we had, the indications upon which we had acted had been confirmed by events.

Similar indications came the next month. Wilson strode into Churchill's office around noon on January 23, 1915, and said, "First Lord, those fellows are coming out again."

"When?"

"Tonight. We have just time to get Beatty there," he said, referring to Vice Admiral Sir David Beatty, commander of the battle cruisers. Wilson explained that the codebreakers had read a message sent at 10:25 that morning to Hipper, ordering a reconnaissance of the Dogger Bank, a sandy shallows in the North Sea about sixty miles east of Britain.

Britain elected to use the same tactics as before, and units under Beatty sailed to block the German homeward trip. This time they were luckier. Contact was made at 7:30 A.M. on January 24 at a point on the Dogger Bank. When Hipper saw the numerous English forces, he followed directives, collected his ships, and ran. The British, in their faster, superdreadnought-class battleships, gave chase. By 9 A.M., the *Lion,* carrying Beatty, opened fire at 20,000 yards (eleven miles). The action soon became general between the four British and four German capital ships. The *Blücher* was sunk and the *Seydlitz* and *Derfflinger* heavily damaged. Confusion in the British squadron after a shell crippled the flagship permitted the German ships to escape. Nevertheless, the Germans staggered into port, flames leaping above their funnels, their decks encumbered with wreckage and crowded with the wounded and the dead. The German ships did not stir out of port again for more than a year.

The codebreakers had by this time expanded slightly and taken up the quarters in the Admiralty's Old Building that soon gave them their unofficial name: "Room 40, O.B." The Battle of the Dogger Bank earned them the confidence of the Admiralty, and shortly afterward the terrifying Lord John ("Jackie") Fisher, the builder of the dreadnought fleet who had just returned as first sea lord, gave Ewing carte blanche to get whatever he needed for the betterment of his work. Ewing augmented his staff, added to his intercept and radio direction-finding stations, and improved their equipment.

But some of Room 40's effectiveness was lost due to excessively tight control by the director of the operations division, Captain Thomas Jackson. Boorish and self-opinionated, Jackson distrusted civilians' ability to deal with naval affairs and was unpleasant to them. He hardly visited Room 40 at all, and on one of those occasions came only to complain that he had cut his hand on one of the red boxes in which the intercepts were circulated. Another time, when a change of cipher key temporarily interrupted the flow of solutions, he called to express his relief that he would not be further bothered by such nonsense. This attitude was to have grave effects.

In the late spring of 1916, the new commander of the German High Seas Fleet, Vice Admiral Reinhard Scheer, was chafing at his inactivity. He decided to try to repeat, with a variation, some of the tactics that sought to bring parity between his fleet and his enemy's. He would attempt to entice the British Grand Fleet to where his submarines could attack it and his High Seas Fleet fall upon a section of it without risking a general engagement.

His orders, however, lay at the mercy of British radio intelligence. Cryptanalysis was part of this; another was radio direction-finding. In this, radio stations take bearings on the emissions of a transmitter from two or more points; a control center plots these bearings on a map, and the transmitter is located where they cross. Successive plottings can determine the movement of a transmitter—its direction and speed.

It seems to have been such intelligence that led the Admiralty to inform its forces at 5 P.M., May 30, 1916, that the High Seas Fleet was apparently about to put out to sea. At this news, virtually the entire Grand Fleet, that mighty armored pride of England, built up steam and sallied forth majestically from Scapa Flow, Invergordon, and Rosyth. It sought a major fleet action that would give England the undisputed control of the seas on which her strategy in the war so heavily depended.

There then occurred one of those trifling errors on which history so often turns. On sailing, Scheer had transferred the call sign DK of his flagship *Friedrich der Grosse* to the naval center at Wilhelmshaven in an attempt to conceal his departure. Room 40 was aware of this procedure, but it was the insufferable operations director, Captain Jackson, who came in on May 31 to ask where call sign DK was. He was not the sort of person to whom one offered unsolicited advice, so he was merely told, "In the Jade River." Jackson passed along this message, and the Admiralty thereupon radioed Jellicoe that directional wireless placed the enemy flagship in the harbor at 11:10 A.M. Three hours later, with Jellicoe believing that the Germans were still in port, the two fleets made contact in the middle of the North Sea.

This rather shook Jellicoe's faith in Admiralty intelligence. It was further jolted when he plotted the position of the German cruiser *Regensburg* as given by the Admiralty report and found that it appeared to be in almost the very same spot as he himself then was! At the time no one knew that the *Regensburg* navigator had made an error of ten miles in his reckoning and that blame for the absurd result lay with the German officer, not with the cryptanalysts of Room 40 reading the German report of the ship's position.

After the brief flurries of action, damaging but inconclusive and unsatisfactory to both sides, that constituted the Battle of Jutland, Scheer at 9:14 P.M. ordered: "Our own main body is to proceed in. Maintain course SSE 1/4 E; speed 16 knots." At 9:46 he altered it slightly to south-southeast 3/4 point east. Both messages were decoded with almost unbelievable alacrity by Room 40, and by 10:41 a summary of them had been received aboard the flagship.

But Jellicoe had had enough of Admiralty intelligence. Furthermore, the summary had omitted Scheer's 9:06 call for air reconnaissance off the Horn Reefs, which would have confirmed his intentions to head for home, and thus there was nothing to contradict a battle report from the *Southampton* that suggested a different enemy course. Jellicoe therefore rejected the Admiralty information, which this time was right. As a result, he steered one way, Scheer fled another, and Britain's hope of a decisive naval victory evaporated in a welter of errors, missed chances, and distrust.

But if Room 40, through no fault of its own, did not enable Britain to win a major naval battle, it did play a critical role in helping her to win the war.

In 1917, Germany on one side and Britain and France on the other were gasping in exhaustion from a war that both had thought would be over—as the kaiser said—"before the leaves fall" in 1914. Germany thought she saw a way to win: Unrestricted submarine warfare would starve the Allies into submission. She recognized that this would probably bring the United States into the conflict against her. But her new foreign minister, Arthur Zimmermann, thought of a way to neutralize this danger. He would distract America by getting Mexico to wage war on her. And he would persuade Mexico to do this with an offer she could not refuse: Upon victory, Mexico would get back the territories she had lost in the Mexican-American War of 1846.

He put his proposal into code and cabled it on January 15 via Sweden to the Western Hemisphere. But the cable touched British soil. The British intercepted the message, and Room 40 deciphered it. The director of naval intelligence, Captain Reginald Hall, whom the American ambassador called a genius ("all other secret service men are amateurs by comparison"), saw that he had a propaganda weapon of the first water. With permission, he gave it to the Americans. President Woodrow Wilson, stunned by the German proposal, gave it to the Associated Press. The story made headlines in papers all over the nation on March 1. The isolationist Midwest, previously unconcerned with the distant poppings of a war in Europe, jerked awake at the thought of a German-officered Mexican army advancing up toward Chicago.

Five weeks later President Wilson—who had been reelected just months earlier on the slogan "He kept us out of war"—went up to Capitol Hill to ask Congress to "make the world safe for democracy" by declaring war on Germany. Congress complied. And soon the fresh strength of the young nation was pouring into the factories and trenches of the Allies. The Germans were driven back and back until they had no choice but to surrender. The codebreakers, who had gotten their start with a codebook recovered from a stricken German warship at the beginning of the war, had played a major role in bringing that war to an end.

Postscript: For the twenty-fifth anniversary of the *Magdeburg*'s stranding, the old battleship *Schleswig-Holstein* was sent to Poland to commemorate the cruiser's dead, who were buried in a Danzig cemetery. The ceremonies lasted a day, but the battleship remained moored at the port as tension between Poland and Nazi Germany mounted. At 4:48 A.M. on September 1, 1939, her 11-inch guns roared, shattering and setting ablaze some Polish installations on the Westerplatte, a sandy tongue of land. The shots were the first of World War II.

Jutland

by JOHN KEEGAN

John Keegan's inspiration has been to focus on something too often overlooked: the experience of the individual soldier on the battlefield. How much terror and pain and confusion is embodied in those unavoidable map arrows showing unit and ship movements, so like the anonymous shuttling of boxcars in a railyard? Keegan's *The Face of Battle* (Viking) has become one of the most influential works of military history in the past two decades, and justifiably so. He has lately added a naval version, *The Price of Admiralty* (Viking), from which the following account of Jutland is excerpted. Nineteen sixteen was the year of the huge matériel battles—Verdun and the Somme as well as Jutland—in which the brute industrial force of the Western Allies began to wear Germany down in a way that their uninspired military leadership could not. Jutland was the first—and also the last—great clash of dreadnoughts, technological marvels of their age; the mechanized havoc inflicted on their crews was appalling. Though the entire confrontation lasted just twelve hours, it was for thousands involved a nightmarish ordeal. In terms of comparative losses in ships and men, the German High Seas Fleet was the victor, narrowly. But sometimes even indecisive battles can be decisive, and in this case decisive, that worsened word, may apply. Why was it that the High Seas Fleet would never fight again?

Admiral Reinhard Scheer, the commander of Germany's High Seas Fleet during World War I, proved a sailor of Nelsonian stamp. Reserved in expression and unassuming in manner, Scheer achieved high command only because fatal illness removed his predecessor. Once established in office, however, he showed a marked capacity for dismissing difficulty, concentrating on the strengths rather than the weaknesses of the German navy. A torpedo specialist, he believed that his surface and submarine forces had the capacity to inflict unacceptable damage on the British Grand Fleet if it could be maneuvered into unfavorable circumstances. Throughout the spring of 1916, he worked on refining plans for an extended operation that would run his opponents' battleships and battle cruisers onto a series of submarine-laid minefields, and allow his capital ships to pick off casualties and detached units at small cost to himself.

In 1916 the High Seas Fleet counted sixteen dreadnoughts (revolutionary new turbine-driven battleships that were more heavily armed and armored than any ship then afloat) and five battle cruisers to the Grand Fleet's twenty-eight dreadnoughts and nine battle cruisers; it also had six pre-dreadnoughts (the heaviest battleships carrying mixed-caliber batteries before development of the dreadnought). The balance of force, given what was then being built, could not improve in Scheer's favor. He therefore concluded that the time to act was now or never; and in the early morning of May 31, 1916, he ordered his squadrons to sea in the hope of returning to port with losses fewer than those he inflicted.

Altogether twenty-two battleships, five battle cruisers, eleven cruisers, and sixty-one torpedo boats of the High Seas Fleet put to sea. The modern capital ships were organized into two battleship squadrons of eight dreadnoughts each, as well as the 1st Scouting Group of five battle cruisers. Scheer commanded the battleships; Vice Admiral Franz Hipper was in command of the battle cruisers. Hipper's ships began to leave their North Sea ports at one o'clock in the morning; Scheer followed at 2:30 A.M. The best speed of the dreadnought squadrons, determined by their slowest ships, the *Posen, Rheinland, Nassau,* and *Westfalen,* was twenty knots; but it was further reduced to eighteen knots by six pre-dreadnoughts that Scheer had included to bulk out numbers. The 1st Scouting Group had a maximum speed of twenty-six knots and was committed to the role of finding and "fixing" the location of the enemy's fleet until the heavier ships came up.

Scheer's plan did not envisage a decisive action. Realistically he recognized that his inferiority in numbers of ships and in weight of broadside (400,000 to 200,000 pounds, reflecting the lighter calibers of his ships' main armament) ruled out a German Trafalgar. He hoped nevertheless to come off the better by entangling the Grand Fleet with a U-boat line he had deployed off the British bases and by inflicting losses on ships and squadrons temporarily separated from the main body. The High Seas Fleet was to steer due north, toward the outer mouth of the Baltic, the Skagerrak, by which the Germans were to name the ensuing battle. News of its sortie was trusted to draw the Grand Fleet southward to a rendezvous.

However, the news came to the Grand Fleet much sooner than Scheer had expected. Through the capture of three cipher books, the Admiralty had acquired the key to the whole German maritime and overseas cipher system—a priceless advantage that enabled the Admiralty to detect Scheer's intention to "come out" as early as May 16, when his U-boats departed for their patrol lines. It was confirmed on May 30, and Admiral Sir John Jellicoe, commanding the Grand Fleet, was immediately warned. As he had on hand plans for a "sweep" of his own, the third undertaken that year, he rapidly translated his scheme for a probe into orders for a major action. Two hours before Hipper left Jade Bay, the Grand Fleet, including its Battle Cruiser Fleet, was already at sea, heading for an encounter off the west coast of Danish Jutland.

The battle that followed is conventionally divided by naval historians into five phases: the battle-cruiser action, encompassing two of the phases—a "run to the south" and a "run to the north"; the first and second encounters of the battleships; and a night action, involving many clashes between light forces, in which the High Seas Fleet made its escape to the Elbe River and Jade Bay.

The Battle Cruiser Fleet, commanded by Vice Admiral Sir David Beatty, comprised his six fastest ships—the *Lion, Tiger, Princess Royal, Queen Mary, Indefatigable,* and *New Zealand*—and was accompanied by the fast battleships of the 5th Battle Squadron, the *Barham, Valiant, Warspite,* and *Malaya.* These were the most formidable ships on either side, heavily armored, mounting 15-inch guns, and capable of twenty-five knots—as close to the kaiser's cherished ideal of a "fast capital ship" as was then possible. They were superior to any other battleship and barely slower than the fastest battle cruisers, which were safe against them only by taking flight.

The Battle Cruiser Fleet passed undetected through Scheer's U-boat patrol line (as Jellicoe's battleships later would), thus robbing the High Seas Fleet's sortie of much of its point—and gravely compromising its security. But the Admiralty staff had perversely misinterpreted the cipher intelligence, and so assured Jellicoe that the enemy was still in port nine hours after it had put to sea.

In consequence, Beatty's and Hipper's battle cruisers managed to arrive within fifty miles of each other, some ninety miles west of the mouth of the Skagerrak, at two o'clock in the afternoon, without either having knowledge of the other's proximity. Chance drew them together: Light forces on each side detected a neutral merchant ship lying between their axes of advance and blowing off steam. Diverting to investigate the unknown vessel, they found each other. Fire was exchanged, signals were sent (HMS *Galatea:* "Enemy in sight. Two cruisers probably hostile in sight bearing ESE course unknown"), and the battle cruisers were ordered by their commanders to change course and steer for each other.

By the sort of mischance that would have been excusable at Trafalgar, when flags were the only medium of intercommunication, but not at Jutland, where radio provided a means of duplication, Beatty's fast battleships missed his hoist directing them toward the Germans and persisted in a prearranged turn northward to rendezvous with Jellicoe. The result was that Beatty led his lightly armored battle cruisers to challenge Hipper's ships unsupported. And when action was joined, at 3:45 P.M., it did not go the British way.

Hipper, on sighting Beatty's ships, ordered a turn to draw them down onto Scheer's battleships following forty miles in his rear. The British, silhouetted by the sun in the western sky, showed up crisply in the German range finders. "Suddenly my periscope revealed some big ships," recorded Georg von Hase, gunnery officer of *Derfflinger.* "Black monsters; six tall, broad-beamed giants steaming in two columns." A few minutes later Hipper signaled "open fire" and the German battle cruisers began observing and correcting their fall of shot. Beatty, whose range takers had overestimated the distance separating the two lines, was busy getting a radio message off to Jellicoe and did not yet respond. Some five minutes after the Germans had begun to engage, Beatty's flag captain ordered the "open fire" on his own responsibility and also began to observe effects.

Because British range-finding was inferior to German (due to the better quality of German optics), the Battle Cruiser Fleet, which outranged the 1st Scouting Group, had allowed itself to run within the fire zone of the enemy's guns. Hipper's 11- and 12-inch armaments were therefore straddling and scoring hits on Beatty's 12- and 13-inch-gun ships when more prudent ship-handling would have denied them the opportunity. Bad signaling also misdirected British gunners so that one of the five ships in Hipper's line (*Derfflinger*) was spared altogether from attack by Beatty's ships for nearly ten minutes. The consequences were not long delayed. Gunnery control officers on both sides were trying to hit hulls and particularly turrets that, even if heavily armored, were the access points to magazines, detonation of which was the quickest way to put an enemy out of action.

Such a direct hit on a lightly armored and unprotected sector of the ship normally killed or wounded everyone who was in the vicinity. On armor, however, shells exerted erratic effects. In Q turret of HMS *Tiger,* which was hit on its armored roof at 3:55 P.M. by an 11-inch shell from the *Moltke,* two men were killed outright and a midshipman was mortally wounded. Four other sailors were wounded, but three of them were able to help bring the turret back into action. "The dead were placed to one side," according to one report, "the wounded given first aid, and necessary substitutes were brought up from below to replace casualties."

A quick survey of the damage revealed that the more fragile machinery and instruments had been disabled but that the guns and loading gear still were in working condition; as the directors of strategic bombing were to discover during World War II, it is almost impossible to destroy high-grade steel machinery with explosive, however accurately it is delivered.

But there was one thing that put the German guns at an advantage: All the British capital ships had a fundamental design defect—an insufficiency of "antiflash" devices between the turrets and the magazines. The Germans had learned a lesson from the battle cruiser *Seydlitz*'s near-fatal internal fire after a direct hit on a turret the year before at the Battle of Dogger Bank. The fire had traveled down the turret trunk—the tube for bringing shells up from the magazine. Consequently the High Seas Fleet's ships had been modified to avert the passage of flash down their turret trunks. The British ships had not. A subsequent investigation revealed that the British crews, in their determination to achieve the highest possible rates of fire in gunnery competitions, had removed antiflash devices from the trunks without realizing that cordite flash in the turret labyrinth posed the gravest danger to dreadnoughts. A third of the British battle cruisers would be destroyed as a result.

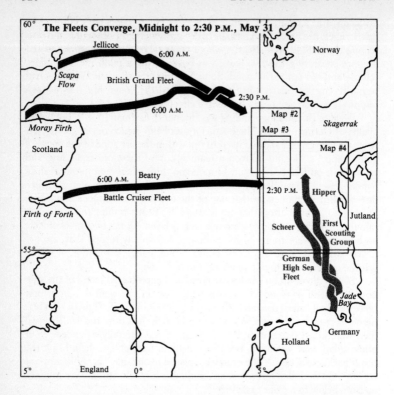

This nearly happened to Beatty's flagship, the *Lion*. Her Q turret was hit by a 12-inch shell from the *Lützow* at four o'clock, killing everyone in the gunhouse. But one of the gun's numbers, as he died, involuntarily sent the loading cage of the right gun down into the working chamber. A fire, apparently spreading down the turret's electrical cables, ignited the cordite in the cage and the working chamber; and fire passed thither down the turret trunk toward the magazines. The turret officer, Major F. J. W. Harvey, managed with his dying breath (he had lost both his legs) to order that the magazine doors be closed and the magazine flooded. In giving this order, for which he was posthumously awarded the Victoria Cross, he saved the ship.

The fire that the shell started below the turret was fatal to all the crew in the workspaces above the magazine. As was stated in a later report:

[It] passed down the main trunk into the shell room and handling room and up the escape trunk into the switchboard compartment. In this latter compartment were stationed, beside the switchboard men and certain of the electrical repair party, the after medical party under the charge of a surgeon. All these men, together with the magazine and shell-room crew, were killed by the cordite fire. . . . [Their] bodies and clothes were not burnt and, in cases where the hands had been raised involuntarily, palms forward, to protect the eyes, the backs of the hands and that part of the face screened by the hands were not even discolored. Death to these men must have been instantaneous.

Beatty's flag captain pulled the ship out of the line to take her from the danger zone. The Germans believed her finished.

Shortly afterward, the *Indefatigable,* which had been exchanging salvos with the *Von der Tann,* also suffered hits. The *Lion*'s were to prove survivable; the *Indefatigable*'s were not. One salvo penetrated her thinly armored deck. Another, hitting near her fore turret, set off a fatal internal explosion, and at two minutes past four she turned over and sank.

In terms of battle cruisers, numbers were now equal. "I gazed at this in amazement," remembered Beatty's flag captain. "There were only five battle cruisers in our line. . . . I glanced quickly toward the enemy. How many of them were afloat? Still five." Beatty now ordered his light forces into action in the 15,000-yard space separating the two battle lines. Light cruisers and destroyers, engaged by the German battle cruisers' secondary armament, tried to launch torpedoes against the enemy's heavy units; Hipper's light forces swung into action against them. And then, while light cruisers and destroyers fired their 6- and 4-inch guns against each other, the four battleships of the 5th Battle Squadron, redirected at last onto their proper targets, began to fire their shells, tossing columns of water larger than any that had yet been seen around the German battle line. Suddenly the odds among the heavy ships were again in Beatty's favor: nine against five, with greater range and weight of shell on his side.

But German gunnery achieved one more success: A full 12-inch salvo hit the *Queen Mary,* consort of the *Tiger* and *Lion.* She did not survive. About 4:26 P.M., after several earlier hits, she was struck on one of her forward turrets. A cordite fire entered the forward magazine, and the resulting explosion blew off the forepart of the ship. Shortly afterward a hit on X turret blew up the after magazine, and the remains of the ship capsized. Gunner's Mate E. Francis, a survivor of the X turret crew, described the sequence:

Then came the big explosion [the detonation of the forward magazine], which shook us a bit, and on looking at the pressure gauge I saw the [hydraulic] pressure had failed. [Hydraulic power trained the turret, elevated the guns, and worked the ammunition lifts and loading rammers.] Immediately after that came . . . the big smash and I was dangling in the air on a bowline, which saved me from being thrown onto the floor of the turret. . . . Numbers two and three of the left gun slipped down under the gun, and the gun appeared to me to have fallen through its trunnions and smashed up these two numbers. Everything in the ship went as quiet as a church, the floor of the turret was bulged up and the guns were absolutely useless. . . . I put my head up through the hole in the roof of the turret and I nearly fell back through again. The after four-inch battery was smashed right out of all recognition and then I noticed the ship had an awful list to port. [X turret, behind the bridge, gave no view of the missing foreparts of the ship.] I dropped back inside the turret and told Lieutenant Eward [the turret officer] the state of affairs. He said, "Francis, we can do no more than give them a chance; clear the turret." "Clear the turret," I called out, and out they all went.

Francis and Midshipman Lloyd-Owen of X turret were to be among the *Queen Mary*'s 20 survivors, of a crew of 58 officers and 1,228 men. The *Indefatigable* sank with the loss of all but two of her crew of a thousand. These catastrophes, with the later loss of the *Invincible*, were to be the great tragedies of Jutland, because of their unexpectedness. The vulnerability of the *Invincible* and *Queen Mary* to long-range, armor-piercing fire was the most unsettling outcome of all the events of the Jutland encounter. It was the *Queen Mary*'s loss that prompted Beatty's notorious remark, "There seems to be something wrong with our bloody ships today."

Meanwhile, however, under the cumulative effect of Beatty's much heavier gunnery, Hipper's line was now running ever deeper into danger. Well-aimed salvos were falling about his ships every twenty seconds; some were scoring hits, and the British officers on the bridges of the battle cruisers and battleships who could see enough to judge the course of the action were now certain that the destruction of the 1st Scouting Group was at hand.

Then, at 4:30 P.M., Beatty received a signal from one of his advance light cruisers that she had "sighted enemy battle fleet bearing approximately SE, course of enemy N." The implication was clear: If Beatty continued making his "run to the south," he would arrive under the guns of Scheer's battleships, against which his Battle Cruiser Fleet, even with the support of the 5th Battle Squadron, could not hope to stand without devastating consequences. At 4:40, therefore, he signaled a turnaway, toward Jellicoe's approaching squadrons, and the "run to the north" began.

Commodore W.E. Goodenough, commanding the British light cruisers that had sighted Scheer's ships—it was the dense clouds of black smoke from their coal-burning engines, working at full revolutions, that had drawn his attention toward the eastern horizon—held on far into the danger zone while he established their number and bearing. When he at last turned away, he was followed by torrents of shells, any one of which could have obliterated him or a consort. Forty large shells fell within seventy-five yards of the cruiser *Southampton* as she made her escape at twenty-five knots toward Jellicoe, zigzagging between the shell fountains to confuse the German range takers.

Beatty's battle cruisers had meanwhile put enough distance behind them to be out of danger. But the fast battleships of the 5th Battle Squadron, once again misled by a signal, had not. They were five minutes late in turning away, and in the interval the *Barham* and *Malaya* were hit by German fire, the *Malaya* heavily. One of her secondary batteries was knocked out and she was holed beneath the waterline. But the fast battleships' advantage in gunpower told in reply. Several German battleships and battle cruisers were struck by salvos from the retreating British ships, the *Seydlitz* so hard that she risked sinking.

But the *Seydlitz* herself scored hits, notably on the battleship *Warspite*. At about 5:30 the *Warspite* was hit several imes. In the next few minutes a shell burst in the starboard secondary battery. Commander Walwyn reported that "a sheet of flame came down through the slits of sliding shutters . . . [and he] heard a lot of groaning." When he went forward, he found that the burst had started a fire in the ready-use cordite among the guns of the starboard secondary battery. The fire had "frightfully burnt" two gun crews and was also blazing around the conning tower, through the slot of which "signalmen and messengers peering out . . . looked like thrushes in a nest, gaping and shouting, 'Put the fire out.' We eventually got a steam main connected and got water."

The fire had also taken hold below, in the navigating officer's cabin, burning a store of 400 life jackets nearby.

> The stench of burning rubber being perfectly awful . . . smoldering wooden uprights of doors kept on breaking out again . . . decks were all warped and resin under corticine [deck covering] crackling like burning holly. . . . [E]verything in the fore superstructure was wrecked and it looked like a burned-out factory all blackened and beams twisted everywhere. . . . [A] twelve-inch had come through the after funnel, through the beef-screen [meat-storage area] and smashed the second cutter to matchwood. On its way through the beef-screen it had carried a whole sheep with it, which was wedged into the gratings. At first I thought it was a casualty.

That a sheep's carcass could be mistaken, even briefly, for a human casualty testifies to the appalling nature of wounds that high-explosive projectiles frequently inflicted in the confined spaces of armored ships.

But the "run to the north," though a withdrawal, had scored hits on German ships and reunited Beatty with Jellicoe. It was therefore as much a British success as the "run to the south" had been a British setback. Still, both had been preliminary engagements. Shortly after 6:00 P.M. the battle fleets themselves at last drew within range of each other. Their covering screens of cruisers and light cruisers had already been in action and the Germans had fallen under the guns of Beatty's battle cruisers with disastrous results: Three cruisers—the *Wiesbaden*, *Pillau*, and *Frankfurt*—had suffered crippling damage. But so too had a British destroyer, the *Shark*, overwhelmed by heavier fire, and a cruiser, the *Chester*, in which the boy hero of Jutland, Jack Cornwell, had been killed. (The sixteen-year-old Boy First Class, though wounded, remained at his post and received the Victoria Cross posthumously.) And there were to be more losses before the dreadnoughts began their artillery duel. Two British armored cruisers, supporting Jellicoe's battleships, came under fire from Scheer as they steamed ahead of the Grand Fleet; the *Warrior* was rapidly wrecked and the *Defence* blown up, both hit by shells against which their thin sides offered no protection, at ranges too long for their 8-inch guns to straddle.

And there was to be another catastrophe before Jellicoe's and Scheer's battleships saw each other. Three battle cruisers, the *Indomitable*, *Inflexible*, and *Invincible*, oldest and weakest of their type, were accompanying the Grand Fleet. At 6:01 P.M., the *Lion*, which had returned to the fight, had come within sight of Jellicoe, who signaled to Beatty, "Where is the enemy's battle fleet?" The answer was ambiguous, but it persuaded the commander that he must now anticipate imminent action and deploy from column into line—the formation best suited for the concentration of maximum gunpower on the enemy. As his six columns began their fifteen-minute deployment, the *Invincible*, steaming ahead of the main formation, out of sight of Jellicoe but in sight of Beatty, also came within view of the Germans.

It was an unlucky rendezvous. Cloud and mist, which until now had concealed their presence, suddenly parted to reveal the isolated squadron of three battle cruisers to the leading German battleships, which opened fire instantly. The *Invincible*, the leading ship, was the focus of the attack and was hit repeatedly. At 6:33 P.M. a shell penetrated the roof of Q turret amidships and blew her into halves. Among the six survivors of her thousand men was the composer Richard Wagner's godson, who had been observing the fall of shot from the highest point in the ship.

Fortunately the surviving battle cruisers were not to bear the brunt of the ensuing action, while the battleships, which were, had external armor sufficiently thick to keep out the projectiles that had damaged the *Invincible* and Beatty's ships so fatally. Moreover, Jellicoe's battleships were to join action with Scheer's on highly advantageous terms.

Ambiguous and intermittent though the signaling of his advance forces had been, Jellicoe was the more fully alerted of the two commanders to the approach of his opponent. Hipper had been able to warn Scheer of the imminence of fleet action with no clearer signal than "Something lurks in that soup. We would do well not to thrust into it too deeply." Scheer, who had thitherto believed he had the British Battle Cruiser Fleet in a trap, now had to grapple with the anxiety that it might be supported by the rest of the Grand Fleet, yet without clear indication of its location. Jellicoe, on the other hand, not only knew Scheer's positions and heading but also could calculate that his own heading put him between Scheer and his line of retreat to the North German ports, and therefore that he could "Trafalgar" the enemy if daylight and the accuracy of his gunnery availed.

The Grand Fleet's twenty-eight battleships, deploying from columns to line as they passed the wreck of the *Invincible* (many British sailors thought she was a German ship and cheered as they saw her), now enjoyed the advantage of the light—an advantage that earlier in the day had been the enemy's—and could see their targets clearly on the western skyline. To Scheer's range takers, Jellicoe's ships were "indicated on the horizon ahead of us [only] by the firing of heavy-caliber guns. The entire arc stretching from North to East was a sea of fire. The muzzle flashes were clearly seen through

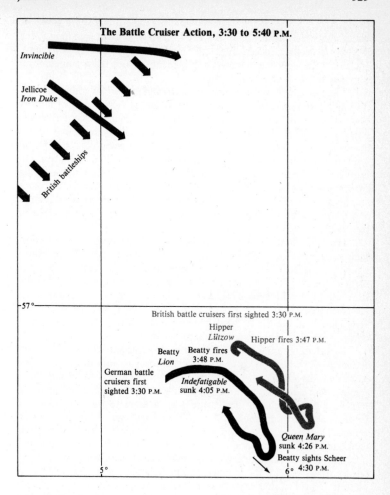

The Battle Cruiser Action, 3:30 to 5:40 P.M.

Invincible

Jellicoe
Iron Duke

British battleships

-57°-

British battle cruisers first sighted 3:30 P.M.

Hipper
Lützow   Hipper fires 3:47 P.M.

Beatty   Beatty fires
Lion   3:48 P.M.

German battle
cruisers first   *Indefatigable*
sighted 3:30 P.M.   sunk 4:05 P.M.

Queen Mary
sunk 4:26 P.M.
Beatty sights Scheer
6° 4:30 P.M.

5°

the mist and smoke on the horizon, though there wasstill no sign of the ships themselves."

The opening range was about 12,000 yards, well within the reach of the guns on the leading British ships, which, by classic tactics, had "crossed the T" of the German line and were pouring fire at its head. British obervers were convinced they were scoring a succession of hits and sinking ships. Several German battleships—and battle cruisers, leading the fleet—were hit in this exchange; twenty-two shells struck altogether. The Germans inflicted thirty-three in return, all on British battle cruisers, cruisers, and fast battleships of the 5th Battle Squadron; Jellicoe's line of dreadnoughts was not touched. As it steamed imperturbably onward, steadily closing the range and interposing itself more deeply between the High Seas Fleet and home, Scheer's nerve cracked. After only ten minutes' engagement, he ordered a simultaneous turnaway to take his fleet out of danger.

The German ships disappeared instantly and mysteriously from the British range takers' field of vision as the smoke and gathering dusk of a misty evening enclosed them. They might have turned south. Jellicoe correctly guessed that Scheer had chosen the quickest way out of danger and turned due west, toward the English coast. He ordered an alteration of course southward, to better his chances of cutting off the enemy's retreat, and held onward. So, too, for some ten minutes (6:45–6:55 P.M.) did Scheer, until, hoping to escape across the rear of the Grand Fleet, he signaled a reversal of course and began to steer due east. His intention was to reach the coast of Jutland and then work his way home behind the minefields fringing it in German territorial waters.

His order, however, was timed too early. Overestimating the speed of Jellicoe's advance, he suddenly found himself at about 7:10 under fire once more from the British battleships, his T crossed again, his weakest ships—the battle cruisers—in the van, and last light silhouetting his line while it hid the British ships from his guns. This "second encounter" of the battle fleets went far worse than the first for the Germans. They scored only two hits on Jellicoe's line (both on the *Colossus*) while the British scored twenty-seven in return, on the already heavily stricken battle cruisers.

Less than ten minutes of this treatment persuaded Scheer to break off action. At 7:18 he signaled another simultaneous reversal of course to his battle line, having meanwhile ordered the battle cruisers to "charge" the enemy and his light cruisers and torpedo boats to lay smoke and mount a torpedo attack. Hipper's "death ride"—an allusion to the last charge of Prussia's armored horsemen in 1870—put all but one of his ships out of action. The torpedo attack was more profitable. Jellicoe deployed his own light cruisers and destroyers against it as the Germans approached and caused most to launch at extreme range, or not to launch at all. Nevertheless twenty-one torpedoes traveled the distance, forcing Jellicoe to order a general turnaway and individual ship captains to maneuver sharply. No hits were scored, but by the time Jellicoe resumed his pursuit, Scheer had put himself at extreme range of the Grand Fleet—some ten to eleven miles—and was heading south for home with the British abreast of him to the east and slightly to his rear.

Light was failing fast as the last phase of the battle—later to become known as "the night action"—opened. The sun set at 8:24 P.M. At 8:30 Scheer ordered his squadron of six pre-dreadnoughts to go to the aid of his battle cruisers, which, lying to his east, were still under fire from Beatty's ships; his, in turn, were running ahead of Jellicoe's line of advance. While the pre-dreadnoughts exchanged fire with Beatty's fleet, Hipper's battle cruisers were able to make good their escape; eventually, as Beatty's range takers lost definition on the darkening horizon, so did the pre-dreadnoughts, which were able to disengage unscathed.

While the darkness grew thicker, the battle fleets converged on southerly courses in complete ignorance of each other's whereabouts. In the six miles of sea that separated them, there were to ensue nine encounters between German and British light forces, and between British light forces and the German battle fleet. In the first, none of the four torpedoes fired struck a target. In the second, the British destroyer *Castor* was hit a number of times and in the confusion failed to report the German position to Jellicoe for half an hour. In the third, the British cruiser *Southampton* sank the German cruiser *Frauenlob* by torpedo. In the fourth and largest engagement, the destroyer *Tipperary* was sunk with heavy casualties, and the *Elbing*, the ship that had opened the battle hours earlier, was fatally crippled; it sank four hours later. In the fifth, British destroyers attacked the German dreadnoughts at ranges that closed to a thousand yards and damaged one by ramming. In the sixth, a British destroyer put a torpedo into the German pre-dreadnought *Pommern*, found its magazine, and blew it up. In the seventh, a British armored cruiser, the *Black Prince*, was set on fire by salvos from a German dreadnought and also blew up. The eight and ninth were destroyer actions, in which one German torpedo boat was lost.

While these brief and chaotic encounters, the last timed at 3:30 A.M. on June 1, were taking place, the High Seas Fleet, holding to its southerly course and making several knots less than the Grand Fleet, had passed behind the British and gotten safely to the coast of Jutland and its minefields. It was in sore straits. One of its battle cruisers, the *Lützow*, had sunk; of the four remaining, only one, the Moltke, was still capable of fighting.

The *Lützow*'s captain described her end, which came early on the morning of June 1:

> After it became clear that it was not possible to save the ship, because she had 8,300 tons of water in her and was on the point of heeling over, I decided to send off the crew. . . . She was so down by the bows that the water came up to the control tower and the stern was right out. On my orders the ship was sunk by a torpedo fired by G-38 [a German torpedo boat]. She keeled over and after two minutes swiftly sank with her flag flying.

The only other German capital ship not to return from Jutland was the pre-dreadnought *Pommern*, which had been blown up during the night action by a torpedo fired from the destroyer *Onslaught*. The German pre-dreadnoughts were not elaborately subdivided and had no underwater protection. The explosion broke *Pommern* in half. There were no survivors from her crew of 844.

That terrible toll is largely explained by the near impossibility of finding survivors on the surface of the sea during the hours of darkness. That some initially did survive her wreck is suggested by the aftermath of the *Queen Mary* and *Invincible* disasters, in which twenty-six were picked up; even from the *Indefatigable,* two crewmen survived and landed in German hands. The *Pommern's* broken hull remained afloat for at least twenty minutes after the torpedo strike. The surmise is that the ship was destroyed by a succession of explosions, beginning in the magazines of the secondary armament and spreading to where the 11-inch charges and shells were stored. Men in the tops and on the bridge must have been thrown into the sea, and others in the upper decks would probably have been able to make an escape. All were subsequently lost, however, to the darkness and the cold.

Those most imperiled by internal explosion—indeed without hope of escape at all—were the ammunition and engine-room crews. Ammunition handlers, if at the flash point, suffered instantaneous extinction. Stokers and mechanics might undergo a protracted and awful agony. That must certainly have been the fate of the engine-room crews on the *Pommern,* as well as on the *Indefatigable* and *Queen Mary,* trapped in air pockets belowdecks, plunged into darkness, engulfed by rising water, perhaps also menaced by escaping superheated steam and machinery running out of control.

The details of the last minutes of those engine-room spaces are mercifully hidden from us. Some impression of what the victims underwent is conveyed by the experience of the engine-room crew of the *Warrior,* the British armored cruiser attacked by *Derfflinger* and other German battle cruisers at about 6:00 P.M. The *Warrior,* which was quite inappropriately attempting to support the British battle-cruiser line, suffered hits by fifteen heavy shells, one of which struck at the waterline, causing flooding in the whole engine-room space.

The damage trapped the survivors among the engine-room crew in the working spaces. There were initially eight of them. The engineer officer in charge attempted to lead the others out of the engine room, but he was defeated. He "found by the glimmer of the sole remaining oil lamp that the water was coming over the floor plates, and the crank pits were full up and the cranks were swishing round in the middle of it." The *Warrior* was not a turbine ship but a reciprocating-engine one—massive pistons worked in cylinders that were as tall as the engine-room ceiling, perfectly safely while the ship was proceeding normally, but at great risk to the engine-room crew as soon as anything went awry. According to a later report, the engineer officer first

> tried to ease the engines and shut off steam, fearing further accidents, but by this time the water was breast high over the floor plates, and he decided the only thing to do was to clear out. But by this time the ladders were inaccessible as the floor plates were dislodged, and there was every chance of being drawn into the racing cranks. They climbed up over pipes and condensers, holding hands to prevent the swirling water carrying them away. Unfortunately their chain was twice broken, with the result that several men were jammed somehow and drowned. The remainder climbed from one vantage point to another as the water rose until they reached the upper gratings, but by this time it was quite dark, and having no purchase anywhere they could not dislodge the gratings overhead, and apparently found themselves doomed to certain death.

Not only were they expecting to be drowned, but escaping steam almost suffocated them, and they kept splashing oily water over their faces to keep themselves from being peeled. Some men had wrapped scarves round their heads to protect themselves, and all kept as much of their heads as they could in the water. The surprising thing was that the engines went on working till the water was halfway up the cylinders and only stopped then because the boilers were shut off. . . .

[T]his agony of terror went on for nearly two and a half hours in pitch darkness and apparent hopelessness. . . . A stoker petty officer . . . absolutely refused to recognize the horror of the situation and kept talking and cheering them all up. . . . [T]hey kept hold of each other to save their lives as long as possible, but one by one they kept dropping off and getting lost and drowned in the water, till at last there were only three of them left. (The engineer officer himself would have been lost, having slipped from his hold and finding himself being drawn into the machinery, but the petty officer held on to him and kept him up until he recovered somewhat.) They thought at one time that the ship had been abandoned . . . then they felt a noticeably cold stream of water coming in . . . and from this they apparently had the idea that the ship must be under way, and therefore in tow of someone, which encouraged them. At last they heard some order being "piped" round the ship and they all shouted together and this led to their rescue.

There was to be no rescue for the engine-room crew of the battleship *Pommern*, any more than there had been for those of the battle cruisers *Queen Mary* and *Indefatigable*. The crews of the turbine-driven battle cruisers were spared the horror of crushing and dismemberment by cranks and pistons as the shattered hulls of their ships carried them down into the deeps. The older *Pommern*, a juggernaut of the sea, must have mangled many of her stokers and mechanics as she made her last plunge. And in all three ships the escape of propulsive steam would have flayed men alive before drowning deprived them of life.

By 6:30 A.M. on June 1, most of the ships in the High Seas Fleet had reached the safety of the Jade estuary; the last casualty was the battleship *Ostfriesland*, which at 5:30 A.M. struck a mine laid by HMS *Abdiel* but managed nevertheless to limp home. The *Seydlitz*, which twice grounded on the approach to the Jade, had to be hauled ignominiously into harbor stern first. The Battle Cruiser and Grand fleets, with their accompanying shoals of destroyers and cruisers, had returned to Scapa Flow and Rosyth by June 2. At 9:45 that evening Jellicoe reported to the Admiralty that his warships were ready to steam out again on four hours' notice.

That signal writes the strategic verdict on Jutland. Brtain's navy remained fit for renewed action, however soon it should come. Germany's did not. The kaiser preferred to ignore this fact. He exulted that "the magic Trafalgar has been broken," distributed Iron Crosses wholesale to the crews of the High Seas Fleet when he visited it on June 5, and kissed many of the captains. He promoted Scheer to full admiral and invested him with the Pour

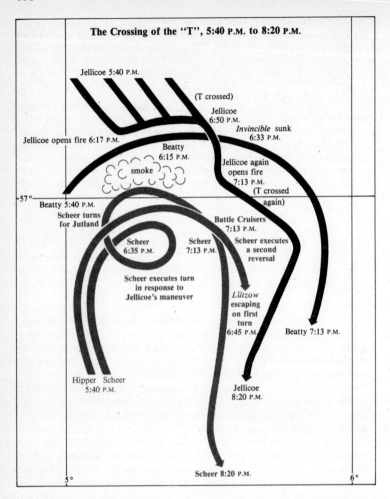

The Crossing of the "T", 5:40 P.M. to 8:20 P.M.

Jellicoe 5:40 P.M.

(T crossed)

Jellicoe
6:50 P.M.

Invincible sunk
6:33 P.M.

Jellicoe opens fire 6:17 P.M.

Beatty
6:15 P.M.

smoke

Jellicoe again
opens fire
7:13 P.M.

(T crossed
again)

-57°

Beatty 5:40 P.M.

Scheer turns
for Jutland

Battle Cruisers
7:13 P.M.

Scheer
6:35 P.M.

Scheer
7:13 P.M.

Scheer executes
a second
reversal

Scheer executes turn
in response to
Jellicoe's maneuver

Lützow
escaping
on first
turn
6:45 P.M.

Beatty 7:13 P.M.

Hipper Scheer
5:40 P.M.

Jellicoe
8:20 P.M.

5°

Scheer 8:20 P.M.

6°

le Mérite, Germany's highest military honor. Scheer himself, however, was much less convinced of his "victory." Shortly after the battle, reflecting on its conduct to fellow admirals, he conceded that "I came to the thing as the virgin did when she had a baby," and in his official report on Jutland to the kaiser on July 4, he warned that "even the most successful outcome of the fleet action," which he implicitly conceded Jutland had not yielded, "will not force England to make peace."

"The High Seas Fleet," Scheer said in his report to the kaiser, "will be ready by the middle of August for further strikes against the enemy." However, contemplating and acting are two different things.

True to Scheer's word, the High Seas Fleet did put to sea, on August 19, and steamed north to bring the English east coast town of Sunderland under bombardment. Scheer's approach was covered, however, by ten of the zeppelins he had not been able to take to Jutland, and when one reported that the Grand Fleet was bearing down on him from the Scottish anchorages, he reversed course and raced for home. The Admiralty cryptographers had detected his sortie, and were to do so again when he next put to sea, in October, with the same humiliating outcome. That was to be the High Seas Fleet's last open challenge to the Royal Navy. In April 1918, when it slipped out of port once more, its mission was mere commerce raiding against the Scandinavian convoys. An engine-room accident in one of the battle cruisers, causing the battleships also to reduce speed, then obliged Scheer to call off the operation and return to port.

For more than half the war, therefore—from June 1, 1916, until November 11, 1918, twenty-nine months in all—the High Seas Fleet had been at best "a fleet in being," and for its last year scarcely even that. Much explains its inactivity: the growth of the Grand Fleet's strength relative to its own (Britain launched nine capital ships between 1916 and 1918, Germany only three), the addition of the Americans to the British dreadnought fleet after April 1917, and the kaiser's increasingly neurotic opposition to taking any naval risk whatsoever. But the central factor in the reduction of the High Seas Fleet to an inoperative force was the action of Jutland itself. Germany had built a navy for battle. But in the only battle fought by its united strength, the navy had undergone an experience it did not choose to repeat.

Germany could publicly celebrate Jutland because the raw "exchange ratio" was in its favor. The High Seas Fleet had inflicted far greater damage than it had suffered. Three British battle cruisers, the *Indefatigable, Invincible,* and *Queen Mary,* were sunk, as were three armored cruisers, the *Black Prince, Defence,* and *Warrior,* and eight destroyers. And five British capital ships had suffered hits by 11-inch shells or heavier, notably the *Lion, Tiger,* and *Warspite.* The High Seas Fleet, by contrast, had lost only one battle cruiser, the *Lützow;* the other ship casualties were either pre-dreadnoughts like the *Pommern* or secondary units like the four light cruisers and five torpedo boats.

Three to one, in rude terms, did make Jutland look more like a German than a British victory. But calculated in refined rather than crude terms, the "exchange ratio" was very much more in Britain's than Germany's favor. Three of her fast battleships—*Warspite, Barham,* and *Malaya*—had suffered damage requiring dockyard attention. But the battleship fleet itself was almost unscathed; and despite losses, the Battle Cruiser Fleet on June 1 still outnumbered the German 1st Scouting Group, which moreover was crippled by damage. The German dreadnought battleships had also suffered grievously. *König, Markgraff,* and *Grosser Kurfurst* all needed major refits when they returned to port, and the German battle line could not have met the British at four weeks' notice, let alone four hours', except at risk of outright defeat. The balance of forces had not been significantly altered by relative losses. The Grand Fleet still outnumbered Scheer's, twenty-eight dreadnoughts to sixteen.

The human cost, however, had fallen far more heavily on the British. True, her long tradition of "following the sea" and her large seafaring population made her losses easier to replace than the German. But the truth was that over 6,600 British officers and sailors had gone down with their ships or been killed on their decks while the Germans had lost only a few more than 2,000.

The casualties of ironclad warfare, as compared with those of woodenwall warfare, were gruesome. The solid shot exchanged by the ships at Trafalgar dismembered or decapitated, and tossed showers of wooden splinters between and across decks. But if the missiles did not kill outright, their victims retained a chance of clean and quick recovery, even under the hands of surgeons whose only tools were the probe and the knife. The casualties at Jutland suffered wounds almost unknown to an earlier generation of naval surgeons: metal fragmentation wounds, scouring trauma by shell splinter, and, most painful and hardest of all to treat, flash and burn effects and flaying by live steam. An officer on the destroyer *Tipperary* described coming across a sailor "with a large portion of his thigh removed, probably the result of scouring by a shell splinter. 'What can I do with this, sir?' asked the torpedo gunner who was attempting first aid. . . . I merely covered the wound with a large piece of cotton wool and put a blanket over him. 'Feels a lot better already,' said the wounded man." He was among the majority who drowned when the *Tipperary* foundered two hours later.

Even the wounded who came for care where care was organized—as well as it could be—did not find great comfort. The medical officer of the battle cruiser *Princess Royal* described a surgical center in which wounded men were wounded again by incoming German shells ("the next day about 3 lbs weight of shell fragments . . . were swept up from the deck") and where fumes from explosions elsewhere in the ship, sinking through the internal spaces because heavier than air, forced staff and patients to don respirators.

> Casualties began to arrive, amongst them a gun-layer from the after turret, which had been put out of action by a direct hit. He . . . had a foot nearly blown away. . . . This gun-layer had developed German measles about two days previously, and should by rights have been landed, but owing to the mildness of his complaint, and because he was an important rating, he had been isolated on board and permitted to come to sea. Later on I amputated his leg. . . . I proceeded to operate on a . . . marine who had been brought down bleeding seriously from a punctured wound of the face. . . . We had hardly started operating before rapid firing developed, and the tray with all my instruments was deposited on the deck . . . [but we] proceeded to operate on the gun-layer. The light was most trying [gunfire had forced the doctors to depend on barely adequate oil lamps], the securing of arteries during the operation being particularly difficult. . . . The dressing of large numbers of burns, some very extensive ones, now fully occupied the time of the whole staff. . . . Most of the wounded, who numbered exactly 100, were seriously burned.

Aboard the cruiser *Southampton,* which was a smaller ship, the doctors had to work under even more makeshift conditions. The operating room, according to one of her lieutenants,

> was the stokers' bathroom . . . about eight feet high, twelve feet broad, and twelve feet long. The centre of the room was occupied by a light portable operating table. A row of wash basins ran down one side and the steel walls streamed with sweat. . . . Stepping carefully between rows of shapes who were lying in lines down each side of the passage-way, I put my head inside the narrow doorway. Bare-armed the fleet surgeon and a young doctor were working with desperate but methodical haste. They were just taking a man's leg off above the knee. . . .
>
> I went aft again and down to the ward-room. The mess presented an extraordinary appearance. As it was the largest room in the ship we placed in it all the seriously wounded." [The *Southampton* had suffered forty killed and forty to fifty wounded.] The long table was covered with men, all lying very still and silently white. As I came in (the doctor) signalled to the sick-berth steward to remove one man over who[m] he had been bending. Four stokers, still grimy from the stokehold, lifted the body and carried it out. Two men were on top of the sideboard, others were in arm-chairs. A hole in the side admitted water to the ward-room, which splashed about as the ship gently rolled. In the ankle-deep flood, blood-stained bandages and countless pieces of the small debris of war floated to and fro. . . . [T]he most dreadful cases were the burns—but this subject cannot be written about.

Both fleets, as they made their way back to harbor from their inconclusive North Sea encounter, were encumbered belowdecks with "dreadful cases" that "cannot be written about." The first—it was to be also the last—great clash of dreadnoughts had inflicted appalling human damage on their crews. But the toll of casualties is not to be compared with the bloodlettings of the western front. Exactly one calendar month after Jutland, the British Expeditionary Force was to attack the German trench line on the Somme and suffer 20,000 killed in a single day of action. There had been such massacres before, and others would follow before the exhaustion of the combatant armies would bring the agony of trench warfare to an end. Set against the 5 million deaths in action suffered during the First World War by the British, French, and German armies alone, Jutland is small beer. As a proportion of crews present, some 110,000 in all, the total of fatal casualties, approaching 9,000, is high, but it must be set against the consideration that the event was unique. Earlier actions had not been costly in lives, and there were to be no major fleet actions after May 31, 1916.

Jutland ranks among the costliest naval battles ever fought. Not until the great Japanese-American clashes of the Second World War in the Pacific would action at sea bring death to so many sailors. And there is another dimension to the engagement: It called into question all the presumptions on which the great ironclad fleets—the dreadnoughts being their ultimate embodiment—had been built.

As Ernle Chatfield, Vice Admiral Beatty's staff commander in the Battle Cruiser Fleet, put it in retrospect:

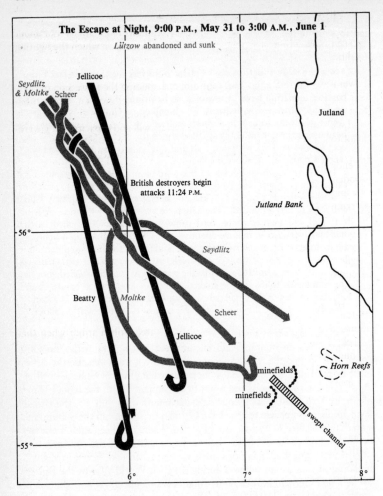

The Escape at Night, 9:00 P.M., May 31 to 3:00 A.M., June 1

Lützow abandoned and sunk

Jellicoe

Seydlitz & Moltke Scheer

Jutland

British destroyers begin
attacks 11:24 P.M.

Jutland Bank

56°

Seydlitz

Beatty   *Moltke*

Scheer

Jellicoe

minefields}

( ) *Horn Reefs*

minefields}

swept channel

55°

6°   7°   8°

What would happen [in Nelson's time] when two ships met and engaged
was, as far as material was concerned, known within definite limits from
handed-down experience and from a hundred sea-fights. [Nelson] knew exactly the risks he ran and accurately allowed for them. He had clear knowledge, from long-considered fighting experiences, how long his ships could
endure the temporary gunnery disadvantage necessary in order to gain the
dominant tactical position he aimed at for a great victory.... We had to buy
that experience, for our weapons were untried. The risks could not be measured without that experience.... Dreadnoughts had never engaged, modern massed destroyer attack had never taken place.

The passing of the wooden walls and the coming of the iron, steam-driven warship had wrenched naval strategy from its foundations. For about two centuries, admirals had manipulated a naval system in which the fighting qualities of their ships and the rare "clash transaction" of battle—Clausewitz's term—had been but two among the factors by which the balance of sea power was struck. There were many others, including the possession of overseas bases at strategic points, the availability of trained seamen, the distribution of ports that were adaptable to naval operations, the interoperability of land with sea forces, and, besides all these, the will and capacity of a government to maximize its material avantages for military purpose in great waters.

The British had proved supremely successful at the adjustment of means to ends in the pursuit of national power through the maintenance of a wooden-wall navy. But the supersession of wood by iron and sail by steam in the middle of the nineteenth century had consigned the Royal Navy to the working-out of an invisible crisis that, though it would take decades to emerge in its plenitude, threatened to undermine all the assumptions on which wooden-wall supremacy had been established. Ironclad navies, vulnerable to defeat "in an afternoon," as Winston Churchill percipiently put it, were fragile instruments of national supremacy. They were expressions of the strength not of a whole national system—social, financial, and industrial—but of no more than a single one of its technological aspects.

Germany's naval technology was proved by Jutland to be superior to Britain's. Her ships were stronger, her guns more accurate, her ordnance more destructive. German shells had usually penetrated British armor when they struck; the reverse had not been the case. Because the German navy took second place in national life to the German army, on which the bulk of the state's wealth was spent, Germany's admirals could not transform technological into strategic advantage over their British counterparts. But because Britain's admirals were themselves the servants of a naval technology supported by a financial and industrial power that since the 1870s had been in relative and irreversible decline, their strategic posture was also defective. In the years from 1914 to 1916, the Grand Fleet, and its battle-cruiser appendix, was perhaps the largest embodiment of naval strength the world had ever seen—in weight of firepower, it unquestionably was. But it was a pyramid of naval power trembling on its apex, at risk of being toppled by any new technological development that threatened its integrity.

The Tunnels of Hill 60

by ROBERT COWLEY

With the Yser and the frantic struggles that go by the name of the First Battle of Ypres, the last gaps in the western front closed. From November 1914 on, siege warfare took over along the 470-mile front. Think of the opposing trench systems as vast citadels turned upside down. Traditional siege methods seemed the appropriate way to breach those inverted walls. They included the mine—tons of explosive planted under enemy trenches at the end of a tunnel. The mine would be blown, sometimes vaporizing hundreds of men in a matter of seconds, and troops would rush to occupy the smoking crater: Often as not, it only provided another obstacle to be gotten around. Mine warfare tended to center on high ground that had local tactical value. One such feature just to the south of Ypres was Hill 60—its height in meters—an insignificant but dominating mound of railroad spoil. The struggle to win and hold Hill 60, most of it conducted underground, swayed back and forth for the entire war. Its lamentable history is a case, you might say, of how to make a molehill out of a mountain.

The hills around Ypres come as a shock. Their groundswells roll inland and even rise abruptly from the plain, a mirror image of the North Sea close by. Covered by rich pastures and bursts of woodland, they don't fit the flat and sodden stereotype of the First World War Salient. As elevations go, they are hardly overpowering. The ridge system that dominates the old town, with its rebuilt towers and star-shaped fortress walls, rarely exceeds 200 feet above sea level, or 60 meters and change. But elevations are relative, and you constantly have the sensation of being higher up than you actually are. Perhaps it is the long views that those hills command. The Germans had seized them by the middle of 1915, and the Allies spent the next three years trying to recover them—with siege methods that Marshal Vauban, the seventeenth-century builder of those Ypres walls, would have applauded.

A homely simile recurs in the diaries and memoirs of British soldiers, and you have to believe that it was passed around as part of everyday conversation. "Very little rest from shellfire and none at all from the perpetual and eerie feeling of always being watched whatever one is doing, by the Germans on the hills around," wrote an architect turned artillery officer named P.H. Pilditch. Then comes the obsessive image: "It was like living in the bottom of a huge flat soup plate."

On the western front, generals willingly sacrificed lives in obscene numbers to take and hold high ground. The rationale, explains the geographer Douglas W. Johnson, was that an observer on a hill could "save tens of thousands of his comrades by directing artillery fire against enemy . . . objectives easily located from his point of vantage but absolutely hidden behind a wall of trees to one who stands on the plain itself." Topography, in World War I, was destiny.

All this goes far to explain the melancholy history of Hill 60, a modest eminence that overlooked the southeastern flank of the salient. The struggle that made Hill 60 notorious began as a local action late in April 1915 and initially had nothing to do with the monthlong convulsion following the German army's first release of poison gas a few days later and a few miles away. Before long, though, the Hill 60 battle was incorporated into what came to be known as the Second Ypres (the first having been fought the previous autumn, when the British and French stopped the Germans practically at the gates to the town). The brief taking of Hill 60 by the British (and its retaking by them in 1917 as a prelude to the Third Ypres) involved a method of siege warfare—tunneling and mining—that seems incredible given those famously swampy conditions.

Today, the fact of tunnels seems as much a surprise as the hills. It shouldn't be. Consider one recent discovery near the town of Ypres itself. Some years ago workers at a local brickworks were excavating for the characteristic blue Flanders clay—London clay, the British call it. They had dug through the bed of sand just below the surface, exposing indentations filled in with darker topsoil. What looked like geological liver spots were telltale blemishes of shell holes. The men reached the clay and were beginning to remove it when they struck a line of wooden beams. It was the roof of a long, fortified dugout from 1917—not a true tunnel, but the next thing to it. How could one exist? The answer was that once you dug deep enough, the clay, that impervious Flanders clay, would keep out the worst of the water. (It also prevented water from seeping down, which partly explains why conditions on top were so miserable.) The workers found an entire gallery complex with bunks for 180 men and, wedged in between the ceiling beams, the petrified corpse of a rat.

The accepted way to take a hill on the western front was to tunnel under it and blow it up. Against the machine gun there was no better solution. The operation at Hill 60 would be duplicated many times, especially (but not exclusively) in 1915. The results are still scattered over the landscape of Belgium and northern France. Take the Butte of Vauquois in the Argonne— which mine explosions so cut apart that even now it looks like a melon with a great slice hacked out—or Les Éparges, southeast of Verdun, where the tourist road to the much-disputed overlook known as Point X positively teeters amid craters. A Messines Ridge mine that failed to explode in 1917 went off during a thunderstorm in 1955, producing an instantly ideal place to dump farm rubbish. (It took some thirty years to fill the crater up; only a shallow dip remains amid the beets.) Agriculture, more often than not, is the chief beneficiary of the Great War.

Hill 60 was an artificial mound, a spoil heap formed by the earth removed in the nineteenth century when a single-track railroad was cut through the Messines Ridge, some three miles south of town. The "60" referred to the height of the hill, 60 meters, or 197 feet, above sea level—but in these parts it might as well have been the Matterhorn.

There is a photograph of the hill that I return to constantly. It was taken from a lesser spoil heap known unceremoniously as the "Dump" to the British troops who clung to it. The date is April 10, 1915, a Saturday, and the Germans have held Hill 60, just a few hundred yards away, for four months, since they wrested it from the French in December. The time, to judge from the lie of the light and shadow on ruined walls, is early afternoon. A cluster of cumulus clouds—they remind me of a school of whales—is passing -overhead: Their dark undersides indicate an approaching cold front.

The railroad cutting angles, ravinelike, across the foreground of the photograph; and a ragged reserve line, belonging to the British, cleaves to the far embankment. In a corner by a concrete bridge abutment is a scattering of crosses, an improvised cemetery; nearby, a tiny figure in a greatcoat seems to be looking for something at the sandbagged entrance to a dugout.

The single living creature observable, he tantalizes. So does the subject of the photograph, Hill 60, its short, bare, steep slopes rising to a crown of sandbags—the German positions, all but unapproachable. (You can scarcely make out the British fire trenches, situated at the foot of the hill.) The place has the look of a gravel bank in a farmer's back acres. A dark line of trees, not yet turned to wooden corpses, seems to form up in the shelter of the hill. Except for the immediate fighting areas, the western front was still amazingly green in 1915 and would remain so well into the next year, when artillery became the dominant, landscape-altering weapon. This early in the war, blackthorn hedges are more in evidence than barbed wire.

But what you can't see that afternoon is as noteworthy as what you can. It is not just the sense of an overriding nervous silence, but the fact of other lurking potentials. Buried amid those German earthworks on the crest and as far as a couple of miles to the east are 6,000 cylinders full of chlorine. Hill 60 was supposed to be the site of the first gas attack. Like steel bulbs, the cylinders had been planted late in February, but the predicted winds from the south had refused to cooperate in their blooming. The German high command grew increasingly fearful that its intentions would be found out and by April 10 had ordered the installation of more cylinders along the opposite face of the salient, where the gas would be released twelve days later.

There is, meanwhile, another unseen element in the photograph, and one fully as dramatic—the mine shafts that are, at this moment, probing in both directions. The invisible tunnelers, German and British, work in muddy water, clawing and hacking at the dripping clay. (The favored method is known as "clay-kicking," by which a miner on an adjustable seat drives his spade with both feet.) The air is so bad and so thin that the candles that provide the only illumination often go out, and matches burn cherry red without flaming. Men breathe with a painful and labored rasp. Blacksmith bellows blowing fresh air through hosepipes hardly help; more effective but noisier mechanical devices good for mining operations at home might tip off the enemy. Men emerge from a shift preternaturally exhausted and nauseous with headaches; some have permanently damaged eyesight. In the infancy of mine warfare, progress of ten feet is a good average for a day—though as the fear quotient rises, the tunnelers push that to fourteen, even once to a desperate sixteen and a half feet.

Menace is very much in the stiff wind of early spring. The Germans may still hope that they can coordinate mine explosions with the gas attack. At the very least, they can obliterate those trenches at the bottom of the hill and force the British backward a few hundred yards. The farther the enemy is from that crucial heap, the greater the difficulty in reaching it, either underground or over. The Germans have every reason to worry about that threat. By April 10 the British have already run three shafts under Hill 60 and are ready to charge them with explosives.

On a front of no more than 300 yards, the opposing mine operations are inescapably close. Men try to work as quietly as possible; they can sometimes hear the sounds of digging nearby, and the muffled voices of their less cautious neighbors. Discovery, they know, can result in the explosion of a small defensive mine known as a camouflet and entrapment at the end of a collapsed tunnel—burial alive.

In March two British tunnelers actually broke into a German shaft. They immediately snuffed out their candles and crouched in the water, listening. They heard a foot splash on the other side. Scrambling back through the low passage, they reached a vertical shaft and climbed a ladder into the sunlight of their front line. (Safety was relative. At this point they were only 50 yards from the German trenches.) An hour or so later, they returned with an officer, who shone a torch through the hole in the wall. There was a single reverberating crack as a bullet ripped through the officer's sleeve. The three of them managed to get away in the dark. They forced themselves to return, and this time found that the Germans had left a canister of explosive. They cut the wires and replaced it with a small explosive device of their own. Digging stopped. After a week, the British resumed work, but apprehensively, carving out a short fork at the end of the tunnel. The Germans, for reasons that will never be known, did not challenge them. When the time came to set the main charges, the British miners dumped two 500-pound stashes of easily portable guncotton and got out.

The two other British tunnels were longer, about 100 yards, and branched into more substantial Ys, the explosive chambers. A pair of 2,000-

pound charges of gunpowder, old-fashioned even by the primitive standards of 1915, went into one tunnel, and a 2,700-pound pair into the other. The charging probably began several hours after the taking of the photograph, on the night of April 10-11. The British needed five nights to lug up the 100-pound sacks of gunpowder, 94 in all, winch them down the shafts, and haul them forward to the waterproofed boxes under the German lines. But the attack was not scheduled to go off for another two days, on April 17. Men checking and rechecking the wiring and fusing could hear the sounds of enemy miners overhead. They, too, were setting charges, and there was no way of telling who had the advantage. The German mines, as it turned out, were supposed to blow on April 19, two days too late.

So much grace under pressure for such a nasty conclusion: That was the Great War in a nutshell. I find it hard to put the brash voice of a Major John Norton Griffiths out of mind. Norton Griffiths, who supervised the early British mining operations on the western front, was a newly rich contractor turned Conservative politician, who dashed around in his own Rolls; he comes through as a younger version of Boss Mangin in Shaw's *Heartbreak House*. He boasted of the Hill 60 scheme, "This will prove the biggest mine yet exploded," and added some grisly advice: "If advantage is taken of the dust (bricks, mortar, and Germans!) by sending forward an attacking party the same time the button is pushed . . . it should give ample cover . . . Wiser to get a few men hit with falling . . . Germans than to get a larger number hit by machine guns." In the event, one man who poked his head above the trench as the mines were exploding was smacked in the face, and killed, by a flying piece of "dust."

April 17, a Saturday, was one of those spring days memorable for its sunlit softness. Even the casually ceaseless rifle fire, a background noise as natural as birdsong on the western front, subsided toward evening. An unnerving stillness settled on the landscape. At five minutes after seven, the plungers descended at ten-second intervals, blowing up the three pairs of mines. Columns of earth spurted up, black veined with damp gunpowder that had failed to explode, while artillery opened on the approaches to the hill, blocking both escape and reinforcement. The survivors of the company that held the hill stampeded for the rear, their panic occasioned not only by the shock of the explosion but by the fear of ruptured gas cylinders. The attacking infantry reached the considerably reduced and rearranged summit in a few bounds and occupied the six smoking craters. There was some scattered bayoneting. Regimental buglers added an invigorating nineteenth-century touch to the proceedings. In fifteen minutes the attack was over. The Germans had suffered 150 casualties, the British, 7—and the permanent alteration of the topography of Hill 60 had begun. (Was it even "60" any longer?) When Prime Minister Asquith learned of its capture later that night, he considered the news important enough to warrant disturbing the king.

The next two and a half weeks would contribute immeasurably to the postwar reputation of Hill 60 as the premier tourist attraction of the salient. Even as Asquith was delivering his happy message to the king, German reinforcements were forming up in the trench-seamed fields behind the hill; after midnight, counterattacks began. There were four of them in the darkness, the last at 4:30 A.M. The Germans, meanwhile, set to grinding down the defenders under a millstone of artillery. For hours on end the slopes of Hill 60 were hidden in dust and black smoke from exploding Jack Johnsons (after the first black heavyweight champion), or coal boxes, as the 5.9mm shells were also known. The sounds of the Hill 60 battle could be heard for miles around. Lulls in the bombardment only signaled fresh attacks. It didn't help that enfilade fire came from another spoil heap across the tracks that the British had nicknamed the "Caterpillar," after its peculiar shape, a wriggling inverted S. (The Germans called it, simply, Hill 59, though its summit now looked down on that of its recently higher neighbor.) The British recognized too late that they should have taken the Caterpillar as well, instead of leaving themselves exposed on a bump of earth little more than a few hundred yards wide. "All traces of trenches had . . . disappeared," said the Official History. "The surface of Hill 60 was a medley of confluent mine and shell craters, strewn with broken timber and wire: and in this rubbish heap it was impossible to dig without disturbing the body of some British or German soldier." Four Victoria Crosses were earned in the first five days. "The men who are lucky enough to come back," Captain William LaTouche Congreve, a later (and posthumous) VC winner, noted in his diary, "say that it is the worst fighting in the war."

In their reports the defenders constantly mentioned "gas vapors." Though the Germans did fire some tear-gas shells, the irritating odor referred to probably came from leaking chlorine cylinders. The Germans did not actually use poison gas on Hill 60 until the evening of May Day, when the battle had become part of the general salient struggle. This time the wind was right; they released the gas from positions less than a hundred yards from the cavities that passed for British fire trenches, a distance that seemed on the broad side by 1915 standards. The British beat them back-barely. Those who were not incapacitated managed with rapid rifle fire to check the bombing parties that attempted to squeeze them from the flanks. They held the Germans off long enough for support troops, dashing through the lumbering cloud, to tip the balance.

Talk of some desperate glory: Moistened masks of cotton, extemporized respirators, were the only protection, and the gas killed close to 150 British, more than half of whom dropped where they fought. But the harrowing episode was not without value, as the British *Official History* points out, because "The forbidden cloud had been faced and defeated for the first time." Congreve encountered some of the Hill 60 gas victims at a clearing hospital the next morning: "They looked very bad indeed, so bad that the doctors are hardly able to save a single case. Oxygen is but little use, and they just get more and more acute and die. Some turn quite purple—horrid to see. It was fearful seeing the rows and rows of stretchers in the yard, all gasping and in misery."

Four days later, on May 5, the luck of the British ran out. The Germans literally caught them napping. It was 8:45 A.M., and most of the trench garrison were catching a few moments of sleep after another night of shelling. The Germans had chosen a different direction of release, from the flank by the railroad tracks, and the gas, instead of billowing over the trenches, drifted across the hill and along them. One sentry gave the alarm, but exhaustion had taken its toll on defensive reflexes.

The *Official History* describes what happened next. "The gas hung about the trenches so thickly that even with a cotton respirator, that had constantly to be redamped, it was impossible to stay in them. Some men ran back to the support line and those who remained were overcome: thus when the Germans advanced after the gas had been flowing fifteen minutes, they secured all but a small portion of the front line on the lower slopes of the hill." Presently, that, too, fell. The battle continued all day and into the night, but Hill 60, with its superlative views of the salient, was firmly in German hands and would remain so for the next two years.

The most memorable feature of the nineteen-day struggle had less to do with its details than with its density. As Captain Congreve put it, thousands of men had died for "a heap of broken earth . . . a place about the size of the center part of Trafalgar Square." What had started for the British as a small operation had cost them 100 officers and 3,000 men; but the Germans, attackers for most of the time, no doubt suffered comparable losses. Even such mean eminences as Hill 60 were considered worth the price. On the western front, height always made right.

The taking of Hill 60 did have more than a passing local significance. The Germans now controlled almost every major elevation along the entire 470-mile line, and there was hardly a place where the Allies did not have to attack uphill. On the western front the Germans had erected a kind of serpentine wall which their opponents would have to climb over. Only one gap remained, the Meuse heights above Verdun—a gap the Germans would attempt to brick up the following year. So, by the end of the spring of 1915, they could concentrate on standing fast and wearing down the French and British, who persisted in cranking up one "war-winning" battering-ram effort after another, while they pursued the more immediate prospect of victory on the eastern front. For the moment, the Germans were postponing any thought of a decision in the West; time would take care of that. As they would demonstrate so convincingly, not to act was to act, and it almost won the war for them.

During the next two years, the most arresting events involving Hill 60 took place underground. It was a case, you might say, of making a molehill out of a mountain. Hill 60 became a monument to man's trial by earth. At levels varying from 15 to 100 feet, an intricate network of galleries reached out from both lines. (On the Allied side, the miners were often tall Canadians or Australians, who considered 25 feet of a 6-by-3-foot passage a good day's average, with a record 41 feet for a 24-hour period and 212 feet for a week. The tunnels dug by British miners, smaller men, were lower and narrower— but were also more carefully constructed. One reason that the Australians went faster was that they didn't always bother to prop their diggings.) If maps of the colliding systems make little apparent sense, the reason is that digging tunnels and countertunnels had become an end in itself. You might hear suspicious sounds nearby and burrow in that direction with the object of blowing a camouflet or of pushing a torpedo, an 8-foot-long pipe packed with 100 pounds of ammonal, into a hole bored quietly with a hand auger. The effect was of a chess game between moles.

But the stakes were bigger. If you were to enter a certain opening in the side of the railroad cutting, 220 yards behind the British front line and out of sight of the eyes prying from Hill 60, you would find yourself at the beginning of the most extensive tunnel system in that part of the western front. The main tunnel, more than a quarter of a mile long, its walls and ceiling shored by timber supports every foot or so, was known as the "Berlin Sap" because, as the miners said with industrious hopefulness, it would lead to Berlin. No place for a claustrophobe, the Berlin headed steeply and narrowly downward until it leveled off at a depth of 90 feet. Your torch lighting a tight, bobbing oval in the abyssal darkness, you sloshed through dirty water, with trepidation now, knowing that German workings were somewhere above. You were under no-man's-land. Every so often you would have to squirm by bogies on rubber wheels, which miners pushed silently over wooden rails; the carts carried sandbags filled with blue clay, bound for the surface. (The bags would be deposited far behind the lines, so as not to give away the location of the diggings—nor the fact, which was considered Most Secret at the time, that the British had managed to reach down through the mushy topsoil to the deep clay, something the Germans had not yet accomplished.) Presently you would pass a multitude of side galleries, which the 1st Australian Tunnelling Company had christened with such nostalgic names as Brisbane, Melbourne, and Adelaide. Some of those branch tunnels were as long as the Berlin itself, and two of them, known simply as A and B, had special destinations. Branch A led, as it were, to the bowels of Hill 60. There, by August 1916, a charge of 53,000 pounds of ammonal and guncotton had been stacked in waterproofed boxes in a widened and heightened chamber, and tamped—that is, blocked behind a blast wall of bags filled with dirt brought from B branch. B branch veered off toward the Caterpillar, under which, by October, there were 70,000 pounds of high explosive. The British would leave the two great charges for the better part of a year, waiting for the right offensive moment to set them off.

That moment nearly did not come. In the autumn of 1916, rising water filled the entire Berlin Sap. Technology eventually prevailed: the use of electric pumps and steel caissons where the leaks were worst. (Geologists helped, too, by figuring out the seasonal rise and fall of the underground water table.) But as opponents, the Germans proved as formidable as Nature. They were convinced that the British were up to something. On April 9, 1917, 600 men raided the British trenches in front of Hill 60. The Germans hoped to destroy the mine system. They penetrated 200 yards, not quite far enough, remained for an hour, and blew in the entrances of some shallow "subways"—long, fortified dugouts—asphyxiating 25 infantrymen trapped inside one of them. The miners who were captured "appear to have held their tongues," says the Australian official historian, although "a sample of earth brought back proved that the British must have sunk a sap far below the level of the German workings. . . . The enemy had accordingly pushed on with a deep shaft, using concrete in getting through the soft stratum which had previously impeded him."

The tension increased. "Listeners all a bit windy," an officer reported. Despite all the false alarms from a timber settling or earth failing, there was no mistaking the sound of German digging near the Hill 60 mine. The Australians blew camouflets; the Germans blew them back. They actually collapsed a portion of the tunnel leading to the explosive chamber, trapping two listeners. One, a sapper named E.W. Earl, "coolly went on listening and heard a German walk down an enemy gallery apparently directly over the great mine." The date was May 25, just two weeks before it would at last be exploded. Earl wrote to his mother, made a will, and continued to listen. Two days later the Australians rescued the listeners (Earl died eventually from the effects of asphyxia), repaired the tunnel, and decided to take no more countermeasures, which might only tip off their concern. So they waited while the Germans came closer and closer.

The mines at Hill 60 and the Caterpillar went up, as scheduled, on June 7, 1917. They were the northernmost of the 19 fired before dawn that morning along the Messines Ridge, part of General Sir Hubert Plumer's siegework masterpiece that tore the first breach in the German hill wall around Ypres. Ten officers and 677 men of the German 204th Division died in the explosions at the two spoil heaps and, except for some token resistance from pillboxes still intact, the British infantry pretty much walked over what remained. The summit and the side of Hill 60 closest to the railroad cutting had completely disappeared, along with the remains of several hundred humans.

Hill 60 became, after the war, something of a tourist trap. "This hill of heroic memory," wrote one Beatrice Brice in 1929, "is now desecrated beyond any place in the Salient by horrible erections of booths and shanties." The novelist R.H. Mottram visited the place at about the same time and came away with "an impression that more souvenirs have been produced from Hill 60 than ever fighting put there." For years a local man had a little museum on the lower slopes, complete with a trench system. Every spring, though, the trenches seemed to move. In his unremitting search for artifacts, he would simply make new excavations and fill in the old ones.

The souvenir stalls and the museum and the "trenches" did survive a second world war, but not the relentless sprawl of small factories and suburban villas at the foot of the hill. The place itself has become a permanent park—a kind of unnatural preserve maintained by the Commonwealth War Graves people. With its proliferation of monuments, it is about the closest thing you'll find on the western front to the commemorative passion of Americans for their battlefields. On a summer afternoon, in what could be a corner of Gettysburg, children kick a soccer ball around a rough stonework post that seems like half a gateway, a gateway to a vanished underworld. It is the monument to the 1st Australian Tunnelling Company. If you look carefully, you will detect nicks in it, bullet marks from a 1944 gun battle between German troops and local resistance fighters, two of whom were killed here. Could there be better evidence that the two wars were really a continuous conflict, with an armistice, in its true sense, intervening? The Gettysburg monuments, of course, don't bear scars from later wars, and that may be the signal difference between European and American history.

A path passes through a grove and runs up an abrupt embankment, the way littered with bulletlike sheep pellets. Just below the crest, a little girl yips in disgust, scrapes her sandals on a rock, and asks her father to carry her the rest of the way. You glance at what appears to be a giant bite out of the hillside: the crater of 1917. The walls have crumbled and the base has filled in; it isn't particularly impressive. The crater, curiously, never did fill with water, perhaps because surviving tunnels acted as drainage conduits.

You puff on to the top, where sheep swirl languidly. But the pastoral effect soon dissipates: You are always conscious of that backdrop of clustered roofs. Even with the trampling of decades of sightseers, the hard earth remains not just bumpy but positively chaotic, a relief map of forgotten suffering. A flat stone in the dry grass proves to be a slab of concrete concealing a low dark opening, a collapsed dugout. There are piles of concrete rubble everywhere.

You hear an onrushing roar from the railroad cutting below, an eerie sound effect. It is an afternoon train heading south in the direction of the French border. You forget how close that border is, only a few miles from this point. Across the tracks is the Caterpillar crater, which is impressive, a huge round carbuncle dent, tree ringed and water filled. You begin to sense the enormous power of those explosions. If you didn't know differently, you might mistake the crater for a pond cleverly sited at the summit of a wooded ridge.

The real attraction of Hill 60 is not its ancient marks of destruction but a tidy little pillbox. It was originally built by the Germans and rebuilt by the British after the 1917 walkover. That rebuilding mainly entailed reversing its gun slits southward in the direction of the German lines. The vertical corrugated imprints of a cement mold have not crumbled. The pillbox has the look of a Templar's flat-topped helmet subsiding into earth long ago crusaded out, but with narrow slits still ominously vigilant. You peer into them: nothing but musty darkness inside.

An aged throat clears itself at your shoulder. A man, pipe in one hand, cane in the other, explains how "Les Boches" used this pillbox in both wars. He returns the pipe to his mouth, lifts the cane and, holding it like a rifle, noiselessly traverses the fields beyond. You remember the dictum of an Imperial War Museum battlefield expert about seeking out eighty-year-olds for information: "If I've got one, I know I'll find what I want." This chap seemed only in his seventies. It was the British, in fact, who held the pillbox during the brief battle fought here in May 1940, just before Dunkirk—what you might call the Fifth Ypres (count 'em). This time the Germans took the town. Until recently a German 37mm tank shell was half embedded in the concrete. The Germans did use the pillbox four years later—in the Sixth Ypres—when the 1st Polish Armored Division liberated the area during a dash that took them, in less than twenty-four hours, from the French frontier to the Dutch. You wonder if, in both fights, men took shelter in the "trenches" across the road? Did they finally become real ones?

Up on Hill 60, not even the wraiths of displaced earth linger. Except for a momentary glimpse of the towers of Ypres, rising over revived woodland, it's hard to understand why the spot was so fought over. Remember, though, that this blasted bit of raised heath was once considerably higher. It is said that Hill 60 lost 18 meters, or almost 60 feet, during the Great War. If we could put aside a feeling of sinister nostalgia, we would call it Hill 42 today.

FDR's Western Front Idyll

by GEOFFREY C. WARD

Franklin D. Roosevelt never did get a chance, as he so ardently desired, to see action as a combatant; he spent the duration of the Great War (or at least the U.S. part of it) as assistant secretary of the navy, shackled to a Washington desk. He envied the sons of his distant kinsman, Theodore Roosevelt, who managed to get themselves respectably wounded and killed. FDR's only direct contact with the fighting was an eight-week European inspection tour in the summer of 1918. He raced around the western front in a gray touring car, visiting battlefields and deliberately trying to expose himself to enemy fire; he loved every minute of his brush with war. He also found time to do a lot of shopping, make a hash of a diplomatic mission to Italy, and meet Winston Churchill for the first time. Churchill was not impressed. This account comes from Geoffrey C. Ward's National Book Award–winning *A First-Class Temperament: The Emergence of Franklin Roosevelt,* which Harper & Row published.

While running for his second term in August 1936, President Franklin Delano Roosevelt made an appearance in the great outdoor pavilion at Chautauqua, New York, where William Jennings Bryan had often preached pacifism before America entered World War I. Domestic issues were uppermost in the minds of most voters in that depression year, but the president felt it necessary at least once during the campaign to pledge his determination to isolate the American people from any new war in Europe.

"I have seen war," said FDR, with great solemnity:

> I have seen war on land and sea. I have seen blood running from the wounded. I have seen men coughing out their gassed lungs. I have seen the dead in the mud. I have seen cities destroyed. I have seen two hundred limping, exhausted men come out of the line—the survivors of a regiment of one thousand that went forward forty-eight hours before. I have seen children starving. I have seen the agony of mothers and wives. I hate war.

But if hatred was the emotion the sights and sounds of war kindled in Franklin, they did so very slowly. During his eight-week inspection tour overseas in 1918 when he was assistant secretary of the navy—his only direct contact with the fighting in World War I—he seems to have had a uniformly grand time. Nowhere in the jaunty diary kept by Livingston Davis, Roosevelt's Harvard classmate and worshipful special assistant, describing what he and Franklin saw and did, or in Franklin's own carefully selective day-by-day account of what he was up to, sent home to be read aloud to the family, is there so much as a hint of anything but enthusiasm.

The trip enabled Franklin at last to see for himself the battlefields about which he had been so excited and on which other Roosevelts were distinguishing themselves. And it gave him an opportunity to meet and talk with a whole series of his heroes. On July 7, Captain Edward McCauley, Jr., his chief of staff, and his orderly, Marine Sergeant W.W. Stratton, accompanied Franklin aboard a brand-new destroyer, the USS *Dyer*, which was helping to escort a troop convoy through the war zone. The rest of his party—Livy, as Livingston Davis was nicknamed; another friend, Elliott C. Brown; Captain Victor S. Jackson; and a stenographer, R.F. Camalier—were to find their way to London aboard another vessel.

Franklin took over the captain's cabin, setting up a framed photograph of his children on the dresser and wearing what he called "my destroyer costume—my own invention—khaki riding trousers, golf stockings, flannel shirt & leather coat—very comfy & warm [and] does not soil or catch in things!"

Franklin exulted in being at sea:

> [T]he good old Ocean is so absolutely normal—just as it has always been—sometimes tumbling about and throwing spray like this morning—sometimes gently lolling about with occasional points of light like tonight—but always something known—something like an old friend of moods and power. . . . But now though the Ocean looks unchanged, the doubled number on lookout shows that even here the hand of the Hun False God is reaching out to defy nature; that ten miles ahead of this floating City of Souls a torpedo may be waiting to start on its quick run; that we can never get our good Old Ocean back again until that God and the people who have set him up are utterly cut down and purged.

Somewhat to FDR's disappointment, the torpedoes never materialized, though there were two nighttime alarms during the stormy, zigzag crossing. Each time, Franklin eagerly raced to the bridge, barefoot and wearing his silk pajamas, to scan the dark sea. On another occasion the captain mistook a floating keg for a periscope and fired three shots at it before realizing his error. The only real dangers Franklin faced were a near-miss with a second Allied convoy in the fog and the accidental detonation of a four-inch gun aboard the *Dyer* itself during a drill. "I am more than glad that I came this way," he wrote home on July 13. "I have loved every minute of it."

The next day was Sunday, July 14, Bastille Day. That morning, as Franklin "read much, slept much and ate much" aboard the *Dyer*, Lieutenant Quentin Roosevelt, just twenty years old and a distant cousin of FDR's, took off from Orly field just outside of Paris at the controls of his Nieuport 28. With him flew seven other planes from the 95th "Kicking Mule" Aero Squadron of the 1st Pursuit Group. Their mission was a sortie behind the German lines in the Marne salient.

Quentin was the youngest and perhaps best loved of Theodore Roosevelt's four sons, ardent, high-spirited, and, despite severe nearsightedness, eager to equal or surpass the achievements of his older brothers. He had begun officer training at Plattsburgh at just seventeen while still a Harvard sophomore and was already engaged, to Flora Payne Whitney, the lovely young daughter of Harry and Gertrude Vanderbilt Whitney. His parents thought the elder Whitneys showy, but they liked Flora, whom Quentin called "Fouf," and TR had tried to arrange for her to travel to France so that before his son went into combat the young couple might marry and have "their white hour together." Regulations had defeated him: Women without specific tasks to perform were barred from traveling to Europe.

On July 5, nine days before this morning's takeoff, Quentin had survived his first dogfight. "You get so excited," he wrote home afterward, "that you forget everything except getting the other fellow, and trying to dodge the tracers, when they start streaking past you." On the 10th he shot down his first enemy plane, just north of Château-Thierry, then toasted his success at dinner with his brother Ted's wife, who was stationed with the Red Cross in Paris. His squadron mates called him "the Go and Get 'em Man" because of his eagerness for combat. "Whatever now befalls Quentin," his proud father told his mother when he got the news, "he has now had his crowded hour, and his day of honor and triumph." In a letter to Ted, Jr., he was still more exultant: "The last of the lion's brood has been blooded!"

Now, as Quentin's squadron flew above the battlefield near the little red-roofed village of Chamery, seven German planes appeared. "They came out of nowhere," one American airman remembered. "Christ, but the air was full of Fokkers." The squadrons roared toward one another. Precisely what happened next is unclear: "To tell you the truth," the same pilot recalled, "each pilot was busy looking out for his own hide."

Somehow, Quentin split off from his comrades. Two German planes flew at him at once, firing as they came. His engine sputtered and his plane rolled over, then plunged downward, spiraling until it smashed into a rutted field below. There had been no smoke or flame; perhaps, his fellow pilots hoped, he had survived, to be taken prisoner.

On the morning of the 16th, a reporter ran up the steps at Theodore Roosevelt's Oyster Bay, Long Island, home with a puzzling telegram his office had just received: WATCH SAGAMORE HILL FOR—. TR came outside to read it, then closed the door so his wife would not be alarmed and told the reporter he feared it meant "something has happened to one of the boys."

No further news came until early the next morning when the newspaperman, tearful now, returned with word that Quentin had been shot down. He had in fact been dead before he hit the ground, two machine-gun bullets through his head.

The colonel paced the piazza with the reporter. "But Mrs. Roosevelt," he said at last. "How am I going to break it to her?"

He straightened his shoulders and went inside. After half an hour, he returned with a prepared statement: "Quentin's mother and I are very glad that he got to the front and had a chance to render some service to his country, and show the stuff that was in him before his fate befell him."

TR later expressed both his pride and his private anguish in a letter to an old comrade-in-arms, Robert Ferguson:

> Well, Bob, when you and I had the chance we did our duty, altho it was on such an infinitely smaller scale; indeed, if I had not myself gone to war in my day I don't think I could have borne to send my sons to face death now. It is bitter that the young should die; [but] there are things worse than death, for nothing under Heaven would I have had my sons act otherwise than as they acted. They have done pretty well, haven't they? Quentin killed, dying as a war hawk should . . . over the enemy's lines; Archie crippled, and given the French war cross for gallantry; Ted gassed once . . . wounded seriously, and cited for "conspicuous gallantry"; Kermit with the British military cross, and now under Pershing. Dick [Derby, one of TR's sons-in-law] knocked over by a shell. . . .

In a letter to Ferguson's wife, her friend Isabella, Eleanor Roosevelt sounded very like her uncle: "The family has been wonderful about Quentin," she said. "He was instantly killed by 2 bullet holes in the head . . . so he did not suffer & it is a glorious way to die." To Franklin, she revealed more: Her heart ached for Uncle Ted and Aunt Edith, she said; "Think if it were our [youngest son] John, he would still be a baby to us."

The family learned later that German aviators had seen to it that Quentin was buried with full military honors because he was the son of Colonel Roosevelt, whom they believed to be a great American, and they had marked his grave with a simple cross and the wheels of his airplane. (The Germans were not uniformly gallant, however. One soldier carved souvenir cigarette boxes from parts of Quentin's plane, and another photographed his sprawled body, then had the picture printed up as a postcard for sale back home. Several copies of this ghastly photograph eventually found their way back to the Roosevelt family.)

Franklin landed at Portsmouth on July 21, 1918, and was delighted to be met on the quay by a large group of officers that included Admiral William Sowden Sims and Rear Admiral Sir Allan Frederick Everett, naval secretary to the first lord of the Admiralty. ("I am told it is a very great honor to have had Everett sent down to meet me," he told Eleanor. "Personally, I think it is because they wanted to report as to whether I am house-broken or not.")

Rolls-Royces took Franklin and his party to London and the Ritz Hotel, where he had "a magnificent suite as the guest of the British admiralty." It was a heady time for an American official to be in the British capital. The streets with which Franklin was so familiar from his many boyhood visits were now filled with Americans in uniform, and newspapers reporting on the western front, where a German thrust had just been blunted, were full of praise for American troops: "The counterattack in the Rheims salient has heartened everybody enormously," Franklin reported; "our men must have undoubtedly done well. One of my Marine regiments has lost 1200 and another 800 men."

Franklin's orders from his chief, Secretary of the Navy Josephus Daniels, were "to look into our Naval administration" and help coordinate its efforts with those of other American agencies. But he was also authorized "for such other purposes as may be deemed expedient by you on your arrival." Within hours of reaching London, he was volunteering to take on a delicate diplomatic assignment that he hoped would be good for both the war effort and his own career.

Sir Eric Geddes, first lord of the Admiralty, evidently planted the idea in his mind. Geddes "has awfully nice eyes and a smile," Franklin wrote, "but is more like a successful American business man than any British Cabinet Officer one is accustomed to picture." Geddes flattered his young visitor and accompanied him on an inspection tour of British and American bases— "Geddes inspects a yard very much as I do—he walked them off their feet & took a special interest in the wood saws." Geddes also let slip selected British secrets, made a show of seeking out Franklin's opinion on matters already decided, and joined with him in issuing joint radio messages that Franklin cabled to Daniels "in the interests of the *entente cordiale.*" ("I hope he gave them to the press," Franklin wrote home.)

The British were alarmed at conditions in the Adriatic, where the enemy was now sinking more Allied shipping than they were in the Atlantic. The Italians insisted simultaneously upon total control of Allied naval activity in that region and near-total passivity. The British wanted action, Geddes explained, and believed the only way to get it was to create a unified naval command, with a Briton in overall command.

Franklin, as impatient as the British for aggressive action and always eager to find a larger role to play than his superiors had envisioned for him, volunteered to go to Rome and press for the British plan. He needed little urging to bring the matter up with other British officials as he made his rounds in London. Not surprisingly, they were uniformly enthusiastic, promising to get approval for his mission from the French. Franklin was shrewd enough, however, to deflect Geddes's hint that he accompany Franklin to Rome. He told Eleanor:

> I am convinced this would be just the wrong move, as the whole situation
> is . . . deadlocked . . . and my business
>   is to find a way out or a compromise. I cannot do this if the Italians think
> the British are bringing me along as 'Exhibit A' to prove that America takes
> wholly the British line. . . .

To Daniels, whose inbred suspicion of the British Franklin always had to keep in mind, he explained things slightly differently:

> The trouble seems to be chiefly with the Italians themselves and a certain amount of jealousy of the French in regard to the Atlantic and of the British in regard to their rather condescending attitude about things in general. . . . The Italians may not love us . . . [but] at least they know that we have no ultimate designs in the Mediterranean.

On July 29, Franklin was received at Buckingham Palace by King George V, an event he reported in proud detail to his mother, whose fascination with royalty he fully shared:

> The king has a nice smile and a very open, quick and cordial way of greeting one. He is not as short as I had expected, and I think his face is stronger than photographs make it appear. This is perhaps because his way of speaking is incisive, and later on, when he was talking about German atrocities in Belgium, his jaw almost snapped. . . .
> I . . . remarked something about having been to school in Germany and having seen their preparation for the first stages of the war machine. The king said he went to school in Germany, too, for a year; then, with a twinkle in his eye—"You know I have a number of relations in Germany, but I can tell you frankly that in all my life I have never seen a German gentleman. . . ."
> He was a delightfully easy person to talk to, and we got going so well that part of the time we were both talking at the same time. I understand that this type of interview is supposed to last only fifteen minutes, but it was nearly three-quarters of an hour before the king made a move. . . .

That evening he attended a dinner for the war ministers at Gray's Inn, where, to his horror and without warning, he was called upon to speak after Lord Curzon, General Jan Smuts, and other senior Allied statesmen had all offered their views. He did his best, but it was not enough to impress at least one of the guests to whom he was introduced: the minister of munitions, Winston Churchill, who evidently did not bother to disguise his disdain for the tall, breathless young visitor from Washington. "I have always disliked [Churchill] since the time I went to England in 1918," FDR told Joseph P. Kennedy, his ambassador to the Court of St. James's, at the White House in 1939. "He acted like a stinker at a dinner I attended, lording it over all of us. . . ." In a subsequent conversation with Kennedy, he added that Churchill had been "one of the few men in public life who was rude to me."

Franklin did better the next evening when he attended a dinner at the House of Commons and afterward had a "long talk with Mr. [Arthur] Balfour [then foreign minister] . . . while we walked up and down the terrace in the dark." Balfour assured him that "everyone understands" it was the U.S. Marines who "stopped the rush at Château-Thierry" and that the British cabinet had warmly endorsed his trip to Rome.

Franklin clearly felt himself at the heart of things in London: "In spite of all people say," he wrote, "one feels much closer to the actual fighting here." But there was also time to go to the theater, visit old family friends, and enjoy a "great old talk" at the St. James Club with Livy and another Harvard classmate, Ned Bell.

Franklin and Livy also found opportunities for a good deal of shopping, using an admiralty car with a uniformed chauffeur to do the driving and guard their packages. "My old friends, the silk pajamas, have gone up from 30 to 60 shillings," Franklin wrote home, "& I only got 3 pairs instead of the 6 pairs I wanted!"

"I do wish you would write me," Franklin had urged Eleanor in a shipboard letter, "if you can think of any small thing Mama or the children would like me to get. I would ask you to do the same thing in regard to yourself, but I fear you would suggest table-cloths or feather-dusters. If you *could* by way of a change think of yourself, I *would* perhaps find it in London or Paris." James, then ten, replied that he would like "the kaiser's helmet and, if possible, the kaiser himself," but Eleanor's response was characteristically practical: Sara, her mother-in-law, wanted a black bag from Paris, Anna needed "6 new nightgowns and 6 prs of drawers," and the boys required "knit stockings with turn-over tops." She wanted nothing for herself except two pairs of gloves.

With Franklin overseas, Eleanor carefully divided her summer between her children and her war work. She had at least toyed with the notion of going abroad herself that spring; the Red Cross had asked if she would be willing to organize a canteen in England, as Mrs. Theodore Roosevelt, Jr., had already done in Paris. "I really won't go abroad," she had reassured Sara, "but it is a fearful temptation because I feel I have the strength and probably the capacity for some kind of work and one can't help wanting to do the real thing instead of playing at it over here." And she was frankly envious of Franklin for being able to go: "I hate not being with you and seeing it all," she told him after his visit with the king. "Isn't that horrid of me!"

But if she could not go overseas, she would not abandon her new life outside her home. War work "was my emancipation and education," she told a friend years later. "I loved it. I simply ate it up." She went to Hyde Park, New York, to settle the children in with Sara at the family estate before Franklin left. "Hot though the Hudson River was, I felt the children were old enough to stand it," she wrote; there would be no time for summering at far-off Campobello. Then she returned to Washington to work for a month at the Red Cross canteen.

"I . . . spent all day and most of the night at the canteen. I had nothing else to do . . . and in the heat to which I was quite unaccustomed, I was anxious to keep busy. No place could have been hotter than the little corrugated-tin shack with the tin roof and the fire burning. . . . It was not an unusual thing for me to work from nine in the morning until two or three the next morning, and be back again by ten. The nights were hot and it was possible to sleep only if you were exhausted."

Franklin worried that she would do too much and damage her health.

"I've come to the conclusion that you only feel heat when idle," she assured him. She had promised Franklin and his mother that she would spend the entire month of August with the children at Hyde Park. But faced with that claustrophobic prospect—and with Franklin safely overseas and unable to tease her—she took still another step toward independence: She learned to drive, steering the Roosevelt family's Stutz through the streets of Washington, D.C., from her home to Union Station every morning while Huckins, the patient family chauffeur, offered rapid-fire suggestions from the running board. And during August, Eleanor attempted to free herself in another way: She sought to conquer her deep childhood fear of water and learn to swim, struggling to keep afloat as she dangled from a long pole held by her mother-in-law's butler.

On July 31 Franklin and his party set out from Dover for Dunkirk aboard a British destroyer with the assistant secretary's flag fluttering from the mainmast—"the first time this sort of thing has ever happened on a British ship." He was at last on his way to the western front, where, thanks again in part to U.S. troops, the Allies had just driven the Germans north of the Marne River.

Two "magnificent limousines, each with two Poilus on the front seat and rifles in a rack in front of them," met Franklin and his party at Dunkirk and roared toward Paris at high speed, through Calais and Boulogne and Beauvais, along roads pocked with bomb craters and so dusty that Franklin stopped to "change from my sea-going suit to khaki trousers, leather puttees and a gray coat."

In Paris the French government put them up at the Hotel Crillon in "wonderful rooms on the troisième, southwest corner." Franklin had instructions from his mother to look in on various members of the family living in and around the city. His first telephone call, made as soon as he got into his room, was to his aunt Dora Forbes, Sara's oldest sister, who had refused to leave her Paris flat even when the Germans shelled the city and seemed on the verge of seizing it. Franklin had breakfast with her before beginning his first round of official visits and later took her for a daylong drive to Versailles and back, just as he had on his honeymoon thirteen years earlier.

Franklin also paid his respects to the Oyster Bay Roosevelts present in Paris: "I went out at tea time to see Ted and [his wife] Eleanor and found them in a nice little house just beyond the Arc de Triomphe," he noted. "Archie was there also, looking horribly badly." Both of TR's sons were recuperating from serious wounds: Ted, Jr., had been hit in the leg; Archie's arm had been broken and his knee shattered by shrapnel. "They both have really splendid records," Franklin wrote, records he still yearned somehow to equal.

Meanwhile, he had to content himself with official business. He was received by the minister of marine, the minister for foreign affairs, Marshal Joseph Joffre, and the president of France, Raymond Poincaré—to whom he found he had to introduce himself, since no one had bothered to tell him "who I was." The high point of his visit was an interview with the premier, Georges Clemenceau:

I knew at once that I was in the presence of the greatest civilian in France. He did not wait for me to advance to meet him at his desk, and there was no formality such as one generally meets. He almost ran forward to meet me and shook hands as if he meant it; grabbed me by the arm and walked me over to his desk and sat me down about two inches away. He is only 77 years old, and people say he is getting younger every day. . . . He launched into a hair-raising description of the horrors left by the Boche in his retreat—civilian population—smashing of furniture—slashing of paintings—burning of houses—and he said—"These things I have seen myself. . . ."

Then still standing, he said—"Do not think that the Germans have stopped fighting or that they are not fighting well. We are driving them back and will keep them going back because we are fighting better and every Frenchman and every American is fighting better because he knows he is fighting for the Right. . . ." He spoke of an episode he had seen while following just behind the advance—a Poilu and a Boche still standing partly buried in a shell hole, clinched in each other's arms, their rifles abandoned, and the Poilu and the Boche were in the act of trying to bite each other to death when a shell had killed them both—and as he told me this he grabbed me by both shoulders and shook me with a grip of steel to illustrate his words, thrusting his teeth toward my neck.

That evening, Franklin reported to his family, he and his party dined quietly at their hotel. He did not detail what happened afterward. The House Naval Affairs Committee had arrived and was also staying at the Crillon. After dinner Franklin accompanied them on a lively tour of Parisian nightclubs, beginning at the Folies-Bergère but soon moving on in the wake of a knowing midget hired as a guide. When they got back to the hotel, around 4 A.M., they found the entrance barred by an iron gate. Republican Congressman Sidney Mudd of Maryland, a massive man and drunker than his companions, leaned heavily on the bell, setting off a loud, insistent gong that roused the staff and woke many guests. (One of them was Herbert Hoover, staying on the floor above Franklin and his party; he later demanded to know who the noisy revelers had been.)

The following evening Franklin, Livy, and the rest plunged back into Paris nightlife, dining this time at the Café de Paris. Franklin described this dinner to his wife and mother, solemnly assuring them that since no alcohol could be served to any man in uniform, their fellow diners had been "extremely happy, no rowdiness and wonderfully little intoxication." But these strictures evidently did not apply to Franklin or his staff, for when they left for the front at last at 6 A.M. the next day, August 4, Livy was badly hung over and so were most of the others in his party.

A French naval officer named Pamard and the U.S. naval attaché at Paris, Captain R. H. Jackson, rode with Franklin in the first of three big gray touring cars assigned to his party, each with a tiny pair of American and French flags snapping from its radiator cap. Captain Jackson had already annoyed Franklin by trying to shepherd him through his formal appointments in Paris at a brisker pace than Franklin had liked. Now he made things worse. Ordered to ensure Franklin's safety, he was determined that the assistant secretary visit only areas securely in Allied hands. This was to be Franklin's one opportunity to see the fighting for himself, and he was no less determined to get as close to it as he could.

As the little convoy moved eastward toward Château-Thierry, winding its way among wounded soldiers and the overladen carts of refugees returning to their newly liberated villages to see if their homes were still standing after four years of war, the two men clashed angrily. Franklin was not interested, he said, in "late rising, easy trips and plenty of bombed houses, thirty miles or so behind the front." When Jackson continued to argue, Franklin relieved him of further responsibility for his travels; from then on, Franklin told Eleanor, "for four days I ran the trip."

He pushed his party from one battlefield to the next, curious, keen, tireless: "I managed to get my boots and leggings off and fell in," he wrote by flashlight one night after finding a place to sleep in an empty, battered house, ". . . 1:00 A.M. and a thoroughly successful day."

"Such tireless energy as Roosevelt's, I have never known," Captain McCauley remembered later, "except perhaps for his kinsman, Theodore Roosevelt. I thought I was fairly husky, but I couldn't keep up with him. In a letter to my wife I complained bitterly that it didn't seem to matter to him what he ate, where or when he slept or if he ever got a bath."

Franklin insisted on walking partway into Belleau Wood. He later wrote:

> In order to enter the wood itself we had to thread our way past water-filled shell holes and thence up the steep slope over outcropping rocks, overturned boulders, down trees, hastily improvised shelter pits, rusty bayonets, broken guns, emergency ration tins, hand grenades, discarded overcoats, rain-stained love letters, crawling lines of ants and many little mounds, some wholly unmarked, some with a rifle stuck, bayonet-down, in the earth, some with a helmet, and some, too, with a whittled cross with a tag of wood or wrapping paper hung over it and in a pencil scrawl an American name.

And he took elaborate pains to enhance the reputation of the men he continued to call "my" marines: He made a point of noting a dinner conversation with a French general who, he said, "told me with his own lips" that he had personally ordered Belleau Wood renamed "Bois de la Brigade de Marine," rather than "Bois des Americains," as unnamed "jealous individuals" in the army were now claiming. He also issued orders that the 5th Marines be permitted to wear their corps buttons on their collar points so that their khaki uniforms could instantly be distinguished from those worn by army troops.

He reviewed troops, called upon senior officers unannounced, dashed inside village churches to survey the damage "done deliberately and maliciously by the Huns," contrasted the "stolid, stupid look" of German prisoners with the "awake and intelligent" ones of their French captors, and longed for a chance to strike a blow at the enemy himself. Not far from Reims, at the battered village of Mareuil-en-Dôle, which the enemy had abandoned just twenty-four hours earlier and where dead horses and "a little pile" of unburied German corpses offended "our sensitive naval noses," he finally got his wish. The 6th U.S. Gun Battery was shelling the German lines only seven miles away, and "Just as we descended from the motors," he wrote, "a loud explosion went off very close by."

Much later he told a friend what had happened next:

> We were walking along, that is picking our way through what we were told was a quiet sector in no danger from the big German guns . . . now and then stopping to use the glasses so as to see more plainly what was all intensely interesting, when an explosion . . . seemed to plant a shot right in our midst. . . . Commander Brown jumped clear of the earth by a couple of feet. Captain McCauley made a sound like nothing earthly. I danced. . . . From the bushes on our right came wild howls of laughter, shrieks and screams of glee which upon investigation proved to be a gun crew of our own army. . . . They had seen the group of American Naval officers coming up and just wanted to see how the Navy would stand fire.

After Franklin and his companions got over their fright, the gun crew invited them into the thicket, where, as he told Eleanor, "We visited the other guns of the battery of 155s [and] fired one of the guns." The memory of this proximity to combat remained vivid all his life. Visiting France in 1931, he himself drove his son Elliott to Mareuil-en-Dôle to show him just where it had happened, and later he would claim to have scored a direct hit on a busy junction, thereby causing the enemy "much confusion. I will never know how many, if any, Huns I killed."

"The members of my staff have begun to realize what campaigning, or rather sight-seeing, with the Assistant Secretary means," Franklin wrote home, "and Captain Jackson is still visibly annoyed because I upset his comfortable plans for an inspection of regions fought over a month ago."

Approaching Verdun, he stopped his caravan again to survey the scene of fighting that had yielded nearly 1 million casualties:

> For a few moments it didn't look like a battlefield, for there was little or nothing to see but a series of depressions and ridges, bare and brown and dead. Seen even from a short distance there were no gashes on these hills, no trenches, no tree trunks, no heaps of ruins—nothing but brown earth for miles upon miles. When you look at the ground immediately about you, you realize that this earth has been churned by shells, and churned again. You see no complete shell holes, for one runs into another, and trench systems, and forts, and roads have been swallowed up in a brown chaos.

Within the battered citadel itself, where he and his party were entertained at "a splendid dinner" that included fillet of beef with truffles, he was shown the original signboard with the defiant message—"Ils ne passeront pas"—that had inspired its French defenders during the long German siege.

He insisted upon exploring the fetid underground passages himself, "although . . . I could not help feeling that it is the same air being breathed over and over again."

Later, near Fort Douaumont, and still closer to the fighting, he was issued a steel helmet and gas mask and stood out in the open so long, at a sharp turn in the road called "L'Angle de Mort," snapping pictures of all that remained of the village of Fleury, that German observers had time to call in artillery. A colonel hurried his important visitors out of harm's way, "and sure enough, the long whining whistle of a shell was followed by the dull boom and puff of smoke of the explosion at Dead Man's Corner we had just left." In his excitement, he left a suitcase filled with important papers on the running board of his car; a French soldier later found it by the roadside and returned it to him at his Paris hotel.

On August 8 Franklin traveled to Rome by private railroad car. Again he enjoyed the attentions of senior officials: Baron Giorgio Sonnino, the foreign minister, "did a very unusual thing in not only receiving me but in talking to me for half an hour. [An American diplomat] said he had never known him to be so chatty and cordial, as he has rather the reputation of a bear." He held a forty-five-minute press conference—"an unusual occurrence for Italy," he told Eleanor—"and they loved it, apparently, and it did good."

In a meeting with the Italian chief of staff and minister of marine, he did not hesitate to encourage greater naval aggression in the region. Austria was near collapse, he argued; concerted action by the combined Allied fleets could destroy the Austrian ships and open the Dalmatian coast to attack. He found the younger Italian officers eager for battle but their older superiors adamantly opposed to it. At one point he wondered aloud at the wisdom of keeping the whole Italian battleship fleet within the harbor at Taranto for an entire year, not allowing it to steam into the open sea even for fleet drill or target practice.

"Ah," said the chief of staff, "but my dear Mr. Minister, you must not forget that the Austrian fleet has not had any [practice] either."

"This is a naval classic," Franklin told Eleanor, "which is hard to beat, but which perhaps should not be publicly repeated for a generation or two."

He thought he had done better with the prime minister, Vittorio Orlando. "Things have worked out all right," he reported to Daniels before boarding the train back to Paris; he had persuaded Orlando to agree to "a commander in chief for the naval forces in the Mediterranean." But he had not so persuaded him; Orlando had agreed merely to a chairman of a joint naval staff and had gone *that* far only when promised that Italy would continue to have the final say over operations in the Adriatic.

FDR's chief was not pleased. The French complained that Franklin's impetuous attempt at negotiating among the Allies had undercut them. Daniels assured the secretary of state that he had never authorized his assistant to "say who should command" in the region. Woodrow Wilson himself sent a terse note to the Navy Department, asking that henceforth he be told of any civilian missions to Europe, as "too many men go over there assuming to speak for the government."

Franklin's first venture into diplomacy had been an embarrassment rather than the triumph he had hoped for. By the end of the month, he realized it himself: "Frankly," he confessed to Geddes, "I have not reached the milk in the cocoanut [sic]."

Only momentarily daunted, he took his party southwest to inspect all the antisubmarine bases along the Atlantic coast from Bordeaux to Brest. "[A] frightfully busy week," he wrote Eleanor, "—on the road each day from 6 A.M. to midnight—& and we have done all manner of interesting things . . . all by auto—flying stations, ports, patrols, army stores, receptions, swims at French watering places, etc. etc."

Livy was more succinct: "FD having joy ride."

They bought lace at Quimperlé, had "a delicious swim" at dawn on a deserted beach, and "all had a fly" in a dirigible tethered to the U.S. naval station at Paimboeuf. At Pauillac on the 14th, Livy noted, "5,000 men [were] drawn up for us . . . several thousand were eating & [we] had lunch on a raised dais while a band of singers entertained. FD made them a very good speech." In it he told the enlisted men "they must always realize that hundreds of thousands of other men . . . at home would give anything in the world to change places with them."

"It is hard for me to go back to a dull office job at Washington," Franklin added, "after having visited the lines where our boys are making history."

More than ever, Franklin wanted to make that kind of history, too, and as they drove from port to port, he and Livy talked seriously of resigning their posts for active duty.

The previous year, back in Washington, Franklin had urged that a naval battery of 14-inch, 50-caliber guns—originally intended for use aboard battle cruisers and with an effective range of twenty-five miles—be mounted on railroad cars for use against the Germans on the western front. That battery was at last being readied near St.-Nazaire, and on the 17th Franklin drove up to inspect it.

The battery commander, Rear Admiral Charles P. Plunkett, hurried to welcome him. Plunkett, a wiry veteran with a gray mustache, wore an army officer's hat and uniform with two stars on his shoulder, indicating the rank of either rear admiral or major general, depending upon the branch of service to which he belonged.

"Captain McCauley," Franklin said, turning and winking broadly to his aide, "who is this major general?"

"Mr. Secretary," McCauley said, "that is Admiral Plunkett."

"Admiral," Franklin continued, looking Plunkett up and down, "you are out of uniform." The assistant secretary was himself dressed in tie and tweed jacket and puttees, wearing a soft hat and leaning on a cane.

The admiral, "much perturbed," tried to explain: Regulation whites were too conspicuous and easily soiled for work on land, he said, and navy blue was far too heavy for this hot work. Repeated letters to the Navy Department requesting permission to make the change had gone unanswered.

Franklin threw back his head and laughed. He had only been joking, he said; permission was hereby granted. The two men inspected the first train of thirteen cars, each with "U.S.N." painted on its side, ready at last to move toward the war after six weeks of argument with French authorities, who had feared that the ninety-ton guns would destroy the railroad bridges over which they had to pass.

Franklin yearned to go too: By signing on he could simultaneously fulfill two long-standing dreams—to take part in frontline combat and to be a naval officer. He asked the admiral if he might join the battery. He later said Plunkett wanted to know first "if I could swear well enough in French to swear a French train onto a siding and let his big guns through. Thereupon, with certain inventive genius, I handed him a line of French swear words, real and imaginary, which impressed him greatly, and he said that he would take me on . . . with the rank of Lieutenant Commander."

Franklin wrote Eleanor from Brest three days later:

> Somehow I don't believe I shall long be in Washington. The more I think of it, the more I feel that being only 36 my place is not at a Washington desk, even a Navy desk. I know you will understand. . . . Kiss the chicks—I wish I could see them each day and tell them of the wonderful things their country is doing here. A great deal of love from your devoted F.

Back in Paris again, Franklin held a press conference to report on the Allies' rapid progress in combating submarines. The members of the press "were all in full dress suits, with white ties," he reported to Eleanor, and "nearly all of them were the *rédacteurs*—the editors—of the papers. They were having the privilege of being received by 'Monsieur le Ministre.' Apparently, it caused the most awful furor." Determined to make the story "just as big as I possibly could," Franklin was in his element: He dispensed with his translator, sat on the edge of a table, and told the newspapermen that he would address them in the overconfident language made famous by his cousin Theodore, "Roosevelt French." The reporters were dazzled, and made much of his assurances that the war effort was "over the hump."

The assistant secretary had hoped for a formal invitation for his party to visit British headquarters at the front, Captain McCauley remembered, but "the invitation was not as cordial as it might have been, and the trip was called off" in favor of a quick courtesy visit to General Douglas Haig by Franklin alone. He and Livy and two officers then sped north along the coast to Belgium, where they watched an inconclusive battle between destroyers and submarines just off the beach, inspected a home for 500 war orphans, lunched with King Albert I at his château near his headquarters at La Panne, and took a drive with him to a nearby village where one wall of the town hall had been torn off by a shell the previous day. The old town records lay exposed to the weather, hundreds of brittle pages tied with tape.

That night, returning to Paris along unfamiliar, twisting roads and without lights, Franklin shook with fever. Livy took his temperature: It was 102 degrees. Roosevelt chose to ignore it, continuing to charge around Paris, even finding time to shop for books in the little stalls along the Seine across from

Notre Dame, until it was time to leave for Britain once again.

At the end of August, Franklin and Livy were in Scotland, where they inspected the North Sea mine barrage and the battleship squadron at the Firth of Forth, fished for salmon, and drank like undergraduates. At Strathpeffer, a former spa whose hotels had been commandeered as hospitals for wounded sailors, Livy noted, they "had a few rounds of Scotch," followed by "a wonderful dinner," after which their host "brought out some real Chartreuse. Had private parlor, so sang and told stories till 1 A.M. Wonderful time going to bed, FDR finding a fox in his bed, Jack dressed up and Brown coasted downstairs."

The next morning Franklin insisted everyone turn out for fishing. Livy described the day:

> Brown, FDR, Jack and I with Wallace drove out to Black Water belonging to Sir Arthur Mackensie in pouring rain in a dos-à-dos. Gillis late in coming so all had some Scotch and had a fine sing-song. All in regular clothes, low shoes, etc., but no one got a strike. Weather was so dour all had to keep it out with copious draughts of sublime Scotch so all sang all the way home. While clothes were drying, Wallace concocted a brew of hot Scotch, honey, and oatmeal served in beakers. All had at least two, and on descending found all guests and servants assembled so all hands to parlor formed circle and sang *Auld Lang Syne*.

All this conviviality—plus an ill-timed flat tire—made the party nearly four hours late for an inspection at Inverness. The men had been waiting in the rain since 10:00, and when Franklin finally drove up at 1:45, Livy Davis noted, their commander, Admiral Joseph Strauss, was "spitting mad." After what must have been a somewhat tense official luncheon, Franklin and his party drove on fortified with still "more Scotch and all got out at Perth for delicious and extremely jolly dinner. Had sing-song in train till bed time at 10:30. One of the jolliest days of my life!"

Franklin pushed on alone the next day to visit old family friends while Livy and the rest of the party went back to London. They joined forces again on September 6 for one last round of good times before heading home. Livy again noted some details:

> Worked at hotel, then went to Coliseum to see Russian dancers in "The Good Humored Ladies." Thence . . . at 6 FD, Lt. Heyden and I went to American Officers Club in Lord Beaconsfield's house on Curzon Street. Several delicious rounds of c.t.'s [cocktails] and saw many friends. Returned to hotel where had a very rough dinner. . . . Lt. Com. Jack Garde, and John Roys brought in Prince Axel [nephew of the king] of Denmark and his staff. . . . Everybody got drunk. All finally faded away except FD, Brown, Jackson and I. Stayed up until 4:30 pitching coins, playing golf, etc.
>
> Sept 7—Up at 7 to pack. All feeling very rocky.

Langdon Marvin, Roosevelt's law partner, who happened also to be in London as part of a Red Cross unit, helped him pack his bags before dawn.

Franklin was weak and pallid, but he did confide to Marvin that he was going to hurry right home, resign his post, and at last "get assigned to the big guns at the front."

Meanwhile, back in America, Uncle Theodore used the occasion of a family funeral to take his favorite niece, Eleanor, aside to speak to her about Franklin. He had no wish to wound her, but the death of his son had made still more stern his views about a young man's obligations. It was Franklin's plain duty to get into this war, he told her. She must use her influence as his wife to persuade him to enlist. Eleanor flushed with anger—she felt it was her husband's choice, not hers; besides, Franklin had tried to join the navy and been told to stay where he was by the president himself—but she did not openly disagree with her uncle.

A wire from Franklin, sent before he embarked for home, finally arrived at the Roosevelt estate: UNDER NEW DRAFT LAW PLEASE REGISTER ME AT HYDE PARK PERIOD ALL WELL.

All was not well, however. Shortly after the USS Leviathan set sail from Brest for New York on September 12, Franklin collapsed in his cabin, suffering from double pneumonia. Livy and McCauley fell ill, too; so did Prince Axel and most of his suite. Spanish influenza, the pandemic that would take 20 million lives worldwide that year, raged through the ship. Several officers and men died during the five-day voyage and were buried at sea. Franklin caught the disease later at home while still weak from pneumonia, but recovered.

As soon as he was well enough, at the end of October, he told both Secretary Daniels and President Wilson that he intended to leave the Navy Department for active duty. But it was too late. At 5 A.M. on November 11, the conflict that had taken the lives of 10 million young men ended in Marshal Ferdinand Foch's railroad car in the forest of Compiègne.

For Eleanor, "The feeling of relief and thankfulness was beyond description." But for Franklin, relief and gratitude were mixed with disappointment: He had missed the Great War.

Gamblers on the Turkish Brink

by DAVID FROMKIN

If you remember the Greco-Turkish war of 1921–22 at all, it may be for Ernest Hemingway's description of the Greek evacuation of Smyrna, from *In Our Time*. ("All those mules with their forelegs broken pushed over into the shallow water. It was all a pleasant business. My word yes a most pleasant business.") This was the war that created the modern state of Turkey out of the wreckage of the Ottoman Empire. That wreckage, as David Fromkin tells us, attracted the political high rollers of Europe. For Mustafa Kemal the stakes were nothing less than a new nation. But they were equally high for the Greeks and David Lloyd George, the British prime minister, who bet everything on maintaining the empire's hold on Constantinople and ruined his career in the process. As the twenties began, a war-weary Europe contemplated the unhappy prospect of a nasty regional conflict that seemed to be spreading out of control, even as another one had done in 1914. This account is taken from David Fromkin's much-praised study, *A Peace to End All Peace: Creating The Modern Middle East 1914–1922*, published by Henry Holt.

As the twentieth century closes, Turkey plays an increasingly visible role on the world stage. With her large and rapidly growing population, she may join and powerfully influence the European Community. Yet in the earlier part of the century, it was an open question whether any such country would come into existence: whether an independent Turkish nation would emerge in any part of the dying Ottoman Empire, the Arabic and Turkish-speaking Muslim sultanate that had ruled the Middle East for centuries.

Should the Turks be granted a country of their own? And if so, where? These questions were seriously considered by British prime minister David

Lloyd George, whose preeminence in Allied councils with regard to such matters was due to Britain's leading role in the wartime conquest of the region —and to the fact that a million-man British army was still in place there when the armistice halted the First World War in late 1918.

Most of the Turks of the Ottoman Empire lived in Anatolia, sometimes called Asia Minor, which corresponds roughly to present-day Turkey. (The other large Turkish-speaking population in the region was ruled by the Russian Empire and also sought independence unsuccessfully in the years after the overthrow of the czar in 1917.) Large numbers of Greeks and Armenians lived in Anatolia, too, as did Kurds, Jews, and others. The Armenians, their historic homeland partitioned between the Ottoman sultan and the Russian czar, lost about half their population in the massacres and forced deportations of 1915. The Greeks, however, retained a strong position based around the coastal metropolis of Smyrna (now Izmir), which had been a center of ancient Greek civilization.

Lloyd George, who presided over a coalition government of Liberals and Tories, was strongly anti-Turkish and heir to the Liberal foreign-policy tradition supporting Christian Greece against the Muslim Turks. The Armenians were Christians, too, and in theory equally deserving of support, but they were in a difficult situation—outnumbered and wedged between hostile Turks and Russians—so he pushed onto the Americans the burden of protecting and possibly governing them, a burden later rejected by the U.S. Senate. For his own country, Lloyd George reserved the role of sponsoring claims to less perilous areas of Anatolia.

Several of the Allies asserted claims. The United States, which had not been at war with the Ottoman Empire and was technically an associated power rather than an ally, asked for nothing, and czarist Russia no longer existed; but France and, even more so, Italy and Greece harbored territorial ambitions in Anatolia, some of which wartime Britain had pledged to support.

In the spring of 1919, Italy angered the other Allies by moving unilaterally to occupy points she coveted along the Anatolian coast: first Antalya and then Marmaris. Fearing that Smyrna would be next, the other Allies deputized the nearby Greeks to occupy the city and its environs until the Allies could consider to whom Smyrna would be awarded. Although the Greek occupation was supposed to be temporary, in practice it decided the issue in favor of Greece.

The landing of the Greek forces ignited spontaneous resistance in Turkey. Ex-Ottoman soldiers took back the weapons they had laid down under the terms of the armistice. Not until the summer of 1920 did Britain and France, with a reluctant Italy in tow, reach an agreement on the peace terms to be imposed on the Ottoman Empire. By then, as War Minister Winston Churchill had warned Lloyd George all along, the large British conscript army had been demobilized and Britain had lost the troops to enforce her terms. When even the tame Ottoman sultan, living in Constantinople in the shadow of the British fleet's guns, balked at signing the crushing treaty, the Allies were obliged to ask the Greeks to send troops to the city. In exchange, the

Greeks were allowed to press an offensive deep into Turkey. The many-pronged Greek offensive launched in June 1920 overwhelmed resistance to the treaty at the sultan's court.

The treaty was signed at the suburban French city of Sèvres, outside Paris, on August 10, 1920. Designed to satisfy not only Greece and the other Allies but also the Kurdish minority and the much-martyred Armenians, it was understandably anathema to the Turks. It partitioned Asia Minor, which the Turks claimed entirely for themselves, awarding independence in the northeast to the Armenians and autonomy in the east to the Kurds, and in the west giving Smyrna and its hinterland to the Greeks to administer with the plan of incorporating it into the kingdom of Greece. The south was to be divided into French and Italian economic zones. The Straits of the Dardanelles were to be placed under an international regime, while Constantinople was to be held hostage for the good behavior of the sultan in such matters as the treatment of minorities. Even in what remained to them of Anatolia, the Turks would not have full independence; their public finances were placed under European control.

Since only Greece still had the military resources available to enforce the treaty, Sèvres set the stage for a final duel between the two combatants still standing on the field of battle: the triumphant Greeks, based on the coast, and the dissident remnants of the Ottoman Turkish Army, who were gathering on the plateau of the interior.

It was to be a duel not merely of two armies but of two powerfully attractive visions: a reborn Hellenism and a new Turkish nationalism. The modern Greeks had for decades been reclaiming their past, harking back to their greatness in the ancient world. In pursuit of this vision, they took back one after another of the historic Hellenic lands from the Ottoman Empire during the nineteenth and early twentieth centuries. Classical Greece had not been a country but a collection of city-states, and its real frontier was not political but cultural—its language and civilization. The coast of Asia Minor was part of it. Settled by Greeks thousands of years ago, the coast and its offshore islands had emerged in the seventh and sixth centuries B.C. as the flourishing center of Greek civilization—the land of Homer; of the philosophers Pythagoras and Thales; of Hippocrates, the father of medicine; and of Herodotus, the father of history.

Eleuthérios Venizélos, the charismatic pro-Ally Greek prime minister who returned to power toward the end of World War I, was a foremost exponent of a Hellenic renaissance in Asia Minor. With his forceful personality, he developed an almost mesmeric hold over the imaginations of American, British, and French leaders at the Paris peace conference and won them over to the Greek cause. When he fell from power soon after the Treaty of Sèvres, pro-German politicians returned from exile to replace him, and the pro-German King Constantine reclaimed the throne. Together, they set out to prove they were equally capable of achieving the Hellenic dream. Unlike Venizélos, however, they could not command Allied support; their return to power thus proved a gift to their Turkish opponent, General Mustafa Kemal (better known today as Atatürk, "Father of Turks," a name he acquired in 1937).

Kemal's program for Asia Minor was largely his own brand of narrowly defined Turkish nationalism. A lean, tough, hard-living, hard-drinking officer in his late thirties, he had won fame as the victor at Gallipoli (1915) and had been the outstanding general on the Turkish side of the world war. Though he had been an early activist in the Young Turkey party that had ruled the Ottoman Empire since just before the war, he disagreed with its leaders: He thought them mistaken in bringing Turkey into the war on Germany's side; thought the empire a source of weakness rather than strength to the Turks of Anatolia; was opposed to having a state religion; and wanted Turks to become more like Europeans.

Kemal's chance had come in 1919, just after the war, when a friend in the war ministry got him an appointment from the sultan to serve as inspector general, with wide-ranging powers to go out into the anarchic countryside and restore order. Taking full advantage of his appointment, Kemal assumed command of Ottoman forces in the interior. Among the diverse groups responding to his appeal were Muslim mullahs crusading against the Greek Christians, and underground cadres of militant Young Turks who dreamed of multinational empire over much of the Middle East. In rallying behind him, they were obliged to set aside their own agendas and support Kemal's: the creation of a Turkish national state in a territory consisting mainly of Anatolia.

When the Allies occupied Constantinople in March 1920, Kemal declared the sultan their prisoner and the sultan's decrees therefore invalid. Escaping from Allied-occupied Constantinople, about 100 members of the Turkish Chamber of Deputies, elected in 1919, joined some 200 others elected from what they termed "resistance groups" to form a parliament. This body created a Government of the Grand National Assembly in the provincial capital city of Angora (today called Ankara), and Kemal was elected president.

Kemal prepared the ground for the military campaign against the Greeks by adroit diplomacy aimed at detaching them from their former allies. His first move was to establish a working relationship with Soviet Russia. It took careful diplomacy, for Kemal was openly and fiercely anticommunist, but eventually Nationalist Turkey became the first country to receive Soviet military aid—weapons and supplies—on a large scale. Together the Soviet Russians and the Turkish Nationalists defeated Armenia's bid for independence and confirmed the partition of Armenia between Turkey and Russia.

Italy, angered at the pro-Greek policy of England and France, unnerved by skirmishes with the Kemalists, ideologically in sympathy with Turkish nationalism, and lured by Kemal's promises of economic concessions, was the first of the Western Allies to change sides. France, similarly motivated, was the next to shift to a pro-Turkish policy when Venizélos fell and Constantine returned to the Greek throne. Italy and France then began negotiating to supply arms and other aid to Nationalist Turkey, though whether they actually did so remains disputed.

Even Great Britain felt obliged to modify her position and join France in a limited economic blockade of Greece to protest the return of the pro-German King Constantine, who was surrounded by such other wartime enemies of the Allies as the politician Dimitrios Gounaris. The British prime minister remained prepared to back Greece, but other members of the government felt otherwise, so Lloyd George was unable to offer Greece more than moral support.

Between the summer of 1920, when the Allies imposed the Treaty of Sèvres on a prostrate Turkey, and the winter of 1921, the situation was therefore entirely transformed. Indeed the reversal was so complete and so swift that it has few if any parallels in modern history. The Allies were now officially neutral with regard to the treaty that they themselves had conceived, written, and imposed a mere six months earlier.

Would Greece, abandoned by the Allies, try anyway to singlehandedly enforce the terms of the treaty? Constantine's ministers felt they had little choice but to do so. In terms of domestic politics, it was impossible for the new Greek government to withdraw from Asia Minor. A second option, recommended by Venizélos, was to dig in, holding the territories awarded to Greece at Sèvres and adopting a defensive strategy. That, however, would have been politically unpopular and would have committed Greece to the economic strain of maintaining a substantial military presence in Asia Minor indefinitely—for Kemal showed no disposition to oblige the Greeks by descending from the Anatolian plateau anytime soon to attack them.

Constantine's government thus opted to launch a quick knockout blow against the Kemalists. Since Kemal's forces would not descend to the coastal plain, the Greeks would come up the plateau after them and pursue them into the interior with the aim of bringing them to battle. The Greeks, with roughly 120,000 troops against Kemal's approximately 30,000, were confident that they would prevail. Lloyd George encouraged them to proceed.

They launched their attack on March 23, 1921, and despite faulty staff work and stiff opposition succeeded in moving up along difficult ground toward the plateau. Arnold Toynbee, the historian, accompanied the Greek army as a reporter for the *Manchester Guardian.* He noted that as his vehicle moved up the rough terrain, he "began to realize on how narrow a margin the Greeks had gambled for a military decision in Anatolia, and how adverse were the circumstances under which they were playing for victory over Kemal." At the end of the week, the Greeks were repulsed by Kemal's general Ismet at the village of Inönü and retreated.

The Greek government blamed its military commanders, and on April 7 Gounaris—now prime minister—and his colleagues asked retired general Ioannis Metaxas, Greece's outstanding military figure, to lead the next offensive in Anatolia. He refused, saying the war could not be won. The Turks had developed a national feeling, Metaxas said, and would fight hard for their independence. The politicians replied that it would be politically impossible to abandon the war. Despite the risk, they felt compelled to gamble everything on the success of one last offensive, scheduled for the summer.

On June 22 the Allies sent a message to the Greek government offering mediation in the war. Greece politely refused, saying that preparations for an offensive were so far along that it would be impractical to call them off.

Constantine and Gounaris had left themselves with no option but to launch their crusade, and Lloyd George's fortunes rode with them. His secretary and mistress (whom he later married) noted in her diary that he

> has had a great fight in the Cabinet to back the Greeks (not in the field but morally) and he and Balfour are the only pro-Greeks there. . . . [He] has got his way, but he is much afraid lest the Greek attack should be a failure, and he should have proved to have been wrong. He says his political reputation depends a great deal on what happens in Asia Minor. . . . [I]f the Greeks succeed the Treaty of Versailles is vindicated, and the Turkish rule is at an end. A new Greek Empire will be founded, friendly to Britain, and it will help all our interests in the East. . . .

On July 10, 1921, the Greek army launched a brilliant three-pronged attack. Greek commanders had learned from their earlier mistakes and did not repeat them. The offensive was crowned with the capture of Eskisehir, a rail junction considered to be the strategic key to western Anatolia.

Lloyd George was jubilant. Near Eskisehir, however, the Turkish commander, General Ismet, though overwhelmed by the enemy, could not bring himself to retreat. Kemal assumed the burden and personally ordered the Turkish forces to fall back.

When Kemal's people learned that he was going to abandon western Anatolia to the enemy, there was an uproar in the National Assembly; political enemies, personal rivals, and defeatists joined hands against him. After a time Kemal called the Assembly into secret session and proposed a Roman course of action: that the delegates elect him dictator for three months; should he fail as supreme commander, the blame would fall entirely on him. The proposal appealed both to those who believed in victory and to those who were certain of defeat, and was adopted.

Employing a strategy similar to that used by the Russians against Napoleon, Kemal pulled his forces back to within fifty miles of his capital at Angora and deployed them behind a great bend in the Sakarya River. In the time available to him, he requisitioned resources from the entire population, commandeering 40 percent of household food, cloth, and leather supplies, confiscating horses, and preparing for total war. He ordered his troops to entrench in the ridges and hills that rose steeply from the near bank of the river toward Angora. By mid-August his army had dug into this powerful natural defensive position, circling Angora for sixty miles behind the loop in the Sakarya and dominating from high ground the passage of the river.

On August 14, 1921, the Greek army started the long, difficult march on Angora. The chief of the supply bureau warned that the army's extended line of communications and transportation would break down if it advanced beyond the Sakarya; but his colleagues at headquarters were not concerned since they did not intend to push much beyond that. The Greek commanders

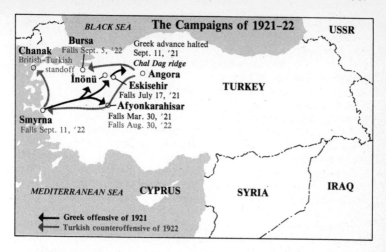

believed they had already beaten the enemy and would merely finish him off at this last stand. They invited the British liaison officers who accompanied them to attend a victory celebration in Angora after the battle.

But the nine-day march was arduous, across desert and wilderness that provided neither food nor water. In the sand and dust, motor vehicles broke down and there were persistent problems of supply. At the end of the march, as the Greeks moved toward Angora, Turkish cavalry dashed in behind them to raid their supply lines.

The advancing Greek army made first contact with the enemy on August 23 and attacked all along the line on August 26. Crossing the river, the Greek infantry, under intense Turkish fire, fought its way slowly up toward the heights, driving the enemy from one ridgetop line of entrenchments to another above it. The fierce combat went on for days, with the Greeks advancing about a mile a day. By September 2 they had gained control of the commanding heights, a long, broad ridge called Chal Dag.

The Greeks were poised to seize victory, and the Turks were on the verge of retreat; but both armies were too exhausted to move. A curious calm descended on the battlefield. What became clear only gradually in the days that followed was that Kemal's strategy had succeeded: He had lured the Greeks into overextending their supply lines, which had been disrupted by his cavalry raids. For days the bone-weary, hungry, thirsty Greeks at the front had been deprived of food and ammunition; they had kept going on sheer courage. Now they could no longer go on.

It was one of those astonishing moments when the truth becomes visible. Both the tactical victory and the strategic defeat of the Greek army could be seen at a glance: Greek troops dominated the field of battle from Chal

Dag; yet their position was one in which soldiers never want to find them-selves—fatigued, bereft of supplies, and deep inside enemy territory.

The Turks were exhausted, too, and down to their last supplies of ammu-nition; they were also badly demoralized after losing Chal Dag. Yet Kemal held off from retreating, sensing that if he could hold firm long enough, the other side would retreat first. Neither army could go on fighting for more than a few days, so it came down to a contest of wills in which the Turks held the advantage as soon as the Greeks began to realize the peril of their position.

On September 8, after nearly a week of calm, Kemal took all of his remaining ammunition and threw it into one last attack. By September 11, unable to continue fighting, the Greek troops at the front finally received the order to retreat. They descended from the heights that they had won with so much bloodshed and, unhindered by the Turks, crossed back over the Sakarya River, retreating to Eskisehir, where they had started their march a month before. The campaign was over.

Between the summer of 1921 and the summer of 1922, a lull prevailed in the Greco-Turkish War. During this time Kemal gathered arms and supplies to launch an attack; Greek prime minister Gounaris and his foreign minister journeyed west to seek aid from the Allies. They were met with little sympa-thy. In London they sat in the ambassadors' waiting room at the Foreign Office, hat in hand, hoping Foreign Secretary Lord Curzon would somehow solve their problems. They called upon the prime minister, too; but Lloyd George told them, "Personally I am a friend of Greece, but . . . all my colleagues are against me. And I cannot be of any use to you." He urged them to fight on nonetheless, in hopes that things would change for the better. In the spring of 1922 he told Venizélos, who had come to see him in the House of Commons, that when Constantine eventually disappeared from the scene, public opinion in the Allied countries would swing back toward support of Greece. "Meanwhile Greece must stick to her policy," he said.

Lloyd George found himself increasingly isolated, even within his own government, and the foreign secretary took effective control of efforts to resolve the crisis. In collaboration with the Allies, he sought an accommoda-tion with Nationalist Turkey.

Fearing that the Allies were about to betray him that summer, King Constantine withdrew a vital force of three regiments and two battalions from the Greek army in Anatolia, where they had been standing guard against the Turks, and sent them to Thrace, the European province of Turkey oppo-site Constantinople. His government announced that Greece would occupy Constantinople in order to bring the war to an end. His desperate calculation was that this threat would impel the Allies to take some action to resolve the conflict, presumably in favor of Greece. He gambled that at the very least the Allies would let his forces in Thrace pass through Constantinople to rejoin his weakened armies defending the Asia Minor coast. But instead, the Allied army of occupation in Constantinople barred the road to the Greeks, assert-ing an armed neutrality. As a result, the Greek troops withdrawn from the front line in Asia Minor could not return.

Meanwhile, Constantine's withdrawal of units from the coast of Asia Minor prompted Kemal to hasten his attack on the weakened and overextended Greek defensive lines there. Secretly massing his forces, he launched an attack on the southern front at dawn on August 26. Following two days of fierce fighting, the Greeks were forced to retreat in disorder.

Greece hastily assembled a fleet to evacuate her army. Racing the coming September rains and the advancing, vengeful Turkish army, soldiers all along the coast thronged toward the ships, traversing a countryside in which perhaps a million people had been left homeless. The ancient Greek community of Asia Minor was seized with dread. The archbishop of Smyrna wrote to Venizélos on September 7 that "Hellenism in Asia Minor, the Greek state and the entire Greek Nation are descending now to a Hell from which no power will be able to raise them up and save them. . . . It is a real question whether when Your Excellency reads this letter of mine we shall still be alive, destined as we are . . . for sacrifice and martyrdom." He ended with an appeal for help.

Appeals were in vain. Venizélos was powerless to give aid, and two days later the archbishop was sent to the martyred death he had foreseen: A mob of Muslims tortured him to death.

Since the beginning of the war, atrocities between the Muslim and Christian communities had escalated. When the Greek army first landed in Smyrna in 1919, soldiers had butchered unarmed Turks. In *The Western Question,* Arnold Toynbee reported that in visiting Greek villages destroyed by the Turks, he noticed that the houses had been burned to the ground one by one, as if the Turks had savored doing it. King Constantine also claimed Greek corpses had been skinned. In the 1921 campaign, Toynbee charged, the Greek army deliberately drove whole villages of Turkish civilians from their homes. By 1922 the destructiveness had become so widespread, and pain and death were inflicted so casually, as almost to defy description. Some sense of the horror is conveyed by such firsthand accounts as Ernest Hemingway's "On the Quai at Smyrna."

Long-smoldering religious and national tensions erupted in Smyrna, the greatest city of Asia Minor, at summer's end in 1922. The Armenian quarter went up in flames on September 15, and the fires spread—or were spread—to the Greek and European quarters. Between 50 and 75 percent of the ancient metropolis was destroyed; only the Turkish quarter remained untouched. Hundreds of thousands of people had lived in the Christian city; it proved impossible to calculate how many of them died in its final agony. A *Chicago Daily News* correspondent, John Clayton, was the first to describe the devastation, pounding out the story on his portable typewriter amid the ruins: "Except for the squalid Turkish quarter, Smyrna has ceased to exist. The problem of the minorities is here solved for all time. No doubt remains as to the origin of the fire. . . . The torch was applied by Turkish regular soldiers." To this day, however, pro-Turkish scholars deny this widely believed accusation.

U.S., French, English, and Italian naval vessels hurried to evacuate their own nationals. The Americans and the British at first refused to aid anyone else, but the Italians accepted on board anyone who reached their ships, and the French accepted anyone who claimed to be one of their citizens—if he or she could say it in French. As the crisis deepened, the Allies were driven to a more general evacuation. When Kemal threatened to treat all Greek and Armenian men of military age as prisoners of war, Greece and the Allies organized the evacuation of masses of civilians as Greece completed her military evacuation as well.

By the end of 1922, about 1.5 million Greeks had fled Turkey or been driven out. Ernest Hemingway, then a war correspondent for the *Toronto Star*, wrote that he would never forget the procession of destitute Greek refugees, perhaps twenty miles long. His Croatian landlady, more familiar with such sights, quoted a Turkish proverb to him: "It is not only the fault of the ax but of the tree as well." In the weeks to come, it was echoed in various forms by Allied statesmen who searched their consciences and discovered, each in his own way, that blame for the catastrophe should be placed on somebody else.

Constantinople and European Turkey—Eastern Thrace—were the next and final objectives on Kemal's line of march. The neutral Allied army of occupation—whose purpose in occupying Constantinople had long since disappeared—stood in his way. But as the Nationalist Turkish armies advanced to their positions, the Allies panicked. The war had been far away from them; but if Kemal attacked, they too would have to fight the Turks. For Italy and France, who had no quarrel with Kemal and indeed had become his supporters, the position was absurd. For England, whose prime minister did have a quarrel with Kemal, the position was alarming—and the news of it surprising. As late as September 4, the *Times* had reported that "the Greek army unquestionably sustained a reverse, but its extent is unduly exaggerated." By mid-September, however, headlines such as NEAR EAST PERIL and NEAR EAST CRISIS were appearing regularly, and photos of Smyrna in flames replaced society weddings and theater openings. Britons, four years after the armistice, were shocked to be told suddenly that they might have to fight a war to defend far-off Constantinople. Their immediate inclination was to get rid of the government that had gotten them into such a situation.

But Constantinople and the Straits, because of their world importance for shipping, and Eastern Thrace, because it is in Europe, had special status in the minds of British leaders. Winston Churchill, hitherto pro-Turkish, came to the rescue of Lloyd George's policy and told the cabinet in September,

> The line of deep water separating Asia from Europe was a line of great significance, and we must make that line secure by every means within our power. If the Turks take the Gallipoli Peninsula and Constantinople, we shall have lost the whole fruits of our victory.

By mid-September 1922, the last Greek troops had been evacuated and a direct armed clash between Britain and Turkey seemed imminent. The cabinet met in a series of emergency sessions commencing September 15, when Churchill told his colleagues that the Allies' misfortunes were due to the fact that they had let their armies melt away. They needed armies, he said, and they also needed to secure support from the Dominions (who, after the world war, had wrung from Lloyd George a concession that in the future the question of war or peace was to be decided by each of them for herself) and from France in reinforcing the British troops facing Kemal's armies.

On September 15, the cabinet instructed Churchill to draft, for Lloyd George's signature, a telegram informing the Dominions of the British decision to defend the neutral zone in Turkey and asking for their military aid. Shortly before midnight the telegram, in code, was sent to each of the Dominion prime ministers.

The cabinet also decided that the public should be informed of the seriousness of the situation, and to this end Churchill and Lloyd George prepared a press release on September 16 that appeared in that evening's newspapers. It expressed the government's desire for a peace conference with Turkey, but said none could convene under the gun of Turkish threats. It expressed fear that if comparatively weak Muslim Turkey could be seen to have inflicted a major defeat on the Allies, the rest of the Muslim world would be encouraged to throw off colonial rule. The communiqué mentioned consultations with France, Italy, and the Dominions regarding joint military action to avert the Kemalist threat.

The belligerent tone of the statement alarmed the British public and also caused alarm abroad. Furious that the British government appeared to be speaking for him, French premier Raymond Poincaré ordered his troops withdrawn from the front line of the neutral zone; the Italians followed forthwith, leaving the British forces to face the enemy alone.

The Dominion prime ministers also were offended. The communiqué was published in Canadian, Australian, and New Zealand newspapers before the prime ministers had time to decode the cables they had received, which led them to think Churchill and Lloyd George were trying to rush them into something without giving them time to think. British Dominions had never refused to follow the mother country into war, but now Canada and Australia refused to send troops, and South Africa remained silent. Only New Zealand and Newfoundland responded favorably.

On September 22, Lloyd George asked Churchill to chair a cabinet committee to oversee military movements in Turkey. Churchill's brilliant friend F.E. Smith, now Lord Birkenhead and serving as lord chancellor, had been critical of Churchill for changing to an anti-Turkish position, but at the end of September he joined Lloyd George and Churchill as a leader of the belligerent faction. It was a question of prestige, Birkenhead felt; England must never give in to force.

The British press, however, continued its campaign against the war, and public protests were held. Labor-union delegates went to Downing Street to deliver their protest to the prime minister personally.

Lord Curzon crossed over to Paris to concert a strategy with the Allies.

On September 23 he finally agreed with France and Italy on a common program that yielded to all of Kemal's demands—Eastern Thrace, Constantinople, and the Straits—so long as it could appear to be a negotiated settlement rather than a surrender.

Meanwhile, the British and Turkish armies confronted each other at Chanak (today's Çanakkale), a town on the Asiatic side of the Straits from which tours now depart for the ruins of Troy. The French and Italian contingents having retired to their tents, a small English contingent stood guard behind barbed wire, with orders not to fire unless fired upon.

Once again Kemal demonstrated an ability to unnerve the other side at the psychologically right moment. The first of his troops advanced to the British line on September 23 but did not open fire; they stood their ground. A few days later more Turkish troops arrived. By the end of September, there were 4,500 in the neutral zone, talking through the barbed wire to the British and holding their rifles butt-forward to show that they would not be the first to fire. It was an eerie confrontation. On September 29, British intelligence reported to the cabinet that Kemal, pushed on by Soviet Russia, planned to attack the next day. The false report was believed. With the cabinet's approval, England's military chiefs drafted a stern ultimatum for the local British commander to deliver to Kemal, threatening to open fire.

The local British commander did not deliver the ultimatum. Instead he reached an agreement with Kemal to negotiate an armistice—and so brought the crisis to an end. For many reasons—including fear of what Lloyd George and Churchill might do—Kemal accepted a formula that allowed the Allies to save face by postponing Turkey's occupation of some of the territories she was eventually to occupy.

Had Kemal invaded Europe, it would have meant war. The belligerent posture of the British leaders appeared to have stopped him. Given the actual weakness of their position, this represented a brilliant triumph for Lloyd George and Churchill. (The British electorate, however, did not see it in this light. In the flush of what he believed to be a victory, Lloyd George decided to call a snap election—and as a result the Tories left his coalition and brought down his government. The subsequent election was a disaster for him, and he never held office again.)

After much difficult bargaining, an armistice was worked out at the coastal town of Mudanya on the morning of October 11. It was to go into effect at midnight October 14. Significant issues were left unresolved, but consideration of them was postponed until a peace conference that concluded at Lausanne the following year. Essentially Kemal was able to obtain the terms that he had always demanded: an independent Turkish nation-state to be established in Anatolia and Eastern Thrace. Before long, Kemal's Turkey took physical possession of Constantinople, the Straits, and Eastern Thrace from the departing Allies.

In Greece and Turkey, vanquished and victor reaped the respective rewards of failure and success. A military revolt swiftly overthrew Constantine, who was sent into exile. Gounaris and other ex-ministers of the deposed monarch were court-martialed and convicted of high treason. Gounaris and five others were executed by firing squads.

Constantine and his ministers had committed no crime in the ordinary sense. They had done something worse: They had brought about a historic catastrophe for their nation. Greek influence in Asia Minor, after thousands of years of existence, had been lost forever in the autumn of 1922 by the government of King Constantine.

As Greeks departed those shores, Turks began the task of creating a new country to the design of Mustafa Kemal. Victory soon brought Kemal something close to absolute power in his domains. He abolished the sultanate, the caliphate, and the empire; brought in the Western alphabet and Western dress; imposed a secular nation-state on a population that found such notions alien; and set his people on a road intended to lead them into the European community.

Joint Plan RED

by THADDEUS HOLT

So far, these pages have been almost totally concerned with the management of violence, and it is with relief that we turn to an exercise that today smacks of pure whimsy. In 1931, U.S. planners conjured up a threat that could have relegated the coming depression to the shadows: war with the British Empire. Before the Second World War, foreign powers were designated by colors in contingency plans: Britain was RED; Japan, ORANGE; Canada, CRIMSON; and so forth. Joint Plan RED, involving the army and the navy, may be an improbable scenario, but it actually exists. A British drive down the Hudson Valley (shades of Burgoyne)? A landing near New Bedford and a thrust to gain the port of Boston? The massing of a U.S. offensive along the Vermont-Quebec border? If that sounds outlandish, then only consider that the Canadians, too, had a plan to hold off the U.S. until the British came to the rescue. Thaddeus Holt, a lawyer, a writer on military subjects, a former deputy undersecretary of the army, and a member of the *MHQ* Advisory Board, describes his surprising catch during a fishing expedition in the National Archives.

Get off the elevator on the fourth floor of the marble palace on Pennsylvania Avenue that houses the National Archives. Turn left and walk into a big dim room with row after row of microfilm-viewing machines. Squeeze apologetically past the prim genealogist and the glassy-eyed graduate student, and stake your claim to an unused machine. Go into the adjoining low-ceilinged room filled with racks of flat steel drawers. You want rack number 10-20, the seventh drawer down. It glides out easily on ball bearings. In it are ninety little square blue boxes, each containing a reel of 35mm film. Fish out box number 1421/10 and take it back to your machine. Switch it on, thread up your film, start cranking the reel. Projected pictures of old letters, memoranda, documents of all kinds whiz past on the white metal plate in front of you. When you reach a page marked—

SECRET
DECLASSIFIED BY: JCS DECLASSIFICATION BRANCH
DATE 4 Feb 74
JOINT ARMY AND NAVY BASIC WAR PLAN-RED

—then stop

You have before you what was once among the most sensitive and closely held documents on earth.

Prepared by the old Joint Board of the Army and Navy, predecessor of the Joint Chiefs of Staff, this is the American contingency plan, with supporting "Estimates of the Situation," for war between the United States and the British Empire.

Before the Second World War, foreign powers were designated by colors in army and navy contingency plans. RED meant Great Britain; CRIMSON meant Canada; and SCARLET meant the Anzac dominions, Australia and New Zealand. After 1918, a RED war was most improbable, but planning for that contingency went on—partly, no doubt, to give colonels and captains something to do; and specifically, perhaps, to give the army something to work on that would call for millions of citizen-soldiers, since the navy was expected to have the leading role in the really serious contingency plan, Joint Plan ORANGE, a war with Japan. So this last full-dress joint RED plan—approved by the secretaries of war and the navy in May 1930—which, with its supporting estimates of the situation, constitutes a hefty document of ninety-four legal-size, single-spaced pages, was never more than an exercise.

But suppose it had been real.

It is early 1931, and you are President Hoover. The United States and Britain have somehow drifted into enmity. Public opinion in both countries has turned ugly. Hearst and McCormick are howling for King George to be punched in the snoot, and Beaverbrook is howling for the tricky Yankees to be taught a lesson. You are visited in the White House by your secretary of state, the patrician Wall Street lawyer Henry L. Stimson; your secretary of war, tough Oklahoma oilman Patrick J. Hurley; your secretary of the navy, Brahmin banker Charles Francis Adams; the chief of staff of the army, young, handsome, flamboyant General Douglas MacArthur; and a mild, dry Down Easter, the chief of naval operations, Admiral William V. Pratt.

Stimson confirms that if it comes to shooting it will be just the United States against the British Empire, with no allies on either side; Japan is busy in Manchuria, Mexico is digesting her revolution, the Europeans want only peace. Now, Mr. President: These gentlemen have come to brief you on their estimate of the situation and their war plan. And they ask you to make one basic decision at once, a decision that they say could itself precipitate war but is imperative to protect the country.

This is what you would hear:

The first question, Mr. President, is what strength the RED powers have and what we have. The answer, to begin with, is that they are stronger than we are: on land, on sea, and in the air. We can catch up, but we must move swiftly and play for time.

We have barely 100,000 officers and men in the regular army (including the Air Corps) at home, in nine divisional organizations; another 40,000 are in Panama, the Philippines, Puerto Rico, and Hawaii, and we need to keep them there. The National Guard has 175,000 men, in eighteen divisional organizations plus components of nine cavalry brigades. The Organized Reserve is about 113,000 officers and 5,000 men; they provide the officer complement and cadre for a possible thirty-three more divisions and for expanding regular and Guard divisions to war strength. We have calculated everything, Mr. President, from the day you order mobilization—M-Day. We estimate it will take at least till M + 60 (days) to mobilize the twenty-seven regular and Guard divisional organizations, with corresponding support troops. We can have relatively strong covering forces on the frontiers by M + 4, and all initially available forces concentrated in frontier commands by M + 10. With a draft law in operation by M + 60, we could have 2.1 million men in service by M + 120, but of course it will take time to train and equip them. Our mobilization plan anticipates ultimately, with a draft law in force, a trained army of 4.6 million men, but that could take two years under war conditions. At the outset we would have to work with the regulars and get whatever use we can out of the Guard.

On their side, the Canadian army has an active peacetime strength of 52,000. Canada could have 120,000 men, eleven divisions, under arms in thirty days. In England, there is a 100,000-man "Expeditionary Force" of four infantry divisions and two cavalry brigades, ready for worldwide emergencies; this force could be in Nova Scotia in thirty days. By an imperial agreement made in 1926, Britain undertakes to mobilize eight regular divisions in two weeks and thirteen divisions of the Territorial Army (their equivalent of our National Guard) in six months, while the Dominions and India would mobilize thirteen divisions swiftly to bridge the gap till the Territorials are ready. We calculate that they could have 270,000 men—twenty divisions—in Canada available for field service in sixty days. All told, assuming the whole empire joins in the war, they could have, net of battle losses, 460,000 men, or twenty-eight divisions, in the theater in six months, over 1 million in nine months, a maximum of nearly 2.5 million men, seventy-seven divisions, by M + 480. They already have the shipping tonnage to support such an effort.

As for sea power, we have eighteen capital ships, all battleships; they have twenty, including four of their fast battle cruisers. They have six aircraft carriers and we have only three, though in fact ours carry more planes in total. [Nobody in 1930 really knew how much that mattered, because nobody then knew how effective aircraft would be against warships.] They have sixty-two cruisers to our eighteen, and sixty-eight subs to our fifty-seven; we, however, have 221 destroyers to their 175. Our fleet is divided: Our Main Battle Force, including twelve battleships and all three carriers, is on the West Coast, where it has normally been based since 1922; only four of our battleships are in the Atlantic. Theirs is divided, too, between the Home Fleet and the Mediterranean, but in five days they could concentrate in the Channel, and the Grand Fleet, with 13 battleships, three battle cruisers, and five carriers, could be at Halifax by M + 13. Overall, their navy is better balanced than ours, with greater speed and gun range; but their radius of action is inferior, meaning they cannot operate at great distances from their bases. For a major enterprise in North America they would have to assemble a great fleet of commercial tankers; that would take time.

They have much greater land-based air power than we do. In the United Kingdom, the Royal Air Force has thirteen squadrons of bombers, twelve of fighters, and five for observation; there are another eleven bomber squadrons overseas. They have nearly 4,000 active and reserve pilots. They can have thirty-four land-based squadrons in Canada by M + 30. (If they used aircraft carriers to transport the planes, they could have seventeen there by M + 10.) We have only a very weak air force in the continental United States with which to meet a major emergency: only three squadrons of pursuit planes, two of bombers, two of attack planes, and nine of observation planes. With the Guard and the reserves, we could perhaps double this number by M + 120.

The bottom line: Eventually we can be stronger than they are, but not overwhelmingly so. It will take time.

The next question, Mr. President, is what *they* might do.

The British and the Anzacs would probably concentrate an "Asiatic Fleet" at Singapore and take the Philippines with troops from India. Guam we can write off; Samoa, too. The Anzacs would occupy them early. Alaska will probably see only raids from Canada. Hawaii is a long way from British bases and strongly defended; they probably would not attack it except in the later stages of a war in which they were overwhelmingly successful. We could accept all these losses if we had to, plus the raiding that is likely to take place across the border in Minnesota, North Dakota, and Montana and along the southern Atlantic coast. We could even accept an invasion of the West Coast by Indian and Australian troops by way of British Columbia. For the industrial heartland and war-making power of the United States—the main prize for any enemy, which we must defend at all costs—lies northeast of a line drawn from Norfolk to Chicago. The vital theater is thus the Atlantic one.

The only outlying possession whose loss would be unacceptable is the Panama Canal. That would gravely burden the transcontinental rail system, and it would be an irretrievable disaster if it were closed before our Main Battle Force reached the Atlantic side. It is vulnerable, especially to air attack. The year before last, in the Caribbean maneuvers called Fleet Problem IX, planes from our new carrier *Lexington* evaded all the defenses, including planes from *Lexington*'s sister ship *Saratoga*, and "struck" the canal locks. Many officers think this shows that if planes get within range they will always get through.

Canada is crucial. Only from Canada can the forty-eight states of our homeland be seriously attacked; and occupied Canada would be a big bargaining chip at the peace table. Even if Canada should declare neutrality, we urge you not to recognize that neutrality—certainly not unless they allow us to occupy at least Halifax, Nova Scotia; St. Johns, Newfoundland; Victoria, British Columbia; and bridgeheads at the Soo (the canal locks at Sault Ste. Marie), at Detroit/St. Clair, and at Niagara Falls along the line of the Welland Canal.

For us the most sensitive point on the border is the Soo locks; 87 percent of our iron ore passes through the Great Lakes. For them, the most sensitive point on the border is the Niagara power-generating complex; if it were knocked out it would not affect us much, while its loss, combined with stoppage of coal from western Canada and our control of Quebec, would strangle the Canadian industrial base in the Ontario peninsula. But the real key to North America is Halifax, Nova Scotia, with its naval base. It is a warm-water port, open year-round, whereas the St. Lawrence is frozen several months a year. It is two days' sailing from Boston, four from Norfolk. With control of the western Atlantic, the British could build up a major force at and through Halifax, and from that base launch an amphibious invasion of our northeastern industrial core.

The prime British consideration must be an early invasion of the United States to prevent the full development of our power. With their stronger navy, they will therefore probably bring across troops in force and large elements of air power before they have managed to destroy or contain our fleet and have actually gained control of the western Atlantic. (They are probably already quietly augmenting their light naval forces at Halifax, readying Canadian bases to receive the RAF, and strengthening the garrisons at Jamaica, Trinidad, and Bermuda.) Especially if our fleet has not been concentrated in the Atlantic when war begins, we should expect an effort to close the Panama Canal.

At the earliest possible date, the RAF will start bombing all industrial centers within range of Canadian bases in order to paralyze our industrial effort, retard our mobilization, and force a concentration of our Air Corps to defend those areas and force air combat in which they may gain clear air superiority. British naval forces will try to get control of the Great Lakes as soon as possible and interrupt our ore transport.

As soon as they have the forces for it in place, a major invasion attempt based on the Montreal-Quebec line seems inevitable. It is only 180 miles from the Canadian border to Albany, and if they could reach and occupy that city it would have a far-reaching effect on our industrial region and system of communications.

Then, once the United States Fleet is decisively defeated or effectively contained and there is a sufficient build-up of British forces in North America, in conjunction with the offensive down the Hudson we expect an amphibious landing aimed at capturing a major port to serve as a base for large-scale warfare. Boston is the most probable target. We have studied every possible landing site from the beaches east of Portland, Maine, down to Virginia Beach, and we conclude that the landing area most advantageous to the British would be the coast just to the east of Narragansett Bay. Heavy equipment could be offloaded by lighters at the Westport River, southwest of New Bedford, and at the small harbors of Buzzards Bay, until New Bedford with its docks was captured. New Bedford would serve as a base until Narragansett Bay was cleared. It, in turn, would afford a base for operations against either New York or Boston. Boston with its great port would be the logical first big objective. The loss of Boston, followed by a penetration of our vital industrial area, might be the determining factor of the war. The British have the strength to mount such a campaign—if they can hold on to Halifax and Quebec.

So, Mr. President, we turn at last to our own plan. We envisage denying the British the bases from which to invade the United States by seizing Canada as quickly as possible.

The first crucial step, if the situation permits, will be to seize Halifax. By M + 4 we can have a three-division corps of 25,000 men—probably the 1st Division (the Big Red One) and the 26th Division (the Massachusetts National Guard), plus some other units and a brigade of Marines—at Boston with enough shipping and naval escort to send them against Halifax. By M + 10 they can land in Nova Scotia. Actually capturing Halifax may not be easy; the lakes and rivers in Nova Scotia will let them organize successive defensive lines. If the British have reinforced the garrison, it will be a very tough fight.

As for the campaign on the land frontier: Assuming that the Army command structure is set up according to the new Four-Army Plan that we are preparing now, General MacArthur will put on his second hat as commanding general, 1st Army Group, and set up GHQ at Harrisburg, Pennsylvania. 1st Army Group will consist of four field armies. The Halifax expedition will be one corps of First Army. First Army will have two other corps, which as soon as possible will mount a two-pronged operation targeted on Quebec City, one by way of Colebrook, New Hampshire, the other by way of Sherbrooke, Quebec. Third Army, two corps, will operate on First Army's left, its main effort a corps-size operation to Three Rivers, isolating Quebec City from the west and supporting First Army in the attack on Quebec City if necessary, with its other corps (less one division sent to reinforce Panama) covering the left flank of the main effort and threatening Montreal.

Second Army's front will be the Great Lakes area; one corps will seize bridgeheads at Niagara and Detroit/St. Clair, while another corps (less one division kept in GHQ reserve) will seize a bridgehead at Sault Ste. Marie. A corps of Fourth Army, less one division to cover the Pacific coast, will cover the Northwest; another corps will be shipped out to reinforce Hawaii and the Philippines.

Those will be our initial moves with the units we have active or can activate rapidly. When our build-up permits, First Army's mission will be to occupy the city of Quebec and all Canadian territory east thereof and south of the St. Lawrence. Third Army will occupy the province of Quebec west of the city of Quebec and south of the St. Lawrence and Ottawa rivers, and the province of Ontario south of Lake Nipissing. Second Army will have a triple mission. It will help Third Army seize southern Ontario. It will expand the

Sault Ste. Marie bridgehead as far as Sudbury, Ontario, which is an intensely strategic spot, for 90 percent of the world's nickel comes from there. And it will capture and hold Winnipeg. This will cut Canadian transcontinental communications, shutting off eastern Canada (and the United Kingdom) from the wheat of the Canadian prairies, and shutting the main front off to reinforcements from India and the Anzac dominions by way of the Pacific; it will also close Canada's warm-season back-door route from Britain via Hudson Bay and the railroad from Churchill down to the transcontinental rail system. Fourth Army will invade British Columbia, capture and hold Vancouver, and reinforce Hawaii and the Philippines further if that is feasible.

The Navy, meanwhile, will establish control over the western North Atlantic and the Strait of Juan de Fuca, and blockade the Pacific coast of Canada. As soon as consistent with priority operations in Canada, it will seize and hold Jamaica, the Bahamas, and Bermuda—plus, later on, Trinidad, St. Lucia, and other British West Indian and Central American possessions. It will establish control over the Great Lakes. It will safeguard vital American seaborne trade. And it will keep in mind its primary mission, which is to destroy the Royal Navy's main battle fleet. Our plan does not envisage actively seeking a decisive fleet action at an early stage, but we would not refuse the opportunity if it were offered. We believe that British strategy will be to seek such an action.

Assuming we win a decisive fleet action, we will have permanent control of the Atlantic and our goal will be to effect economic exhaustion of the United Kingdom by naval warfare—including submarine warfare—and by seizure of whatever British territory may be necessary to carry out that purpose. If the British should win such an action, they would then have permanent control of the Atlantic and may be expected to carry out the invasion strategy we have described.

So, Mr. President: That is Joint Plan RED. Everything depends on speed—to seize the key points in Canada before the British can reinforce them. Absolutely everything in the plan hinges on our Battle Force being in the Atlantic on M-Day. If the British were able to shut the Panama Canal before that concentration could be effected—as, to repeat, they very possibly could do—they could readily establish control over the Atlantic and bring reinforcements into Canada at will. Even if our Halifax expedition were initially successful, the force there would wither on the vine. In thirty days from mobilization they can have thirteen battleships at Halifax, over thirty land-based aviation squadrons at Canadian bases, and the Expeditionary Force on its way or on the scene. It takes twenty-three days to get the Battle Force from San Pedro–San Diego to the New York–Narragansett Bay area. That could make it a neck-and-neck race to Halifax against the Grand Fleet and the British Expeditionary Force.

Therefore, Mr. President, we urge you to order the Battle Force concentrated in the Atlantic at once.

And we have to tell you that such a move under present tense conditions would probably precipitate war: a war of long duration, involving the maximum effort of the armed forces and civil power of the United States.

Fifteen years ago, as Herbert Hoover, private citizen, you were in charge of the great relief effort in Belgium; you have seen enough of the most horrible of modern wars to last many lifetimes. A year, even less, could see Boston a major hostile base under enemy occupation and millions of men locked in trench warfare all across the Northeast. To order the Battle Force to weigh anchor could precipitate war, your advisers tell you; yet they tell you that if you do not do it, the country is desperately vulnerable.

What do you do?

Joint Plan RED, of course, does not tell us that.

Joint Plan RED assumed that Britain was also drawing up such contingency plans. It stated flatly, "While there has been no act of Parliament since the World War designed to produce national plans for war, . . . the Chiefs of Staff of the three [British] fighting services may be assumed to have well considered war plans for the conduct of any probable war ready at any time to present to the Prime Minister." There the American planners seem to have been mistaken; or perhaps the operative word is "probable." For Great Britain seems to have had no contingency plan at any time in this century, certainly at any time since 1918, for war with the United States. The First Sea Lord, Admiral of the Fleet Sir Charles Madden, assured Admiral Pratt in 1930 that there was no such plan, and one of his predecessors, Admiral of the Fleet Viscount Jellicoe, sometime commander of the Grand Fleet and victor (more or less) of Jutland, told the Canadian government in 1919 that the possibility of an American war was so small that it should not affect Canadian planning.

But in armed forces the world over, there is always somebody who doesn't get the word. One Canadian who evidently did not get Jellicoe's word was Colonel J. Sutherland Brown, known as "Buster" Brown, who from 1920 to 1927 served as a sort of one-man G-2 and G-3 for Canada's modest military forces (his title was director of military operations and intelligence). Buster Brown disliked and distrusted the Yanks and rejected the argument "by many people who should know about international affairs that war between the United States and the British Empire is unthinkable"; so he prepared "Defence Scheme No. 1," a detailed 200-page plan for Canadian action in the event of a war with the United States. It remained the official Canadian plan for an American war until rescinded in May 1931.

Defence Scheme No. 1 envisaged that, if the Americans did not succeed in sweeping into Canada at the outset by a swift coup de main, "there would be a period elapsing of perhaps a couple of weeks before a determined effort would be made to advance on Canada by Divisions of all Arms." Hence, Brown's plan called for swift spoiling attacks into the United States by "Flying Columns" of whatever force was on hand in the first three or four days of a war, augmented by hastily assembled militia forces. The "Flying Columns" would drive as deeply into the United States as they could, followed by a fighting retreat in the face of superior American counterattacks, burning bridges, carrying off rolling stock, and a wrecking railroads along the way—all in order to disrupt American activity as much as possible and buy precious time for help to arrive from Britain.

Under this scheme, the Canadian Maritime Command would invade Maine and try to cut the east-west railroad system (this would help hold Sydney, St. John, and Louisburg for the disembarkation of troops from England). Quebec Command would take the offensive on both sides of the Adirondacks and in Vermont—via Malone, Plattsburg, and Burlington, respectively—with a view toward converging at Albany and hoping to reach the line of the Mohawk Valley and east to Rutland and Montpelier, meanwhile destroying the locks at Oswego and Rochester. Great Lakes Command would conduct raids and try to establish bridgeheads at Niagara, Detroit/St. Clair, and Sault Ste. Marie, from which all movable resources, including trucks, would be carried off to Canada, while the rail lines from Buffalo and the locks of the Erie Canal would be destroyed. Forces of the Prairie Command would converge toward Fargo via Minot, Grand Forks, and Red Lake Falls, followed by a general advance toward Minneapolis-St. Paul; and the Pacific Command would try to seize Spokane, Seattle, and Portland, and then move east to capture Great Falls and Butte.

Fanciful, maybe, given the relative strengths of the two combatants. But who is to say that the desperate dash of Buster Brown's "Flying Columns" in all-out defense of their homeland would not have bought the precious days necessary for British reinforcements to reach the scene—especially since the authors of Joint Plan RED seem not to have envisaged such aggressive action by the Canadians?

Joint Plan RED was never formally and completely rescinded; like old soldiers, it just faded away. The Navy continued sensibly to focus on an ORANGE rather than a RED war, though hypothetical problems at the Naval War College sometimes involved a fight with the Royal Navy. Finally, in 1939, the Joint Board officially recognized that Joint Plan RED was "wholly inapplicable" to the existing international situation and directed that no further planning under it be done. It was ordered kept in the files, however, since it had useful elements for Atlantic defense in general. By that time, planning had gone beyond the old contingencies involving single or double "colors" to the new polychrome realities of worldwide coalition warfare involving the Axis and the democratic powers: a series of plans called RAINBOW.

So whether you were President Hoover or President Roosevelt, you were never called upon to order Joint Plan RED into execution—except perhaps in one special sense: One of the basic lessons of RED and RED-ORANGE planning had been that, no matter how grave the situation might be in the Pacific, the Atlantic theater was the decisive one for the United States. And it was this planning experience that underlay the fundamental decision of the Second World War, embodied in the plan called RAINBOW FIVE, which was ordered into execution on December 11, 1941: to go for victory in Europe first.

Guernica: Death in the Afternoon

by DAVID CLAY LARGE

As a tool of modern warfare, propaganda has become not just increasingly effective but indispensable. The Great War proved that beyond question: A neutral United States was the great plum ripened for harvest by Allied propaganda. But few have used propaganda better than the Communist-dominated government of Republican Spain. It often seemed that the Communists were more concerned with winning support beyond Spain's frontiers than with winning the civil war within them; that may have been Stalin's intention all along. In Guernica, the Republic achieved a matchless coup—even if it suffered yet another military reverse. The bombing of the holy city of the Basques by Hitler's Condor Legion in April 1937 set off a worldwide storm of protest, and a well-orchestrated one. Picasso's most famous painting came out of Guernica. General Francisco Franco's rebel government first tried to deny that the bombing had taken place. Later it changed its story: Red arsonists had destroyed Guernica. But then everybody was busy honing myths. What really did happen is Professor Large's story, adapted from his *Between Two Fires: Europe's Path in the 1930s,* published by W. W. Norton.

On the evening of April 26, 1937, in the tenth month of the Spanish Civil War, the British war correspondent George Steer was having dinner with some colleagues at a restaurant in Bilbao, Spain. Suddenly a Spanish government official ran into the restaurant shouting, "Guernica is in flames!"

Steer and several other journalists immediately jumped into a car and raced toward Guernica, a town in the Basque country of northern Spain about fifteen miles northeast of Bilbao. When they were still ten miles from their destination, they noticed that the night sky was beginning to glow a fleshy pink, "the sort of pink that Parisians have dreamed of for centuries." In the town they found "a trembling, wild red disorder." Roofs and windows of houses trailed "locks of fire"; tattered telephone wires rolled "drunkenly, merrily" across the main street; four sheep lay in a pool of blood.

Skirting numerous bomb craters and huge mounds of "volcanoed fresh earth," they encountered Basque militiamen laying out bodies "riddled with bullet holes" and townspeople walking around in a daze, their "spent open faces" lit up by the fires. When pressed to relate what had happened, the people made "the funny noises of bombers poising, fighters machine-gunning, bombs bursting, houses falling, the tubes of fire spurting and spilling over the town." As he listened to these accounts, Steer examined some silver cylinders he found on the ground. Their stamps indicated German manufacture; thermite, an incendiary agent, leaked from their bases.

After interviewing several people, Steer climbed a small hill to check on the fate of El Árbol, an ancient oak tree under which the kings of Spain had traditionally vowed to respect Basque liberties. The tree, which had been partially burned in Napoleon's Peninsular campaign, had survived this latest onslaught. It "stood there in its mummified death, untouched between thick white pillars. . . . A few rose petals lay on the stones around—pink confetti blown there in the twilight by the bombardment of Guernica."

On April 28 the *Times* of London and the *New York Times* carried a long story by Steer about what he had seen and learned in Guernica. The article related how Junkers and Heinkel aircraft attached to Germany's Condor Legion, which Hitler had sent to Spain to help General Francisco Franco overthrow the Popular Front regime in Madrid, had bombed and strafed the town for some three and one-quarter hours. But Steer did not content himself with describing the raid and its grim results; he went on to offer explanations calculated to give this brief moment in the Spanish Civil War a prominent place in the annals of modern warfare. His report said, in part:

> In the form of its execution and the scale of the destruction it wrought, no less than in the selection of its objective, the raid on Guernica is unparalleled in military history. Guernica was not a military objective. A factory producing war matériel lay outside the town and was untouched. So were two barracks some distance from the town. The town lay far behind the lines. The object of the bombardment was seemingly the demoralization of the civil population and the destruction of the cradle of the Basque race. Every fact bears out this appreciation, beginning with the day when the deed was done.
>
> Monday was the customary market day in Guernica for the country round. At 4:30 P.M., when the market was full and peasants were still coming in, the church bell rang the alarm for approaching airplanes, and the population sought refuge in the cellars and in the dugouts prepared following the bombing of the civilian population of Durango on March 31st, which opened General [Emilio] Mola's offensive in the north. . . .
>
> The tactics of the bombers, which may be of interest to students of the new military science [of terror-bombing], were as follows: First, small parties

of airplanes threw heavy bombs and hand grenades all over the town, choosing area after area in orderly fashion. Next came fighting machines which swooped low to machine-gun those who ran in panic from dugouts, some of which had already been penetrated by 1000 lb. bombs, which make a hole 25 ft. deep. Many of these people were killed as they ran. A large herd of sheep being brought in to the market was also wiped out. The object of this move was apparently to drive the population underground again, for next as many as 12 bombers appeared at a time dropping heavy and incendiary bombs upon the ruins. The rhythm of this bombing of an open town was, therefore, a logical one: first, hand grenades and heavy bombs to stampede the population, then machine-gunning to drive them below, next heavy and incendiary bombs to wreck the houses and burn them on top of their victims.

Steer's colleagues on the scene in Guernica sent out similar reports, although they were not as thorough or graphic. Nor did they interpret the event as a terror attack designed to annihilate "the cradle of the Basque race." Steer was willing and anxious to advance this thesis because, like so many journalists and other writers who covered the Spanish Civil War, he saw himself less as a reporter than as a combatant, his weapon a typewriter rather than a rifle. This does not mean that he knowingly twisted facts, only that he placed them in a context that would reveal the full truth behind a war he saw as an apocalyptic contest between good and evil, light and darkness. He would have agreed with his colleague Martha Gellhorn (later Ernest Hemingway's third wife), who wrote: "We knew, we just *knew* that Spain was the place to stop Fascism. This was it. It was one of those moments in history when there was no doubt."

The fascist forces that Steer was hoping to skewer with his pen immediately advanced their own interpretation of what had happened in Guernica on that fateful April afternoon. On the 27th, as the first news stories from Guernica were beginning to circulate in western Europe, the Spanish Nationalist command in Salamanca issued a declaration flatly denying that the town of Guernica had been bombed at all. Franco's chief press spokesman, Luis Bolín, a former correspondent for the Monarchist paper *ABC*, insisted that "our planes, because of bad weather, have not been able to fly today [sic] and consequently could not have bombed Guernica." Bolín's statement also cleared the Germans, on the grounds that "there is no German or foreign air force in National Spain. There is a Spanish air force, a noble, heroic Spanish air force, which constantly fights against Red planes, Russian and French, piloted by foreigners."

How then did Bolín explain the fires that ravaged Guernica? He said that the Reds themselves had set them! "The incendiarists are those who, last summer, burned Irún, and yesterday, Eibar. Unable to hold back our troops, the Reds have destroyed everything. They accuse the Nationalists of deeds that are but the realization of their own criminal intentions."

During the next two days, the Nationalist command repeated these charges, insisting that their "data" showed that the fires in Guernica came from below, not from above, and that there were no holes in roofs or craters in the streets that might point to a bombing attack. Embellishing upon its original theme of Red culpability, the rebel press office insisted that the destruction was "carried out by Asturian dynamiters, employed by the Marxists, in order afterward to attribute the crime to us." Another Nationalist statement added that Franco forces had no reason to bomb Guernica, because the town was far from their lines and not a military target—the one point on which their story agreed with Steer's.

The dispatch by Steer and the riposte from Salamanca were the first salvos in a war of words and images, a war that lasted as long as the Spanish Civil War—and indeed well beyond. (As late as 1973 a senior editor of the *National Review,* Jeffrey Hart, used the 1967 memoirs of Luis Bolín to argue that Guernica had been destroyed primarily by Red arsonists, not by bombing. Communist propagandists, he said, created "The Great Guernica Fraud.") Though virtually all efforts to interpret Guernica were sharply partisan, there soon emerged intriguing modifications of both the Republican and Nationalist positions. It became gospel in Republican circles (and even in some later scholarly studies, most notably Hugh Thomas's classic *The Spanish Civil War*) to argue that the Condor Legion bombed Guernica not just to terrorize the civilian population but also to test the effectiveness of new aircraft and ordnance. The Nationalist press office eventually admitted that *some* rebel planes *might* have bombed Guernica, which it began to depict as a significant "military target" after all. But the press office and its foreign supporters continued to insist that the bulk of the destruction was carried out by Red arsonists on the ground.

Given the polemical and highly political press coverage of the Guernica episode, it is not surprising that the historian and journalist Phillip Knightley offered it as a prime example of the "myth-making" proclivities of modern war correspondents. But if this event was indeed extensively mythologized— first in press reports, then in poems, novels, and paintings like Picasso's celebrated *Guernica*—can we nonetheless, some fifty years after the fact, dig out deposits of historical reality from the layers of historical myth? More precisely, on the basis of contemporary evidence, can we reasonably reconstruct what happened and also find answers to the knotty questions of motivation and responsibility?

Any effort of this kind must begin by examining the Guernica episode against the backdrop of the Nationalist offensive in the north, which Generals Franco and Mola launched after the rebel forces failed to take the city of Madrid in early 1937. The Basque country was now entirely cut off from the Loyalist enclaves in Madrid and Catalonia. Victory in the north would give the Nationalists control over Spain's largest coal and iron-ore reserves, its most productive steel mills, and key port facilities still being used by the republic. Bilbao, in the center of a highly fortified area called the Iron Ring, would be the primary goal; but to get within striking distance of Bilbao, the Nationalists needed to establish footholds in the rugged mountains of Vizcaya. On March 22 Franco ordered Mola to prepare a devastating attack on the Basque country, using every airplane and artillery piece the Nationalists could spare. "The entire northern front," said Franco, "has to be obliterated before the autumn."

To achieve this goal, Franco expected to make extensive use of the men and machines that his two fascist allies, Italy and Germany, had sent to his aid. Though both these powers had already rendered Franco invaluable assistance, Italian intervention struck some of the Nationalist Spaniards as a mixed blessing. "The Germans behave with dignity and avoid showing off. The Italians are quarrelsome and despotic bullies," declared a Nationalist officer. Italian unwillingness to work closely with the Spaniards resulted in a stinging defeat for the fascist forces in the battle of Guadalajara in mid-March. Hemingway, newly arrived in Spain, promptly declared it the "biggest Italian defeat since Caporetto." The jubilant Republicans renamed the Italian Corpo Di Truppe Volontarie (Corps of Voluntary Troops) "Cuándo Te Vas?"—"When are you leaving?" Even Nationalist officers toasted the success of their Republican adversaries who "had demonstrated that Spaniards, even Red Spaniards, could always get the better of Italians." For Mussolini, who had expected to win the war for Franco in one swift campaign, Guadalajara was a defeat that needed to be avenged with all possible speed and at all costs. He vowed that no Italian commander would return home alive if Italy did not win a major victory in the immediate future.

Franco's German allies were also anxious for quick success. Their contingent in Spain, the Condor Legion (so called because Air Marshal Hermann Göring, who oversaw its creation, liked bird names and could identify with the world's largest vulture), was made up of the Luftwaffe's crème de la crème. Most of the roughly 5,000 pilots and supporting ground personnel were young (average age twenty-two) and all were enthusiastic soldiers. Their commander, General Hugo Sperrle, a shaven-headed giant who, Hitler bragged, was Germany's "most brutal-looking general," spent much of his time urging the Nationalist command to fight the war more aggressively. Sperrle's chief of staff, Colonel Wolfram von Richthofen (cousin of the legendary World War I ace Manfred von Richthofen), looked more like a diplomat than a soldier, but he shared Sperrle's pit-bull mentality. For him there was "no higher calling than that of warrior," no greater pleasure than "fighting for the führer and the people." Both of them strongly supported Franco's decision to conquer the north in short order. Sperrle promised to commit all of the Condor Legion's resources to the campaign.

On March 31, General Mola issued a statement: "I have decided to terminate rapidly the war in the north. Those not guilty of assassinations and who surrender their arms will have their lives and property spared. But if submission is not immediate, I will raze all Vizcaya to the ground, beginning with the industries of war."

On this same day the Condor Legion bombers put Mola's threat into practice. Against the town of Durango, a rail and road junction southeast of Bilbao, they launched what U.S. ambassador Claude Bowers called "the most terrible bombardment of a white civil population in the history of the world up to March 31, 1937." (When he used the word *white*, he was obviously distinguishing it from Mussolini's 1935 air attacks on civilian targets in Abyssinia.) Though the figure is disputed, German bombs killed at least 127 people, including 14 nuns in the Chapel of Santa Susana and 2 priests, one of whom was blown apart while he was elevating the Host in the Church of Santa María.

Nationalist ground troops, however, had difficulty following up on the successes of the Condor Legion pilots. The terrain in Vizcaya was treacherous, and coordination between air and ground forces poor. The Germans became convinced that the Spanish were being too cautious. Von Richthofen went to see Mola and (according to his diary) "demanded stronger action and accused him of want of energy." Eventually von Richthofen worked out an agreement with Mola's chief of staff, Colonel Juan Vigón, that placed control of all air forces in German hands and ensured that German and Italian bombers would attack enemy troop concentrations "without concern for the civilian population."

Through the first three weeks of April, German and Italian planes divided their time between support operations and assaults on Bilbao. The Bilbao bombing, however, was hampered by cloud cover, while the ground offensive continued to proceed more slowly than the Germans had hoped. Sperrle, frustrated, proposed that the Nationalists temporarily break off the northern offensive and return to the Madrid front. But Franco insisted on continuing the Bilbao offensive. Von Richthofen now concluded that if the Spanish command was serious about taking the Basque country, it might be necessary "to reduce Bilbao to soot and ashes."

By late April, however, it became clear that the Basques were in trouble. The Nationalist command noted extensive retreat movements in the direction of Bilbao. On April 25 von Richthofen, studying his battle map, thought he saw an opportunity to prevent the retreating Basque units from reaching the heavily defended area immediately around Bilbao. The map showed that the three main roads leading toward Bilbao from eastern Vizcaya converged at one point: the Rentería bridge near the town of Guernica. Von Richthofen marked this site as a "possible target." That same evening Nationalist troops stood fifteen kilometers from Guernica. "Our hopes have risen a great deal," wrote von Richthofen in his diary.

What happened next can best be chronicled by referring to additional von Richthofen diary entries, operation orders of the Italian Air Legion, commentary by Condor Legion pilots, and accounts by survivors in the town.

Von Richthofen's diary contains the following entry for April 26, 1937:

Deploy immediately: A/88 [reconnaissance squadron] and J/88 [fighter squadron] over roads in the area of Marquina-Guernica-Guerricaiz. Deploy K/88 [attack-bomber squadron] (after return from Guerricaiz), VB/88 [experimental bomber squadron], and Italians against roads and bridges (including suburb) hard eastwards of Guernica. That [area] must be closed off if we are finally to achieve success. . . . Vigón agrees to advance his troops in such a way that all roads south of Guernica are closed. If that works, we'll have bottled up the enemy around Marquina.

On the same day, the commander at the Italian air force headquarters at Soria issued the following orders to three "Savoia-Marchetti 79" pilots: "Bomb the bridge at Guernica. This bridge, just to the right of the town, is the convergence point for several roads from the east now being used by enemy troops retreating toward Bilbao. The town itself, for political reasons, should not be bombed. . . ."

At about 4:40 P.M. two nuns on the roof of La Merced Convent in Guernica rang a bell and shouted, "Avión! Avión!" According to witnesses, within a few moments of that warning a single plane appeared over the eastern end of town. The aircraft, a Heinkel 111, passed once over the city, then returned and dived in the direction of Rentería bridge. Though there was no flak—Guernica had no antiaircraft guns—the plane's bombs landed not on the bridge but about 300 meters to the southwest in a plaza fronting the railroad station. One bomb blew up the Julián Hotel across the plaza. A volunteer fireman saw women and children blown high into the air and then raining down in "legs, arms, heads, and bits and pieces everywhere."

About twenty-five minutes later, three more Heinkel 111s appeared low in the sky. Their bombs, released at about 2,000 feet, hit a candy factory near the Rentería bridge, igniting caldrons of sugar syrup and turning the factory into an inferno. Young female workers, some of them on fire, began stampeding from the building. The central marketplace, not far away, was also hit. Two bulls, sprayed with burning thermite, charged through the canvas-walled stalls, setting the entire market ablaze. Next, five pairs of Heinkel 51 fighters zoomed in very low over parts of the town not yet obscured by smoke. According to one witness, two of the planes "just flew back and forth at about one hundred feet, like flying sheep dogs rounding up people for the slaughter." One plane zeroed in on a woman and her three small children, killing them all in a single burst. Another wiped out the town band.

At about 6 P.M. the first bombers—Junkers 52s and Italian Savoys— neared their target. They came in groups of three, wave after wave, carrying among them almost 100,000 pounds of high explosives. These they dropped helter-skelter through the smoke and dust hanging over the town. One bomb hit a *pelota frontón*—a jai alai court; another blew up the Bank of Vizcaya; and still another demolished an orphanage. By the time the last of the bombers had headed back to their bases, roughly two-thirds of the buildings in Guernica were leveled or on fire.

People were now streaming from the town into the nearby fields and hills. Among them was a Basque priest who provided the following account of the next phase of the raid.

The airplanes came low, flying at two hundred meters. As soon as we could leave our shelter, we ran into the woods, hoping to put a safe distance between us and the enemy. But the airmen saw us and went after us. . . . We heard bullets ripping through the branches. . . . Meanwhile women, children, and old men were falling in heaps, like flies, and everywhere we saw lakes of blood.

Four days after the raid, with Guernica occupied by Nationalist troops, von Richthofen wrote in his diary:

> Guernica, city of 5,000 inhabitants, literally leveled. Attack was launched with 250kg [high-explosive] bombs and fire bombs, these about one-third of the total. When the first Ju's [Junkers 52] arrived, there was already smoke everywhere (from the experimental bomber squadron, which attacked first with three planes). Nobody could see roads, bridges, or suburban targets anymore, so they just dumped their bombs in the midst of it all. The 250s knocked down a number of houses and destroyed the municipal fire system. The fire bombs now had time to do their work. The type of construction— tile roofs, wooden decks, half-timbered walls—facilitated their destruction. Inhabitants were generally out of town because of a festival; most of those [in the town] fled at the outset of the attack. A small number died in wrecked shelters. Bomb craters in the streets are plainly to be seen—absolutely fabulous! City was completely closed off for at least twenty-four hours; that would have guaranteed immediate [conquest] if troops would have attacked right away. But at least [we had] a complete technical success with our 250s and EC.B1s [fire bombs].

Colonel Hans Henning von Beust, leader of the Condor Legion's Bomber Squadron 1, stated in 1955 that his unit had bombed Guernica from an altitude of 3,500 meters—just under 12,000 feet. Because there was so much smoke and dust, he said, the pilots could only "estimate" where the bombs would fall. He added that a strong easterly wind blew the bombs from the primary target area over the city center. Lieutenant Colonel Karl von Knauer, leader of Fighter Squadron 1, wrote in his diary for April 26, 1937, that a sortie carried out against a "bridge at Guernica" had a "good effect." After visiting the site on May 1 and viewing the devastation, he opined that some of the bombs might have set off ammunition dumps in the town.

This evidence alone should be enough to prove that planes under the Nationalist command indeed bombed Guernica. It also shows that the German pilots were proud of what they had achieved. Since none of the "military targets" had been hit, the "success" and "good effect" noted in the German sources can only refer to the destruction of the town itself.

These sources tell us yet more. The bomb mixture von Richthofen describes—two-thirds high explosives and one-third incendiaries—suggests that the Condor Legion wanted to knock out more than a bridge (which was made of stone and steel) and road crossings: Clearly, buildings were to be smashed and burned. The stated goal of the attack—"closing off" Guernica to retreating troops—could be achieved only through large-scale devastation; a few craters in the roads would not have been adequate. (The Condor Legion pilots knew, in any event, that their bombers lacked bombsights accurate enough for pinpoint bombing; von Beust admitted it was "a wonder that we hit anything at all.")

Having had the chance to view the Guernica ruins on April 30, von Richthofen said nothing about *any* (not to mention *most*) of the destruction having been caused by Republican troops on the ground. Both von Beust and von Knauer stated explicitly that in their opinion the Reds had not burned the town. Could the Germans simply have missed the "data" cited by the Nationalist command? It is impossible to state categorically that *no* fires were set. But it is highly improbable that any were. Why would the Red soldiers want to destroy the haven in which hundreds of their number had found refuge and toward which other Republican forces were retreating? Furthermore, if the Republicans wanted to impede the Nationalist advance by burning Guernica, why not destroy the bridge at the same time? And if they were aiming at a propaganda coup, why not torch the sacred oak, El Árbol?

While evidence from the German and Italian side makes it clear that their planes bombed Guernica, it does not suggest—as Steer and other pro-Republican commentators have claimed—that annihilating the entire town was the goal from the outset. Rather, it suggests that the mission was to close off the town by knocking out the Rentería bridge, the incoming roads, and the eastern suburbs. The Italians, as we have noted, were under orders not to bomb the city itself.

German and Italian sources also make clear that the raiders saw Guernica as a legitimate military target, not a candidate for an experiment in terror-bombing helpless civilians. They attacked on April 26 not because it was a market day but because it was the first day they could organize sorties to cut off the Republican retreat toward Bilbao. Some historians have claimed that Hermann Göring admitted at his Nuremberg trial in 1946 that he regarded Guernica as a "testing ground," but he said only that he saw the Spanish war *in general* as an opportunity to test new machines and techniques.

As for the charges that Guernica was bombed because it was the "cradle of the Basque race," it seems probable that Vigón, who planned the raid with von Richthofen, understood the town's historical significance and welcomed the opportunity to strike a blow at Basque autonomy. However, there is no evidence that this was a primary motive for the attack or that the German and Italian pilots who carried it out were aware of the town's symbolic significance. They were imported military technicians, not *students* of Spanish history.

On the other hand, terror and psychological warfare cannot have been entirely absent from the pilots' minds as they approached their target. They had bombed and strafed defenseless civilians often enough in the past—the Italians had done so in Barcelona (on orders from Mussolini), the Germans in Durango. The Condor Legion command, we know, was frustrated with the Nationalists' slow progress in the north; it was looking for a quick breakthrough. As for the Italians, they had a recent humiliation to avenge, and a warning from *Il Duce* that they had better do so quickly. It seems reasonable to assume that when the main strike force arrived over Guernica and found the primary targets obscured by smoke and dust, the bombardiers had no compunction about dumping their bombs "in the middle." Nor, apparently, did the fighter pilots hesitate to machine-gun people—and even sheep—running helplessly on the ground.

If it is clear that German and Italian planes carried out an attack against Guernica, is it equally clear that Franco's fascist allies bear sole responsibility for what happened? Undoubtedly they bear a large share of it, for the Condor Legion command had demanded and received a "significant influence" over Nationalist tactical operations in the north. But all sorties were cleared through the Nationalist command in Salamanca, and the Guernica attack was no exception. Mola himself apparently did not participate in the planning session with Vigón and von Richthofen, but he must have known that Guernica (or its environs) was on the list of targets. This town stood between his forces and Bilbao, the great prize, which in fact the Nationalists occupied on June 19, after weeks of systematic bombing. (The Iron Ring had proved to be of less durable metal.) Before starting the northern campaign, Mola had signed leaflets dropped on Basque towns warning that he would "raze all Vizcaya to the ground" unless submission was immediate.

A related question concerns General Franco's role in this affair. Two historians of the raid have insisted that von Richthofen and Vigón made their decision "without reference to higher authority." Franco's English biographer, George Hills, claims (very plausibly) that the Germans attacked Guernica without consulting any Spaniard at all. He says Franco first learned about the bombing from foreign news reports and initially dismissed these as "Red propaganda." When informed by his own command that the Condor Legion had in fact carried out the attack, he allegedly told the Germans that he would "not have war made on my own people." (An odd comment, if true: What did he think he had been doing since the rising in July 1936?)

While it may be plausible to argue that Franco did not personally order the attack on Guernica, or even know of it in advance, it is not plausible to insist, as many of Franco's defenders have done, that he bears no responsibility for the atrocity. He had authority over the Nationalist campaign and was the only Spanish general to whom the Condor Legion and the Italian Air Legion were responsible. He had made the decision to conquer the Basque country and had held to this goal even when the Germans wanted to break off the offensive. Though in January 1937 he had ordered all rebel air units to avoid attacking civilian population centers "without prior permission" from himself, he had done nothing when his fascist allies ignored this injunction. If he indeed was "pale with anger" over the bombing (as Hills insists he was), perhaps his anger stemmed less from sympathy for the victims than from a perception that Guernica was a public-relations fiasco of the first order.

This would explain the alacrity with which Franco's press office mounted its countercampaign charging "Red arson." Eventually even the Germans understood that they might have been overzealous in "closing off" Guernica. Berlin ordered Condor Legion personnel to say nothing of the affair. Sperrle, anticipating an international investigation, sent Condor Legion teams into the town to clear away telltale dud bombs and bomb fragments.

Nationalist officers in the field, however, sometimes spoke with embarrassing candor about what had happened to Guernica. In August 1937 a Franco staff officer told U.S. correspondent Virginia Cowles: "Of course [Guernica] was bombed. We bombed it and bombed it and bombed it, and *bueno,* why not?" A Nationalist press officer who was traveling with Cowles said to her later, "I don't think I would write that if I were you."

The bombing of Guernica has since emerged as the best-known atrocity in a war filled with atrocities. Within the broader framework of modern military history, it is often cited both as a precedent-setting example of "terror-bombing" and as a harbinger of more devastating urban infernos to come.

Yet, tragic as this event was, in some ways it is surprising that it should have taken on such symbolic weight. Despite claims to the contrary, it was by no means the first large-scale bombing of a civilian population. In the Ethiopian War, for example, the Italians had frequently bombed undefended towns and even Red Cross centers. And the earlier bombing of Durango in the Spanish Civil War was another precursor to Guernica. Although the Guernica raid certainly took on terrorist dimensions, "demoralization of the civil population" was not its initial or primary purpose, as it was in many World War II attacks.

What makes the Guernica case special is primarily the historical and symbolic significance of the target—even though the pilots and bombardiers who laid waste the city had little or no notion of this significance. Nor, obviously, could they have known that their raid would shock the world and become the subject of the twentieth century's most celebrated painting. Picasso's *Guernica* helped make this Basque town's destruction emblematic of the horrors of modern warfare. But it seems to me that the Guernica episode—both the event and its subsequent interpretation—ought to stand not just for war's horrors but also for its ironies.

"They Can't Realize the Change Aviation Has Made"

by RICHARD M. KETCHUM

Has any American hero soared quite so high or fallen so low in the public esteem as Charles A. Lindbergh? In 1938, firsthand observation of the German aircraft industry convinced him that the airplane had given the Nazis an unbeatable edge, and that the coming war was one the United States couldn't win. When, on the evening of September 15, 1939, he stepped before the microphones to begin a crusade against our involvement, Lindbergh enjoyed a celebrity (and a popularity) equal to President Franklin D. Roosevelt's. His fears would set the tone—and the terms—of the war debate in America. As the months went on and his passionate speeches multiplied, he came to personify the isolationist cause. And yet within two years, Lindbergh would find himself discredited, and then forgotten, a colonel forbidden to command. In an adaption from his book *The Borrowed Years 1938–41: America on the Way to War* (Random House), Richard M. Ketchum tells of the fatally earnest error that destroyed Lindbergh and the America First movement.

On the same September day in 1938 that Neville Chamberlain returned in triumph to London from the Munich Conference waving a scrap of paper before his countrymen and telling them it meant "peace for our time," Charles A. Lindbergh arrived at the U.S. embassy in Paris. Ambassador William Bullitt had invited him to a conference and thoughtfully offered him the same room in which he had stayed on the momentous night of May 21, 1927. It seemed strange, Lindbergh thought, to see once again the familiar surroundings of the embassy—the court, the staircase, the corner parlor he remembered—and he noticed that there was now a brass plate on the bed he had slept in eleven years earlier.

Surely other memories flooded back: of a hundred thousand deliriously happy Frenchmen swarming onto the field at Le Bourget to greet him when he landed after the thirty-three-hour flight, some of them ripping pieces of fabric off the *Spirit of St. Louis,* others dragging him from the cockpit and carrying him away on their shoulders until he escaped to the pilots' quarters, identified himself self-consciously—"I am Charles A. Lindbergh"—and handed letters of introduction to then-Ambassador Myron Herrick. Then came the medals, the speeches, the crowds—always the crowds—and the trip home to the States aboard the cruiser *Memphis,* to be greeted with half a million letters, 75,000 telegrams, two railroad cars filled with press clippings, the engulfing admiration of his countrymen, and promotion from captain to colonel in the Air Corps Reserve. President Calvin Coolidge, awarding him the congressional Medal of Honor and the nation's first Distinguished Flying Cross, told throngs in Washington that the transatlantic flight was "the same story of valor and victory by a son of the people that shines through every page of American history." Then there was New York, a city gone berserk, with some 4 million ecstatic people cheering their hearts out during an incredible ticker-tape parade up Broadway.

Of all the public figures who captivated America in that decade of noise and hero worship, only Lindbergh retained his almost magical hold on the public through the thirties, perhaps because he embodied the youthful, unquenchable spirit Americans felt they had left behind, the national belief that the unattainable was somehow within reach. His achievement alone would have caught the imagination of the entire world—and did—but the fact that he was a boyish Galahad out of the West, a guileless, modern-day knight in aviator's helmet and goggles, with tousled blond hair and a smile that melted the heart, brought him such adoration as few men in history have known.

He maintained that he had no wish to be a celebrity, but America would not allow him *not* to be one, and in a perverse sort of way he abetted the process. He flew the *Spirit of St. Louis* to all forty-eight states after his transatlantic flight; he went to Mexico and South America; he wrote a book, *We,* about his famous adventure, and this plus a series of newspaper and magazine articles brought him wealth along with additional fame; he flew from coast to coast, setting a new speed record; he had a whirlwind romance with Anne, the lovely daughter of Dwight Morrow, a prominent lawyer, partner of J.P. Morgan, and ambassador to Mexico; and he and his bride flew off the next year to Canada, Alaska, Siberia, Japan, and China—a journey chronicled in Anne Morrow Lindbergh's best-selling *North to the Orient.* It seemed that he was never out of the news, was constitutionally unable to avoid being the public figure, all the while insisting that he wanted only privacy and to be let alone. The paradox was that he appeared to be sustained in a curious way by these frequent forays into the public eye, even as he denied that it was so and raged at reporters and photographers who considered it their job to document the doings of the famous man.

Then came the dark time, the hour of lead, as Anne Lindbergh would call it. On March 1, 1932, their firstborn child, Charles Augustus, Jr., was kidnapped from his nursery crib in their home near Hopewell, New Jersey. A

$50,000 ransom payment was delivered to a cemetery in the Bronx, but the baby was not returned; on May 12 his body was found in a shallow grave not far from their house. To the Lindberghs it seemed that the newspaper and radio publicity, the reporters' morbid curiosity about every personal facet of the tragedy, would never end. And when Bruno Richard Hauptmann, a Bronx carpenter, was arrested and tried in 1934, their nightmare had to be relived in agonizing detail, imposing an almost unendurable strain on the family.

Believing that the only escape from the "tremendous public hysteria" surrounding him in the United States was to leave the land of his birth, Lindbergh took his wife and second son to England in December 1935 to seek sanctuary and peace. He found both, and during this self-imposed exile he probably had a better opportunity to see what was going on behind the scenes in Europe than any other American private citizen. The British and French treated him with respect, allowing him the privacy he so much desired, and because he was a distinguished aviator he was sought out by Europe's public figures and invited by government officials to inspect the aircraft, factories, and aviation facilities of the major nations on the Continent.

His trip to Paris on September 30, 1938, persuaded Lindbergh to make a personal study of Europe's general situation during the approaching winter. "I don't know how much I can do here," he wrote, "but I feel that if anything can be done to avoid European war, it must be based upon an intimate understanding of conditions in Europe."

Before going to France, Lindbergh had heard from Ambassador Bullitt about the parlous state of that nation's air force. France did not have enough modern military planes even to "put up a show in case of war," Bullitt told him, and in a conflict between France, England, and Russia on one side and Germany on the other, the Germans would have immediate air supremacy. Lindbergh had suspected as much. "Germany has developed a huge air force," he said, "while England has slept and France has deluded herself with a Russian alliance." From Guy la Chambre, the French minister of air, he learned how desperate the situation was. France was producing just forty-five or fifty warplanes a month, compared with Germany's five or six hundred.

When Lindbergh arrived in Paris, Bullitt said he hoped he would take part in a discussion with la Chambre and Jean Monnet, the French banker and economist, to consider the possibility of establishing factories in Canada to manufacture planes for France. The idea, of course, was to circumvent the terms of the U.S. Neutrality Act, which was designed to prohibit the shipment of arms to belligerents, and Monnet was talking about a production potential of 10,000 planes a year. (Bullitt's opinion was that it should be 50,000.)

In the course of that day and the next, Lindbergh discovered that French intelligence put the existing German air fleet at 6,000 modern planes, plus 2,000 to 3,000 older models, and estimated that the Reich had the capability of building 24,000 planes a year—versus France's existing potential of 540 and predicted capacity of 5,000 a year. It was believed further that Britain—which had 2,000 aircraft (only 700 of them modern types)—might be producing 10,000 planes annually in a year's time; but this left an immense gap of 10,000 aircraft a year between Germany's output and the combined expectations of Great Britain and France.

France had not a single modern pursuit plane available for the defense of Paris, and indeed no aircraft of any type as fast as the new German bombers. It would be impossible to obtain planes from the United States because, apart from the restrictions of the Neutrality Act, the U.S. Army, Navy, and commercial airlines were absorbing virtually all of America's productive capacity. Pondering these seemingly insurmountable problems, Lindbergh ventured an astonishing suggestion to the group: Why not purchase bombers from Germany?

At first the Frenchmen laughed, assuming he was joking, but he argued that such an arrangement might quickly smoke out Germany's military intentions and could be in the interest of both parties. While giving France the aircraft she needed, opening up some trade between the two countries, possibly decreasing tension, and reducing the arms disparity, it would also afford Germany a measure of relief from the staggering cost of constructing warplanes.

The meeting broke up without a decision, but in the months to come the French began taking Lindbergh's proposal ever more seriously. Several months later la Chambre asked him to ascertain whether or not the Germans would sell planes to France, and Lindbergh undertook this mission when he went to Berlin. In mid-January 1939, a surprised Lindbergh was informed by General Erhard Milch, who was responsible for Luftwaffe production, that Germany *would* be willing to sell 1,250-horsepower Daimler-Benz engines to France, provided absolute secrecy was observed while negotiations were taking place and provided further that France paid in cash, not goods.

When Charles and Anne took off from Le Bourget in Paris on October 10, 1938, headed for Berlin's Tempelhof Airport, it was their third trip to Nazi Germany in as many years. Thanks to Major Truman Smith, the U.S. military attaché in Berlin, the couple had been invited there in 1936 and 1937 by Hermann Göring, Reich minister for air and, after Hitler, the most powerful man in the nation. Smith, an infantryman by trade, was responsible for reporting to Washington on developments in aviation as well as those in land warfare, and he was not satisfied with the quality of intelligence he was receiving. At the breakfast table one morning, his wife read him a news story about Colonel Lindbergh inspecting an airplane factory in France, and it occurred to Smith that an official visit to Germany by the famous aviator might uncover information the United States wanted.

So the trips were arranged, resulting eventually in more than Smith ever dreamed of obtaining—a full and detailed "general estimate" of German air strength. Sent to Washington over Smith's signature, it was based entirely on Lindbergh's firsthand inspection, expert analysis, and experience of the factories, airplanes, personnel, research, and command structure that constituted Germany's air establishment. That nation, the report declared, had outdistanced France in all respects and was generally superior to Great Britain, except for aircraft engines. By 1941 or 1942, it was estimated, Germany's technical development would equal that of the United States—a "phenomenon of the first diplomatic importance." Lindbergh himself put the case even more strongly, writing to a family friend: "The growth of German military aviation is, I believe, without parallel in history. . . ."

When the Lindberghs first visited Berlin, correspondent William Shirer grumbled that "the Nazis, led by Göring, are making a great play for them," but that was nothing compared to the reception that greeted them on their return in 1938. During the course of a month, the American flier was given an opportunity to talk with all the principals of the aviation establishment—General Milch; General Ernst Udet, a World War I ace who developed the dive-bombing technique first employed in Spain; Heinrich Focke, the aeronautical engineer; and Marshal Göring—not to mention scores of pilots and technicians. He met members of the diplomatic circle in the capital, visited aircraft factories, inspected bomb shelters and antiaircraft batteries, was permitted to fly many of the latest German planes—including the Junkers Ju 90 transport and the Messerschmitt 108 and 109 fighters—and was the first non-German to see the secret new Ju 88 bomber.

Neither Lindbergh nor the Americans to whom he was supplying information seem to have given much thought to the possibility that they were being used, but his seeming freedom of access to Germany's secrets was very carefully planned. Like Lindbergh, high-level visitors from other countries were taken on conducted tours to see the impressive Messerschmitt assembly lines, the performance of the latest planes, the exhibitions of precision bombing. Understandably, this thoroughly memorable experience was guaranteed to make visitors return home and speak with awe of what they had beheld.

On the night of October 18, a Tuesday, Ambassador Hugh Wilson gave a stag dinner at the embassy, and the occasion was the scene of an incident that was to plague Lindbergh for years to come. In addition to German officers and members of the U.S. embassy staff, Wilson's guests included the Belgian and Italian ambassadors, Generals Milch and Udet, Heinkel and Messerschmitt, and Göring. As an aviator, Hermann Göring ranked at the top of Germany's pantheon: A World War ace, he had succeeded to the command of Baron Manfred von Richthofen's "Flying Circus" after the Red Baron was killed. Under his leadership, the Luftwaffe had become the most fearsome weapon of the Third Reich. Vain, arrogant, and complex, Göring was a diplomat, economic planner, art connoisseur, gourmand, dandy, morphine addict, and Hitler's most powerful associate in the high command.

Given the nature of the ulterior motive Ambassador Wilson had in mind, he could be forgiven for using Charles Lindbergh as bait to lure Göring to this dinner. Wilson was eager to establish friendly relations with the number two Nazi in hopes that he would do something to ameliorate the financial plight of Jews who were being forced to emigrate from Germany in a penniless state. Göring was no humanitarian and he lacked the courage to stand up to Hitler, but at least his attitude toward the Jews was ambivalent, which was more than could be said of other top Nazis. It was known that he opposed the use of indiscriminate violence and had helped his actress wife get her Jewish friends away from the Gestapo on a number of occasions.

Lindbergh was standing at the back of the room when Göring arrived, and he noticed that the marshal was carrying a red box and some papers in his hand. Göring chatted briefly with several other guests and gradually made his way over to Lindbergh, handed him the box and the papers, and spoke a few sentences in German, which Lindbergh did not understand. Afterward, the American said, "I found that he had presented me with the German Eagle, one of the highest German decorations, 'by order of *der Führer.*' "

Perhaps a man accustomed to receiving medals does not give much thought to their political significance, but Lindbergh's wife did when he spoke to her about it later that night. She called it "the Albatross," and an albatross it would be, as he learned to his lasting discomfort.

In the journal he kept, Lindbergh described the encounter rather casually, but one gets the impression that he considered it an event of more than usual significance, which indeed it was. For when he and Anne left Germany at the end of October, he could say that he had a fairly clear picture of the overall situation in Europe. "I had seen the strength of Germany," he wrote, "and I knew the weakness of England and France." In his opinion the Germans were a great people whose welfare was inseparable from the rest of Europe, and he was certain that the only hope of avoiding war and preserving Western civilization was to establish a rapport between Britain and Germany. If that failed, and if war should come, America must stay out of it.

Less than twelve months after the poor bargain of a truce that was Munich, when Czechoslovakia was abandoned by its allies, Britain and France, Europe was at war for the second time in twenty years, and most Americans—like Charles Lindbergh—wanted no part of it. In the wake of Hitler's brutal attack on Poland on September 1, 1939, a Roper public-opinion poll revealed that 30 percent of Americans wanted nothing whatever to do with any warring nation, while another 37 percent wished to "take no sides and stay out of [any] war entirely" but would agree to sell arms to belligerents on cash-and-carry terms. These two groups represented two-thirds of the American public. They were folk of just about every persuasion, and all of them felt intensely about an issue that might easily alter the lives of their families and the future of their country.

Their fervor was fueled by long-standing disillusionment and political consequences of the First World War, an ingrained suspicion of "foreigners," and an all but universal belief that the United States—secure behind two oceans—was big enough and powerful enough to go it alone and had no business bailing out the French and English, whose stupidity at Munich had produced what looked like 1914 all over again.

The great debate that was beginning to cut across all levels of American society was now to be governed by an entirely different set of premises. The question was no longer "What do we do if war comes?" War *had* come. It was here. The chessmen were on the board, and the first move had been made. This meant that arguments about intervention or nonintervention were no longer theoretical. On the outcome of the debate would hinge the nation's peace and security and the lives of all those who might be sent into battle in what still seemed to just about everyone to be Europe's, not America's, war.

Charles Lindbergh was acutely aware of this. On April 14, 1939, he had arrived in New York aboard the liner *Aquitania*, one of a passenger list that included numerous refugees. Becauseof his incisive knowledge of Europe's air fleets, he was immediately sought after by government officials, among them Congressman Sol Bloom, chairman of the House Committee on Foreign Affairs, who hoped Lindbergh would testify on the neutrality legislation then under consideration. Lindbergh declined that invitation, but accepted one to meet with General Henry H. Arnold, the popular chief of the U.S. Army Air Corps, to whom the flier had for months been supplying information on the present and potential air strength of the European nations, particularly Germany. (One of "Hap" Arnold's beliefs—which he said he had learned from the Wright brothers, who also taught him to fly in one of their twelve-horsepower planes—was that nothing was impossible. Fortunately for his country, he put that belief into practice by doing everything in his power to encourage the buildup of production facilities that would enable U.S. factories to turn out the planes so desperately needed in the war ahead.)

Just now, Arnold was eager to learn about the Luftwaffe, and the two aviators arranged to get together at the Thayer Hotel at West Point. They talked for several hours in the dining room, which was closed to the public to ensure their privacy, before strolling out to the military academy's baseball diamond. The Army team was playing Syracuse, and the two men continued their discussion while the game went on. What he obtained from Lindbergh, Arnold said later, was "the most accurate picture of the Luftwaffe, its equipment, leaders, apparent plans, training methods, and present defects" he had yet received. Not incidentally, it heightened his determination that the U.S. Air Force must surpass and be capable of overpowering the Germans.

The two met again at Arnold's house in Washington, where Lindbergh was asked if he would be willing to make a study of American aeronautical research and manufacturing operations with an eye to improving their efficiency. He accepted, and went on active duty as a colonel almost immediately. On April 20 he met with Harry Woodring, the isolationist secretary of war whose resignation President Franklin D. Roosevelt would request a year later. Then—after pushing his way through a crowd of press photographers and "inane women screeching" at the door—he entered the White House to meet Roosevelt for the first time.

Lindbergh found both interviews disquieting: the one with Woodring because the secretary asked him not to testify before any congressional committees; the one with Roosevelt because he thought the president "a little too suave, too pleasant, too easy." He was predisposed to like Roosevelt, who was an accomplished, interesting conversationalist, but he believed that since the president was "mostly politician," the two of them "would never get along on many fundamentals." He also got the impression that the chief executive was a very tired man who seemed unaware of how fatigued he was.

In the months that followed, Lindbergh talked with the men who constituted the U.S. aviation establishment, he visited the drafting rooms and factories where aircraft were being designed and built, and he reported to Arnold and other Air Corps chiefs his conviction that only by instituting a significant research-and-development program could the nation catch up with the European countries, even in five years. As August wore on, his thoughts were continuously on Europe and the imminent likelihood of war: He was reminded of the tense hours before Munich, except that now, in the United States, he did not sense the same atmosphere of apprehension and depression he had felt in England a year earlier.

On August 28 he received a telegram from his friend Truman Smith, who was now in Washington after four years as military attaché for air with the U.S. embassy in Berlin. The message read simply, "Yes, 80," which was Smith's estimate of the percentage probability of war. It started Lindbergh wondering if anything he might say in a radio broadcast would be constructive, perhaps helping in some way to halt Europe's rush to war. But then came Friday, September 1, and the huge headlines: GERMAN TROOPS ENTER POLAND.

Along with millions of people everywhere, Lindbergh speculated about what Britain and France would do. He concluded that if they tried to break through Germany's defensive Westwall in an effort to support Poland, they would surely lose the war unless America entered the fight. What in the world were the two allies thinking of? he wondered. Why, if they wanted to prevent the Germans from moving eastward, had they chosen this particular set of circumstances as an excuse to go to war? He had heard that Chamberlain had not even consulted his general staff before entering into an alliance with Poland, and now people everywhere were asking why the governments of Britain and France had not yet declared war. Lindbergh spoke about that to his wife, Anne, who replied, "Maybe they've talked to a general."

What stand should the United States take? Lindbergh kept asking himself. He and Anne listened to Roosevelt's radio talk on Sunday evening, September 3, and the next morning read in the paper that the Cunard liner *Athenia,* carrying 1,400 passengers, had been torpedoed off the Hebrides and that German troops were overrunning Poland. On September 7 Lindbergh made up his mind. "I do not intend to stand by and see this country pushed into war if it is not absolutely essential to the future welfare of the nation," he wrote in his journal. "Much as I dislike taking part in politics and public life, I intend to do so if necessary to stop the trend which is now going on in this country." On September 10 he made a brief entry: "Phoned Bill Castle and Fulton Lewis. Decided to go on the radio next week."

William R. Castle was a conservative Republican who had served in the State Department during the Harding and Coolidge administrations, to become undersecretary of state under Hoover. At Castle's home Lindbergh had met Fulton Lewis, Jr., a conservative (some thought reactionary) commentator who appeared nightly on the Mutual Broadcasting System, and had heard him describe an instance in which "Jewish advertising firms" threatened to remove their sponsorship if a certain feature were carried by Mutual. The network, Lewis added, had decided to drop the feature. "I do not blame the Jews so much for their attitude," Lindbergh observed, "although I think it unwise from their own standpoint." When Castle suggested that Lindbergh speak out against U.S. involvement in the European war, Lewis said he could make arrangements for a network broadcast, and it was later agreed that the address would be carried on Friday evening, September 15, by Mutual. When this news was released, NBC and CBS also decided to carry the speech.

The day before the broadcast, Lindbergh informed Hap Arnold of his plans, and the Air Corps chief suggested he go on inactive duty while actively involved in politics. Arnold read the speech Lindbergh was going to deliver, agreed that it contained nothing that could be considered unethical, and asked if he planned to show it to Woodring. The colonel replied that he had no confidence in the secretary of war, and as he said so he "could tell from Arnold's eyes that he was on my side." He decided not to let Woodring read the talk.

The following day Arnold reported this conversation to Woodring and let Lindbergh know that the secretary was "very much displeased." Woodring's reaction had been to state sourly that he "had hoped to make use of" Lindbergh in the future, whatever that might mean, but that any such plans were out of the question now. The next day Truman Smith told him that the administration was deeply troubled by his intention to take an active role in this touchy political matter, and Smith had been authorized to inform Lindbergh that if he did not make the broadcast, a cabinet post of secretary of air would be created and he would be appointed to the job.

Having sized up Roosevelt as a political animal, Lindbergh was not surprised that he would resort to such a ploy; what astonished him was that the president would think that he, Lindbergh, might be influenced by it. Since the offer had come from Woodring to Arnold to Smith, it was evident that word of it would get around, and Lindbergh thought it a great mistake for the president "to let the army know he deals in such a way." (When Arnold told Smith to take the offer to Lindbergh, Smith asked the general if he thought Lindbergh would accept it. "Of course not" was Arnold's immediate reply. Arnold knew his man.)

And so, at 9:45 on Friday evening, September 15, 1939, the only man in the United States who could rival Franklin Roosevelt for the public's attention stood before six microphones in the Carlton Hotel and made the first broadcast in what would become his crusade against American intervention in the war. In a clipped, slightly nasal tone, he declared that the war just begun was a continuation of "an age-old struggle between the nations of Europe." His voice sounded unnatural to Anne, even though it was "strong and even and clear." She was sitting in the hotel room with a group of friends and network technicians, praying that the American people might understand, that they might realize how difficult it was for her husband to give this speech, turning his back on France and England, two nations that had given their family sanctuary.

"Our safety does not lie in fighting European wars," he was saying. "It lies in our own internal strength, in the character of the American people and of American institutions." Western civilization itself was at risk, he went on, and if Europe was prostrated by war, then the only hope for the survival of those rich traditions and culture lay in America's hands. "By staying out of war," he said, "we may even bring peace to Europe more quickly. Let us look to our own defenses and our own character. . . ." Behind this view lay his certainty that Germany was far more powerful militarily than either France or Great Britain, and that the only way Hitler could possibly be defeated would be in a long, exhausting war. Lindbergh was by nature a questioner and a seeker, and when he asked himself whether the consequences of such a terrible struggle could be measured in terms of winning or losing, he was sure that victory could not be worth what it would cost the United States.

Elaborating again and again on this basic theme during the course of the next year, Lindbergh would make a dozen major addresses, four of them on network radio; speak at major public rallies; write several magazine articles; testify before congressional committees; and devote countless hours to discussions with leaders of the noninterventionist movement (most of whom he considered hopelessly conservative and incapable of assuming positions of national leadership). Almost as important as the dedication he brought to his self-appointed task, according to a man who shared speakers' platforms with him, was the way in which he "evokes a fervor, a tension, such as an ambitious politician would give anything to arouse."

In September 1940, when a group of noninterventionists formed a national organization—the America First Committee—to oppose U.S. entry into World War II, they immediately turned to Charles Lindbergh for assistance. He became their most successful, most sought-after speaker, the very personification of the isolationist cause, capable of attracting more than 30,000 people to a rally.

As a result of his increasing involvement in the debate, he was soon to be one of the most controversial figures in American politics, feared and reviled by the administration, which perceived him—quite accurately—as the most forceful opponent of the president's foreign policy and the man most likely to appeal to and influence the public. Indeed, the immediate reaction to Lindbergh's first speech had been overwhelmingly favorable: It was front-page news in the New York and Washington papers; telegrams and letters from all over the country greeted the colonel and his wife when they returned home from Washington, including one from Herbert Hoover congratulating him on a "really great address" and a polite note from General Arnold saying that he and Secretary Woodring thought the speech "very well worded and very well delivered."

There were brickbats as well as roses: It was only a matter of days before the opposition was in full cry. Dorothy Thompson lashed out at Lindbergh in her column, calling him the "pro-Nazi recipient of a German medal." And that was just the beginning. As the wrangling over America's neutrality grew ever more passionate and strident, Lindbergh and his wife would discover that old friends dropped them, that streets honoring the hero of the first solo transatlantic flight had been renamed. To cap it all, the president of the United States would insult him publicly by likening him to Clement Vallandigham, the Ohio congressman who spoke, during the Civil War, for a group called the Copperheads and predicted the North would never win.

In one of those remarkable coincidences that fate sometimes concocts, the great debate came to a head on the night of September 11, 1941, with the two chief protagonists confronting each other. Lindbergh had agreed to speak to an America First crowd in Des Moines, Iowa, that evening. President Roosevelt was to have addressed the nation after the U.S. destroyers *Greer* and *Kearny* were attacked by German submarines, but his mother died and the radio speech was rescheduled for September 11.

Rather than change plans, the America First Committee decided on the unusual approach of broadcasting the president's talk to the 8,000 Iowans attending the rally, with the scheduled speakers to follow. So what the crowd heard first was a stirring "shoot-on-sight" speech by Roosevelt, and when the America First speakers filed on stage they were greeted with a mixture of boos and applause, with hecklers shouting from the gallery.

When Lindbergh came to the lectern, he promised to speak "with the utmost frankness" about who was responsible for trying to force the United States into the war, and then named "the British, the Jewish, and the Roosevelt administration."

In the contest between isolationists and interventionists, the administration was fair game; so to a lesser degree was Britain. But even to name the Jews—whose danger to America, he said, lay in their dominant influence over the motion-picture industry, the press, radio, and government—and to segregate them *en bloc* from the rest of American society as "other peoples," was to introduce something altogether different into the equation. It was a reminder of the horrors perpetuated inside Nazi Germany, no matter how carefully Lindbergh tried to argue his case. It was, in short, the unmentionable topic, a sacred taboo, and no matter how he might explain his position, it was a political blunder from which America First never recovered.

While it would be improper to blame the demise of that organization on Charles Lindbergh—after all, the Japanese attacked Pearl Harbor less than three months after his speech—it was evident that the heart went out of the movement after the night of September 11. For one thing, the president struck a responsive chord with his "shoot-on-sight" message; events in Europe had made the public increasingly ready for tough talk, if not action. But Charles Lindbergh, a courageous man who never shied away from speaking the truth as he saw it, who had warned his country about the threat from Germany and had then become the noninterventionists' most powerful and persuasive voice, had an equal share in sending America First from the stage of history.

Until then, Lindbergh and the isolationists had profoundly affected

Franklin Roosevelt's tactics concerning foreign policy. As FDR's speech-
writer Robert Sherwood put it, their campaign had so put the president on
the defensive that "whatever the peril, he was not going to lead the country
into war—he was going to wait to be pushed in."

The Battle of Britain: How Did "the Few" Win?

by WILLIAMSON MURRAY

In June 1940, after Dunkirk, it seemed to the victorious Germans, poised at the edge of the English Channel, that the war for Western Europe was all but over. Their high command was confident that the Luftwaffe would soon break the will of their last enemy. A landing on the coast of England—Operation Sealion—would be merely a coup de grace. "Never in the field of human conflict was so much owed by so many to so few." The few to whom Winston Churchill referred were, of course, the RAF fighter pilots. But you could also say that they were Hitler, Göring, and the German high command. As Williamson Murray, the author of *Luftwaffe,* makes clear, what really saved England was a combination of German blunders, intelligence failures, and arrogance on an epic scale. And by the end of 1940 the British were producing far more military aircraft, and on the whole, better ones than the Germans. Lindbergh's premise no longer held true.

On June 18, 1940, a little more than two weeks after the last British ship left Dunkirk, a tired but defiant Prime Minister Winston Churchill announced to the House of Commons:

> What General Weygand called the Battle of France is over. I expect that the Battle of Britain is about to begin. Upon this battle depends the survival of Christian civilisation. Upon it depends our own British life, and the long continuity of our institutions and our Empire. The whole fury and might of the enemy must very soon be turned on us. Hitler knows that he will have to break us in this island or lose the war. . . . Let us therefore brace ourselves to our duties, and so bear ourselves that, if the British Empire and the Commonwealth last for a thousand years, men will still say, "This was their finest hour."

These words, today familiar to every student of World War II, reflect a national determination among the British people to make a desperate stand on their island. While the British braced themselves in June 1940 for the Battle of Britain, the Germans had little sense that they confronted a serious opponent. After it was all over, in the shambles of the Luftwaffe's defeat, Adolf Hitler and his chief henchman, Hermann Göring, stood out as the villains of the piece. What has not been so clear in the historical record, however, is the degree to which the German high command deserves a major share of the blame for the Wehrmacht's first defeat in World War II.

In the glow of victory, the Germans concluded that anything was possible for Hitler's Third Reich. The French army—the very same army that had fought the Reich to a standstill over four long years in World War I—had this time collapsed in barely a month. Hitler himself concluded that the war was over. After playing to Joseph Goebbels's film crew at the signing of the armistice at Compiègne, on June 22, the führer went on vacation. Accompanied by his court, he arrived in Paris for an early-morning visit, then took a picnic tour up and down the Rhine and visited World War I battlefields with his closest associates. He maintained only the loosest contact with his military staff, and that state of affairs resulted in the removal of the chief driving force behind the Nazi war machine. By its very nature, the German high command that Hitler had created was incapable of making critical strategic and planning decisions on its own.

Göring, self-styled Renaissance prince of the Third Reich, had even less interest in pushing the German war machine toward its next confrontation. It was a time to bask in the glories of victory, to add to his collection of Flemish masterpieces, and to dream of medals and other new honors—certainly not a time to worry about the nasty business of digging the British out of their island refuge. Britain could be bluffed and bullied into accepting German peace terms. The attitudes of the rest of the German military leadership reflected those of the führer and his paladin. General Alfred Jodl, chief of operations of the Armed Forces High Command (the OKW—Hitler's military staff, noted on June 30 that "the final victory of Germany over England is only a question of time."

Yet had the German leadership looked at the strategic situation, they would have realized that the difficulties involved in finishing Britain off before autumn were daunting. The German navy had managed to get its only two battle cruisers, the *Scharnhorst* and the *Gneisenau*, badly damaged in operations off Norway's North Cape in June. These operations served no strategic purpose—in fact the German navy's war diary admitted that the purpose of the June battle-cruiser raid was to influence the postwar debates over service budgets. As a result of the Norwegian campaign, the German navy was left with only one heavy cruiser and four destroyers at the beginning of summer 1940. The army, meanwhile, had done no thinking about the complexities of a massive amphibious operation such as crossing the English Channel and landing on the British coast. As an overconfident Field Marshal Wilhelm

Keitel, chief of the OKW, commented in June, such an operation represented nothing more than an enlarged river crossing.

As a result, the responsibility for removing Britain from the war fell to the Luftwaffe—fully in accordance with Göring's view of himself and *his* air force. But the Luftwaffe now faced strategic problems and issues that had never before existed in history: in sum, how to fight and win a great aerial campaign independent of ground and naval forces. There had been much theorizing about such a "strategic" bombing campaign before the war (including the writings of Trenchard, Douhet, Mitchell, and the Air Corps Tactical School in the United States, all of whom had argued that the proper role of bombers was to attack population centers or industry, certainly not to support armies or navies). But there was no actual experience from which one could draw lessons. How easy would it be to find and identify targets? What kinds of targets should one attack? How would national will and morale stand up to bombing? How tenacious would enemy air defenses be? Could an air defense interfere with or even thwart "strategic" bombing attacks?

Besides having few lessons from past wars to plot out a campaign strategy, the Luftwaffe confronted the coming campaign with a force that had lost heavily in the Battle of France. Between May 10 and the fall of France, the Luftwaffe had lost nearly 30 percent of its bombers, 30 percent of its twin-engine fighters, and 15 percent of its single-engine fighters. The fighting had been concentrated almost entirely within a three-week period, straining German pilots and aircraft to the limit.

The Luftwaffe of summer 1940 reflected the traditional strengths and weaknesses of German military institutions. Contrary to the postwar myth that the Germans had neglected their "strategic" bombing force, they in fact had the only air force in the world that was technologically and operationally prepared for such a campaign. Although their twin-engine bombers lacked the range and payload capabilities of the four-engine bombers that came later in the war, the Germans felt that their air force was capable of destroying nearby targets such as Prague, Warsaw, and even London. Meanwhile, like the British, they were working hard to design and build a four-engine bomber. Fortunately, the Heinkel He 177 prototype turned out to be a technological disaster.

Two other factors are also notable in comparing the Luftwaffe to the Royal Air Force and, later, the U.S. Army Air Force. The Germans took the protection of their bombers seriously, and therefore possessed not only a short-range fighter, the Messerschmitt Me 109, but a long-range escort fighter, the Me 110. Moreover, of all the world's air forces, the Luftwaffe was the only one that had done substantial development work on a blind bombing and navigation system—code-named Knickebein ("dog leg")—in which radio impulses would guide a plane to its target. Fortunately for Britain, the Luftwaffe's long-range fighter, the Me 110, proved inferior to both the Spitfire and the Hurricane, and British intelligence learned about Knickebein in time to develop countermeasures, such as listening posts and jamming aparatus, before the Battle of Britain.

The Luftwaffe faced the challenge of the unknown with remarkable blitheness. Throughout the war, the Germans gave intelligence a low priority; thus the Luftwaffe's estimate of British defenses was thoroughly inadequate. General Josef ("Beppo") Schmidt, Göring's chief of intelligence, wrote the basic appreciation, entitled "Study in Blue," that the Luftwaffe issued on July 16. This document arrogantly overestimated German capabilities and British weaknesses.

Schmidt did get some of the numbers right—calculating that with 50 fighter squadrons the British possessed approximately 900 fighters, 675 in commission (in fact, the RAF had 871 fighters, 650 operationally ready in 59 squadrons)—but from there his estimates fell off the table. He characterized both the Hurricane and Spitfire as inferior to the Me 109 in combat, and said that only a "skillfully handled" Spitfire was superior to the Me 110. He calculated that British industry produced 180 to 300 fighter aircraft per month (actual production reached 496 in July, 457 in August, and 660 in September) and said British production would soon drop due to German air attacks and British raw-material shortages.

Schmidt's greatest error, however, was his evaluation of Fighter Command's defense system. According to him, the British at the highest levels were

> inflexible in [their] organization and strategy. As [fighter] formations are rigidly attached to their home bases, command at medium level suffers mainly from being controlled in most cases by officers no longer accustomed to flying. . . . Command at low level is generally energetic but lacks tactical skill.

Reflecting the Luftwaffe's lack of technical intelligence, Schmidt's report made no mention of the British radar system and its implications for the attacking German forces. His report ended with the confident assertion that

> the Luftwaffe is clearly superior to the RAF as regards strength, equipment, training, command, and location of bases. In the event of an intensification of air warfare, the Luftwaffe, unlike the RAF, will be in a position in every respect to achieve a decisive effect this year if the time for the start of large-scale operations is set early enough to allow advantage to be taken of the months with relatively favorable weather conditions [July to the beginning of October].

While the Luftwaffe was gathering its forces for an aerial assault on Britain, the German high command began planning an amphibious assault on the coasts of Britain. Of all the unrealized campaigns and battles of World War II, this was one of the most unlikely. Even the German services seem not to have taken Operation Sealion seriously: The army planned for a landing on nearly ninety miles of beaches, far in excess of what the British and Americans, with their vast resources, would achieve in June 1944. This would have made it virtually impossible to break out of the initial beach lodgment. It is well worth noting that the Allies had two years of massive preparation behind them before they landed at Normandy. A reasonable explanation would seem to be that the German army commanders, knowing the German navy had virtually no surface force left after Norway, had no expectations of making such a landing.

Overall German strategy can be reduced to a formula: The Luftwaffe would break the back of the RAF early in the battle; after two months of air attacks on British industrial and population centers, British morale would crack; then, in the confusion of civil strife and governmental paralysis, Sealion would deal the death blow to British participation in the war.

If the Luftwaffe had achieved such a level of success, Sealion might have had a chance. But as a combined-arms operation against any kind of resistance, it had no chance at all. The Germans had no navy, the army had no experience in combined operations, and the lift for the invading troops and their equipment consisted largely of Rhine River barges. Considering that the Royal Navy had thirty-plus destroyers stationed at each end of the Channel, Sealion would have represented a desperate risk with small chance of success. It is clear that Hitler had serious doubts about the operation from the beginning. Indeed in July 1940 he was more interested in terminating the Soviet Union in the coming year. Thus, Germany's effort to drive Britain from the war had to come from the air.

There, the Germans confronted a more dangerous opponent than the one pictured in their intelligence documents, In addition to its up-to-date fighters, the RAF's command and control system for the air defense of Britain was the most modern in the world—thanks largely to the foresight, drive, and imagination of Air Chief Marshal Hugh Dowding, one of the great commanders of World War II. In the early 1930s Dowding, as Air Council member for supply and research (later, research and development), was responsible for the development of radar and the advanced fighters with which the RAF reequipped its squadrons in 1938 and 1939. In 1936 Dowding became the commander in chief of Fighter Command, where he oversaw the introduction of radar, Spitfires, and Hurricanes into the air defense of Britain. At the same time he also oversaw creation of a command and control system that tied fighter, ground controller, and radar together in an effective air defense system.

Dowding's first contacts with Winston Churchill during the French debacle were not auspicious. The prime minister, desperate over the plight of France (a plight he fully recognized as having resulted from the strategic policies of previous British governments), argued forcefully for a massive diversion of England's fighter strength to the Continent. Dowding argued with equal vehemence against any further reductions in the strength of his command, a portion of it having already been committed to the battle on the Continent. Dowding won. Legend has it that Churchill browbeat his senior military leadership into a number of foolhardy schemes and punished those who disagreed with his policies. It is clear that Churchill did not suffer fools, but those who disagreed with his policies received a fair, if tough-minded, hearing. In early July 1940 the minister for air, Sir Archibald Sinclair, reflecting a cabal within the Air Ministry, reported to the prime minister that he was considering relieving Dowding of his position. (It is not clear why the ministry had it in for Dowding—perhaps simply because he was not a bomber boy; perhaps because his success was showing British prewar bombing theories to be false.) Churchill's reply to Sinclair was brief and to the point:

> Personally, I think he is one of the very best men you have got, and I say this after having been in contact with him for about two years. I have greatly admired the whole of his work in the Fighter Command . . . and especially in resisting . . . the immense pressure to dissipate the Fighter strength during the great French battle. In fact he has my full confidence.

Churchill's confidence in Dowding was to prove justified.

The burden of defending Britain from the Luftwaffe fell chiefly on Dowding's subordinate, Air Commodore Keith Park, commander of 11 Group in the southeastern corner of the British Isles. Backing up Park's forces was 12 Group in the Midlands, which could support 11 Group in defending London. Separate fighter groups defended western England, as well as Scotland and northern Ireland. Fighter Command thus covered the entire British Isles—a fact that German intelligence had missed entirely. This coverage allowed Dowding to replace fought-out squadrons in the south with fresh squadrons from the north.

In all, Fighter Command's strategic position was not so dangerous as it appeared in the summer of 1940. The British air industry had already overtaken German fighter production; by late summer, under the demanding pressure of the minister for aircraft production, Lord Beaverbrook, the ratio favored the British by a two-to-one margin. In France, the Luftwaffe deployed two Luftflotten (equivalent to air forces in U.S. terms): Luftflotten Two and Three. Together, on July 20, those Luftflotten controlled 1,131 bombers (769 in commission), 316 dive bombers (248 in commission), 809 single-engine fighters (656 in commission), and 246 twin-engine fighters (168 in commission). In addition, the Germans deployed 129 bombers and 34 twin-engine fighters with Luftflotte Five in Norway to launch flank attacks on northern Britain. On the basis of their intelligence estimates, the Germans believed there was no fighter defense for the northern portion of Britain.

In microcosm, the strategic problem the Luftwaffe faced was similar to the one the United States confronted in its daylight bomber offensive against Germany in 1943. For maximum effect, bomber raids had to be carried out by day—when the risk to bombers was greatest. Due to the Me 109's limited range, escorted German bombers could strike targets only in southern England (although at night, when they had less need of fighter escort, the bombers could reach farther north); any raids beyond the range of Me 109s would drive bomber losses up to unacceptable levels. This allowed the RAF to use a sizable portion of the British Isles as a sanctuary. Free from the threat of air attack there, the RAF could establish and control its reserves, and protect much of Britain's industrial production, particularly in the Midlands.

By mid-July the Germans were deep into operational planning. In a speech to senior air force commanders, Reichsmarschall Göring enunciated the Luftwaffe's task in the coming battle. He emphasized that the RAF and Britain's aircraft industry would be the critical targets for winning air superiority over Britain. In contrast to the position he took later in the battle, when he demanded that fighters accompany bombers closely, he argued that Luftwaffe fighters should possess maximum operational latitude in protecting bomber formations. Bomber raids would bring up Spitfires and Hurricanes, and the Me 109s would destroy them. The initiative would thus remain with the German fighters, since they would not be tied exclusively to the protection of the bombers.

Unfortunately for the Germans, by summer 1940 Göring was neither consistent nor firm in his command of the Luftwaffe, and Luftwaffe subordinate headquarters had aims other than gaining air superiority. Fliegerkorps I placed support for an invasion, attacks on ports and merchant shipping, and terror raids against major cities on an equal footing with air superiority. The explanation undoubtedly lies in German overconfidence about the coming battle as well as in Göring's loose control. Luftwaffe estimates were that just four days of air attacks over southern England would break Fighter Command; and four more weeks would suffice to eliminate the remainder of the RAF and destroy aircraft factories on which an RAF recovery would depend. Then, completely vulnerable, the British would see the wisdom of accommodation with Nazi Germany; after removing Churchill, they would surrender and accept a subservient position within Europe's new order.

The Battle of Britain was supposed to open with a massive aerial assault. The date, code-named Eagle Day, was first postponed from August 10 to August 13, and then at the last moment the Germans again delayed—both times due to weather—but they were unable to recall their bombers already in the air. Initial attacks thus crossed the Channel without fighter cover. Already by mid-July, however, the Luftwaffe had embarked on heavy air operations to drive the RAF from the English Channel and to shut down the coastal convoys in the south. This the Germans managed to do by early August without unbearable losses, but their success was offset by the experience that Fighter Command picked up in managing the early air battles. The British worked the technological weaknesses out of their radar system, and the slow buildup in the size of Luftwaffe operations gave radar operators considerable practice in estimating the size and course of approaching raids. There were some significant errors at first: For example, on July 11 Fighter Command controllers scrambled six Hurricanes to meet a lone raider making for Lynne Bay; to their shock, the Hurricanes ran into a major raid of fifteen dive bombers escorted by thirty to forty twin-engine fighters. But such unpleasant surprises became less frequent.

Dowding and Fighter Command gained two other important advantages from these early battles. First of all, Fighter Command began discarding outmoded, interwar tactics; British fighters adapted to the nasty world of the dogfight. (They had forgotten the lessons of World War I, assuming that airplanes were simply too fast for traditional dogfighting.) Second—and perhaps most important—Dowding had time to reorganize and refashion Fighter Command after the heavy losses of the French campaign. The units that had suffered most in France during May and early June were now recovering in Scotland and the Midlands, while Dowding's freshest units lay in southern England with a substantial number of experienced aircrews. By the end of July, Fighter Command was better off than it had been at the end of June.

The Germans, on the other hand, not only made few inroads against the British defenses but, as an early August intelligence summary suggests, had failed to learn much about the enemy they had been fighting for nearly a month:

> As the British fighters are controlled from the ground by radiotelephones, their forces are tied to their respective ground stations and are thereby restricted in mobility, even taking into consideration the probability that the ground stations are partly mobile. Consequently, the assembly of strong fighter forces at determined points and at short notice is not to be expected. A massed German attack on a target area can therefore count on the same conditions of light fighter opposition as in attacks on widely scattered targets. It can, indeed, be assumed that considerable confusion in the defensive networks will be unavoidable during mass attacks, and that the effectiveness of the defenses may thereby be reduced.

That the Luftwaffe incorrectly estimated what was going on behind the Straits of Dover was more than a mere intelligence failure. Conceptually the Germans were considerably behind the RAF in developing an air defense system. While they possessed radar, they had not yet developed a real air defense system and thus were unable to recognize the effectiveness of their opponent's system. In fact they failed even to recognize that their own radar might prove useful in estimating how the British were reacting to their attacks. Had the Jafüs, the officers responsible for fighter operations, possessed radar plots of air operations over Britain, they might have played a more significant role in the battle. Instead, with little active or passive intelligence, they spent a dismal summer trying to make some sense of pilot reports.

By early August, Keith Park and Dowding had a fair picture of the parameters within which they would have to conduct the air battle. On the strategic level, Fighter Command had only to hold out until autumn brought bad weather. On an operational level, RAF fighter squadrons in the south would have to meet enemy bomber attacks with sufficient strength to impose a heavy rate of attrition on the attackers and to tie the Me 109s closely to the defense of vulnerable bomber formations. Meanwhile, beyond the Me 109's limited range, Fighter Command's reserves would rest and refit. They would be in position to savage whatever German bomber formations moved beyond Me 109 range.

In some respects, August 13, the official Eagle Day, came as an anti-climax. On August 11 the British lost nearly thirty fighter pilots—7 percent of 11 Group's total. On August 12, German bombs severed power to the radar stations at Dover and Rye; it took the British almost all day to get them back in working condition—though the latticework towers themselves withstood the pounding. But it was not until the afternoon of the 13th that the Germans attacked the RAF and its support structure. Raids on airfields, sector stations, and aircraft factories began in earnest. Almost inexplicably, German intelligence misidentified the parent factory for Spitfire production in South-ampton as a bomber factory, and not until much later did German bombers attack it. These raids hit the British hard. Fighter Command suffered severe attrition of fighter pilots—losses that put in question how long the RAF could sustain the battle for air superiority.

While the pressure on Fighter Command was intense, Luftwaffe units also took a beating. The effectiveness of British resistance came as a nasty shock—especially on August 15, a day that Luftwaffe aircrews (the surviving ones) refer to as "Black Thursday." Luftflotte Five's first appearance in the battle resulted in catastrophic losses that prevented it from launching another daylight raid on northern England: so much for intelligence estimates that the RAF had no fighter defenses in the north. In the south, German raids failed to destroy Fighter Command's radar network. While a number of RAF airfields were badly damaged, most were soon back in working condition. By mid-August the Luftwaffe had lost nearly 300 aircraft (including 105 Me 109s), while the British had lost 148 fighter aircraft. Compounding the attrition of German strength was the fact that aircrews shot down over the British Isles, even if they survived, were lost for the remainder of the war—in the words of one fighter pilot, felled in October 1940, "We were one-way fliers." Many British fighter pilots returned immediately to active duty.

It didn't take long for Göring to become discouraged by the heavy losses. On August 15 he called his senior air force commanders to his Berlin estate, Karinhall, to discuss the failure of the initial air attacks on Britain. Göring berated his generals for everything from faulty target selection to weak leader-ship. But he provided precious little advice and few solutions to their prob-lems. He also made a serious error: On the basis of inadequate damage esti-mates, he removed British radar stations from Luftwaffe target lists.

Within the week, Göring further handicapped the Luftwaffe's ability to break Fighter Command. On August 19 the operations staff stated that Dowding's fighters were the primary objective of the German air campaign and urged that the ground support structure, the aircraft industry, and alumi-num-production facilities therefore be the major targets of German attacks. At the same time, however, Göring ordered the Me 109s to guard bomber formations closely and no longer to seek out Fighter Command in free-chase missions. He thus robbed his fighters of the advantages of surprise and flexi-bility. As a result the British generally dictated the tempo of fighter opera-tions, and the Me 109s found it even harder to protect the German bombers while they themselves were at greater disadvantage in air-to-air combat.

By late August the RAF's tenacious resistance and the resulting German losses had reduced Göring to slandering the courage of his fighter crews. The fighter ace Adolf Galland recalled after the war a conference with the Reichsmarschall:

> [Göring] had nothing but reproach for the [German] fighter force, and he expressed his dissatisfaction in the hardest of terms. The theme of fighter protection was chewed over again and again. Göring clearly represented the point of view of the bombers and demanded close and rigid protection. The bomber, he said, was more important than record bag figures. . . . We received many more harsh words. Finally as his time ran short he grew more amiable. He asked what were the requirements for our squadrons. [Werner] Molders asked for a series of [Me] 109s with more powerful engines. The request was granted. "And you?" Göring turned to me. I did not hesitate long. "I should like an outfit of Spitfires for my squadron."

In fact, Dowding's Fighter Command was under serious pressure. German bomber formations had devastated its frontline airfields and severely stressed its command and control system and maintenance structure. Churchill, in his memoirs, recalled the British difficulties:

> Extensive damage had been done to five of the group's forward airfields, and also to the six sector station. Manston and Lympere on the Kentish coast were on several occasions and for days unfit for operating fighter aircraft. Biggin Hill Sector Station, to the south of London, was so severely damaged that for a week only one fighter squadron could operate from it. If the enemy had persisted in heavy attacks against the adjacent sectors and damaged their operations rooms or telephone communications, the whole intricate organization of Fighter Command might have broken down.

Dowding was almost out of fresh squadrons in the north, and the new pilots coming into Fighter Command had virtually no experience in flying operational fighter aircraft. In August, Fighter Command had lost one-quarter of its pilot strength; it was clear to Dowding that it could not afford losses much longer. The question of the hour was which of the two adversaries could last out the battle of attrition.

In early September the Germans made their final mistake. Discouraged by Luftwaffe failures to break RAF resistance, Hitler and Göring switched the air campaign's emphasis from an air-superiority strategy to a "strategic" bombing offensive against the British capital. The change was prompted by two factors. First, the Nazi leadership was outraged by Britain's temerity in bombing German cities, particularly Berlin. Second, the führer was undoubtedly eager to see whether he could break the "soft" British plutocracy. Interestingly, Field Marshal Albert Kesselring, often regarded by Anglo-American historians as one of the more effective German military leaders, enthusiastically supported the shift to terror attacks. "Smiling Albert" argued that Fighter Command was toppling, that major air attacks on London would finish the job and also break the will of the British people to continue the struggle. His counterpart, Field Marshal Hugo Sperrle, disagreed, but it was an argument he could not win.

The shift in Luftwaffe strategy came with startling suddenness after Berlin was first bombed. On September 7 the pressure on Dowding's forces relaxed. That afternoon Kesselring launched nearly 1,000 bombers and fighters against London. The move caught 11 Group so much by surprise that the British almost entirely missed the raid. They responded as if the massive attack were aimed at 11 Group's defensive structure. Consequently, British fighter attacks hit the German formations, if at all, after they had dropped their bombs on London. The East End docks suffered catastrophic damage, and the great fires there served as beacons for further nighttime attacks. The damage was terrible, but the population did not break.

The easing of pressure on Fighter Command came as a great relief to the hard-pressed fighter pilots and to the strained support structure of Fighter Command itself. And barely one week later the British showed how valuable that respite was. Luftwaffe intelligence, adding to its dismal record, suggested that the RAF was through. But when Kesselring's forces returned for a repeat performance on September 15, their bomber and fighter formations met a resolute and prepared fighter defense. A massive, swirling dogfight covered southern England from the coast to London and resulted in roughly equivalent fighter losses: The British lost twenty fighter pilots, the Germans seventeen. But Fighter Command also savaged the German bombers: Besides Me 109 losses, the Germans lost forty-one other aircraft in the day's fighting.

Pushed to the limit, Dowding's forces bent but did not break. Winston Churchill spent the day at 11 Group's command center at Uxbridge. His memoirs, often so eloquent, fully capture the strain of the day:

> Below us was the large-scale map-table, around which perhaps twenty highly trained young men and women, with their telephone assistants, were assembled: Opposite to us, covering the entire wall . . . was a gigantic blackboard divided into six columns with electric bulbs, for the six fighter stations. . . . Presently the red bulbs showed that the majority of our squadrons were engaged. A subdued hum rose from the floor, where the busy plotters pushed their discs to and fro. . . . In a little while all our squadrons were fighting, and some had already begun to return for fuel. All were in the air. There was not one squadron left in reserve. At this moment Park spoke to Dowding . . . asking for the three squadrons from Number 12 Group. . . . Hitherto I had watched in silence. I now asked, "What other reserves have we?" "There are none," said Air Vice Marshal Park. . . . Afterwards, he said that at this I "looked grave." Well I might. . . . The odds were great; our margins small; the stakes infinite.

As we now know, British fighters did not come close to their claims for German aircraft. Instead of 183, Fighter Command shot down only 60 German aircraft on September 15. The numbers, however, are irrelevant. On September 15, Luftwaffe morale cracked. Faced with serious opposition, a significant number of German bombers dumped their bomb loads over southern England and fled for France. Why this happened is not difficult to understand in light of two factors. First, the Luftwaffe had been engaged in major, sustained air operations since early May, a five-month period. Equally important, there came a point where smooth assurances by Luftwaffe intelligence that Fighter Command was almost through lost credibility in the minds of those who flew, especially since the opposite was so palpably the case.

The postbattle period held considerable irony. Dowding, so instrumental in the victory, was almost immediately retired. Despite Churchill's effort to employ him again, the RAF resolutely refused to give him an important assignment. Even more astonishing was the fact that the British failed to award Dowding any significant honors. Keith Park's treatment was not much better. Despite his contribution to the victory, he found himself shuffled off to a subsidiary, nonoperational command. On the losing side, interestingly, those responsible for the defeat suffered no repercussions: Beppo Schmidt continued as Luftwaffe intelligence chief and soon received a major operational assignment. Göring and Kesselring, of course, remained as senior military leaders to the end of the war. But then, they continued to provide the führer with the optimistic reports he so loved to hear.

Not only was there little correlation between battle performance and reward, but the two combatant air forces learned little from their clash. Luftwaffe chief of staff General Hans Jeschonnek summed up the German response when he remarked shortly before the invasion of Russia the following spring, "At last a proper war!"

For the British, the Battle of Britain confirmed what they had learned over the Heligoland Bight the previous December, when German fighters had savaged a raid of Wellington bombers: that daylight operations in the face of enemy fighters would involve prohibitive losses. But the RAF largely ignored the lesson suggested by the solidity of British morale in the face of the German air assault when it began the area-bombing campaign on Germany.

The U.S. Army Air Force, a major observer of the activities in summer 1940, also misread virtually all of the combat lessons. Its observers in Britain attributed high Luftwaffe losses to inadequate defensive armament, small bomber size, and bad formation discipline. By summer 1941 U.S. air planners were predicting that "by employing large numbers of aircraft with high speed, good defensive power, and high altitude," U.S. bombers without fighter escorts could penetrate deep into Germany without suffering serious losses. The U.S. Army Air Force's lack of interest in a long-range escort fighter is, in the words of the official historians, "difficult to account for." In light of the Battle of Britain, indeed it is.

In one respect, however, British and U.S. airmen did draw an essential, war-winning lesson: Both air forces, unlike the Germans, concluded that numbers would play the crucial role in winning the air war over the Continent. The resulting great aircraft-production programs drawn up in 1940-41 by both nations eventually won control of the air in 1944.

The Battle of Britain was one of the most uplifting victories in human history. "The few" had triumphed, but they had triumphed because of outstanding leadership in the RAF and sloppy, careless execution on the German side. The major reason for the Luftwaffe's failure was overconfidence. Its task admittedly presented operational problems wholly beyond those that had confronted military commanders before. But a cavalierly incompetent intelligence service understated the difficulties, causing the Luftwaffe to dally in July while its opponent, inspired by his desperate situation, rallied his forces. By engaging in irrelevant operations over the Channel in July and early August, the Luftwaffe built up Fighter Command's confidence and expertise.

The muddled execution of Eagle Day was a fitting anticlimax to a bad beginning. With its commander in chief and senior commanders far removed in their comfortable mansions, the Luftwaffe moved from one operational concept to another with no clear overall strategy. Ignorant of the importance of the radar system, misguided as to the locations of British factories supporting fighter production, the Luftwaffe nevertheless managed to inflict excruciating pain on Fighter Command. But that pain, without the discipline of a strategic concept (in the classic sense), could not be turned into a decisive victory.

When all is said and done, Winston Churchill's elegant tribute to Fighter Command underlined the fact that even in the "modern" and "civilized" twentieth century, such virtues as courage and sacrifice are essential to the maintenance of civilization: "Never in the field of human conflict was so much owed by so many to so few."

There is considerable irony in the Battle of Britain. Throughout the interwar period, airmen had argued that air power would allow nations wise enough to invest in air forces to escape the horror of the trench battles of World War I. Moreover, they argued that the past lessons of war and military history were irrelevant to the future employment of air power. They were wrong. The conduct of air operations in the Second World War resembled the strategy of the previous conflict except that the attrition was now in terms of aircraft and aircrews rather than mud-stained infantry. In a larger sense the traditional factors and lessons of war governed the conduct of air operations throughout the war. To quote one of the premier air historians, Anthony Verrier:

> Thus we are left with one clear reminder of a painful truth: The laws of war applied as much to the strategic air offensive waged over Europe's skies through five-and-a-half bitter years as they did to the sailors and soldiers on the distant seas or in the mud or the sand below. Occasionally the airman may have felt himself living or fighting in a new dimension, just as the air commander may have sometimes felt he employed a freedom of maneuver denied to admirals and generals. But the airman died, and the air force commander was defeated and stalemated unless the laws were kept. When

they were kept, success came; until they could be kept, hope was kept alive by courage alone.

For all the newness of the arena in which it was fought, the Battle of Britain reflected war in the modern world, and the air war for the next five years would follow the path so clearly marked out in the summer of 1940.

From Light to Heavy Duty

by PAUL FUSSELL

"Wars are all alike in beginning complacently," Paul Fussell writes, and the Second World War would be no exception. Though the horrors of the First still remained in the minds of millions of men in their early middle age, a kind of collective amnesia affected the next generation. You think of the final image in Richard M. Ketchum's *The Borrowed Years*, of the Yale students snake-dancing through the lobby of the Taft Hotel in New Haven the night of Pearl Harbor. Would many be seeing familiar faces for the last time? But the young would have to learn all over again that wars, once started, take on a monstrous life of their own, that what they are in the beginning bears little resemblance to what they are in the end. Inevitably there will be, as Fussell puts it here, "an inexorable progress from light to heavy duty." What follows is excerpted from his *Wartime: Understanding and Behavior in the Second World War*, published by Oxford University Press. A professor of English at the University of Pennsylvania, Fussell won the National Book Award for *The Great War and Modern Memory* (Oxford University Press). He is the editor of *The Norton Book of Modern War*.

Watching a newsreel or flipping through an illustrated magazine at the beginning of the American war, you were likely to encounter a memorable image: the newly invented jeep, with an elegant, slim-barreled 37mm gun in tow, leaping over a hillock. Going very fast and looking as cute as Bambi, it flies into the air, and behind, the little gun bounces high off the ground on its springy tires. This graceful duo conveyed the firm impression of purposeful, resourceful intelligence going somewhere significant, and going there with speed, agility, and delicacy—almost wit.

That image suggests the general Allied understanding of the war at its outset. Perhaps ("with God's help") quickness, dexterity, and style, a certain skill in feinting and dodging, would suffice to defeat pure force. Perhaps civilized restraint and New World decency could overcome brutality and evil.

"Meet the Jeep," said the *Scientific American* in January 1942. "The United States Army's Answer," it went on without irony, "to Schickelgruber's Panzer Divisions."

At first everyone hoped, and many believed, that the war would be fast-moving, mechanized, remote-controlled, and perhaps even rather easy. In 1940 Colonel William Donovan, later head of the American Office of Strategic Services, was persuaded—as he wrote in a pamphlet titled *Should Men of Fifty Fight Our Wars?*—that "instead of marching to war, today's soldier rides to war on wheels." For this reason, he conjectured, older men could easily fight the coming war, this time sparing the young. Still hidden in the future were Bataan and Guadalcanal, Saipan and Iwo Jima and Okinawa, Dieppe, Normandy, Cassino, and the virtual trench warfare of the European winter of 1944-45. This optimistic vision of Donovan's is especially curious in light of his having won the congressional Medal of Honor while commanding the 69th Infantry in the Great War and earning there the sobriquet Wild Bill. Had time softened his memory of the way ground combat works, the way men will attack only if young, athletic, credulous, and sustained by some equivalent of the buddy system—that is, fear of shame?

But by 1940 the Great War had receded into soft focus, and no one wanted to face the terrible fact that military successes are achieved only at the cost of insensate violence and fear and agony, with no bargains allowed. An American woman married in the 1940s to a B-26 tail-gunner for eighteen months, after which he was killed, speaks for virtually everybody when she recalls in 1984, "I was naïve about pain and suffering." Even the official history of the U.S. Army's Quartermaster Corps admits how innocently far off the mark were early estimates of the number of graves registration units ultimately needed. It would take a skilled pessimist and satirist like Evelyn Waugh to estimate more properly what the war would mean. He notes in his diary in October 1939: "They are saying, 'The generals learned their lesson in the last war. There are going to be no wholesale slaughters.' I ask, how is victory possible except by wholesale slaughters?"

At the start of the war the little light tank, all bolted plane surfaces of one-inch armor plate with smiling men looking out, was standard equipment in the U.S. Army's four "mechanized cavalry" divisions. One model had only machine guns; the most heavily armed carried the 37mm gun. This light tank, the ten-ton "Stuart" or "Honey," was the one with which George Patton established his reputation as a genius with armor. Assistant Secretary of War John J. McCloy, speaking at Amherst College on June 14, 1941, said many more mechanized divisions were needed, but saw no need for heavier equipment. "More like Baby Austins than bloody tanks," commented an experienced British tanker as he watched a shipment of Honeys unloaded at a North African port.

Cavalry mounts were an idea inseparable from the tanks in the first place, as can be inferred from the early American tankers' high laced boots. But at the beginning the cavalry itself still seemed a not implausible arm of the service. In 1941 the U.S. War Department announced with satisfaction that the army had just supplied itself with 20,000 horses, the most since the Civil War, and in April 1941 *Life* magazine devoted its cover to a photograph of an earnest "U.S. Cavalryman," Private Buster Hobbs, standing at attention beside his horse, Gip. Inside, an eight-page "photo essay" celebrated the U.S. 1st Cavalry Division, then training at Fort Bliss, Texas. Over half its 11,600 men were mounted, the rest driving armored cars, jeeps, and motorcycles. Their antitank defense was the 37mm gun. When the *Life* reporter visited the division, the troops were hoping for the ultimate delivery of heavier equipment—thirteen light tanks.

In England the situation was even more touchingly archaic. There, John Verney's yeomanry (i.e., cavalry) regiment was not mechanized until the summer of 1941. Before then it had been quite prepared to fight with lances and sabers. (And as late as 1949 you could buy a military saber in the cutlery department at Harrod's.) At the outset British armor was as dainty as American, depending on little light tanks dating in design from the 1920s and on such vehicles as a rubber-tired, light-machine-gun-equipped armored car called Ironsides. Many of the tanks were armed with machine guns only.

Paul Edwards, a Red Cross representative at a number of American cavalry posts, recalls that at first the "romanticism of the cavalry was still very strong. Officers hated giving it up." During the rout of the British on the Malay Peninsula in 1942, one colonel, says Edwards, "pounded the table" and asserted, "Goddamn it, they'll never [re]take a square foot of it until they get our men down there on horses and donkeys." In this respect the Americans were little more unimaginative than most other victims of the Axis. The Polish cavalry in September 1939 set out with impressive élan to repel the invading panzers. "In a few minutes," one commentator has observed, "the cavalry lay in a smoking, screaming mass of dismembered and disemboweled men and horses." When in spring 1940 the Germans swept through Holland, Belgium, and northern France, the Allies, one Briton recalls, simply "gaped, and said, 'What big tanks they've got.'" To help the British deal with the expected German invasion, the United States sent a million rifles. They would have been as effective as the Home Guard's former arms, wooden imitation rifles, against tanks, artillery, bombs, and flamethrowers.

At the beginning, military usages in many respects resembled civilian, as if the distinctions between those two worlds could be comfortably reconciled. American soldiers were issued white underwear and white towels, as if they were expected to be like other people—civilized and decent. Thus on Guadalcanal an isolated marine unit was able to signal HELP by laying out its T-shirts on a hillside. This would be impossible very soon, when the new experience in camouflage dictated that everything be olive drab—not just underwear and towels but handkerchiefs, pipe cleaners, and even toilet paper. The U.S. Army's initial innocence is registered in Field Manual 21-100, *The Soldier's Handbook,* issued in July 1941. By this time France had been conquered and London, Plymouth, Portsmouth, and Liverpool devastated by bombing, and the Germans had captured Crete with paratroops and invaded Russia with thousands of twenty-ton panzers. But Field Manual 21-100 was addressing the problem of shelter for the individual infantryman this way:

At the command FORM FOR SHELTER TENTS TO THE LEFT (RIGHT), the second in command moves to a position on the right of the guide, who is on the right of the right man of the front rank. . . . On direction of the platoon leader, the odd numbers draw their bayonets and thrust them into the ground alongside the outside of the left heel near the instep. The bayonet indicates the position of the front tent pole. . . . At the command PITCH TENTS, each man . . . steps off obliquely with his right foot a full pace to the right front. . . . Each odd-numbered man places a pin in the ground on the spot which he previously marked with his left heel . . . , the odd-numbered man driving the rear guy pin two-and-a-half tent pin lengths from the rear triangle pin.

You will normally pitch your tent where you will be concealed from enemy observation. . . . [In combat situations] the principles of tent-pitching will apply, but there may be no attempt to align the tents.

In the face of such Boy Scoutism, who could imagine the troops in the forests of Europe crouching in freezing holes roofed with logs or railway ties and mounds of dirt to protect against artillery tree-bursts?

As the war advanced, the armies reluctantly sloughed off such amenities as two-man tents. Early to disappear was the Sam Browne sword belt, and as *The Officer's Guide* reported, "The War Department announced on November 8, 1940, that until further instructions the use of the saber by officers on duty with troops . . . will be discontinued." Indeed, before the war was over, officers would become accustomed to accepting unpleasant facts and dressing like their men, both to raise enlisted morale by lessening the apparent distance between leaders and led and to avoid instant identification by snipers. In the United States Army, shiny metal insignia would retire from shoulders to shirt collars, where, in combat, they could be concealed with a scarf. Officers would abjure telltale pistols for rifles. In the British forces, battle dress would become the uniform of all classes, although not without objection from snobs. At the time of Dunkirk, some officers refused to wear battle dress, arguing that they would not "stand out enough." From an official photograph taken on a balustraded patio in Vincennes in October 1939, you could almost predict that the British were going to be thrown out of France and the French totally defeated. Every one of the six high officers depicted there is wearing a spiffy uniform with ribbons. Four are wearing Sam Browne belts; three, light-colored cavalry breeches with boots. No one has a weapon. The duke of Windsor is there, together with such other losers as General Richard Howard-Vyse and General Maurice Gamelin. All look entirely inadequate to the cynicism, efficiency, brutality, and bloody-mindedness that will be required to win the war. As General Dwight D. Eisenhower recognized in May 1942, thinking specifically of the U.S. War and Navy departments, "The actual fact is that not one man in twenty in the Govt . . . realizes what a grisly, dirty, tough business we are in." Hence, as late as April 1943, when the American plan to shoot down Admiral Yamamoto's plane was being considered, some scruples were felt, and the secretary of the navy was reluctant to proceed with this assassination until, as John Costello says, he had "taken the advice of leading churchmen on the morality of killing enemy leaders."

The inexorable progress from light to heavy duty can be read in the history of the posters issued on behalf of the American war effort. One 1942 poster depicts Joe Louis charging with a slim, long bayonet (soon to be replaced by the less graceful but more effective short and stocky version) attached to a long, slender Springfield rifle. He wears a clean field jacket, properly buttoned. We half expect a necktie. The caption reads: "Pvt. Joe Louis says—'We're going to do our part . . . and we'll win because we're on God's side.' " But a year later who is on God's side seems no longer to matter much, for now open depictions of corpses begin to displace considerations of moral right. A poster of 1943 shows a drowned sailor cast up on a beach: "A careless word . . . A NEEDLESS LOSS." A poster a year later delivers the same message ("CARELESS TALK GOT THERE FIRST") but now with more-shocking imagery: a dead paratrooper's body just settling to earth, his head hanging with closed eyes, his toes just beginning to drag across the dirt. Blood is conspicuous on his jacket and his hand. And finally, posters would venture the ultimate revelation—that the war is so brutal, bloody, and terrible that it must be ended (that is, won) quickly and by any means, moral or immoral. Thus a poster of 1945 depicts with a harsh photograph, not a painting, the awkward, ugly cadaver of a tank crewman sprawled amid realistically messy battle detritus—discarded web equipment, unused clips of rifle ammunition, this man's submachine gun. His helmet is violently tipped forward, revealing the vulnerable back of his head. Unlike Joe Louis's field jacket, this man's is rumpled and torn, covered with spots of dirt—or blood. The point? "This happens every three minutes. STAY ON THE JOB AND GET IT OVER."

By the end, finesse, accuracy, and subtlety had yielded to the demands of getting the job over at any cost. If early on the soldiers had spent many tedious hours practicing "marksmanship," by the end it was clear that precision would never win the war—only intensification would. Thus the troops abandoned aiming at precise targets and simply poured "assault fire" in the general direction of the enemy while moving toward him. Because the shapely Thompson submachine gun took too much time to manufacture, it was replaced by the crude, pressed-metal M-3 "Grease Gun"—which it looked like—since what was wanted, it was finally realized, was a weapon to spew out .45-caliber slugs with more regard for quantity than accuracy. At first, company officers in the ground forces were equipped with the little lightweight carbine. It was handy and cute, resembling, one authority has observed, "a sporting arm" more than a military rifle. But before the war had run its course, many officers abandoned it in favor of the heavyweight M-1 rifle. It was less chic, but its bullet could penetrate many more feet of wood and many more enemy bodies.

The proximity fuse, devised initially for antiaircraft use, betokens a similar coarsening of technique. Where formerly you had to aim accurately to hit a plane, now you could achieve the same end by hitting roughly near it. Similarly, "tactics" became a casualty as the war went on, to be replaced by mass wipings-out, bombings, artillery stonks, and frontal flamethrower assaults. The Japanese "defense" of islands like Tarawa, Saipan, and Iwo Jima could hardly be called "combat" at all in the traditional sense. It was suicide stubbornly protracted, and for the Americans the experience argued the uselessness of agility and cunning when sheer overwhelming force was available. More than the Japanese and the Americans died on those islands. Cleverness died too, and fine distinctions. Outmoded now, hopelessly irrelevant, were such former military values and procedures as the alertness of the scout; the skill at topographical observation from a tethered balloon; the accurately worded message written out (with carbon copy) in the nifty little book of Field Message Forms. Instead, what counted was heavy power, and it is the bulldozers, steamrollers, and earth graders of the Seabees that constitute the appropriate emblems of the Second World War. "Perhaps there was once a time," says the historian Geoffrey Perrett, "when courage, daring, imagination, and intelligence were the hinges on which wars turned. No longer. The total wars of modern history give the decision to the side with the biggest factories." In Europe the industrial basis of "victory" was even clearer. As Louis Simpson puts it in his poem "A Bower of Roses," in one battle near Düsseldorf

> For every shell Krupp fired,
> General Motors sent back four.

Archibald MacLeish was more precise than perhaps he intended when in the *Atlantic Monthly* in 1949 he declared that the United States had "engineered" a "brilliant victory." One Canadian has remembered: "I knew we were going to win the war when I saw the big Willow Run aircraft factory outside Detroit. My God, but it was a big one." In 1940 Roosevelt called for the building of 50,000 planes. "Asked for a time limit," says Len Deighton, "[he] blandly said that it was the number he wanted each year." Before the war was over, the United States had produced almost 300,00 planes, 11,000 of which were in the air over France on D Day alone.

Thus, abetted by engineering and applied science, the war by its end bore little resemblance to the war at its beginning. It had begun with concern about the bombing of civilians (BOTH SIDES AGREE NOT TO BOMB CIVILIANS—*Washington Post,* September 3, 1939) and it ended with not just Hamburg and Dresden but Hiroshima and Nagasaki. If the rubber truncheons issued to British units to repel German invasion of the British Isles were weapons of the beginning, the Tiger tank, the Superfortress, the V-2 rocket, and finally the atom bomb were weapons of the end, after intensification, the "theme" of the war, if it has one, had done its work.

"A singular fact about modern war," we are reminded, "is that it takes charge. Once begun it has to be carried to its conclusion, and carrying it there sets in motion events that may be beyond men's control. Doing what has to be done to win, men perform acts that alter the very soil in which society's roots are nourished." That's Bruce Catton, and he's referring not to World War II but to the American Civil War. At its beginning—say, the Battle of Bull Run (July 21, 1861)—light duty was the expectation. A day or two before the battle, congressmen, society ladies, and various picnickers and pleasure-seekers came out from Washington in coaches to watch from the nearby hills what they assumed would be a gratifying rout of the impudent Southern forces. Some women even brought along evening dresses, expecting a ball at Fairfax Courthouse after the day's successes. But the battle proved a stinging defeat for the North, and now facts had to be faced: The war would be long, brutal, total, and stupid.

The women who brought along their nice formal dresses were not especially unimaginative. Wars are all alike in beginning complacently. The reason is psychological and compensatory: No one wants to foresee or contemplate the horror, the inevitable ruin of civilized usages, that war will entail. Hence the defensive exercise of the optimistic imagination. When in April 1940 a Heinkel bomber crashed in Clacton-on-Sea, East Anglia, causing great damage on the ground and killing, among others, its crew of four Germans, the war was so new that as the German dead were borne to the local cemetery with full military honors supplied by the RAF, women sobbed for them, and, according to historian Derek Johnson, "the gallant foe were laid to rest amidst numerous floral tributes, their coffins being covered with wreaths of lilies, irises, and other spring flowers." Some of these wreaths bore the words "From All Ranks of the Royal Air Force" and "With Heartfelt Sympathy from a Mother." But it wasn't long before soldiers and civilians would be killed in quantity and without scruple, their bodies cremated en masse or tipped into lime pits, and only a couple of years more before A-bombs and the remorseless hanging of German officers convicted of terrible crimes would exemplify the heavy duty the war had necessitated.

Severe trauma was often the result of the initially optimistic imagination encountering reality. For all her tough-mindedness, the twenty-four-year-old American journalist Marguerite Higgins was appalled when, after years of pleading, she was finally designated a war correspondent and allowed in March 1945 to inspect the European combat zone. She was delighted that the Allies were winning and anxious to examine the process up close, but as her biographer notes, nothing in her previous experience or knowledge had prepared her for the "mosaic of misery" she was horrified to encounter. Cities ruined and stinking. Dead bodies everywhere, some torn apart, the American and German equally awful. "More shocking were the wounded, many her own age or younger. Some were blinded, others cruelly disfigured. . . . Many people had lost hands or feet to frostbite." The faces of the Allied soldiers, which she had expected to register at least a degree of satisfaction over their victories, were only "weary" and "bitter."

Marguerite Higgins cannot be blamed for not knowing the truth in advance of experience. The pamphlet "War-Time Prayers for Those at Home," prepared by the U.S. Army and Navy chaplains and published in February 1943, does a remarkable job of glossing over the distinct possibility of soldiers' deaths and mutilations. The featured prayer, displayed on the back cover, is "A Parent's Prayer for a Son in Service." After asking that all anxiety for the soldier be banished from the heart of the petitioner, it solicits God's help in keeping the boy faithful and victorious in struggles with temptation and sin (sex and liquor are meant), as well as "strong, manly, and cheerful." And the prayer goes on to speak of a just peace and to envisage the troops' happy homecomings. Notably absent is a clause that could be expected by the time of the heavy-duty spring of 1945 and that might go like this: "If it be Thy will that he shall lose his life, receive his soul into Thy safekeeping; if it be Thy will that he shall be maimed, provide him and us with comfort and with hopeful hearts."

Journalists more experienced than Marguerite Higgins tried to perform a public service by exploding the hope that some sort of light duty would suffice to win the war. In late November 1943 the U.S. Marines secured Tarawa Atoll—less than three square miles—by expending in a three-day assault more than 1,000 dead and 2,000 wounded. Instructed by photographs of marine corpses drifting in long rows along the shore and of smashed pillboxes and twisted landing craft, those at home began to perceive what sort of heavy duty the war would ultimately demand. Most were horrified, like the mother who wrote Admiral Chester Nimitz, "You killed my son on Tarawa." "This must not happen again," said one editorial, quoted by the *Time* magazine correspondent Robert Sherrod, whose book *Tarawa: The Story of a Battle* (1944) was one of the first to deliver war news that was less than cheerful. His account does full justice to the inescapable horrors, and in a final chapter he deals with the problem of the American innocence that kept such truths about the war pleasantly obscure for so long. Deep deficiency of imagination—that had been the cause of the home-front shock. Like the boys they educated, says Sherrod, "the people had not thought of war in terms of men being killed. . . ." Tarawa had finally made clear one terrible truth: "There is no easy way to win a war; there is no panacea which will prevent men from being killed."

The End in North Africa

by HANS VON LUCK

There seems little of the Second World War in Europe and Africa that Hans von Luck did not take part in. A professional soldier who joined the German army in 1929 at eighteen, he was taught battle tactics by Erwin Rommel and later became one of Rommel's favorite line officers. Luck "viewed the rise of Hitler at first with hope," he admits, "but then with growing misgivings." But he was trained as a fighting man, and fight he did with honor. He received two of his country's highest awards, the Cross in Gold and the Knight's Cross. Luck and his reconnaissance battalion could usually be found in the van of major actions: charging across Poland to the Vistula in 1939, across France to the Channel in 1940, across Russia to the outskirts of Moscow in 1941. (Only one German patrol, apparently, got closer to the Soviet capital than Luck.) The thirty-one-year-old major was rescued from the eastern front when his mentor, Rommel, who was now a field marshal, had him transferred to the Afrika Korps. In the excerpt that follows, taken from Luck's remarkable memoir, *Panzer Commander* (Praeger), we find him in the Egyptian Siwa Oasis, close to the Libyan border. It is October 1942. The German offensive in North Africa, deprived of men and matériel, has sputtered to a halt. Rommel himself has been temporarily invalided home, and the British, under Bernard Montgomery, are about to strike.

On October 23 the expected inferno broke forth with 1,000 guns and sustained attacks by the Royal Air Force around the coastal town of El Alamein. General Montgomery opened concentrated fire on our positions and blasted a hole in our minefields. Our counterattack was ineffective. Under the hail of bombs and the rockets used for the first time by the British fighter planes, and in face also of a defensive line of tanks, it broke down.

Rommel's HQ told me that he would soon give the order to retreat. Though still suffering from a tropical disease, the general had gotten out of a sickbed in Germany and flown back to Africa. By giving up Cyrenaica, that region of eastern Libya that bulges into the Mediterranean, he planned to reach Tripolitania and the Tunisian border and set up a line of defense there. In so doing, it seemed to him important to bring to safety, over a distance of nearly 2,000 kilometers, as many units as possible.

In the midst of these considerations, a brief "fuhrer-order" reached Rommel just before midday on November 3 to the effect that "there is no other choice for our soldiers but victory or death." Retreat was thus forbidden by the highest authority.

As he told me a few weeks after the event, Rommel wavered between absolute obedience to the oath he had taken, and the reality at the front, with the implied destruction of the whole Afrika Korps. That same afternoon of November 3, he decided to pass on to his commanders the führer-order to hold fast; the men, however, were not to be informed. Rommel was sorely frustrated, but for the present he obeyed.

On the morning of November 4, after strong artillery preparation, the British launched another attack. By using 200 tanks, including many of the superior American-made Shermans, and against bitter resistance from the twenty tanks left to us, deep breaches were made. But the Afrika Korps still held out and inflicted considerable losses on the enemy, mainly with our 88mm guns. While the enemy could make good his losses immediately, we lacked any replacements of tanks, heavy weapons, and ammunition.

Toward ten o'clock the British moved against the front of the XX Italian Corps, which, with its poorly equipped defensive weapons, stood no chance of stopping the attack. I tried to give the Italians as much help as possible, but with my armored reconnaissance vehicles and their equally weak antitank guns, any help I could offer was more moral than effective.

It was heartrending to have to witness how the Ariete Division (our most loyal allies) and the remains of the Trieste and Littorio divisions fought with death-defying courage—also how their tanks (the "sardine tins" so often mocked by us) were shot up and left burning on the battlefield. Although I was engaged in actions myself, I kept in contact with the XX Italian Corps until it was almost surrounded. At about 3:30 P.M., the commander of the Ariete Division sent his last radio message to Rommel: "We are encircled, the Ariete tanks still in action." By evening, the XX Italian Corps had been destroyed. We lost good, brave friends, from whom we demanded more than they were in a position to give.

The British now stormed through a breach twenty kilometers wide and threatened a southern outflanking of the Afrika Korps. At that, Rommel decided to ignore Hitler's order and begin an immediate retreat. I received orders to disengage from the enemy and transfer, first, to the area between Siwa and the Giarabub oasis, which was in Libyan territory west of Siwa. My assignment was to reconnoiter in every direction and report, or prevent, any outflanking attempt.

The following morning, November 5, I reached an area north of the Siwa and Giarabub oases without coming into contact with the enemy. Our patrols were positioned in a wide fan, with observation to the east, the southeast, and the south. As a result of sandstorms and heavy downpours, many tracks were made almost impassable for the elements of the Afrika Korps that were now falling back.

On the morning of November 8, Rommel flew into my command post—now east of the Egyptian-Libyan border—and gave me a review of the discouraging general situation. The Afrika Korps was in full retreat toward the Libyan border. We were resisting the British advance with our last resources. I could see the profound disappointment in Rommel's face.

"Through Hitler's crazy order to hold out, we lost a vital day, which cost us losses that cannot be made good. I can't hold Cyrenaica. So with the remains of the Afrika Korps, under General Bayerlein, I shall cross southern Cyrenaica, despite the rains and the sandstorms, in order to set up a first line of defense at Mersa el Brega [just south of Tripolitania].

"I have information," he continued, "that the British, by means of reconnaissance detachments and scout cars, are trying to prepare a southern outflanking of the whole Afrika Korps. This is a deadly danger. So I'm going to send you the Voss Reconnaissance Group [Panzer Reconnaissance Battalion 580 under Major Voss and Panzer Reconnaissance Battalion 33 under Major Linau]. You will then be strong enough to prevent any outflanking."

One couldn't fail to notice how disillusioned Rommel seemed. What had become of his proud Afrika Korps? How depressing it must have been for him to have to give up in a matter of days all that had been conquered in unprecedented operations of the past year.

Also on November 8, HQ informed me by radio that the Americans had landed in Morocco and Algeria and there was a danger that the Afrika Korps could be shut in on two sides.

By day it was very hot, and at night so cold that everyone was glad to have his coat and scarf on hand. Contact with the enemy was resumed. We came upon our old "friends," the Royal Dragoons and the 11th Hussars, led by the legendary Lieutenant Colonel Stirling; we had already been involved with them during our advance on Alamein. The prevailing atmosphere was one of respect: We "understood" each other. Although we knew we were shielding the withdrawal of the Afrika Korps to the west, we had no feeling of being in flight. We operated to all quarters of the compass with the object of maintaining contact with the enemy and getting a clear idea of his intentions. Prisoners had to be taken in order to learn something of the enemy's plans.

Our armored patrols developed their "net" tactic: In flat terrain, with visibility of more than fifteen kilometers, our fast and nimble eight-wheelers formed a large circle, into which they lured the slow but well-armed British Humbers and other scout cars, in order to close the net from two sides. This tactic usually worked, though we sometimes lost isolated scout cars to the more powerful cannon of the Humbers.

The first prisoners were brought in, and some of them greeted me with "Glad to meet you again." The British kept their sense of humor in all eventualities. After the usual small talk, we learned that the main job of the two British reconnaissance battalions was to prevent us from trying to interrupt Montgomery's supply routes by attacking them from the depths of the desert. We found out the names of the commanders of the two British battalions. I also found that some of the prisoners knew me by name: "You are Major von Luck. We'd have been glad to catch you."

We quickly developed a routine. Toward 5 P.M. each day the reconnaissance patrols broke off their operations. In the treeless desert with no landmarks, it was impossible to find one's way back to base in the dark. To avoid betraying our position, light signals were used only in an emergency. The two British battalions carried on in the same way, so that from 5 P.M. all reconnaissance and combat activity was suspended, to be resumed the following day at sunrise. "We could really agree to a cease-fire with the British from 1700 hours until the next morning," I joked. "Why not?" agreed one of my subordinates, Lieutenant Wenzel Luedecke, who had been a moviemaker in civilian life. "We ought to suggest it to them."

Chance came to our aid. One evening, when all our patrols were back, my intelligence officer came by. "The Royal Dragoons are on the radio," he said, "and they would like to speak to you."

"Hallo, Royal Dragoons here. I know it's unusual to make radio contact with you, but Lieutenant Smith and his scouting party have been missing since this evening. Is he with you, and if so, how are things with him and his men?"

"Yes, he is with us. All of them are unhurt and send greetings to their families and friends." Then came the brainstorm: "Can we call you, or the Eleventh Hussars, if we have anyone missing?" I asked.

"Sure," he replied. "Your calls are always welcome."

It was only a matter of days before we arrived at a gentleman's agreement: At 5 P.M. precisely, all hostilities would be suspended. We called it "teatime." At 5:05 P.M. we would make open contact with the British to exchange "news" about prisoners, etc. From a distance of about fifteen kilometers, we could often see the British get out their Primus stoves to make their tea.

Our "teatime agreement" had some remarkable consequences. One evening, a patrol came back with two men and a jeep captured in the desert. A tall, fair-haired young lieutenant and his driver were brought before me. The lieutenant was snobbish and arrogant. Very correctly he gave me his service number only, no other details. I tried to get into conversation with him and told him of my prewar visits to London. He gradually thawed and turned out to be the nephew of one of the owners of Players cigarettes. My officers whispered a suggestion and I had to laugh.

"Lieutenant, what would you say to our swapping you and your driver for cigarettes? We're a bit short."

"Good idea," he said.

"How many cigarettes do you think you are worth? What should I suggest to your commander?"

His answer came without hesitation: "A million cigarettes—that's a hundred thousand packets."

My radio officer made contact with the Royal Dragoons, and I passed along our proposal.

"Please wait, we'll come back to you at once" was the reply. Then, after a bit: "Sorry, we're a bit short ourselves, but we could offer six hundred thousand cigarettes. Come in, please."

To my great astonishment, I received a flat refusal from the young lieutenant. "Not one cigarette less than a million, that's final!" was his answer. So the young man had to pay for the high value he set on himself with captivity.

A week later, shortly before dark, our doctor disappeared behind a rise for the indispensable "spade trip."

"Doctor," I called out to him, "don't go too far—it'll soon be dark." He didn't seem to hear me and went on. When he didn't come back after half an hour, we began to worry. The doctor was not only very popular but also vital to us. We sent out some men and fired prearranged light signals. The doctor remained missing. Had he lost his way, or been caught by the British? We got on the radio.

"Yes, we've got your doctor," the answer came back right away. "He ran straight into our patrol on its way back. This time *we* have a suggestion. The Japanese have cut our communications with the Far East. We can't get quinine anymore and are suffering badly from malaria. Can we exchange your doctor for some of your synthetic Atabrine? Come in, please."

A moral issue now presented itself: Which was more important, to weaken the fighting strength of the British by letting them suffer from malaria, or to get our doctor back? I quickly made up my mind.

"Okay, we'll do business. How many packets do you want for the doctor?"

We agreed on a quantity we could spare, and the next morning, from either side, a jeep with a white flag drove between the lines for the ceremonial handing-over.

"An expensive spade trip, doctor. Good to have you back."

The "teatime agreement" ended later, somewhere in the Tunisian desert. For some days we had lost contact with the two British battalions. Then an orderly came to my command car one evening. "There's a bedouin here who wants to talk to you, major."

With a deep bow, the bedouin came in. "I have a letter for you. I will wait for an answer."

A bedouin with a letter, here, in the desert, where by rights no one should be able to find us? The bedouins always seemed to know where we were. I opened the letter.

From C.O.,
Royal Dragoons
Dear Major von Luck,
  We have had other tasks and so were unable to keep in touch with you. The war in Africa has been decided, I'm glad to say, not in your favor.
  I should like, therefore, to thank you and all your people, in the name of

my officers and men, for the fair play with which we have fought against each other on both sides.

I and my Battalion hope that all of you will come out of the war safe and sound and that we may find the opportunity to meet again sometime, in more favourable circumstances.

With the greatest respect.

I sat down and wrote a similar note to the Royal Dragoons. "Give this letter to the man from whom you received the one to me," I told the bedouin. "Say to him, 'Many thanks,' but don't betray where you found us."

On November 20, I was ordered to go to Rommel. He looked exhausted. His uniform was worn and dusty. The hard withdrawal actions, his deep disappointment, and illness had left their mark on him. He greeted me and took my arm. "Come, we'll go for a little walk." We strolled along the edge of the airfield.

"I no longer know how to cope with the supply problem," Rommel began. "First, the loss of Stalingrad, with two hundred thousand battle-tried men; now we're losing Africa, too, with elite divisions. What we need is to create a German 'Dunkirk.' That means flying out as many officers, men, and specialists as possible to Sicily, leaving the matériel behind. We need the men for the decisive struggle in Europe."

"How will you ever put that to Hitler?" I asked.

"I shall fly to Hitler at Rastenburg and make my opinion clear to him. My word still counts for something; I am still respected among the people and by my men. I don't believe anymore that we shall get what we need in further divisions, aircraft, and supplies in order to turn the wheel yet again."

His face was lined, his shoulders drooping. He was the picture of dejection. "Luck, the war is lost!" he said.

I was appalled. Was everything to have been in vain?

"We're still deep in Russia," I protested. "Most of Europe is occupied by us. Bitter though the loss of North Africa will be, we can carry on the fight and bring about a change of fortune."

"Luck, we've got to seek an armistice, precisely because we still have a lot of pawns in hand. If possible, an armistice with the Western Allies. We still have something to offer. This assumes, of course, that Hitler must be forced to abdicate, and that we must give up the persecution of the Jews at once and make concessions to the Church. That may sound utopian, but it is the only way of avoiding further bloodshed and still more destruction in our cities. Luck, one day you will think of my words. The threat to Europe and to our civilized world will come from the East. If the peoples of Europe fail to join forces to meet that threat, Western Europe will have lost. At the moment, I see only one 'warrior' prepared to champion a united Europe: Churchill."

The next time I visited headquarters, at the beginning of December, Rommel's chief of staff, General Gause, told me that on November 28 Rommel had flown to Rastenburg in East Prussia to see Hitler. But the crucial meeting had the opposite effect of that for which Rommel had hoped: Hitler regarded Rommel as sick and run-down and his report on the situation as greatly exaggerated. He angrily refused even to consider evacuation of the Afrika Korps. Although it was suggested that Rommel take treatment for his tropical disease, he went back to "his" men instead, bringing with him only empty promises of support.

Rommel's retreat through southern Cyrenaica was a masterly achievement. In the meantime, except for a great deal of matériel, we suffered hardly any losses. The danger of a fresh attempt to outflank us remained great, however. Christmas 1942 arrived, and deep in the desert, without a tree or a bush and in the heat of day, our thoughts turned to home. Once, on New Year's Eve, Rommel arrived in his Fieseler Stork to brief me on the situation, and the need to protect the remains of the panzer divisions in the North. He was convinced that the British were about to launch another attack.

Until the middle of January 1943, things remained quiet. To my surprise, my battalion was transferred to the area southwest of Tripoli for a few days to be restored to strength. The quiet spell in a palm grove did us good; in addition, replacements of men, ammunition, and petrol arrived. I used the opportunity for a brief visit to Tripoli. In the bar of the Ouadan Hotel, the Italian bartender served me a cocktail: "I shall probably have to serve the next one to Montgomery," he said. The Italians took things more lightly than we did.

On January 13, I was back with the Reconnaissance Group. The following day, with massive artillery and air support, the British moved against our southern flank, and on January 23 occupied Tripoli without a fight. It was about this time, as we were covering the disengagement of our units, that a patrol reported: "Gathering of high military personnel about six to eight kilometers to the northeast, believe Monty identified, strong protection with tanks and scout cars."

I went there at once and scanned the scene with binoculars. It really did seem to be Montgomery, and, much more sensationally, Churchill appeared to be with him, wearing a safari helmet. It was too far to open fire; 88mm guns and artillery were not available. I immediately sent a radio message to Gause: "Churchill and Monty believed located at great distance, no action possible." Actually, I thought of what Rommel had said about Churchill: That, more than distance, caused me to hold my fire.

Later, I heard that it could well have been Churchill, who, on his way from the conference at Casablanca, had stopped off to see Monty and his troops. However that may be, we never saw Hitler in this theater of war, nor (with the exception of Field Marshal Albert Kesselring) senior officers of the Wehrmacht High Command.

Shortly after, an orderly officer arrived from Rommel with an antiaircraft platoon and one of light artillery. "Major," he said, "your task is as follows: Since Rommel still considers it possible that the British may attempt a wide, outflanking movement from the south, or that the French combat group may turn up, your reinforced battalion is to advance on Foum Tatahouine in southeast Tunisia, capture the French garrison, and reconnoiter to the south and southeast. If no enemy is observed, your combat group will return at once to the Mareth position in Tunisia. [The Mareth defensive line, originally built by the French and somewhat grandiloquently referred to as the "Desert Maginot," was no more than a few dozen pillboxes near the coast and some fortified positions in the mountains inland.] You will set off for the south tomorrow morning; radio contact must be maintained without fail."

Well spread out, we made good progress at first, until a British reconnaissance plane flew over us, circled, and flew off again. That was sinister. I sent off a radio message to Gause: "Expect air attack on my combat group. Can you alert our fighters? Progress toward Foum Tatahouine otherwise good."

Then they came: Flying out of the sun and low over the ground, the Hurricanes attacked, protected by Spitfires, which kept watch high above them. No special orders were needed: All movement ceased; every man left his vehicle and lay flat on the sand thirty yards away. My motorcycle escorts opened fire with their machine guns, but without success. We didn't know that the Hurricanes were armored on the underside. Their target was the flak platoon [the antiaircraft platoon], which was eliminated before it could fire a shot. On their second run up, the artillery platoon was hit and its vehicles badly damaged. As fast as they had come, the fighters turned away. Everything had lasted only a few minutes.

The Hurricanes had to have seen my armored reconnaissance vehicles, so again I radioed. "Have been attacked by Hurricanes. Flak and artillery platoons largely out of action. Reckon on fresh attack. Send Messerschmitts."

The British bases must have been close behind the front. After barely an hour, they were back again. This time, it was the turn of our armored vehicles. With dismay, I saw the Hurricanes fire rockets that went straight through our armor. That was new to us.

The only one to remain in his vehicle was my radio operator, who was sending off my messages. Next to the vehicle stood my intelligence officer, who passed on to the operator what I shouted across to him.

Then a machine—I thought I recognized the Canadian emblem—approached for a low-flying attack on the armored radio station. At twenty yards, I could clearly see the pilot's face under his helmet. But instead of shooting, he signaled with his hand for the radio officer to clear off, and pulled his machine up into a great curve.

"Get the operator out of the vehicle," I shouted to the intelligence officer, "and take cover, the pair of you!"

The machine had turned and now came at us out of the sun for the second time. This time he fired his rockets and hit the radio car, fortunately without doing too much damage.

This attitude of the pilot, whether he was Canadian or British, became for me *the* example of fairness in this merciless war. I shall never forget the pilot's face or the gesture of his hand.

We immediately moved off once more toward Foum Tatahouine. We were now in the middle of the desert, which in this part was flat and provided easy going. And then we spotted the little desert fort lying before us: a heap of stones piled on top of each other; not a tree or a bush in sight. We were met by machine-gun fire, which we very quickly silenced. Then a French captain came toward us; his soldiers had laid down their weapons and raised their hands.

"Why are you still here," I asked him, "now that the front has moved on to Tunisia?"

"We've been stationed here for over a year," the captain replied. "Our task is to keep the fort manned. I have no other orders."

I went with him into his bare office, where I saw a radio set. At a sign from me, it was put out of action by my intelligence officer.

"Regard yourself and your men as prisoners," I said. "Pack whatever you need; I shall have to take you with us." I radioed Gause: "Foum Tatahouine occupied, garrison taken prisoner, radio destroyed. Reconnaissance far to the south, no contact with enemy. Am returning to Mareth position with combat group and several vehicles in tow."

At the beginning of March, I heard from Gause that Rommel intended to fly to Führer-HQ to save what there was to save. As I happened to be in reserve—my battalion had hardly any armored cars or ammunition left—I went to Rommel's nearby command post.

"May I speak to Rommel and say good-bye to him?" I asked Gause.

"Of course. He will be glad to see the commander of his favorite battalion."

As always, Rommel sat in his "Mammoth"—a monster truck seized from the British—with his campaign maps before him. I hadn't seen him for some weeks and was shocked at how unwell he looked—weak, sick, and completely worn out. Still, he had that unique sparkle in his eyes.

"Field Marshal, I have heard that you intend flying to HQ. I don't think you will be coming back. In the name of each individual member of my battalion, I say good-bye to you, till we meet again, sometime, somewhere. We'll hold out here as long as we can, always after the example you have given us."

Rommel stood up; he had tears in his eyes. He went to a cupboard on the wall and came back with a large photograph, which showed him as a healthy and successful man. He signed it with a dedication and handed it to me. "Here, Luck, take this in gratitude and appreciation of your brave battalion. Keep well. I hope we shall see each other again at home. God be with you."

On March 9, he flew to Germany.

At the end of March, an order reached me to report at once, in person, to General Jürgen von Arnim, who had taken command in Rommel's absence. I had no idea what was wanted of me.

General Gause received me. "Rommel has got nowhere with Hitler," he said. "We shall not receive adequate supplies, nor does the führer want to hear anything about a German Dunkirk. Rommel has been sent for treatment and forbidden to return to Africa. Come, the commander in chief is expecting you."

A tall, slim man with sharp features awaited me. "Good to meet you,

Luck. I have the pleasure of presenting you, in the name of the duce, with the Medaglia d'Argento, a decoration that corresponds roughly to our Knight's Cross." General von Arnim pinned the order to my chest and handed me the certificate.

I was naturally pleased. Associated with the order, there was even a small monthly pension and free first-class travel for two on all Italian railways for life. But von Arnim had not sent for me merely because of the order. "Luck, I have decided, in agreement with Rommel and Gause, that you will fly at once to Führer-HQ to lay before Hitler a detailed plan for the evacuation of as many elements as possible of the Afrika Korps. You will first fly to Rome and have the plan countersigned by Marshal Kesselring. You will then fly on to Berlin and report to Colonel General Guderian [chief of the army general staff] and General Schmundt [responsible for the personnel side of the evacuation], likewise for countersigning. You then fly to Berchtesgaden, to Führer-HQ, and report to Keitel or Jodl to be given an appointment with Hitler. Wherever you go, you will keep in contact with us through a thousand-watt radio and a special code."

"I am honored by the task," I replied, "but how should I, an insignificant frontline soldier, get anywhere with Hitler? Besides, I should like to be with my men in the final phase."

"We've thought of all that. The army generals are extremely suspect to the führer; even Rommel is apparently to be left out in the cold. Despite the loss of Stalingrad, Hitler sticks to his message of 'victory or death, but no retreat.' That means we shall lose about 130,000 men in North Africa, too. Hitler is more likely to listen, if at all, to an 'insignificant' major straight from the front. You will travel, and appear before him, in your dusty, faded uniform. That can't fail to have an effect."

The next day I packed the essentials; my main baggage, including the picture of Rommel, I left behind.

In Rome I was allotted a room in the famous Hotel Excelsior on the Via Veneto, and given an appointment with Kesselring for the following morning. The city seemed almost undisturbed. There was no blackout as in Germany, hardly any military vehicles to be seen, and the Via Veneto was pulsating with life as in peacetime. In my faded tropical uniform, I felt out of place.

The next morning a car from the liaison office took me to Frascati, the wine center near Rome, where Kesselring had his HQ. I was admitted at once to Kesselring, who apparently had been fully informed. He was a charming man of medium height with warm and sympathetic eyes. We respected him, as he was the only high commander who had come to Africa.

"I haven't much hope of getting our plan through with Hitler," Kesselring said, "but we must try it. You can fly to Berlin today by courier plane. Every day counts. Good luck." He shook my hand and I left.

Still in my dusty uniform, I landed in Berlin, after sending off a report to von Arnim from Frascati.

What a contrast to Rome! The German city presented a picture of destruction. Many houses were just ruins, and the faces of the once busy

Berliners were gray. One could see they no longer believed in the "Final Victory" of Hitler and Goebbels, though no one dared say as much; the danger of denunciation was too great.

General Schmundt signed the plan that evening without even reading it. The next morning I met with Colonel General Guderian, the newly appointed chief of the army general staff. I had not seen him since the beginning of the war. He looked tired, but his eyes were still lively.

"Luck, I'm glad to see one of the old hands of the panzer force again, alive and well. How many from the early days of our proud force have already gone! We've just lost Stalingrad. You know, perhaps, how many experienced officers and men have fallen there, or have been taken prisoner. And now the same thing is looming in Africa.

"That is why I agreed at once to Rommel's evacuation plan, though we all had little hope that Hitler would agree to it. Your opinion, as an old trooper from the front, carries more weight than ours, which is regarded by Hitler as 'defeatist.' You can still go today, by the night train, and be in Berchtesgaden tomorrow morning."

Through the night I rolled south in a sleeping car, undisturbed by air raids.

The first person I met in Berchtesgaden was a Lieutenant Colonel von Bonin, whom I had last seen on New Year's Eve, 1942, when he accompanied Rommel to my command post in the desert. "What are you doing here?" he greeted me. "I thought you were fighting your last battle in Tunisia."

In confidence, I told about my mission and asked through whom I could best get to make my plea to Hitler.

"My dear chap," the lieutenant colonel replied, "we're not on the battlefield. Here, even Rommel has no say. Here, bureaucracy rules. That means you must first go to the 'officer-in-charge, Africa,' a certain Colonel X, who will announce you to Colonel General Jodl. He will get the OK from Field Marshal Keitel as to whether and when you will be allowed in to the führer. Come—as a start, I'll take you to the colonel. Then from 1230 hours to 1400 hours there's the midday break, when no one at all can be seen. That's the way things are. In Africa, well over a hundred thousand men are bleeding and fighting for their lives, but here the midday break must be observed while the war comes to a stop!"

Colonel X received me in very friendly fashion. I stated my business and asked to be announced at once to Jodl.

"Listen," he answered, "you can forget about the evacuation plan; the North African theater of war has already been virtually written off. We are still trying, of course, to send over as much matériel as possible, but we have no great hopes. Be glad that you are out of the mess."

"Have you any idea," I replied somewhat sharply, "how things look down there, what we've been through, and that we are losing the war only because we have never received adequate supplies? Please arrange an appointment for me with Colonel General Jodl for this afternoon."

It was fixed for three o'clock. Over a meal in the bare mess, Bonin gave me Rommel's address and telephone number. Whatever happened, I wanted to tell him of the outcome.

Soon, with my large envelope containing the evacuation plan, I was standing before Jodl. We knew he was an experienced staff officer, but we frontline troops didn't like him—he was such a toady to Hitler. I explained my mission to him and why von Arnim had chosen me as intermediary. "Things look very bad," I said. "We're no longer equal to the pressure of the British and the Americans. The RAF, in particular, hinders almost all our movements, except when it's raining. The long front cannot anywhere near be covered by us. To prevent a disaster, as many men as possible should be evacuated at once, to be available on fronts where the Western Allies are sure to land. The evacuation plan has been carefully worked out by Rommel and von Arnim and countersigned by Kesselring, Guderian, and Schmundt."

Then I handed him the envelope.

Jodl looked at me for a long time without opening the envelope. "Listen, Luck," he finally said, "there is absolutely no question of evacuating elements of the Afrika Korps, or of considering a German 'Dunkirk,' as you call it. The führer is not ready to think of retreat. We shan't even let you see him personally. He would have a fit of rage and throw you out." Without pausing, Jodl took my arm and led me to a huge campaign map that covered one whole wall. "What do you think about Stalingrad?" he asked.

"Colonel General, we have so much trouble with our own theater of war that we have no time to concern ourselves with Stalingrad. We merely ask ourselves whether it is necessary to abandon so many battle-tried men. The word Stalingrad is for us a provocation: We fear a similar fate."

Jodl was silent for several moments. Then he gave me his hand. "I understand. But your mission is of no avail. Inform von Arnim to that effect." I saw in his eyes a helpless sympathy for the Afrika Korps.

Deeply disappointed, I radioed von Arnim: "Not admitted to führer, plan rejected by Jodl, flying back to Rome and from there to Tunisia." There was nothing more to keep me in Germany; I wanted to be with my men. In Rome I was told that strict orders were in force to allow no further personnel to fly to Africa; only supplies were to be flown to Tunis, within the bounds of what was still possible. I didn't give up, however. I stayed in Rome and went to the liaison office every day, looking for permission.

The daily news from the front was alarming. By the end of April 1943, the front in the south was on the point of collapse; hardly any ammunition, petrol, or replacements were getting across. Then, suddenly, an order from Führer-HQ arrived in Rome: "A start is to be made at once with the evacuation of German and Italian troops from Tunisia; all available means of transport are to be employed." What followed was the very evacuation plan that I had delivered to Jodl weeks before. Junkers, torpedo boats, and ferries were brought into action. My battalion was still in the desert; it would have had no chance of getting through to the north to the Cape Bon Peninsula, where the main evacuation was taking place. I received a last radio message from Captain Bernhardt, who was now in command of the battalion. "Have no petrol or ammunition left, immobile awaiting decisive attack. We greet our commander and our families, Panzer Reconnaissance Battalion 3."

When the first officers and men arrived at the airfields for evacuation, U.S. tanks were already there.

On May 6, after an all-out offensive by the Allies, the remains of the proud Afrika Korps surrendered; more than 130,000 German soldiers alone went into captivity. It was all over.

EPILOGUE: Hans von Luck never did recover the autographed photograph of Rommel, but he did serve with the field marshal again, this time as commander of a panzer regiment in France. He fought the British in Normandy and the Americans on the Maginot Line. In the final confused days of the war, Luck, by now a colonel, was taken prisoner by the Russians near Berlin. He spent the next five years in a labor camp in the Caucasus. Today, in his early eighties, he remains active as a coffee importer—and, every summer, lectures on the Normandy campaign to groups from institutions such as the British Staff College at Camberley and the Swedish Military Academy. "Opponents," he writes, "have turned into friends, who together, and without emotion, try to draw lessons from the events of that time."

Bill, Willie, and Joe

by DAVID LAMB

Bill Mauldin was just twenty-three when he came home from the war in the summer of 1945, and already he—and Willie and Joe, his cartoon dogfaces—were famous. They still are, but he feels no urge to disown them, even though he gave up his brief attempt to follow their peacetime careers. He wasn't comfortable drawing them without beards. Mauldin eventually went on to become a notable political cartoonist, and today lives in semiretirement near Sante Fe, New Mexico. In 1989, David Lamb, a national correspondent for the *Los Angeles Times,* went to visit him. Their conversation touched on subjects as varied as the nature of war humor, getting wounded, Humphrey Bogart, fame, George Patton, and how close Mauldin came to killing off Willie and Joe on the last day of the war. Lamb is the author of *The Africans* and *The Arabs: Journeys Beyond the Mirage,* and, most recently, *Stolen Season: A Journey through America and Baseball's Minor Leagues,* all published by Random House.

It's hard to imagine Willie and Joe being old. But if they were alive today—and mind you, Bill Mauldin has never announced their deaths even though he hasn't drawn them in years—they would be pushing seventy, like Mauldin himself, and I suspect they wouldn't have led very eventful lives since coming home from Europe at the end of World War II.

The Willie and Joe I remember—bearded, sunken-eyed, unsmiling, and somehow both heroic and tragic—looked older and sadder than the GIs I encountered in Vietnam in the late 1960s, and in fact the GIs in both Korea and Vietnam were much younger on the average. Perhaps that's why Mauldin had the good sense not to bring America's two most famous privates back into the army in those wars. By leaving Willie and Joe undisturbed, he succeeded in making them ageless.

"You know, I had planned to kill Willie and Joe on the last day of the war," Mauldin recalled when I visited him at his home in Santa Fe, New

Mexico. "That's the one thing every soldier dreads, getting killed on the last day. I wasn't sure how I was going to do it. Most likely I would have had a shell land in their foxhole or had them cut down by a machine gun. I wouldn't have drawn their corpses. I'd just have shown their gear with their names on it, or something like that."

Mauldin figured he had better warn Bob Neville, the *Stars and Stripes* editor, of their impending death. Neville had never rejected one of Mauldin's drawings, but this time he said, "Don't do it. We won't print it." Neville may have been the only person—editor or general—who ever got Mauldin to back down. "In the end I guess it worked out about right," he said, "but there are still times I wish I had done it. It would have been a very dramatic thing."

When the war was over, Mauldin brought Willie and Joe home with him. He gave them a shave, put them in civvies, and found them jobs in a gas station. "That lasted three or four weeks," he recalls. "Then I said, 'Screw it.'" Mauldin didn't feel comfortable drawing them without beards. He didn't even know who they really were anymore. And much to the horror of his syndicate, Willie (who had appeared on the cover of *Time* magazine in June 1945) and Joe vanished into obscurity. Except for appearing at the funerals of General George Marshall in 1959 and General Omar Bradley in 1981, the two dogfaces who had made Mauldin rich and famous before his twenty-third birthday haven't been seen since in a Mauldin cartoon.

To find Bill Mauldin today, you drive out of Santa Fe a few miles on the Old Santa Fe Trail, head up the hill by the Anthropological Museum, and turn right on the first dirt road. It is 10 A.M., and Mauldin, shoeless and laughing, is out back, trying to prove to his newest batch of kids—Kaja and Sam—that he can get airborne on a Pogo Ball—a jumping ball with a ring. "If you break it, Dad, you owe me twenty bucks," Kaja says. Mauldin has raised eight children in three marriages, and Kaja refers to herself, with proud glee, as "Kid Number One, Litter Three."

Every nook of Mauldin's ranch home bears his stamp. The dining room is lined with books on World War II. The sewing room has been turned into a studio, where he still draws three political cartoons a week that are syndicated by King Features. The garage has been turned into a machine shop, and a spare bedroom is now a darkroom. A master tinkerer, he has put in new bellows and fixed the gears on his old eight-by-ten-inch Saltzman enlarger—"Crank it and see how smooth it turns," he challenges—and soon plans to take a look at the kitchen door that presently swings shut with the help of a weighted Clorox container on a piece of rope. The walls of the breakfast alcove display many framed drawings, among them the only Willie and Joe original Mauldin has left and a Rube Goldberg strip, dated 1942 and signed, "To Bill Mauldin. Good luck in the Service."

Out in the backyard are a snow-blower, a lawn mower older than his wife, a mobile home rigged into a darkroom for desert trips, a worn Chevy pickup, and a 1946 Willys jeep that Mauldin bought new in a Manhattan showroom for $1,180. Except for the spark plugs and points, every part is original, and as he clambers into the jeep's front seat and turns the key, a bottle of beer balanced beside him, I see in my mind's eye, like a black-and-white photograph, the young Bill Mauldin of three wars past (or four). In this photo he wears an impish grin and his eyes speak of mischief. He looks no older than a teenager. His left hand—his drawing hand—holds a cigarette and his right arm is draped over the steering wheel of a muddy jeep named for his then wife, "Jeanie." He is on the Anzio beachhead bound for Cassino. It is the winter of 1943-44.

Willie and Joe took on their final identities in the Italian campaign. Mauldin gave them beards, put bullet holes in their helmets, and began working with a brush instead of a pen, producing stark, bold lines that captured the grimness of the mountain war and the fatalistic exhaustion of the men who fought it. Willie and Joe weren't gung-ho heroes and weren't really very funny. They were simply two undistinguished GIs, inseparable only because of their shared experience, who told us what it was like to live in foxholes, get hassled by officers and MPs in the rear, and fight for survival, not ideology. They were smelly and bored and they wanted to go home.

"War humor is very bitter, very sardonic," Mauldin says. "It's not ha-ha humor. I asked Tad Foster, a cartoonist I admired a lot from the Vietnam War, if people came up to him and said, 'I loved your stuff from the war—it kept me laughing all the time.' Foster said, 'Yup, the sons of bitches.' I feel the same way. When someone says Willie and Joe made them laugh, I get pissed off every time. I tell them, 'You're not supposed to laugh.' Maybe you grin or nod, but it's not ha-ha humor.

"My shtick was this. I never drew dead soldiers, but I always implied that they were lying just off stage. You felt their presence. Another thing, I didn't treat the Germans as monsters. I drew the German soldier as a poor unfortunate who didn't want to be there, which could be said of our boys, too.

"Psychological warfare didn't interest me. I don't ever remember hearing a soldier in Europe or anyplace like Sicily refer to the Germans as Nazis or fascists or anything like that. They were krauts. It was the same in Korea and Vietnam. They weren't commie rats or any of that shit. They were gooks. They were slopes. But they weren't mentioned in political terms."

We had moved inside and were sitting on the sofa in his living room. I had brought along a copy of his book *Bill Mauldin's Army*—which has sold 20,000 copies since being reissued in 1983 by Presidio Press—and he was thumbing through the pages, critiquing himself. "This is Anzio. It's a great drawing. I wish I knew where the original was. . . . I did this one the day I got hit. . . . Here's Willie. I think it's the first time I drew him with a beard." Willie and Joe are climbing a cliff, holding on for dear life, and the sergeant yells, "Hit th' dirt, boys!"

"The main thing about Willie and Joe was that I always felt they were like two cops operating together as partners," Mauldin points out. "They don't particularly like each other. They aren't cut from the same cloth. They don't have the same friends. But they're damned good at what they do together, and each is the other guy's life-insurance policy. They're not devoted to each other, but they need each other. And that makes for a damned good relationship."

Mauldin was on the fast track by the time Willie and Joe were climbing those Cassino hills together. He had once written: "My drawing had become my Rock of Gibraltar. With it, I was still convinced the world might be mine. Without it, I felt like an insignificant jerk." Now the war was bringing that world within his reach. He was talented, dedicated, ambitious, and his earthy depiction of the war was earning him wide recognition—even from General George Patton, who threatened to "throw his ass in jail" if Mauldin showed up in the Third Army area.

Just before Christmas in 1943, in the high mountains above Venafro, Mauldin was wounded by a German mortar while visiting the 179th Regiment of the 45th Division. It was a minor injury, to the shoulder, but it changed both him and his drawings. On the way back to Naples one of the airmen, who had a stack of green leatherette boxes, handed Mauldin a Purple Heart. He accepted it, but with considerable guilt, even anger, knowing that most of his friends in the unit he had shipped over with—K Company of the 45th Division's 180th Infantry—were already dead. The next day Mauldin drew Willie at an aid station telling a medic, "Just gimme an aspirin. I already got a Purple Heart."

"I was hit very lightly, but it was a shock," Mauldin says. "It's always a shock to anyone who gets hit. It's like kids with automobiles: It can't happen to you. But something *did* happen to me. It was something about these guys I knew really getting killed, me really getting hit, and suddenly the war became very real to me.

"So I would say that it was in the fall of 'forty-three that I really sobered up and started realizing there were some things bigger than me and my ambition. Suddenly the drawings grew up, too. Southern Italy became sort of a Valley Forge scene for me. I was privileged to watch it as a guy who could visit a foxhole and not have to stay. I could watch a patrol take off and not have to go with it. And this fills you with—maybe not guilt but a great sense of respect for these guys and what they were going through.

"I remember Humphrey Bogart came over on a USO tour about that time and laid the biggest egg I'd ever seen. He came out on the stage of the San Carlo Opera House [in Naples] and there was this whole goddamned crowd of guys who'd come down off the mountain for four days' R-and-R. I think he was a little bit in the bag, and he got up on the stage and said something dumb like, 'I'm going back to the States to put my mob back together. Any of you guys want to go with me?'

"He was greeted with stony silence. He went on with his tough-guy act and they gave him a nice hand, but they just didn't think he was very funny. Because not one of those guys had a prayer of going home. They knew they were going to stay right there on that mountain until they died. It was a pretty gruesome proposition, and here's Bogart out there trying to make jokes. I got to know him later and he was really a good guy—I liked him. You know, years afterward he told me, 'I'll never forget all those eyes looking at me. I really put my foot in it.' "

Although Mauldin and his colleagues at *Stars and Stripes* were in the army, they lived a privileged existence: They moved with the freedom of civilian correspondents, and their newspaper enjoyed a remarkable degree of editorial independence. Mauldin, a nocturnal worker by choice and habit, lived and worked in a third-floor room overlooking the Galleria shopping arcade in Naples. His room had a chair, a large table against which he leaned his drawing board, and a canvas cot.

The title of his cartoon was "Up Front . . . with Mauldin," a name he was never quite comfortable with because it implied that he was always on the fighting lines, which he wasn't. "Anyone who can draw in a foxhole has my hat off," he told *Time* magazine in 1945. Just after he was hit by the mortar fragment, *Stars and Stripes* received a letter from a soldier in the headquarters of the 179th Infantry. Mauldin still remembers his name—Blankenship. What did Mauldin know about being "up front" anyway? the soldier asked. The editors printed the letter and added a note saying Mauldin had recently received a Purple Heart for a wound received while visiting I Company of the soldier's own regiment. Mauldin's wound was among the first the *Stripes* staff suffered, and it did the paper's image no harm.

"I have very strong ethics about taking things or getting things you don't deserve," Mauldin says. "It's one of the things my parents did for me. I was pissed off when the medic gave me the Purple Heart. My bandage wasn't much bigger than a Band-Aid. But getting hit was probably the most fortuitous thing that could have happened to me. It established me as a guy who went out and got his material the hard way."

Ernie Pyle (later killed in the war) caught up with Mauldin and wrote a column mentioning Blankenship's letter and stating, "Sergeant Bill Mauldin seemed to us . . . the finest cartoonist the war had produced. And that's not merely because his cartoons are funny, but because they are also terribly grim and real. Mauldin's cartoons . . . are about the men in the line—the tiny percentage of our vast army who are actually up there doing the dying. His cartoons are about the war."

It was the exposure from Pyle—not the Pulitzer Prize or his highly publicized confrontation with Patton—that really put him in business, Mauldin says. Soon, syndicates were after him, and in a few months he signed with Pyle's syndicate, United Feature. *Stars and Stripes* printed Mauldin's cartoons first but let him own the copyright. His monthly wages as a sergeant were $66; his weekly income as a syndicated cartoonist, about $250.

"All of a sudden Bill was a blazing success," recalls Jack Foisie, a *Stripes* writer who went on to a distinguished career as a foreign correspondent for the *Los Angeles Times*. "I mean, he was making all this money. But he never lorded it over us. He was droll in his success. Most of us, if not in awe of him, were jealous of his success, in a good-natured way. But he was always popular, sort of one of the boys."

Mauldin's growing fame increasingly enabled him to throw barbs at the top brass and the military police. Patton wondered aloud if Mauldin wasn't an unpatriotic anarchist. In one of Mauldin's most famous drawings, two officers are admiring the Italian mountains, and one says, "Beautiful view! Is there one for the enlisted men?" Another drawing shows an officer in a freshly pressed uniform writing up the slovenly looking Willie and Joe. Willie tells him, "Them buttons was shot off when we took this town, sir."

That one still makes Mauldin grin. "No matter what Patton thought, I never disliked officers. If I'd had my druthers, I'd probably have been a smart-ass little lieutenant. I'd have gone to OSC or something, because I liked the army. I never objected to the concept of discipline, but if you're a leader, you don't push wet spaghetti, you pull it. The U.S. Army still has to learn that. The British understand it. Patton understood it. I always admired Patton.

"Oh, sure, the stupid bastard was crazy. He was insane. He thought he was living in the Dark Ages. Soldiers were peasants to him. I didn't like that attitude, but I certainly respected his theories and the techniques he used to get his men out of their foxholes. You wait around in a foxhole and you're going to get killed. We had a lot of good officers who understood that, who knew how to lead in combat. They didn't say, 'Go here, go there.' They said, 'Come here.' "

While Mauldin's dogfaces were scruffy and disheveled, Patton's clean-shaven troops wore neckties and polished boots (at least Patton tried to keep them that way). Why, Patton asked the Supreme Command, should *Stars and Stripes* make heroes of Willie and Joe? At the "suggestion" of his superiors, Mauldin headed up to the Third Army headquarters in Luxembourg one day early in 1945 to discuss the matter with the general who wore ivory-handled pistols. Patton threw down a drawing of Willie and Joe tossing tomatoes at their officers during a liberation parade. What was Mauldin trying to do, incite a goddamn mutiny? Patton's dog, a bull terrier named Willie, glowered at the young sergeant as the general ranted on.

"The whole thing was just so funny, really hilarious," Mauldin recalls. "The only guy who failed to see the humor was Patton. I didn't even try to give him any lip. I knew it was going to be an embarrassment for him. I think he died without any idea that he'd lost that little battle."

The meeting lasted forty-five minutes, of which Mauldin had been given a minute or so to lay out his artistic response. "All right, Sergeant," Patton said, cutting him short, "I guess we understand each other now."

Six months later, the man who made the cover of *Time* magazine was Mauldin's Willie, not Patton, and a reporter asked the general what he thought of Mauldin's cartoons. "I've only seen two of them and I thought they were lousy," he said.

Few Americans agreed. By the time Mauldin came home in the summer of 1945—with a Purple Heart, a Pulitzer Prize, and a Legion of Merit—his drawings were appearing in hundreds of papers and his Willie-and-Joe book Up Front was a best-seller. "I haven't tried to picture this war in a big, broad-minded way," he wrote in the text. "I'm not old enough to understand what it's all about." He was twenty-three. *Up Front* sold 3 million copies and was number one on the *New York Times* best-seller list for eighteen months.

"You know, Willie and Joe weren't really based on anyone," Mauldin says. "They just evolved as prototypes. But once, about fifteen years after the war, a shrink came up to me at a party in Rockland County, where I was living in New York. He was sort of practicing without permission and he said, 'Do you know who Willie and Joe were?'

"I said, 'Who?' He said, 'Have you looked recently at a picture of your father?' And, my God, he was right. Willie was a caricature of my father, and Joe was a caricature of me—the round-faced, jug-eared kid. I had never thought of it. I'm not sure I appreciate the guy pointing it out to me, but who knows what family things I worked out through those cartoons?"

Mauldin had grown up poor in the hills of southern New Mexico. His father had been an artilleryman in France during World War I, and his grandfather had served as a civilian cavalry scout during the Apache Wars, so Mauldin was raised on war stories, many of them embellished over the years. He joined ROTC in high school and, as a ninety-seven-pound weakling, marched with a 1903 Springfield rifle, unloaded. "I took to ROTC like a duck to water," he once recalled. He also was a natural artist and a feisty needler who knew early on that he wanted to be a political cartoonist. "I was a born troublemaker and might as well earn a living at it," he wrote in his informal 1971 autobiography, *The Brass Ring*.

But after the war and the disappearance of Willie and Joe, Mauldin's career stalled. His drawings became erratic and bellicose. He took on the Ku Klux Klan, the House Committee on Un-American Activities, and conservative veterans' organizations. (In 1971 he suggested publicly that militant veterans' organizations be drafted to finish the Vietnam War.) His syndicate started censoring him, and newspapers started dropping his cartoon.

"Military service is one of those things you do as a duty," Mauldin says. "If you get wounded, crippled, or lose your life, the government owes it to your family to take care of you, but otherwise I don't think anyone's entitled to a goddamn thing. Some guy counts socks for three months at a quartermaster depot and then he's looking for a ride on the gravy train for the rest of his life. He's nothing but a professional sponger. At one point I joined the American Veterans Committee, which was considered very leftish. It no longer exists, but I liked its motto: Citizens first, veterans second."

Mauldin's old buddy Jack Foisie remembers seeing Mauldin at a *Stars and Stripes* reunion in New York in 1947. "There seemed to be some deflation for Bill," Foisie recalls. "He was very high during the war, and now he had other factors to face besides generals. He had a lot of irons in the fire, but Bill looked a little frustrated."

Foisie was right, and at the age of twenty-seven Mauldin retired to pursue other interests. He learned to fly a plane, went hunting, free-lanced for *Life* magazine, and published four more books. He also went out to California and acted in a couple of Hollywood movies, including *The Red Badge of Courage* with war hero Audie Murphy, and then moved back to New York, where in 1956 he became the Democratic candidate for Congress from the Twenty-eighth District. He was trounced by the incumbent—"a rather formidable broad"—in a campaign that personally cost him $50,000. His decade of drifting left him broke, but not washed up. He loved riding the career roller coaster.

He jumped at the chance to join the *St. Louis Post-Dispatch* in 1958, won another Pulitzer, and was the subject of a second *Time* magazine cover piece. He briefly covered the Korean War (as a writer, not an artist) for *Collier's;* spent a few weeks in Vietnam (where a communist mortar attack on his son's base in the Highlands made him a hawk for a few months) and reported on the Six Day Arab-Israeli War for the *Chicago Sun-Times.* But none of these wars was his war as World War II had been, and in 1973 he wrote an article for the *New Republic* entitled "Ain't Gonna' Cover Wars No More." He had lost his emotional perspective and objectivity. "One of the startling things you learn in wars," he wrote, "is how much blood can come from a human body."

So Bill Mauldin came home, home to his roots in the peaceful silence of New Mexico. It is night now and we are mixing martinis in the kitchen. His wife, Chris, twenty-seven years his junior, has sent out for Mexican food. Mauldin seems a contented man in a young family full of love. He passes a bottle of vermouth over the chilling gin and marvels at his creation. He is, he says, "playing out the string" on his career, and that doesn't bother him a bit. The number of papers taking his cartoon has fallen to about seventy-five, and he has not tried to renew his expired contract with the *Chicago Sun-Times.* The arthritis in his hands is troublesome, so he no longer answers his fan letters. In growing old he has found that he is no longer in a hurry.

"I never felt I was all that talented or all that good at what I did," he says, "but I exploited whatever talent I had and gave it a good ride. That's the important thing. I think that's probably the reason I'm getting mellower. I don't have that desperate feeling of *What the hell have I been doing all my life? How can I make up for all this time I've been wasting?* I don't have any of that anymore."

He tells me about returning to the Anzio mountains in 1967. He set up his camera on a tripod in Cassino, on the very spot where the German artillery had been, and his lens swept over the distant American positions where Willie and Joe and thousands of other GIs fought their toughest battles. "What a position the Germans had!" he recalls. "Standing up there at the abbey, you could see why nobody in history ever took Rome from the south."

He also tells me about his return to Rome in 1984, at the invitation of the American ambassador to Italy, for the fortieth anniversary of Rome's fall to the Allies. He flew from Andrews Air Force Base outside Washington as a guest of the Pentagon in a "brass-hat" special—a red-white-and-blue Boeing 707 emblazoned with the words *United States of America* on the fuselage. The plane carried only four passengers, one of whom was the chairman of the Joint Chiefs of Staff, Jack Vessey.

Flying through the darkness high above the Atlantic, meal finished and drink in hand, Bill Mauldin settled back in his upholstered seat and said to himself on that night of memories, "Soldier, you sure have come a long way."

A Lousy Story

by VLADIMIR LEMPORT

Translated from the Russian by Richard Pevear *and* Larissa Volokhonsky

In this time of political chaos, the memory of the Great Patriotic War against the Nazis still unites the new states that were once the Soviet Union. Yet, except for a handful of semiofficial "memoirs" by the leading military actors, elaborate scenery-moving for the most part, precious little from the Soviet side has reached the West. And we have heard even less from the common soldier—the "cucumbers," as the Soviet GIs called themselves, after their green uniforms. The following is a former second lieutenant's account of life (and needless death) on the Don and Stalingrad fronts in the summer and fall of 1942. What Vladimir Sergeyevich Lemport describes as his "notes" are by any measure remarkable, but all the more so for their scathing view of the murderously detached way in which Stalin conducted the war. (Lemport's original title was "The Invisible Enemy"—and he was not just referring to the Germans or his tiny parasitic tormentors.)

    The author was born in 1922, commanded an artillery unit, and was much decorated. He is today a sculptor living in Moscow. Lemport's memoir was written in the early 1980s but did not come out until the end of the decade, in the prominent Russian-language emigré journal *Konti-nent.* Its translators, Richard Pevear and Larissa Volokhonsky, live near Paris; their new translation of Fyodor Dostoyevsky's *Brothers Karamazov* has been published by North Point Press and Vintage.

War is a great mess. Try sorting it out when you're lying there pressing yourself as close to the ground as you can. If you're on the front line, that is exactly what you do. And when you get up and go into an attack, there is one thought in your head: "Will the cursed one blow by me or not?" To distinguish yourself, to perform some great deed, is no more possible in war than it is in peacetime in a factory. The director has the plan and the vision of the final product in his head, and you are screwing in bolts on the assembly line. Of course, you can become a Hero of Socialist Labor and get a gold star pinned to your chest, but for that you have to be recommended by the board, the union, and the party organization.

It's the same at the front. Screw in your bolts and don't poke your nose into someone else's business. Wait till you're recommended. The regimental commander has maps and orders from above, and you have nothing but a rifle and an entrenching tool. Somewhere up above, a general looks at a map and it seems reasonable to him to change the front line. He sends down an order: "At such-and-such point, move five kilometers forward!" As luck would have it, there turns out to be a river just at that point, the White Sturgeon, deep and swift, in open terrain. It would be convenient and relatively safe to sit in trenches behind this natural obstacle. But an order is an order, and you can't say "It's impossible to cross here!" Though from any normal man's point of view it is indeed impossible to cross, because there are no boats, no planks, no trees, and the soldiers all come from the steppes, and not only can't swim but have never even seen a river.

And so it starts:

"Comrade Lieutenant, sir, I can't go in the water: I don't know how to swim!"

But you won't be moved to pity. It's better to drown a soldier than to show irresoluteness or insubordination. All the more so since you've already reported to the battalion commander that there are no boats. You pull out your service revolver, cock it, and yell, "Get into the river at once, you sonofabitch! I'll count to three! Or else you'll never go anywhere!'

The soldier goes into the water, the current seizes him, he drowns—as do all the rest that are forced in. You report to the battalion commander: "Comrade Major, there are only five men left in my company!"

The major is furious. "What did you do to them? I didn't hear a single shot!"

"They all drowned crossing the river, Comrade Major."

"What do you mean, drowned? I'll shoot you right there, like a dog!"

"As you will, Comrade Major. But I did report to you that there were no planks or logs to be found in this area, and the river is deep and swift, it can't be forded. You told me to stop arguing and obey orders."

"You blockhead! What a stupid way to destroy a whole company!"

The major also feels at fault and calls the colonel, his regimental commander.

"I gave you five hours to cross the river!" the latter shouts without listening to the major. "Have you carried out the order?"

No, Comrade Colonel, we've sustained heavy losses!"

"Losses? That's fine! If there weren't any losses, our heads would roll!

What happened? Everything's quiet, not a single shot—did they all get knifed, or what?"

"No, drowned. The company that was to cross over was all slant-eyes, never saw a river before—naturally they drowned, since there was nothing to float on."

"You sonofabitch! Why didn't you take some pontoons? We've been dragging a whole transport of pontoons around. I can give you as many as you want."

"I no longer need them, Comrade Colonel: There are five cucumbers left in the first company, ten in the second, maybe twenty in the third. There's no one to cross."

"You'll have to cross anyway," the colonel says after some pondering. "What counts is the fact that the order has been carried out, even if only one man makes it!"

"All right, send us the pontoons. We'll build a bridge!"

In an hour four American Lend-Lease Studebakers drive up loaded with pontoons. These are quickly unloaded and thrown into the water. Field engineers begin trying to align them. Pale flares whiz up and hang over the river. The Germans open fire with all the artillery at their disposal.

"How's the crossing going?" the colonel asks over the phone. "Are they pounding away?"

"Nonstop! The engineers are all drowned already, and there's no bridge yet," says the major.

At this point the general, the division commander, calls the colonel. "What's with the crossing?"

"Bad! I have almost no cucumbers left, Comrade General! They fell heroically fording the White Sturgeon River!"

"To hell with them, they'll send us more. Get a group of at least five men across and let them hold on until headquarters is convinced that the crossing has been made."

Just as in peacetime, the main thing is to report.

A group of men gets to the other side, holds on for two hours, and perishes without yielding an inch. Headquarters reports to the Center [Stalin, in effect] that the crossing of the White Sturgeon River has been accomplished. The general, the division commander, is awarded the "Banner"; the major gets the "Little Star."

These days we often see brave boys on our movie screens—Red Army soldiers, well fed, dressed in trim uniforms, with decent haircuts—and the audience thinks: "Generally speaking, it wasn't so bad in the war." People compare them with soldiers now and don't see much difference. Of course, there was that kind. There were all kinds. In the rear, in headquarters, in supply. But they weren't the ones who created the atmosphere of the war. The general frontline masses were deprived of everything: food, drink, sleep, soap, baths, respite, and illusions about surviving. No makeup, no artistic metamorphosis is capable of reproducing the emaciation that distinguished the populace of the front lines. Totally faded uniform blouses, shrunk and torn (from crawling over thistles), with white salty patches on their backs from continual sweating, so stiff they would stand up by themselves when taken off. Hair hacked short with whatever instruments were lying around— tufts, bald spots, scabs from constant scratching. Unwashed black faces, bleached eyebrows and lashes, colorless empty eyes.

The front was picturesque and inimitable. No one wants to remember the petty discomforts so tormenting for frontliners. Foot sores, calluses, toes rotting from fungus that nothing can get rid of. Those black, ten-foot-long leg wrappings instead of boots—humiliating, uncomfortable things! And that rather shameful but universal calamity—a sore crotch from ceaseless sweating and the lack of newspaper or any other means of cleaning oneself after fulfilling one's natural, everyday needs. Sweaty armpits, neck chafed by the regulation celluloid collar.

It was just such spots that the lice chose to attack! Oh, those lice! A man infested with them felt constantly worried and anxious. To my great regret, despite my officer's rank, I did not escape this misfortune. They say that in the First World War officers did not have lice, because they wore silk underwear—nothing to hold on to.

I began feeling somewhat out of sorts. But that did not trouble me too much. July 1942: We had retreated. The Don River. Sun. Naturally, a man wearing flannel underwear under his field shirt and breeches sweats more than the average civilian; besides, since he does not undress before going to bed as other people do, he has no idea what's happening inside. Once, however, I scratched behind my collar and caught something that felt like a barberry. Coming out of the shelter, I looked this object over and became convinced that, huge as it was, it was nonetheless a louse. A dirty louse! Then it became clear to me why all the soldiers were swearing the way they were!

Our trench was a long one, but I still did not dare conduct an examination for lousiness right there. I went behind some blackberry bushes, though it wasn't very safe: The place was in view of the Germans and they had it well covered. Taking off my field shirt, I ascertained that my flannel underwear, which had not been washed since May, was thoroughly infested. That was the source of my constant, strange anxiety! And I thought I was worrying over the fate of my fatherland! Not without difficulty, I separated the underwear from my shirt and breeches, squeamishly rolled it into a ball, and hid it in the bushes. When my friend Lev Khokhlov, also a second lieutenant, saw it he said, "You shouldn't have done that. With luck you can always change to clean underwear, but if the lice transfer to your shirt and breeches, there'll be no way to exterminate them. On whipcord they become invisible to the enemy, like us in our trenches!"

Maybe he was right, but just then, on that hot July day, I felt enormous relief and happiness.

"I know what," said Lev. "Let's make ourselves a little louse-popper!"

We collected some empty howitzer shells—big ten-liter brass cylinders—stuck them into the breastwork of our trench, parallel to the ground, and made a fire under them. There were plenty of dry branches in the woods. This was somewhat counter to the requirements of camouflage, but the sun was bright, the fire couldn't be seen, and the wind was blowing in our direction. The brass cylinders became almost red-hot. We undressed, put our clothes over them, and heard a low crackling sound as the lice started popping on the hot shells.

"Well," said Lev, "that's the end of them. Now it's our turn."

He took a tarpaulin and covered the trench with it. The fire had already gone out. We got under the tarp and started sweating violently in our homemade sauna—it was roasting hot. We had also stolen a pot of water from the cook. This was great because we lived without water, though near it. To get water from the river was extremely difficult: The Germans had excellent observation instruments and good snipers who would pick off anyone who dared even in the dark. They were afraid we'd cross the river; besides, they realized what the impossibility of drawing even a bucketful of water meant for us. They themselves sent women to get water from a village they had captured on the other side of the river.

Water was brought to us in cisterns from a long way off and delivered to regimental headquarters. The company cook fetched our portion in an iron barrel on a cart. The cook fed us dinner, gave us tea, but it was impossible to extort even a drop of water from him. He used to give a pot to our captain to wash and shave. We always shaved with dry razors. I didn't mind, but the dark-haired Khokhlov howled with pain during the procedure.

"We've got to call Larissa Ivanovna," he suggested now.

"You think she'll agree?" I wondered. "She's a proud lady."

"Of course she will," said Lev. "Lice bite her as much as us."

We got dressed and went through the connecting trench to the dugout where Lev and I and Larissa Ivanovna lived. We had a bed with a spring mattress for the three of us. Lev was a good homemaker; with my help he had brought this bed from across the river in a boat, before the Germans arrived. A village schoolteacher used to sleep on it; now the three of us took turns, trying to find about three hours in a day. At that moment, Larissa Ivanovna, a senior medical assistant, was exercising her right to rest. There was a mingled smell of earth, dry grass, Larissa's medications, long-unwashed underwear, and woman. Larissa Ivanovna raised her head from the rolled-up trench coat that served as her pillow. "Have they sent for me?" she asked.

"No, we have a proposal to make you," said Lev.

"Depends on what. . . ."

"We propose some disinfestation. . . ."

"I haven't got any bugs!" she snapped.

"That's strange," I said. "Lev and I have millions of them, we all sleep in the same bed, and yet they avoid you! Aren't your feelings hurt? Maybe they're misogynists?"

"Maybe it's because I'm clean," she said.

"Interesting!" said Lev. "I suppose you've got a portable shower in your doctor's bag, or you take baths somewhere in the bushes? Larissa Ivanovna!

We're not concerned with you so much as with our own safety. We've just gotten rid of them. We beg you to do the same."

Larissa's beautiful face . . . However, to talk about the beauty of a frontline woman is like discussing the same quality in some soot-covered village icon. Black skin, white wrinkles, dry and peeling. And so Larissa's dark face with its white wrinkles expressed a lively interest. "But how did you do it?"

"We set up a real Finnish sauna. Besides, I filched a pot of water from the cook while he was seeing the captain," Lev laughed. "Hurry up, the Germans will start shelling in half an hour, and they've got a bead on that place. Put your clothes over the shells, and yourself under the tarp; do the most necessary washing-up with the pot of water—it's warm—and we'll stand guard on both sides so that some loafer doesn't bump into you. . . ."

Apparently lice were bothering Larissa Ivanovna, too, because the tall, thin blonde ran straight where she was told with all the gracefulness of a giraffe. We instructed the senior medical assistant in the use of the Finnish sauna, and stood guard as befitted true knights.

Either the Germans started their shelling earlier that morning or our watch was slow—we had one for the three of us. In any case, before our medical assistant had spent even fifteen minutes in the sauna, a many-voiced howling, from treble to bass, was heard—snakes and dragons of various caliber flew over our heads. They exploded with a clanging and grinding roar; shrapnel shrieked and whined. The second round already fell quite near our guard-post.

Larissa Ivanovna, naked, her clothes in her arms, rushed out. "Don't look at me, you rogues!" she shouted. "Turn away at once!"

"So you're not a mulatto, you're a white girl! But we're not looking," Lev said with perfect coolness.

The shelling went on for about an hour. The ground was covered with cut branches—the work of the shrapnel. The banks of the Don were lined with century-old lindens, oaks, and maples.

When the shooting stopped, we went to look at our "bathhouse." It was covered with dirt and green leaves, and there was a big shell hole next to it.

Lev bent down, poked in the loose dirt, and pulled out his tarp, which had several holes in it. "Well, well . . . ," he said pensively, "we really could have lost our medical staff."

"It's worth risking your life to do what we did," I replied.

"We've been here a month, and it looks like this was our first military operation," said Lev. "How many of the enemy did we destroy, in your estimation?"

"Must be a whole regiment," I guessed. "About five hundred for each of us, times three, that's about a whole wartime regiment."

"Do you remember where you threw your underwear? Go get it and give it a scorching! You won't get any new! It'll be cold in a month. I went through a winter in this war, I know how cold it gets even in the fall."

I ran to the blackberry bushes where I'd left my underwear, but unfortunately there was nothing there.

We were transferred to the Stalingrad front and arrived to join our regiment at 3 A.M., exactly one hour before the guns of the 1st Guard Army were to fire their opening salvo.

Dawn revealed all the inconvenience of our position. Even the Sahara would have been more suitable for military action than that naked steppe sloping in the direction of the Germans. We were in full view of them, which allowed them to conduct precision shelling while they themselves stayed hidden in a deep ravine, aided by skillful camouflage and our own muddleheadedness. We had no modern viewing devices, just some antediluvian spyglasses and ten-power Zeiss binoculars. The Germans had everything except astronomical telescopes, owing to which they knew us all by face. We were too far advanced into their defensive line and almost completely surrounded. They would open fire at us first from in front, a bit later from the left, then from the right.

At headquarters our position was understood differently: It was a mighty breakthrough from the northwest to link up with Stalingrad. And a similar breakthrough from the south.

Strategically, it was all brilliantly conceived, with unheard-of quantities of artillery; but the cost in human resources was too great. And they weren't spared, they were thrown at the enemy with purely Russian generosity. Here surely lies the secret of our victory!

It was impossible to advance in the face of such ceaseless defensive fire. But we advanced. By whole divisions. It could have been done at night, but the order was to advance by day, and so all those divisions were destroyed and new ones followed in their tracks.

Just then an order came through that horrified even the Stalingrad front, which could no longer be surprised by anything.

An order for the liquidation of lousiness.

A wonderful notion had occurred to the chief surgeon of the Red Army—that cleanliness would ease the life of the soldier masses. Since Stalin liked the idea, he issued an order: "Liquidate this disgustingness at once!"

What do I know personally about this order? On September 20, 1942, during the most intense fighting, the commander of our regiment, Colonel Bogdanov, summoned all officers to his headquarters. Under the circumstances, such a gathering was a great luxury: Nonstop artillery fire made any movement difficult. The field was completely bare. As a result a few officers were wounded and one was even killed. His family was informed that he had died heroically.

The colonel looked puzzled. "Comrade officers," he said, "I have received an order marked 'strictly confidential.' That is why I have summoned you all here. Listen: 'In view of the lousiness that has appeared in some units, and the threat of an epidemic posed by cases of typhus, I order all units of the Soviet Army to carry out an immediate disinfestation and take baths. Those guilty of shirking will be punished according to the laws of wartime.' "

The officers were silent.

Finally the commander of the 1st Battalion, Captain Pughin, asked, "How can we do it when we haven't been issued a piece of soap for three months and there is no water for washing, shaving, or drinking?"

"Ask me something simpler," the colonel replied. "I, too, have not been issued any soap, nor the beer that's due the commander of a regiment, but I don't want to go before the tribunal for that! The order says to use the village of Kotluban as a bathhouse. Light the stoves, get them properly heated, and let the men roast their clothes and have a good sweating. Everyone must go through the village; you will report on it afterward."

"Alexander Ignatievich," said Odyn, a broad-nosed Latvian with puffy eyes, "being the oldest man here, I will allow myself to draw your attention to one unpleasant circumstance: The village of Kotluban is an orientation point; we will be an easy target for the Germans. As soon as a significant number of men enter it, we'll be swatted like flies. Am I right or not?"

Colonel Bogdanov, a man with a hard cossack face, listened attentively and said, "You're right, Captain Odyn, that's how it will be. But don't think I'm any stupider than you are! So that you will not think so, I will read you another order from the people's commissar of defense [Stalin]. Listen:

" 'At especially dangerous and strategic locations on the front, in order to avoid discussion of orders from Central Headquarters, disorganization, provocation, cowardliness, profiteering, the sowing of panic, I prescribe the following: The commanders of all frontline units, divisions, separate regiments, battalions, and companies are personally to shoot all persons caught in the aforementioned crimes. This has enormous propaganda significance. I further order that a series of show executions be carried out in all units. Strictly confidential. September 20, 1942.'

"As you see, this is quite a fresh order. You don't think it makes sense to start such a series with me, do you? If Zhukov or Koniev descends on us, they'll ask about the Kotluban operation. What shall I tell them? That I regard it as unnecessary, or dangerous? I'm afraid they'll start the series of show executions with me. Or perhaps, with all due respect, Odyn, we ought to start with you?"

Odyn, though he bent his head in displeasure, raised his hands in a sign of surrender.

Captain Voron, commander of the fourth battery, middle-aged and bald, asked for the floor. "Comrade Colonel of the Guard, our batteries have barely been remanned, after we were surrounded. The loss of even one gunner will harm our combat efficiency. Perhaps we can conduct the battle against lousiness on the spot. There are plenty of shells around. Let's heat them up and roast the lice in the trenches, and then write our official report!"

"And what will your battery stoolies say?" the colonel coldly objected. "And what will the special department say? And can you imagine how the army observers will yell if they're deprived of such a show?"

The assembled officers, to a man, all stared at the ground.

"No one is interested," said Bogdanov, "in whether you have lice or not; what matters is that everyone strictly carry out the order of the people's commissar of defense."

Essentially, it was clear to us all that there was no way to avoid carrying out this order, absurd under the circumstances, and we were already counting the losses in our minds.

"You, for example!" the colonel said, pointing at me. "What's your name?"

"Second Lieutenant Lemport, sir."

"With your unit—which, by the way, I have never seen—you will heat up cottages ten and twelve on Uritzky Street, twenty-five and thirty on Karl Marx Street, and one, two, and three on Krupskaya Street; the rest will be done by other units. Is that clear?"

"Yes, Comrade Colonel of the Guard!"

"Carry out the order. Comrade officers, wait another half hour until the end of the heavy shelling, then return to your units."

The village of Kotluban consisted of black, almost windowless buildings made of rough-hewn boards. Not a tree, not a bush. One well for the whole village. No supplies of firewood to be found in any of the cottages—apparently they used dung or straw for heat. And so we artillerymen started breaking up furniture, porches, barns, and stuffing the big Russian stoves with wood. We took precautions so as not to give ourselves away, and the Germans were quiet, too—apparently having understood our intentions. They dealt out the usual round of shells from time to time. Along with the stokers from other units, we emptied the well and a small pond, filled all available pails, pots, and pans with water, and set them on the stoves.

By 6 P.M. we had finished the heating-up, roasted our clothes, and even washed ourselves. I reported to the colonel.

"Send the First and Second battalions to occupy the houses on Uritzky, Karl Marx, and Krupskaya streets. I'll hold back the Third Battalion. As soon as it's dark, send them in, too," he ordered.

At 7 P.M. the soldiers entered the cottages, and the army observers and representatives of the special department took up their positions to view the operation. In half an hour the irrevocable occurred. The outcome was exactly as Captain Odyn had described it, only more tragic. As soon as the men entered the cottages-turned-into-bathhouses, the Germans hit the village with every kind of artillery they had. Being a man of fantasy, I always pictured an artillery attack as an onslaught of dragons and snakes, because of their long, trailing flight with an explosion at the head. These serpents and dragons now fell on the village until the last cottage was reduced to splinters.

Then [as in Mikhail Lermontov's poem "Borodino"] "we began counting the wounds."

Of the three battalions in the regiment, two were so thoroughly destroyed that they lost all combat potential; but to make up for that, the lice were destroyed together with the men. This was reported to headquarters. They were apparently pleased with our diligence, since there were no reprimands for the human losses. . . .

As a result of this bathing operation, there were also fifty wounded, including two women—our medical assistant, Larissa Ivanovna, and the head doctor of the 1st Battalion, who were trying to save wounded men from the burning cottages. The wounded were the lucky ones—they stayed alive. As they were taken away to the hospital in a truck, all of them were cursing, including the women. They were annoyed to have been wounded while washing. Captain Voron shouted from under his bandage: "Assholes! Didn't I warn them? Lunkheads! Fools! They can fight by themselves now! Without me!"

I'm grateful to our regimental commander, Colonel of the Guard Bogdanov, for deciding to make an example of me and my gunners by sending us to heat up the bathhouses so as to ease the suffering of the lice-ridden men, thereby saving me from a first-class German drubbing when everyone was undressed and steaming. Of our three battalions, only one remained, which the colonel decided to hold back along with their lice. We who had heated up the baths were the only ones who escaped in time.

You gaze into the mists of the past, into a depth of forty years, and cannot get hold of anything instructive, interesting, or grand in this great Battle of Stalingrad, which you witnessed.

Something wrong with your memory?

But you remember perfectly well what happened a year before and a year after.

A psychological problem?

I don't think so. It's hard to unhinge a basically normal psyche. And if something does happen to it, it's hard to set it right again.

I remember some trifles, conversations in the headquarters dugout, running, falling down, the smell of dry earth. I remember soldiers' jokes, and our guffawing whether they were funny or not. We weren't crazy with fear. But for the life of me I cannot put together any coherent memory of what we were doing at that location for almost a month. I don't remember what we ate or drank, or how we did it. I remember some nonsense, some phone conversations, some orders, the enemy tanks in the distance, no bigger than matchboxes. Can it be that life at that most strategic location of the front was so lacking in substance?

Finally, I understood. All of us were incredibly busy saving our lives. That is an extremely serious and difficult occupation. Let me tell you how it went hour by hour.

From 4 to 5 A.M. our opening salvo—along the entire front line, from all kinds of guns. Then, from 5 to 8 A.M., the answering fire of the German artillery. You can't raise your head; everyone lies in his place praying to God that it will blow by. Plowed-up red earth flies into the air, shrapnel screams, we choke with dust, sneeze and cough. From 8 to 10 A.M. we have a visit from the German aircraft—a thousand of them. Hold on! They dump all their explosive loads, then drop down and start strafing anything that moves or looks like a trench. At this point you're seized with such fear that you find yourself digging into the wall of your trench like a mole. What else can you do?

From 10 A.M. to noon, all our guns must fire their allotted four rounds, each at a specific target. This is a strict limit. By that time I am supposed to have presented the battalion commander with a chart showing the targets: here a cannon, there a tank, there a machine gun, and so on. From 2 to 4, the

Germans conduct a massive shelling, primarily of our observation points. These two hours are devastating. You dig yourself into the ground and press yourself as close to it as you can. German mortar fire is expert—dense and precise. Then come our "Katiushas" [multibarreled rocket launchers]. The covers are taken off their skyward-looking barrels; they produce thick clouds of smoke and set fire to the German front line.

In response, the German heavy artillery, 152mm to 200mm, starts shooting. It removes whole cubic meters from our shelters. After that, our guns again fire four rounds each, and during this time we are expected to dig a new connecting trench twenty meters forward. This is called advancing. The new position may be worse for observation and defense, but still we absolutely must advance.

An interesting day, yet it's hard to describe it coherently. Maybe because of a total lack of sleep? And then, you're underground all the time. But while you're underground, you're relatively safe. People die mostly on the surface, where there is no salvation.

I was wounded on one such day. I knew I'd be either wounded or killed when they dragged me out of my dear mother earth like a worm and sent me to man an advanced observation post. I sensed acutely how naked, soft, vulnerable my whole being was! Before the day was over, with three wounds from bullets and shrapnel, and good, officially stamped documents, I was on my way to the rear, to live, to love, to work, to eat and drink and do other simple, joyful things that life consists of. What happiness to be getting farther away every moment from death, from cannon, machine guns, mortars, aircraft, rifles, and all such loathsome human inventions. You race through a million centuries of evolution, from Worm to Man, the king of the universe!

You are a Man again, and your superiors are no longer battalion and regimental commanders who have it in their power to send you to the other world for the sake of the general victory, but doctors whose task is first of all to bring you back to life and then to restore you to health.

War is violence and does violence to everything: reason, logic, human dignity, and first of all to such a naturally human feeling as self-preservation—that is, fear for one's only, inimitable life; war declares this fear shameful, and killing the chief virtue. War is a creature broken loose from the pack of human feelings and concepts.

If the subordinates were to follow common sense and experience, the commander in chief, to his order to move five kilometers forward, would eternally get such answers as

"It's impossible—there's a river there!"

"It's impossible—there's a swamp there!"

"It's impossible—there's a cliff there!"

"It's impossible in broad daylight—the enemy has everything covered!"

"It's impossible at night—it's pitch-dark!"

With the result that it would be impossible to advance.

This the commander in chief prevented by saying: "Pay ten times more with your lives and all will be possible!"

So losses were valued, and sparing men's lives was considered suspicious.

... If people die, it means they're trying hard. If they stay alive, they must be slackers. And so today, when I pass by the memorial with its eternal flame and the loudspeakers announce that the Great Fatherland War cost us 20 million lives, I always think: Didn't we pay ten times too much for that victory?

Conscripting the Queens

by JOHN MAXTONE-GRAHAM

That the Cunard luxury liners *Queen Mary* and *Queen Elizabeth* spent the duration as troopships may seem a curiosity of history, but it is more than that. Can there be any greater evidence of the total mobilization of World War II? As John Maxtone-Graham tells us, the ships were painted battleship gray, steel mess tables crowded the former first-class dining rooms of the *Queens*, men in uniform and the ubiquitous Mae West life jackets milled around empty shopping arcades, and ballrooms and swimming pools became bunkrooms and on the return hospitals. The *Queens* carried up to 16,000 men (the normal complement of passengers and crew was 3,200), but there were lifeboats for only a fifth that number. In spite of wartime alterations, voyages on the *Queens* remained a special experience, and no one is better equipped to describe them than John Maxtone-Graham. He is the author of the classic *The Only Way to Cross,* a history of transatlantic liners.

When writer Walter Lord was with the U.S. Office of Strategic Services (OSS), his chief, William Donovan, advised him on how to conduct himself during wartime passage to Europe. "Wear civilian clothes," suggested Wild Bill, "and remain as inconspicuous as possible."

Though sound advice for OSS operatives almost anywhere else, on board the *Queen Elizabeth* in 1944, a ship awash with khaki, wearing civilian clothing was about as inconspicuous as wearing no clothes at all.

The wholesale movement of troops to theaters of war in those days was never achieved by air. When war broke out in September 1939, the largest and fastest ocean liners ever built crowded the sea lanes. Many would soon be pressed into war duty. Sadly, a great deal of superannuated tonnage including the *Mauretania, Majestic, Berengaria, Homeric, France,* and *Leviathan*—had been scrapped during the thirties, considered of no further use; they would have proved invaluable as transports only a few years later. Fortunately, none could have been put to better use than two brand-new Cunard White Star giants: the *Queen Mary,* which had entered service in the summer of 1936, and her sister, the *Queen Elizabeth,* completed in 1940.

The *Queens* had been designed to provide long-anticipated weekly transatlantic sailings: One would steam from Southampton, the other from New York, every Wednesday. That dream, however, would not be put into practice until 1947, long after hostilities had ceased. Meanwhile, the *Queens* served as one of the Allies' most useful and flexible weapons of global war: reliable, fast, and each able to embark an entire infantry division. The two vessels would join other famous liners in the business of trooping, among them a new *Mauretania* and the *Nieuw Amsterdam,* the venerable *Aquitania* (which had seen identical service in World War I), and the *Île de France.*

Conversion from liner to transport meant, first, a new coat of paint, though not the dazzle-painting camouflage of World War I. Instead of the *Mauretania*'s harlequin paint scheme of 1916, the *Queens*' orange and black funnels, white upperworks, buff deck gear, and black hulls would become battleship gray, profoundly changing their appearance from across the water. All detail vanished under that monochromatic wash. And with good reason: Nothing is more conspicuous on the horizon than the gleam of sunlight on a white bridge screen.

Their only armaments were defensive. Neither *Queen* qualified as a fighting ship, nor did any liner. There has been only one conclusive armed encounter between merchant vessels in the history of naval warfare: the celebrated engagement between the little Cunarder *Carmania* and the German *Cape Trafalgar* off Trinidad at the start of World War I. The British vessel managed to sink the other, but at fearful cost to itself. Ever since, naval strategists on both sides in both wars understood that liners, the faster the better, were most effective as built. Even token armaments were pointless; liners had not enough armor, maneuverability, or firepower to be warships, and their fragile hulls were perilously vulnerable.

In fact, token 4- and 6-inch naval ordnance were mounted fore and aft. Later, Bofors and Oerlikon antiaircraft batteries were added. Once, during a refueling stop in the Marquesas, soldiers with rifles were stationed along the *Queen Elizabeth*'s promenade-deck windows in the event Japanese aircraft appeared. The *Queens*' only armor plate covered engine-room skylights. As a final defensive measure, all troopship hulls were girdled with degaussing cables, a wartime invention for repelling magnetic mines.

Both the *Queen Mary* and the *Normandie* were stranded in New York at the outbreak of hostilities in September 1939. They stayed there throughout the "phony" war of the fall and winter, which was conducted largely by the press and ministries of propaganda. The gray-painted *Queen Elizabeth* left port in early 1940, her destination shrouded in wartime secrecy; and it was only after her surprise arrival in New York in March that the *Queen Mary* sailed on the urgent business of war. Watchers along Twelfth Avenue saw busloads of Cunard White Star crewmen roll onto the pier (they had crossed from Britain on the little *Antonia* in convoy); they also saw lifeboat davits being tested. On a late March afternoon, the *Queen Mary* slipped out of New

York, destination unknown to those on shore; in fact, she was bound for Sydney via the southern oceans.

Unlike the movements of conventional troopers, the *Queen Mary*'s solo passage to Sydney was one of the safest she undertook. It set the pattern for both *Queens*' ultimate wartime use: traveling alone at thirty knots, too fast for accompanying vessels and enemy warships alike. Only the luckiest U-boat commander could have been in position to ambush her. Slow port approaches, however, were dangerous—and inevitable, for both *Queens* carried only 6,000 tons of fuel, enough for an Atlantic crossing but not for a Far Eastern voyage. From New York, the *Queen Mary* had to refuel at Trinidad, zigzag out of the Caribbean, sail to Cape Town and then to Fremantle on Australia's western coast; five days later she entered Sydney heads.

It is curious that German naval intelligence could have plotted these stops as easily as the Admiralty, yet didn't; or perhaps it did but lacked the capacity to implement an attack, though the South Atlantic was, in both wars, a favorite German hunting ground. (Less than a year earlier, the *Graf Spee* had been scuttled in Uruguay's river Plate.) At Trinidad as well as Cape Town, no attack materialized. Nevertheless throughout the war, approaching port, all watertight doors on both *Queens* were closed remotely from the bridge.

At Sydney, within a frantic fortnight, the Cockatoo Docks and Engineering Company understood the first of what would be several refits to increase troop capacity. The *Queen Mary*'s first wartime load was a mere 5,000 Australian and New Zealand troops, men of the 6th ANZAC Division, destined for the mother country. The vessel functioned more or less as in peacetime. The forward observation bar was open, as were the two indoor swimming pools. Since there were no large compartments, existing cabins were used, their capacity enhanced. A first-class double accommodated six in either hammocks or newly installed double-deckers. Later, that same space would hold a dozen men, and larger suites would hold an astonishing twenty-one! On lower decks, cabins without adjoining bathrooms had shower and toilet rooms constructed nearby. Enlisted men ate in three sittings in the first-class dining room, in a surreal charade of peacetime shipboard life.

When the *Queen Mary* left Sydney first carrying troops, she sailed, atypically, in convoy with the *Aquitania, Empress of Japan, Empress of Britain, Mauretania,* and *Andes.* Convoy code names for the six liners were X1 through X6; pride of place—X1—went to the *Queen Mary.* Their destination was the little Scottish port of Gourock at the mouth of the Clyde, within miles of both *Queens*' birthplace at John Brown's Yard. Southampton and Liverpool alike were too close to Luftwaffe surveillance, and Gourock would remain both *Queens*' British terminal throughout the war. Troops were unloaded onto Clyde steamers and taken ashore to trains for Glasgow and the South. A fleet of Dutch lighters would tie up on the opposite side, embarking supplies and an army of cleaning women as the troops disembarked. The presence of those Dutch vessels caused the waters off Gourock to be known informally as Rotterdam Harbor.

The Queen Mary sailed, again in convoy, back to the Far East, where in Singapore's dry dock additional renovations were made, inching up her capacity yet again. Meanwhile, back in New York Harbor, the *Queen Elizabeth* was finally getting up steam. She had arrived in haste from the Clyde after a desperate transatlantic dash, still unfinished, without sea trials, and with some of her launch gear still affixed beneath the hull. While berthed safely at Manhattan's Pier 90 for seven months, some interior work had been done, but, in adherence to U.S. neutrality, nothing remotely warlike.

She sailed to the Far East in November 1940, in the wake of her sister, and went immediately into Singapore's dry dock. In one sense, the *Queen Elizabeth's* conversion was simpler than the *Queen Mary's*, for she lacked a peacetime interior patina—no paneling, carpeting, or furnishings. The second great Cunarder then steamed south to Sydney for further refitting. It was there, in February of 1941, that the two gray-painted *Queen*s met at sea for the first time, an encounter far removed from the peacetime North Atlantic rendezvous their builders had envisioned.

During those early Far Eastern sailings, the *Queen Elizabeth* and the *Queen Mary* alike traveled across what was described as the Indian Ocean ferry, carrying Australian troops as far west as Bombay or Trincomalee, but no farther; until the Battle of El Alamein, Suez was too dangerous. Troops bound for the western desert were transshipped onto smaller vessels while the *Queen*s returned to Australia, sometimes carrying prisoners of war. Heat in the Red Sea and Indian Ocean was appalling belowdecks, and there were some fatalities from heat prostration on both vessels. Troops waiting to disembark in the Gulf of Suez and suffering from heat prostration were revived in the *Queen Mary's* barbershop, the only air-conditioned room on board.

The entry of Japan into the Western war in December 1941 halted the carriage of troops from Australia to European and African theaters. Indeed, the very reverse obtained; now, American troops were desperately needed in Australia. The *Queen Elizabeth* made an eastbound Pacific crossing (refueling at the Marquesas) to the Canadian naval base at Esquimalt, British Columbia, for dry docking; the fall of Singapore had eliminated the *Queen*s' only Far Eastern dry-dock option. From there, the *Queen Elizabeth* sailed south and picked up her first contingent of American troops from San Francisco's Pier 35, the only call either Cunarder would ever make there. (No one could have guessed that thirty years after the war, the *Queen Mary* would end her days retired at Long Beach, California.) As the *Queen Elizabeth* raced back to Sydney, front-page articles in the *Ocean Daily News*, published on board, deciphered the intricacies of Australian currency for mystified GIs.

The *Queen Mary*, meanwhile, was on America's eastern shore, embarking more than 8,000 troops at Boston and sailing around the cape back to Sydney. Her Boston stopover had included more work toward the relentless escalation of her passenger load. As the Far Eastern voyages were concluded early in 1942 and a shorter transatlantic schedule initiated, it was agreed that during summer crossings even more than 8,000 troops could be carried. the ultimate record was 16,683, carried eastbound on the *Queen Mary*.

The most dangerous aspect of this overcrowding was the shortage of lifeboats. Since the *Titanic* tragedy of 1912, British Board of Trade regulations required a seat in a lifeboat for every soul on board, passengers and crew. The *Queen Mary*'s peacetime passenger capacity was 1,948. With an additional 1,260 in officers and crew, lifeboat capacity for 3,208 was mandated. A total of twenty-four lifeboats were spaced along the sides of the vessel above the boat deck. But even though six more were added during the Boston refit, they could accommodate only 3,000. Carley floats would hold the rest, if—and it was a big if—swimming soldiers could reach them. Abandoning ship would mean that most of the troops on board would be thrown into the sea with nothing more than life jackets at their disposal.

It was a calculated wartime risk, mentioned only indirectly in a recorded conversation between Prime Minister Churchill and General George C. Marshall, the U.S. Army's chief of staff and an understandable advocate of raising both *Queens*' capacities to their maximum. He asked Churchill how many passengers could be carried on each *Queen* if Board of Trade regulations were ignored. The prime minister hazarded 16,000. "You must judge for yourselves," he cautioned, "the risks you will run."

The risks were, as everyone knew, appalling; but the rewards outweighed them. One of the almost quaint conventions of a GI crossing on either of the packed *Queen*s was a lifeboat drill the first morning at sea, just as in peacetime except that now boat decks were solid with moiling troops, only a fraction of whom would be able to enter a lifeboat if a torpedo or bomb struck. As with so many wartime conundrums, there was no solution. Cunard's masters and marine superintendents turned a blind eye, capacity was increased, and the Plimsoll line—that prudent-maximum-load mark on the ships' hulls—was painted over and forgotten for the duration of the war.

To saturate existing space, planners made use of an infamous U.S. Navy invention, standee bunks. Each bunk was a narrow canvas rectangle, laced within a steel frame. Stacked five high, they were hinged to a pair of vertical stanchions welded to deck and deckhead. It was crowded, claustrophobic, and ruthlessly efficient. Standee bunks could be put anywhere: along promenade decks, in cabins, in the observation lounge, even in the swimming pools. They were not the roomiest accommodations those involuntary passengers had ever known, and it was a further shock for them to discover that they would have the use of their berths for only half the day. "Hot sack," it was called, or "musical bunks." Sleep rotation was the order of the day. On crowded summer sailings, each berth might be occupied by three eight-hour shifts, and hundreds of troops would have to make do on the open decks.

Feeding those thousands required radical catering techniques. Long steel tables and benches were crammed into the first-class dining room, and only two meals were served—breakfast and dinner; lunch aboard the *Queen*s became a wartime casualty. The men were fed in eight sittings of forty-five minutes each. Sittings lined up in corridors several decks above until directed to descend to the dining room by military police. They brought their own mess gear and, after the meal, left by a forward entrance and washed their gear in hot, soapy salt water. Nine canteens scattered all over the vessel did a brisk trade in Coca-Cola and candy but no chewing gun: Careless GIs used to leave it on the decks, and it was consequently outlawed.

As it turned out, the risk was less a matter of torpedoes or bombs than stability and draft. Passenger loads of 16,000 involved a staggering topweight load of 2,000 tons, allowing for each embarking soldier and his kit an approximate weight of 250 pounds. Those additional tons exacerbated an already critical problem aboard both Queens. They were terrible rollers. (Stabilizers would not be installed until long after the war.) The Queen Mary, in particular, had a tendency to hang on the roll, to stay at the far end of a 10- or 12-degree roll for nerve-racking seconds before recovering sluggishly, returning upright, and then heaving over to the opposite end. Thousands of peacetime Queen Mary passengers had been made uneasy, queasy, and in some cases terrified by their vessel's unfortunate predilection; for GIs during heavily laden crossings, it was far worse.

The Queens were loaded far more lightly in the winter, not merely because of the severity of Atlantic storms but because the heated promenade decks were too cold to house troops. Winter routine throughout the ships was to use only the bottom two standee bunks, leaving topmost tiers empty and hinged up out of the way. Even so, damage could be catastrophic. The Queen Elizabeth, plowing eastward through mountainous seas near Greenland on a northern deviation, had her foredeck badly buckled by two consecutive monster waves inundating the bow. The same onslaught shattered all of the bridge windows as well, a hundred feet above the sea. Near Iceland once, the Queen Mary rolled to port so far, it was said, that her main-deck railings went under.

Before they reached New York, embarking regiments assembled at New Jersey's Fort Dix and Camp Kilmer. They even rehearsed, using giant plywood mock-ups of the Queens' C-deck entry ports. Guides from each unit went to the piers early to familiarize themselves, as much as possible, with the vessel's geography before their units arrived by bus or ferry from across the Hudson. Embarkation proceeded throughout the night. As each man boarded, he was presented with a metallic disk indicating one of three zones —red, white, or blue—in which he would be berthed. There was no reason for him ever to leave that zone throughout the crossing, and military police— headquartered in the former Austin Reed clothing ship on Promenade Deck Square—enforced that segregation throughout the voyage.

Even within these zones, movement was prescribed: forward on the starboard side, aft on the port. Waiting on each man's bunk was a kapok-filled life jacket, nicknamed Mae West because of its swelling front. (They could as well have been called Quasimodos, for they bulged in back, too.) They were supposed to be worn everywhere at all times, except in the bunk, and the punishment for failure to do so was confiscation of boots; crossing wet winter decks in stocking feet for a day was an effective Mae West reminder. Also distributed to the troops was a small booklet about the crossing; it began by saying, "The voyage, while short, will be extremely difficult for all."

The daily tedium was such that the captain of the troop-laden Nieuw

Amsterdam said he dreaded sighting anything at sea, because the men would list his vessel dangerously by crowding to one side or the other for a better view. He solved the problem by ordering everyone below for "an air-raid drill" whenever the crow's nest reported anything on the horizon. The same ruse was never used on the *Queens*, perhaps because it would have taken too long to get the men off the decks. But the decks did have to be cleared for bona fide air-raid drills; otherwise gun crews literally could not get to their guns. Sailing out of New York Harbor overloaded with GIs was tricky for the *Queens*, because if their square-bottomed hulls listed only slightly to either side, the appreciable increase in their forty-two-foot wartime drafts made contact with the top of the Holland Tunnel a distinct possibility.

Walter Lord and his OSS draft, doing their best to look "inconspicuous" in mufti, boarded the *Queen Elizabeth* at Pier 90 on July 19, 1944. All twelve were assigned to cabin M-104. Lord carried a musette bag, like all his fellow passengers; but, he remembers, his was not government issue; it came from Abercrombie & Fitch. "OSS was just like that," he recalls. At the Brooklyn Army Terminal, he had been inoculated and given a gas mask, steel helmet, and solemn instructions to say nothing to anybody about the vessel's probable destination. Once on board, he discovered that everyone knew.

Extracts from letters Lord wrote at the time suggest that there were only three activities during the crossing: "sleep, read or play cards, usually standing up." Junior commissioned officers (Lord held the "assimilated rank of captain") dined in the original second-class dining room; Lord's was the third sitting, and he sat at table 35, waited on by Cunard stewards (whom he would tip at crossing's end) and choosing dishes from a not-bad menu. Since there were only two meals a day, all the OSS draft had been advised to bring cookies and candy from New York. Chocaholic Walter Lord had two dozen Hershey bars in his musette bag and, sealed in his footlocker in the baggage room, six bottles of whiskey held in reserve for the parched U.K.

They sailed at noon, their only escort out of the harbor a watchful blimp that droned overhead until abandoning them off Staten Island. The five-day crossing was uneventful, the weather either gray or sunny but the seas always calm. They went far south, near the Azores, then north up the center of the Atlantic to Gourock.

In the main lounge there was a mishmash of battered furniture, with a velvet rope down the center to segregate the sexes—there was a detachment of nurses on board. Also on board was Glenn Miller's orchestra, without their leader but full of music. They played concerts every day, indoors and out on the afterdecks. There was no daylight in the lounge, because all promenade-deck windows, as well as the clerestory windows looking out onto the boat deck, were painted over. The gloom was heightened by a continuous fog of cigarette smoke. All that could be heard apart from the conversation were Coke cottles being opened, the riffle of shuffled cards, the jingle of coins, and the rattle of dice. (Throughout the war, in addition to poker, rummy, and blackjack, the most riveting of all *Queens* troop games was, curiously, hearts.) There was no traditional midocean gaming such as bingo or "horse racing."

No drink was available on board, save those warm Cokes that Lord remembers having the appeal "of vintage wines." By crossing's end, he recalls, a combination of seasickness, cigarettes, and overcrowding had made the *Queen Elizabeth* smell to high heaven. The thing he found most amusing was the curious dichotomy of peace and war shipboard. For example, he had to fill out a landing card, on which a line still inquired politely if he planned to disembark at Cherbourg before Southampton—a common peacetime itinerary. On that very day, however, the *Ocean Daily News* carried the headline AMERICANS BATTLING INTO CHERBOURG.

The war ended, and the *Queens* were restored to peacetime service, fulfilling their owner's and builder's fondest expectation. They sailed well into the late sixties. Then the *Queen Mary* was retired to Long Beach, California, and the *Queen Elizabeth*, after an unsuccessful layover/retirement at Fort Lauderdale, Florida, was bought and renovated by a Hong Kong shipping man. He was to have returned her to service, but she burned on the day that work was completed—January 9, 1972—resulting in a total loss.

But a third *Queen, Queen Elizabeth 2,* had already entered the Atlantic lists, carrying Cunard's tradition into the present. It seemed unlikely that she would ever know conversion to trooping, but in May 1982 the unlikely happened. She was called up for war, dragooned by the Ministry of Defence to transport 3,500 British soldiers down to retake the Falklands.

This time there was no lengthy stopover in dry dock, no months of preparation. Within a fortnight the *QE2*'s peacetime furnishings had been off-loaded and shipyard workers had added helicopter flight decks fore and aft; modern strategy demanded this vital structural modification, never part of the original *Queens*' wartime capability.

There was no need for standee bunks, for the troop contingent of slightly over 3,000 would number only twice the vessel's passenger complement. Additionally, many stewards did not go, and their cabins could be used to berth soldiers. There was no paint job, either Cunard's colors remained as they were. The only change was the altered profile caused by the added helicopter decks.

Once again, refueling points were needed. Freetown, in Sierra Leone, was used, the same port at which both her predecessors had often bunkered during the war. South of Ascension Island, the vessel was blacked out at night, and a ship's officer boarded a helicopter to circle the darkened *QE2*, hunting for telltale chinks of light. The radar was shut down, too, although Captain Peter Jackson turned it on and off periodically—far too quickly for any Argentine watchers to get a fix—to assess the position of nearby icebergs.

At South Georgia Island, the *QE2* met with the P&O's *Canberra*, transshipped the troops and equipment on board, and embarked the crews of sunken Royal Navy vessels for the trip home to England. So the *QE2* fulfilled the great dual functions of wartime passenger liners troopship outbound, hospital ship homebound.

En route home from South Georgia, the *QE2* was RASsed—a Royal Navy acronym for Refueling at Sea. This was harder than it sounds, since a liner's fuel ports, used only at a pier, are low down in the vessel. Extensions to the fuel intakes had to be brought up as far as two deck, and 100 men along a passenger corridor ran forward with a line to haul the refueling hose on board from the tanker. It worked splendidly.

The Falkland voyage was an occasion for intense pride among the young civilian crew members. Although there were still a couple old-timers on board —men who had served on the *Queen Mary* or the *Queen Elizabeth* during World War II—to most of the crew, having their ship turned into a trooper, even if only for one suspenseful voyage, was a new, exhilarating adventure. They were participating, after all, in a glorious tradition. Though this was doubtless a final chapter of Cunard war service, it was a story that had started with other Cunarders chartered to take troops to the Crimea, the Boer War, World Wars I and II.

It will probably never happen again. Or could it? Perhaps decades from now, the pair of golden scissors used by three successive queens to launch the first three *Queen*s may be retrieved from Glasgow's Museum of Transport. At a shipyard, Her Majesty Queen Diana may cut the launch cord that will send her namesake thundering down the ways into the oceans of the world, a fourth *Queen* that might someday serve, somewhere, as a trooper herself.

The Secrets of Overlord

by STEPHEN E. AMBROSE

Modern military leaders have come to recognize that surprise can be critical to victory. Just consider the role of surprise, along with an awesome technical superiority, in the Coalition's Desert Storm destruction of the Iraqi army. Ways have to be found to overcome a defender's natural edge. This was never so true as in the invasion of Europe in 1944—Operation Overlord—when its commander, Dwight D. Eisenhower, faced daunting obstacles: Hitler's Atlantic Wall fortifications, crack German divisions that actually outnumbered the Allied landing force, and the enemy's certainty of when the invasion would take place—but not where. Eisenhower had to mask his true intentions both before the battle and after it was joined. Were the Normandy landings merely a diversionary assault? The elaborate deceptions of Overlord would include faked radio traffic, turned agents, pâpier-maché tanks, phony oil docks built by Hollywood stagehands, preparations for landings that would never take place, and the conspicuous movement of armies that didn't exist. This remarkable story is told by Stephen E. Ambrose, the biographer of Eisenhower and Richard M. Nixon, professor of history at the University of New Orleans, head of the Eisenhower Center there, and a distinguished military historian.

On June 6, 1944, the United States, Britain, and Canada launched the largest force of warships in history across the English Channel. It escorted the largest concentration of troop transport vessels ever assembled, covered by the largest force of fighter and bomber aircraft ever brought together, preceded by a fleet of air transports that had carried tens of thousands of paratroopers and glider-borne troops to Normandy.

Not one German submarine, not one small boat, not one airplane, not one radar set, not one German anywhere detected this movement. As General Walter Warlimont, deputy head of operations of the German Supreme Headquarters, later confessed, on the eve of Overlord the Wehrmacht leaders "had not the slightest idea that the decisive event of the war was upon them."

In World War I, surprise on a grand scale was seldom attempted and rarely achieved. In World War II, it was always sought and sometimes achieved—as with the Japanese attack on Pearl Harbor and the German invasion of Russia, both in 1941, and the German attack in the Ardennes in 1940 and again in 1944. One reason for this difference between the wars was that World War II commanders judged surprise to be more critical to victory than a preattack artillery bombardment. In the age of machine guns, other rapid-fire artillery, and land mines, the defenders could make almost any position virtually impregnable, no matter how heavy the preattack bombardment. Another reason for the increased emphasis on surprise was that the much greater mobility of World War II armed forces made surprise more feasible and more effective. Because of improvements in and more imaginative use of the internal-combustion engine (especially in tanks and trucks), the geographic area in which the conflict was fought was much larger in World War II. The preinvasion bombardment for Overlord, carried out by aircraft, was spread all across France and Belgium. It may have wasted a lot of bombs, but it also kept the Germans from discerning a pattern that would indicate the invasion site.

None of the surprises achieved in World War II was more complex, more difficult, more important, or more successful than Overlord. To fool Hitler and his generals in the battle of wits that preceded the attack, the Allies had to convince them not only that it was coming where it was not but also that the real thing was a feint. The first objective could be achieved by attacking in an unexpected, indeed illogical, place, and by maintaining total security about the plan. The second required convincing Hitler that the Allied invasion force was about twice as powerful as it actually was.

That there would be landings in France in the late spring of 1944 was universally known. Exactly where and when were the questions. To learn those secrets, the Germans maintained a huge intelligence organization that included spies inside Britain, air reconnaissance, monitoring of the British press and BBC, radio intercept stations, decoding experts, interrogation of Allied airmen shot down in Germany, research on Allied economies, and more.

The importance of surprise was obvious. In World War I it was judged that to have any chance at success, the attacking force had to outnumber the defenders by at least three to one. But in Overlord the attacking force of 175,000 men would be outnumbered by the Wehrmacht, even at the point of attack, and the overall figures (German troops in Western Europe versus Allied troops in the United Kingdom) showed a two-to-one German advantage. Doctrine in the German army was to meet an attack with an immediate counterattack. In this case, the Germans could move reinforcements to the battle much faster than the Allies, because they could bring them in by train, by truck, and on foot, while the Allies had to bring them in by ship. The Germans had storage and supply dumps all over France; the Allies had to bring every shell, every bullet, every drop of gasoline, every bandage across the Channel.

Allied intelligence worked up precise tables on the Germans' ability to move reinforcements into the battle area. The conclusion was that if the Germans correctly gauged Overlord as the main assault and marched immediately, within a month they could concentrate thirty-one divisions in the battle area, including nine panzer divisions. The Allies could not match that buildup rate.

In the face of these obstacles, the Allies managed to maintain a deception about their true intentions even after the battle began. How they did so is a remarkable story.

Thousands of men and women were involved, but perhaps the most important, and certainly the most dramatic, were the dozen or so members of BI(a), the counterespionage arm of MI-5, the British internal-security agency. Using a variety of sources, such as code breaking and interrogation of captured agents, the British caught German spies as they parachuted into England or Scotland. Sir John Masterman, head of BI(a), evaluated each spy. Those he considered unsuitable were executed or imprisoned. The others were "turned"—that is, made into double agents, who sent messages to German intelligence, the Abwehr, via radio, using Morse code. (Each spy had his own distinctive "signature" in the way he used the code's dots and dashes, which was immediately recognizable by the German spy master receiving the message.) The British kept the double agents tap-tap-tapping, but only what they were told to send out.

This so-called Double-Cross operation, which had come into being in the dark days of 1940, managed to locate and turn every German spy in the United Kingdom, some two dozen in all. From the beginning the British had decided to aim it exclusively toward the moment when the Allies returned to France. Building up this asset over the years required feeding the Abwehr information through the spies that was authentic, new, and interesting, but either relatively valueless or something the Germans were bound to learn anyway. The idea was to make the agents trustworthy and valuable in the eyes of the Germans, then spring the trap on D Day, when the double agents would flood the Abwehr with false information.

The first part of the trap was to make the Germans think the attack was coming at the Pas de Calais. Since the Germans already anticipated that this was where the Allies would come ashore, it was necessary only to reinforce their preconceptions. The Pas de Calais was indeed the obvious choice. It was on the direct London-Ruhr-Berlin line. It was close to Antwerp, Europe's best port. Inland the terrain was flat, with few natural obstacles. At the Pas de Calais the Channel was at its narrowest, giving ships the shortest trip and British-based fighter aircraft much more time over the invasion area.

Because the Pas de Calais was the obvious choice, the Germans had their strongest fixed defenses there, backed up by the Fifteenth Army and a majority of the panzer divisions in France. Whether or not they succeeded in making the position impregnable we will never know, because the supreme Allied commander, Dwight D. Eisenhower, decided not to find out. He chose Normandy instead. Normandy had certain advantages, including the port of Cherbourg, the narrowness of the Cotentin Peninsula, access to the major road network at Caen, and proximity to the English ports of Southampton and Portsmouth. Normandy's greatest advantage, however, was that the Germans were certain to consider an attack there highly unlikely, because it would be an attack in the wrong direction: Instead of heading east, toward the German heartland, the Allies would be heading south into central France.

The second part of the trap was to make the Germans think, even after the attack began, that Normandy was a feint. Geography reinforced Eisenhower's choice of Normandy in meeting this requirement, too: If there were major Allied landings at the Pas de Calais, Hitler would not keep troops in Normandy for fear of their being cut off from Germany—but he might be persuaded to keep troops in the Pas de Calais following a landing in Normandy, as they would still stand between the Allied forces and Germany.

The deception plan, code-named Fortitude, was a joint venture, with British and American teams working together; it made full use of the Double-Cross system, dummy armies, fake radio traffic, and elaborate security precautions. In terms of the time, resources, and energy devoted to it, Fortitude was a tremendous undertaking. It had many elements, designed to make the Germans think the attack might come at the Biscay coast or in the Marseilles region or even in the Balkans. Most important were Fortitude North, which set up Norway as a target (the site of Hitler's U-boat bases, essential to his offensive operations), and Fortitude South, with the Pas de Calais as the target.

To get the Germans to look toward Norway, the Allies first had to convince them that Eisenhower had enough resources for a diversion or secondary attack. This was doubly difficult because of Ike's acute shortage of landing craft—it was touch and go as to whether there would be enough craft to carry five divisions ashore at Normandy as planned, much less spares for another attack. To make the Germans believe otherwise, the Allies had to create fictitious divisions and landing craft on a grand scale. This was done chiefly with the Double-Cross system and through Allied radio signals.

The British Fourth Army, for example, stationed in Scotland and scheduled to invade Norway in mid-July, existed only on the airwaves. Early in 1944 some two dozen overage British officers were sent to northernmost Scotland, where they spent the next months exchanging radio messages. They filled the air with an exact duplicate of the wireless traffic that accompanies the assembly of a real army, communicating in low-level and thus easily broken cipher. Together the messages created an impression of corps and division headquarters scattered all across Scotland: "80 Div. request 1,800 pairs of crampons, 1,800 pairs of ski bindings," they read, or "7 Corps requests the promised demonstrators in the Bilgeri method of climbing rock faces." There was no 80th Division, no VII Corps.

The turned German spies meanwhile sent encoded radio messages to Hamburg and Berlin describing heavy train traffic in Scotland, new division patches seen on the streets of Edinburgh, and rumors among the troops about going to Norway. Wooden twin-engine "bombers" began to appear on Scottish airfields. British commandos made some raids on the coast of Norway, pinpointing radar sites, picking up soil samples (ostensibly to test the suitability of beaches to support a landing), and in general trying to look like a preinvasion force.

The payoff was spectacular. By late spring, Hitler had thirteen army divisions in Norway (about 130,000 men under the German military system), along with 90,000 naval and 60,000 Luftwaffe personnel. In late May, Field Marshal Erwin Rommel finally persuaded Hitler to move five infantry divisions from Norway to France. They had started to load up and move out when the Abwehr passed on to Hitler another set of "intercepted" messages about the threat to Norway. He canceled the movement order.

To paraphrase Winston Churchill, never in the history of warfare have so many been immobilized by so few.

Fortitude South was larger and more elaborate. It was based on the First U.S. Army Group (FUSAG), stationed in and around Dover and threatening the Pas de Calais. It included radio traffic; inadequately camouflaged dummy landing craft in the ports of Ramsgate, Dover, and Hastings; fields packed with pâpier-maché tanks; and full use of the Double-Cross setup. The spies reported intense activity in and around Dover, including construction, troop movements, increased train traffic, and the like. They said that the phony oil dock at Dover, built by stagehands from Hollywood and the British film industry, was open and operating.

The capstone to Fortitude South was Ike's selection of General George S. Patton to command FUSAG. The Germans thought Patton the best commander in the Allied camp (a judgment with which Patton fully agreed, but which Eisenhower, unbeknownst to the Germans, did not) and expected him to lead the assault. Eisenhower, who was saving Patton for the exploitation phase of the campaign, used Patton's reputation and visibility to strengthen Fortitude South. The spies reported his arrival in England and his movements. FUSAG radio signals told the Germans of Patton's comings and goings and showed that he had taken a firm grip on his new command.

FUSAG contained real as well as notional divisions, corps, and armies. The FUSAG order of battle included the U.S. Third Army, which was real but still in the United States; the British Fourth Army, which was imaginary; and the Canadian First Army, which was real and based in England. There were, in addition, supposedly fifty follow-up divisions in the United States, organized as the U.S. Fourteenth Army—which was notional—awaiting shipment to the Pas de Calais after FUSAG established its beachhead. Many of the divisions in the Fourteenth Army were real and were actually assigned to General Omar Bradley's U.S. First Army in southwest England.

Fortitude's success was measured by the German estimate of Allied strength. By June 1, the Germans believed that Eisenhower's entire command included eighty-nine divisions (of about 15,000 men each), when in fact he had forty-seven. They also thought he had sufficient landing craft to bring twenty divisions ashore in the first wave, when he would be lucky to manage five. Partly because they credited Ike with so much strength, and partly because it made such good military sense, the Germans believed that the real invasion would be preceded or followed by diversionary attacks and feints.

Security for Overlord was as important as deception. As Ike declared, "Success or failure of coming operations depends upon whether the enemy can obtain advance information of an accurate nature." To maintain security, in February he asked Churchill to move all civilians out of southernmost England. He feared there might be an undiscovered spy who could report the truth to the Abwehr. Churchill refused; he felt it was too much to ask of a war-weary population. A British officer on Ike's staff said it was all politics, and growled, "If we fail, there won't be any more politics."

Ike sent Churchill an eloquent plea, warning that it "would go hard with our consciences if we were to feel, in later years, that by neglecting any security precaution we had compromised the success of these vital operations." In late March, Churchill gave in; the civilians were put out of all coastal and training areas and kept out until months after D Day.

Eisenhower also persuaded a reluctant Churchill to impose a ban on privileged diplomatic communications from the United Kingdom. Ike said he regarded diplomatic pouches as "the gravest risk to the security of our operations and to the lives of our sailors, soldiers, and airmen." When Churchill imposed the ban, on April 17, foreign governments protested vigorously. This gave Hitler a useful clue to the timing of Overlord. He remarked in early May that "the English have taken measures that they can sustain for only six to eight weeks." When a West Point classmate of Ike's declared at the bar in Claridge's Hotel that D Day would be before June 15, and offered to take bets when challenged, Ike reduced him in rank and sent him home in disgrace. There was another flap a week later when a U.S. Navy officer got drunk and revealed details of impending operations, including areas, strength, and dates. Ike wrote Chief of Staff George Marshall, "I get so angry at the occurrence of such needless and additional hazards that I could cheerfully shoot the offender myself." Instead, Ike sent the officer back to the States.

To check on how well security and deception were working, SHAEF (Supreme Headquarters Allied Expeditionary Force) had another asset, the Ultra system. This involved breaking the German code, Enigma, enabling SHAEF to read German radio signals. Thanks to Ultra, the British Joint Intelligence Committee was able to put together weekly summaries of "German Appreciation of Allied Intentions in the West," one- or two-page overviews of where, when, and in what strength the Germans expected the attack. Week after week, the summaries gave Ike exactly the news he wanted to read: that the Germans were anticipating an attack on Norway, diversions in the south of France and in Normandy or the Bay of Biscay, and the main assault, with twenty or more divisions, against the Pas de Calais.

But Fortitude was an edifice built so delicately, precisely, and intricately that the removal of just one supporting column would bring the whole thing crashing down. On May 29, with D Day only about a week away, the summary included a chilling sentence: "The recent trend of movement of German land forces towards the Cherbourg area tends to support the view that the Le Havre-Cherbourg area is regarded as a likely, and perhaps even the main, point of assault."

Had there been a slip? Had the Germans somehow penetrated Fortitude?

The news got worse. The Germans, in fact, were increasing their defenses everywhere along the French coast. In mid-May the mighty Panzer Lehr Division began moving toward the Cotentin Peninsula, while the 21st Panzer Division, which had been with Rommel in North Africa and was his favorite, moved from Brittany to the Caen area—exactly the site where the British Second Army would be landing. More alarming, Ultra revealed that the German 91st Division, specialists in fighting paratroopers, and the German 6th Parachute Regiment had moved on May 29 into exactly the areas where the American airborne divisions were to land. And the German 352nd Division moved forward from St.-Lô to the coast, taking up a position overlooking Omaha Beach, where the U.S. 1st Division was going to land.

Ike's air commander, British Air Chief Marshal Sir Trafford Leigh-Mallory, was so upset by this news that he recommended to Ike that the airdrops be canceled. Ike refused, but the German movements and Leigh-Mallory's reaction badly stretched his nerves.

Eisenhower did not, however, give up on Fortitude. At about midnight on June 5-6, even as Allied transport planes and ships began crossing the Channel for Normandy, the supreme commander played the ultimate note in the Fortitude concert: He had the spy the Germans trusted most, code-named Garbo—actually a resourceful spy for the British from the start—send a message in Morse code to the Abwehr giving away the secret. Garbo reported that Overlord was on the way, named some of the divisions involved, indicated when they had left Portsmouth, and predicted they would come ashore in Normandy at dawn.

The report had to be deciphered, read, evaluated, reenciphered, and transmitted to Hitler. Then Hitler's lackeys had to decide whether to wake him with the news. They did, but then the whole encoding and deciphering operation had to be reversed to get the word to the German forces in Normandy. By the time it arrived, the defenders could see for themselves—there were 6,000 planes overhead and 5,000 ships off the coast, and the first wave of troops was coming ashore.

In short, Garbo's report, the most accurate and important of the entire war, arrived too late to help the Germans. But it surely raised their opinion of Garbo—and this was vital. For now that Fortitude had helped the Allies get ashore, the question was, could the deception be kept alive long enough to let the Allies win the battle of the buildup that would follow?

Garbo was the key. On June 9 he sent a message to his spy master in Hamburg with a request that it be submitted urgently to the German high command. "The present operation, though a large-scale assault, is diversionary in character," Garbo stated flatly. "Its object is to establish a strong bridgehead in order to draw the maximum of our [German] reserves into the area of the assault and to retain them there so as to leave another area exposed where the enemy could then attack with some prospect of success." Citing the Allied order of battle as the Germans understood it, Garbo pointed out that Eisenhower had committed only a small number of his divisions and landing craft. He added that no FUSAG unit had taken part in the Normandy attack, nor was Patton there. Furthermore, "the constant aerial bombardment which the sector of the Pas de Calais has been undergoing and the disposition of the enemy forces would indicate the imminence of the assault in this region which offers the shortest route to the final objective of the Anglo-Americans, Berlin."

Within half a day, Garbo's message was in Hitler's hands. On the basis of it, the führer made a momentous decision, possibly the most important of the war. Rommel had persuaded Hitler to sent two Fifteenth Army panzer divisions to Normandy. The tanks had started their engines, the men were ready to go, when Hitler canceled the order. He wanted the armored units held in the Pas de Calais to defend against the main invasion. He also awarded the Iron Cross, second class, to Garbo. (Garbo, a young Spaniard whom the British, secretly, also honored, ended a long silence about his elaborate and risky activities only in 1985, with the book *Operation Garbo*.)

The deception went on. On June 13 another spy warned that an attack would take place in two or three days at Dieppe or Abbeville. A third spy reported that airborne divisions (wholly fictitious) would soon drop around Amiens. In late June a fourth agent, code-named Tate, said he had obtained the railway schedule for moving the FUSAG forces from their concentration areas to the embarkation ports, thus reinforcing from a new angle the imminence of the threat to the Pas de Calais. One Abwehr officer considered Tate's report so important that he said it "could even decide the outcome of the war." He was not far wrong.

The weekly intelligence summary on June 19 read: "The Germans still believe the Allies capable of launching another amphibious operation. The Pas de Calais remains the expected area of attack. Fears of landings in Norway have been maintained."

July 10: "[T]he enemy's fear of large-scale landings between the Seine and the Pas de Calais has not diminished. The second half of July is given as the probable time for this operation."

July 24: "There has been no considerable transfer of German forces from the Pas de Calais, which remains strongly garrisoned."

By August 3, when Patton came onto the Continent with his U.S. Third Army, most German officers realized that Normandy was the real thing. By then, of course, it was too late. The Germans had kept hundreds of their best tanks and thousands of their finest fighting men (a total of fifteen divisions in France) out of this crucial battle in order to meet a threat that had always been imaginary.

There were delicious ironies at the heart of Fortitude's success. Surprise in war often depends on the defenders underestimating the strength of the attacking force, but in Overlord that was reversed: Fortitude made the Germans overestimate Eisenhower's strength. Surprise also usually depends on exploiting the defenders' weaknesses, but this, too, got turned around: As in jujitsu, Eisenhower employed German strength to German disadvantage.

The Germans in 1944 held three major conceits as articles of faith. The first was that their spies in the United Kingdom were the best in the world. The second was that their Enigma was the best encoding machine ever developed, literally unbreakable. The third was that their own code breakers were the best available. Fortitude used these German conceits to do the Germans in.

Twenty-two years after the event, in 1966, when the author was interviewing Eisenhower on the subject of Fortitude, the supreme commander explained various parts of the operation, then gave one of his big, gutsy laughs, slapped his knee, and exclaimed, "By God, we really fooled them, didn't we?"

When the Maquis Stood and Fought

by TED MORGAN

The resistance in occupied France was on the whole successful, especially when it limited itself to sabotage and guerrilla operations. Only when it tried to fight conventional actions in the open with veteran German units did it suffer humiliating routs. In 1944 there were two such pitched battles between a German mountain division and the maquis. Maquis means "scrubland," and these irregulars were truly fighters of the scrub, hiding in rough country, always on the move, pausing only long enough to hit the enemy and run. But in these instances the maquis violated a cardinal rule of guerrilla warfare: never take on regulars unless, and until, they are in total disarray. Both battles, in the Alpine foothills of Glières and the Vercors, were similar, taking place in mountainous redoubts that seemed impregnable. They weren't, as the Germans easily proved, but the Allied propaganda machine turned them into victories anyway. Both were situations that were ready-made for instant legends. (The second battle was, incidentally, an attempt to deceive the Germans about Allied intentions after D Day.) This tale of pride unrewarded and promises unkept is told by Ted Morgan, a former Pulitzer Prize–winning journalist who is the author of numerous works of history and biography. The present article was adapted from Morgan's book *An Uncertain Hour: The French, the Germans, the Jews, and the City of Lyon, 1940–1945,* published by Arbor House.

"The French are good at turning their defeats into victories," Luigi Barzini once told me, "and the Italians their victories into defeats." A defeat is turned into a victory through a trick of memory, when it is remembered as a great feat of arms. The vanquished soldiers are eulogized as heroes. The shame of defeat is papered over with the rhetoric of martyrdom.

What every French schoolboy remembers about the Battle of Waterloo is that Napoleon's personal guard stood and fought to the last man: "La garde meurt et ne se rend pas" ("The guard dies and does not surrender"). The nation's schools and textbooks conspire to produce a patriotic version of war.

In occupied France in 1944, there were two pitched battles between the Germans and the maquis (resistance), which ended disastrously for the maquis but were pumped up into great heroic actions that the resistance could be proud of. The two operations were remarkably similar. They both took place in mountainous areas, one near Grenoble, the other near the Swiss border. They both began with the maquis occupying high ground and ended with their being encircled and wiped out.

The word *maquis* means "scrub" or "scrubland," and brings to mind irregular units hiding in the countryside, staying on the move, adopting hit-and-run tactics. But in these two cases, the maquisards gathered on the plateaus, which they tried to hold and defend, and were eventually spotted, surrounded, and attacked. For the Germans, these were textbook exercises in taking a badly fortified high ground. For the maquis, they were humiliating routs with high casualties.

The Plateau des Glières is a tableland in the Haute-Savoie area of France, between the French city of Annecy and the Swiss city of Geneva. Twelve miles long and seven wide, at an altitude of 4,500 feet, with no roads and a steep approach of rock cliffs, the plateau seemed inaccessible, particularly in the winter, when it was snowed in.

In early 1944, the Haute-Savoie was already in a state of insurrection. A profusion of maquis groups—fugitives from the recruitment of young Frenchmen for forced labor in Germany; anti-Franco veterans of the Spanish Civil War; communist *francs-tireurs* (resistance units); and Secret Army units with allegiance to Charles de Gaulle—had found favorable conditions for their activities in this mountainous and sparsely populated area. As a result, there were daily skirmishes, daily *attentats* (armed attacks) and reprisals.

The Free French in London wondered to what extent they should encourage these activities. The Allied landing in Normandy was believed to be still months away, and the Allied strategy was to time serious maquis operations with the landing, creating diversions that would keep the Germans busy. Thus a Free French broadcast on February 7 said: "Mobility is the essential element for the maquis. . . . The aim of the Germans is to trap and destroy you. The answer is to disperse and avoid a pitched battle."

At the same time that such messages were sent, the maquis in the Haute-Savoie was promised massive parachute drops of weapons. The resistance leader for the area, Henri Romans-Petit, had to find an appropriate terrain where the drops could be made and the arms could be collected and dispatched to the various groups. It had to be a safe, remote place, outside the valleys patrolled by the Germans, with an escape route to neighboring villages.

The Glières Plateau was the obvious choice, and at the end of January, Romans-Petit sent a "reception team" of 200 maquisards there to prepare the drop zone and organize delivery of the matériel. He had no intention of turning the plateau into a fortress, to be held against an attack; he saw it merely as a suitable drop zone that a mobile unit could man when necessary and evacuate if observed. But in February, Romans-Petit left the Haute-Savoie to direct the maquis operations in the neighboring department of the Ain. Chosen to lead the force of 200 in his place was Théodose ("Tom") Morel.

Morel was a regular-army lieutenant and graduate of the French military academy at St.-Cyr who had gone over to the maquis but retained the qualities developed by his military training: a high sense of honor, a deep desire to avenge the shame of occupation, and a burning ambition to be the initiator of a major feat of arms.

The idea came to Morel from the Free French slogan on the BBC: "In Europe, three countries are resisting: Greece, Yugoslavia, and the Haute-Savoie." The idea was to occupy a piece of the Haute-Savoie and proclaim it Free France. He told a fellow officer, Louis Jourdan-Joubert: "We must decide, in the face of German pressure, whether to exist or not to exist. Not to exist means dissolving the maquis camps. To exist, now that the snow prevents or slows down enemy movements, means regrouping in a zone that is easy to defend."

Morel's plan was to occupy the Glières Plateau and hold it with 1,200 men. He convinced himself that in the winter the plateau could not be attacked. He further believed that with all the maquis activity in the area, the Germans were demoralized. Finally, he wanted to show London that the maquisards were not a bunch of layabouts who did nothing but send radio messages; they were a force to contend with, capable of a major action that could create serious problems for the Germans.

By February 10, Morel had moved 460 men onto the Glières Plateau and was organizing its defense. Abandoned cabins were found to house them, and food was brought from nearby villages. Igloolike machine-gun emplacements were built in the snow. A team was sent to the nearby ski resort of Mégève to "requisition" skis from vacationers. The drop zone was made ready, with four bonfires that were to be lit as soon as they heard the planes that would come from England. Bad weather delayed the planes until February 14, when fifty-four containers landed deep in the snow outside the cleared drop zone; but Morel's men managed to retrieve most of them. There were other drops on March 4 and March 10. They now had more weapons than they could use—enough, in fact, for 5,000 men. The drops boosted morale, showing the men that they were not completely isolated, that London was thinking about them. But the drops also alerted the Germans, giving them the impression that there were many more maquisards on the Glières than was actually the case.

In the meantime the maquis had reached a sort of modus vivendi with the unit of gendarmes of the collaborationist Vichy regime stationed in the village of Petit-Bornand, where the maquisards often went for supplies. Why, at this late date, should Frenchmen fight Frenchmen? On February 18 a detachment of gendarmes led by the highest-ranking officer in Petit-Bornand, Major Jean Raulet, also out of the St.-Cyr academy, went up to the approaches of the plateau and met with Tom Morel to establish an agreement, which was almost stillborn due to one of those disputes that prickly, protocol-conscious graduates of St.-Cyr are prone to.

"Good morning, monsieur," said Morel, who was wearing a less-than-regulation uniform consisting of a leather jacket, ski pants, and the floppy beret of the *chasseur alpin.*

Annoyed at not being addressed by his rank, Raulet said, "I'm in uniform. You can see I'm a major."

"But you don't know my rank in the resistance," Morel replied.

"You're right, but you will call me *mon commandant* or, I am sorry to tell you, this meeting will be over."

But then, as they talked, they became less formal, and worked out a system wherein the maquisards and the gendarmes would avoid each other. They would take different paths at different hours, and when the maquis went to Petit-Bornand for supplies, the gendarmes would look the other way. The point Morel made was: "We are fighting the Germans, so leave us alone." When Raulet was sent to the Glières a few days later on a reconnaissance mission, he informed Morel where he was going, and on his return reported to the Germans that he had seen nothing.

The agreement between the gendarmes and the maquis, however, was imperfectly observed. On March 1 a medical student named Michel Fournier, who was working in the Glières infirmary, went into Petit-Bornand for medicine and was arrested. Unable to obtain his release, Morel on March 9 took a hundred men to the village of Entremont, where sixty gendarmes were stationed, to collect hostages he could exchange for "Michou" Fournier. He surrounded the Hôtel de France, where the gendarmes were garrisoned, and they compliantly allowed themselves to be disarmed—all but their commander, Captain Paul Lefevre, who refused to be taken prisoner. As in the dispute over rank with Major Raulet, this was a matter of honor between officers, a matter of stubborn pride, tones of voice, an escalation in the wrong things said. Lefevre and Morel got into a shouting match and finally Morel said, "So this means war." "Yes, this means war," replied Lefevre, pulling a revolver from his pocket and firing it point-blank, killing Morel. Lefevre was then killed by a submachine-gun burst from one of Morel's men.

Morel's body was brought back to the Glières on a sled, along with about thirty gendarmes as hostages. He was buried on the plateau on March 11 with full military honors, in a coffin draped with red, white, and blue parachutes from the drops. The next day, March 12, the Glières was bombed by Heinkel 111s based in Dijon. The fifty-kilo bombs didn't do much damage, but Morel's leaderless men were demoralized. Some thought the plateau should be evacuated. But when they radioed London, they got back this message: "Consider Glières a bridgehead. Parachuting one battalion. If operation succeeds, parachuting massive troops." The policy in London had changed with the prospect of a bridgehead and its propaganda value.

With all the weapons they had received, the men of Glières were sure more fighters were on the way. They were in a sense the dupes of those weapons, and of the promises from London.

Captain Maurice Anjot, a career army officer like Tom Morel, took command. He was soon attacked by General Karl Pflaum's 157th Alpine Division of about 7,000 men, plus SS units and 1,000 men of the Vichy Milice. Pflaum's men were armed with mountain artillery and heavy mortars, and had air support. On March 23 the general visited the approaches to the plateau and said he was satisfied with the preparations.

On March 26, after artillery shelling and an aerial bombardment, the attack up the plateau began. The German Alpine troops in their white winter uniforms maneuvered through the trees, blending in with the snow. Anjot's men covered the paths with machine guns, but the Germans got through at Monthievret and poured through the breach, a tide of men in white trudging upward in the thigh-deep snow. They took some losses, and the maquisards could hear the German wounded calling *"Mutti"* ("Mommy").

But it was a hopeless situation. Forty-three maquis died on the first day of fighting. As night fell, Captain Anjot ordered a retreat. Some got through the mountain passes to Annecy. Some came across German patrols and surrendered. Captain Anjot was killed in a skirmish. The Germans took 180 prisoners, most of whom were deported to POW camps. Eleven appeared before a court-martial on May 4, and five of those were shot. Losses reported by the Germans were six dead and fourteen wounded.

London radio turned the Glières battle into a propaganda victory: The maquis had fought off 12,000 Germans for two weeks, inflicting, on a single German battalion, losses of 400 dead and 300 wounded. This would have amounted to a 99-percent casualty rate, since a battalion in Pflaum's division consisted of 708 men. The battalion commander was quoted as saying, "The men of the maquis fought like lions."

By 1973, when André Malraux, a resistance hero himself, came to the Glières Plateau to inaugurate a monument to the memory of the fallen, the 12,000 Germans had grown to 20,000. "It took 20,000 Germans to dislodge 500 Frenchmen from this plateau," Malraux said, "where this great white bird now stands, with one wing of hope and one wing amputated in battle . . . for then, we were waging guerrilla warfare—and remember that France does not choose among her dead who was right and who was wrong—and these men of the Glières directly affronted the *milice*, directly affronted Hitler's army."

But if they were wrong to stand and fight superior forces in an untenable position, who encouraged them with false hopes and broken promises?

Five months later, the same scenario was repeated on a larger scale on the Vercors. Once again there was the mistaken notion that a prolonged defense of a mountain redoubt could be undertaken with a limited number of troops. Once again there was faith in the promises from London. The Vercors was a V-shaped plateau between Grenoble and Valence, with the Rhone and Isère rivers forming the two sides of the V. It was thirty miles long and fifteen miles wide, twice as big as the Glières, with steep limestone cliffs that gave the maquisards a feudal sense of safety, as though they could repel an attack by throwing boiling oil down on their enemies. Deep ravines indented the cliffs like the fingers of a hand, and outcroppings of rocks with strange shapes contributed to the massive, fortresslike appearance. It was mistaken, however, to think of the Vercors as impregnable, for there were a number of approaches, in the form of dirt roads, mule tracks, and mountain passes. The Vercors was a natural fortress with natural and man-made breaches.

It was first used as a hiding place for *réfractaires*—young men escaping forced labor in Germany. In early 1943 there were eighty-five réfractaires hiding in the Ferme d'Ambel, an abandoned farm, and by the end of 1943 there were fourteen such "camps." The idea arose among some of the resistance leaders in the Grenoble area that the plateau could be held. A plan called Operation Montagnard was drawn up, positing that there were only eight ways into the Vercors, five of them up canyons and three cut through solid rock—all easy to defend, and impassable by tanks. The Vercors could be likened to a landlocked aircraft carrier from which planes and troops could be launched. The role of the maquis would be to occupy and defend it until the main body of troops could be flown or parachuted in.

This plan was presented to Jean Moulin, the resistance leader for all of France, in January 1943. He went to London and sold de Gaulle on it. By November 1943 there were about 1,000 maquisards in the Vercors, and on November 13 the first drop came, aluminum cylinders packed with small arms. The Vercors leaders asked for mortars and heavy machine guns, but London replied that "guerrilla tactics do not require heavy weapons."

As word got out that a maquis redoubt was forming in the Vercors, men began to arrive from surrounding cities—from Grenoble and Romans, from Die and Voiron, even from Lyons—until by May 1944 there were roughly 4,000. From London and Algiers, where de Gaulle was now based, came messages of encouragement. The plan called for dropping 4,000 paratroopers into the Vercors. On May 30 a directive from Algiers said, "Go ahead with Vercors operations." This implied that requests for heavy weapons and more troops would be honored.

Then came the Normandy landing on June 6, which was followed by an order for mobilization in the Vercors. It later turned out that this order was part of a greater plan: The Allies wanted the Germans to think the Normandy landing would be followed almost at once by a landing in Provence, so that German troops would remain south of Lyon. The Free French were asked to send the mobilization order, which they expected would be intercepted by the Germans and confirm the Germans in this opinion. The Free French agreed on condition that they be allowed to countermand the mobilization order within a few days. This they did, telling the Vercors leaders that the time was not ripe for immediate operations, that the Allies were throwing all their resources into the Normandy pocket and had nothing left over for the maquis.

But it's one thing to countermand an order, and quite another to break

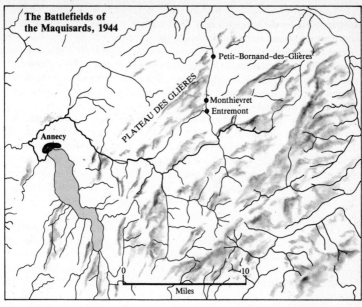

The Battlefields of the Maquisards, 1944

Petit-Bornand-des-Glières

Monthievret
Entremont

PLATEAU DES GLIÈRES

Annecy

0   10

Miles

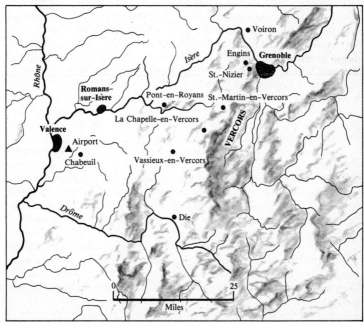

Voiron

Isère

Engins   Grenoble
St.-Nizier

Romans-sur-Isère

Pont-en-Royans   St.-Martin-en-Vercors

Rhône

La Chapelle-en-Vercors

VERCORS

Valence

Airport

Chabeuil

Vassieux-en-Vercors

Drôme

Die

0   25

Miles

the momentum built up in the euphoria of events. The men of the Vercors were mobilized and ready for action. Their momentum, fueled by promises of heavy weapons and more troops, could not be reversed. By this time the Germans had realized what was going on, and on June 13 a German column of 400 men was observed marching up the eastern approach. This was in fact the breach in the Vercors rampart, a winding road with hairpin turns from Grenoble up to the village of St.-Nizier. The only solution was to mass enough men there to defend it.

Defend it they did, beating back the Germans. But two days later the enemy returned with 2,000 men and took St.-Nizier. To the military leader of the Vercors, Major François Huet, a regular-army officer, this was not a major blow. To the contrary, it meant a shorter defense perimeter. One of the problems of the Vercors Plateau was that it was so big that to defend all of it thinned out his troops, a few men here, a few men there. This was the time to change tactics, to disperse and regain mobility, rather than try to defend the entire vast mesa.

The pull of the heroic defense was still great, however, and a cautionary message saying "Situation catastrophic" was sent to Algiers in hopes of prodding de Gaulle into sending the clamored-for bazookas, mortars, mountain guns, and reinforcements from the sky. Each night they listened for the message that meant a drop was coming—"Le petit chat est mort" ("The little cat is dead"). But the little cat did not die.

On June 22 the men on the plateau looked down and saw troop movements on the ring road, départementale 93. It was one of those cloudless days when the men on the plateau could see the shadows cast by trees on the road 3,000 feet below. Besides what they could see, they had a good flow of information from all over the region. Toward the end of June, there was bad news and good. The bad news was that German gliders had arrived at the Montélimar airport, using tail parachutes to check their speed on landing. The good news was that a few days later, on June 25, thirty-six Liberator bombers dropped 800 containers near Vassieux-en-Vercors, one of the maquis headquarters. To celebrate, they held a parade. The nurses from the Vercors field hospital wore their starched caps and aprons.

As the men of the Vercors now saw it, their biggest threat was the airfield near the town of Chabeuil, on the western edge of the plateau. The Germans were five minutes by air from the heart of the Vercors, which they could bomb at will. On June 26, Junkers 88s taking off from Chabeuil bombed and strafed the Vercors villages of Saint-Martin and Vassieux. Chabeuil became an obsession. Every day a message was sent to Algiers: "For God's sake, bomb Chabeuil."

They now realized that they were surrounded and at the mercy of bombardments, but they lived on hope—of massive troop drops and of the expected Allied landing in the south of France, which they did not know had been put off until August 15. On July 3 the Republic of Vercors was proclaimed, with its own courts and government, and the French flag flew on the plateau.

Meanwhile, the Germans were mounting the biggest operation ever seen in France against the maquis, spearheaded by those veterans of the Glières victory, General Karl Pflaum's 157th Alpine Division. Pflaum also had under his command a unit of SS glider troops, an elite regiment of Alpine commandos, or *Gebirgsjager*, two batteries of mountain guns, air support from the Chabeuil air base, and tanks from the 9th Panzer Division out of Valence—in all, about 10,000 men.

Pflaum's plan was a dawn attack from all points of the compass—from the town of Die in the south up toward Vassieux; from Pont-en-Royans in the west and St.-Nizier in the east; and over the mule-track passes to the north and northeast. Two hours after launching the ground attack, glider troops would be dropped on Vassieux. Then there would be serious mop-up operations. As a trump card, General Pflaum had a map of the Vercors water sources, from which the maquisards would have to supply themselves.

London and Algiers were responding to the pleas of the men on the plateau, but in a small way. In early July an OSS team of eleven Americans and four Canadians was dropped, and on July 7 the airstrip team finally arrived, an engineer and his men, who started leveling a 300-foot runway. The engineer spent his days peering through his surveyor sextant, and promised to have the job done in a week.

On July 12 La-Chapelle-en-Vercors, another maquis headquarters, was bombed. On July 14 seventy-two Flying Fortresses dropped 800 containers over Vassieux in broad daylight, leading to more German bombing and strafing. When it was all over, the Vercors survivors wondered: Had the daylight drop been ordered so the Germans would think the Vercors was about to be reinforced? Was this more disinformation, tied to the slow progress in Normandy?

On July 15 the Germans blew up a bridge over the Isère River to the west of Pont-en-Royans, and a tunnel at Engins, closing off two exit roads. The 157th Alpine Division was on the move from Chambéry to Grenoble, and the panzers were moving up from Valence. The horse-drawn mountain artillery was positioned near the passes. On July 18 the Germans laid mines, set up their machine-gun emplacements, and methodically sealed off the remaining escape routes. On July 20 fifteen heavy guns arrived by train from Lyon.

The men of the Vercors could actually watch themselves being boxed in. They were the observers of their coming demise. They knew they were about to be attacked by a division-strength force armed with tanks, artillery, mortars, and air cover. They knew that only a massive troop drop or an Allied landing in the south could save them, and they also began to realize that it was too late for either. A message went out to Algiers: "If you want to save the Vercors you must act quickly."

On July 21, as the dawn sun touched the Vercors peaks with purple, the German attack was launched. About 200 maquisards were at work on the landing strip at 7 A.M. when they heard planes. Looking up, they saw forty unmarked aircraft in the sky, towing gliders. Just in time, they thought. They took off their caps and cheered and waved, and the antiaircraft machine guns on the airstrip held their fire. But when the gliders were released and swooped down on the strip, 400 SS men jumped out, ten per glider, firing submachine guns and flamethrowers. They quickly overwhelmed the maquisards in Vassieux and took control of a central point on the plateau even as it was being besieged from all four sides.

On July 22 the big three-engine Junkers 88 bombers landed on the airstrip that had been meant for Allied Dakotas, bringing in fresh troops and supplies and taking out the German wounded. On July 23 General Pflaum sent his Alpine commandos up the steep western slope, the slope that was dubbed "the French Dolomites." They surprised the maquisards at two poorly defended passes. The French were now caught in an east-west pincer, with the Germans also holding the center of the plateau. It was hopeless, and Major Huet ordered dispersal by small groups. They would try to get off the plateau by slipping through the German lines.

The maquisards' last message, on July 24, expressed all their anger and frustration: "We consider that those in Algiers who have understood nothing of our situation are criminals and cowards."

Among those who evacuated the plateau were the wounded, doctors, nurses, and chaplain of the Vercors field hospital, who found a hiding place in a huge cavern with a twenty-foot ceiling, the Grotte de la Luire, five miles north of Die. There were twenty-six wounded, among them four German prisoners and an American OSS man. On July 25, the mop-up operations came so close to the grotto that the wounded heard dogs bark, and at night saw flares in the sky and tracer bullets being fired into the underbrush.

That day it was all over. In Grenoble, General Pflaum congratulated himself: "It's *wunderschön,* it's only taken five days." Now they were combing the Vercors for the maquis remnants, some of whom were shot on sight. Many others, however, including Major Huet, escaped. The French losses were 639 dead, while the Germans lost a total of 159.

On July 27, a gray-capped German soldier, with fifteen more behind him, peered into the opening of the Grotte de la Luire. The four German wounded, recognizing men from their unit, started shouting, "Nicht schiessen! Hier ist ein Krankenhaus! Wir sind Gefangene! Sie haben uns gepflegt!" ("Don't shoot! It's a hospital! We're prisoners! They took care of us!"). The SD lieutenant in charge took the wounded to an abandoned farm nearby and had all but one of the wounded non-Germans shot. Those who could stand were lined up against a wall. The others were shot on their stretchers. The OSS man was spared—he was a curiosity, the first American they had seen in the war. Two of the three doctors and the Jesuit chaplain were shot, and the seven nurses were deported to Ravensbruck.

I don't want to imply that the maquis conducted only strategically unsound, doomed operations. The Vercors and Glières actions were exceptions, not the rule. In most areas of France, the maquis held itself to the standard guerrilla tactics of surprise attacks and sabotage. Their harassment of the occupiers grew so much in 1944 that the Germans retaliated with exceptional brutality. When two German soldiers were shot in Lyon on January 10, twenty-two hostages paid "the well-known forfeit." When grenades were thrown at a detachment of German troops in Clermont-Ferrand on March 8, killing one and wounding thirty-two, fifty hostages were shot.

And if the maquis was defeated on the plateaus of Glières and Vercors, it also scored some major victories. For example, on June 8, 1944, the SS Panzer Division Das Reich moved out of its Montauban garrison in the south of France to reinforce the German troops on the Normandy front. This 450-mile trip, which should have taken three days, lasted more than two weeks, owing to the guerrilla attacks of various maquis groups. The delay was crucial to the Allies, helping them to secure the Normandy bridgehead. But French civilians paid the price—642 men, women, and children massacred by the SS in the village of Oradour-sur-Glane.

In the case of the Vercors, however, as in the case of the Glières, defeat was inadmissible. On the same day that General Pflaum expressed his pleasure at the outcome, General de Gaulle in Algiers spoke before the recently formed French Consultative Assembly, the embryo of a postwar French government. It was important to present to this group a rosy picture of maquis activities, and so he said:

> Even at this moment, the enemy is attacking the Vercors massif with forces of every service and major air support. According to unimpeachable reports, the Germans have already lost, in this incessant struggle since the beginning of June, at least 8,000 dead, more than 2,000 prisoners, and a very large number of wounded.

What were these "unimpeachable reports"? In reality, there was only the final cry of distress from the Vercors on the previous day. De Gaulle knew that the Vercors was lost; however, the situation required a legend. No other maquis unit had the distinction of having been attacked by the Germans in such numbers. Today in the Vercors, tourist buses chug through the tunnels, and guides point out the places where battles were fought. The plateau is sprinkled with white crosses; one comes upon them not only in cemeteries but in fields and woods, on mule tracks and mountain passes, and on the banks of streams—wherever men fell.

Casey's German Gamble

by JOSEPH E. PERSICO

There are few figures in recent American history so deviously—some would say malevolently—influential as William J. Casey, the CIA director under Ronald Reagan. Casey did not come into the job without experience in intelligence. As the chief spymaster of the OSS in Europe during the last months of the war against Hitler, he had brought off a genuine coup, and one that few thought possible: the penetration of Nazi Germany by American spies. Casey's operatives really were versed in the dark arts that we associate with fictional espionage thrillers. Where is the best place for a parachutist to land? How do you deal with a suspicious policeman? How do you kill with a newspaper? What is an L pill? Or a Joan-Eleanor? Casey was by disposition a gambler, and for the most part, as Joseph E. Persico tells us, his German gamble worked. But forty years later it was the same instinct that would lead him to the grief of Iran-Contra. This article was adapted from Persico's biography, *Casey: The Lives and Secrets of William J. Casey from the OSS to the CIA,* published by Viking Penguin.

In December of 1944, William J. Casey, who thirty-seven years later would become the most controversial director in the CIA's history, was a navy lieutenant JG attached to the London headquarters of the Office of Strategic Services. Casey, at that point, was about to cross a divide: From serving essentially as an espionage paper-pusher, he would author one of the lesser-known clandestine triumphs of World War II, the penetration of Nazi Germany by American spies.

The thirty-one-year-old Casey had come to America's fledgling spy service by a circuitous but typical route. A law-school classmate had joined the prestigious New York firm of Donovan, Leisure, Newton & Lombard. The senior partner was William ("Wild Bill") Donovan, "father of the OSS." Casey worked this old school tie to have himself transferred from the navy—where he was slowly going mad reviewing shipbuilders' contracts for landing craft—to the OSS. His credentials were neither better nor worse than those of most neophyte U.S. spies: graduation from Fordham University in 1934; a brief stint as a depression-era social worker; law school; and a rapid flowering as one of the youngest and best-informed authorities on wartime mobilization while working for an organization called the Research Institute of America.

Casey could easily have ridden out the war in this role, but he itched to be in the fight. Hence the wire pulling that brought him to the OSS. His formal title in London was chief of the OSS Secretariat for the European theater of operations. More accurately, he had become Donovan's man, one of the general's roving cage rattlers, an extension of his eyes and ears.

It seemed, however, that Casey's war would soon end. By the fall of 1944, with the Western Allies at the German border and the Russians closing in from the east, Germany's defeat was foreordained. In the last war the Germans had been sensible enough to quit before bringing destruction down on their own homeland. Allied leaders expected self-interest and reason to prevail again. In the fall of 1944, American GIs were talking "home by Christmas."

Instead, Adolf Hitler struck back. All along the Siegfried Line, resistance stiffened. General George Patton's headlong race across France stalled along the Moselle River. Field Marshal Bernard Montgomery's rash gamble, Operation Market Garden—a northerly bypass of the Siegfried Line and a dash through Holland, straight on to Berlin—failed utterly. And then, on December 16, the Germans launched an offense of blitzkrieg scale through the Ardennes: the Battle of the Bulge. Winston Churchill told the British people, "The truth is, no one knows when the German war will be finished."

From the moment Casey had first heard Donovan mention the desirabilty of infiltrating agents directly into Germany, during a plane ride earlier that summer up the Loire River, he had started turning the idea over in his mind. In September he had sent Donovan a secret cable headed "An OSS Program Against Germany." Casey described what he saw as a Trojan horse:

> There are some two million Russians, more than a million and a half Poles, a million and a half Belgians, between 300,000 and 400,000 Dutch, and on and on inside Germany, an explosive potential for us that we must not overlook.

On December 17, the day after the U.S. First Army was caught flat-footed by the German drive through the Ardennes, Casey sent Donovan another message, urging him to shift gears:

> It must be assumed that the Germans will be able to maintain resistance throughout the winter. . . . Intelligence on order of battle, defense installations, air targets, morale, military plans and other conditions inside Germany should carry the highest intelligence priority. Controls over movements and food are now so tight that the establishment of agents inside Germany is likely to be an extremely slow and uncertain process. However,

when these controls begin to break down, OSS must be ready to place agents within Germany.

The London OSS office was divided into two major branches: Secret Operations (SO), the blow-up-the-enemy-bridges end of the business; and Secret Intelligence (SI), the clandestine collection of information, traditional spying. SI was now paramount. Joe Haskell headed SI in London. But Haskell, a West Pointer, had grown weary of espionage and wangled a combat command. By December 1944 the SI job was vacant. Haskell's deputy, Alan Scaife, was his presumed successor. Casey's judgment of Scaife was brutal: "He was one of the original white shoe boys. He'd done it all in a day. He'd married one of the Mellon heiresses. And that took care of Alan. The guy didn't have much steam. His people were rattling around with nothing to do. SI was falling apart."

Just before Christmas, while the Battle of the Bulge was still raging, Donovan came to London with Whitney Shepardson, the worldwide SI chief. The two closeted themselves with David Bruce, the OSS commander for Europe, and other London brass. The meeting went on for most of the afternoon. "When they finally came out," Casey recalled, "Donovan took me aside and said, 'Bill, you're the new chief of SI for Europe. I'm giving you carte blanche.' To do what? I asked him. Those blue eyes of his twinkled and he said, 'Why, to get us into Germany.'"

As a still junior partner of the British, the OSS had dropped over a hundred teams into France in advance of D Day. But these agents had landed in friendly lands and were welcomed by an occupied people eager to drive out the Nazis. By contrast, an agent sent into Germany would be parachuting into the enemy heartland. No resistance fighters would greet him on the ground. No safe houses would be waiting. No communications channels existed. And in the wake of the plot against Hitler, the Gestapo had tightened its control over the German people like a garrote.

Even the Allies' grand strategy worked against penetration of the Reich. The Allies demanded unconditional surrender. Roosevelt had further asked his confidant and treasury secretary, Henry Morgenthau, to devise a plan for pacifying Germany after the war. Morgenthau had come up with a scheme for dismembering Germany and turning her into "a country primarily agricultural and pastoral in character." The Allies thus had handed Nazi fanatics a powerful reason to spur the German people to fight on. What was to be gained by surrender? Total prostration before the victors, while, in Joseph Goebbels's phrase, their country was reduced to "a potato patch."

Casey moved into the office vacated by Joe Haskell and began to inventory his assets. "We had nothing at all on Germany," he later recalled.

Until now, all we had thought about was how the hell did you get on those Normandy beaches without being thrown off? We had not thought beyond France. Then, all of a sudden, that war is over. We had this apparatus and didn't know what to do with it. The army hadn't always wanted our help. But they saw what we could do in southern France. And they were taking a beating in the Ardennes. Terrible casualties. And why? A colossal intelligence failure. So now the brass was more receptive to us.

As soon as I had SI, while the Bulge was still being fought, I went to see two top Brits in intelligence—Sir Stewart Menzies, who later became "C," the head of MI6; and Sir Gerald Templer, who headed up the German desk for Special Operations, Executive. I was disappointed. "It can't be done, Mr. Casey. We're sorry. You won't be able to get your people in—and if you do, you won't be able to get their intelligence out. This is Germany, not Holland or Yugoslavia."

But Donovan wanted it. Penetrating Germany was to be our first totally OSS show. We'd lose people, sure, but nothing compared to the casualties our troops were taking along the Siegfried Line. It didn't matter what the British said. It didn't discourage me. I never entertained for a minute any thought of not going ahead. And I accomplished one thing at least: I got the Brits to lift their ban on operations by us against Germany. At least they wouldn't stand in the way.

Casey realized that he already had the skeleton of a German operation upstairs, over his office: the Labor Division. One of the early casualties of Nazism had been the German trade-union movement, which Hitler replaced with a paper organization. The deposed trade unionists, mostly socialists and Communists, had been herded into concentration camps or had fled the country. Arthur J. Goldberg, general counsel for the CIO at the beginning of the war, had persuaded Donovan that these labor refugees represented priceless intelligence assets. They possessed an unrivaled knowledge of Germany's economic infrastructure; workers knew what made a country work. Donovan had immediately grasped the point and persuaded Goldberg to exploit this potential by creating a labor organization within the OSS.

While the other units at 70 Grosvenor parachuted spies and saboteurs into occupied Europe, the Labor Division went about its humdrum chores. It was run by George Pratt, who, before the war, had been chief trial counsel for the National Labor Relations Board. Pratt would give a few pounds to some half-starved Düsseldorf railroad-union exile who could tell him exactly how coal cars were loaded in the Ruhr. His people studied bills of lading, which revealed what sorts of German war matériel was moving on Rhine River barges. The staff of the Labor Division pored over German newspapers, smuggled in through neutral Sweden and Portugal. They filed away odd bits of information that slowly began to yield an X ray of daily life inside Germany— the ration cards issued, curfew hours, travel permits required. A news story about a woman who had been arrested for selling cigarettes to a foreign worker revealed the location of a conscript labor camp, a possible site for harboring an agent.

Pratt was an ancient by OSS standards, then in his mid-forties, a small, neat, sandy-haired man with a little half-smile that suggested a secret understanding of life. Casey called him down to his office. "George," he said, "those Reds you're harboring upstairs are the only people around here who know a damn thing about Germany. I'm going to use the Labor Division as the cadre for the German operations. I'm going to create a whole new organization around it. We'll call it the Division of Intelligence Procurement. Nobody will know what the hell that means. But the DIP is going to put agents inside Germany. And you're going to run it under me. Anything, anybody you want, you get. You're going to have to learn how to recruit, how we train agents, how we invent cover stories, how we paper the agents, how we get them into Germany, and how we get the intelligence out."

Casey gave him the priorities passed along by the army. "First, we want troop movements through rail centers. The next thing we need are targets for the Eighth Air Force. After that, we want to know industrial output, especially anything on new Kraut wonder-weapons. And if you've got any time left, anything that will tell us if the Nazis are serious about the Alpine Redoubt, this last-ditch stand in Bavaria we keep hearing about."

It was as if a man and a mission had been waiting a lifetime to be mated. Richard Helms, then an OSS navy lieutenant, one day to be the director of Central Intelligence himself, roomed with Casey at the time. "The man had a natural bent for what the Germans call *Fingerspitzengefühl*," Helms remembered, "a feel for the clandestine. He had enormous drive, too. Bill could set a goal, get people fired up to do it, and then give them their heads."

Casey may have inspired those under him, but he still wore only the uniform of a navy lieutenant, and he now had to deal on equal terms with men who were ranks above him—army generals, Air Corps brass, chiefs of Allied intelligence services. Casey took his problem to Lester Armour, who, as a captain, was the senior OSS naval officer in the London office. "Let's go see Admiral Stark," Armour suggested. "He's just across the street. Maybe we can get you a little more braid."

Harold Stark was not eager to put navy noses out of joint by jumping Casey over scores of officers with actual naval experience. He had another solution. As Casey recalled, "The admiral took one look at me and said, 'The best thing we can do for him is put him in a gray suit.' So Captain Armour walked me around the corner to Selfridge's, and I bought two gray suits." On January 5, 1945, Casey was mustered out of the navy, but he retained his OSS position as a civilian. He was Mr. Casey again, a supple enough rank to deal with any amount of brass.

His first concern was the potential agent pool. Americans, no matter how fluent in German, were out of the question. If young and healthy, why weren't they in the Wehrmacht? If old or unhealthy, how could they parachute? More-promising sources were the prisoner-of-war cages. Here were tens of thousands of native Germans—and among them, inevitably, anti-Nazis. But General Dwight Eisenhower, as supreme Allied commander, had forbidden the recruitment of POWs as secret agents; it violated the Geneva Conventions. The best single source was the pool of exiles in London who could be infiltrated into that huge body of foreign conscript workers in Germany. They did not have to be German. They did not have to speak German. But their cover as workers limited them to a low-level perspective of the Reich.

Far more ticklish was the question of using German communist refugees living in England. On the one hand, they possessed model credentials: They were German; they hated the Nazis; and they had brawled with Hitler's brownshirts for years to see who would rule Germany. When they lost, the least lucky Communists wound up in concentration camps, and the more fortunate escaped Germany.

On the other hand, Casey gagged at the prospect of using Communists as American spies. On one of his trips to Paris, he had met Albert Jolis, a dashing and sophisticated scion of an old diamond-merchant family. Jolis had been recruited into the OSS because his business had given him a wide acquaintance with European labor leaders. Jolis, too, was horrified at the prospect of recruiting German Communists as agents. At the end of the war, they would be in place, positioned to seize power. The affinity between the two men was instant. "Here," at last, Jolis thought, "is someone who sees communism the way I do."

In the end, Casey's trust in Donovan proved stronger than his abhorrence of the Left. It was all too clear what Donovan felt in his heart, but he had said he would deal with the devil to beat Hitler. Was Casey to be more Catholic than the pope? "Look," Casey told a disappointed Jolis, "I think it's wrong. But the old man wants it." And so Casey began to prepare communist exiles for a trip home to Germany as U.S. spies.

Casey also managed to find a way around the ban on recruiting prisoners of war. German-speaking OSS officers would go into the POW cages and strike up conversations. They might profess a grudging admiration for Hitler and wait to see who disagreed. Prisoners who had served in *Strafbataillon* (German army punishment units) were often receptive. But no matter what the approach, the Americans in the end always asked, "Are you saying you want to volunteer to fight against the Nazis?" An answer in the affirmative left a legalistic crack of light between recruitment and volunteering.

The agent pool was now defined: Europeans who could pass as foreign workers; anti-Nazi German prisoners of war; and willing refugee Germans.

Casey found two men in the Labor Division to manufacture cover stories. Privates Lazare Teper and Henry Sutton were unlikely soldiers, two soft-looking men, already in their thirties. Teper was big, dark-haired, shambling, with an engaging lopsided smile. Sutton was fat, with apple cheeks, undisciplined tufts of blond hair, and a high-pitched Viennese accent. (He had been born Heinrich Sofner.) It was left to Teper, the senior private, to choose a name for the new cover-story unit—of which he and Sutton were the entire roster. He called it the Bach Section, after his favorite composer.

The section's cubicles were jammed with files containing alphabetized facts on hundreds of German cities. From this mass of minutiae, Teper and Sutton began to construct a person, giving him or her a family history, an authentic address, schools attended, a profession, dates and places of employment. They included such details as the color of the buses in the agent's hometown, and the burial place of deceased parents (a favorite question that the Gestapo posed to suspected enemy agents).

The identity chosen dictated what papers the agent would need: a foreign worker's passport for a conscript laborer; a paybook for an ersatz soldier; a hospital pass for a phony nurse. In addition, there were ID and ration cards for everybody. The Bach Section passed along these requirements to Willis Reddick, Casey's chief counterfeiter. Reddick was a neat, mustachioed man who had run a printing business in Springfield, Illinois, before the war. He had a simple, useful approach to his work: Anything that could be printed could be counterfeited. Reddick would locate servicemen who had previously worked for the U.S. Bureau of Printing and Engraving and the American Bank Note Company, as well as commercial artists from the staffs of *Collier's* and the *Saturday Evening Post.* Casey would arrange to have them transferred to London. Actual forgers who could have been sprung from prison held no interest for Reddick: "How good could they be?" he said. "They got caught."

Reddick's people never lacked for cigarettes—they simply counterfeited ration stamps. Carl Strahle, who ran the printshop, once came worriedly to Reddick. "Suppose these guys decide to start knocking out the British five-pound note?" Strahle asked. "They could do it, you know."

Reddick's models were authentic German documents scavenged by OSS teams from captured towns, from POWs, from the enemy dead. To give the documents an aged patina, the forgers left them on the floor, where they were walked on all day, or wore them for a time in their armpits.

Nearby, on Brook Street, was the OSS clothing depot, a brownstone with an interior that looked like a thrift shop run by the Salvation Army. Some of the clothes literally came off the backs of refugees from Germany. OSS people asked if they would be willing to sell their suits, dresses, shoes, hats, combs, razors, shaving brushes, wallets, even the suitcases they carried— anything made in Germany. German uniforms could be found among the detritus of battle or acquired in POW cages. OSS officers would enter a cage and have the prisoners fall in for "inspection." The demands of the Geneva Conventions were technically observed: If a man's tunic or cap was taken, he was given a replacement. The item might not fit, but the conventions were not specific about sizes.

For the last, most critical link in the chain of penetration, where error meant almost certain capture or death, Casey relied on a former Brooklyn photographer. Lieutenant Anthony Turano's job was to choose the pinpoints where the agents were to be parachuted. The ideal pinpoint, Turano learned through hard experience, was a flat field, away from antiaircraft batteries, near a woods where an agent could hide, near a back road he could travel, and with a major feature visible from the air by night—a lake, a bend in a river, the ever-burning lights of a German POW camp. Turano's chief headache was the Army Air Corps. Pilots hated dropping agents. They dreaded flying low enough or slow enough to make safe, accurate drops—which from their perspective felt like playing sitting duck to German guns.

Casey liked to go out to Area F, the training facility outside London, to see it all coming together. Area F was part trade school and part Fagin's classroom. The curriculum included burglary, bribery, and blackmail. Agents were taught how to use shortwave radio, how to remember what they saw and how to report it, how to copy a signature from a real document to a false one by using the damp surface of a freshly hard-boiled egg, how to parachute (taught in three days, compared to six weeks for army airborne units). They also learned how to kill with a newspaper: Fold it into a square, then fold it diagonally to make a point; shove the point into the soft flesh just under the chin. And they learned that if a policeman seemed to be watching them, the best thing was to ask him for directions to allay his suspicions. If captured, agents were to endure torture for forty-eight hours so their accomplices would have time to get away. If they could not stand the torture, their alternatives were escape or the L pill—a dose of cyanide encased in rubber; a captured agent could bite into it and be dead in minutes. If an agent did not survive, the U.S. government would pay his designated beneficiary a $2,500 death benefit.

Casey lived in an incongruous world in London. OSS personnel there were safe from the front, yet exposed to the occasional earth-shuddering blasts of the V-2s. Casey's Division of Intelligence Procurement put in eighteen-hour days while the white-shoe boys partied all night in Mayfair salons on PX scotch and black-market luxuries. He himself was either lunching with Stewart Menzies at the Travellers or sharing cold rations with agents in a hut at an airfield.

Unlike Donovan, Casey was a man whose sense of adventure was vicarious. Watching the trainees, he was filled with a mixture of awe and puzzlement. What made them do it? What would induce a man to jump out of an airplane to spy inside Nazi Germany? Their cover was thin at best—10 percent hard fact, the rest invention, often pure guesswork. Given little enough inquiry, any cover story would collapse. In the end, the agent's greatest protection lay in his mind—in quick-wittedness, in a talent for lying, in the vigilance, fear, and loneliness that honed his instinct for self-preservation.

As Casey left Area F, he would tell the agent handlers, "Give these guys anything they want. They're the kings around here. We work for them."

On a moonlit evening late in January of 1945, Casey and Pratt climbed into an army panel van at Area O, the staging area. The two men made desultory small talk. Reddick, Pratt said, was having trouble getting the watermarks right on foreign worker passports. The Polish recruits were an undisciplined lot, but they were tremendously eager. It looked like a clear night. If the weather held over Germany, finding the pinpoint should be no problem.

Leon Grell, an OSS escort officer, appeared with two men. They were dressed in mismatched suit jackets and pants, dingy white shirts buttoned at the neck, worn cloth caps—in all respects the uniform of working-class Europeans. Grell introduced the agents to Casey and Pratt as the "Doctor" team, the code name for their mission. They were two Belgians going in as conscript workers.

They began the two-hour drive to Harrington airfields, guided in the pitch-black night only by parking lights. As they rode, Casey studied the men out of the corner of his eye. One kept up a stream of gallows humor, each joke followed by a nervous giggle that died in the unresponding silence. The other agent remained grim-faced and said nothing.

At Harrington, Grell led them into a Quonset hut and ordered the agents to empty their pockets, to make sure they were not taking British railway ticket stubs, matchbooks advertising the Kit-Kat Club, or Players cigarettes into Germany. He sealed their personal possessions—money, letters, photographs, and keys—in an envelope and told the men cheerily that he would return everything soon, when they came back. Next, he went through a checklist of their forged documents. Then he gave each man a money belt with the equivalent of $700 in reichsmarks and two gold pieces. Each also received a Smith & Wesson .45. The pistols had little practical value, but they boosted the agents' morale. Finally, they were issued three packets of pills. The blue pills were to overcome fatigue; the white were knockout pills; the third was the L pill.

Grell told the agents to take off their shoes. He bandaged their ankles and fixed rubber cushions under their heels to help break the force of the jump. They were handed jumpsuits, baggy affairs that fit easily over their clothes. A zipper ran the length of the suit, so the agent could step out of it in an instant. In the roomy pockets were a flashlight, a knife to cut the chute if it got hung up in a tree, and a short spade to bury the parachute and the jumpsuit. The two men slipped on helmets lined with sponge-rubber cushioning, then goggles, leather gauntlets, and finally their parachutes. Grell fluttered around them, tugging at the straps, like a mother dressing a bride. When he finished, he nodded to Casey, who shook hands with the men. He watched them climb into a B-24 painted black to melt into the night sky. And he watched the plane take off. Casey's first mission was on its way to Germany.

Months before, in autumn 1944, Casey had had dinner with a navy lieutenant commander named Stephen Simpson. They had talked about a key obstacle that would have to be overcome if they ever penetrated Germany—communications. Spies in occupied Europe were able to communicate via shortwave radio from safe houses. The signal was diffuse and could be picked up by German radiogoniometry vans that cruised city streets and the countryside, but agents solved this problem by frequently changing safe houses. In Germany, however, there were no assured safe houses. Shortwave radio would be terribly risky.

Simpson, an RCA engineer before the war, had told Casey of a solution. Since joining the OSS, he had been working on a system that would let an agent on the ground communicate directly to a plane flying overhead. He had wanted to see Casey because he knew that the man had a reputation for getting things done. "You give me the people, the equipment, and the right plane," Casey remembered him saying, "and I can give you a way to communicate from Germany."

Casey had managed to get Simpson the support he needed, and early in 1945 the engineer produced his system. The agent on the ground carried a battery-powered transmitter/receiver that fit into the palm of his hand. Its signal rose on a beam no wider than a pencil at the point of origin, widening gradually until it reached the plane circling overhead. The narrow signal was virtually undetectable on the ground. Aboard the plane a radio operator talked directly to the agent and recorded their conversation on a new gadget, a recorder that captured sound on a spool of wire. Simpson called his invention Joan-Eleanor, Joan for a WAC officer he admired and Eleanor for the wife of a colleague.

Casey assigned a young, quietly effective officer, Lieutenant Colonel John Bross, to get Simpson the aircraft he needed. Bross cajoled, wheedled, begged, and finally managed to get the air force to provide a lightweight attack bomber, the A-26, which had a range of 1,400 miles.

"Do you know what that means?" Simpson had asked Casey.

"Sure," Casey said. "It means we can drop a team into Berlin."

By now Casey had resigned himself to consorting with Communists. The first attempt to parachute agents near Berlin was assigned to a team of two German Communists who had worked together in an anti-Nazi labor organization. They had ultimately made the Gestapo death list but managed to escape to England. Pratt had designated their mission "Hammer," which Casey liked to refer to as "Hammer and Sickle." The team, equipped with Joan-Eleanor, flew an A-26 out of Watton airfield on March 1, 1945.

The missions had begun to clog the pipeline. Over fifty teams were backlogged, waiting for the next moonlit period. Casey became impatient and decided to take a calculated risk: He tried test-dropping agents by the dark of the moon. The result was a surprise: Virtually the same percentage of teams hit the pinpoint whether they jumped in the dark or by moonlight. From then on, agents parachuted every night that the weather permitted planes to fly. By May, Casey had fifty-eight teams inside Germany.

The job became his graduate education in geopolitics. He had formed sixteen teams of highly motivated Poles, men who had witnessed Nazi barbarism in their homeland. Then, in February of 1945, at Yalta, the Western Allies ceded part of Poland to the Soviet Union. Allied leaders buckled to Soviet pressure and backed away from the democratic Polish government-in-exile in London in favor of Stalin's proxies, the Lublin provisional government. Overnight, Casey recalled, "the morale drained right out of our Poles. I could see it happening before my eyes. After that, they just went through the motions. They weren't worth a damn. I never forgot what caving in to the Russians did to those people."

Dropping agents was roughly comparable to planting a garden: One sowed seeds, then waited for something to come up. The DIP dropped a team near Bochum, or Regensburg, or Stuttgart, then waited for the first shortwave transmission, the first message to be brought out by courier, the first successful Joan-Eleanor connection. The seeds began to sprout, some to flower, some to be crushed underfoot, some to disappear entirely. The first team that Casey had seen off, Doctor, had set up in Kufstein in the Alps and become downright garrulous, transmitting more than fifty messages to London. The Doctor team reported that Allied fears that the Germans were preparing to hole up in an Alpine redoubt appeared to be unfounded.

Eleven days after being dropped near Berlin, the Hammer team began talking via Joan-Eleanor to an A-26 circling overhead. The agents identified a power plant on the Rommelsbergsee still feeding key war industries despite daily bombing raids over Berlin. The agents also pinpointed for the Eighth Air Force two tank factories still functioning in the suburbs.

The Chauffeur mission established itself in Regensburg, where the agents recruited two French girls who had been forced into prostitution by the German army. The girls slipped the agents into their closet to eavesdrop on the postcoital revelations of German officers. Later, from a field outside of town, the team reported via Joan-Eleanor the movement of units heading west to meet the Allied advance. They also located the headquarters of the general staff in Regensburg as a possible bomber target.

A team called "Luxe" virtually ordered up a bombing raid on the railhead in Weilheim. The Air Corps sent in P-38 Lightning dive bombers and the after-action report read: "Heavy damage to tracks, rolling stock on the Munich-Garmisch-Partenkirchen line. . . ." What the Luxe team saw on the ground was that one building of an aircraft plant had been slightly damaged, but the rest of the American bombs had struck houses in a residential neighborhood and hit a clearly marked hospital train, further injuring or killing over 350 wounded men.

In February, George Pratt reported to Casey on Crocus, the code name for Hilde Meisl. She had been recruited in London, where she was living as a refugee member of a puritanical sect of German socialists who did not eat meat and did not smoke or drink. She was a plain woman in her early thirties with a scrubbed face that had never known makeup. She pulled back her hair into a bun and wore drab dresses of the type favored by American Shakers. She had been flown to a point near the French-Swiss frontier, where she was able to slip into Switzerland. Eventually she made her way over the Austrian border to Vienna and succeeded in setting up an intelligence network among fellow socialists there. She had been returning over the Austrian-Swiss border when an SS patrol spotted her and brought her down with a shot that shattered both her legs. Before any of the SS could reach her, Meisl bit into her L pill. Pratt remembered that Casey seemed surprised at the news. Clearly, the activities at 70 Grosvenor could have deadly consequences.

The Chisel team was dispatched during foul weather in an A-26 with a defective navigation system, and the plane vanished. Another team, dropped prematurely by a pilot impatient to get home, parachuted into the full view of an SS unit that was watching an outdoor movie.

The missions ran from useless to priceless; their fate from the farcical to the heroic. Casey knew it and accepted early on the essential nature of warfare: a messy, disorderly tragedy tinged with black comedy.

On April 12 he boarded a DC-3 to Paris. The mood among the passengers and crew was subdued. Just hours before, news had reached London that Franklin Roosevelt was dead. The conservative Casey had been no champion of Roosevelt and the New Deal. He also thought Roosevelt's insistence on unconditional surrender was righteous bluster elevated to misguided military policy that was only lengthening the war. Nevertheless, Casey had a history student's eye for the value of charismatic leadership. And it was Roosevelt who had had the vision to back Donovan in creating a U.S. intelligence service when virtually every other element of his administration was ready to choke the OSS in its cradle. At the news of Roosevelt's death, Casey had watched tears stream down the faces not only of Americans at 70 Grosvenor but of Poles, Czechs, Frenchmen, and the ordinary Londoner in the street. A great figure on the stage of history had passed on, and Casey found himself choking back tears.

Less than a month later, the war in Europe was over. The London staff applied its considerable ingenuity to an appropriate celebration. They drafted the Norwegian chef at Claridge's to prepare a victory banquet. The turnout of white-shoe boys was nearly 100 percent. The party went on for a night and a day, and for the first time in years Casey permitted himself to get slightly drunk.

On a day in the middle of July, he went into his office and disappeared behind masses of after-action reports, debriefings, statistical analyses, bombing surveys, and agent interviews. He fired out copy around the clock to WAC secretaries working in shifts and finally emerged two sleepless days later with a document that was classified Secret and entitled "Final Report of SI Operations Inside Germany."

Given his gift for embellishment, Casey's document is remarkable for its understatement and for demonstrating the triumph of the analyst over the promoter in himself. He made no heroic claims. He was, he said, submitting the report with a mixed sense of "satisfaction and dissatisfaction." Of 102 missions that had originated under his command, he rated 62 as successes, 29 as failures, and 11 as "results unknowable." Although 5 percent of the agents dropped had become casualties, this figure was actually far below expectations. He later remarked, "When I'd see those guys off, I have to admit, I never expected to see any of them again." Knowing what he knew now, he said, the OSS could have attempted the penetration of Germany earlier, possibly by as much as a year. That had been his greatest disappointment.

He described the bombing raids, the bomb damage, the enemy troop movements revealed to Allied ground forces, the identification of local Nazi leaders, all achieved through intelligence procured by agents inside Germany. But he made no claim that the enterprise he had commanded had shortened the war by a week, a day, even an hour. The most he would say was "We probably saved some lives." The greatest value of these operations, he concluded, was that "for the first time, we operated under our own steam."

America's entrance into clandestine warfare had been late. The recruitment, training, documentation, and dispatch of nearly 200 agents into the enemy heartland, a police state in the grip of the Gestapo, marked the arrival of the OSS as a professional intelligence service. Donovan's determination that the United States could and ought to maintain its own intelligence service, Casey wrote in his final report, "has been vindicated in Germany."

Long years afterward, Casey was asked by an interviewer what the war had meant to him. "Maybe it was because I was young," he answered, "but

I'd never known such responsibility. I had five hundred people under me, a couple of air force squadrons at my disposal, a dozen French châteaus where we kept agents. I could walk into Patton's or Bradley's briefings anytime I wanted to. I felt part of something larger than myself. I was making decisions that were a part of history." A Casey not given to visible displays of emotion looked out the window of his home and across Long Island Sound. His eyes clouded over. "It was the greatest experience of my life."

And in that experience lay one key to his behavior as the director of Central Intelligence nearly forty years later: the belief that he was fighting a clear-cut "enemy" in communism, that all indeed is fair in war, that rash gambles such as the Iran-Contra affair must be taken. Whether these gambles would succeed was another matter.

The Tragedy of Unconditional Surrender

by CHARLES STROZIER

Once again, let us beware the "lessons of history." As that eminent historian Gordon A. Craig of Stanford writes, "A good number of our politicians, our pundits, and our self-styled experts are . . . adroit in finding spurious historical justification for their own purposes." To them, history is "a vast medicine cabinet filled with patent nostrums for all ills, and when crises arise they rummage about frantically in it until they come up with something that seems to fit the current case, all too often making things worse than they might have been." There is no better case in point than the distressing history of unconditional surrender. The concept, as practiced by the United States and her allies at the end of World War II, was based on Franklin D. Roosevelt's misreading, perhaps deliberate, of U.S. Grant's terms to Robert E. Lee at Appomattox. In the Civil War, absolute capitulation served a moral end. But in 1945 it threw a cloak of virtue over a savage and—Charles Strozier contends here— unnecessary act: the dropping of the atomic bomb. There are those who feel—William J. Casey, as we remember, was one of them—that FDR's insistence on an unconditional surrender rather than a negotiated settlement may have added crucial months to the war in Europe. Those months may not only have cost hundreds of thousands of lives but may also have given the Soviets a foothold in Central Europe they might not have been able to gain otherwise. Strozier is a professor of history at John Jay College of Criminal Justice, City University of New York. He is the author of *Lincoln's Quest for Union,* among other writings on Lincoln and the Civil War.

The term *unconditional surrender* has come to describe a way of ending war in which the loser must capitulate without stipulation. As a technical (and popular) term, *unconditional surrender* most frequently contrasts with the idea of *negotiated settlement,* in which agreement on terms precedes the cessation of hostilities.

Unconditional surrender played a special role in the American Civil War, linked to the humane and moral task of ending slavery. In the twentieth century, however, leaders of a more imperial America applied the rhetorical heritage of Lincoln and Grant to the notion of stamping out the enemy once and for all with an unparalleled nuclear brutality. In attempting to carry over nineteenth-century concepts of how to end a war into a time of vastly advanced technology, they tragically misapplied what they perceived to be the lessons of history. My story, which I will tell in reverse chronological order, begins in the waning months of World War II.

Harry Truman became president on April 12, 1945, determined to abide by the policies of Franklin Delano Roosevelt. On the day he took office and only hours after FDR's death, Truman declared: "The world may be sure that we will prosecute the war on both fronts, east and west, with all the vigor we possess to a successful conclusion." At the time, it seems, Truman viewed the war as nearly over anyway, and he understandably saw it as his responsibility to pursue the struggle to its logical—and previously agreed upon—end. He reiterated his views on this issue four days later: "Our demand has been and it *remains*—Unconditional Surrender! We will not traffic with the breakers of peace on the terms of the peace."

A number of factors prompted Truman's immediate affirmation of unconditional surrender. He was apparently committed to seeking retribution for Japan's bombing of Pearl Harbor. "When you have to deal with a beast," he once said, "you have to treat him as a beast." As a new president in wartime, Truman felt compelled to follow, at least initially, the policies of his predecessor. Prudence dictated quick adoption of Roosevelt's policies. Truman also came to power unprepared to govern. Roosevelt had consulted with Truman only three times in private and those were brief, uninformative visits. The only basis for action Truman possessed was existing ideas. He was in no position to alter a doctrine as popular and entrenched as that of unconditional surrender.

Nothing Truman soon learned of the atomic bomb changed his views. He simply folded his knowledge of the bomb's imminence into his strategic planning. Atomic weaponry, to the extent he understood it, was simply a technical military advance that could help realize quick victory. Furthermore, Truman found support for this attitude from the experts. An eerie sense of inevitability about the bomb's use, together with a deep curiosity about it, surrounded all those close to the seat of power. General Leslie Groves, the overall coordinator of the Manhattan Project, never questioned that the bomb would be used when it was ready. Robert Oppenheimer felt that the decision to drop the bomb "was implicit in the project. I don't know whether it could have been stopped." Henry Stimson later said: "At *no time* from 1941 to 1945 did I ever hear it suggested by the president or any other responsible member of the government that atomic energy should not be used in the war." Churchill supported use of the bomb, as did the other Allied officials who knew of its existence.

There were dissenters, to be sure. First, a group of Manhattan Project scientists in Chicago, inspired by Leo Szilard, wrote a report in June 1945 that vigorously opposed the use of the bomb on a civilian target and called instead for a technical demonstration of its enormous power. This so-called Franck Report, however, never reached beyond the scientific experts advising the Interim Committee that in turn advised Secretary of War Stimson, who finally advised the president. All that remained of the Franck Report, by the time it worked its way through the bureaucracy, was the plea to Truman to tell Stalin of the bomb's existence before it was used. No other group or individual among the small number of scientists or advisers to Truman who knew about the bomb seems to have even made the argument *then* that there was anything intrinsically wrong in using the atomic bomb on civilians as part and parcel of the war effort.

Second, there was some potential opposition within the army to using the bomb. General Dwight D. Eisenhower reportedly told Truman at Potsdam that he opposed its use. But how and when to use the atomic bomb were never really debated by military experts. The focus of army dissent, to the extent it existed, was on the goals of the war, especially the doctrine of unconditional surrender, and most immediately on whether to invade the Japanese mainland. The two were related. After the Germans were defeated, it was not entirely clear to the military that the probable costs of invading Japan justified the demand for unconditional surrender.

These "probable costs" have become an issue of some dispute in recent years. In various memoirs and statements after the war, Truman, Stimson, and Churchill all reported that they believed an invasion would have cost the Americans a million casualties and the British half that number. It seems Roosevelt first vaguely suggested the figure of a million casualties at Yalta in February. As with other things, the figure may have originated in his fertile imagination. For a number of revisionist historians, the meeting of the Joint Chiefs of Staff and several secretaries of the military with Truman on June 18 has become a matter of significance. At that meeting the military representatives asked for approval to begin an invasion of Kyūshū on November 1. They estimated that casualties would be in the range of 30,000 to 50,000.

This is the only time that the military ever generated precise figures in connection with any aspect of the invasion of Japan, and they were obviously low. However, several factors must be kept in mind. The purpose of that meeting was only to discuss the invasion of Kyūshū, which it was proposed should begin on November 1, 1945. At Yalta, Roosevelt had estimated that the war could easily continue until 1947, which is why he was so eager for the Soviets to commit themselves to entering the war in the East as soon as possible. By June, however, things had changed. Japan was devastated by the war, and many observers believed Japan would surrender when Kyūshū fell. But that was by no means certain. In the back of everyone's mind was the Okinawa campaign. It had begun on April 1, 1945, and dragged on until June 21, incurring some 65,000 casualties and damaging 350 ships.

Despite the June 18 meeting, it seems the prevailing wisdom among military experts was that the final defeat of Japan would incur huge casualties. Truman reported in 1953:

> I asked General [George C.] Marshall at Potsdam what it would cost in lives to land on the Tokyo plain and other places in Japan. It was his opinion that such an invasion would cost at a minimum a quarter of a million American casualties, and might cost as many as a million, with an equal number of the enemy. The other military men agreed.

There is no reason not to believe Truman's report. Perhaps he and the generals he consulted were wrong (and it appears they were), but one must distinguish between retrospective wisdom and contemporary realities. Their false beliefs obviously influenced their behavior. In a sense, therefore, as the military leaders understood the situation, the atomic bomb saved the army. Victory came complete without a costly campaign.

Third, and last, potential disagreement about the decision to drop the bomb existed in the State, War, Navy Coordinating Committee (SWNCC), which had been created in February 1945. Joseph Grew, former ambassador to Japan and now undersecretary of state, was potentially the pivotal figure in proposing alternatives to use of the bomb. The State Department presided over the SWNCC. Several factors, however, cut short SWNCC's possible role as the vehicle for generating an alternative to dropping the bomb.

Within the committee itself, it seems the military figures dominated discussion and forced their initiatives. But the crucial factor was undoubtedly that James Byrnes, Truman's trusted adviser who became secretary of state, stood firm on the use of the bomb. Byrnes was politically astute, a hard-liner on making no concessions to the Japanese, and he was closer than anyone to Truman. In fact it hardly mattered what Joseph Grew or other State Department officials felt in the hectic few weeks before August 6. They had no access.

Opposition to the bomb's use was thus muted or compromised. Saying that, however, is not the same as explaining why the bomb was dropped. A number of arguments have been offered. The bomb undoubtedly saved some American lives, probably many, and it shortened the war. Atomic weaponry was also a logical means of seeking revenge for Pearl Harbor. Americans had generally endorsed the war warmly since that attack, though their fervor was undoubtedly heightened by a decided racism toward the Japanese. Furthermore, Truman, like Roosevelt before him, felt strongly that a goal of the war should be a kind of ideological cleansing. Free society seemed to depend on the elimination of fascism from the earth. Initially, of course, the primary target for the bomb had been the Germans. But the war in Europe had been resolved by the time Truman became president, and America's attitudes toward Nazism easily carried over to the Japanese. The awesome power of the bomb encouraged Truman to think of eliminating the source of Japanese militarism by a complete and utter defeat of Japan in the war. As a result, none of the mistakes of World War I and the Treaty of Versailles, which many believed had caused the second war, would be repeated.

The bomb also got tied indirectly to affairs in Europe, giving Truman what he hoped would be a trump card with the Soviets, of whom he was darkly suspicious. By the summer of 1945, when it was clear Japan would surrender before too long, Truman wanted to keep the Soviets out of the war in the East and away from potential spoils. Truman, as the revisionists argue, wanted to assert the enormous power of this new American weapon—Churchill called it a Second Coming in wrath—primarily to influence events in Eastern Europe. Revisionist historians who make this argument are baffled by the apparent absence of a valid military reason for dropping the bomb in the summer of 1945 and thus look elsewhere to understand Truman's motivation in deciding to use it. The revisionist interpretation is thus highly indirect. It argues essentially that the Japanese became pawns in the struggle over Poland, and that Hiroshima began the cold war much more than it ended World War II.

But up close, these arguments, offered as explanations for why we dropped the bomb, are inadequate. First, the idea that we saved American lives by dropping the bomb—whether the appropriate casualty figure to use is 10,000 or a million as the cost of an invasion—is a profoundly misleading way of formulating the issue. Throughout June and July of 1945, the Japanese were suing for peace via their ambassador in Moscow. There was no need to invade Japan or drop the bomb. We had won. The Japanese asked only that before surrendering they be guaranteed the right to keep their emperor. In other words, they wanted to negotiate their surrender. We refused; dropped two atomic bombs, causing untold suffering; forced unconditional surrender on the Japanese; and then let them keep the emperor.

Second, popular support for the war was different from a universal popular demand to annihilate whole cities. The great joy among civilians and soldiers alike that followed V-E Day suggested that support for an invasion of Japan might have eroded quickly in the face of determined Japanese opposition.

Third, it can be reasonably claimed—as several military advisers argued at the time—that it is not the purpose of fighting armies to root out obnoxious philosophies.

The argument, finally, that our real target was the Soviet Union rather than Japan hinges on a misperception of the attitudes Americans held in 1945. The argument also depends on a distorted view of Truman as malevolent, devious, and perhaps paranoid. At the urging of first Stimson and then Byrnes, Truman tried to maximize the diplomatic benefit of the bomb. But the attempt to harvest diplomatic benefits from the bomb was possible only because it was a foregone conclusion that it would be dropped on Japan. There is no doubt Truman hoped to contain Soviet expansion in Eastern Europe (and Asia) by demonstrating the new American weapon and cutting short the war. When Churchill learned of the bomb, he was similarly delighted at the prospect of curbing Soviet expansion. But it is wrong to regard that perceived benefit as an explanation of why Truman gave the go-ahead to bomb Hiroshima. The president would have dropped the bomb even if he had not been distrustful of the Soviets. The bomb in Asia was connected with European affairs and certainly was to have a separate future in relation to the cold war. But it must be clearly distinguished from its past and the reasons it was dropped.

"The atomic bomb," Truman said later, "was no great decision, not any decision you had to worry about." And he did not worry, because it flowed naturally from the doctrine of unconditional surrender that he had inherited from Roosevelt. Given that doctrine, the surprise would have been if he had *not* dropped the bomb. It informed, even shaped, every decision he made after April 12 regarding Japan and the bomb. The potential casualty figures for an invasion of Japan were meaningful for Truman and the others only because it was an unquestioned assumption that a negotiated surrender (which the Japanese were requesting before August) was not acceptable. Surrender first had to be complete and without precondition, as unconditional surrender was understood, and then terms, even generous ones, could be worked out.

In the complicated military and political situation of that summer of 1945, the bomb made it possible to realize rather easily these goals of war. And so Japan, asking only to keep her emperor, which in the end we were willing to allow, had to be bombed. Certain things were very clear for Truman, who sought meaning for the bomb in Scripture. He noted in his diary at Potsdam on July 25, 1945: "We have discovered the most terrible bomb in the history of the world. It may be the fire destruction prophesied in the Euphrates Valley Era, after Noah and his fabulous Ark."

The question, therefore, of why we dropped the bomb turns into a far more provocative and difficult question: Where did unconditional surrender come from? Most immediately, the answer is that it originated in the wartime leadership of Franklin Delano Roosevelt. The story he liked to tell is that at a rushed news conference in January 1943, it spilled out quite by accident. "We had so much trouble getting those two French [Charles de Gaulle and Henri Giraud] together that I thought to myself that this was as difficult as arranging the meeting of Grant and Lee—and then suddenly the press conference was on, and Winston and I had no time to prepare for it, and the thought popped into my mind that they had called Grant 'old Unconditional Surrender,' and the next thing I knew I had said it."

In fact, things were more complicated than that. Soon after Pearl Harbor, the State Department had set up an advisory committee on postwar problems. This blue-ribbon committee spawned a subcommittee on security problems, chaired by Norman Davis, former ambassador-at-large. On May 21, 1942, the committee recommended that the goal of the war should be unconditional surrender rather than a negotiated armistice. This recommendation Davis communicated directly to Roosevelt, apparently without even telling Secretary of State Cordell Hull. In August Roosevelt instructed Oliver Lyttelton to tell Churchill that he, Roosevelt, would be satisfied with nothing but the unconditional surrender of Germany.

The question was then discussed in the fall of 1942 by the Joint Chiefs of Staff, who recommended that no armistice be granted Germany, Japan, Italy, or their satellites until they agreed to "unconditional surrender." Roosevelt told his staff on January 7, 1943, that he intended to argue for those terms at the forthcoming conference in Casablanca. Finally, he consulted with Churchill on the issue at Casablanca, for Churchill wired his cabinet during the conference for advice on how to approach unconditional surrender in relation to Italy.

So it was quite a misrepresentation for Roosevelt to pretend that he pulled the idea of unconditional surrender out of thin air. However, two points are worth stressing. First of all, once the idea was formulated and announced, Roosevelt became solidly wedded to it. He wanted to avoid the mistakes of 1918, when an ambiguous surrender in the field was followed by a stringent war-guilt clause in the peace treaty. He also felt it was important to root out and destroy "a philosophy in Germany, Italy, and Japan which is based on the conquest and subjugation of other peoples."

Some generals doubted the wisdom of unconditional surrender, feeling it was not needed to justify an occupation, that it might inspire last-ditch fighting, and that an army could defeat an enemy but not necessarily change their political views. General George A. Lincoln said later that the doctrine of unconditional surrender lacked "practical horse sense." But Roosevelt would brook no opposition. The slogan gained wide appeal throughout the nation as a moral and political commitment to firm antifascism.

Roosevelt's understanding of the doctrine was that the Axis powers had to surrender without condition. It would then be up to the Allies, who in his mind were decent, to decide how best to reconstitute the vanquished enemy and restore peace to the world. But there were to be no restrictions on the surrender itself. It could not be negotiated. Somehow that was crucial to the process of achieving a victory that would justify the war and ensure a lasting peace. "Please note," Roosevelt once said angrily, "that I am not willing at this time to say we do not intend to destroy the German nation."

The second point worth stressing is that Roosevelt's use of the Civil War as a precedent for unconditional surrender was neither frivolous nor accidental. He returned to it often after Casablanca. Thus, to give one example, on July 24, 1944, at the conclusion of a conference in Hawaii on Pacific war strategy, Roosevelt held a news conference. A reporter asked whether the goal of war with Japan was still unconditional surrender. Roosevelt bristled. He said that certain high-minded people objected to unconditional surrender because it was too "tough and rough" and would prolong the war. Well, he said, I'll explain it this way:

> Back in 1865, Lee was driven into a corner back of Richmond, at Appomattox Courthouse. His army was practically starving, had had no sleep in two or three days, his arms were practically expended. So he went, under a flag of truce, to Grant. Lee had come to Grant thinking about his men. He asked Grant for his terms of surrender. Grant said, "Unconditional surrender." Lee said he couldn't do that he had to get some things. Just for

example, he had no food for more than one more meal for his army. Grant said, "That is pretty tough." Lee then said, "My cavalry horses don't belong to us, they belong to our officers and they need them back home." Grant said, "Unconditional surrender." Lee then said, "All right, I surrender," and tendered his sword to Grant. Grant said, "Bob, put it back. Now do you unconditionally surrender?" Lee said, "Yes." Then Grant said, "You are my prisoners now. Do you need food for your men?" Lee said, "Yes. I haven't got more than enough for one meal more." Then Grant said, "Now about those horses that belong to the Confederate officers. Why do you want them?" Lee said, "We need them for the spring plowing." Grant said, "Tell your officers to take the animals home and do the spring plowing. There you have unconditional surrender. I have given you no new terms. We are human beings—normal, thinking human beings. That is what we mean by unconditional surrender."

Precedent, it might be said, is everything in human affairs. Roosevelt's inventive reading of the surrender at Appomattox draws us back into that most curious of American events, the Civil War, as the crucible in which the doctrine of unconditional surrender was forged. In this first of modern wars, a new technological capacity to kill and destroy emerged, along with a strikingly new set of ideas about military strategy, the relationship between a fighting army and noncombatant civilians, and the criteria that determine when war is over. The latter are of enormous significance and relate directly to the brutality, length, and totality of twentieth-century warfare.

Clausewitz, whom Lincoln did not read, long ago pointed out that the political objectives in war "determine both the military objective to be reached and the amount of effort it requires." War, he stressed, "is a continuation of political activity by other means." War is not senseless passion, is not crazy, "but is controlled by its political object."

Few historical figures understood the inner logic of these ideas more clearly, more sensitively, or, one might add, more mournfully than Abraham Lincoln. Even as he left Springfield as president-elect on February 11, 1861, he spoke to his assembled friends and neighbors about the task before him, which he said was "greater than that which rested upon Washington." And no wonder. At that point all the states of the Deep South had seceded, a Confederate government had been formed, and a new president, Jefferson Davis, had been elected. Federal forts had been seized, and everywhere people were preparing for war.

Lincoln considered the Union sacred and indissoluble. "Physically speaking," he said, "we cannot separate. . . . A husband and wife may be divorced, and go out of the presence, and beyond the reach, of each other; but the different parts of our country cannot do this. They cannot but remain face-to-face. . . ." No one was clearer in his mind than Lincoln about the dangers of Southern aims to spread the odious institution of slavery to the territories, or even, as he argued in 1858, to nationalize it. But he also felt strongly as the newly elected president that the Constitution unequivocally protected slavery in the South. The North had no business in a war to end slavery. What he would do is prevent rebellion aimed at dissolving the Union.

But surely, he argued in his first inaugural address, the disagreements between North and South could be ironed out without resorting to bloodshed. He claimed only the legitimate powers conferred upon him as president under the Constitution. Beyond that, he said, "there will be no invasion—no using of force against or among the people anywhere." And Lincoln concluded, hoping to assuage bitter feelings:

> In *your* hands, my dissatisfied fellow countrymen, and not in *mine*, is the momentous issue of civil war. The government will not assail *you*. You can have no conflict, without being yourselves the aggressors. *You* have no oath registered in heaven to destroy the government, while *I* shall have the most solemn one to "preserve, protect, and defend" it.

Lincoln hated the idea of war, but he was insistent that he would not compromise away the Union. He drew the line at Sumter. The South fired the first shot, and the war came. Lincoln treated it at first as a narrowly limited problem, conceiving of the war as a kind of large-scale police action. Thus his April 15, 1861, call for 75,000 state militia was to deal with "combinations too powerful to be suppressed by the ordinary course of judicial proceedings. . . ." As he told Congress in July, he had acted only to prevent an attempt to destroy the federal Union. "A choice of means to that end became indispensable," as he put it. He vowed then not to use the army to destroy property or bother peaceful citizens. He believed that Southern sentiment against the war, except in South Carolina, would prevail.

In the course of the next year, several interrelated developments turned a small-scale domestic rebellion into a huge civil war. Most important, the North, beginning with Bull Run in July 1861, discovered this was to be a serious war indeed, one they could easily lose unless their greater economic and demographic resources were fully mobilized. Even then, ineffective leadership among Northern generals nearly lost the cause. Lincoln himself, with no military experience to speak of, quickly boned up on nineteenth-century strategic thinking, found it lacking in relevance, and began to direct his own war, something he continued until 1864, when he could at last turn the task over to Ulysses S. Grant.

Once Lincoln realized the war was not to be short and swift, he adjusted his tactics. General Winfield Scott's basically passive Anaconda Plan, in which the South's ability to survive would be squeezed off as the Confederacy was pounded on three fronts, remained his overarching strategic conception. But his implementation of it became total, aggressive, and active. The blockade of Southern ports tightened. Containing the South gave way in time to an invasion of Georgia and the total defeat in the field of Lee's army in Virginia.

In the process, the overall military effort vastly expanded. The army's size went from under 100,000 in the summer of 1861 to over 400,000 men in a matter of months; in the end, some 2 million men served in the Northern armies, not to mention another 900,000 to a million who fought for the

Confederacy. One huge Northern army engaged Lee over four long and deadly years in Virginia. A second pushed across Tennessee after many setbacks and eventually managed to turn south from Chattanooga and topple Atlanta, then march unvexed to the sea. A third army drove south from Cairo, Illinois, and in July 1863, with the defeat of Vicksburg, opened up the Mississippi.

This last Northern army interests me greatly, for until the summer of 1863 it was led by Ulysses S. Grant. Slouched on his horse, gnawing the end of an old cigar, Grant, like Lincoln, sensed the need early on to adjust strategic thinking about the war to the realities of what the North faced. His importance is far more complicated than simply demonstrating a will to fight, incessantly and brutally, if necessary. He saw, however vaguely, that the military *and* the political objectives of the war had to be altered.

It began inauspiciously at a Southern fort located in the extreme western region of Tennessee. This fort was named Donelson, and it seemed likely to float away in the hard rains of February 1862. Grant attacked the fort that month and won a decisive victory. Vastly overshadowed in significance by later battles, Donelson should be seen as one of the turning points of modern history. For it was not the mere taking of the fort that mattered, but the manner in which it was taken.

The fort was besieged, and with Grant preparing a final assault, hope dimmed for the Southern troops. Out came a messenger under the protection of a white flag, asking for terms. Grant wrote, "No terms except unconditional and immediate surrender can be accepted. I propose to move immediately upon your works." They surrendered, though their commander, General Simon Bolivar Buckner, said in his reply that the terms were "ungenerous and unchivalrous."

That first *formal* use of *unconditional surrender* in American history, indeed in the modern history of the West, resonated loudly, with the public —Grant soon became known after his initials, as "Unconditional Surrender" Grant. Now, it should be noted that there is a history of the idea of unconditional surrender that precedes the taking of Fort Donelson. Most immediately, the term itself had surfaced casually and somewhat ambiguously a few days earlier when Grant and Admiral Andrew Hull Foote took Fort Henry. As the *New York Times* reported on February 12, 1862: "The firing on the port of the gunboats immediately ceased, and a boat was sent over from the flagboat, which found, upon landing, that the rebels were completely disposed to an unconditional surrender."

It also seems that the obscure Battle of Lexington, Missouri, on September 20, a small Confederate force led by General Sterling Price surrounded Union troops and demanded surrender. A flag came out asking for terms. The word that came back was "Unconditional, by G-d, and five minutes to decide in!" The Federals surrendered but retained their private arms and personal effects. Earlier, in surrendering Fort Sumter, Major Robert Anderson insisted on certain conditions. According to the *New York Times* report, "The terms were not, therefore, unconditional."

More broadly, however, in the period before the Civil War, there was also what might be called an emerging rhetoric in which notions of immediacy and unconditionality pervaded the language and thought of Americans. It affected the way people thought about the Union, secession, slavery, the territories, and perhaps themselves. For someone like William Lloyd Garrison, the concern was slavery's abolition. In a letter written on September 6, 1855, Garrison noted: "Though we have differed somewhat as to means, we have never been divided on the vital question of immediate and unconditional emancipation." Southerners spoke vehemently of their unconditional right to secede.

During the winter of 1860–61, an important but now obscure political movement took shape in the upland South. It was called the Union party—by which it showed its distaste for dissolution—and had "conditional" and "unconditional" wings. In political circles, the Unconditional Unionists throughout eastern Tennessee and western Virginia enjoyed some prominence. Finally, the actual words *unconditional surrender* seem to have been first used by Abraham Lincoln in his Cooper Union Address on February 26, 1860, in relation to the territories. Will the South be satisfied, Lincoln asked, "if the Territories be unconditionally surrendered to them?"

The more specific military use of the concept of unconditional surrender was a practice known to the Romans. But in the West, for at least the last 500 if not a thousand years, the idea that your enemy must be brought to his knees and forced to give up unconditionally *before* any negotiation can proceed had dropped out of the theory and practice of war. Fighting before the Civil War was in general a deadly game held away from population centers and leading to negotiated settlements. Clausewitz, writing after the Napoleonic Wars, did not use the term *unconditional surrender* and only vaguely understood the meaning of total war. In any event, he was not read widely for several decades, and he was translated into English only in 1874. It was Lincoln, Grant, and the Civil War that incorporated total war into modern experience.

There is a clear connection here between the emerging nation-state, a new type of deadly warfare, and an ending in which an enemy capitulates completely. To put it epigrammatically, the totality of the modern state seems to require unconditional surrender as a necessary correlative of its total wars. The American Civil War brought that into focus.

Grant moved like an elemental force, powerful but uncritical, an unreasoning, unreflective happening without explicit meaning. It was Lincoln's job to supply meaning and purpose, to turn a tendency toward demanding the unconditional surrender of the enemy into national policy. Given slavery, the mere preservation of the Union was inadequate to the task at hand. By the spring of 1862, the war was already an ordeal by fire. At the single Battle of Shiloh in April 1862, there were more casualties than in all previous American wars. At Antietam in September 1862, more Americans died in one bloody day than have died in any other day of battle at any time or in any place (including Normandy).

For Lincoln and others, the mere return to the Union as previously constituted, with slavery as an integral part, seemed an inadequate reason by itself to justify such carnage. Pressures were mounting everywhere to link the war to ending slavery—pressures from Congress, from articulate blacks such as Frederick Douglass, and most of all from within Lincoln himself. The issue was not to forestall English recognition of the South. That old idea is incorrect.

Lincoln had to move cautiously to expand the goals of the war. Northern racism was virulent, and he was still anxious to keep the border states quiet. In the summer of 1862, he therefore maneuvered broadly. In a public letter to Horace Greeley, he tried to calm Northern fears by stressing that emancipation would occur, if at all, simply as a way of realizing the war's *only* goal— preservation of the Union. He talked to a delegation of black ministers about returning freed blacks to Africa, an old idea of his that he soon abandoned. In December he presented to Congress a constitutional amendment to indemnify Southerners after emancipation. And, of course, he wrote the Emancipation Proclamation itself in dry language meant to inspire no one; it is certainly the least quotable of all important Lincoln documents. He also made emancipation apply only to areas over which the North had no control—deliberately preserving slavery in the border states.

And yet these were ruses. From July 1862, Lincoln was firmly committed to emancipation and merely sought an effective means to make it happen. That came basically after the Battle of Antietam in September, when emancipation was announced with the provision that the formal proclamation would actually be issued 100 days later. In this delay, typically, Lincoln gave the South a way out: The announcement specifically gave the South the opportunity to preserve slavery, *if* it stopped fighting by the end of the year.

Lincoln was thus flexible and cautious in expanding the goals of the war. But having taken that crucial step, he never looked back and never wavered. He also worked through the implications—personal, political, economic, social, and military—of emancipation. After January 1, 1863, he never again publicly mentioned black colonization. He equalized pay for black and white soldiers and used the power of his office and his personal stature to push through Congress the Thirteenth Amendment, abolishing slavery in early 1865 and ending the tenuous legal status of the Emancipation Proclamation.

Lincoln also blended his enlarged sense of the war with an implicit affirmation of the unconditional surrender of the South. He seems never to have actually used the term (during the war, at least), probably to avoid giving unnecessary offense to prickly Southern sensitivities. But it hardly mattered. The idea was in the air, everywhere. And everything he did as commander in chief was to pursue a firm policy that the South must stop fighting without preconditions. He elevated Grant to his top general and turned him loose to fight and fight and fight some more to end it all.

Grant needed no prodding. He again used unconditional surrender against General John C. Pemberton at Vicksburg in July 1863; and Lee did in fact surrender unconditionally at Appomattox in 1865. On April 7, 1865, Lee had tried to goad Grant into negotiations before the end of hostilities, which would have forgone unconditional surrender. Grant, however, helf firm; on April 9 Lee stopped fighting, in accordance with Grant's demand that surrender must precede discussion of terms. The two generals then ment, and at that point Grant made several important concessions to Lee and his armies. That sequence, however, was exactly the way Grant and Lincoln understood unconditional surrender to work.

Earlier, Lincoln had approved of actions like Sherman's March to the Sea, that demonstration to civilians and a helpless "defending" army in Georgia and South Carolina of the massive power of the North. At Hampton Roads, furthermore, the secret peace conference in January 1865, Lincoln said he could entertain no proposal for ceasing military operations against the South unless they stopped fighting and agreed to the restoration of the Union. He listened patiently while the Southern representatives objected that such terms amounted to unconditional surrender or submission (the terms were used interchangeably), then added that he personally would be liberal in exercising the power of the executive, once the Union was reconstituted. "Trust me" was the message.

Jefferson Davis reported to his Congress on February 5, 1865, that "the enemy refused to enter into negotiations with the Confederate States or to give our people any other terms than unconditional submission to their rule."

In the end, Lincoln, groping for meaning himself and full of doubts, even brought in God to justify his policies. I say, "even" because that was not Lincoln's style. But in the eloquent second inaugural address, Lincoln, speaking for God, explained why the war, now all but over, had been fought:

> The Almighty has His own purposes. "Woe unto the world because of offences! For it must needs be that offences come; but woe to that man by whom the offence cometh!" If we shall suppose that American Slavery is one of those offences which, in the providence of God, must needs come, but which, having continued through His appointed time, He now wills to remove, and that He gives to both North and South, this terrible war, as the woe to those by whom the offence came, shall we discern therein any departure from those divine attributes which the believers in a Living God always ascribe to Him? Fondly do we hope—fervently do we pray—that this mighty scourge of war may speedily pass away. Yet, if God wills that it continue, until all the wealth piled by the bond-man's two hundred and fifty years of unrequited toil shall be sunk, and until every drop of blood drawn with the lash, shall be paid by another drawn with the sword, as was said three thousand years ago, so still it must be said "the judgements of the Lord, are true and righteous altogether."

Was it worth 600,000 dead to end slavery? Did God will it? Lincoln thought so, and the heart of his military policy as commander in chief was to pursue unconditional surrender of the South, to insist that his (actually liberal) terms of reconstruction would *follow* the end of fighting and could never be the basis of negotiations. I daresay in our romanticized notions of the Civil War and genuine admiration for the integrity of Lincoln, we have failed to note the complicated and ambivalent meanings of his leadership for twentieth-century wartime presidents, especially lesser men like Truman with atomic bombs in their arsenal. Lincoln helped give moral and historical meaning to the concept of unconditional surrender.

In context it is hard not to affirm that meaning. The Civil War began with a limited goal (saving the Union) and at first had few casualties. As the war changed into a huge and bloody affair, however, unconditional surrender emerged almost spontaneously in the field, and Lincoln's explanation for why the North was fighting expanded to include the abolition of slavery. The war, including the way it was fought to the bitter end, ensured freedom for blacks.

The war also made the nation-state triumphant. Lincoln became a sacred and secular national hero. The moral integrity of freeing the slaves blended necessarily with the explicitly political and national outcome of the war, because they were linked in time and place. Unconditional surrender was a critical part of the kind of war that had to be fought to realize these goals. Over time, however, the linkage was undone, and the defense of the nation became its own moral imperative, even if that meant obliterating whole cities of innocent people for no good military purpose. Hiroshima and Nagasaki have their analogues in the fire storms of Dresden and Tokyo (though the atomic bomb created a much more complicated future, connecting unconditional surrender with a new fearsomeness). Great men can be confusing touchstones of wisdom.

First Strike

by ABRAHAM RABINOVICH

A classic tactical maneuver is the disruptive expedient known as the "spoiling attack." A spoiling attack is a largely preventive measure calculated to delay and thwart, to gain the initiative before it can be gained from you. Surprise is an important element, and often the decisive one. It's hard to think of a spoiling attack more decisive than the Israeli preemptive air strike on Egyptian airfields that began (and all but ended) the Six-Day War of June 1967. Here, tactics were elevated to strategy: The destruction on the ground of much of its air force took away the offensive edge Egypt had enjoyed until then. Though the story of the raids is well known, nobody had been able to get to the actual participants until Abraham Rabinovich, a features writer for the *Jerusalem Post*, tracked them down. He revealed details of preparation for the raid, and its execution, that had remained classified for more than twenty years. Rabinovich is the author of an account of another secret Israeli operation, *The Boats of Cherbourg* (Seaver Books/Henry Holt).

The normally crowded streets in the center of Tel Aviv were almost deserted when General Mordecai Hod, commander of Israel's air force, drove out of the General Staff Headquarters compound on Sunday evening, June 4, 1967, and headed for home. For three weeks virtually all able-bodied men in Israel had been deployed along the nation's borders waiting for the signal to go to war.

Only cabinet ministers and a few senior officers knew that war would be launched the next morning. General Hod believed that with a bit of luck it would be over, in effect, by midday.

His prediction would have struck almost any Israeli who heard it as bizarre, particularly those—including not a few in high places—who were gripped by apocalyptic visions about Israel's fate in the coming conflict. Even Israel's most renowned war hero, General Moshe Dayan, was pessimistic about what lay ahead. Just before he was named defense minister three days earlier, he had told the commander of the army of the south confronting the Egyptians that in the coming battles against the massed Arab armies, tens of thousands of Israelis would be lost.

The crisis had appeared from an unexpected direction three weeks earlier, when Egyptian troops began moving through the heart of Cairo toward the Sinai Desert in a display of force. It was Syria, not Egypt, with whom Israel had been experiencing tension over border clashes in recent months.

Egyptian president Gamal Abdel Nasser had felt impelled to aid the Syrians and demanded that the U.N. buffer force in Sinai be removed: It had been there since the last Arab-Israeli clash, in 1956. The Egyptian army began to take up forward positions along the desert roads to Israel. Egyptian planes made reconnaissance flights over Israel, especially over the nuclear reactor at Dimona. The Arab noose tightened: Jordan reinforced its West Bank positions, Syria's Golan Heights forces went on full alert, and Saudi Arabia, Iraq, Morocco, and other nations organized expeditionary forces. Western powers made it clear that they would not intervene militarily. On May 19, Israel began mobilization. When Nasser blocked the Strait of Tiran—effectively isolating Israel from the Red Sea—and concluded a mutual defense treaty with Jordan, the stage was set for war.

The air force had played a marginal role in both of Israel's two previous wars—the War of Independence in 1948–49 and the weeklong Sinai campaign in 1956. But by the eve of the Six-Day War, Israel had 172 fighter-bombers in flying condition and 45 jet trainers, in addition to helicopters and auxiliary craft. The Egyptian air force numbered 420 planes, of which 240 were fighter-bombers or long-range bombers. If Syria and Jordan entered the war and Iraq dispatched part of its air force—which it would—Arab air supremacy over Israel in combat craft would be 2.5 to 1.

Among Israel's ground generals, the air force's primary role in a future war was seen as providing support for the land forces and protecting Israel's vulnerable cities from enemy air attack. The latter would be no easy task, given the sheer number of planes in Arab hands and their deployment in a broad arc around Israel's borders within half an hour's flying time of Tel Aviv.

For a decade, however, the air force had been developing its own idea about its role in any future war. It had begun as a whimsical notion that became a concept, then slowly evolved into an operational plan with a name, Moked, the Hebrew word for "focus." Moked had been largely developed by Hod's predecessor, General Ezer Weizmann. The notion was to break the back of an enemy's air force with one blow at the opening of a war by catching it on the ground. The concept was to achieve the necessary surprise by flying low to avoid enemy radar and maintaining absolute radio silence. The plan, built up over years of painstaking intelligence and staff work on one hand and of pilot training on the other, consisted of the myriad nuts and bolts needed to turn the concept into an operational reality.

While combat planes had often eluded radar by flying low, no nation had ever attempted to throw an entire air force at an enemy using that ploy—close to 200 jet aircraft flying at treetop level over hundreds of miles toward targets scattered over thousands of square miles. It would take only one random sighting, even from a solitary soldier on the ground with access to a radio, to alert the antiaircraft defense network and send the enemy's planes aloft—not only forewarned but forearmed with the advantage of altitude over the low-flying attackers.

To achieve surprise, initial targets would have to be hit simultaneously. Egypt, Israel's major opponent, had a score of air bases scattered from the upper Nile to the delta to the breadth of Sinai. The bulk of the Egyptian air force was concentrated at about half of them. Faultless coordination would be needed to bring the planes to these targets at the same time.

The closest field, at El 'Arīsh in the Sinai Peninsula, was only fifteen minutes' flying time from central Israel, while the farthest that could be reached in a first strike was almost an hour away, at Beni Suef. The Israeli aircraft were all of French make but differed greatly. The modern Mirage 3s could reach deep into Egypt and match the modern, Soviet-made MiGs and Sukhois in the Egptian air fleet. About a third of the planes were slow-moving Ouragans. Their range was limited to the Sinai Peninsula and they were easy prey for Egypt's advanced interceptors. There were also Mystères, Super-Mystères, and Vautours, the latter capable of long-range bombing.

To arrive at their targets simultaneously at zero hour, the planes would have to take off from Israel's four military air bases—and from the country's international airport, to which some fighter-bombers had been shifted—at carefully staggered times. Since Israeli intelligence had established that it took the Egyptians at least five minutes to get planes aloft in an emergency, some bases could be hit as late as zero plus five. Routes would have to avoid locations where the formations might be seen from the ground by Egyptians likely to report the sighting. In short, the operation would require prodigious planning, immaculate performance, and a large measure of good luck.

Amid extremely tight secrecy, work began on making the plan operational. Every few months Israeli photoreconnaissance planes appeared over air bases in Egypt, Jordan, and Syria to take low- and high-altitude photos. Each military airfield in these three countries was assigned its own file in the offices of Israeli intelligence, and these files were regularly updated.

Simultaneously, air training for the operation got under way. Over and over again pilots practiced taking off on precise schedules in foursomes, forming up and flying in close formation in total radio silence close to the ground. Group leaders practiced navigating with compass and watch at low altitude, with the landscape flashing by at dizzying speed and the view restricted by lack of height.

Pilots were among the first reservists mobilized. They immediately began refreshing themselves in the basic skills needed for Moked as well as for more conventional missions, such as ground support and air-to-air combat. The training exercises were held mostly over the Negev desert bordering Sinai. Periodically the pilots staged mock low-level attacks on each other's air bases. Whereas other air forces had modernized by arming their planes with missiles and rockets, Israeli air commanders were convinced that, at this stage of missile development at least, the old-fashioned aerial cannon should remain the backbone of the air force's armament for both air-to-air combat and ground support. When the Mirage 3s arrived from France, they contained no cannon at all; Israeli technicians promptly installed them.

The go-for-broke first-strike plan was only one of many in the air force drawer, but as the crisis deepened, it was the one that seemed increasingly appropriate to General Hod. The massing of the Arab armies around Israel's borders and the bellicose statements of Arab leaders made it more and more apparent that Israel was facing not just a bloody skirmish but a battle for its very existence.

Hod, weighing the odds against Israel, dismissed the option of a passive, Battle of Britain-type defense. Strong as such a defense might be, some enemy planes were bound to get through to the coastal plain, into which 70 percent of Israel's population and most of its industrial infrastructure were crowded. The chances of such penetration increased markedly if the attack initiative was left to the Arabs.

Early in the crisis period, Hod was summoned to a meeting with Prime Minister Eshkol, who also served as defense minister, and General Yitzhak Rabin, the chief of staff. For the first time the air force chief outlined Moked in detail to a non-air force forum—of two—and requested approval of its implementation should war break out. Some misgivings were expressed about committing virtually the entire air force to an attack on Egypt and leaving the country open to an attack from the east—but approval was granted.

At Eshkol's request, Hod told the ministers that the air force had a plan for a first strike at Egypt; but he gave no details. Even in meetings of the general staff, Hod went little further than that, to reduce the risk of leaks. He was obliged, however, to reveal one key element of Moked—zero hour. If Israel launched a preemptive attack, the ground generals wanted it to begin at night to exploit the army's skill at night fighting. Hod insisted that zero hour be 7:45 A.M. Israeli time, and with Rabin's backing he got his way.

The air force had chosen this odd hour precisely because of its oddness. Intelligence reported that the Egyptians maintained a dawn patrol over their bases from first light, the classic time for air attacks out of the rising sun, until about 7 A.M. It was also known that senior Egyptian air commanders lived off the air bases and arrived for work at 8 A.M. (9 A.M. Egyptian time). At 7:45, it could safely be assumed, they would be in their cars, unable to react in the decisive first moments of the attack. By that hour, too, morning mists would lift and Israeli pilots would be well rested.

The three-week "waiting period," as it came to be called, was a nerve-racking time for the nation as a whole. On Thursday night, June 1, in response to public pressure, Dayan was appointed defense minister. He had been army chief of staff during Israel's highly successful Sinai campaign against Egypt in 1956 and was one of the most charismatic figures in the country. With Dayan, decisiveness could be expected. The very next morning he persuaded Eshkol and other leaders that there was no choice but war. If the cabinet gave its approval at its regular Sunday morning meeting, zero hour should be the following morning. The general staff, including Hod, was informed of the decision Saturday night. On Sunday the cabinet gave its approval.

Hod summoned his base commanders Sunday afternoon. He announced that Moked would be executed the next morning. In the first wave, 160 planes would go up—almost 95 percent of Israel's operational fighter-bombers—and they would hit at nine targets. Six bases would be struck at 7:45, two others five minutes later. The ninth, Beni Suef, would not be reached by the Vautours until 8:10, but given enough confusion, the bombers there should still be on the ground.

Only twelve planes would remain behind in Israel to provide air defense—four in the air and the others on ground standby. Intelligence had calculated that it would take the Syrians at least three hours to respond after being informed by Egypt of the attack. By that time the first wave would be back and capable of dealing with them. There would be total electronic silence until the first wave hit. If a plane developed trouble before zero hour and the pilot had to bail out, he would do so without reporting by radio; his wingmates would make note of his position. Hod told the base commanders to inform squadron leaders of the pending attack, but not to inform the other pilots lest tension keep them awake.

During this day Hod was informed that the latest air reconnaissance photos showed the Egyptians had moved additional squadrons into forward air bases in Sinai. The news delighted the general: The more planes the Egytians moved into Sinai, the more his short-range Ouragans could chew on.

Instead of bedding down at headquarters, Hod drove to his home in the suburb of Zahala, east of Tel Aviv, on Sunday night; it was part of the general deception plan that had been set in motion. At a press conference that morning, Dayan had said that a diplomatic solution to the crisis must now be sought. With the Soviet embassy in Tel Aviv closely monitoring Israeli preparations—and radioing coded information to a spy ship about seventy miles offshore—it was quite possible that the return of Hod, Rabin, and other senior officers to their homes would be noted and taken as a sign that nothing unusual was in the offing. Hod had no trouble falling asleep at 11 P.M., calmed by the fact that if there was still something he had not thought of doing, it was too late now to do it.

Major Ron Pecker, commander of a squadron of Mirages at the Tel Nof base south of Tel Aviv, was notified of zero hour Sunday evening when the base commander summoned all squadron commanders. When the major returned to his men, he tried to keep his eyes from flashing the news.

Pecker stayed late in his office, preparing the briefing he would give his men in the morning and going over the details of the mission once again. Every squadron had been assigned several bases. Each foursome in the squadron had a flight leader, who would guide the planes to target. Copies of the files on the Egyptian airfields had been distributed to the squadrons during the waiting period. Each pilot knew what his specific targets were. The pilots had studied air photos and models of their target fields every day until they knew every revetment and gun position by heart. Photo-interpretation experts had told them which of the planes in the photos were dummies.

They would hit in waves, five to seven minutes apart. Each wave would make three passes. Three was considered optimal for maximum damage before the guns and missiles on the ground began to get the range. The SAM antiaircraft missiles that the Soviets had begun installing at Egyptian air bases were a new and unknown factor.

Pecker would lead his own foursome in the first strike against Inchas near Cairo, one of the main bases for advanced MiG-21 interceptors. It would be essential to prevent them from pouncing on the slower planes in the Israeli air fleet. Close to midnight the squadron commander went down to watch the mechanics arm the planes, as they did each night. In his apartment, he set the alarm for 4 A.M. and went to bed. He, too, had no trouble falling sound asleep.

Major Yaacov Terner, commander of an Ouragan squadron, would not manage to sleep at all. He was, at thirty-two, the youngest squadron commander in the air force. His planes would attack Sinai bases, and he himself would lead the attack on El 'Arish, the base closest to the Israeli border. Most of the pilots in his unit were from kibbutzim—collective settlements—and their average age was twenty-three. For two weeks they had been practicing within their foursomes the attacks on their specific targets—the order in which the planes would attack, the angle of attack, the direction in which they would break after the first run.

The pilots were awakened early and, entering the briefing room at 5 A.M., clearly sensed something. When they were all seated, Terner wrote "zero hour—0745" on the blackboard. "We're going to war against Egypt today," he said. There was total silence. One or two younger pilots seemed to pale. Terner spoke briefly and they listened to a report on weather conditions over Sinai: There was a little mist near the Suez Canal, but it would clear soon. Before the session broke up to let the foursomes review their separate attack scenarios, Terner told the pilots: "When you look though your gunsights this morning, remember that the entire nation will be looking through them with you. Don't miss."

The air bases roared into life as the pilots mounted their planes and ignited engines to check systems. The pilots signaled readiness to their flight leaders with thumbs up. Ground controllers now became the key figures as the planes began to taxi in carefully staggered order toward the runways. With strict radio silence in force, the controllers at some fields signaled to flight leaders on the tarmac by flashes of light from the control tower. At other fields, signalers on the ground, with flags and clipboards listing the takeoff time of each foursome, moved the planes into position. Fuel trucks at the end of the runways topped off planes whose missions would be taking them to the very edge of their fuel capacity—even fuel lost in taxiing and idling would be replenished. At 7:14 A.M. a green light flashed from a control tower and the first plane lifted off.

In his underground command post, General Hod heard the terse code words on the telephone indicating that the squadrons were up. The room had filled with high-level visitors, including Rabin and Weizmann.

The deception stage of the operation had begun more than an hour before, when dozens of small Fouga jet trainers rose from their bases and headed south to the Negev air space in which the fighter-bomber squadrons had been training so intensively for the past three weeks. The Fouga pilots deliberately flew high, where they would be picked up by Egyptian radar in Sinai, and they communicated with each other and with their control centers on the radio in the open as if on a routine training exercise. "Cat One calling Cat Four"—the pilots identified themselves by the code names that the Egyptian electronic monitors had become accustomed to hearing every morning since mid-May. The Fougas' mission was to continue painting lulling pictures on Egyptian radar screens until 7:45, when they were to land and be armed with rockets that would permit them to provide close support to the ground forces attacking the Gaza Strip.

Meanwhile, the first attack planes headed out to sea and turned toward the Egyptian coast. Flying just above the waves, Pecker felt as if he were in the cabin of a high-speed boat. The routes of the over-water squadrons were carefully plotted to take them out of the radar range of the Soviet spy vessel. The possibility that the Soviets would become aware of the sudden burst of activity at the airfields could not be discounted. Around 7:15 A.M., radio transmissions between the Soviet embassy in Tel Aviv and the spy ship were suddenly rendered inaudible by electronic interference. Precisely at 7:45, as suddenly as it had started, the interference disappeared.

Major Terner sat in his cockpit at the end of the runway at Lod watching the other foursomes from his squadron lifting off on precise schedule. The three other planes in his flight were echeloned behind him, their cockpit canopies still raised. His group would be the last to go since it had the shortest distance to cover. At 7:30 the control tower flashed *go.* Terner gave the thumbs-up signal to the three other pilots and started down the runway. Rising over electrical lines, the planes leveled off at 100 feet and turned south, keeping well to the east of the Egyptian-controlled Gaza Strip. The trees and electricity pylons flashing below soon gave way to the sere landscape of the semiarid Negev.

Suddenly they were over an army—masses of tanks, half-tracks, and trucks deployed in attack formation. This was the northern prong of the Israeli Southern Command—the force that would have to batter through the powerful Egyptian defenses on the northern Sinai coast road. Camouflage nets still covered the vehicles, and the fliers could see soldiers waving at them. When the planes reached their targets, the code words Red Sheet would be flashed to the ground forces, sending them into action.

Terner held a map in his left hand at eye level so that he could read it and keep an eye on the sky at the same time. On the map were lines indicating where he was supposed to be at fixed times. He wore his watch with its face on the underside of his left wrist so that he could see at a glance both the map in his hand and the time. He confirmed his whereabouts on the map by glancing out of the cockpit at landmarks such as gulleys or ridgelines, and he adjusted speed accordingly between 325 and 370 miles per hour by playing with the throttle.

They turned west toward the Sinai border. Straight ahead on the ground was a small group of men. He was over their heads almost before they heard him. They were bedouin squatting around a campfire making coffee. In the split second that he had in which to take in the scene, Terner saw that the smoke from the fire was being blown by a west wind.

His greatest fear now was missing the precise point where he was to pull up and find the airfield below him. If the airfield was not there, it could not be far away, but the pilots would have to circle until they found it, alerting the Egyptians and giving their antiaircraft gunners time to man their weapons and get their range. Ahead he saw the final major landmark—a row of flat-topped hills alongside a broad, dry riverbed. His watch read 7:44. In half a minute he would pull the stick back.

The Nile delta rushed at Major Pecker's foursome streaking across the last sliver of sea. As they closed on the coast, the planes rose slightly to clear land obstacles. Below, small villages, green fields, and irrigation ditches flashed by. Farmers were looking up in one of the fields. Pecker realized they were waving at him.

In the silence pervading the war room, the large clock facing General Hod from the opposite wall seemed to him to be stuck. He stood at a large table covered with a map of the region. Lines on the map depicted the routes being taken by each foursome on its way to its targets. Atop each line was a toy tower representing the location of that attack group at any given moment.

Young female air force controllers leaned over the table periodically to advance the towers toward the Egyptian air bases. Since the pilots could not report their locations, the women positioned the towers on the basis of a previously drawn schedule showing where the planes ought to be. The towers were converging steadily on their targets. Finally, six controllers placed their towers squarely on the Egyptian air bases. The clock read 7:45. All eyes were focused on Hod. Suddenly the radio hookup to the air-control centers crackled.

"Pull up," said a distant voice.

"Pull up," said another.

The attack groups had reached their target areas and the flight leaders were ordering their planes to rise off the desert floor. There was no longer need for radio silence.

"Pull up."

The El 'Arish airfield was exactly where it was supposed to be, over his right shoulder, when Yaacov Terner gained altitude. But the runways did not stand out black as they had in the air photos; they were grayish and difficult to see against the desert landscape. He leveled off at 1,500 feet and led his group toward the field. Their first objectives were the three antiaircraft batteries. Only one battery was manned, and its gunners opened fire on the approaching planes.

Terner's own target was the main battery of six radar-controlled 57mm guns. As he dived, he could see the gunners racing out of a nearby tent in an attempt to reach the guns before he did. Remembering the bedouin campfire, he aimed slightly to the right of the battery to allow for windage. The cannon shells exploded dead center.

Of all the airfields hit this morning, El 'Arish was the only one whose runways would not be bombed. If all went according to plan, the Israeli army would capture it by nightfall and the air force would be using it as an advanced base by the next morning. The Ouragans formed into two pairs and began strafing runs. Two MiGs sat at the end of the runway with canopies closed. Their pilots had ignited engines, but they required a minute to warm up and the Ouragans were upon them before the MiGs could get moving. Terner's men hit every plane they saw, and the field was soon covered with black smoke.

Out of the corner of his eye, Major Pecker could make out greater Cairo on the western horizon, but he was focused on the air base at Inchas spread out below. He knew every revetment, and they were full of Egypt's best planes. Pecker's Mirages were each fitted with two 1,000-pound bombs, which they planted on the runways at one-third and two-thirds their lengths, effectively blocking any chance of takeoff. That accomplished, they began their strafing runs. Within moments the airfield was chaos as MiG-21s loaded with fuel exploded.

The Mirage pilots were oblivious to the antiaircraft fire. Instead of confining themselves to the planned three passes, they made five. As Pecker led his flight away from the field, he estimated that there were fifteen planes burning on the ground. But plenty were left for the next foursome, scheduled to arrive in a few minutes.

At other airfields, planes were holing the runways with a special bomb developed by Israel's military industries. Dropped from 100 meters, it was slowed by a parachute that turned the bomb downward at a sixty-degree angle to the ground. A rocket was then fired in the bomb's tail, driving it deep through the runway concrete, where it exploded after several seconds, leaving a five-yard-wide crater. Only occasionally would an Egyptian plane manage to maneuver around the craters and take off to engage the attackers or to flee.

General Hod began hearing the first radioed reports from returning flight leaders at 8:15. As each reported the number of Egyptian planes estimated to have been destroyed, Hod tallied them up. It came to almost 200 planes, half the Egyptian air force—and twice what he'd anticipated. He suspected that it was exaggerated in the confusion of battle, but the actual tally, according to Israeli sources, was 204.

First reports also began to arrive of Israeli planes down. Eight planes had been lost, half in air battles with Egyptian fighter planes that had managed to get off the ground. Four others had been shot down by antiaircraft fire. One flight group had not found its target. Altogether, however, it was apparent that the operation had been an astonishing success.

Within less than ten minutes of landing at their bases, the Israeli planes had been turned around by their ground crews, fully rearmed and refueled.

With the Syrian and Jordanian air forces still showing no signs of responding, the air force command decided to throw its weight against the Egyptians once again in a second wave. While some of the planes attacked airfields hit earlier—this time flying at normal altitude and guided by the smoke rising from the fields—planes with longer ranges were dispatched to six other airfields in Upper Egypt and on the Red Sea. At Luxor, near the Valley of the Kings, eighteen planes were destroyed, including eight Tupolov-16 bombers, some of which had managed to escape the first-wave attack on Cairo-West Airfield. In all, 107 planes were destroyed in this wave; only one Israeli plane was downed. Second-wave aircraft were also assigned to hit radar stations and other installations.

Additional waves would be launched against some of the Egyptian bases as well as against Syria, Jordan, and Iraq, whose air forces by late morning had begun to launch their own, largely ineffective strikes against Israeli targets. On this first day, Israeli pilots averaged three combat sorties and destroyed most of the 469 planes lost by Egypt, Syria, Jordan, and Iraq in the Six-Day War. Of these, sixty were downed in aerial combat. The Israeli air force would lose forty-six planes in the war, mostly to antiaircraft fire, and twenty-four pilots. By the second day, the bulk of the air force was being used in ground support.

On the ground the Egyptian army, stripped of support, reeled back before Israeli armored spearheads and was soon in headlong flight toward the Suez Canal. Jordan's king Hussein, honoring a pledge of support to Nasser, opened fire with artillery and small arms all along his border with Israel late on the morning of June 5, in total ignorance of the fact that the Egyptian air force had effectively been wiped out. Within two days he had lost the West Bank and the Arab sector of Jerusalem. On the Syrian front, Israeli motorized infantry scaled the Golan Heights and drove the defenders from their formidable positions.

It had been the air force's first strike that broke the back of Arab resistance—psychologically no less than physically—and opened the way to Israel's stunning victory in the Six-Day War. The trauma suffered by the Egyptian air force would leave its impact on air forces around the world. Planes would no longer be left on the tarmac in neat rows or in unroofed revetments but would be tucked safely into bombproof shelters. Runways would no longer cross each other, creating an intersection that offered a convenient target for a bomb that would paralyze both runways. New impetus was given to the development of modern air-defense systems, including a range of ground-to-air missiles and sensors better able to detect approaching aircraft.

In the Middle East, the victory changed the parameters of the Arab-Israeli dispute. Israel's display of national will and technical capability, particularly in the air force's first strike, shocked the Arab world and largely dispelled the notion that Israel could be swept into the sea. Within Israel, the victory unleashed a new national vitality—but the territorial gains also created a political and moral dilemma that persists until this day.

Much of this far-reaching impact could already be sensed by the pilots returning to Egypt for the second strike on the morning of June 5. In the wastes of Sinai below, they could see clouds of dust thrown up by the tank armies wheeling in the desert, as well as flashes of artillery. The war and the dying were only beginning, but the columns of smoke rising over the Egyptian airfields to the west signaled that a tremendous victory had already been won and that things would no longer be as they had been.

A Very Long Night at Cam Lo

by RONALD H. SPECTOR

Ronald H. Spector's memories of his quest to find out what happened in a forgotten (but hardly forgettable) Vietnam engagement is a little epitome of the problems military historians face. It is also a humbling reminder that the study of history has never been, and can never be, an exact science. How can it be when unpredictable human beings are involved—and people under extreme stress? In 1968 Spector (who is now a professor of history and international affairs at George Washington University and the author of five books) was a newly promoted lance corporal working in the historical section of the 3rd Marine Amphibious Force near Da Nang. He was assigned to ferret out the details, or what remained of them after five months, of a Tet offensive struggle for the town of Cam Lo. His commander wanted to know if any of its marine defenders deserved medals. Spector did his best to reconstruct the event, but it was only through a chance discovery, twenty years later, that he would learn what really happened. This "short, bloody, confused, sometimes desperate" small-unit action was more typical of the battles of Tet than much-publicized episodes such as Khe Sanh and Hue. In battle, whether it is night or day, warriors must forever grope their way through the dark.

This all began as a result of my promotion. In the spring of 1968, I was promoted from private first class to lance corporal in the Marine Corps at the large headquarters of the 3rd Marine Amphibious Force, outside Da Nang in Vietnam. I worked in the historical section.

If pressed, I would have had to admit that there *were* a few other noteworthy developments occurring at the time. Peace talks between the Americans and the North Vietnamese were getting under way in Paris. Saigon was receiving a steady rain of rockets, which would eventually kill or injure more than 5,000 people and leave an estimated 100,000 more homeless. Just south of the Demilitarized Zone (DMZ) near the Cua Viet River in eastern Quang

Tri Province, marines and South Vietnamese troops were fighting an entire North Vietnamese division in what would become the biggest battle of the war. In still another part of Vietnam, a C-130 transport plane, taking off with a load of women and children being evacuated from a besieged Special Forces camp called Kham Duc, was hit by heavy ground fire and crashed, killing everyone aboard. Back home, cities such as Washington, Detroit, and Chicago were still recovering from the shock of the riots that followed the murder of Dr. Martin Luther King, Jr. Senators Robert Kennedy and Eugene McCarthy were battling it out in the Oregon and California presidential primaries, and Columbia University students were busy waging guerrilla warfare against the faculty and the cops.

I was vaguely aware of all this on that hot, dusty morning in 1968, but none of it seemed particularly important measured against my promotion. I was mentally calculating how much extra cash it would bring me for my forthcoming R & R trip to Bangkok as I listened to the general's speech congratulating me and two other newly promoted marines. The general was the chief of staff, or the assistant chief of staff, or the vice chief of staff, or something or other in the maze of desks, typewriters, communications equipment, telephones, worried-looking officers, and harried clerks that constituted our headquarters. We stood at parade rest facing his desk, trying to look humble and dedicated.

The general told us that everyone appreciated the great job we were doing, and he knew that our families and friends were very proud of us. (Actually, my mother was worried sick; my sister was telling her friends at Boston University that I was really hiding out in Canada; and my father wondered why I couldn't have joined the Public Health Service. As for my friends, most were busy building an antiwar coffeehouse in New Haven "for working-class soldiers" and seldom expressed an opinion on my military career.)

I was just beginning to speculate about whether the price of a massage in Bangkok was likely to be affected by inflation when I became aware that the general had concluded his speech and was now addressing me. He had something he wanted me to check into, he said, handing me a large manila folder. He thought the historical section could clear this up. Inside the folder was a single sheet of paper with some map coordinates, a few unit designations, and the date 2 February. "Find out who was involved in this thing at Cam Lo," said the general. "Get all the names and the units involved. I want to write them up for some awards."

I carried the folder into the cubicle occupied by the travel section. "I want to go to Cam Lo," I said.

"You don't want to fly into Cam Lo," replied one marine travel agent. "They've been getting incoming the last three days. Why not go to Dong Ha and then catch a ride to Cam Lo?"

Dong Ha International Airport, as some air force wit had dubbed the primitive airstrip just south of the DMZ, was within range of North Vietnamese artillery. I'd had the pleasure of being kicked down the ramp of a

C-130 there, its engines roaring as it continued to taxi slowly down the runway to present a minimal target to communist gunners. "No thanks," I said. "How about if I go to Quang Tri?" Quang Tri was the 3rd Marine Division's rear headquarters, located a few miles outside artillery range.

"He can't fly fixed wing to Quang Tri," observed another travel agent.

"No, but he can take the army chopper to Phu Bai and then catch a helo into Quang Tri," replied the first. "He can take the army courier flight right from our helo pad."

"Sounds good," I said.

Travel arrangements completed, I returned to my quarters to get my gear together. Although I spent at least half my time behind a desk in our relatively safe and comfortable headquarters compound—which boasted such amenities as electricity, beds, and indoor plumbing—I still thought of myself as a field marine, far different from the contemptible clerks and communicators with whom I was obliged to share living quarters. My source of greatest satisfaction was to return from one of my infrequent forays into the bush, utilities covered with mud and red dust, boots unbloused, rifle sans sling, and be met by the awed stares and respectful queries of the office clerks, to which I replied with studied casualness, "Been out in the boonies," or, "Been up north." Short silence, followed by "Get into any shit?" Answer (even more casually): "A little."

Nevertheless on this particular morning I failed to experience the satisfaction I usually felt on leaving the world of partitioned cubicles, clicking typewriters, and headquarters rigamarole. This assignment, collecting fodder for a general in a mood to give awards, seemed beneath my dignity. As a matter of fact, the whole damned war had begun to seem beneath my dignity. Up until now, most of what I had done, as one of the best and brightest of the historical section, had at least appeared to have some serious purpose.

I was relatively new at the job. Many of my "oral history interviews" were disorganized, incomplete, or trivial, and my knowledge of what was actually going on in Vietnam was so rudimentary that I missed many important developments. It was also true that at one point in my career as the Samuel Eliot Morison of the Vietnam War, I had left $500 worth of new recording equipment sitting on a pile of sandbags when the Vietcong paid an unusual daytime call to the hamlet south of Hoi An where I was interviewing. Our gunnery sergeant later suggested I change my report on the lost equipment from "Lost due to enemy action" to "Abandoned while trying to save my ass."

Still, I felt that this latest assignment was too much. Awards and medals were not exactly scarce commodities in Vietnam in 1968. Although the highest awards for valor, such as the Navy Cross and the Silver Star, were still pretty rare and commanded great respect, many medals at the lower end of the scale had become plentiful. For example, by the end of the Vietnam conflict, the Marine Corps would have awarded fifteen times as many Navy Commendation medals as it had in World War II, although only about 20 percent more marines served during the Vietnam era than during World War

II (and only about 60 percent of the Vietnam-era marines actually got to Vietnam). A story making the rounds concerned a captain who allegedly received the Bronze Star for running a PX. As I dragged my flak jacket and helmet out from under my bunk, I reflected that while some marines might have died trying to win a medal, I'd undoubtedly be the first killed trying to get someone else a medal.

My mood began to improve as I boarded the army courier chopper for Phu Bai. This had to be one of the great free trips in Vietnam. I rode as one of the door gunners, but there was seldom anything to shoot at, and the view from the narrow bench in the waist of the Huey was superb. A short stop at the Da Nang air base to pick up the mail, then out across the Gulf of Da Nang, dotted with sampans and ships, up over the long strings of truck convoys picking their way across the blue-green mountains of the Hai Van Pass, then down into the narrow strip of flat rice paddies of Thua Thien Province.

We landed at the sprawling army and marine base complex at Phu Bai, near the city of Hue, and adjourned for lunch at the nearby army mess. The mess sergeant had recently received a large shipment of blue food coloring and was trying it out in various recipes. Today's piéce de résistance was cake with blue icing. There was also much talk of his recent blue stew, and blue soup had been reported as well.

Forgoing the opportunity to sample these delicacies, I hiked across the Phu Bai airstrip to the marine air group to hitch a ride to the Quang Tri base. I was met at the helo pad by Staff Sergeant Juisto, the chief of the 3rd Marine Division's historical team. He was in one of the rare and sought-after headquarters jeeps, a sure sign that the general had been on the phone with someone at Quang Tri and that my mission was regarded as important.

I already knew a little about Cam Lo from the past few weeks in Da Nang, where I had been assigned to collate and summarize the after-action reports of the Tet offensive, which were now coming into our headquarters. From the brief references in these reports, it was apparent that something nasty had happened there. There was mention of an attack by an entire Vietcong main force battalion and of most of the South Vietnamese defenders running away; and the gossip around Da Nang was that most of the Americans had been killed or wounded.

Staff Sergeant Juisto suggested we begin our research at Dong Ha, in the division operations center, before going on to Cam Lo and the units involved in the battle. So early the next morning, still in possession of the coveted jeep, we rode into Dong Ha and began poring through the division's spot reports, after-action reports, and journals. By late morning we had found very little, and Juisto suggested we leave Dong Ha before lunchtime—the favorite hour for North Vietnamese gunners to lob a few rounds into the base in hopes of upsetting our digestion.

As if to illustrate the wisdom of this advice, three loud explosions rocked the base, and two of the clerks in our hard-backed tent office abandoned their typewriters to disappear through the trapdoor leading to the bunker beneath the wooden floor. A more experienced clerk glanced up impatiently and observed, "That's outgoing, not incoming, dick-heads. When it's incoming you'll know it." I allowed as to how I wasn't very hungry anyway.

Over the next few days, Staff Sergeant Juisto and I drove from one sandbagged outpost to another, checking the journal files and situation reports and searching through flimsy carbon-paper messages that, although only three or four months old, were already covered with the ever-present red dust and turning brittle from heat and humidity.

The story of the battle was like that, too. "Some individuals," the duke of Wellington once wrote, "may recollect all the little events of which the great result is the battle won or lost; but no individual can recollect the order in which, or the exact moment at which, they occurred, which makes all the difference." The attack on Cam Lo had occurred less than five months before, but might as well have taken place in the last century. The well-known one-year tour (actually thirteen months for marines), together with R & R trips, redeployments, changes of command, reassignments, and casualties, guaranteed a constantly changing cast of characters at any given place and time in any unit in Vietnam. This, plus the fact that the Tet battles had produced an unusually large number of casualties, meant that few of the participants in the Cam Lo battle were still around. Several marines claimed to know people still in the area who had been at Cam Lo, but most of them could not be found, and those we did find turned out not to have been there.

Toward the end of our search, in a small, dusty, sandbagged command post near a highway, we finally found a few records that enabled us to reconstruct some of the battle. The records gave the names of most of the units and many of the individuals involved, the time of the attack, and the casualties on both sides. It wasn't much, but it was sufficient to fill in the blanks in the awards forms. Still, I wondered what had really happened.

I was still wondering twenty years later, when I was a professor at the University of Alabama, doing research for a book about Vietnam. While going through material about American GIs' relations with Vietnamese, I saw a reference to a battle in which most of the Vietnamese had run away. It came from an oral history tape. The date seemed right, so I requested the tape from the Marine Corps Historical Center.

The tape was indeed about the fighting at Cam Lo, and to my surprise it had been done by one of our marine historians, Staff Sergeant Ed Evans. He had visited Cam Lo the morning after the battle and interviewed some of the survivors. Evans and his team normally sent their tapes directly to Marine Corps Headquarters in Washington, and since he rotated home a few weeks after doing the interviews, neither Staff Sergeant Juisto, who had replaced him, nor I had ever found out about them.

Had Evans not left Vietnam when he did, I might have learned about his interviewing at Cam Lo. Members of the historical teams usually let me know if they had something good, as I did for them. But Evans may not have thought his interviews with the Cam Lo survivors were any big deal. He had been in Vietnam almost a year by that time; he had just come from Khe Sanh and was on his way to interview a unit of the 9th Marines who had also had a bad night defending a bridge. On the tape, there is nothing to indicate that he believed anything unusual had happened at Cam Lo. He sounds crisp, professional, a little bored, more than a little tired. His subjects sound much the same, though their voices also reveal that combination of elation, relief, and nervousness that comes after a narrow escape.

My interest heightened by listening to the tape and I went to the U.S. Army Center of Military History in Washington to check the reports of Advisory Team 4, Cam Lo District, in the files of the monthly reports made by province senior advisers to General William Westmoreland's deputy for pacification. What I found gave me a fairly clear picture of what had happened on that night more than twenty years ago.

The fight at Cam Lo on February 2, 1968, appears a rather minor episode in the bloody panorama of raids, sieges, battles, and bombardments that are remembered as Tet 1968. Cam Lo was only one of sixty-four district headquarters attacked by about 50,000 communist troops during less than three days in January and February 1968. In addition, the Communists attacked five major cities and thirty-six provincial capitals. In Saigon, the Tan Son Nhut airfield, the Vietnamese General Staff headquarters, the president's palace, police posts, the radio station, and even the American embassy compound came under attack.

Reporters and camera crews, never scarce in Saigon, covered the fighting around the city and then moved north to Hue, the old imperial capital. There, South Vietnamese and American troops battled for twenty-six days to dislodge some 7,500 North Vietnamese regulars, killing 5,000. Whatever time reporters could spare from covering Saigon and Hue, they devoted to the remote outpost of Khe Sanh near the Laotian border. At Khe Sanh, 40,000 communist troops were squaring off with some 6,000 marines and Vietnamese rangers in what was to become the most widely reported battle of the war.

With all these other things going on, it is not surprising that the battle at Cam Lo has failed to find its way into the history books. Yet it might have if the outcome had been different. Cam Lo was only a few miles from the DMZ and a short distance from the large American bases at Dong Ha and Quang Tri. It was directly on the overland route to Khe Sanh. A communist unit firmly lodged there in those early days of February might have given American generals a first-class headache.

Cam Lo District was in the east-central part of Quang Tri Province, the northernmost province of South Vietnam. The town of Cam Lo occupies both sides of the Cam Lo River. In the two years since the province had become a major battleground, the district's population had been swollen by more than 20,000 refugees, who had taken up residence in squalid camps. Removed from their traditional villages, most could find little work except as occasional day laborers at American or South Vietnamese military bases. The district chief, Captain Phan Dinh Caos, was a lame duck, scheduled for replacement. Since mid-January he had been seriously ill and absent from duty. The acting district chief, a first lieutenant, was considered by American advisers to be wholly ineffective.

As North Vietnamese forces closed on Khe Sanh to the west, the district's already shaky security situation further deteriorated. Neighboring Hong Hua District was swallowed up in a massive invasion of North Vietnamese regulars, sending an additional 1,200 refugees streaming into Cam Lo. Ambushes, sniper fire, and mines became almost daily occurrences along Route 9, the road connecting Cam Lo with Khe Sanh in the west and with Dong Ha and the main north-south artery of Vietnam, Route 1, in the east. In clandestine Vietcong meetings, the people of the district were told that in any future political settlement between the Americans and the North, Quang Tri would go to the Communists. During Tet, every town and city in the province was to come under attack.

In January, South Vietnamese security forces captured Doan Cu, the Vietcong district chief, along with documents detailing communist plans for a major offensive in Quang Tri Province. The intelligence section of the South Vietnamese Army's 1st Division at Hue promptly sent a courier to scoop up the documents before local officials and their U.S. advisers could thoroughly examine them. (An understandable reaction, since the division's intelligence section was penetrated by communist agents.) Yet enough was learned from these and other sources to put the small U.S. Army advisory detachment at Cam Lo District on alert. If Major James C. Payne, the district senior adviser, had required any further evidence of imminent danger, he received more than enough when the province exploded in the first Tet attacks on January 30 and 31.

The district's only defenders were two platoons of Vietnamese Popular Forces (PFs). The Popular Forces, a kind of part-time South Vietnamese militia, were considered the most poorly led, trained, and equipped in the Vietnamese armed forces. During six months in 1966, a quarter of all PF troops had deserted. Working with some of the PFs in Quang Tri were marine combined action platoons (CAPs), fourteen-man marine rifle squads integrated into a PF platoon of thirty to forty men. One of these platoons, CAP-1-1, was a few hundred yards northwest of the district headquarters compound; the CAP company headquarters was in the compound.

Feeling less than overwhelming confidence that his forty-odd PFs and his dozen or so Americans could hold the district headquarters, Major Payne had requested help, and on January 30 the first platoon of D Company, 1st Battalion, 4th Marines, had arrived to reinforce the headquarters' defenses.

The headquarters compound was located along Route 9 in the center of a broad valley just south of the Cam Lo River. Less than three miles to the west, the mountains began, stretching farther west to Khe Sanh and Laos. To the east, relatively level land paralleled the road to Dong Ha. To the south, rice paddies extended to the hills about a mile and a half away. North of the river, the terrain became more rugged, with thick, high brush.

February 1 was the marines' third night at Cam Lo. The weather was calm but the sky heavily overcast. The marines expected trouble, but they had not had time to reconnoiter the area and build deep bunkers or even dig deep fighting holes. The platoon had been reinforced with additional machine guns and a 3.5-inch rocket-launcher team but lacked one of its three squads.

And like other marines in Vietnam at that time, they were experiencing problems with their M-16 rifles.

Problems with the M-16—particularly the weapon's tendency to jam—had become widespread since 1966, when the M-16 had begun replacing the old M-14. The main cause of the jamming was the rifle's failure to eject spent rounds. Marines had various theories about it. In a report, the generals stressed "the absolute necessity of keeping the weapon immaculately clean, mainly because of the extremely fine tolerances of its moving parts and the tendency of rounds to bend in the chamber." But they conceded that even when clean some M-16s "still developed microscopic pits in the chamber" that would lead to jamming. A congressional committee would later claim that the jamming was due to faulty propellant supplied by the Army Ordnance Corps. Others called for the substitution of new chrome-coated chambers in the rifles. A marine in one of the combined action platoons near Cam Lo had a more succinct explanation, as reported in the *Marine Corps Gazette*. After a firefight in which all rifles in his squad had jammed, he "melodramatically threw his M-16 on the ground, denouncing it as 'a piece of shit.' "

At about 2:15 on the morning of February 2, the compound at Cam Lo was suddenly hit by more than a hundred rounds of recoilless-rifle, rocket, and 82mm mortar fire. Major Payne immediately ran to the main command and communications bunker, a heavily sandbagged building in the center of the compound. His assistant, Captain Raymond E. McMaken, went to the bunker beneath the advisory team quarters to maintain communication with the marines on the perimeter. Major Payne's calls to Dong Ha brought almost immediate artillery support; but when Captain McMaken requested help from air force "Spooky" gunships—specially modified AC-47s carrying parachute flares and electrically driven Gatling guns capable of firing 6,000 rounds per minute—he was advised that the weather was too overcast to permit air support.

Then, at about 2:35, a recoilless-rifle round slammed into the command bunker, killing two Popular Force soldiers and fatally wounding Major Payne. Picking his way into the rubble of the command bunker, Captain McMaken found John Cleary, a Department of the Army civilian adviser, requesting additional artillery support over the still functioning radio. Instructing Cleary to stay on the radio, McMaken moved outside the bunker to have a better field of vision for adjusting artillery. Relaying his adjustments to Cleary, McMaken directed artillery rounds all around the compound.

About 3:00 A.M., more than 200 Vietcong launched their main attack on the compound from the north and east, supported by heavy fire from recoilless rifles, rocket-powered grenade launchers, B-40 rocket launchers, and heavy machine guns. (Some marines later claimed the Vietcong had even had pack howitzers.) The PF soldiers manning the listening posts on the approach to the compound promptly fled.

The Americans had planted claymore mines along the likely routes of attack leading to the compound. These small devices sprayed deadly metal pellets across a wide area when detonated by a trip wire. But they failed to detonate—either they were too old or their wires had been cut by the heavy communist and American fire.

As the Vietcong approached the barbed wire that ringed the compound, McMaken brought the supporting artillery rounds ever tighter—so tight that some landed inside. At the same time, Sergeant Donald Key Sellers's two squads of marines from 1st Platoon, D Company, opened fire on the Communists to their front and left.

Positioned in one of the compound's sentry towers, Private First Class Marlin Resinger fired round after round from his M-79 grenade launcher. From his vantage point in the tower, Resinger "could see Vietcong soldiers running everywhere." Incredulously, he noted that the enemy even carried a large flag and a bugle.

Private First Class Larry E. Herwig, who had had the 10:00 P.M. to midnight watch, was asleep in a bunker at the far end of the marine lines when the attack came. Reacting instinctively to the sound of gunfire, rockets, and mortars, Herwig, still wrapped in his poncho liner, began rolling toward his fighting position. Momentarily disoriented in the darkness, however, he soon discovered that he had actually rolled outside one strand of the perimeter wire. He managed to free himself from the poncho liner and get back inside the wire, but he still lacked his rifle and flak jacket. Crawling into the nearest building, he found more than a dozen Popular Force soldiers in a state of near panic. All ignored Herwig's exhortations and gestures to get outside and man the perimeter. Finally, one soldier handed Herwig a grenade, patted him on the back, and pointed him at the door. Convinced by this eloquent gesture that his efforts were fruitless, Herwig ran around the building and into the marine lines yelling, "Marine coming in!" There he was met by his squadmates with his rifle and helmet.

In the northeast corner of the compound, the PFs proved no more determined than those Herwig had found in his building: They all abandoned their positions and hid in bunkers. Lance Corporal Lawrence M. Eads and three or four other marines of the combined action company, together with a navy corpsman, took over their positions in a small building opposite a portion of the perimeter where the enemy had made a twenty-foot-wide breach in the wire. Armed with an M-60 machine gun and their M-16 rifles, they managed to keep most of the Communists from passing the breach in the wire. Almost immediately, however, two of the M-16s jammed. The marines were obliged to make the hazardous run from their fighting position back to their "hooch" for wadding gear to clear their jammed rifles.

After about a half hour of close-up fighting, a Vietcong soldier managed to lob a Chinese-made grenade at the marines. Eads, the navy corpsman, and another marine were wounded by shrapnel from the grenade but continued to fire. Shortly afterward they were able to pin down the grenade thrower and kill him with a burst of machine-gun fire. But now the marines had begun to run short of ammunition.

From his tower, Private Resinger had fired over 600 rounds from his M-79 grenade launcher. Toward dawn, however, the M-79 was blown out of his hand by a round that passed through the barrel and out the side of the grenade launcher, knocking him to the ground. Around this same time, the heavy overcast finally began to clear, enabling aircraft and artillery to provide better illumination of the battlefield. Although the Vietcong continued their assaults on the compound until daylight, their best opportunity had ended with the arrival of the illumination and the failure of their assault on the northeast corner of the compound.

Just prior to daylight, a reaction force from the 2nd Battalion, 9th Marines, with a platoon of tanks, arrived at the northwest corner of the compound. Their arrival sealed the fate of the Communists, who withdrew, leaving behind over sixty dead and two dozen prisoners—a small portion of the 30,000 to 50,000 soldiers the Communists were to sacrifice in their Tet attacks. The unusually large number of prisoners captured was attributed by most Americans to the fact that many were as new to the area as the marines who had been moved up as reinforcements to Cam Lo. When things began to go wrong in the attack, the Vietcong had nowhere to go and no knowledge of the terrain to help them hide.

Later, examining the enemy casualties, the marines were impressed by the fact that the Vietcong had "better equipment than we did. Their equipment was new, their utilities were new, it looked as if they hadn't been in the field very long." To Private Resinger, it "seemed like they were prepared to stay. . . . The VC know their stuff, and their weapons never jam."

It remains unclear how many Americans and South Vietnamese fought at Cam Lo that night. Assuming that the two squads of 1st Platoon, D Company, were up to full strength (a highly improbable assumption for the winter of 1967–68 in Vietnam), the total for all American servicemen could not have been much more than forty. Of these, seven Americans—Major Payne and six marines—were killed. Twenty others were wounded, fifteen seriously enough to require evacuation. Of the forty-odd PFs assigned to Cam Lo, many ran away, but at least a few are specifically mentioned in Staff Sergeant Evans's tape as having held their positions throughout the battle, no small achievement in the face of the better-armed, better-trained Vietcong. Two PFs were killed and five more wounded.

The fight at Cam Lo was only a footnote to the stubborn and protracted fighting that engulfed Vietnam in those bloody months of 1968, when the rate of marine casualties rose to equal and exceed those in some of the island battles of World War II; when thousands of South Vietnamese were killed, maimed, or made homeless by the fighting in the cities; and when thousands of People's Liberation Army and Vietcong soldiers were cynically fed into hopeless assaults and futile offensives by their North Vietnamese masters.

Yet Cam Lo is an important footnote, for it illustrates—far better than the media extravaganzas in Saigon or the grim, almost World War II–style sieges at Khe Sanh and Hue—what most of the hundred-odd battles of Tet were like: short, bloody, confused, sometimes desperate. "A very near thing" was how Joint Chiefs of Staff Chairman General Earle Wheeler later described the Tet offensive to President Johnson. South Vietnamese soldiers did the bulk of the fighting in these more obscure battles, and unlike the PFs at Cam Lo, they usually acquitted themselves well.

I returned to Da Nang in 1968 with the details of the battle still hazy, but I was confident that I had more than enough unit names, date-time groups, journal extracts, and other military minutiae to write up even Mao Tse-tung for a citation. After ambling around our small compound a few times to ensure that my officemates could see that I had been "out in the bush," I went to see the general's admin chief.

"I got that stuff the general wanted on Cam Lo," I announced triumphantly. "I was up north for almost a week tracking it down."

"Cam Lo?" He looked at me blankly for a second and then smiled. "Oh, yeah, we found out all about that."

"What do you mean *you* found out all about that?" I spluttered. "I just got the story together now."

"No, about the awards I mean," replied the admin chief. "Somebody wrote them up for some awards right after they got hit, but the assistant division commander, or the division commander, or somebody, disapproved it, said they hadn't done anything any other marines hadn't done. Want a Coke?"

Looking back on it twenty years later, I think perhaps the general who turned thumbs down was correct, or at least appeared to be at the time. The war, especially along the Demilitarized Zone, had grown so grim and bloody by that winter and spring of 1967–68 that the extraordinary began to seem ordinary; unreasonable demands and exceptional efforts began to seem routine. Compliments were few and complaints even fewer. It had been a long war, and it was getting worse every day.,

I left Vietnam more than fifteen months after the fight at Cam Lo. By that time, most of the survivors of that night had long since returned home. Some had probably been killed or wounded in other fights. Many, doubtless, received awards and decorations for other achievements. However, I know of only one case where I can say for certain that someone received an award connected with the actions at Cam Lo. That person was myself. Shortly after I returned home, I was awarded a Navy Achievement medal. That was pretty close to the bottom in the hierarchy of medals—but the citation did mention my good research work on the Tet offensive.

Twilight Zone at the Pentagon

by THOMAS B. ALLEN

If you thought the war game in Thaddeus Holt's article about Joint Plan RED was unlikely, then savor some of the strange emanations from Room 1D-957 in the basement of the Pentagon one week early in December 1962. War gaming, as has been pointed out, is about as old as war itself. Chess came out of war games. Before Midway, Japanese admirals dismissed the results of games that showed that they would put their carriers at risk. In this age of ever-increasing technical complexity, war games are essential to combat-team training, especially in the U.S. Navy. But still, we've probably never witnessed war games quite like those played by such celebrity guests of the Defense Department as TV's Rod Serling, Hollywood director John Ford, and cartoonist Milton Caniff (*Steve Canyon, Terry and the Pirates*), among others. There was an element of paranoid wackiness about the proceedings that was undeniable, but remember that when those grandees of the world of mass entertainment entered the fifth dimension of Olympiad I-62, the Cuban missile crisis was barely a month behind them. Thomas B. Allen is the author of the book *War Games* and, with Norman Polmar, of an encyclopedia compilation, *World War II: America at War 1914–1945*.

As Rod Serling used to say, "There is a fifth dimension beyond that which is known to man. It is a dimension as vast as space and as timeless as infinity. . . . It is an area we call the Twilight Zone." And once, in real life, the popular television dramatist took the Pentagon into "The Twilight Zone."

Imagine, if you will, Serling in Room 1D-957 in the basement of the Pentagon for five days at the end of 1962, at the invitation of the Joint Chiefs of Staff. He and other civilians have been asked to participate in a series of games in which they are developing secret scenarios of America's future.

Urged on by high-ranking military officers, the civilians are producing their own Twilight Zone: The Soviet Union conquers the United States; in a face-to-face confrontation with Nikita Khrushchev, President Barry Goldwater poises his finger over a nuclear button. But sometimes their fantasies are eerily prophetic: The president is impeached; the shah of Iran is toppled and flees into exile.

Besides Serling, the Olympians (as game reports call them) include Milton Caniff, the creator of the comic-strip hero Steve Canyon; John Ford, the Oscar-winning director whose classics included movies set in every American conflict from the Revolution to World War II; mystery writer Harold Q. Masur; and representatives from organized labor and industry. All the players have signed nondisclosure statements and been told to say, if asked why they are in Washington, simply that they are "attending a conference." The games are highly secret, as is the existence of the Joint War Games Control Group of the Joint Chiefs of Staff, which manages the games. Serling and the others have been invited to the Pentagon to play Olympiad I-62, a series of politico-military war games that start on Monday, December 3, 1962, and end on Friday, December 7—a date that seems a bit freighted with irony.

Such policy-planning games, imported from academia early in the Kennedy administration, still go on today. The players in these games usually are military officers and middle-level or high-ranking civilian officials drawn from the Department of Defense, the Department of State, the Central Intelligence Agency, and the White House.

In a typical war game, the thirty to thirty-five players are divided into player and control teams. Each team is put in a room that contains little more than a long table, chairs, and equipment for viewing videotapes. On the walls are maps (usually the sort published by the National Geographic Society) and whatever printed material needs to be displayed. A video camera, attached near the ceiling, is aimed at the table.

The basic game scenario—"believable; real and projected world tensions, activities, and policies," according to a Pentagon description—sets up a crisis situation, which is generally a year or more in the future. The staff may work as long as six months developing the basic scenario. Researchers often go overseas to interview U.S. ambassadors, senior military commanders, and experts on the region that is the setting for the scenario. They may even gather information on the performance of specific weapons—"to the trench level."

The final scenario is in two parts: a "world scene," usually presented documentary-style on a video screen; and the "crisis," in written form. The world scene—maps, clips of news broadcasts—thrusts the players into the future and lays out the situation in which the crisis is taking place. The staff strives to make the video presentation realistic. "We get support from the Defense Communications Agency, which as a matter of course records all the news programs, and they save that, and we can go and raid those clips," says a Pentagon briefing officer. "The world scene creates synthetic history to bring participants forward. We project into the future to change history a little bit and to get participants away from current-day policy restraints and let them freewheel."

Players are assigned to a U.S. Blue Team or a Soviet-bloc Red Team, with a Control Team presenting the scenario—typically, a description of a potential crisis just over the horizon—and running the game. Control might be represented by a military officer from the War Games Control Group or an Ivy League professor of political science.

The game does not move rapidly. It can last four days, from about eight in the morning to about four in the afternoon, with occasional overtime. A typical move takes three or four hours to make and report to Control. "When they begin to address the new situation, time is stopped. The four hours fit on one tick of the clock," the briefing officer says. "There are no late-breaking news flashes, no demarche from the Soviets. The reason is because we want them to achieve consensus and discuss the policy aspects of it. We don't want them to prove how they can respond with the right actions."

Olympiad was different, for its principal players were merely civilians with imaginations. And they played not one game over three or four days, as was usual, but four separate games, each seemingly designed to stimulate extreme reaction.

Assassinations of world leaders, for example, occur frequently in the Olympiad scenarios. Most of the assassinations are the work of the scenario writers, but sometimes they originated with the players. (For some time, I was told, assassinations had become quite the vogue in game playing.) West German chancellor Konrad Adenauer is poisoned. Soviet agents posing as anti-Gaullists kill French president Charles de Gaulle in one scenario and gravely wound him in another. Indian prime minister Jawaharlal Nehru and British prime minister Harold Macmillan are also assassinated. Serial regicide, in a Pentagon-sponsored game eleven months before the assassination of President Kennedy, undoubtedly helps to explain why the Department of Defense kept Olympiad I-62 classified as top secret for more than a quarter of a century.

But even when a game is pried from the Department of Defense through the Freedom of Information Act, the document bears the "sanitizing" black streaks of a Pentagon censor who blots out not what was said but the names of the speakers in war-game dialogue. The words of players are not attributed lest rash comments during a game come back to haunt them.

The same courtesy was extended to the Olympians. So although a slip of the censor's pen revealed that Serling and Caniff were on the Blue Team, there is no way of knowing who said what. Nor are there any authors' credits for the initial scenarios or the teams' reactions to the events in the scenarios. What emerges from the released report on Olympiad is a series of anonymous, interlocking narratives. But when compared to records of other games, Olympiad stands out as unique. There can be no doubt of the credits:

Produced by the Pentagon
Dramatization by Rod Serling

Directed by John Ford
Starring Steve Canyon

The Olympians warm up on three relatively routine games: negotiations for a disarmament treaty; simultaneous crises in Berlin and Cuba; and turmoil in the Middle East. The games introduce the Olympians to a world in which the United States is threatened by Communists around the globe. (Playing the third warm-up game, the Blue Team decides to explode a nuclear bomb 100 miles off the Soviet coast as a warning. The game report notes that the Olympians did not balk at any action "even though it means full-scale nuclear war.") The crucial fourth game, dubbed DAFT (for "decade after"), departs from the Blue-Red team format; instead, the Olympians are asked to respond to three scenarios that might have come straight out of the Twilight Zone. Each scenario breaks off at a crucial moment. The Olympians must produce an ending that will help guide planners of U.S. strategy in the decade ahead.

The first scenario envisions America's defeat in a nuclear war in the early 1970s. Enraged, one of the players says, "The real reason why we lost the war was the failure of the President." Criticism of President Kennedy punctuates the scenarios. Those same scenarios had circulated among Kennedy's military and civilian policy planners but had not been played. "I tried unsuccessfully for several months to get anyone to use them," an anonymous Control tells the Olympians. "You were a heaven-sent opportunity."

As the first scenario opens, NATO has begun to crack following 1963 elections of communist governments in France and Italy. West Berlin mayor Willy Brandt (who really would become chancellor of West Germany in 1969) makes a deal with East Germany, and a united Germany is reborn.

The scenario continues:

Desperate conferences between England, Canada and the US ended when England agreed to withdraw all troops from the European Continent, but insisted on the free passage of US, Canadian, and English troops and equipment to their homelands. The ensuing evacuations resembled Dunkirk; women and children were flown out, minus nearly all personal possessions; every available ship was pressed into service to evacuate the streams of military convoys converging on the western European ports, through crowds of jeering or crying people.

The United States and Canada, expecting a Soviet nuclear attack, evacuate all cities. Soviet missiles knock out early-warning radar and then destroy Detroit, Pittsburgh, Seattle, San Francisco, Los Angeles, and other U.S. cities. Khrushchev telephones the U.S. president, unnamed but presumably Kennedy, to say: "This is not nuclear blackmail. This is it. Only one-quarter of my force was launched. If you retaliate, I'll wipe out the rest of the U.S." The president, who has sent Strategic Air Command bombers on retaliatory strikes, calls them back and agrees to negotiate with Khrushchev.

But, says the scenario, "two squadrons of B-52s, either through communication garble or madly enraged, pushed on—delivering 100 megatons on Moscow, Minsk, and Pinsk." The Soviets answer this Steve Canyonesque mutiny with another wave of missiles. The United States sues for peace.

Soviet troops and officials arrive in the United States, which is divided for occupation. The old Confederacy states east of the Mississippi, plus Kentucky and Tennessee, are turned over to Castro. Texas, New Mexico, and Arizona are put under control of Mexico, which is a communist nation. Alaska and Hawaii are directly annexed by the Soviet Union, along with the states of the Pacific Northwest. The Northeast and Midwest as far as the Rockies are largely a nuclear wasteland and are occupied by Soviet troops until a puppet government is set up.

The Cuban Confederacy, as it is called, gives American blacks new status as Cuban "blood brothers." There are wholesale executions of whites in the Orange Bowl. But in this scenario there is hope—at least for the white Americans—for within a year a "strongly organized underground of firm discipline" and "growing power" challenges the rule of the Cubans and the blacks. The new organization calls itself the Centennial Ku Klux Klan.

In the Democratic Peoples Federation of Mexico, "Spanish-speaking Americans of intelligence and standing" become local officials. In the Democratic Republic of Mid-America, an underground movement called the Sons of Liberty II has developed ray guns that can "stop nuclear and internal-combustion engines, paralyze or kill life, and possibly influence weather." But freedom for them and all other Americans is only a dream. *The End.*

"Too downbeat," one of the Olympians, presumably John Ford, says of this scenario, adding: "I'm not buying it for a motion picture. . . ." Another brushes aside the dismal vision. Americans, he declares, "are not going to quit, and we are going to have arms all over that are hidden." We must begin caching arms right now, the Olympians urge as they quickly veer from the hypothetical future to a present threatened by the enemy "at our doorstep."

No weapon, an Olympian passionately declaims, "is better than the hand or the heart of the man who carries it. We urge that while one American lives who can pull a trigger, it is his duty to do so." Only two months before, Khrushchev had been caught putting Soviet missiles in Cuba. Most Americans believed that Kennedy had won the nuclear showdown with Khrushchev, but the DAFT scenarios reflect a fear that Khrushchev's bold move in Cuba was far more significant than his retreat. The futures presented to the Olympians are haunted by nuclear confrontations even more ominous than the real Cuban missile crisis. The United States is imperiled on every side. Besides the Soviets, with their missiles, there is also "the indistinct shadow of the sleeping Chicom giant . . . a menace that needed to be chained."

Caught up in this vision, the Olympians make recommendations that seem more suited to the 1962 present than the 1972 future. They want "subterranean armories of small arms scattered throughout the country and available to any civilian population." They suggest that the United States go beyond its shores to set up "great secret armories." The Olympians want missile-equipped submarines hidden in the Antarctic and remote "supersecret bases" manned by covert troops "who can retaliate" from overseas if "we are shot down in the street." They advise the immediate building of "basic vaults of production units" to preserve vital apparatus, such as communications equipment, along with the ingredients and blueprints for manufacturing nuclear weapons. Resistance forces, aware of these caches, then can make their own nuclear bombs to use against the Soviet occupiers.

To stave off this looming conquest, the Olympians say, American youth must be taught that "in case of enemy invasion," everyone is "expected to carry on the fight," from "the ash cans of the lower East Side of New York to the apple orchards of Oregon." Special Forces and the CIA should "arm those who are with us behind the iron and bamboo curtains." And America must prepare to "mercilessly introduce biological and meteorological warfare" against our enemies.

To preserve civilization, the Olympians create a new form of citizenship—"Canambrian," which encompasses the people of the United States, Canada, Great Britain, Ireland, and Australia. Canambrian citizenship could even be extended to Latin Americans, as long as there are "educational safeguards."

The second DAFT episode, weaving domestic politics with world affairs, opens in August 1963, when "the shamed representatives of the new African states went into virtual hiding" at the U.N. because "most Caucasians south of the Sahara to the Union of S. Africa had been wiped out in a gruesome cannabalistic [sic] orgy of Inter-tribal MauMau murder more shocking than anything in history."

The U.S. ambassador to the U.N. (then Adlai Stevenson) "introduced only an insipid motion of censure against the responsible African governments." So "the US Congress, Press and public, surfeited with our namby-pamby reactive policy (dubbed 'shrinkmanship' by ex-governor Tom Dewey), blew up."

Congress demands U.S. withdrawal from the U.N. and impeaches the president, who, since this is happening in 1963, is presumably Kennedy. In the new cabinet, United Auto Workers leader Walter Reuther is secretary of state and Teamster boss Jimmy Hoffa is secretary of labor. (In real life, Hoffa, just convicted of jury tampering, was the major target of Attorney General Robert Kennedy's investigation of labor racketeering.) General Matthew B. Ridgway is recalled to active duty to head the new War Department as the one chief of staff. The scenario abolishes the office of the Joint Chiefs—the game's sponsor.

Under a resolute new president (presumably Lyndon Johnson), the U.S. Air Force destroys Cuba for no apparent reason. Panama and Puerto Rico jointly become the fifty-first state. All foreign aid is stopped. Taiwan is "turned over to Japan, with the concurrence of China." American technicians help China build nuclear weapons. "Senator Wayne Morse made an impassioned plea for liberalism, claiming neutralism was really only isolationism, but retired, visibly shaken by his colleagues' roaring boos."

Europe, with both NATO and Eastern bloc troops withdrawn, forms

United Western Europe. A Syrian Muslim known as Saladin II forges a new Saracen Empire that encompasses the Arab world. "The Mid-African continent was again 'Darkest Africa,' practically out of touch with the rest of the world, consumed by inter-tribal battles."

Saladin, backed by the Soviet Union and China, conquers Israel. Senator Jacob Javits of New York, a firm supporter of Israel in real life, is mocked in the scenario, which has him demanding that "the United States immediately invade the Saracen Empire and restore a free Israel stretching from the Suez to the Dardanelles." Only one nation, the Dominican Republic, offers asylum to Israeli refugees. The Saracens take over Israeli nuclear facilities and manufacture small weapons so that individual Arabs are able to carry nuclear bombs into the cities of the West.

When the Olympians respond to DAFT II, laughter greets one remark: "The Kennedy dynasty has been broken." In that post-Kennedy America, fallout shelters and domed cities guarantee the nation will survive even with "tens of millions of casualties from a massive nuclear attack." U.S. scientists are working on "a global satellite-borne anti-ballistic missile boost and mid-course intercept system" that uses laser beams to stop enemy missiles. And the Saracens who are toting nuclear bombs will be detected by "cheap portable fluoroscopes for surveillance in guarding against suitcase weapons."

The Olympians also come up with a "substitute for aid funds": an antifertility powder that can be secretly slipped into a needy nation's drinking water "if it is to our advantage somewhere to check the growth of a population."

The Olympians revise the U.S. educational system. Old-fashioned patriotic messages are emphasized: "It's a wonderful thing to have the hackles of your neck come up when you see the Stars and the Stripes in front of you." All high-schoolers of a certain IQ level are required by law to go to college or trade school. A national physical-fitness program will "make a potential Ranger out of every American boy and out of all American girls that are willing to go for it." At the age of eighteen or nineteen "this lad can be a Ranger just by putting on the uniform." Then, say the Olympians, "we . . . give them their practice in using knives."

DAFT III, the wildest of all, focuses directly on the man who is the commander in chief of all the military men in the Pentagon's Room 1D-957. In 1964 the Democratic party,

> committed to the candidacy of President Kennedy, could not inject any suspenseful counter to the battle royal joined between the Republican prospects. . . . Then, suddenly, . . . the Southern Democrats and Conservative Republicans agreed to hold a non-partisan convention in Dallas in September to discuss "National policy and the threat of the 'far left' to American existence."

President Kennedy is reelected in 1964, but his running mate is Nelson Rockefeller. Vice President Lyndon Johnson has resigned and is running as the presidential candidate for the newly organized Constitutional Democrats party; Johnson's running mate is Barry Goldwater.

In his second term, President Kennedy drives up the national debt and launches several apparently meaningless small-scale wars in which 34,407 U.S. servicemen are killed and 107,743 wounded. Robert McNamara continues as secretary of defense, but his Pentagon is caricatured as a building full of record-keeping machines and civilians concerned with motion studies and management analyses. Steve Canyon's beloved Strategic Air Command is put under civilian control.

In the 1968 election Goldwater defeats Rockefeller, and subsequently he meets Khrushchev at summit conferences in Moscow and Washington. The two leaders cease competitive aid to other nations, embargo military arms exports to China and Africa, and agree to negotiate a peace treaty. In November 1969 Goldwater and Khrushchev meet again in Moscow, along with leaders of Warsaw Pact and NATO nations.

At a grand ball in the Kremlin,

> [a]s the music of the Moscow symphony swelled, and the Bolshoi Ballet began its intricate and beautiful symbolism of Swan Lake, a disheveled subminister rushed in to Khrushchev and whispered something. The Premier, almost apoploctic [sic], removed his shoe and began beating on the arm of his chair. The music stopped. Khrushchev shrieked, "I've been betrayed! The capitalist war mongers have started a revolution in Hungary! It is supported by the Chinese from Albania, and aided by the traitorous Yugoslavs, who proclaim that they are going to restore the old Austro-Hungarian Empire with the help of the West!"
>
> In the stunned silence that followed, communists and westerners edged apart; women fainted; into the ballroom came burp gun-carrying Red Army soldiers in field uniforms. In a wild rage, Khrushchev pointed at President Goldwater, "You have gone too far," he hissed. "This time the American dogs are not in their kennels. They are here in my house. Remember Beria's death; declare yourselves now, before you die!"

The Olympians react to this cliff-hanger by finishing the scene: President Goldwater—"his white hair gleaming, his black tortoise shell glasses shining"—takes from a briefcase a black box manufactured by Westinghouse (one of whose executives is an Olympian). On the box are rows of buttons, including four labeled *Homeland China, Albania, Hungary, Yugoslavia*. Other buttons are labeled *Total Destruction by Nuclear Devices, Partial Destruction by Conventional Means, Temporary Immobilization by Nerve Gas*. (An Olympian later explains that in playing out their game they had Kennedy secretly approve the development of earth-orbiting satellites "containing nerve gases, permanent death-dealing chemicals, nuclear and conventional weapons.")

Goldwater shows the black box, which controls the satellites, to Khrushchev and says, "Mr. Chairman, as you can see, the capabilities for stopping the reported actions lies [sic] between the choices you see before you, and I now offer you, as a gesture of good faith, the opportunity of choosing the method of ending the circumstances which have caused your gore [sic] to rise."

The report does not say which button Khrushchev selects.

The gaming ended on the afternoon of December 7 with Paul Nitze, assistant secretary of defense for international security affairs, speaking to the Olympians. War games like this are important, he says. "We've done what you've just been doing: gone through several Berlin war games, several disarmament war games. . . . We're going to read with interest the results of the work you've done."

Nitze was not just being polite. War games—officially, politico-military simulations—were considered so important for policy planners that lengthy reports on them were sent directly to Nitze and other high-ranking officials. During the game the Olympians heard from General Maxwell D. Taylor, chairman of the Joint Chiefs of Staff; General Earle G. Wheeler, army chief of staff; General Curtis E. LeMay, air force chief of staff, and Admiral C.V. Ricketts, vice chief of naval operations.

The chiefs' remarks are not recorded in the Olympiad report, but the words of a Pentagon general are. He tells the Olympians that this game "is the initial effort to get some fresh and uninhibited minds from the leading walks of American life in here to add fresh ideas to the Department of Defense in the effort to enhance our US interests."

We know that the Pentagon has continued to enter the Twilight Zone of imaginary futures on the march toward Vietnam, toward Star Wars, toward whatever still lies beyond. The joint chiefs of staff and commanders of U.S. forces use computer-run games for contingency planning. Grenada was gamed long before the actual invasion, and so was Panama. Gaming played an important part in General Norman Schwarzkopf's strategic planning in the war against Iraq. But because of the secrecy shrouding the games, we do not know the identities of other "fresh and uninhibited minds" who may have been summoned to Room 1D-957 and asked to help construct the American future.

"Thats Ocay XX Time Is on Our Side"

by GEOFFREY NORMAN

As long as the Vietnam War lasted, the plight of the U.S. POWs came through as one of the most depressing and humiliating episodes in our recent history. But, as we now learn, their experience was something else entirely. *"THATS OCAY XX TIME IS ON OUR SIDE."* Armed with that ironic epigram and their own considerable skills and wits, the POWs endured their years of lonely confinement with ingenious grace, digging in for the psychological long haul. Isolated and forbidden to communicate, they taught themselves the age-old prisoner skill of the "tap code"—for communication was the foundation of resistance. How do you frustrate rats without poison or traps, mend clothes without needles or thread, strengthen a broken arm without doctors, or play bridge with men several cells away without cards? It's true that these were a special group of men, highly trained and well educated, the cream of the military crop who benefited from a shared sense of purpose and a secure chain of command, all qualities that gave them a better than normal chance to survive. But their captors did everything they could to neutralize these strengths, and they too had time on their side. The following article is adapted from Geoffrey Norman's *Bouncing Back* (Houghton Mifflin). Norman, who is himself a veteran of Vietnam, based much of what you might call his American *Papillon* on interviews with men who had been held in a prison they nicknamed the Plantation.

On March 31, 1968, President Lyndon Johnson told the American people that he was suspending bombing of North Vietnam above the 21st Parallel. At the conclusion of his speech, he also announced that he would not be running for reelection. Johnson had been defeated by the North Vietnamese; he was quitting and going home. It remained to be seen if the

U.S. prisoners of war, mainly airmen who had been shot down, would be so lucky.

The news was broadcast over speakers in every prison camp. And when there was nothing said about their release, many of the POWs drew the darkest conclusion. In a camp called the Plantation, on the outskirts of Hanoi, Lieutenant Commander Richard Stratton, the senior ranking officer, said to the three other men in his cell, "If we weren't part of some deal—no more bombing in exchange for our release—then we are going to be here for a long time. Probably until they start bombing again." Stratton's prediction was accurate. He and the others would spend five more years in North Vietnam.

While Hanoi was no longer being bombed, the air war continued in the Panhandle of North Vietnam, and new shootdowns arrived with the unwelcome news that the war was still going on. There were no negotiations yet and no reason to believe that peace and repatriation were at hand.

A single rail line ran outside the Plantation, just beyond the back wall of the old building that the men called the Warehouse, which had been divided into cells. In his cell, designated Warehouse One, Stratton and his cellmates could lean a pallet bed against the wall, climb the ladderlike studs that held the boards together, and look through the gunports at the passing trains. Even after Johnson's decision to halt the bombing of Hanoi, the passing cattle cars were full of young men in uniform on their way to the fight. More than any information from recent shootdowns or the small seeds of truth amid the propaganda of the camp news, this was the most vivid proof that the war was not winding down.

Guards still came to take prisoners out for interrogations, but these increasingly became what the POWs called "temperature quizzes." Instead of being pumped for military information or pressed for propaganda, they were asked how they were getting along and how they felt about their captors and the war. Most of the POWs maneuvered to avoid head buttings. They answered vaguely and were eventually returned to their cells. They began to suspect that in many cases the quizzes were merely a pretext for interrogators to practice their English. Still, to see the door open and the guard point his finger at you was a frightening experience.

There was no way of knowing, when you left the cell for the walk up to headquarters, if you were in for a temperature quiz or something a lot more serious. Delegations were still coming into Vietnam for tours; prisoners in all the camps were still being pressured to make statements, sometimes with the promise of early release; punishments were still being inflicted on men caught violating camp rules. In short, the weeks and months that followed the Tet offensive of early 1968 were not better by any objective measure.

The POWs began psychologically digging in, adjusting to the long haul. Most were in their twenties or early thirties. A few were barely old enough to have voted in one election before they were shot down. Some were fathers of children they'd never seen; husbands of women they had lived with for only a few weeks. It seemed increasingly possible—even probable—that they would be middle-aged or old men before they left Vietnam. Their survival now included facing this hard reality. Somehow, they had to find ways to fill those years, to salvage something from their youth.

At all of the POW camps in North Vietnam, communication between prisoners was strictly forbidden. Roommates managed to communicate without being overheard, but a man could not shout through walls or windows, or leave messages, or try in any other way to make contact with the other prisoners in the camp. Men were thrown into solitary, locked in irons, hung by ropes, and beaten when they were caught trying to communicate.

Still, it was worth the risk, since communication was the foundation of any kind of resistance. The senior man had to get his orders out to everyone in the camp, and everyone had to be tied in; four men alone in a room were not part of a unified resistance. With something called the "tap code," prisoners were able to communicate and establish an organization. Working together helped them overcome feelings of isolation and boredom, and ultimately enabled them to resist.

The principle of the tap code is ancient, at least as old as Greek civilization. In modern dress, it appears in Arthur Koestler's descriptions of life in the Soviet gulag in his novel *Darkness at Noon.* POWs believed that it had been invented by an air force captain named Smitty Harris, who came up with it while he was in survival school and remembered it in Hoa Lo after he had been shot down. Although the POWs may have been wrong about the origins of the tap code, no group in history ever employed it more successfully or more enthusiastically. Learning the tap code was like getting a telephone: It opened a world.

The basis of the code is a grid that looks like this:

ABCDE
FGHIJ
LMNOP
QRSTU
VWXYZ

The letter c could be substituted for k, and the code was read like the coordinates on a map—down and right. For example, the letter m would be three down and two across. To transmit an m through the wall, a prisoner would tap three times, pause, then tap twice.

Most men learned the code from a roommate, but it was possible to teach it through a wall to a man who was all alone and needed it worse than anyone. A man who knew the code would simply tap on the wall until he got a response. He might tap out the familiar rhythm of "Shave and a Haircut" until the man on the other side came back with "Two Bits." Once that happened, they were in communication. Then the tedious business of teaching a language began, first using a more primitive system. The first man would tap once, pause, tap twice, pause, tap three times, pause . . . and so on, until he reached twenty-six. Then he would do it again. Eventually the other man would understand that the twenty-six taps represented the alphabet. a was one, b was two, and so on.

When this had been established, a few messages would be transmitted. The men would exchange names, perhaps, and shootdown dates. It was exceedingly slow and tedious, but it established the link and the rudiments of the method. The next step was to tap out the message "Make a matrix." That done, the newcomer was instructed to fill in the alphabet. In this way the first code was used to explain the much shorter, more efficient one.

At the Plantation, as well as the other camps, the walls were alive with the sounds of men urgently tapping out messages.

When it became clear to the men at the Plantation that they were not going home in return for an end to the bombing of Hanoi, they began trying to improve the physical conditions of their captivity. They would never be comfortable—the cells were crowded and unventilated, and the men slept on boards and wore the same clothes day after day—but they could try to keep clean, and they could improvise several other ways to reduce their misery.

In Warehouse Four there was a lieutenant (j.g.) named Tom Hall who gained a reputation among his fellows as an especially gifted improviser. A farmboy from outside of Suffolk, Virginia, who had grown up learning how to doctor animals, fix cars, and make all of the endless repairs necessary to keep a farm running, he knew how to "make do." After graduating from Virginia Tech, he had gone into the navy and learned to fly fighters. He had been stationed on the *Bonhomme Richard*, on Yankee Station, when his F-8 was hit by a SAM. He had gone to afterburner and pointed the plane toward the beach. Over the Gulf of Tonkin, safely out of reach of the patrol boats and fishing junks, he ejected. The rescue helicopter picked him up and flew him back to the carrier, whose captain was waiting to greet him. A photographer caught the moment, and the picture made the papers back in the States.

Like any pilot who has ejected, Hall was ordered to stand down for a day. The following morning, the weather was so bad over North Vietnam that no missions were flown from the ship. The next day Hall was flying again and he caught another SAM. This time he bailed out near Hanoi—and the North Vietnamese got him. That was June 1966.

To the men who shared space with him in North Vietnam, Tom Hall was the perfect roommate. He knew how to be quiet, but when he talked, he always had something interesting to say. He told them stories about life back home on the farm, including one about how his family kept a hummingbird flying free in the house to keep the bugs down. The other pilots loved this story; the idea of a hummingbird in the house was somehow otherworldly.

Hall never got too high or too low. He maintained an even strain, as pilots say, and he looked after his comrades first and himself second. He didn't bitch and he didn't quit and he knew, by God, how to cope. It was Hall who figured out how to ease the problem of the drafty cells in the winter of 1968, when the men would wake up in the morning close to hypothermic and spend the first hour or two of the day trying to warm up. HATS, he tapped through the wall. Use extra cloth or, better, a sock to make a hat. Stretch it until it fits over your head like a watch cap. You lose most of your body heat through your head, he explained, and this would help. The men tried it, and it did help. Nevertheless, it was cold, especially during the night.

MOSQUITO NETS, Hall tapped. When it is below forty outside, he explained, you do not need to guard against mosquitoes, but the net can be turned into a kind of insulation, like the fishnet material that Scandinavians use for underwear. Before you lie down to sleep, wrap your upper body in your mosquito net. Like the hats, the improvised underwear was a help. The men were not exactly warm, but they weren't chilled to the bone any longer.

Tom Hall improvised sewing needles from fish bones, or from pieces of wire picked up in the yard. The POWs could now mend their clothes, and they even amused themselves by learning to do a kind of needlepoint. The favorite pattern was, far and away, the American flag.

Hall was also given credit for discovering that a man could use his sandals, which were cut from old rubber tires, as a toilet seat by laying them across the cold, sharp, dirt-encrusted edges of the bucket before he squatted. This, in the minds of many POWS, was the most inspired bit of improvisation in the entire war.

Another persistent, seemingly unsolvable problem at the Plantation was the rats. They were abundant and they were bold. You could chase them out of your cell during the day, but they returned at night. Men were frequently awakened by the pressure of small feet moving across their chests.

Using items that he scrounged—pieces of metal, string, and an empty tin can—Hall built a working mousetrap that kept his cell rat-free. He could not use the tap code to teach the other men how to build such a trap from odds and ends, but he could tell them how to improvise a substitute for plaster out of brick dust and water and use that to seal the ratholes. The other prisoners went to work plastering the holes, and for a while this worked as well as all of Hall's other ideas. But the rats were not pushovers. They began to gnaw their way through the weak plaster barricades, and soon the men had to struggle to replaster the holes faster than the rats could gnaw them open again.

Once more, Hall came through. The Vietnamese grew a kind of bell-shaped pepper, which they ate with their rations. The pepper was fiercely hot, hotter than any jalapeño the Americans had ever eaten. It was possible to sneak one or two of these peppers out of the mess hall when you were on food detail, and Hall advised the other prisoners to plug the ratholes with them. Checking the holes a day or two later, the men noticed that the rats had tried gnawing through the new plugs but had given up before breaking through. The peppers were too hot even for them.

The rats remained a problem—there were no complete, unequivocal victories for the POWs—but Tom Hall had made it into a fight, and the POWs got their innings.

Housekeeping was humdrum stuff for men who flew supersonic fighters and were accustomed to turning their dirty uniforms over to a laundry run by enlisted men. But it became vastly important at the Plantation and the other camps. The camp was dirty, and sanitation was nonexistent. Spiders, roaches, and flies were everywhere. One man tapped out a message designating the housefly as the national bird of North Vietnam. Keeping clean was important not only for its own sake but because it represented a challenge, however small. It wasn't the stuff of a fighter pilot's dreams, like shooting down a MiG, but under the circumstances it would do.

In their weakened condition, the POWs were prey to all sorts of infections and parasites. They worked hard at keeping their cells, their clothes, and themselves clean. Each man was issued a small bar of lye soap every week, and since it seemed to be almost as abundant as pumpkins, they washed their uniforms vigorously with it when they were taken out to bathe. But they still got sick. Medical lore was dredged up from memory and passed through the wall. When you had diarrhea, you should drink only the broth from your soup and leave any greens or meat it might contain. If you were constipated, you should eat whatever solids were in the soup and leave the liquid. It was not much, but it was a regimen and they followed it.

Boils were a constant, painful problem, as were abscessed teeth. One man remembered a doctor telling him an old piece of medical shorthand—"piss and pus must come out"—so he sneaked razor blades from the shower and used them to lance the boils and open the abscesses. It was painful and messy, but it seemed to work.

Many of the prisoners had been seriously injured when they ejected, and there was a lot of discussion through the wall about how to treat those injuries. What could you do about a broken bone that had not been set properly and was healing crooked?

Al Stafford—one of Stratton's roommates—had suffered a broken upper arm when he was blown out of his plane. The arm seemed to be mending, after a fashion, but he could not raise it to the level of his chest or move it laterally beyond an arc of about 30 degrees. He improvised slings and used his good arm for support, but this only increased the stiffness. He imagined himself returning home—whenever that day came—as a cripple.

Down the line of cells somewhere, another POW learned about Stafford's problem and tapped back that he should begin exercising the arm as much as possible to prevent muscle atrophy and to break up the deposits of calcium that were forming around the break. It was something he'd learned after a football injury.

This led to a debate within Stafford's cell about exercise in general. Should prisoners exert themselves? Dick Stratton, never a man for fitness regimes even before he was shot down, was against strenuous exercise programs. In Stafford's case, he thought it would merely aggravate the injury. As for the other men, he said exercise would burn calories, and they could not afford to waste a single BTU. They were on starvation rations; sit-ups and push-ups would only exhaust whatever small reserves they had. But Stratton was careful not to overexert his authority in this matter. He did not order the men not to exercise strenuously; he merely recommended against it. (Later, he began exercising himself.)

Stafford tried some simple flexing movements. How much worse, he asked himself, could it make his arm? So he would raise it, tentatively, until he reached the point where pain told him to stop. Then he would raise the arm another inch or two, stopping when he could hear something inside begin to tear. It sounded almost like a piece of paper gently ripping. Tears would fill his eyes and he would feel himself growing faint. He would lower his arm until the pain had passed and he had his breath. Then he would slowly raise the arm again, until he reached the same point, and then he would bite down on his back teeth and go another inch, and one more. . . .

After a couple of weeks, he noticed that the arc of mobility had grown by a couple of degrees. So he massaged the arm and kept on. He set goals: Get the arm loose enough that he could use it to drink a cup of water; then enough that he could touch the top of his head. Every day he worked the arm until he could hear that sound of tearing paper and he was on the edge of passing out. The other men in the cell would look away while he was exercising. Now and then, one would say, "How's the arm, Al?"

"Better. Lots better. I can touch my nose."

"That's great, man. Really great. Hang in there."

Other prisoners, desperate for some kind of physical activity, began doing calisthenics. This was tricky, since the sounds of a man running in place or counting off push-ups would alert guards. They would open the cell's little judas window, wave a finger at the man, and tell him to stop. If he was caught repeatedly, he might be taken up to the headquarters building, which the POWs called the Big House, for interrogation and punishment. Prisoners were to sit quietly in their cells, eat their two bowls of soup a day, come out for a bath and a shave once a week, and otherwise do nothing.

So prisoners who wanted to do calisthenics had to depend on the "clearing system." Along the line of cells, men would watch—and if a guard approached, they would bang on the walls hard enough to alert everyone along the line. When a heavy thud sounded along the wall, men would scramble up from the floor to sit on their bunks with their hands folded in their laps, like subdued children waiting silently in church for services to begin. Between the warning thuds, they did their push-ups and their sit-ups and kept meticulous records of their repetitions. Scores were tapped through the wall, and competitions inevitably followed.

The sit-up count reached into the thousands. A man would fold his blanket into the shape of an exercise mat, get down on his back on the floor, and begin knocking them out with the easy rhythm of a metronome—up and back, up and back, up and back . . . breathe in, breathe out, breathe in, breathe out. . . . Soon the steady, repetitive flexing of his own body would shut out everything else and he would be alert to nothing except movement and the possible thump from a man in another cell, clearing. Up and down . . . six hundred, six hundred one . . . two . . . Time seemed to slide by when a man was doing his sit-ups. And when he finished, or had to quit, he would feel an overall exhaustion that seemed so much better than the angry tension that grew tighter and tighter inside, like a rope being slowly twisted, when he simply sat on his bunk, hands folded in his lap, waiting for time to pass, feeling his life go by, leaving behind it a trail of . . . nothing.

For some men, calisthenics were insufficient. After thousands of push-ups, tens of thousands of sit-ups, miles of running in place, they wanted something more challenging. For some reason, it seemed essential to start lifting weights.

There were, of course, no weights available, and nothing in the cells even came close. The sawhorses and pallet beds were too big and cumbersome. The only other things in the cells were the buckets. So the physical-fitness fanatics began curling buckets full of human waste to develop their arms. Some days the buckets were heavy and some days they were light. They always stank, but that seemed less and less important to men who had learned to share space with rats and sit on those buckets with absolutely no privacy. They did their curls, concentrating to make the lifting motion smooth and fluid so the contents of the buckets would not slop around too much inside or spill over the edges.

Years later, when he was home, one of the men went to a movie about weight lifting and bodybuilding. The movie was *Pumping Iron,* and it occurred to him that hour after hour, day after day, for almost six years of his life, what he had been doing was pumping shit. It seemed the perfect description.

It was not enough to work on housekeeping, health, and fitness. Even after you had done all you could to keep the cell and yourself clean, exercised until you were exhausted, and taken your turn tapping or clearing, there were still long, empty stretches of time that had to be filled. Somehow, you had to keep your mind occupied; otherwise you would dwell on your situation and sink into a swamp of self-pity. The POWs found they had more resources than they could have imagined for keeping themselves diverted. It came down to discovering what they already knew.

Stafford was on the wall one day when someone from the next cell tapped out a riddle. You are on a path, the message read, and you come to a place where the path goes off in two directions. There is a guard at the head of each new path. If you take one path, you will meet certain death. If you take the other path, you will live. One guard always lies and the other always tells the truth. You do not know which is which, and you may ask only one question of one of them. What is the question that will allow you to proceed safely?

It took a long time for the man in the next cell to tap out that message. It took much longer—months, in fact—for Stafford, who had never been good at math and logic and the other empirical disciplines, to figure out the answer. But this was the point. When one of his roommates, who knew the answer, tried to coach him, Stafford said, "No, goddammit. Don't ruin it. I'll get it."

Like virtually all of the prisoners, Stafford finally gave up and asked someone to tell him the answer—which was simplicity itself. You ask either guard, "If I ask the other guard which is the road to safety, what will he tell me?" And then you take the opposite path. This was the best of many brain-teasers that went through the wall.

Killing time was not an altogether new experience for the aviators. They had always had time on their hands while waiting to fly—especially in the days before the war. One way of killing time had been with card games that could be put down before takeoff and resumed when the planes were back down. Ready-room and alert-room bridge games could last for weeks. It took some resourcefulness, however, to get a rubber going in prison when all four players were in different, and not always adjacent, cells.

First, you needed cards. The Vietnamese were not handing any out. Although they were included in Red Cross and other packages sent to the POWs, these were not distributed until very late in the war. So the POWs had to make the cards. Toilet paper was available. A quill could be made from broom straw, ink from ashes and water. The cards were made small so they could be easily concealed.

Next came the fundamental problem of how to play the game. The men who decided to make up a bridge foursome would each arrange their cards the same way. Then the instructions for how to shuffle would be tapped through each wall. Sometimes these instructions would be relayed by a man who did not play bridge but was willing to help keep the game going and do a little tapping to pass the time.

CUT . . . DECK . . . TEN . . . CARDS . . . DEEP
CUT . . . LARGE . . . PILE . . . FIFTEEN . . . CARDS . . . DEEP
PLACE . . . THIRD . . . ON . . . FIRST . . . PILE . . . and so on until the deck was shuffled.

Then every man would deal four hands, pick up the one that was his, and begin the bidding. Once the bidding was complete, the dummy hand would be turned over. The other hands would remain facedown, and as a card was played, the man making the play would identify the card and its place in the original pile by tapping, so the other players could find it without looking at the rest of the cards in the hand. It would have been easy to cheat, but also, under the circumstances, utterly pointless.

A hand of bridge that probably would have taken no more than ten minutes to play under normal conditions could last for two or three weeks when every play had to be laboriously tapped through several walls. Now and then a new man would decline an invitation to play, saying that it couldn't be done, that tapping all the bidding and the rounds and the scorekeeping through several walls would just take too much time. The other men had an answer, which went back to a time when Dick Stratton had been thrown into a totally darkened cell for punishment.

Light deprivation for long periods of time is known to cause disorientation and severe emotional distress. Stratton had been kept in that cell for nearly six weeks. His only lifeline was the wall and the man on the other side, Jack Van Loan. At first, simply to give Stratton some kind of reference point, Van Loan would estimate the passage of time and give Stratton a hack every fifteen minutes. It was something. Then, as time went on, Van Loan began asking Stratton to explain things to him: books that Stratton had read, courses he had taken in college, anything that he could remember and describe in detail. After a while they came to the subject of philosophy, and Stratton was trying to tell Van Loan, through the wall, about a course he had taken in existentialism. That word alone was tough to get across, and Van Loan missed it several times. Each time, Stratton would patiently tap it out again. When they had finally gotten that single word straight, Stratton began tapping out the name Kierkegaard. It seemed to take hours. At one point, Stratton tapped out an apology: SORRY THIS IS TACING SO LONG

Van Loan tapped back: DONT WORRY ABT IT XX I THINC TIME IS ON OUR SIDE XX CEEP TALCING

From then on, whenever a man protested that a bridge game would take too long to tap through several walls of the Warehouse, the man on the other side would tap back: THATS OCAY XX TIME IS ON OUR SIDE

Card games and chess were good for filling time, but they were not enough to engage fully the minds of college-educated men accustomed to learning as a routine discipline. So they began memorizing lines from poems or plays that they might have been taught to recite as children and had never forgotten, even if they had to work hard at the job of recall. When a man had the lines, he would tap them out to a prisoner in the next cell, who recited them over and over until he had memorized them himself. The music of the lines, the hard cadences—especially of Kipling—provided a kind of solace.

> *For it's Tommy this and Tommy that*
> *And Tommy how's your soul?*
> *But it's thin red line of heroes*
> *When the drums are on the roll.*

Men who had never cared much for poetry began to crave the verses, waiting eagerly for them to come through the wall. The POWs in one cell were in the midst of learning *The Highwayman,* line by painstaking line, when they were ordered to move. The order came just as they were reaching the climax of the poem and Bess was prepared to "shatter her breast in the moonlight" to warn the highwayman. It was like losing a mystery novel when you are three or four chapters from the end. From their new cell, which had no common wall and could not receive messages by tap code, the men smuggled a message asking what had happened. A message was smuggled back to them—at some risk—and it read: HIGHWAYMAN AND BESS—KIA

As in some old, preliterate society, storytelling became an important art. The stories and myths of their generation were often films, so after the evening meal and the order to put up nets and lie down on the hard wooden pallets, it would be time for movies. A cellmate who could remember a film would lie on his bunk and begin patiently narrating the action, scene by scene, going into character for dialogue and adding as much detail to the physical descriptions as he could remember or invent. Many of the men had favorite movies they had seen more than once, so they were able to relate a passable summary. Some had a real talent for the work and, with the help of other men who had seen the movie, could assemble a fairly complete account. Certain movies became very popular. Dr. Zhivago was easily the best-loved movie at the Plantation.

Still, there were long stretches of dead, empty time when nothing happened and a man was reduced to simple, mute awareness of his situation. He was hungry. In the summer he was hot and eaten up with skin infections; in the winter, cold and shivering. He was desperately uncertain about the future. He did not know if he would be hauled out for a quiz in ten minutes, still be a captive in ten years.

Almost all of the POWs learned to fantasize. There was a distinction, however, between idle daydreaming and disciplined fantasizing. No one needed to be told that simply crawling under a blanket and dreaming childhood dreams of mother and dog and painless innocence was unhealthy. That kind of random, formless escape would lead a man further and further into passivity, self-pity, arid isolation. Instead, when you fantasized, you tried to create real situations and solve real problems. Properly done, a good session of fantasizing would tire you out, leave you with a sense of having accomplished something.

Al Stafford had always loved to sail, so he would sit up straight with his eyes closed and imagine himself out in Chesapeake Bay. He would decide on the season and then try to remember just what the prevailing weather would be. In the summer, when the cell was stifling and full of bugs, he would picture himself out for a winter sail on the bay, with the water the color of lead, the wind blowing whitecaps off the tops of the swells. He saw himself wearing oilskins, and except for a lone freighter moving up the channel, he had the bay to himself. In the winter, while he huddled under his blanket, he would imagine himself stripped down to a bathing suit, skimming past crab boats and other craft scattered across the mild green expanse of the bay.

At the end of an hour or two of sailing, Stafford could taste the salt on his lips and feel the sun on his skin. He sailed for hours and hours. He used real checkpoints and kept a real logbook. "Five knots equals a mile every twelve minutes. . . . I'll be at the Oxford lighthouse by 1610. . . ."

In another cell, farther down the Warehouse, another man played golf. He would spend two hours a day playing a course he remembered hole by hole. He concentrated so hard on his shots that he could feel the tick of the ball when he made contact with the sweet spot. When his mind wandered for a few moments, he would feel the ugly, metallic sensation all the way up his arms and into his shoulders. A goddamned duck hook, he would tell himself, and trudge off into the rough, hoping that he would be able to find his ball and learn not to use too much right hand.

During his golf games, his cellmates left him alone. It was easy to tell when he was playing, because he would be sitting on his pallet in something like a lotus postion, with his eyes closed and his lips moving just slightly as he talked himself through the round. Then, after a couple of hours, he would open his eyes and begin to stretch, as though to relieve the tension. One of the other men in the room would say, "How'd you hit 'em today, Jerry?"

"Not bad. I was two under when I made the turn, but I pushed my drive on fifteen, a long par-five. Had to play safe out of the rough and double-bogeyed the hole. Then I three-putted seventeen from twelve feet out. Really blew it. So I was one over for the round."

"That's not bad."

"No, it was a good round. Great weather, too."

"So what about the handicap?"

"I'm still sitting on a two."

"Little more time on the driving range and you'll be a scratch golfer."

"Putting green is more like it. That three-putt killed me."

There was only one limit to this kind of fantasizing: You had to know enough about the situation or the task to make it realistic. You could not simply decide you were going to be a professional golfer and imagine yourself in a playoff against Jack Nicklaus if you had never played a round in your life. But if you put yourself into a world that you did know and understand, and you took your time and forced your mind to follow the consequences of every single choice, you could create a world of almost tangible reality.

It was an escape, but it was also a discipline. If you were a golfer and you played every day, you might feel yourself actually getting better. Though he had not seen blue water for two years, since the morning he last crossed the coast of Vietnam at 20,000 feet, Al Stafford felt sure he was a better sailor than he had been when he was shot down. He knew so much more now. He had been through certain situations so many times in his mind that he now did the right thing automatically. It was like the time you spent in a flight simulator on the ground, which prepared you for situations you later encountered in the air.

But even if it was a productive way to use long, empty stretches of time, it was still no substitute for the real thing. When it was too hot and he was too dispirited even to fantasize, Stafford wondered when he would see blue water and feel the wind again—or, in his worst moments, if he ever would.

Along the row of cells in the Warehouse, men strained to keep busy, finding the solution in everything from a serious form of make-believe to the most elaborate improvisation. A man named Charles Plumb "played" music on the keyboard of a piano diagramed in brick dust on the floor. He would patiently play the pieces he could remember, practicing until he got them right. Like Tom Hall, Plumb was an innovator. He had grown up in rural Kansas, where he had been an active Boy Scout and 4-H member. Like many boys his age, he had also fooled around with ham radios and had once sent away for a kit to build his own receiver. He remembered enough about it to try building one at the Plantation so he could listen to news from some source other than Radio Hanoi.

The yard at the Plantation was littered with scrap and debris. On his way to a rare and welcome work detail, Plumb would walk in the typical prisoner fashion, head lowered and shuffling his feet dejectedly. Actually, he was looking for wire. He easily found enough for an aerial and a ground.

During interrogations, prisoners used pencils to write out confessions or letters of apology to the camp commander. They routinely pressed too hard and broke the lead. While a guard was sharpening the pencil, the prisoner would sneak the small piece of broken lead into his clothing to smuggle back into his cell. An eighth of an inch of pencil lead set into a sliver of bamboo made a wonderful, highly prized writing instrument. The POWs would care-fully hide their pencils against the possibility of a search. Being caught with a pencil brought punishment for breaking the rule against contraband. Worse, the pencil would be confiscated.

For his radio, Plumb used one of these small pencil points as a detector, balancing it on the edges of two razor blades. For the antenna coil, he wrapped wire around a spool that he made from scrap wood, which he shaped by rubbing it against the rough wall of the cell. He built a capacitor from alternating sheets of waxed paper and aluminum foil smuggled from the kitchen or saved from cigarette packages.

This left the earpiece, which required an electromagnet, diaphragm, and housing. A nail served for the electromagnet. The housing was an unused insulator stuck in the wall, probably dating back to the time the French built the camp. He had worked the insulator loose from the wall and was preparing to wrap the nail with fine wire when the guards conducted a search and confiscated all the parts to his radio. He was taken to the Big House, put in the ropes, and forced to write a letter of apology to the camp commander. He never heard the Voice of America on his little radio.

While Plumb was busy with one of his projects, his roommate, Danny Glenn, concentrated on designing and building his dream house. Glenn had studied architecture at Oklahoma State before going into the navy and was shot down four days before Christmas 1966. At the Plantation he filled the hours working on the plans and blueprints for the house he promised himself he would build—exactly to his specifications, with exactly the materials he wanted—when he finally got out of North Vietnam and went home. He would rough out the plans on the floor, carefully working out the dimensions and noting the placement of headers, joists, and studs. Then he would draw up his materials list, room by room. His lists were exhaustive and specific, down to the precise gauge of the electric wire. The blueprint of a room would stay on the floor for days, then weeks, while he made his corrections and pondered his decisions.

Lying under his mosquito net at night, Plumb frequently was awakened by his cellmate's voice.

"Hey, Charlie?"

"Yeah."

"You asleep?"

"No."

"Listen, if I'm bothering you . . ."

"That's okay. What is it?"

"Well, you know that upstairs bathroom, the little one at the head of the stairs?"

"Uh-huh."

"Well, I've been thinking about it and I've decided to go with Mexican tile. What do you think?"

"I think it would look real good."

"You sure?"

"Absolutely."

"It's not too fancy?"

"No. I'd say Mexican tile would be just right."

"Well, what about the color?"

"Hell, I don't know."

"I was thinking green. That dark green like you see on sports cars. British racing green, they call it."

"I think that would look real good."

"Okay, Charlie. Thanks a lot."

"Sure."

"Goodnight."

In the morning, Glenn would go to his blueprints and materials list and write in green Mexican tile for the upstairs bathroom. Then he would check the dimensions and do the arithmetic to calculate just how many three-inch squares he would need and where he would need to cut to fit. He would memorize as much as he could and make notes in tiny script on a piece of paper from a cigarette package, using one of the contraband pencil points or an improvised pen. Then he would fold the sheet into the smallest possible square and hide it in a crack in the wall, erase the schematic of the room he'd been working on, and start another.

That night, after the mosquito nets were down, he would say, softly, "Charlie, I'm thinking about paneling that family room downstairs. What do you think . . . ?"

Nearly ten years later, after he had come home and started a new life, Plumb got a call at his home in Kansas.

"Charlie, this is Danny Glenn."

"Yeah, Danny, how you doing?"

"Good. How about you?"

"Real good. What's up?"

"Charlie, I want you to come see me. There's something I want to show you."

"Well . . . all right. Where are you?"

"Oklahoma. Let me tell you how to get here."

Plumb wrote down the directions and said he would drive down that weekend.

"Great, Charlie. Can't wait to see you."

Plumb followed the directions and when he made the last of several turns, the one that would take him up to the driveway where he was to turn in, he saw the house. It was the very same house that he had heard described a thousand times and had helped design while his roommate scratched out the plans and prints on the floor of their cell. He stopped the car and studied the house for a long time. It was unbelievable, like something from a dream.

"Hey, Charlie, come on in. Let me show you around."

Everything was there in exact detail. Plumb could walk around the house as if he had lived there all his life. When he came to the end of a hall and opened a door, he knew exactly what would be on the other side, knew where every bathroom was and what kind of tile would be on the floor. Nothing was out of place and nothing had been changed from the way this house was planned, all those years ago.

"It's beautiful," he said. "I can't believe you got everything just right."

"Oh, it was a bitch, let me tell you. They'd stopped making a lot of the materials I had in mind when I designed this baby. I had to go to salvage yards and warehouses all across the Southwest to find some of this stuff. But, by God, I wasn't going to compromise. I had too much invested—you know what I mean."

Plumb understood.

The Gulf Crisis and the Rules of War

by MARTIN VAN CREVELD

This collection began with an essay on the latest theories about the origins of war. It is perhaps appropriate that we end with a murky and disputatious subject, which also goes back to those origins, the rules of war. As Martin van Creveld writes in the provocative article that follows: "From the dawn of history men, far from discarding all restraint when they went to war, have sought to regulate it and subject it to limitations." But van Creveld argues that since the Persian Gulf Crisis those rules, always unofficial but curiously binding, have begun to change in significant ways. What is happening to them is in keeping with the changing nature of war itself. Conventional warfare of the Desert Storm variety is for the foreseeable future an anachronism, and is giving way to the sort of low-intensity conflict in which tribal, ethnic, and religious factions fight each other without the benefit of high-tech weapons or huge state-supported armies. The rules of war will have to deal with these new realities, says van Creveld, a professor at the Hebrew University in Jerusalem, who is one of the most important—and controversial—military historians of our time. He is the author of such books as *Supply and War, Technology and War,* and, most recently, *The Transformation of War* (The Free Press), on which this article was based.

As the Persian Gulf crisis unfolded, the rules of war—as understood by most of the world in this last decade of the twentieth century—were violated in many ways. The very first move in the crisis—namely, the use of force by President Saddam Hussein in order to abolish an existing state, change an international boundary, and conquer territory—already constituted a clear violation of existing *jus ad bello.* Adding insult to injury, the Iraqi government then announced that if war broke out they would resort to a weapon prohibited by international treaty: poison gas. Next, foreign citizens belonging to many different nationalities were detained, refused exit visas, and sent to various strategic installations, where they were made to serve as human shields against attack. Finally, and in what many saw as a justified response to these Iraqi moves, the U.S. government dropped hints that if war broke out—and possibly even if it did not—Saddam Hussein (and his mistress) would be among the first targets.

Whatever one may think of these various deeds, threats, and announcements, there is no question that from the opening days of the crisis, much new ground was broken. In spite of Saddam's eventual defeat, precedents were set, some of which will no doubt be followed in the future.

In modern works on strategy, the rules of war—defining what the belligerents may and may not do—are scarcely mentioned. In this respect they differ markedly from medieval books such as Honoré Bonet's *L'Arbre des batailles* and Christine de Pisan's *L'Art de chevalerie,* which mainly discuss not strategy or tactics but the actions one knight may legitimately take against another, as well as how wars should be declared, whether ruses are permitted, and the like.

The reason behind our modern "strategic" indifference to such problems is that we, like Carl von Clausewitz, see war as an instrument of the state, an organization that, unlike medieval principalities, both makes the law and recognizes no judge above itself. Further, the first chapter of Clausewitz's *On War* defines war as an act of violence carried to the utmost bounds; hence, whatever self-imposed restraints a war may admit are "so weak as to be hardly worth mentioning."

There are three interrelated points to be made. First, what is and is not considered acceptable behavior in war is historically determined, neither self-evident nor unalterable. Second, and however regrettable the fact in the eyes of some, the Gulf crisis may well represent a turning point in what is and is not permissible. Third and possibly most important, in ignoring this problem our present-day military historians and strategists are committing a serious error. Far from being merely a weak "philanthropic" (Clausewitz's term) attempt to mitigate the worst horrors, the rules define what armed conflict is all about—even to the point that without them war itself becomes impossible.

To begin with the question of what war may—and may not—be waged for: The single document most subscribed to by mankind today is the United Nations Charter. That charter expressly forbids the use of force for altering international boundaries, that is, "aggressive war." This prohibition arose from the Allies' experience with Nazi and Fascist aggression. However, during much of history no such ban existed. Between about 1500 and 1789 in particular, altering frontiers and acquiring territory were the main reasons rulers went to war. They were, in fact, expected to go to war over territory.

Then as now, provinces derived their importance from the demographic and material resources they contained, as well as the strategic position they occupied. And, as now, some kind of juridical justification—often in the form of ancient feudal rights—was usually required if a ruler sought to take over his neighbor's property. However, the idea that territory forms an integral part of the state and cannot be formally conceded under any circumstances had not yet been born.

Instead, provinces were viewed almost as pieces of real estate, to be exchanged among rulers by means of inheritance, marriage, agreement, or force. "My generals have lost a war; I pay with a province," commented Emperor Franz Josef after Austria was defeated by Prussia and Italy in 1866. Governments had the right to dispose of territory without considering the inhabitants' wishes or interests. Since borders were the result of historical accident, they were never regarded as sacrosanct.

The modern idea that borders are inviolable has a curious, somewhat twisted history. The French in the revolutionary years 1793–95 were the first to make the annexation of new territories dependent on popular approval. Every time the citizens' army entered some town or district, it drove out the local "tyrant" and held a plebiscite. The inhabitants would express their burning desire to join the glorious republic; their desire would be acknowledged by the Assemblée Nationale and the act of union itself formally accomplished.

While it is true that most of the territorial changes and the revolution itself were later undone, the new doctrine of self-determination refused to die. Having originated in the womb of democracy, it formed an alliance with nationalism toward the middle of the nineteenth century and acquired a new and strident quality that was frequently anything but democratic. As the nationalist gospel told the story, it was not the fact that certain people lived between the river and the mountain that made them into a nation; on the contrary, it was alleged—if only as a historical fiction—that the people in question had *chosen* to live between the river and the mountain *because* they constituted a nation.

The enlightenment of the eighteenth century had emphasized certain commonalities—reason above all—among all peoples. The new doctrine of nationalism, on the other hand, was interested mainly in the differences that separated one people from another. Beginning in the 1860s, there arose an important school of thought that perceived these differences as bound up with the country, its climate, its physical characteristics, and its history. From this it was but a short step to the idea that a people's material and spiritual lives—the very things that made them a nation—were intimately connected with their territory; hence, every inch of that territory was part of the "sacred" patrimony linking past generations with the future.

The most visible outcome of these developments was a change in the status of territory: Territory became inalienable in principle and increasingly in fact as well. Even when military misfortune compelled a state to sign away a province, as France did Alsace and Lorraine in 1871, the people were supposed to treasure its memory in their hearts, forever looking for the opportunity to restore their ownership.

At Versailles in 1919, nationalism achieved its greatest triumph. The collapse of the old multinational empires was followed by an attempt, led by

President Woodrow Wilson, to reconcile might with right by redividing the world in accordance with the principle of self-determination. The redistribution was far from perfect, but once it was completed the victors in particular tended to regard borders as fixed and unalterable. Any attempt to alter them by force—for whatever reason—was labeled "aggression." And countries that refused to accept this new logic—particularly Germany, Italy, and Japan—were considered "revisionist" disturbers of the peace. Their use of armed force to overrun existing frontiers caused them to be confronted by a coalition consisting of virtually the entire world, and their subsequent defeat, as well as the war-crimes trials, confirmed the principle that aggressive war should not be allowed to overturn the territorial status quo. In his death cell, Alfred Jodl, Hitler's chief operations officer, regretfully recalled the days when wars ended with the exchange of a province or two, after which everybody was friends again.

Since 1945 there have been numerous smaller wars, aggressive and other. Often, particularly in the so-called Third World, where most of these wars took place, the borders separating the countries in question were drawn by the old colonial powers and were arbitrary and irrational. Yet to date few countries have succeeded in having their attempts to move borders recognized as legitimate by the international community. On only one occasion has an entirely new frontier been carved out by means of war. That was Israel's War of Liberation in 1948–49, and the amount of trouble *that* has led to does not require recounting. The American victory in the Gulf crisis has merely confirmed the rule. Whatever else Saddam Hussein might have done, he probably would *never* have gotten the annexation of Kuwait recognized by any other state, including even his own closest allies.

In the eyes of many people, the most flagrant violation of international law in the Persian Gulf was Saddam Hussein's use of gas in his war against Iran and his threat to use it against Israel and the Allied forces. Our abhorrence is certainly justified, but it ignores the fact that during most of history the employment of asphyxiating agents has been considered perfectly normal and hardly deserving of comment.

Before the modern age, asphyxiating agents, most commonly smoke, were used in siege warfare. All through ancient and medieval times, mining—tunneling under walls to cause their collapse—was one of the most important means available to a besieging army. As mining led to countermining, subterranean encounters ensued. Both sides used combustibles to smoke each other out of their respective galleries.

There were occasional attempts to use smoke in other situations as well. Early modern military handbooks described all kinds of substances—some of them including strange components like snakeskins, bird droppings, and menstrual blood. These peculiar mixtures were to be put in barrels or on carts, set alight, and rolled toward the enemy with the aim of blinding or asphyxiating him, or driving him away with sheer bad smell. Such substances were rarely used, however—not so much for humanitarian reasons as for technological ones: Only limited quantities could be produced; the fuses for igniting them were unreliable; and even if they were ignited, the wind, temperature, and barometric pressure could cause the resulting smoke to spread unpredictably. The substances were therefore most commonly used in siege warfare, where spaces were constricted and considerable concentrations could be achieved.

The rise of the modern chemical industry in the first half of the nineteenth century changed the situation. Noxious substances could now be made to order and in any quantity. From midcentury on, authors discussed new possibilities, either making suggestions to the military—most of which were examined and found impractical—or incorporating them into tales of imaginary wars, as H. G. Wells did.

Chemicals seemed about to turn war into something new, unprecedented, and even more monstrous. As a result, when Czar Nicholas II assembled the First Hague Conference in 1899, all major countries felt obliged to attend. Admiral Alfred Thayer Mahan, acting as America's representative, said he could see no logical difference between blowing up people in a ship, from which they could scarcely escape, and choking them by gas on land. Nevertheless, it was decided to ban poison gas, and the decision was reaffirmed eight years later at the Second Hague Conference.

The use of gas in World War I is well known. The first to employ it were the Germans at Ypres in April 1915. Though this was initially denounced as Teutonic wickedness, within a few months everybody else followed suit and gas became an acceptable weapon. As the British military historian and strategist B. H. Liddell Hart—himself a gas victim—was later to note, as weapons go, gas is relatively humane. The best available data—collected by the son of the inventor—indicate that gas was responsible for only about 3 percent of all casualties in the war; and compared to those wounded by other means, a greater percentage of gas victims recovered.

The threat of gas made it necessary to encumber soldiers with protective gear and obstructed their work. Moreover, using gas against a line of enemy trenches was one thing; drenching entire districts and even provinces, asphyxiating large numbers of noncombatants, for the purpose of mobile operations is another. This may explain why the prohibition on the use of gas was reaffirmed at Geneva in 1937 and observed during World War II.

While the ban has been violated on a few occasions since then—the Egyptians' reliance on gas in Yemen during the sixties comes to mind—by and large it has achieved its purpose and, what is more, created a situation whereby the use of gas is regarded with horror. Either because Saddam Hussein did not dare to use gas or because he did not feel that his situation was sufficiently desperate to require it, the recent Gulf crisis did not witness its employment. All the same, an objective observer will have to admit that Mahan was right insofar as this horror has neither logic nor history to support it.

When Saddam Hussein announced that Western citizens would not be allowed to leave Iraq but would be held hostage, much of the world was outraged by this violation of the rules of war and, indeed, of the standards of "civilized behavior" in general. Such outrage is certainly justified, but it overlooks the fact that during most of history taking hostages as a guaranty against attack has been a common method of war and diplomacy, at times even more important than strategy.

Greek city-states routinely gave and took hostages from among their most prominent citizens, considering this the best way to guarantee that treaties would be kept and that conquered peoples would not revolt. The practice was continued by Rome. The Greek historian Polybius was the most famous among a group of hostages who, after the destruction of Macedonia in 168 B.C., were taken to Rome; he spent twenty years of his life in the Italian capital. Later during imperial times the Romans (and after them the Byzantines) routinely had the sons of client kings educated in Rome, as was Herod Agrippa, for example. This supposedly imbued them with pro-Roman sentiments while permitting their use as hostages should the need arise.

Throughout ancient and medieval times, the garrisons of besieged towns and fortresses sometimes put captives on the wall and threatened to mistreat or kill them unless the attackers desisted. Medieval princes also continued the practice of giving and taking each other's sons, relatives, and retainers hostage. For example, following the Battle of Poitiers, King John II's brother (Philip of Orléans), his two younger sons (Louis of Anjou and John of Berry), his cousin (Pierre of Alençon), and the dauphin's brother-in-law (Louis II of Bourbon) were detained in England pending the payment of ransom, the surrender of contested territories, and the handing over of certain castles designated as pledges for the execution of the treaty. Similarly, the system by which the sons of vassals were educated in the lords' households continued in force until well into the Renaissance. It permitted those youths to seek advancement and make useful connections and at the same time helped guarantee their fathers' good behavior.

As late as the Thirty Years' War, warfare was conducted not only by states but by independent noblemen, free cities, religious leagues, peasant organizations, and all kinds of freebooters. The Treaty of Westphalia, signed in 1648, finally defined the state as the dominant type of organization that wages war. Thereafter states were understood as abstract organizations possessing independent legal personalities and embracing both rulers and ruled. Their rise led to the idea of government as an institution separate from the people who exercised it, putting an end to the rationale for holding rulers' relatives hostage. Even the most absolute rulers, such as Louis XIV, were increasingly guided by raison d'état, not their personal inclinations. As a symptom of changing attitudes, Frederick II on the eve of the Battle of Leuthen (1757) gave express orders that if he was taken prisoner, the war was to be continued as before. The time came when rulers who behaved otherwise were regarded as corrupt, treasonous, or both. This applied as well to their subordinates.

Simultaneously, the late seventeenth century saw the rise of standing armies clearly separate from the civilian population. These armies claimed, and increasingly obtained, a monopoly in the use of legal armed violence. As war was taken out of the hands of the society at large, rulers began to formalize the situation by concluding mutual agreements that obliged them to refrain from involving each other's citizens in war by taking them hostage or by any other means. From these agreements modern international law, as codified by such men as Emmerich von Vattel around the middle of the eighteenth century, evolved. The idea that taking hostages constitutes a contravention of the rules of war dates from this time. The result was that when the Germans took civilian hostages in connection with antipartisan warfare in Italy, France, and elsewhere during World War II, some of the Germans were subsequently apprehended and punished.

During the past two decades, the convention that forbids hostage-taking has clearly been eroded—for two reasons. First, more and more wars are being waged by organizations that are not states and that do not recognize the distinction between armies and civilian populations. These organizations see no reason to adhere to conventions that states established for their own convenience. Second, when the aim of policy is not war but deterrence, taking hostages, however uncivilized it may appear to modern sensibilities, makes perfect sense. Though Saddam did not carry out his threat of using hostages (or prisoners of war, which is another story) to protect his strategic installations, again it is possible that a precedent has been set, one that may increasingly be followed in the future.

Finally, the Persian Gulf crisis has been remarkable in that both George Bush and Saddam Hussein publicly announced their intention of making the struggle a personal one—either by resorting to subversion in order to kill the opposing leader or by threatening to put him on trial for alleged crimes. Both courses of action fly in the face of modern rules of war, which are based on the fiction that wars are waged by states, not men. Since rulers are supposed to be merely acting on behalf of their states, for some 300 years, between 1648 and 1945, making war per se was not considered a crime and was not supposed to be punished. This applied even in cases when the opportunity to punish did present itself, as when Napoleon III was taken prisoner by the Prussians in 1871. He was merely held for a few weeks and then allowed to leave for England, where he died.

States, however, are a comparatively recent invention. During most of history, rulers, not states, waged war, and were supposed to wage war, on their own behalf. As a result, waging war ad hominem—against the enemy leaders themselves—was not the exception but the rule. The Book of Joshua describes how the Israelites first stepped on the necks of enemy kings whose cities they had conquered and then put them to death. Alexander, during his Persian campaign, pursued Darius relentlessly, and indeed not before the emperor was dead was Alexander's work of conquest really accomplished. Roman soldiers who killed the enemy commander (who in many cases was the ruler) were rewarded with the *spolia opima,* or first spoils; captured enemy leaders were led along in triumph and then, unless the victor chose to exercise clemency, were killed in public and their bodies subjected to all kinds of outrages.

Insofar as medieval warfare was largely a question of class, most feudal rulers did not approve of common soldiers' killing enemy commanders and on occasion reacted sharply to prevent such acts or to punish them. However, acting among themselves they waged war on one another—and indeed, given the structure of medieval society and the absence of any clear distinction between the private and public domains, it is difficult to see what else they could have done.

In this respect, as in so many others, our modern ideas date from the second half of the seventeenth century. As the idea of the state as an abstract organization emerged, an increasingly sharp line was drawn between the rulers' private personas and their public ones. The latter were legitimate targets; the former were supposed to remain inviolate. During the eighteenth century, princes addressed each other as *monsieur mon frère* even as they went to war. Their families were respected; so, by and large, was the private property of enemy commanders. (Frederick the Great in a fit of pique once demanded that a hunting lodge belonging to an Austrian general be burned, and was rebuffed by his commanders.) When Napoleon besieged Vienna in 1809, he took care to direct his artillery fire away from Schönbrunn Palace, where Princess Marie Louise—the future empress—was known to be lying ill.

By 1914, so strongly entrenched had this particular convention become that the state-assisted assassination of an archduke started a world war. But as far as we know, in neither of the great conflicts of this century were there attempts to wage war by murdering enemy rulers.

Since 1945 a growing number of wars have been waged not by states but by all kinds of other organizations. Since these organizations have not been recognized as governments, their leaders do not enjoy immunity and are often hunted by every imaginable overt and covert means. Originating in modern terrorism, this has begun to extend to interstate conflict as well. Conversely, the leaders of these organizations see no reason to grant immunity to their persecutors, with the result that from the White House to 10 Downing Street, high-profile politicians have taken to turning their residences into fortresses.

Judging by the declarations of both sides in connection with recent events in the Persian Gulf, the idea is spreading that rulers should not enjoy immunity but be held personally accountable for their actions. Whether it will be contained or whether we shall witness a return to earlier historical ideas that did not make the distinction and did not seek to avoid war ad hominem, only time will tell.

The above briefly outlines the rules pertaining to the reasons for which war may be made, the weapons that may be used, the question of hostages, and the question of waging war against the leaders themselves. In all four areas, the relevant norms have proved to be neither eternal nor self-evident but the product of specific historical circumstances. Therefore, should circumstances change, so in all probability will the norms. Already as a result of the Persian Gulf crisis it seems that some of the modern rules of war—notably the one that prohibits states from employing violence in order to change international borders—are as strong as ever. Others appear to be on their way out; in October 1990 it was President François Mitterrand who said that France did not take hostages, and in the next sentence placed restrictions on the movements of Iraqi diplomats.

What is more, the four problems discussed here represent only a fraction of a much larger body of conventions and usages. From the dawn of history men, far from discarding all restraint when they went to war, have sought to regulate it and subject it to limitations. Even some of the most primitive societies known to us surrounded armed conflict with rules that defined the way it should be declared and terminated. The same societies also sought to establish procedures by which the two sides could communicate (parleys), ways in which the fighting could be temporarily halted (truces), places that would be exempt from it (sanctuaries), weapons that could not be used (poison arrows), and so on.

Like all rules, those that pertain to war are occasionally—some would say frequently—broken. The purpose of the rules is not, as Clausewitz and most modern "strategists" seem to think, simply to appease the consciences of a few tenderhearted people. Their real function is to protect the armed forces themselves. This is because war, the most confused and confusing of all human activities, is also among the most organized. Armed conflict can be successfully waged only if it involves the cooperation of many men. Men cannot cooperate, nor organizations even exist, unless they abide by a common code. That code should be in accord with the prevailing cultural climate, clear to all, and capable of being enforced. A group of people unclear about just whom they are (and are not) allowed to kill, for what ends, under what circumstances, and by what means is not an army but a mob. Though there have always been mobs, usually when confronted by an effective fighting organization they have scattered like chaff before the wind.

The need for rules of war, however, goes further than this. War by definition consists of killing, of deliberately shedding the blood of fellow creatures. Killing is an activity no society can tolerate unless it is carefully circumscribed by rules that define what is and is not allowed. Always and everywhere, killing done by certain authorized persons, under certain specified circumstances, and in accordance with certain prescribed rules is saved from blame and regarded as praiseworthy. Conversely, killing that ignores the rules or transgresses them usually provokes punishment—often the killing of the transgressor.

Though societies have differed greatly as to the precise way in which they draw the line between war and murder, the line itself is absolutely essential. Some killers deserve to be decorated, others hanged. Where this distinction is not preserved, society will fall to pieces and war will become mere indiscriminate violence.

So far removed is such uncontrolled violence from war proper that Greek mythology, always a good source of insight, had two different deities to represent them. The patroness of orderly, regular war was the virgin goddess Pallas Athena. Springing from Zeus's forehead, she was a powerful warrior who is often represented leaning on her spear, her helmet pulled back, lost in thought. The patron of unrestrained violence was Ares, "mad, fulminating Ares," to quote Homer, an outcast among gods and men. Athena was one of the greatest deities; the largest city in Greece, as well as the Parthenon, was named in her honor. Ares, born to the same father, was a minor deity with few worshipers and fewer temples. The *Iliad* tells how Ares on one occasion met Athena in battle and was soundly defeated. Bleeding and trumpeting his pain as he ran from the field, he ascended to Olympus and complained to Zeus— from whom he received scant sympathy.

Though the rules of previous ages differed from our own, then as today those who broke them were sometimes apprehended and brought to justice. Nor was fate necessarily kinder to those, probably the majority, who never stood trial. Western literature as represented by the *Iliad* begins at the point where Agamemnon, the mighty king, is punished by Apollo for violating the law and rejecting the ransom of a young woman he had captured. In later Greek mythology, warriors who desecrated temples or committed other excesses were persecuted by the Erinyes and overtaken by Nemesis, the monstrous goddess of revenge who made a victim's very food inedible. During the Christian Middle Ages, knights who did not respect the rights of monks, nuns, and "innocent people" in general were destined to be hounded by the devil while they lived and to be carried off to hell after they died.

Although the Persian Gulf crisis is over, the possibility still exists that Saddam Hussein and his associates will one day be made to account for their crimes. Meanwhile, it has already become clear that the rules of war—established by European or European-derived states and codifying their own preferred way of engaging in armed conflict—are changing and will continue to change.